Module No.	Interactive Spreadsheet Module	Page

SIXTH EDITION

MANAGERIAL ECONOMICS

Economic Tools for Today's Decision Makers

Paul G. Keat

Thunderbird School of Global Management

Philip K.Y. Young

Nth Degree Systems, Inc. and Duke Corporate Education

Prentice Hall
Upper Saddle River, New Jersey

Library of Congress Cataloging-in-Publication Data

Keat, Paul G.
  Managerial economics : economic tools for today's decision makers / Paul G. Keat,
Philip K. Y. Young.—6th ed.
    p. cm.
Includes bibliographical references and index.
ISBN-13: 978-0-13-604004-0 (casebound)
ISBN-10: 0-13-604004-7 (casebound)
  1. Managerial economics.   I. Young, Philip K. Y.   II. Title.
HD30.22.K39 2009
338.5024'658—dc22

                                                                2008028750

Executive Editor: Chris Rogers
Editorial Director: Sally Yagan
Editor in Chief/AVP: Eric Svendsen
Product Development Manager: Ashley Santora
Editorial Assistant: Valerie Patruno
Editorial Project Manager: Susie Abraham
Marketing Manager: Andy Watts
Marketing Assistant: Ian Gold
Permissions Project Manager: Charles Morris
Senior Managing Editor: Judy Leale
Production Project Manager: Kerri Tomasso
Senior Operations Specialist: Arnold Vila
Operations Specialist: Carol O'Rourke
Cover Designer: Margaret Kenselaar
Cover Illustration/Photo: Jean Louis Batt/Taxi/Getty Images, Inc. (bottling plant); Steven Hunt/Image
    Bank/Getty Images, Inc.
Composition: Integra
Full-Service Project Management: Thistle Hill Publishing Services, LLC
Printer/Binder: Edwards Brothers
Typeface: 10/12 New Baskerville

Credits and acknowledgments borrowed from other sources and reproduced, with permission, in this
textbook appear on appropriate page within text.

Pearson Education Ltd., London
Pearson Education Singapore, Pte. Ltd
Pearson Education, Canada, Inc.
Pearson Education–Japan
Pearson Education Australia PTY, Limited

Pearson Education North Asia, Ltd., Hong Kong
Pearson Educación de Mexico, S.A. de C.V.
Pearson Education Malaysia, Pte. Ltd
Pearson Education Upper Saddle River, New Jersey

Prentice Hall
is an imprint of

www.pearsonhighered.com

10 9 8 7 6 5 4 3 2
ISBN-13: 978-0-13-604004-0
ISBN-10:   0-13-604004-7

To my wife, Sheilah, our children, Diana and Andrew, and our seven grandchildren—P.G.K.

To Ilse and Adriana, and to Christopher, Allison and Hayden—P. K. Y. Y.

Brief Contents

The following appendices will be found online, www.pearsonhighered.com/keat:

Review of Mathematical Concepts Used in Managerial Economics
Linear Programming
Calculations for Time Value of Money
Solutions to Odd-Numbered Problems
Demand for White Zinfandel in Los Angeles: Additional Data and Analysis

Contents

The following appendices will be found online,
www.pearsonhighered.com/keat:

Review of Mathematical Concepts Used in Managerial Economics

Linear Programming

Calculations for Time Value of Money

Solutions to Odd-Numbered Problems

Demand for White Zinfandel in Los Angeles: Additional Data and Analysis

Preface

One day after class, a student in one of our courses commented on the managerial economics text then being used: "This book is very dry. What it needs is a plot!" To a large extent, the idea for this text stemmed from this remark. This is a text that we believe will excite readers about managerial economics as well as inform them about this vital part of management education. Each chapter begins with a "Situation," in which managers in a fictional company, Global Foods, Inc., must make certain key decisions about their products in the beverage industry. After the relevant economic concepts or tools of analysis are presented, each chapter ends with a "Solution," a suggested way in which these concepts or tools can be used to help managers make the best decision.

The heart of managerial economics is the microeconomic theory of the firm. Much of this theory was formalized in a textbook written over 100 years ago by Professor Alfred Marshall of Cambridge University. Indeed, if readers were to refer to his *Principles of Economics* (1890), they would find many of the diagrams and equations presented in this text as well as in all other texts in managerial economics. To be sure, the world has changed greatly since Marshall's ideas were developed. Market structures other than the "perfectly competitive model" are now much more important. Technology moves at such a rapid pace that the rate of obsolescence of products is now often measured in months rather than years. Competition among firms is frequently conducted on a global scale rather than a local or national one. Multinational firms invest, manufacture, and sell around the world. In so doing, they sometimes buy out their global competitors or form alliances or joint ventures with them. In recent years, the Internet and e-commerce have become critical elements of most businesses.

Yet through all of these changes, basic microeconomic principles such as supply and demand, elasticity, short-run and long-run shifts in resource allocation, diminishing returns, economies of scale, and pricing according to marginal revenue and marginal cost continue to be important tools of analysis for managerial decision makers. In fact, the overall objective of this text is to demonstrate to our readers that the application of microeconomic theory has stood the test of time and continues to be relevant to many facets of modern business decision making.

We are well aware of the reputation that economics courses have among some business students of being "too theoretical and not practical enough for the real world." In our opinion, nothing could be further from the truth. We know that the instructors in managerial economics will agree with us on this matter. We hope that this text will serve as a solid supplement to their classroom efforts to demonstrate to their students the importance and utility of economic theory for business decision-making.

This text is designed for upper-level undergraduate and first-year MBA courses in managerial economics and applied economics. The first two chapters are a general introduction to economics and economic reasoning. A review of the mathematical concepts and tools used in the text has been placed online. In addition to discussing the applications of economic theory to the firm, our text (as is the custom with all texts in managerial economics) includes chapters on various tools of analysis that are helpful to business decision makers but that are not part of the core of traditional microeconomic theory. These are demand, production and cost estimation using regression analysis, forecasting, capital budgeting, and risk analysis. A discussion of linear programming is also available online, along with a review of the time value of money.

IMPROVEMENTS IN THE SIXTH EDITION

In this sixth edition, we sought to improve on the previous editions by incorporating what we continue to learn in our classroom teaching, particularly in the corporate education setting. In addition, we received a number of useful suggestions from the faculty selected by Prentice Hall to review the previous edition. A number of examples that we have used in previous editions continue to be discussed in this text. But we have also added recent examples to ensure that the applications of the theory to business activities and practice are current.

Our examples and applications are presented as integral parts of the chapter narrative. We have deliberately chosen not to use "boxed or shaded" sections of the stories scattered throughout the book. Our reviewers continue to tell us that the use of boxes and shading tend to be distracting to the reader. At end of each chapter, we provide a "Global Application." These days it seems that so much of business and economics is global that it might seem to be unnecessary to single out examples as being global. However, we continue to have this feature, because we want to make sure that our readers see the global implications of the concepts and tools of analysis of managerial economics.

We also continue to use the ongoing case of Global Foods, the hypothetical food and beverage company that faces problems and challenges relating to the topics presented in each chapter. Thanks to a suggestion from one of the professors who uses our text, we will now also include in the Instructor's Guide suggested ways to incorporate a classroom discussion of the "Situations" and "Solutions" for selected chapters of the text.

The following important changes, additions, or updates have been made in this sixth edition. They are listed in order of their importance to this text.

➤ An entirely new chapter on managerial economics in action has been written. We have chosen the beverage industry as the case example, the very industry in which our hypothetical Global Foods is competing. We felt that it would be more relevant and more interesting to our readers to learn what is happening in the actual world of carbonated soft drinks and bottled water. In addition, this chapter shows how managerial economics can be used in helping a company's managers in the business planning process. Student readers will eventually find that the development of a business plan involving forecasting demand, assessing the competitive environment, pricing, and budgeting is a vital task of a business manager. They will see firsthand how the mastery of the concepts and principles of managerial economics can help them in these tasks. The numerical examples are hypothetical but the backdrop in the beverage industry and the planning process are based on the actual business experiences of both the authors and the contributing author, Amy Roman.

➤ The appendix of the above chapter also contains interviews with executives from Coca-Cola and Pepsi-Cola. One of the best ways for readers to learn about how managerial economics can be used to understand and deal with the challenges in the soft drink industry is to hear directly from seasoned executives in the field.

➤ An entirely new section on productivity in the services sector has been added. This can be found as Appendix 6A in chapter 6, "The Theory and Estimation of Production." There is no questioning the increasing importance of the service sector relative to the manufacturing and agricultural sectors, particularly in the United States. To fill in the gap found in our previous editions, we have asked a leading practitioner to write this new section of our text. Matt Denesuk is a Ph.D.

in economics and a specialist in the development of productivity in the services industry for IBM. IBM is, of course, a company that is itself a major example of the shift in a company's focus from manufacturing to services. Today, more than 50 percent of IBM's revenue comes from its global services operations.

➤ The views of another practitioner regarding the outsourcing of goods manufacturing is also incorporated in chapter 6. It is presented in the section on Global Applications (see "Toll Manufacturing in China").

➤ Professor Stephen Erfle of Dickinson College has contributed a valuable new section on the use of Excel in regression analysis. His analysis, found in Appendix 5A, utilizes real data on the consumer demand for wine that was made available for his research by IRI, a leading provider of information on household purchases of consumer goods. Further details about his data and analysis can also be found on this text's Web site.

➤ Whenever appropriate, business examples from the previous editions, including the "Global Applications" found at the end of the each chapter, have been updated or replaced. For example, chapter 4 contains references to new articles on price, income, and cross-price elasticity. In chapter 12, we combine the concept of present value with break-even analysis. Several new examples have been added in the appendix to chapter 4.

➤ Although not new for this edition, we would like to remind readers that references to the mathematical appendix are noted by the symbol ▲ and references to the appendix about the time value of money is noted by the symbol Ⓣ and references to the Excel exercises are noted by ▨.

ANCILLARY MATERIALS

Companion Website: (www.pearsonhighered.com/keat)

The Website contains Internet exercises, activities, and resources related specifically to the sixth edition of *Managerial Economics: Economic Tools for Today's Decision Makers*.

For Students: The **Online Study Guide** prepared by Kim Hawtrey of Hope College offers students another opportunity to sharpen their problem-solving skills and to assess their understanding of the text material. The Online Study Guide grades each question submitted by the student, provides immediate feedback for correct and incorrect answers, and allows students to e-mail results to up to four e-mail addresses.

Instructor's Resource Center

This password-protected site is accessible from www.pearsonhighered.com/keat and hosts all of the resources listed below. Instructors may click on the "Resources" link to access files or may contact their sales representative for further information.

Instructor's Manual: This manual, written by the textbook authors, contains all answers to the questions and problems found in the text. It is available to instructors in Microsoft Word format.

Test Item file: Written by S. Hussain Jafri of Tarleton State University and available to instructors in Microsoft Word format, this Testbank contains multiple-choice questions and a set of Analytical Questions for use in testing students on the material presented in each chapter of the text. Answers are also provided.

PowerPoint Presentation: This lecture presentation tool, prepared by Kim Hawtrey of Hope College, offers outlines and summaries of important text material, tables and graphs, and additional examples. The package will allow instructors to make full-color, professional-looking presentations while providing the ability to create custom handouts for students.

TestGen-EQ software: TestGen-EQ test generating software allows instructors to custom design, save, and generate classroom tests. The software pulls questions from the Test Item File prepared for this textbook and it permits instructors to edit, add, or delete questions from the test banks; edit existing graphics and create new graphics; analyze test results; and organize a database of tests and student results. This new software allows for greater flexibility and ease of use. It provides many options for organizing and displaying tests, along with a search and sort feature.

ACKNOWLEDGMENTS

We wish to thank our colleagues at Thunderbird School of Global Management and former colleagues at IBM and Pace University for their help and encouragement in our work for this and all previous editions. We are particularly grateful to Dr. Jack Yurkiewicz, professor of management science at Pace University, for writing the material on linear programming (now available online); and to Sylvia Von Bostel, of Booz-Allen & Hamilton, who wrote an important part of chapter 14. Special thanks to Professor Shannon B. Mudd, who wrote a major part of chapter 11 for the fourth edition and to Michael Mills, who helped to update material for the fifth edition. We also wish to thank Robin Cole for helping us to write the case used in chapter 6. This case is based on her actual experience in the soft drink industry.

For the preparation of this sixth edition, we want to especially thank Stephen Erfle, professor of economics at Dickinson College, Dr. Mathew Denesuk of IBM, and Amy Roman, marketing consultant, for writing substantial new material in selected chapters of this text. Mr. Xu Feng provided valuable insights on toll manufacturing, as discussed in Chapter 7.

We also thank Professor Kim Hawtrey of Hope College for writing the Online Study Guide and for preparing the PowerPoint presentation, and Professor S. Hussain Jafri of Tarleton State University for preparing the Test Item File.

Our appreciation also goes to the reviewers of the sixth edition. They are: Mina Baliamoune, University of North Florida; Stacey Brook, University of Sioux Falls; Richard Cox, University of Arkansas; Brad Ewing, Texas Technical University; Aric Krause, Westminster College; Alex Orlov, Radford University; Lawrence White, New York University; and Darin Wohlgemuth, Iowa State University.

And we continue to be grateful to all the reviewers of the previous five editions. They are: Michael J. Applegate, Oklahoma State University; Robert Britt, West Virginia University; Peter Brust, University of Tampa; Charles Callahan, III, State University of New York, College at Brockport; John Conant, Indiana State University; Lewis Freiberg, Northeastern Illinois University; Edward H. Heinze, Valparaiso University; George Hoffer, Virginia Commonwealth University; Al Holtmann, University of Miami; Richard A. Jenner, San Francisco State University; Douglas Lamdin, University of Maryland, Baltimore County; Dale Lehman, Fort Lewis College; Jerry Manahan, Midwestern State University; Cynthia McCarty, Jacksonville State University; Yale L. Meltzer, College of Staten Island; L. W. (Bill) Murray, University of San Francisco; Jan Palmer, Ohio University–Athens; Leila J. Pratt, The University of Tennessee at Chattanooga; L. B. Pulley, University of Virginia; Mathew Roelofs, Western Washington University; Roy Savoian, Lynchburg College; Frederica Shockley, California State University–Chico; Ken Slaysman, York College of PA; William Doyle Smith, University of Texas at El Paso; Robert Stuart, Rutgers University; James Tallant, Cape Fear Community College; Mo-Yin Tam, University of Illinois at Chicago; Yien-I Tu, University of Arkansas; Daryl N. Winn, University of Colorado; Richard Winkelman, Arizona State University; Richard Zuber, University of North Carolina at Charlotte; Habib Zuberi, Central Michigan University.

In closing, we would like to express our appreciation to the helpful, encouraging, and patient team at Prentice Hall: Eric Svendsen, editor in chief; Chris Rogers, acquisitions editor; Kerri Tomasso, production project manager; Susie Abraham, assistant editor; and Valerie Patruno, editorial assistant. A special thank you to Angela Urquhart and Andrea Archer at Thistle Hill for keeping us on schedule.

About the Authors

Paul G. Keat has been a member of the Global Business Faculty at Thunderbird School of Global Management for the past 20 years. At present he is an Associate Professor Emeritus. Prior to his coming to Thunderbird he was for many years associated with the International Business Machines Corporation in professional and managerial capacities.

His education includes a B.B.A. in accounting from the Baruch School of the City University of New York, an M.A. from Washington University, and a Ph.D. in economics from the University of Chicago.

Dr. Keat began his IBM career in the department of economic research and then moved into the long-range planning area. Later, as a member of the finance function, he spent several years at IBM's European headquarters in Paris, as manager in the financial planning area, and then as the financial manager for the company's European software business. After his return to the United States, Dr. Keat served as manager in the pricing area of one of the company's manufacturing groups. Before leaving IBM in 1987 he was associated with the company's International Finance, Planning and Administration School (IFPA), where he taught managerial economics, lectured on finance in a number of company-related courses, and managed academic courses. He also taught at IBM's IFPA school at La Hulpe, Belgium.

Dr. Keat has taught at several U.S. universities, including Washington University, CUNY, and Iona College. He was an adjunct professor of finance at the Lubin Graduate School of Business at Pace University, and he also taught in Pace's Executive MBA program.

Philip K. Y. Young is the founder and president of Nth Degree Systems, Inc., a consulting firm that provides customized education and training programs to major corporations around the world. He is also a member of the global faculty network of Duke Corporate Education. He has 30 years of teaching experience as a professor of economics in MBA programs and over 20 years of experience developing and teaching customized education and training programs.

Most of his teaching career was spent in the Lubin School of Business of Pace University in New York. Following this, he was clinical professor of management at Thunderbird School of Global Management. His client list includes a number of multinational corporations in such industries as information technology, telecommunications, fast-moving packaged consumer goods, consulting services, advertising and public relations, pharmaceuticals, semiconductor manufacturing and design, and financial services. He teaches for these companies in the United States, Latin America, Western and Central Europe, Asia, and the Middle East.

He received a B.A. from the University of Hawaii, a master's degree in international relations from Columbia University, and a Ph.D. in economics from New York University.

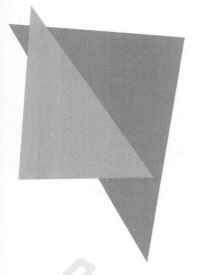

C h a p t e r   1

Introduction

Learning Objectives

Upon completion of this chapter, readers should be able to:

- Define managerial economics and discuss briefly its relationship to microeconomics and other related fields of study such as finance, marketing, and statistics.

- Cite the important types of decisions that managers must make concerning the allocation of a company's scarce resources.

- Provide specific examples of how changes in customers, competition, and technology can affect the ability of a company to earn an acceptable return on its owners' investments.

- Cite and compare the three basic economic questions from the standpoint of both a country and a company.

The Situation

The last of the color slides was barely off the screen when Bob Burns, the CEO of Global Foods, Inc., turned to his board of directors to raise the question that he had been waiting all week to ask. "Well, ladies and gentlemen, are you with me in this new venture? Is it a 'go'? Shall we get into the soft drink business?"

"It's not that easy, Bob. We need some time to think it over. You're asking us to endorse a very major *decision*, one that will have a long-term impact on the direction of the company."

"I appreciate your wish to deliberate further, Dr. Breakstone," Bob responded, "but I would like to reach a decision today. As the president of a major university, you have been especially valuable in advising this company in matters relating to social and governmental policies. But we must diversify our business very soon in order to maintain the steady growth in profits that we have achieved in recent years. As my presentation showed, the manufacturing and marketing of our own brand of soft drink is one of the best ways to do this. It represents a significant diversification, yet it is very closely related to our core business: food.

"The *economics* of the soft drink market tell us that we would be foolish to pass up the kind of *investment return* that the market offers to those newcomers willing to take the *risk*. The food business is generally a mature one. On the other hand, our *forecast* indicates that there is still a lot of room for growth in the soft drink market. To be sure, there is a tremendous amount of *competition* from the 'red team' and the 'blue team.' But we already have expertise in the food business, and it should carry over into the beverage market."

"That's just it, Bob," interjected another board member. "Are we prepared to take this risk? You yourself acknowledged that the *market power* wielded by the two dominant companies in this business is not to be taken lightly. Others have tried to take market share from them and have failed miserably. Moreover, the projections that you have

(continued)

(continued)

shown for a growing soft drink market are based on the *assumption* that the growth rate will remain the same as it has been in the past ten years or so. As we all know, the soft drink market has been growing, but it has also been very fickle. Only recently, Americans were on a health kick, and fruit juices and bottled waters along with health foods were in fashion. Now it seems that soft drinks are back in style again. Who knows what people will want in the future? Maybe we'll all go back to drinking five cups of coffee a day. And what about all the money that we're going to have to spend up front to *differentiate* our product? As you well know, in the processed-food business, establishing brand recognition—not to mention brand loyalty—can be extremely difficult and costly."

"Well, ladies and gentlemen, all your concerns are certainly legitimate ones, and believe me, I have given much thought to these drawbacks. This is one of the biggest decisions that I will have made since becoming CEO. My staff has spent hundreds of hours analyzing all available data to arrive at a judgment. Our findings indicate a strong probability of earning an above-average return on an investment in the soft drink business, a return commensurate with the kind of risk we know exists in that market. But if we could make all our decisions with 100 percent certainty simply by feeding numbers into a computer, we'd all be out of a job. To be sure, details on production, cost, pricing, distribution, advertising, financing, and organizational structure remain to be ironed out. However, if we wait until all these details are worked out, we may be missing a window of opportunity that might not appear again in this market for a long time. I say that we should go ahead with this project as soon as possible. And unanimity among the board members will give me greater confidence in this endeavor."

INTRODUCTION: ECONOMICS AND MANAGERIAL DECISION MAKING

Managerial Economics is one of the most important and useful courses in your curriculum of studies. It will provide you with a foundation for studying other courses in finance, marketing, operations research, and managerial accounting. It will also provide you with a theoretical framework for tying together courses in the entire curriculum so you can have a cross-functional view of your studies.

Economics is "the study of the behavior of human beings in producing, distributing and consuming material goods and services in a world of scarce resources."[1] *Management* is the discipline of organizing and allocating a firm's scarce resources to achieve its desired objectives.[2] These two definitions clearly point to the relationship between economics and managerial decision making. In fact, we can combine these two terms and define **managerial economics** as the use of economic analysis to make business decisions involving the best use of an organization's scarce resources.

Joel Dean, author of the first managerial economics textbook, defines managerial economics as "the use of economic analysis in the formulation of business policies." He also notes a "big gap between the problems of logic that intrigue economic theorists and the problems of policy that plague practical management [which] needs to be bridged in order to give executives access to the practical contributions that economic thinking can make to top-management policies."[3]

William Baumol, a highly respected economist and industry consultant, stated that an economist can use his ability to build theoretical models and apply them to any business problem, no matter how complex, break it down into essential components, and describe the relationship among the components, thereby facilitating a systematic search for an optimal solution. In his extensive experience as a consultant to both industry and

[1]Campbell McConnell, *Economics*, New York: McGraw-Hill, 1993, p. 1.
[2]For books supporting this definition, see Peter Drucker, *Management*, New York: Harper & Row, 1973.
[3]Joel Dean, *Managerial Economics*, Englewood Cliffs, NJ: Prentice-Hall, 1951, p. vii.

government, he found that every problem that he worked on was helped in some way by "the method of reasoning involved in the derivation of some economic theorem."[4]

William H. Meckling, the former dean of the Graduate School of Management at the University of Rochester, expressed a similar sentiment in an interview conducted by *The Wall Street Journal.* In his view, "economics is a discipline that can help students solve the sort of problems they meet within the firm." Recalling his experience as the director of naval warfare analysis at the Center for Naval Analysis and as an economic analyst at the Rand Corporation, one of the nation's most prominent think tanks, Meckling stated that these institutions are "dominated by physical scientist types, really brilliant people." However, he went on to say that "the economists knew how to structure the problems . . . the rest of the people knew a lot about technical things but they had never thought about how you structure big issues."[5]

As it has evolved in undergraduate and graduate programs over the past half century, managerial economics is essentially a course in applied microeconomics that includes selected quantitative techniques common to other disciplines such as linear programming (management science), regression analysis (statistics, econometrics, and management science), capital budgeting (finance), and cost analysis (managerial and cost accounting). From our perspective as economists, we see that many disciplines in business studies have drawn from the core of microeconomics for concepts and theoretical support. For example, the economic analysis of demand and price elasticity can be found in most marketing texts. The division of markets into four types—perfect competition, pure monopoly, monopolistic competition, and oligopoly—is generally the basis for the analysis of the competitive environment in books on corporate strategy and marketing strategy.[6]

There are a number of other examples to be found. The economic concept of opportunity cost serves as the foundation for the analysis of relevant cost in managerial accounting and for the use of the "hurdle rate"[7] in finance. As shown in chapter 2, opportunity cost also plays an important part in understanding how firms create "economic value" for their shareholders. Finally, in recent years, certain authors have linked their managerial economics texts thematically with strategy and human resources.[8] Figure 1.1 illustrates our view that managerial economics is closely linked with many other disciplines in a business curriculum.

Our approach in this text is to show linkages of economics with other business functions, while maintaining a focus on the heart of managerial economics—the microeconomic theory of the behavior of consumers and firms in competitive markets. When clearly understood and exemplified in actual business examples, this theory provides managers with a basic framework for making key business decisions about the allocation of their firm's scarce resources. In making these decisions, managers must essentially deal with the following questions listed in abridged form:

1. What are the economic conditions in a particular market in which we are or could be competing? In particular:
   a. Market structure?
   b. Supply and demand conditions?

---

[4]William Baumol, "What Can Economic Theory Contribute to Managerial Economics?" *American Economic Review,* 51, 2 (May 1961), p. 114.

[5]"Economics Has Much to Teach the Businessman," *Wall Street Journal,* May 3, 1983.

[6]Professor Michael Porter, whose books on strategy have greatly influenced this field of study, is himself a Ph.D. in economics.

[7]Essentially, this is a company's cost of funds expressed as a percentage (e.g., 15 percent). Any project funded by the company should have a rate of return that is greater than this level.

[8]See for example, David Besanko et al., *Economics of Strategy,* New York: John Wiley & Sons, 2004, and James A. Brickley et al., *Managerial Economics and Organizational Architecture,* New York, McGraw-Hill, 2004.

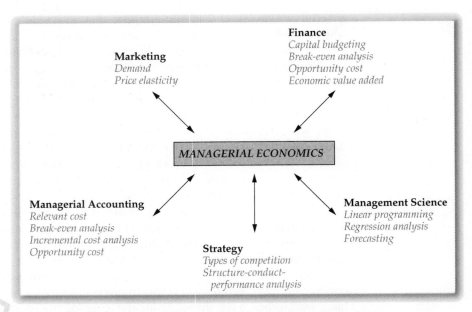

Figure 1.1 Managerial Economics and Other Business Disciplines

    c. Technology?

    d. Government regulations?

    e. International dimensions?

    f. Future conditions?

    g. Macroeconomic factors?

2. Should our firm be in this business?

3. If so, what price and output levels should we set in order to maximize our economic profit or minimize our losses in the short run?

4. How can we organize and invest in our resources (land, labor, capital, managerial skills) in such a way that we maintain a competitive advantage over other firms in this market?

    a. Cost leader?

    b. Product differentiation?

    c. Focus on market niche?

    d. Outsourcing, alliances, mergers, acquisitions?

    e. International dimension—regional or country focus or expansion?

5. What are the risks involved?

Perhaps the most fundamental management question is question 2, which concerns whether a firm should be in the business in which it is operating. This is the very question addressed by Bob Burns and the rest of the board of directors of Global Foods in this chapter's "The Situation" vignette.

Note that question 5 has to do with a firm's risk. Uncertainty pervades our everyday lives, especially when we are considering what may happen in the future, and uncertainty, or risk, is always present in the operations of a business. Of course, some things are fairly certain. A company that buys steel can get a price quote and be certain what it will pay for a ton. A company with temporary excess cash to invest for a short period of time can ascertain the interest rate it will earn. An investor purchasing a U.S. Treasury bill is virtually certain that he or she will be repaid in full at maturity.

However, when it comes to future impacts, few things are certain. We can define risk or uncertainty (we explain the difference between these two terms in chapter 12) as a chance or possibility that actual future outcomes will differ from those expected today. Actually we are usually only concerned with unfavorable results. Thus we can say that risk is the possibility that the outcomes of an action will turn out to be worse than expected. Typical of the types of risk that businesses face would include:

➤ Changes in demand and supply conditions
➤ Technological changes and the effect of competition
➤ Changes in interest rates and inflation rates
➤ Exchange rate changes for companies engaged in international trade
➤ Political risk for companies with foreign operations

You may not literally see the term *risk* in many of the chapters of this book. In some of the chapters we implicitly assume that we know the level of demand, the product price, production cost, and the economic profit resulting from operations. However, we really know that risk is present in most situations. In chapter 12, we show how businesses attempt to quantify risk and how decisions are made under these conditions, but this is not all. Chapter 5 deals with estimating the effects of changes in the variables that determine the demand for products. It also looks at predicting future results based on past experience, assuming we have sufficient historical data. It also talks about the challenges of estimating what may happen in the future if historical data do not exist. Furthermore, in chapter 15, we discuss the risks faced by companies in the semiconductor industry and specifically those encountered by Standard Microsystems Corporation (SMSC). As you see when you study this chapter, public companies such as SMSC must specify the risks they face when they prepare their annual 10-K report to the Securities and Exchange Commission. The more familiar you become with the risk sections of these reports, the more you will realize how difficult it is for managers to avoid risk. We believe that mastering the principles offered in this text will help present and future managers to rationally assess and deal with the various types of business risks that firms must address in the daily operations of their business.

THE ECONOMICS OF A BUSINESS

Another way to appreciate the study of managerial economics in a business curriculum is to consider how the material covered in this text relates to what we call the **economics of a business.** By this we mean "the key factors that affect the ability of a firm to earn an acceptable rate of return on its owners' investment." (See chapter 2 for a discussion of financial goals of a firm such as return on investment, profit maximization, and economic value added.) The most important of these factors are competition, technology, and customers.

The impact of changing economics on well-established companies can be better understood and appreciated within the framework of a four-stage model of change. This model is shown in Figure 1.2.

Stage I can be called "the good old days" for companies such as IBM, Kodak, Sears, and any number of other solid, blue-chip companies whose dominance of the market allowed them to achieve high profit margins by simply marking up their costs to provide them with a suitable level of profit. Then changes in technology, competition, and customers put pressures on their profit margins as well as market share and forced them into Stage II, where they sought refuge through cost cutting, downsizing,

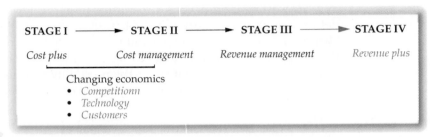

Figure 1.2   Four Stages of Change

restructuring, and reengineering. In the United States, this began to occur in the 1980s and continued on to the early 1990s, when consultants such as Michael Hammer touted the benefits of "reengineering" as a means of dealing with these changes.[9]

From the mid-1990s on, companies sought to enter Stage III when they realized that the continual focus on cost had its limits insofar as its ability to increase profits. After all, there is only so much money that a company can save by reducing its work-force or by becoming more efficient. Therefore, in Stage III "top-line growth" became the major focus.[10] Although companies may have reaffirmed their ability to grow their top line, Wall Street analysts questioned their ability to grow in a *profitable* manner. Thus Stage IV becomes a necessary part of a company's full recovery from the impact of changing economics.[11]

Avon is a good example of a well-established company that has gone through the first three stages and is seeking a firm footing in Stage IV. Stage I for Avon lasted until the latter part of the 1970s. As more and more women began to enter the workforce on a full-time basis, the effectiveness of Avon's vaunted sales force (the "Avon ladies") began to decline. In the 1980s, Avon chose to deal with this change by diversifying rather than taking the full brunt of cost cutting implied in Stage II. In the late 1980s, they were actually faced with the threat of a hostile takeover by Amway. By the early 1990s, Avon divested itself of its acquisitions and started its way through Stage II by consolidating its manufacturing facilities and call centers worldwide. In 1997, just about the time we were beginning work on the third edition of this text, Avon embarked on a substantial reengineering program that aimed to save it hundreds of millions of dollars. Because Avon had to make up for lost time due to its excursions into diversification, its entry into Stage III overlapped that of Stage II. The mid-1990s marked the beginning of Stage III, when Avon expanded aggressively into emerging markets such as China, India, Central Europe, and Russia. It also continued to grow in Latin America, a region of the world in which it had already developed a considerable amount of business. In their U.S. and Western European markets, Avon is spending more on marketing to improve and modernize the image of Avon products. For example, it recently opened "Avon Centre" in the fashionable Trump Tower building on Fifth Avenue in New York City.

In 1999, Avon appointed its first woman CEO, Andrea Jung, to lead the company into Stage IV. By early 2002, both stock analysts and the media seemed to agree that she and her team had done a solid job in improving both its growth and its profitability. Key moves included the development of retail channels of distribution, simplifying its line

---

[9]Michael Hammer and James Champy, *Reengineering the Corporation,* New York: HarperCollins, 1993.
[10]See, for example, Robert G. Cross, *Revenue Management,* New York: Broadway Books, 1997.
[11]See Ram Charan and Noel M. Tichy, *Every Business Is a Growth Business,* New York: Random House, 1998.

of products and focusing on some of its best-selling products. In addition, it launched a new line of cosmetics sold through the J.C. Penney stores and has also started to develop products for younger shoppers. Mindful of the opportunities as well as the threats of online shopping, Avon is trying to straddle its traditional direct sales channel and the "new economy" by encouraging its representatives to set up their own Web sites.[12] More recently, Avon's growth strategy has also involved the boosting of its brand image by using film star Salma Hayek as a spokesperson, heavily promoting the company's line of anti-aging creams and lotions, and launching a line of beauty products particularly for young women 16 to 24 years old. This last initiative involves women in this age group as potential sellers and buyers.[13]

In recent years, Avon's strategy of expanding in emerging markets is continuing to reap benefits. For example, revenue grew at about 25 percent per annum in China. There are now over 130,000 active Avon reps in that country. Avon has also expanded its product offerings in the teen market in mature markets.[14]

There are numerous other examples of well-established corporations that were forced by changes in customers, competition, or technology to go from Stage I to Stage II and have had to change their strategies in order to move on to Stages III and IV. In previous editions, we cited IBM, Sears, and Kodak as three of the more well-known examples of companies that experienced these changes. IBM, under the leadership of CEO Lou Gerstner, has been able to move from Stage II to Stage III primarily because of its expansion into services.[15] In fact, starting in 2003, its service business (including strategic outsourcing, maintenance, and consulting) comprised almost 50 percent of its total revenue. In 2002, it acquired PWC in order to further its aim of increasing the profitability of the service business.

In 1988, Sears was pushed down to the number 3 spot in general retail sales by Wal-Mart and Kmart. Over the past decade and a half, it has tried a number of different strategies to regain its preeminence. Right after it tumbled from number 1, it tried to compete directly with Wal-Mart with an "EDLP" (everyday low price) strategy. That failed and in 1991 it tried to reposition itself as a women's clothing store (e.g., "Come see the softer side of Sears"). In 2002, it purchased Lands' End with the expectation that this acquisition would boost both its in-store product line and its online shopping service.

During this same period of time, Kmart also felt the competitive effects of Wal-Mart to the point where, in January 2002, it had the largest bankruptcy filing in the history of the retail business. But in the next few years, Kmart CEO Eddie Lampert dramatically turned the company around. After taking the company out of Chapter 11, he announced plans to acquire Sears in an $11 billion deal. Some analysts were skeptical about whether this would be enough to compete against Wal-Mart, the warehouse clubs such as Costco and Sam's Club, and big specialty discounters such as Best Buy and Home Depot.[16] Sears still exists today but continues to struggle. Early in 2008,

---

[12]"A Makeover Has Avon Looking Good," *BusinessWeek*, January 22, 2002. Also see a cover story on Ms. Jung in *BusinessWeek*, September 18, 2000.

[13]Transcript of Avon Strategic Update Meeting 2003, reported by *Fair Disclosure*, March 28, 2003.

[14]Recent data on Avon are readily available on its Web site and public statements. See, for example, its Q3 Earnings Conference Call as reported in *Fair Disclosure Wire*, October 2007.

[15]For Gerstner's personal account of his years at IBM, see Lou V. Gerstner, Jr., *Who Says Elephants Can't Dance?* Harper Collins, 2002.

[16]Sears CEO, "Lands' End CEO-Merger Made in Synergy Heaven?," *CNN Financial News*, May 13, 2002. For an excellent summary of the strategic steps that Sears tried to take to fight back against Wal-Mart and the "big box" stores such as Best Buy and Home Depot, see "Sears Roebuck and Co. at Goldman Sachs Retail Conference Final," *Fair Disclosure Wire*, September 9, 2004. For the story on the Kmart-Sears merger, see "Eddie's Master Stroke," *BusinessWeek*, November 29, 2004.

Mr. Lambert announced that major changes in senior management, including the CEO, were going to be made. Plans were also underway for Sears to go through a major reorganization.[17]

Kodak has been struggling for more than a decade to establish a clear-cut strategy to help make the transition from its chemicals-based film business to the era of digital imaging. After undergoing a series of wrenching cuts in its workforce (from a peak of about 50,000 shortly after World War II to the current level of about 15,000) and a series of different strategies, Kodak finally seems to have made the necessary changes to survive and perhaps thrive in the digital era. Essentially, what its CEO Daniel Carp believes is that the winning strategy involves using the strong cash flow still being generated from its film, paper, and photofinishing businesses to build leadership in consumer markets for digital cameras, inkjet paper, online photofinishing, kiosks, and minilabs. The cash is also being used to help it compete in the industrial markets for medical imaging and commercial printing.[18]

In early 2008, Kodak announced a major product launch that its executives hope will propel the company into a new stage of growth. The product is an inkjet color printer that will be up to 50 percent lower in cost of total ownership (particularly the cost of the ink cartridge) than similar products from competitors such as Hewlett-Packard. According to CEO Antonio Perez (who once was the number 2 executive at H-P), "After today, the inkjet market will never be the same. We are changing the rules in this industry to ensure that consumers can affordably print what they want."[19]

The four stages of change model provides more than just a framework to judge current business events. The model also underscores the importance of various topics covered in this text. For example, in Stage I when the company dominates the market, the monopoly model whereby firms are free to price their products using the "MR = MC rule" (you learn about this in chapter 8) would be particularly useful. In Stage II, when the company must engage in cost cutting in response to changing competition, customers, and technology, the material in chapters 6 and 7 on cost and production and in chapter 8's section on highly competitive markets become vital to understand. In Stage III, when the company tries to grow its way out of its decline, chapters 4 and 5 provide critical information. These chapters cover the qualitative and quantitative analysis of demand, the keys to growing revenue. Finally in Stage IV, when the company strives for profitable growth, just about all the material in this text can prove helpful.

A BRIEF REVIEW OF IMPORTANT ECONOMIC TERMS AND CONCEPTS

For purposes of study and teaching, economics is divided into two broad categories: microeconomics and macroeconomics. The former concerns the study of individual consumers and producers in specific markets, and the latter deals with the aggregate economy. Topics in microeconomics include supply and demand in individual markets, the pricing of specific outputs and inputs (also called factors of production, or resources), production and cost structures for individual goods and services, and the distribution of income and output in the population. Topics in macroeconomics include analysis of the gross domestic product (also referred to as "national income

---

[17]See http://managementaschangeagent.blogspot.com/2008/01/lambert-indicates-new-direction-for.html.
[18]See "Kodak CFO Brust to Outline Expanded Digital Strategy," *M2 Presswire,* November 20, 2003, and "Eastman Kodak's Shift to Digital Paying Off," *Toronto Star,* September 23, 2004.
[19]See http://www.dpreview.com/news/0702/07020601kodakallinoneprinters.asp.

analysis"), unemployment, inflation, fiscal and monetary policy, and the trade and financial relationships among nations.

Microeconomics is the category that is most used in managerial economics. However, certain aspects of macroeconomics must also be included because decisions by managers of firms are influenced by their views of the current and future conditions of the macroeconomy. For example, we can well imagine that the management of a company producing capital equipment (e.g., computers, machine tools, trucks, or robotic instruments) would indeed be remiss if they did not factor into their sales forecast some consideration of the macroeconomic outlook. For these and other companies whose businesses are particularly sensitive to the business cycle, a recession would have an unfavorable effect on their sales, whereas a robust period of economic expansion would be beneficial. However, for the most part, managerial economics is based on the variables, models, and concepts that embody microeconomic theory.

As defined in the previous section, economics is the study of how choices are made regarding the use of scarce resources in the production, consumption, and distribution of goods and services. The key term is *scarce resources*. **Scarcity** can be defined as a condition in which resources are not available to satisfy all the needs and wants of a specified group of people. Although scarcity refers to the supply of a **resource,** it makes sense only in relation to the demand for the resource. For example, there is only one Mona Lisa. Therefore, we can safely say that the supply of this particular work of art by da Vinci is limited. Nevertheless, if for some strange reason no one wanted this magnificent work of art, then in purely economic terms it would not be considered scarce. Let us take a less extreme and certainly more mundane example: broken glass on the streets of New York City. Here we have a case of a "resource" that is not scarce not only because there is a lot of broken glass to be found, but also because nobody wants it! Now suppose there were a new art movement inspired by the use of materials retrieved from the streets of urban areas, with broken glass from the streets of New York being particularly desirable. The once-plentiful resource would fast become a "scarce" commodity.

The relative nature of scarcity is represented in Figure 1.3. As seen in Figure 1.3, the supply of resources is used to meet the demand for these resources by the population. Because the population's needs and wants exceed the ability of the resources to satisfy all the demands, scarcity exists.

In an introductory economics course, the concept of scarcity is usually discussed in relation to an entire country and its people. For example, you will probably recall from your first course in economics the classic example of "guns" (representing a country's devotion of resources to national defense) versus "butter" (representing the use of resources for peacetime goods and services). To be sure, scarcity is a condition with which individual consumers and producers must also deal. This text is primarily

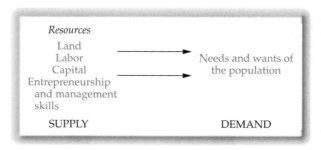

Figure 1.3 Supply, Demand, and Scarcity

concerned with the way in which managers of the producing organizations contend with scarcity. However, before discussing this particular aspect of the problem, let us review the condition of scarcity from the perspective of an entire country.

The intent of the "guns versus butter" example is to illustrate that scarcity forces a country to choose the amounts of resources that it wants to allocate between defense and peacetime goods and services. In so doing, its people must reckon with the **opportunity cost** of their decision. This type of cost can be defined as the amount or subjective value that must be sacrificed in choosing one activity over the next best alternative. In the "guns versus butter" example, one activity involves the production of war goods and services, and the other pertains to the production of peacetime goods and services. Because of the scarcity of resources, the more that the country allocates to guns, the less it will have to produce butter, and vice versa. The opportunity cost of additional units of guns are the units of butter that the country must forgo in the resource allocation process. The opposite would apply as resources are allocated more for the production of butter than for guns.

In the presence of a limited supply relative to demand, countries must decide how to allocate their scarce resources. This decision is central to the study of economics. In fact, economics has been defined as "the science which studies human behavior as a relationship between ends and scarce means which have alternative uses."[20] Essentially, the allocation decision can be viewed as comprising three separate choices:

1. *What* goods and services should be produced and in what quantities?
2. *How* should these goods and services be produced?
3. *For whom* should these goods and services be produced?

These are the well-known *what, how,* and *for whom* questions found in the introductory chapter of all economic principles textbooks.

The first question incorporates the "guns versus butter" decision. Should a country with scarce resources produce guns? Should it produce butter? If so, how much butter and how many guns? The same applies to the countless other goods and services or product groups that a country is capable of producing.

The second question involves the allocation of a country's resources in the production of a particular good or service. Suppose a country decides to produce a certain amount of butter. What amounts of land, labor, capital, and entrepreneurial efforts should it devote to this end? Should it use more workers than machinery (a labor-intensive process) or vice versa (a capital-intensive process)? The important point to remember about this question is that it is an economic and not a technical one. It is not asking which formula or recipe should be used to make butter; it is asking what combination of the factors of production should be used in producing a given amount of the product.

The meaning of the third question should be readily apparent. It is a decision that must be made about the distribution of a country's output of goods and services among the members of its population.

All countries must deal with these three basic questions because all have scarce resources. Scarcity is a more serious problem in some countries than in others, but all have needs and wants that cannot be completely met by their existing resources. Precisely how these countries go about making allocation decisions is the question to which we now turn.

---

[20]Lionel Robbins, *An Essay on the Nature and Significance of Economic Science,* 2nd ed., London: Macmillan, 1935, p. 16.

There are essentially three ways a country can answer the questions of what, how, and for whom. These ways, referred to as *processes,* are as follows:

1. **Market process:** The use of supply, demand, and material incentives to answer the questions of what, how, and for whom.

2. **Command process:** The use of the government or some central authority to answer the three basic questions. (This process is sometimes referred to as the *political process.*)

3. **Traditional process:** The use of customs and traditions to answer the three basic questions.

Countries generally employ a combination of these three processes to allocate their scarce resources. The market process is predominant in the United States, although the command process plays an important role. Hence, the United States is said to have a mixed economy. Based on the levels of spending by the federal, state, and local governments, we can state that approximately one-fifth of the goods and services produced in the United States are influenced by the command process. The command process does not necessarily mean that a government literally orders the production of certain amounts of guns, butter, or other goods or services; rather, a government may use the material incentives of the market process to allocate resources in certain ways, a process often referred to as *indirect command.* For example, the government offers defense contractors the opportunity to earn a profit by producing military goods and services. In addition, the government can control the allocation of resources in a more direct way through various laws governing the actions of both consumers and producers. For example, the government controls manufacturing and distribution through such agencies as the U.S. Food and Drug Administration. It attempts to control consumer use of certain foods and drugs through various laws and regulations. A simple but important example of this pertains to the tobacco industry. Over the past several decades, the U.S. government has made determined efforts to convince people to stop smoking. These efforts range from warnings on cigarette packages to the banning of smoking on airline flights. Prohibition during the 1920s offers another example of the government's efforts to stop the consumption of certain goods or services.

In addition to using rules and regulations and its fiscal power, the government can also influence the allocation of scarce resources through subsidies, tariffs, and quotas. Further discussion of these aspects of the command process in the U.S. economy is found in other sections of this chapter and throughout the text. In fact, Chapter 14 is devoted to a discussion of the role of government in the market economy.

The traditional process is also at work in the U.S. economy, but this process can be better understood by considering its impact on different countries throughout the world, particularly those whose economies are still developing. Examples of the traditional process are found in the eating habits, and in the patterns of work and social interaction, in such countries. Two examples of how the traditional process influences the allocation of scarce resources are religious restrictions on certain foods, such as beef and pork, and hiring practices based primarily on familial relationships. A branch of anthropology called economic anthropology is particularly concerned with the impact of customs and traditions on the economic questions of what, how, and for whom. In the business curriculum, students will find this subject of particular importance in courses on international business.

Because of the predominance of the market process in the U.S. economy, our discussion of the allocation of scarce resources is based on the assumption that managers operate primarily through the mechanisms of supply, demand, and material incentive (i.e., the profit motive). Their decisions about what goods to produce, how they should be produced, and for whom they should be produced are essentially market oriented. That is, firms choose to produce certain goods and services because, given the demand for these products and the cost of using scarce resources, they can earn sufficient profit to justify their particular use of these resources. Moreover, they combine their scarce resources to produce maximum output in the least costly way. Finally, they supply these goods and services to those segments of the population expected to provide the most material reward for their efforts.

Table 1.1 compares the three basic questions from the standpoint of a country and from the standpoint of a company, where they form the basis of the **economic decisions for the firm.** From the firm's point of view, question 1 is the product decision. At some particular time, a firm may decide to provide new or different goods or services or to stop providing a particular good or service. For example, consider Apple's decision to get into the business of music downloading and MP3 players. The Apple iPod is now the most profitable part of its product portfolio. The iPhone is another good example of new product development.

Another major decision involves the incumbent telephone companies such as Verizon, and AT&T entering the market for VoIP (Voice over Internet Protocol) services. This represents a drastically different kind of phone service than the one based on circuit switching that is currently the mainstay of the companies' business. Another good example of a company moving into another line of business is Dell's decision to go head to head with the likes of Hewlett-Packard and IBM in the market for printers. In fact, by changing its name from "Dell Computers" to simply "Dell," the company signaled its intention of going beyond just being a purveyor of PCs and servers.[21] As you see in chapter 2, Global Foods decides to sell bottled water in addition to carbonated soft drinks. Bottled water actually represents the fastest-growing segment of the nonalcoholic beverage market, and certainly our fictional company does not want to get left behind.

Question 2 is a basic part of a manager's responsibility. It involves personnel practices such as hiring and firing, as well as questions concerning the purchase of items ranging from raw materials to capital equipment. For example, the decision to automate certain clerical activities using a network of personal computers results in a more capital-intensive mode of production. The resolution to use more supplementary, part-time workers in place of full-time workers is another example of a management decision concerning how goods and services should be produced. A third example involves the selection of materials in the production of a certain item (e.g., the combination of steel, aluminum, and plastic used in an automobile).

The firm's decision concerning question 3 is not completely analogous to that of a country. Actually, a firm's decision regarding *market segmentation* (a term used in the marketing field) is closely related to question 1 for a country. In deciding on what

Table 1.1   The Three Basic Economic Questions

From the Standpoint of a Country	From the Standpoint of a Company
1. What goods and services should be produced?	1. The product decision
2. How should these goods and services be produced?	2. The hiring, staffing, procurement, and capital budgeting decisions
3. For whom should these goods and services be produced?	3. The market segmentation decision

---

[21] Adam Lashinsky, "Where Is Dell Going Next: After Eating Everyone's Lunch in the U.S. PC Biz, They're Now Aiming at Printers, Storage—and the World. Is Anybody Scared Yet?" *Fortune,* September 18, 2004.

segment of the market to focus, the firm is not literally deciding who gets the good or service. For example, suppose a firm decides to target a certain demographic segment by selling only a "high-end" or premium version of a product. However, the way in which a company markets the product (which includes its pricing and distribution policies) makes certain segments of the market more likely to purchase the product.

Perhaps one of the best ways to link the economic problem of making choices under conditions of scarcity with the tasks of a manager is to consider the view put forth by Professor Robert Anthony that a manager is essentially a person who is responsible for the allocation of a firm's scarce resources.[22]

It is interesting to note that "managers" or "management skills" was not delineated as a separate factor of production by early economic theorists. The four traditional categories of resources are land, labor, capital, and entrepreneurship. The last category can be treated as broad enough to include management, but the two classifications do involve different characteristics or skills.

The term *entrepreneurship* is generally associated with the ownership of the means of production. In addition, it implies willingness to take certain risks in the pursuit of goals (e.g., starting a new business, producing a new product, or providing a different kind of service). Management, in contrast, involves the ability to organize and administer various tasks in pursuit of certain objectives. An important part of a manager's job is to monitor and guide people in an organization. In the words of Peter Drucker, who has been called "the founding father of the science of management,"

> It is "management" that determines what is needed and what has to be achieved [in an organization]. . . . Management is work. Indeed, it is the specific work of a modern society, the work that distinguishes our society from all earlier ones. . . . As work, management has its own skills, its own tools, its own techniques.[23]

Part of being a good manager involves taking risks, so experts have advised managers to become more "entrepreneurial." By the same token, entrepreneurs may require professional management expertise to run their venture more effectively. Michael Dell, founder of Dell Computer Corporation, is perhaps one of the best examples of an entrepreneur who required professional management at some point in the development of his company. Back in the mid-1990s, Dell's rapid growth created serious process and control problems. To his credit, Michael Dell brought in seasoned executives from large corporations to help the company deal with these problems.

After professional managers came in, Dell went on to achieve considerable success. However, interestingly enough, by 2007, the situation seemed to have come full circle. Unfortunately, Dell's senior management did not fully realize the importance of the growth in the home computer market and the differences in buying behavior between businesses and consumers. Dell's success has been mainly in the "B2B" or business to business arena. As more homes began to have broadband connections, more consumers demanded laptops as well as desktop computers. Many people prefer to go to stores to actually try out their computers. Dell's direct sales model did not offer them this opportunity. Dell's main rival, H-P, bolstered by its acquisition of Compaq, came out with

---

[22]Actually, Anthony divided the planning and control process in a firm into three activities: strategic planning (i.e., setting the firm's overall objectives), management control (i.e., making sure scarce resources are obtained and used effectively and efficiently in the firm's accomplishment of its objectives), and operational control (i.e., making sure specific tasks are carried out effectively and efficiently). These ideas were first put forth in R. N. Anthony, *Planning and Control Systems: A Framework for Analysis,* Boston: Harvard Business School, Division of Research, 1965.

[23]Drucker, *Management,* p. xi.

an array of newly designed products that appealed to consumers and used their already established retail distribution network to sell these products. As a result, H-P surpassed Dell in computer sales. This prompted Michael Dell to return to active duty in the company. In early 2007, Dell's CEO Keven Rollins stepped down and Michael Dell once again become the company's CEO.[24]

Some economists cite management skills as a separate factor of production. Others include them in the general category of entrepreneurship. Still others combine entrepreneurship and management skills into one category, as we have done. An interesting treatment of the subject was given by Alfred Marshall, whose work in economic theory about 100 years ago still provides much of the foundation for modern microeconomics. Marshall used the building trade to illustrate certain differences between managerial and entrepreneurial skills and activities. According to Marshall, individuals may well be able to manage the construction of their own homes, even though they are less efficient than would be a professional contractor. However, it is another matter when housing construction is carried out on a large scale.

> When this [housing construction] is done on a large scale, as for instance in opening a new suburb, the stakes at issue are so large as to offer an attractive field to powerful capitalists with a very high order of general business ability, but perhaps with not much technical knowledge of the building trade. They rely on their own judgment for the decision as to what are likely to be the coming relations of demand and supply for different kinds of houses; but they entrust to others the *management of details* [emphasis added]. They employ architects and surveyors to make plans in accordance with their general directions, and then enter into contracts with professional builders for carrying them out. But they themselves *undertake the chief risks of the business* [emphasis added], and control its general direction.[25]

You may be somewhat surprised at the freshness of observations made a century ago. You may also believe that Marshall was referring simply to management tasks and responsibilities at different levels. Putting Marshall's ideas in terms of today's large corporation, what he refers to as "the decision as to what are likely to be the coming relations of demand and supply" most likely involves strategic decisions made by upper management. What he terms "the management of details" is usually carried out by lower levels of management (e.g., by first-line supervisors).

Regardless of how the classification is handled, it is important to be aware of the distinction between the two factors. Obviously, the content of this text is devoted to developing management skills. Nonetheless, a mastery of the economic principles presented in this book could well lead to a sharpening of one's entrepreneurial skills by helping assess the market conditions and risks involved in a particular venture.

THE CASE OF GLOBAL FOODS, INC.: SITUATIONS AND SOLUTIONS

Prior sections of this chapter cited various reasons why an understanding of economics is important to managerial decision making. An effective way of demonstrating this importance is to cite real-world examples gleaned from the popular press and distilled from the findings of research studies on the use of economics in managerial decision making. All other texts in managerial economics do this, and this book is no exception. In addition, we want to show how economic terms and

---

[24]See http://www.computerworld.com/action/article.do?command=viewArticleBasic&articleId=9009944.
[25]Alfred Marshall, *Principles of Economics,* 8th ed., Philadelphia: Porcupine Press, 1920, reprinted 1982, pp. 245–46. (First edition published in 1890.)

concepts can be applied to managerial decision making through the use of a series of hypothetical situations such as the one presented at the beginning of this chapter. In fact, each chapter begins with a *situation* requiring some sort of decision or action relating directly to the subject matter of the chapter. For example, in this chapter, a decision must be made about whether to enter the soft drink market. This is a fundamental business decision involving the allocation of a firm's scarce resources, a major theme of this chapter.

At the end of each chapter, a *solution* for the situation is presented based on the knowledge gained from reading the chapter. We use the term *solution* rather loosely because it may not involve a specific answer, as one might expect in the solution to a mathematical problem. In our view, the ambiguity of a solution is very much in keeping with conditions in the real world. Often in an actual business problem, there is no unique formula that one can use to compute the answer.[26] Either the formula does not exist or is not entirely applicable to the problem, or the problem itself is not amenable to a straightforward quantitative solution technique. Even when a specific numerical solution is achieved—as is the case in chapter 12 on capital budgeting—there may be other considerations of a qualitative nature that temper the acceptability of the solution. Therefore, the solutions offered at the end of the chapters are only suggested outcomes of the situations. (You may want to consider alternative ways for the managers depicted in the situations to deal with their tasks or problems.)

The situations used throughout the book are based on one industry and one firm in that industry. As you have already learned, we use the soft drink industry. Moreover, we follow the trials and tribulations of the managers of Global Foods, Inc., and, in certain cases, the managers of firms that do business with Global. This helps tie together the disparate aspects of economic analysis. Also, we believe that a focus on one firm in one industry creates added interest in the events depicted in the situations, further motivating mastery of each chapter's material.

A number of industries were initially considered. We chose the soft drink industry based on the following criteria:

1. The industry should be one that all readers can relate to as consumers.
2. The goods or services sold in the industry should be essentially nontechnical, and the means of production should be relatively easy for the layperson to understand.
3. The competitive environment should be intense.
4. Information about the industry should be readily available (e.g., from trade journals and research monographs), and news about current activities in this industry should be frequently reported in the popular media.

The soft drink industry closely meets all these criteria. Just about everyone consumes this product, and the product itself is rather simple: carbonated water, sweeteners, and various flavorings. The packaging is also uncomplicated. Soft drinks are sold today in 12-ounce aluminum cans, in 1- and 2-liter plastic bottles, and in glass bottles (particularly in foreign countries). The making of the syrup and the bottling of the beverage involve various manufacturing processes that are relatively easy to understand. The two most important trade publications in the soft drink industry are *Beverage World* and *Beverage Digest*. We found them to be excellent sources of background

---

[26]When Pepsi-Cola bought Quaker Oats primarily to gain ownership of that company's leading beverage brand, Gatorade, in 2001, analysts at first questioned the soundness of this decision because this brand only grew by 6 percent compared with its double-digit annual growth in the years leading up to the acquisition. But as of 2004, Pepsi seems to have made the right choice. Although sales of carbonated soft drinks have declined for both Pepsi and its archrival, Coca-Cola, Pepsi's noncarbonated products led by Gatorade have helped the company achieve a much faster growth rate than Coke. See, for example, Kurt Badenhausen, "Who's Got the Fizz: PepsiCo or Coca-Cola?" *Forbes*, September 18, 2004.

information on the industry. Moreover, the major soft drink companies are constantly reported on in major periodicals. Recent articles from these sources are cited throughout the text.

The situations used in each chapter, along with the characters portrayed at Global, are entirely fictitious. However, the features of each situation closely resemble actual business problems or circumstances that managers must often address. The verity of the issues involved in each situation is based on the authors' experiences in private industry, as well as on extensive interviews with managers from various companies in the soft drink business. The following section gives a summary of the situations and solutions presented in the chapters. The main decisions to be made by the characters portrayed in the situations are included under the heading "Key Question."

SUMMARY OF THE SITUATIONS AND SOLUTIONS

1 INTRODUCTION

Situation: Bob Burns, CEO of Global Foods, Inc., asks the board of directors to approve a decision to enter the soft drink business.
Key Question: "Should we enter the soft drink business?"
Solution: The board approves the decision, and Global Foods enters the soft drink business.

2 THE FIRM AND ITS GOALS

Situation: In an effort to increase the company's revenues, Bob Burns considers entry into the bottled water market, the fastest-growing segment of the nonalcoholic beverage industry.
Key Question: "How can we improve the value of our company when the Wall Street analysts are judging us primarily on our ability to grow our revenue and profit?"
Solution: Bob decides to take Global Foods into the bottled water business.

3 SUPPLY AND DEMAND

Situation: Bob Burns, CEO, and Nicole Goodman, vice president of marketing, consider developing and launching a product line of gourmet tea.
Key Question: "What are the current and future supply and demand conditions in the consumer market for premium and specialty tea?"
Solution: Anecdotal information and a survey of articles in trade journals and business periodicals indicate that tea could be the next "big thing" in the U.S. beverage industry. However, Bob is not completely convinced and asks Nicole to do further quantitative analysis of the supply and demand for tea.

4 DEMAND ELASTICITY

Situation: Henry Caulfield, the proprietor of a Gas 'n Go convenience store, must evaluate the desirability of various pricing schedules for soft drinks set by the major beverage companies.
Key Question: "For what price should I sell this new soft drink?"
Solution: He decides that the relative inelasticity of the products in question makes it difficult to increase sales by lowering the price.

5 DEMAND ESTIMATION AND FORECASTING

Situation: Frank Robinson, newly appointed head of Global's forecasting department, is asked to estimate the next year's sales of Citronade, the company's lemon-lime soda.

Key Question: "What will next year's sales for Citronade be?"

Solution: Frank uses a trend analysis, adjusted seasonally as well as cyclically, to forecast the coming year's sales.

6   **THE THEORY AND ESTIMATION OF PRODUCTION**

Situation: Christopher Lim, production manager, is concerned about the best way to bottle the water that the company now intends to sell. To differentiate Global Foods' product in a highly competitive market, the marketing people want to use glass bottles. In Chris's view, this may help in the marketing of the product, but may well increase production costs significantly.

Key Question: "Should we package the water in glass bottles?"

Solution: Chris recommends that plastic bottles should be used to package both the carbonated soft drink and the bottled water products.

7   **THE THEORY AND ESTIMATION OF COST**

Situation: Shayna Soda Company, an independent bottler of Global Foods soft drinks, is looking for new ways to increase the profitability of its soda production. Adam Michaels, the plant manager, receives a marketing flyer from a new potential supplier in the next state, Lawrence Aluminum Products.

Key Question: "Should the company stay with its current main supplier in the next town, Kayla Containers, Inc., or switch to this new supplier?"

Solution: Shayna Soda Co. decides to stay with Kayla Containers, Inc., after considering all the other factors involved in the switch. Raw material costs were lower with Lawrence Aluminum, but other associated costs resulted in a net increase.

8   **PRICING AND OUTPUT DECISIONS: PERFECT COMPETITION AND MONOPOLY**

Situation: Frank Robinson is appointed product manager of the new bottled water product. One of his first tasks is to recommend a price for the product.

Key Question: "What price should we charge for our new product?"

Solution: After analyzing the demand elasticity and short-run cost structure of the product, Frank recommends a price based on the MR = MC rule.

8   **APPENDIX B   BREAK-EVEN ANALYSIS (VOLUME–COST–PROFIT)**

Situation: Suzanne Prescott, a senior analyst for the bottled water division, is asked to prepare a profit plan for the coming year.

Key Question: "What is the profit outlook for the coming year for our bottled water product, Waterpure?"

Solution: She uses break-even analysis to forecast the coming year's profit for this product. She also uses sensitivity analysis to provide best-case and worst-case scenarios.

9   **PRICING AND OUTPUT DECISIONS: MONOPOLISTIC COMPETITION AND OLIGOPOLY**

Situation: The management committee of Global Foods asks Frank to reconsider his pricing recommendation because his analysis did not take into account certain competitive and market issues.

Key Question: "What is the best price for a product, given its demand, cost, and competition?"

Solution: After much debate, the management committee, with Frank's additional help, decides to set the price of its product slightly lower than the premium-priced competitors but slightly higher than the "value brands."

10   SPECIAL PRICING PRACTICES

Situation: Rebecca James must decide what price bid she should submit to a large airport caterer that wants to award a contract to a single supplier.

Key Question: "How should the bid price be set to give Global Foods a good shot at obtaining the large caterer's contract?"

Solution: Because demand elasticities differ in different markets, the price offered in this price-sensitive market will have to be sufficiently low to give Global a good chance of winning the contract.

11   GAME THEORY AND ASYMMETRIC INFORMATION

Situation: Henry Caulfield's daughter, Erica, believes she can help her father better understand and anticipate the pricing reactions of his closest competitors by applying to his business some of the principles of game theory that she learned in her college business courses.

Key Question: "How can managers deal with dynamic business conditions in which their decisions often trigger reactions by their competitors?"

Solution: Although game theory can help Henry understand the underlying dynamics of his pricing tactics against his competitors, in practical terms it falls short of providing him with a definite solution about what to do.

12   CAPITAL BUDGETING AND RISK

Situation: George Kline, the manager of Global's capital planning department, is considering a proposal for the expansion of company activities into a new geographical region.

Key Question: "Should we expand into a new geographical area?"

Solution: Using capital budgeting techniques involving the calculation of net present value and internal rate of return, George recommends that the firm accept the project. He also performs a scenario analysis to present an optimistic and a pessimistic set of results.

13   THE MULTINATIONAL CORPORATION AND GLOBALIZATION

Situation: Global is interested in investing in a plant in one of the countries that were formerly part of the Soviet sphere. George Kline, manager of Global's capital planning department, is asked to conduct a capital budgeting analysis of an existing plant in the Czech Republic.

Key Question: "Should Global make an investment in a plant in the Czech Republic?"

Solution: George calculates the NPV and IRR for both the subsidiary and for the parent company. Although the results for the subsidiary are favorable, the NPV for the parent is negative. He therefore recommends that the company should not make the investment at this time.

14   THE ROLE OF GOVERNMENT IN THE MARKET ECONOMY

Situation: About five years ago, Bill Adams, the CIO of Global Foods, Inc., was asked by CEO Bob Burns to consider outsourcing the companies' voice and data network. As it turned out, the company signed a ten-year contract with AT&T for this service. About four years into the contract, Bill was not completely satisfied with the way the service was being provided. He asked his staff to reconsider the terms and conditions of the contract.

Key Questions: "Government deregulation has provided more options for a company in certain industries such as telecommunications. Is this always in the best interest of the company? What are some of the costs and benefits for outsourcing that were made possible by government deregulation?"

Solution: After weighing the costs and benefits of the outsourcing that was made possible by government deregulation, Bill decides to stay with AT&T for the balance of the contract.

15   MANAGERIAL ECONOMICS IN ACTION: THE CASE OF THE SOFT DRINK INDUSTRY

Situation: Amy Roberts, Global Foods' newly appointed brand manager for one of its products, Spritz soda, is asked by her boss, Fred Duchesne, to develop a business plan for rejuvenating the growth and profitability of this brand.

Key Question: What are the important factors that affect this brand's production, cost, and consumer demand? Based on this analysis, what steps should Amy and her team take to increase this product's revenue and profit growth?

Solution: Amy develops a plan to grow the revenue of Spritz soda by developing a "high energy" version of this product. Her manager is impressed with her proposal but asks her to provide a more solid economic justification for this new product launch.

GLOBAL APPLICATION: REINVENTING THE CORPORATION THROUGH STRATEGY AND OWNERSHIP

In the previous edition, we introduced in this section the case of two companies, Western Union and VNU, that appeared to be very successful in reinventing themselves as a result of major changes in the "economics of their business." Recall from reading this chapter that by this we mean changes in one or more of the following factors: customers, technology, competition, and in certain industries, government regulation.

Western Union began well over a hundred years ago when long distance communication by telegraph had just begun. The changes in technology since that time are quite obvious, and so if the company had not started to branch out from the telegraph, it soon would have gone out of business. The company eventually went into the money transfer business as a way of diversifying. A brief historical survey of Western Union's activities provides a good illustration of the importance of reinvention in a global environment.

1851: Western Union's predecessor company, the New York and Mississippi Valley Printing Telegraph Company, is formed by a group of businessmen in Rochester, NY.

1856: The New York and Mississippi Valley Printing Telegraph Company changes its name to Western Union Telegraph Company, signifying the acquisition of various competing firms.

1861: Completes the first transcontinental telegraph line, providing fast communications during the Civil War.

1871: Introduces Western Union Money Transfer (registered trademark) service, which soon becomes the company's primary business.

1914: Introduces the first consumer charge card.

1933: Introduces singing telegrams.

1970: Offers next-day delivery via postal service.

1974: Launches Westar I, the first domestic communications satellite.

1989: Launches Quick Collect (registered trademark), a service that provides creditors with a fast and secure method for collecting delinquent accounts via flat-rate money transfers. Also, Rapid Money Transfer service becomes available outside North America.

1992: Initiates Western Union money order service.

1993: Introduces *Dinero en Minutos* (registered trademark), making funds sent from the United States to Mexico available in minutes.

1994–95: Becomes part of First Data Corporation.

2000: Launches www.westernunion.com as a means of transferring funds over the Internet.

2001: Celebrates 150th anniversary, has a network of more than 100,000 agent locations around the world.[27]

As you can see, Western Union was helped immensely when First Data, a major processor of credit card transactions, bought it in 1994. The corporate resources of First Data helped to sustain and grow Western Union's business. Today, it is the leading provider of money transfer services, including transactions over the Internet. Its business is spurred on by the increasing number of immigrant workers in countries throughout the world (particularly the United States) who send their hard-earned money back home to their families. It appears that the saga continues for this success story in corporate reinvention. In 2006, First Data announced that it was going to spin off Western Union. Today Western Union is a separate company whose shares trade on the stock market.

The other company we cited as a success story in reinventing itself is VNU. From a Dutch publishing company, it transformed itself over the past decade into a leading global provider of marketing and media information. The divestiture of much of its book publishing and yellow pages businesses and the acquisition of ACNielsen and Nielsen Media Research provided the foundation for this reinvention. However, in 2005, the company decided to use its surplus cash to buy IMS, a company specializing in the collection and analysis of data involving purchasing of prescription medicine. Leading shareholders of VNU vehemently protested and the CEO was forced to step down from his job. Shortly afterward, VNU was bought by a consortium of private equity companies. Today it is a privately held company. The case of VNU illustrates how difficult it is to sustain the reinvention and growth of a company operating in markets with changing customers, technology, and competition. The case of Western Union illustrates that a company that has experienced quite a lot of change in its economics can no longer count on the corporate support of a larger entity.

The Solution

After about an hour of heated debate, Bob had a suggestion to make to the board. "Look, we've been discussing this to such an extent that perhaps the key arguments I made in my presentation have gotten lost or confused. Let me summarize the seven key reasons why we want to enter the soft drink business, and then let's vote on this matter.

1. *Outlook for the industry:* Prospects for growth in the industry continue to be strong. Therefore, we can expect the demand for our products to be a part of this positive industry trend.
2. *Market size and structure:* Although the industry is dominated by Coca-Cola and Pepsi-Cola, we believe there is still room for the entry of niche marketers. A number of regional and specialty companies have emerged over the past few years, particularly those offering sparkling fruit juices. We believe we can be as successful, if not more successful, than these new entrants.
3. *Manufacturing, packaging, and distribution:* Our experience in the manufacturing of food products will give us a significant head start when we enter the soft drink business. Moreover, we do not plan to build bottling facilities from scratch. Instead, we look to purchase and consolidate existing bottling plants currently owned and operated by independent firms or by multiple franchise operations. We are also encouraged by the number of new cost-

(continued)

---

[27]These were taken, some almost verbatim, from the Western Union Web site. Only certain highlights were selected for this section. For a full listing, click on "About Us" and then "History."

(continued)

reducing technologies that have been introduced and the fact that the cost of the artificial sweetener aspartame should decline now that Monsanto's patent has expired.

4. *Transportation and distribution:*   We already have a well-managed fleet of vehicles that deliver our food products. We also have important influence and contacts in the retail food business. These will be essential in establishing a presence on the shelves of supermarkets and convenience stores throughout the country.

5. *Pricing, advertising, and promotion:*   As the 'new kid on the block,' we recognize that we will have to enter the market as a price follower. However, in time, as our products are developed and marketed, we should be able to establish some independence either to raise or lower our prices in comparison with the rest of the industry. As far as advertising and promotion are concerned, we have an excellent advertising agency that has served us well with our current product line. However, we shall be flexible enough to consider other agencies if the need arises. Moreover, our experience with various promotional programs (e.g., discount coupons through direct mail and magazine inserts) should be transferable to the soft drink industry. Most important, all advertising and promotional efforts should be greatly aided by the fact that our company name—Global Foods—enjoys a high degree of consumer recognition (along with the specific brand names of our products).

6. *New products:*   As you have seen in the detailed report, we have exciting plans for several new products as well as a full line of naturally and artificially sweetened carbonated drinks. Through an independent market research company, we have tested consumer preferences for our new offerings. The results have been most satisfactory.

7. *Financial considerations:*   As stated at the very beginning of this presentation, our main goal is to create value for our shareholders. We must continue to grow in a profitable manner if we are to continue satisfying the financial expectations of our shareholders. We compete in a mature industry that enables us to generate a considerable amount of cash from our current line of products with well-entrenched brand names. We believe that we should use this cash to expand into the soft drink business. As all our financial projections and analyses indicate, this effort should yield a rate of return that is more than enough to compensate us for the investment and its associated risk."

After giving this executive summary, Bob Burns asked the board for a final decision. "All right, let's vote. All those in favor of entering the soft drink market? Opposed? Great, it's unanimous. Ladies and gentlemen, we're going into the soft drink business."

SUMMARY

Managerial economics is a discipline that combines microeconomic theory with management practice. Microeconomics is the study of how choices are made to allocate scarce resources with competing uses. An important function of a manager is to decide how to allocate a firm's scarce resources. Examples of such decisions are the selection of a firm's products or services, the hiring of personnel, the assigning of personnel to particular functions or tasks, the purchase of materials and equipment, and the pricing of products and services. This text shows how the application of economic theory and concepts helps managers make allocation decisions that are in the best economic interests of their firms.

Throughout the text, numerous examples are cited to illustrate how economic theory and concepts can be applied to management decision making. References are also made to business cases and economic events that have been reported in the popular press. However, a unique feature of this book is a unifying case study of a food and beverage company, Global Foods, Inc. Each chapter begins with a situation in which the managers of this firm have to make key economic decisions. The solutions that end the chapters suggest ways that economic analysis can assist in the decision-making process.

IMPORTANT CONCEPTS

Command process.   The use of central planning and the directives of government authorities to answer the questions of *what, how,* and *for whom.* (p. 11)

Economic decisions for the firm.   "What goods and services should be produced?"—the product decision. "How should these goods and services be produced?"—the hiring, staffing, and capital-budgeting decision. "For whom should these goods and services be produced?"—the market segmentation decision. (p. 12)

Economics.   The study of how choices are made under conditions of scarcity. The basic economic problem can be defined as: "What goods and services should be produced and in what quantities?" "How should these goods and services be produced?" "For whom should these goods and services be produced?" (p. 2)

Economics of a business.   The key factors that affect the ability of a firm to earn an acceptable rate of return on its owners' investment. The most important of these factors are competition, technology, and customers. (p. 5)

Managerial economics.   The use of economic analysis to make business decisions involving the best use of a firm's scarce resources. (p. 2)

Market process.   The use of supply, demand, and material incentives to answer the questions of *what, how,* and *for whom.* (p. 11)

Opportunity cost.   The amount or subjective value forgone in choosing one activity over the next best alternative. This cost must be considered whenever decisions are made under conditions of scarcity. (p. 10)

Resources.   Also referred to as *factors of production* or *inputs,* economic analysis usually includes four basic types: land, labor, capital, and entrepreneurship. This chapter also includes managerial skills and entrepreneurship. (p. 9)

Scarcity.   A condition that exists when resources are limited relative to the demand for their use. In the market process, the extent of this condition is reflected in the price of resources or the goods and services they produce. (p. 9)

Traditional process.   The use of customs and traditions to answer the questions of *what, how,* and *for whom.* (p. 11)

QUESTIONS

1. Define *scarcity* and *opportunity cost.* What role do these two concepts play in the making of management decisions?
2. Elaborate on the basic economic questions of *what, how,* and *for whom.* Provide specific examples of these questions with respect to the use of a *country's* scarce resources.
3. Following are examples of typical economic decisions made by the managers of a firm. Determine whether each is an example of *what, how,* or *for whom.*
   a. Should the company make its own spare parts or buy them from an outside vendor?
   b. Should the company continue to service the equipment that it sells or ask customers to use independent repair companies?
   c. Should a company expand its business to international markets or concentrate on the domestic market?
   d. Should the company replace its own communications network with a "virtual private network" that is owned and operated by another company?
   e. Should the company buy or lease the fleet of trucks that it uses to transport its products to market?
4. Define the market process, the command process, and the traditional process. How does each process deal with the basic questions of *what, how,* and *for whom?*
5. Discuss the importance of the command process and the traditional process in the making of management decisions. Illustrate specific ways in which managers must take these two processes into account.
6. Explain the differences between management skills and entrepreneurship. Discuss how each factor contributes to the economic success of a business.
7. Compare and contrast microeconomics with macroeconomics. Although managerial economics is based primarily on microeconomics, explain why it is also important for managers to understand macroeconomics.

8. What do you think is the key to success in the soft drink industry? What chance do you think Global Foods has in succeeding in its new venture into the soft drink market? Explain. (Answer these questions on the basis of the information provided in the chapter and any other knowledge you might have about the food and beverage business.)

9. Essentially, what do you think are the changing aspects of the economics (i.e., customers, technology, and competition) of the following industries?
   a. Telecommunications
   b. Retail merchandising
   c. Higher education
   d. Airlines

10. (Optional) Have you been personally involved in the making of a decision for a business concerning *what, how,* or *for whom?* If so, explain your rationale for making such decisions. Were these decisions guided by the market process, the command process, or the traditional process? Explain.

The Firm and Its Goals

Learning Objectives

Upon completion of this chapter, readers should be able to:

- Understand the reasons for the existence of firms and the meaning of transaction costs.

- Explain the economic goals of the firm and optimal decision making.

- Describe the meaning of the "principal-agent" problem.

- Distinguish between "profit maximization" and the "maximization of the wealth of shareholders."

- Demonstrate the usefulness of Market Value Added® and Economic Value Added.®

The Situation

Bob Burns looked over the last few numbers provided to him in a consultant's report on the soft drink industry, closed the binder, and turned to Nicole Goodman, Global Foods' vice president of marketing. "Looking back, our decision to get into the soft drink industry was a good one, but who would have thought that an industry that showed such strong growth in the early 1990s would start to peak so soon? Also, we should have known that the two leading brands wouldn't stand still while we tried to increase our market share. Coke has been very successful with its Sprite® against Cadbury-Schweppes' 7-Up®, and it seems that they will launch a rival brand to Cadbury's Dr Pepper®. I think we need to get into a growing market.

"An idea occurred to me recently when I was watching the Yankees-Mets baseball game on television. When one of the Yankee players returned to the dugout after hitting a home run, he didn't go to the water cooler, but instead picked up a bottle of water. I already knew that bottled water was the fastest-growing segment of the beverage industry, and statistics I've seen since reinforce this. We must get into this market while it's still growing."

"I hate to say this, Bob, but it may be a case of 'too little, too late,'" said Nicole. "Established companies such as Perrier have been around for a long time; Perrier also owns strong American brands such as Poland Spring, Deer Park, and Calistoga. Evian, which is owned by the French company Danone, has also been quite successful in the United States. I am afraid that if we entered the market we would start way behind."

"I'm not prepared to give up so easily, Nicole," replied Bob. "We have good distribution channels, bottling know-how, and marketing savvy. This business is close to our core competency and it is still growing. We have told analysts that we expect to grow at a 10 percent rate in revenue and even more in profits, given our tight cost controls. At our upcoming shareholder meeting, our shareholders and the analysts will be expecting to hear our plans for further business expansion. In the past, we did it with the help of soft drinks, and now is the time to grow our beverage division with bottled water."

INTRODUCTION

Chapter 1 explains that managerial economics deals primarily with the problem of deciding how best to allocate a firm's scarce resources among competing uses. The best or optimal decision is the one that enables the firm to meet its desired objectives most closely. This chapter elaborates on the process of making decisions under conditions of scarcity by discussing the goals of a firm and the economic significance of the optimal decision. An online appendix explains the role of marginal analysis in economic decision making. This appendix also presents a review of the mathematics used in this text to illustrate key economic concepts and methods of analysis.

The major portion of this chapter is devoted to a discussion of the goals of the firm. However, to carry on this discussion sensibly, we must first define and explain *the firm*.

THE FIRM

The traditional (neoclassical) theory of economics defined the **firm** as a collection of resources that is transformed into products demanded by consumers. The costs at which the firm produces are governed by the available technology, and the amount it produces and the prices at which it sells are influenced by the structure of the markets in which it operates. The difference between the revenue it receives and the costs it incurs is *profit*. It is the aim of the firm to maximize its profit.

The preceding theory assumes the existence of the firm. But this leaves the reason for its existence unanswered. Why does a firm perform certain functions internally and others through the market? It appears that the size of the firm is not determined strictly by technological considerations. Then why are some firms small and others large?

Answers to the preceding questions began to appear in 1937 when Ronald Coase postulated that a company compares costs of organizing an activity internally with the cost of using the market system for its transactions.[1]

If there were no costs of dealing with the outside market, a firm would be organized so all its transactions would be with the outside. However, it is incorrect to assume the marketplace does not involve any costs. In dealing through the market, the firm incurs **transaction costs**.

Transaction costs are incurred when a company enters into a contract with other entities. These costs include the original investigation to find the outside firm, followed by the cost of negotiating a contract, and later, enforcing the contract and coordinating transactions. Transaction costs are influenced by uncertainty, frequency of recurrence, and asset specificity.[2]

Uncertainty, the inability to know the future perfectly, increases transaction costs because it is not possible to include all contingencies in a contract, particularly a long-term contract. Frequent transactions also tend to make it necessary for explicit contracts to exist.

But probably the most important of these characteristics is asset specificity. If a buyer contracts for a specialized product with just one seller, and furthermore, if the product necessitates the use of some specialized machinery, the two parties become tied to one another. In this case, future changes in market conditions (or in production technology) may lead to **opportunistic behavior**, where one of the parties seeks to take advantage of the other. In such cases, transaction costs will be very high.

---

[1]The seminal work in this area was by Ronald H. Coase in "The Nature of the Firm," *Economica*, 4 (1937), pp. 386–405, reprinted in R. H. Coase, *The Firm, the Market and the Law*, Chicago: University of Chicago Press, 1988, pp. 33–55. Coase was awarded the Nobel Prize in Economics in 1991.
[2]Much of this discussion is based on Oliver E. Williamson, "Transaction-Cost Economics: The Governance of Contractual Relations," *Journal of Law and Economics*, 22 (October 1979), pp. 233–61.

When transaction costs are high, a company may choose to provide the service or product itself. However, carrying out operations internally creates its own costs. A major cost is that, in hiring workers to do the work within the firm, the firm incurs monitoring and supervision costs to ensure the work is done efficiently. Quite possibly, employees who work for a fixed wage or salary may have less incentive to work efficiently than an outside contractor.

Employers will try to decrease monitoring costs by using incentives to increase employees' output. Among such incentives are bonuses, benefits, and perquisites ("perks"). Another popular incentive is to provide workers with the possibility of stock ownership, using stock options and employee stock plans. Stock ownership is also used to attract new employees. Such employees will, of course, benefit when the company is profitable and its stock increases in value. However, incentives come with a price tag.

The trade-off between external transaction costs and the cost of internal operations can be shown on the simple graph in Figure 2.1. When a company operates at the vertical axis, all its operations are conducted with the outside. As we move to the right on this graph, the firm substitutes internal for external operations. The cost of external transactions decreases, while the cost of internal operations increases. The total cost is the vertical summation of the two costs, and it decreases at first as the company finds that internalizing some operations is efficient. However, as more of the operations are internalized, some efficiency is lost, and the total cost begins to rise again. The company will choose to allocate its resources between external transactions and internal operations so the total cost is at a minimum, which in this case will occur about midway between the two extremes.

If transaction costs for a specific product or service are higher than the costs of carrying on the activity internally, then a company benefits from performing this particular task in-house. An independent firm may not find it profitable to produce a product if only one or few customers demand it. However, as markets expand, the demand for a product or service, which may have been limited in the past, now

Figure 2.1   Trade-off Between Transaction Costs and Internal Operating Costs

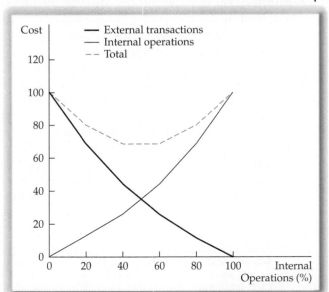

expands. This will permit new firms to specialize in activities that previously had to be performed by the firm that needed this task to be performed. Thus new companies and industries come into existence. This is true not only in the case of products, but also for services that at one time were performed by the firm itself and are now produced by independent firms—for example, cleaning services, security services, and cafeterias are often now run by specialized firms. Another example would be the college bookstore that is operated by one of the large companies in the book industry. This idea is actually rather old. It really started with Adam Smith, who stated that "the division of labor is limited by the extent of the market." George Stigler discussed this point in a 1951 article, and concluded that as industries expand, companies that previously had produced everything internally will tend to experience "vertical disintegration."[3] What has happened, of course, is that transaction costs have decreased and that the possibility of "opportunistic behavior" has also diminished.

Although the outsourcing of peripheral, noncore activities has been around for a long time, the outsourcing of a business's core activities is a somewhat more recent activity. In the past we have seen the outsourcing of private-label or house-brand merchandise. However, now the outsourcing of highly technical products and services is widespread. The term "offshoring" is generally used when a company sources its product in a foreign country.

Thus, for instance, "80 percent of Kodak's reloadable cameras and all of its digital cameras are sourced in Asia." "Compaq computer [prior to its merger with Hewlett-Packard] made only about 10 percent of the computers it sold to consumers." This is a very different situation from that which existed in the earlier part of the twentieth century, when Ford made its own tires, steel, and glass.[4]

At one time, the IBM Corporation's principal and almost exclusive product was computer hardware. This has changed over the past years. Today more than one-half of IBM's revenue derives from services. Its Global Services segment consists of Global Technology Services, which provides outsourcing infrastructure services, and Global Business Services, which provides professional services such as consulting, systems integration, and applications management services. The external revenue of Global Services in 2007 was $54.1 billion, or over 55 percent of total external revenue. At the same time, the company outsources much of its manufacturing to contract manufacturing companies around the world to manufacture IBM-designed products.[5] IBM's personal computers were built and assembled by many different companies before IBM sold its entire PC division to Lenovo Group Limited in December 2004.

Another venue for outsourcing is human relations. Payroll administration has long been handled by outside firms. Now, some companies use third-party services for recruitment, health care, benefits, pensions, and many other activities. Thus, for instance, in 1999 BP Amoco turned over many of its HR functions to Exult, a Texas firm, with a 5-year, $600 million contract. In the fall of 2000, Bank of America contracted with Exult to handle its human relations functions, signing a 10-year, $1.1 billion contract.[6]

An even more recent phenomenon is the transfer of white-collar jobs to foreign countries where salaries and wages are lower. Although the opening of call centers has been occurring for some time, there has been a wave of outsourcing (offshoring)

---

[3]George J. Stigler, "The Division of Labor Is Limited by the Extent of the Market," *Journal of Political Economy*, 59 (June 1951), pp. 185–93.
[4]This paragraph is based on Kerry A. Dolan and Robyn Meredith, "Cover Story," *Forbes*, April 30, 2001, pp. 106–12.
[5]International Business Machines Corporation, *Annual Report*, 2007.
[6]Doug Garr, "Inside Out-Sourcing," *Fortune*, Summer 2001, pp. 85–92.

of some highly technical jobs, particularly in the production of software. New companies have been appearing in many countries that supply software services. India is probably the largest supplier of these services because it has a large, well-educated labor force and salaries tend to be a fraction of those in the United States and other western countries.

Quite recently, U.S. companies and legal firms have started to ship legal work to India. It is estimated that the Indian legal services industry will grow from $140 million in 2006 to $640 million in 2010. Some large U.S. companies even have in-house legal departments in India. A leading Indian legal services company is Pangea3. About 80 percent of its clients are corporations and 20 percent are law firms.[7] Accounting firms are now also transferring some of their less complicated work to foreign countries. In the United Kingdom, Ernst and Young, one of the major accounting firms, announced that it will recruit 200 workers in Bangalore to process tax returns.[8] We return to the subject of offshoring later in this book, in chapters 6 and 13.

Coase and the Internet

When Ronald Coase wrote his article in 1937, he and the rest of the world knew nothing about the advent of the Internet in the last years of the twentieth century. However, his contribution to economic theory turns out to have great relevance to today's business transactions over the Internet. If you should surf the Internet and type in the following keywords, "Transaction costs Coase Internet" you will get a large number of hits attesting to today's popularity of Coase's ideas.

The basic idea of the trade-off between the costs of internal operations and external transactions remains as valid as ever. But the revolutionary event that occurred in recent years is that the Internet has caused transaction costs to decrease drastically, making it easier and more efficient for companies to curtail their own operations and farm out much of the work they would have been performing to outside companies that specialize in specific operations.

As mentioned previously, transaction costs include the cost of search and investigation, contract negotiations, and coordination or enforcement. How has the Internet impacted these transactions and their costs?

Search and investigation have been made significantly easier. Potential suppliers can be quickly and easily identified. Information on their reliability and credit standing is readily available, and so are evaluations of their financial conditions. "Online clearing houses . . . permit a purchaser to contract for price, quality and delivery dates with few clicks of the mouse," making contracting a much easier task. As far as coordinating costs are concerned, it is now much more simple to follow a shipment as it progresses toward its location, and to take action in real time, if this should become necessary.[9]

Although Coase has stated that he is not paying much attention to e-commerce, he believes that understanding transaction costs in the new economy "enables you to have more specialization and greater production, because you are more efficient. You'll get more small firms as a result, but large firms will also get larger, because they can concentrate on core activities and contract out what they can't do well."[10]

---

[7]Cynthia Cots and Liane Kufchock, "India Wins Rising Share of Legal Work from U.S.," *International Herald Tribune*, August 22, 2007.
[8]Vanessa Houlder, "E&Y Sends Compliance Work Offshore," *Financial Times*, July 12, 2007.
[9]This section, including the direct quotation, is based on Don Tapscott, David Ticoll, and Alex Lowy, "Internet Nirvana," *eCompany Now*, December 2000, pp. 98ff.
[10]Bob Tedeschi, "Coase's Ideas Flourish in the Internet Economy," *New York Times*, October 2, 2000.

We end this discussion with the conclusion that a firm will trade off costs incurred in conducting transactions with the outside market with the costs of internalizing such transactions in order to minimize the combination of the two. This is consistent with the overall economic goals of the firm, the subject to which we turn next.

THE ECONOMIC GOAL OF THE FIRM AND OPTIMAL DECISION MAKING

Every business has a goal. Most students would assert that the primary goal of a business is to earn a certain amount of profit (i.e., to "make money"), and, in fact, the economic theory of the firm—the foundation on which much of managerial economics rests—assumes the principal objective of a firm is to maximize its profits (or minimize its losses).[11] Thus, throughout this text, unless otherwise stated, we assume this same objective, known among economists as the **profit maximization hypothesis**.

To be sure, there are other goals that a firm can pursue, relating to market share, revenue growth, profit margin, return on investment, technology, customer satisfaction, and shareholder value (i.e., maximizing the price of its stock). It is crucial to be precisely aware of a firm's goals. Different goals can lead to very different managerial decisions given the same limited amount of resources. For example, if the main goal of the firm is to maximize market share rather than profit, the firm might decide to reduce its prices. If the main goal is to provide the most technologically advanced products, the firm might well decide to allocate more resources to research and development. The added research and development expenses would most likely reduce the amount of profit the firm earns in the short run but may result in increased profits over time as the company increases its technological lead over its competitors. If the main goal of the firm is to carry a complete line of products and services, it may choose to sell certain products even though they might not be earning a profit.

Given the goal (or goals) that the firm is pursuing, we can say that the **optimal decision** in managerial economics is one that brings the firm closest to this goal. For example, as you see in chapter 8, to maximize its profit (or minimize its loss), a firm should price its product at a level where the revenue earned on the last unit of a product sold (called *marginal revenue*) is equal to the additional cost of making this last unit (called *marginal cost*). In other words, the optimal price equates the firm's marginal revenue with its marginal cost.

One additional concept should be presented in our discussion of a firm's goals. In economics, a distinction is made between the "short-run" time period and the "long-run" time period. As explained in greater detail in later sections of this text (see chapters 3, 6, and 7), these time periods actually have nothing directly to do with calendar time. During the short run, we assume a firm can vary the amount of certain resources (e.g., labor hours) but must operate with a fixed amount of at least one of its resources (e.g., factory space). Theoretically, in the long run, a firm is able to vary the quantities of all resources being used. In this text, we look at both short-run and long-run decisions made by the firm. We assume a company's goal is to maximize profits both in the short and long run. However, it must be understood that a business will, at times, sacrifice profitability in the short run with the anticipation of maximized long-run profits.

---

[11]As we see in chapter 8, a firm may lose money in the short run and still be better off than it would be if it were to shut down operations, as long as its losses are less than its fixed costs. However, if it is going to lose money, from an economic standpoint it is optimal to minimize its losses.

GOALS OTHER THAN PROFIT

Economic Goals

The concept of profit maximization has been attacked as incomplete by many writers. They point out that companies may have other economic objectives, such as those mentioned previously.

For the time being, we omit discussion of the objective of "value" or "shareholder wealth" maximization and consider some of the other alternatives concerning a company's activity during a single period of time (such as a year). It is readily admitted that profit maximization is a rather vague term. How does a company know that its profits in a given period are the largest they can be? Or, more correctly (from an ex ante, or planning, viewpoint), how does a company know that the actions it is taking in this time frame will result, if all goes as expected, in the greatest possible profit?

Let us look at the objectives set out by a company's CEO (or a committee representing the company's top management). It is not unusual for the CEO or his or her representatives, having decided on the achievable results for the next fiscal period, to distribute objectives to the various operating heads at the beginning of the planning cycle. Now imagine this memorandum from the firm's CEO to the general manager of one of the company's operating units:

> Dear Alex,
>
> We have had a pretty good year in 2007, and we believe that 2008 should be even better.
>
> I am therefore issuing the following objective for your unit in 2007. Take any and all actions that will ensure your profit is maximized.
>
> Corporate management is confident that you will not disappoint us. We know that the objective we have given you is challenging. We also are convinced that it is achievable.
>
> ERIC, CEO

This memorandum is obviously an extreme simplification, but what is Alex to do with his marching orders to maximize profit? What resources does he have to do this? How can his performance be measured at the end of the year? What is his maximum profit?

Now let us look at another "objective" memorandum:

> Dear Alex,
>
> We have had a pretty good year in 2007, and we expect that 2008 should be even better. We are assigning specific objectives to each of our operating units in such a way that the total result will be a financial posture consistent with our economic and industry forecasts, our available resources, and good increases in productivity. With this in mind, we want you to build your 2008 plan to correspond to the following objectives for your unit:
>
> 1. Your revenue should increase by 10 percent from 2007.
>
> 2. The profit margin of your unit should increase from 8 percent to 9 percent, and your return on assets should be 10 percent.

3. Your division will receive $10 million of company funds for expansion projects whose minimum internal rate of return should be 12 percent.

4. The head count of your unit can increase by no more than 2 percent.

Corporate management is confident that you will not disappoint us. We know that the objective we have given you is challenging. We also are convinced that it is achievable.

ERIC, CEO

Assuming that this memorandum makes more sense (which it certainly should, for otherwise our point has been lost), does this mean that the company's objective is not really profit maximization, but rather a growth rate, a profit margin, or a return on its assets? This is what many writers on this subject say.

Such a conclusion is, however, misleading. Any of these measures in itself is incomplete, and each should be seen as a realistic target consistent with the ultimate objective of maximizing the firm's overall profits. Management, in this example, advised by its expert staff regarding the company's economic environment, competition, technological advances, and market potential, has come to the conclusion that maximum profits can be achieved by the combination of growth and profit measures included in its memorandum.

Thus, the specific objectives assigned to an operating unit are really proxies for the overall objective of profit maximization. The achievement of these proxies is also measurable at the end of the fiscal period; the division executive's performance and contribution toward the company's profits can be evaluated, and rewards in terms of bonuses or incentive plans can then be determined.

Economic Objectives

The following are examples of statements about goals from three leading beverage companies.

COCA-COLA ENTERPRISES, INC.

Company expects strong cash flow from operations . . . capital spending will total about $1 billion in 2007. Based on the company's strategic plan, it is expected that long-term annual revenue growth should be 4–5%, operating income growth 5–6% and earnings per share growth should be in the high single digits. . . . "Return on invested capital is expected to improve by 30 basis points or more annually."[12]

PEPSICO, INC.

The company expects mid-single-digit volume and net revenue growth in 2007 and earnings per share of $3.30. Cash from operating activities should be about $7 billion, and the company anticipates capital spending of $2.6 billion. In 2008 the company will meet its long-term target of mid-single-digit volume growth and at least a 10% increase in earnings per share.[13]

---

[12]"Coca-Cola Enterprises Inc. Reports Fourth-Quarter and Full-Year 2006 Results," *CCE Press Release*, February 13, 2007.

[13]"PepsiCo Reports Strong Sales and Operating Results for 2006 Fourth Quarter and Full Year," *PepsiCo News Release*, February 8, 2007; Betsy McKay, "Pepsi Envisions Challenges Ahead," *Wall Street Journal*, October 12, 2007.

CADBURY SCHWEPPES PLC
The company published a "new financial scorecard" that includes:

Revenue growth of 3–5% per annum
Growth in margins and return on invested capital over time
Dividend growth in line with earnings growth
Maintain an efficient balance sheet[14]

Noneconomic Objectives

In this complex world, companies may have objectives that are not strictly economic or at least do not appear to be governed by economic thinking. Indeed, some large companies have published statements of principles that, if accepted at face value, would indicate that making profits is the last thing for which they strive. Profits may be mentioned as only one of several objectives, and they may actually be listed last. Furthermore, the statements do not mention any maximum but rather concentrate on such measures as "adequate" or "reasonable" return to stockholders. Such modesty is certainly more palatable to the public. What, then, are some of the guiding principles such companies publish?

1. Provide a good place for our employees to work.
2. Provide good products/services to our customers.
3. Act as a good citizen in our society.

These actions are costly, and at first glance may seem to interfere with profit maximization. However, consider the following: Satisfied employees not only tend to be more productive, but will remain with the company longer, thus decreasing expensive labor turnover. Without satisfied customers, a company will not remain in business. Supporting good causes, such as charitable and other nonprofit organizations, will create goodwill and ultimately potential sales. Therefore, it would be worthwhile for a company to spend resources on such **noneconomic objectives** consistent with increases in revenues and profit. If this is the case, then attaining these objectives is not incompatible with profit maximization, and indeed, these objectives could be classified as economic.

We could enlarge this discussion of so-called noneconomic objectives, but the point has been made. Today's markets and institutions constrain companies in many ways that did not exist in the past. Therefore, companies must concern themselves with creating employee and customer satisfaction and maintaining social responsibility to a much higher degree than in the past. But these considerations do not contradict the profit maximization principle. If companies were maximizers in the past, under less restrictive conditions, they are still maximizers today but have to operate within the requirements imposed by current standards and the costs that accompany them.

ONCE AGAIN—DO COMPANIES MAXIMIZE PROFITS?

We discussed some possible alternative objectives to profit maximization and concluded that none of these objectives is necessarily inconsistent with our basic principle. Now let us look at another criticism that has been leveled at the view of profit maximization as the primary objective.

---

[14]Cadbury Schweppes, *Annual Report*, 2006.

The argument is that today's corporations do not maximize. Instead, their aim is to "satisfice." To understand this argument, we have to consider two parts of this idea:

1. The position and power of stockholders in today's corporation
2. The position and power of professional management in today's corporation

Years ago the owner or owners of a business also managed it. Businesses were predominantly quite small and lent themselves to being operated as individual proprietorships, partnerships, or small, closely held corporations. Modern businesses, particularly medium-size or large corporations, of course, cannot be managed by the owners, who are the shareholders and number in the thousands or even hundreds of thousands. Many stockholders own only minute pieces of a corporation. Furthermore, stockholders tend to diversify their holdings; thus, they may hold small interests in many different corporations. The argument asserts that most stockholders are not well informed on how well a corporation can do and will be satisfied with an adequate dividend and some reasonable growth. Because they own different stocks, poor performance on one of their holdings may be offset by some of their other assets. The stockholder is more concerned with the portfolio of stocks than with any individual stock. Shareholders may not be capable of knowing whether corporate management is doing its best for them, and they actually may not be very concerned as long as they receive what they consider a satisfactory return on their investment—hence "**satisficing**."

Second, in a modern corporation professional managers—the chairman of the board, the president, a group of vice presidents, and other high-level managers—direct the operations of a company. Although they are overseen by a board of directors (which often includes a large number of insiders), they are responsible for major decision making. It is claimed by a number of writers that managers (who commonly hold a relatively small number of shares) have their own objectives, which do not include maximization of shareholder earnings. Indeed, it is often said that managers tend to be more conservative—that is, risk averse—than stockholders would be because their jobs will most likely be safer if they turn in a competent and steady, if unspectacular, performance. They could probably benefit stockholders in the long run by taking some well-calculated risks. However, they may be too cautious to do so, and thus they miss out on opportunities. They fear that they may not survive the reverses that could result from risk taking. If stockholders need only be satisfied, this may be the appropriate way for management to go.

Management's interests may actually be contrary to those of stockholders. For instance, management may be more interested in revenue growth than profits. Why? It has been claimed that management remuneration tends to be a function of revenue size rather than profits. Several studies have been made on this subject, but the evidence is considerably less than overwhelming. Also, company management may be more interested in maximizing its own income, may indulge in various perquisites, and in general may not act in the best interest of the widely dispersed, somewhat disinterested and lethargic stockholder population. The divergence in the objectives between owners and management has been the subject of much discussion in economic literature and is known as the "principal-agent" problem or simply as the "agency problem."[15]

---

[15]A formal theory dealing with the potential conflicts between shareholders and management was developed by Michael C. Jensen and William H. Meckling in their article "Theory of the Firm: Managerial Behavior, Agency Costs and Ownership Structure" (*Journal of Financial Economics,* October 1976, pp. 350–60). These conflicts arise whenever managers own less than 100 percent of the stock, which is, of course, the predominant situation in today's large corporation. To ensure managers act on behalf of the stockholder, the latter will have to incur "agency costs," which are expenditures to monitor managers' actions, to structure the organization in such a way as to limit management's action, and so forth.

The two sides in this relationship tend to complement one another. The owners of the corporation—the stockholders—are not interested in maximization, or even if they are, they are not well informed and have too little power. The corporation's management, whose selfish motives lead them to act in their own favor when stockholder and management goals differ, will manage in a way that serves their interest, while keeping the stockholder satisfied with adequate return and moderate growth.

Like all ideas presented by intelligent people, this one probably contains a certain amount of truth. Each of the points seems eminently reasonable and, for all we know, could be valid over limited periods of time. However, let us look at some of the realities of life and some recent events in the business world that tend to contradict this argument.

You, the reader of this book, may be among that group of far-flung stockholders owning a hundred shares in a company with millions of shares outstanding. However, particularly in the case of large corporations, much of the outstanding stock is held by institutions in professionally managed accounts. Among these are banks that manage large pension funds, insurance companies with their extensive portfolios, and mutual funds. These organizations employ expert analysts (who are only human, and therefore, at least occasionally make mistakes) who study companies and pass judgment on the quality of their management and their promise for the future. Of course, they deal mostly with stock prices, but after all, stock prices are a reflection of a company's profitability.[16] These analysts make recommendations to their management on which stocks to buy and which to sell. Companies that underperform would be weeded out of these institutional portfolios, with a consequent drop in their stock prices.

Now, what happens when certain stocks tend to underperform in the market? They become targets for takeovers by others. We really do not have to belabor this point because anyone reading the business sections of daily newspapers or other business publications is very much aware of recent events in the takeover and buyout arenas. In addition to the accumulation of stock and subsequent tender offers by outside financiers, we have also witnessed the existence of proxy fights by dissident large stockholders. Thus, it appears that management in today's corporation is not insulated from outside pressures. Management is constrained to act in agreement with stockholders, who look for increases in stock values and returns and who act to "punish" the managements of those companies that appear to underperform.

Another argument leads to a similar conclusion. Competitive pressures also act to stimulate management to performance. If a company's results lag behind those of competitors, those lethargic stockholders who do not challenge the company directly will tend to sell its shares and turn to those companies providing better returns and better prospects of returns. The price of the company's stock will suffer relative to prices of the others; such a scenario will not go unnoticed in financial markets. Company management will come under the gun to improve performance, and ultimately management may be replaced because of pressure by outside board members, a successful proxy fight, or even a takeover. A very vocal and sometimes effective advocate of shareholder rights has been the California Public Employees' Retirement System (Calpers). With about $246 billion in assets as of April 28, 2008, it has demonstrated that changes in corporate governance can be accomplished. Calpers reviews the performance of companies in its investment portfolio and selects companies that have performed poorly and for which it may seek a change in corporate

---

[16]The connection between profits and stock prices is examined in the next section, when we expand the maximization principle to include the wealth of stockholders.

governance. It listed eleven companies in its 2007 "Focus List." Among the companies listed were Eli Lilly, International Paper, Marsh & McLennan, and Sara Lee. Calpers' "Focus List" for 2008 listed five companies, including Cheesecake Factory and La-Z-Boy.[17] It has been reported that more than 1,340 U.S. chief executive officers left their positions in 2006. This was the highest rate on record.[18]

The Sarbanes-Oxley Act was passed in 2002 in response to a number of corporate scandals. The act sets new, stricter standards on the behavior of public corporations and accounting firms. Since then, shareholders have become much more active in proposing changes in corporate policies in proxies that are to be considered at annual stockholder meetings. Several of these reforms, such as changing the way by which directors are elected and stockholders casting nonbinding votes on executive pay, have received much greater consideration and in some cases actually were adopted.[19]

In addition, there is the managerial labor market. Managers who have performed well for their stockholders will most likely be in greater demand and will be better compensated than managers with mediocre records.

Management has another, more direct, motivation to act in concert with the objectives of stockholders. Parts—frequently large parts—of an executive's remuneration are tied to performance in terms of operating profits for the corporation or for units supervised by the particular executive.[20] Furthermore, an executive's compensation package is usually enhanced by the issuance of stock options. Because the value of stock options depends on the price of the company's stock, which in turn is a function of the company's profit performance, self-serving company managers may find that their objectives (less than miraculously) coincide with those of the stockholders.

Profit Maximization, Restated

It is readily agreed that the existence of the profit maximization objective can never be proven conclusively. We must note, however, that lack of financial success by a company is not necessarily a contravention of the principle. The best of plans may go awry, and management's judgment certainly is not error proof. Under certain circumstances, the aim for loss minimization may replace the goal of profit maximization, but this too supports our basic premise. As difficult as it is to point to acts of profit maximization by management, none of the alternative constructions lends itself as well as a yardstick by which to measure business activity. As long as a corporation strives to do better—that is, prefers higher profits to lower profits and lower costs to higher costs, and acts consistently in those directions—the assumption of profit maximization serves as a better basis for judging a company's decisions than any of the other purported objectives. Incidentally, this "striving to do better" can include a multitude of decisions, including those that lead to a revenue increase greater than a cost increase, a revenue decrease smaller than a cost decrease, or a constant revenue with decreased costs. All these decisions involve an increase in profits.

However, maximizing profits in the very short term (e.g., 1 year) can always be accomplished by management. If, for instance, revenue in the coming year is expected

---

[17]Much information about Calpers can be obtained by visiting www.calpers.org or www.calpers.ca.gov. Information on its governance activities and "Focus List" can be found under www.calpers-governance.org/alert/selection/default.asp.

[18]Francesco Guerrera, "Tough Year Ahead for US Chiefs," *Financial Times*, January 3, 2007.

[19]Jena McGregor, "Activist Investors Get More Respect," *BusinessWeek*, June 11, 2007, pp. 34–35.

[20]The fact that these performance incentives may be tied to near-term profits can create a problem because the executive's horizon may be shortened. More about this is discussed later.

to decline, a company can keep up its profits by cutting expenses. If management seeks to do this without an immediate further reaction on revenue, it can eliminate some development projects. The effect of a lack of new products will not be felt right away, but the shortsightedness of this management decision will come home to roost in a few years. This is the decision area in which the objective of period profit maximization can be attacked more logically. Profit maximization for one period is an incomplete measure from the viewpoint of a business organization that is expected to operate into the infinite—or at least the foreseeable—future.

MAXIMIZING THE WEALTH OF STOCKHOLDERS

Because period profit maximization is an extremely useful way to look at day-to-day decision making in the firm, we use it as our model throughout most of this book. However, there is another view of maximization that is usually adopted in finance textbooks and that takes into consideration a stream of earnings over time. This concept includes not only the evaluation of a stream of cash flows; it also considers the all-important idea of the time value of money.[21] Because it is an obvious fact that a dollar earned in the future is worth less than a dollar earned today, the future streams must be discounted to the present. Both the shape of these streams through time and the interest rate at which they are discounted affect the value of the stockholders' wealth today. The discount rate in particular is affected by risk, so risk becomes another component of the valuation of the business. Financial theorists differentiate various types of risk, with the two major types commonly identified as business risk and financial risk.

Business risk involves variation in returns due to the ups and downs of the economy, the industry, and the firm. This is the kind of risk that attends all business organizations, although to varying degrees. Some businesses are relatively stable from period to period, whereas others incur extreme fluctuations in their financial returns. For instance, public utilities (i.e., suppliers of electricity and gas, as well as the operating telephone companies) tend to have more stable earnings over time than do industrial companies, particularly those in industries that are highly cyclical (e.g., steel, automobiles, and capital goods), or companies in high-tech fields.

Financial risk concerns the variation in returns that is induced by leverage. *Leverage* signifies the proportion of a company financed by debt. Given a certain degree of leverage, the earnings accruing to stockholders will fluctuate with total profits (before the deduction of interest and taxes). The higher the leverage, the greater the potential fluctuations in stockholder earnings. Thus, financial risk moves directly with a company's leverage.

How do we obtain a measure of stockholders' wealth? We do so by discounting to the present the cash streams that stockholders expect to receive out into the future. Because we know today's price of a company's stock, we can—given the expected dividends to be received by the stockholders—determine the discount rate the investment community applies to the particular stock. This discount rate includes the pure time value of money and the premiums for the two categories of risk. The dividend stream is used to represent the receipts of stockholders because that is all they really receive from the company. Of course, a stockholder also looks for a capital gain, but selling the stock at some point involves someone else buying it; thus, this payment represents

---

[21]Time value of money and discounting of cash flows is discussed in greater detail in the appendix found on the Companion Website.

only a trade, an exchange of funds. However, dividends represent the returns on the stock generated by the corporation. In equation form, we have the following:

$$P = \frac{D_1}{(1 + k)} + \frac{D_2}{(1 + k)^2} + \frac{D_3}{(1 + k)^3} + \cdots + \frac{D_n}{(1 + k)^n}$$

where P = present price of stock

D = dividends received per year (in year 1, year 2, . . . year n)

k = discount rate applied by financial community, often referred to as cost of equity capital of company

If it is assumed that the corporation will have an infinitely long life and dividends will remain the same year after year, then the price of each share of stock can be calculated as a perpetuity with the following formula:

$$P = D/k$$

Investors, however, will usually expect dividends to rise. In the case where dividends grow at a constant rate each year, the formula for share price becomes

$$P = D_1/(k - g)$$

where D_1 = dividend to be paid during coming year

g = annual constant growth rate of dividend expressed as a percentage[22]

Multiplying P by the number of shares outstanding gives the total value of the company's common equity.[23]

A simple example will help clarify the previous equation. Assume that a company expects to pay a dividend of $4 in the coming year, and expects dividends to grow at 5 percent each year. The rate at which stockholders discount their cash flows (which is really the rate of return stockholders require to earn from this stock) is 12 percent. There are 1 million shares outstanding. We would expect the price of each share to be

$$P = 4/(0.12 - 0.05) = 4/.07 = \$57.14$$

The value of the company's stock would be $57.14 million. This is the expected market value given the variables that we have assumed. However, this may not be the maximum value the company could achieve. The variables in the equation may have to change. Because k is a function of the company's level of risk (both business and financial), the company may be able to decrease k by lowering the riskiness of its operations or by changing its leverage. It can affect g and D by retaining more or less of its earnings. By retaining a larger portion of its earnings and devoting a smaller portion of its earnings to dividends, the company may be able to increase its growth rate, g.

Thus, under this construction, maximizing the wealth of the shareholder means that a company tries to manage its business in such a way that the dividends over time paid from its earnings and the risk incurred to bring about the stream of dividends always create the highest price and thereby the maximum value for the company's stock.

---

[22]The derivation of these formulas is discussed in greater detail in chapter 12.

[23]The value of a company's equity can also be obtained by calculating the present value of the expected stream of "free cash flows." However, when free cash flow is correctly constructed, it is essentially equal to dividends paid. This subject is discussed at greater length in appendix 12A when the calculation of the value of a corporation is presented.

This **wealth maximization** hypothesis tends to weaken even further the management versus stockholder argument. Corporate executives, for whom stock options represent a significant portion of remuneration, now have an even greater incentive to aim at results that conform to the objectives of the stockholders.

This is a rather complex if quite obvious development of the maximization principle. As stated previously, we work primarily with the profit maximization hypothesis because it is quite sufficient for most of our purposes. We return to the wealth maximization rule in chapter 12 when we discuss a company's investment and replacement decisions involving expenditures for which the resulting payoffs flow into the corporation over a considerable period of time. In that chapter, we also briefly discuss how the market tends to determine the rate of return it requires from a company (and thus sets the discount rate k, the company's cost of capital). In chapter 12, we also examine the question of risk and uncertainty and attempt to find ways to deal with it.

Market Value Added and Economic Value Added

Various publications have measured the wealth of stockholders by taking the price per share quoted in the stock market pages and multiplying it by the number of shares outstanding. The product is, of course, the current value of the shares, and thus reflects the value of the company accorded to it by the market. However, such a measure does not show the wealth that has been created by the company. After all, suppose the stockholders had contributed more capital than the stock was worth currently. Then, actually, the company would have "destroyed" some of the stockholders' wealth. What is really important is how much the stockholders' investment is worth today relative to what they have contributed to the corporation in originally buying the stock and then having earnings retained by the corporation for reinvestment.

A relatively new measure has become popular with the financial community as well as with many corporations. It is called **Market Value Added (MVA®)** and has been developed by the consulting firm of Stern Stewart.[24] MVA represents the difference between the market value of the company and the capital that investors have paid into the company.

The market value of the company includes the value of both equity and debt. The capital includes the book value of debt and equity on the company's balance sheet plus a number of adjustments that increase the basic number. Among these adjustments is the inclusion of research and development (R&D) expense (which accountants treat as expense). Prior years' R&D is cumulated and amortized over a number of years. Another item that is included is the amortization of goodwill. Thus, in the end, the contributed capital of the corporation will turn out to be larger than merely the book value of equity and debt. Although the market value of a corporation will always be positive, the MVA may be positive or negative, depending on whether the market value of the company is greater than the capital that investors contributed. Where a corporation's market value is less than the contributed capital, investors' wealth has actually been "destroyed."

A recent ranking of 1,350 corporations based on June 2007 stock prices showed General Electric at the top with an MVA of $311 billion, followed by Exxon ($264 billion) and Microsoft ($231 billion). At the other end of the scale were JDSUniphase Corporation and Pfizer, which actually showed a negative MVA.[25]

---

[24]This concept was originally introduced in 1990. See G. Bennett Stewart III, "Announcing the Stern Stewart Performance 1,000: A New Way of Viewing Corporate America," *Journal of Applied Corporate Finance*, Summer 1990, pp. 38–59.

[25]"Ranking of Companies by MVA," EVA Dimension LLC, 2007. Such a measure favors large companies and penalizes smaller companies. To show the relative market value added, one could divide the MVA by the company's annual revenue.

Basically, MVA is a forward-looking measure. If market value reflects the financial markets' appraisal of a company's future cash streams, then MVA represents the financial markets' assessment of the company's future net cash flows (i.e., after subtracting the investments the company must make to achieve those cash streams).

Another measurement developed by Stern Stewart is **Economic Value Added (EVA®)**. EVA is calculated as follows:

$$\text{EVA} = (\text{Return on Total Capital} - \text{Cost of Capital}) \times \text{Total Capital}$$

Actually, the calculation of return on capital (profit divided by capital) is nothing new. However, EVA subtracts an estimated cost of capital from return. If the resulting number is positive, then the company has earned more than its investors require, and thus will add to investors' wealth. In contrast, if cost is greater than return, then value is being destroyed.

To avoid distortions created by accounting conventions, Stern Stewart makes numerous adjustments to the return and capital numbers. Actually, EVA could be said to be very much like "economic profits," which are mentioned briefly in the next section of this chapter and are discussed thoroughly in chapter 9. However, when these numbers are calculated they are generally based on past results, and do not necessarily say anything about a company's future profitability. Still, "Stern Stewart says that there is a close correlation between EVA and MVA—if managers improve EVA, the company's MVA is highly likely to improve too."[26]

Over the last few years, many companies have begun emphasizing the EVA measure over more traditional measures such as earnings per share and return on equity, as have money managers such as Oppenheimer, Calpers, and others.[27]

ECONOMIC PROFITS

Throughout this chapter, we use the term *profit* and assume it has some kind of meaning. But we have not defined it. We only said that profit—and its maximization—is uppermost in the company owner's and manager's minds. In a way, profit is easy to define. Every company that closes its books annually and whose accountants construct a statement of earnings (whether this company is public so everybody can see the published statement and its "bottom line," or whether it is private) knows its profits. The accountants report the level of profits, and they also affirm that everything in the financial statements has been done in conformance with generally accepted accounting principles (GAAP).

Unfortunately, things are not quite that simple. Profits as reported on an earnings statement are not necessarily definitive. Accountants have certain amounts of freedom in recording items leading to the "bottom line."[28] A few examples will suffice:

1. There are different ways of recording depreciation. In the past, the straight-line method, the sum-of-the-years'-digits method, the declining balance method, and probably others have been used. Under present tax law, the Modified Accelerated Cost Recovery System (MACRS) is most frequently employed.

---

[26]"A Star to Sail By?" *The Economist*, August 2, 1997, p. 54.
[27]S. Tully, "America's Greatest Wealth Creators," *Fortune*, November 9, 1998, p. 195. The following articles discuss how companies use the EVA concept: "Stern Stewart EVA™ Roundtable," *Journal of Applied Corporate Finance*, Summer 1994, pp. 46–70; S. Milunovich and A. Tsuei, "EVA® in the Computer Industry," *Journal of Applied Corporate Finance*, Spring 1996, pp. 104–15; A. Jackson, "The How and Why of EVA® at CS First Boston," *Journal of Applied Corporate Finance*, Spring 1996, pp. 98–103.
[28]Some writers in this field have said that accountants take too many liberties. Professor Abraham Briloff has written a number of books and articles on this subject.

2. There are various ways of recording inventories, the famous FIFO (first-in, first-out) and LIFO (last-in, first-out) being just two alternatives.

3. Amortization of such items as goodwill and patents can be recorded differently.

This is just a small sample of the better-known alternative treatments by accountants, and any of these are in conformance with GAAP. Moreover, the tax return that a company completes and sends to the IRS may be quite different from the published statement of a public company.

As if the question of what accounting profits really are were not enough, the economist compounds this problem even further. Everybody agrees that profit equals revenue minus costs (and expenses). But economists do not agree with accountants on the concept of costs. An accountant reports costs on a historical basis. The economist, however, is concerned with the costs that a business considers in making decisions, that is, future costs. We concern ourselves with this concept more thoroughly later in this book, but we must touch on the subject now, albeit briefly. Basically, economists deal with something they call *opportunity costs* or *alternative costs*. This means that the cost of a resource is what a business must pay for it to attract it into its employ or, put differently, what a business must pay to keep this resource from finding employment elsewhere. To get down to specific examples, we can mention the following:

1. ***Historical costs versus replacement costs.***   To an economist, the replacement cost of a piece of machinery (and, therefore, the level of periodic depreciation on the replacement cost) is important, whereas an accountant measures cost—and depreciation—on a historical basis.

2. ***Implicit costs and normal profits.***

   a. The owners' time and interest on the capital they contribute are usually counted as profit in a partnership or a single proprietorship. However, the owners could work for someone else instead and invest their funds elsewhere. So these two items are really costs to the business and not profit.

   b. The preceding item is not relevant in the case of a corporation because even top executives are salaried employees, and interest on corporate debt is deducted as an expense before profits are calculated. However, the payments made to the owners/stockholders—dividends—are not part of cost; they are recorded as a distribution of profits. But surely part of the shareholders' return is similar to the interest on debt because stockholders could have invested their funds elsewhere and required a certain return in order to leave the investment with the corporation. Thus, on this account, corporate profits as recorded by accountants tend to be overstated.

It appears, therefore, that an economist includes costs that would be excluded by an accountant. Indeed, the economist refers to the second category of costs—which are essential to obtain and keep the owners' resources in the business—as **normal profits,** which represent the return that these resources demand to remain committed to a particular firm.

Thus, **economic costs** include not only the historical costs and explicit costs recorded by the accountants, but also the replacement costs and implicit costs (normal profits) that must be earned on the owners' resources. In the rest of this book, profits are considered to be **economic profits,** which are defined as total revenue minus all the economic costs we describe in this section.

GLOBAL APPLICATION

The model of a firm's goals discussed in this chapter applies predominantly to firms operating in the United States and possibly the United Kingdom. However, one must ask whether profit maximization or shareholder wealth maximization is also valid for other countries. It is often said that for many reasons (e.g., political, cultural, legal, and institutional), firms in other countries pursue goals that include the interests of other groups, such as labor, community, government, and so on, in addition to interests of stockholders. In some countries, for instance, labor unions are represented on the board of directors. Thus, it may be necessary to consider such interests in our discussions. However, even if such considerations are important, it is possible for us to treat them as constraints on the actions of a firm. Even if profit or shareholder wealth maximization is not the only objective, as long as firms attempt to take actions that will improve their earnings—within specific constraints—our maximization model can still be used.[29] It is important to recognize, however, that multinational firms (e.g., a U.S. parent corporation operating in many different countries through subsidiaries or branches) will encounter restrictions and complications, which they must consider in doing business abroad. We list these and explain them briefly:[30]

1. Foreign currencies and their exchange rates must be considered. Thus, revenues, costs, and other cash flows that are denominated in other currencies must be translated into domestic currencies, and their potential changes must be analyzed for their impact on the business. Under certain circumstances, a profitable activity abroad can become unprofitable from the viewpoint of the domestic parent corporation.

2. Legal differences must be taken into account. Dissimilarities in tax laws can have important consequences on results of transactions between the domestic parent corporation and its foreign subsidiary. Differences in legal systems make the tasks of executives considerably more complex.

3. Most Americans have in the past mastered only their own language, and thus, are often at a disadvantage when dealing with their multilingual counterparts in other countries.

4. The differences in cultural environments influence the defining of business goals and attitudes toward risk. Thus, such differences can greatly affect the way business is conducted.

5. The role of government in defining the rules under which companies operate varies from country to country. Although in some countries market competition prevails, in others the political process dictates the behavior of firms in much greater detail.

6. Corporations operating in different countries may be restricted from transferring corporate resources out of the country and may even face the danger of expropriation. This is political risk, which must be included in any economic analysis of a company's prospects.[31]

The points just discussed, as well as others, must always be considered by companies doing business abroad. Although some of the differences may have adverse effects on a company, participation in a global market is a necessity for most large (and even small) firms today. Profitability, and even survival, can depend on a company entering global markets and competing worldwide.

---

[29]It is interesting to note that, in an interview, Heinrich von Pierer, then chief executive officer of the German electronics firm Siemens, stressed "German corporate values as concern with quality, reliability and long-term thinking." He also made the following statement: " . . . if people think that German businesses have an aversion to shareholder value, we are not a very good representative of such companies. . . . To improve profitability and market capitalisation is the main goal." Peter Marsh, "A Conglomerate with an Air of Confidence," *Financial Times,* January 21, 2002.

[30]We discuss some of these subjects at greater length in chapter 13.

[31]The preceding points can be found in Eugene F. Brigham and Phillip R. Daves, *Intermediate Financial Management,* Thomson Southwestern, 2004, pp. 211–212.

The Solution

It was a lively stockholder meeting. Bob Burns thought to himself that it was a good thing that the speech he prepared with the help of his assistants was short because the stockholders were eager to enjoy the rest of the day with other activities that Global Foods had arranged. After covering the results for the most recent fiscal year, Bob continued:

"Over the past decade, American-based global companies have experienced heightened competition necessitating a restructuring of their operations, and more recently the economic crises in the economies of Asia as well as other areas in the world.

"Throughout this period, your management has maintained as its primary objective to continue to increase the value of your investment in the company. We are well aware that, recently, the price of our stock has not been increasing at the rate it did earlier in this decade. However, throughout this period we have remained committed to a long-run increase in the price of our stock. To accomplish this goal, we need to return to a double-digit annual increase in revenue as well as profits.

"As a part of this growth strategy, we are entering the growing market for bottled water. In the past 10 years, sales of bottled water in the United States have increased by 144 percent, and annual per capita consumption has more than doubled.[32] This is not a fad, but a trend. The quality of the water we drink has become increasingly important, as the confidence of Americans in their tap water is eroding.

"To maintain and increase our profits we have, over the past few years, been extremely diligent and successful in decreasing our production, marketing, and administrative costs. But there is a limit to such endeavors. In the long run, we must find new ways and growing markets to increase our profitability and thus discharge our responsibility to you, our stockholders—increase the value of your investment. Entering the market for bottled water is one of the directions that will bring this about."

SUMMARY

In this text, we generally assume a firm's short-run or long-run objective is the maximization of its profit or the minimization of its loss. Although a firm can select from a number of other goals, both in the short run and in the long run, the assumption of profit maximization provides us with a clear-cut model for explaining how firms can use economic concepts and tools of analysis to make optimal decisions. In presenting these concepts and tools of analysis, a certain amount of mathematics will be employed. Thus, before proceeding to the next chapter, we believe that a brief review of the mathematics used in this text will be helpful. This review is contained in the online appendix.

IMPORTANT CONCEPTS

Business risk.   The variability of returns (or profits) due to fluctuations in general economic conditions or conditions specifically affecting the firm. (p. 36)

Economic cost.   All cost incurred to attract resources into a company's employ. Such cost includes explicit cost usually recognized on accounting records as well as opportunity cost. (p. 40)

Economic profit.   Total revenue minus total economic cost. An amount of profit earned in a particular endeavor above the amount of profit that the firm could be earning in its next best alternative activity. Also referred to as *abnormal profit* or *above-normal profit*. (p. 40)

Economic Value Added (EVA).   The difference between a company's return on total capital and its cost of capital. (p. 39)

---

[32]Corby Kummer, "Carried Away," *New York Times Magazine,* August 30, 1998, p. 40.

Financial risk.   The variability of returns (or profits) induced by leverage (the proportion of a company financed by debt). The higher the leverage, the greater the potential fluctuation in stockholder earnings for a given change in total profits. (p. 36)

Firm.   An organization that transforms resources into products demanded by consumers. The firm chooses to organize resources internally or to obtain them through the market. (p. 25)

Market Value Added (MVA).   The difference between the market value (equity plus debt) of a company and the amount of capital investors have paid into the company. (p. 38)

Noneconomic objectives.   A company's objectives that do not appear to be governed by economic thinking but rather define how a business should act. "Acting as a good corporate citizen" is an example of a noneconomic objective. (p. 32)

Normal profit.   An amount of profit earned in a particular endeavor that is just equal to the profit that could be earned in a firm's next best alternative activity. When a firm earns normal profit, its revenue is just enough to cover both its accounting cost and its opportunity cost. It can also be considered as the return to capital and management necessary to keep resources engaged in a particular activity. (p. 40)

Opportunistic behavior.   One party to a contract seeks to take advantage of the other. (p. 25)

Optimal decision.   The decision that enables the firm to meet its desired objective most closely. (p. 29)

Profit maximization hypothesis.   One of the central themes in economics, the claim that a company will strive to attain the highest economic profit in each period. (p. 29)

Satisficing.   A concept in economics based on the principle that owners of a firm (especially stockholders in a large corporation) may be content with adequate return and growth since they really cannot judge when profits are maximized. (p. 33)

Transaction costs.   Cost incurred by a firm in dealing with another firm, including the cost of investigation, negotiation, and enforcement of contracts. (p. 25)

Wealth maximization.   A company's management of its business in such a manner that the cash flows over time to the company, discounted at an appropriate discount rate, will cause the value of the company's stock to be at a maximum. (p. 38)

QUESTIONS

1. The following is a quote from a *New York Times* article: "If a company makes product donations to the school—computers for instance—then the image of a company goes up as graduate students use the company's products." Does such action square with a company's objective of profit maximization? Discuss.

2. Is the maximization of profit margin (profit as a percentage of total sales) a valid financial objective of a corporation? Discuss.

3. "The growth of consumer information organizations, legal requirements, and warranty requirements has caused significant increases in the cost of customer satisfaction. Thus it is no longer useful to talk about profit maximization as a company objective." Comment on this quote.

4. Discuss the difference between profit maximization and shareholder wealth maximization. Which of these is a more comprehensive statement of a company's economic objectives?

5. Explain the term *satisfice* as it relates to the operations of a large corporation.

6. Discuss the meaning of the term "principal-agent problem." Why does this problem exist?

7. Why may corporate managers not specifically aim at profit (or wealth) maximization for their companies?

8. What are some of the forces that cause managers to act in the interest of shareholders?

9. Do you believe that profit (or shareholder wealth) maximization still represents the best overall economic objective for today's corporation?

10. Because of inflation, a company must replace one of its (fully depreciated) machines at twice the nominal price paid for a similar machine eight years ago. Based on present accounting rules, will the company have covered the entire cost of the new machine through depreciation charges? Explain by contrasting accounting and economic costs.

11. How do implicit costs lead to a difference between accounting and economic profits?

12. You have a choice of opening your own business or being employed by someone else in a similar type of business. What are some of the considerations in terms of opportunity costs that you would have to include in arriving at your decision?

13. Various depreciation methods can be used to arrive at an accounting profit number. From the viewpoint of the economist, how should annual depreciation be determined?

14. Do you believe that the profit maximization model can be applied to the activities of a multinational corporation? Explain.

15. What are transaction costs? How does *opportunistic behavior* tend to increase transaction costs?

16. The outsourcing of important parts of a company's production has been growing in recent years. How would you explain these changes? How has the Internet contributed to these changes?

17. What are some reasons for companies internalizing transaction costs?

18. A company has two million shares outstanding. It paid a dividend of $2 during the past year, and expects that dividends will grow at 6 percent annually in the future. Stockholders require a rate of return of 13 percent. What would you expect the price of each share to be today, and what is the value of the company's common stock?

19. Discuss the difference between the calculation of shareholder wealth and the concept of *Market Value Added*. Which of the two would appear to be more meaningful from the viewpoint of a shareholder?

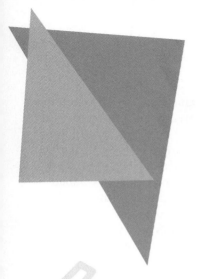

C h a p t e r   3

Supply and Demand

Learning Objectives

Upon completion of this chapter, readers should be able to:

- Define supply, demand, and equilibrium price.
- List and provide specific examples of the nonprice determinants of supply and demand.
- Distinguish between the short-run rationing function and the long-run guiding function of price.
- Illustrate how the concepts of supply and demand can be used to analyze market conditions in which management decisions about price and allocations of resources must be made.
- Use supply and demand diagrams to show how the determinants of supply and demand interact to determine market price in the short run and in the long run.

The Situation

While sipping a cup of green tea laced with honey and ginseng, CEO Bob Burns began to reminisce. It seemed like yesterday, but it was actually more than 10 years ago when he had convinced the board of directors of Global Foods, Inc., to go into the soft drink business. Here he was a decade later, sampling a product that his VP of Marketing, Nicole Goodman, was telling him would be an even stronger "growth engine" for the company than bottled water. She had pointed out to him that in 2003 American consumers spent $5 billion on tea. Although this amount was far less than the $20 billion spent annually for coffee, it was five times as much as people spent on tea a decade ago.[1] "It's obvious," she told him, "Global Foods must get into the tea business." As he poured his second cup of tea, Bob had to admit that even he had begun to prefer tea over coffee. He decided to call Nicole into his office to discuss the matter further.

"Okay, Nicole," Bob began, "You've always had a good instinct for what's new in the market. But before we leap into this, I want a report on exactly why you believe tea will be the real spark to our company's growth in the coming 5 years. After all, in our business it's all about 'share of stomach.' If people are drinking more tea, then they might be drinking fewer soft drinks and bottled water, so we'd be cannibalizing our own products. I'd feel much better if you could help me understand why this wouldn't be the case. Furthermore, what are the key determinants of the demand for tea? Could this be just a fad? Already people are starting to tire of their low-carb diets. Nicole, I want you to provide me with a report on the elements that are driving the demand for tea. How responsive will people be to price changes, to changes in the price of competing products such as bottled water and carbonated soft drinks? Is tea a 'luxury' good, or is it a necessity? The answers to these questions will help us better understand how to price and position our brand in the marketplace."

---

[1]Much of the situation and solution is based on Elizabeth Olsen, "A Tea Party, and All Boomers Are Invited," *New York Times*, October 17, 2004.

45

INTRODUCTION

In this chapter, we introduce the basic elements of supply and demand. Although for some of you, this chapter serves as a review of material covered in an economics principles course, it has been included because it is essential for every reader to have a thorough grounding in supply and demand before proceeding to the particulars of managerial economics. There may be situations—such as those described in this chapter's "The Situation" vignette—in which you may be required to conduct or evaluate a study with a considerable use of supply-and-demand analysis. But regardless of how directly this chapter's material may apply to your work, most of the material covered in this book relates in some way to supply or demand. Indeed, supply and demand can be considered the conceptual framework within which the specifics of managerial economics are discussed.

MARKET DEMAND

The **demand** for a good or service is defined as

> *Quantities* of a good or service that people are ready to *buy* at various *prices* within some given *time period, other factors* besides price held constant.

Note that in this definition "ready" implies that consumers are prepared to buy a good or service both because they are willing (i.e., they have a preference for it) and they are able (i.e., they have the income to support this preference).

Demand can first be illustrated with an example in which we imagine that you, the reader, are part of a simple market experiment. Suppose you were asked to respond to the following survey question: "In a 1-week period, how many slices of pizza would you be prepared to buy at the following prices: $2.00, $1.50, $1.00, $.50, and $.05?" Every reader would obviously have his or her own pattern of response. Let us assume a sample of three readers responds in the following way:

Price (Per Slice)	Q_{D1}	Q_{D2}	Q_{D3}	Q_{DM}
$2.00	0	2	3	5
1.50	1	2	5	8
1.00	2	2	8	12
0.50	3	3	10	16
0.05	4	4	12	20

As you can see, the combined responses of the three individuals make up the total **market demand** (Q_{DM}) for pizza, the sum of all individual demands.

Market demand is illustrated with a simple numerical function, as shown in Table 3.1. This table shows a hypothetical demand for pizza. As the price of a slice of pizza falls from $7.00 to zero, the amount that consumers in this market are willing to buy increases from zero to 700 slices. This inverse relationship between price and the **quantity demanded** of pizza is called the **law of demand**. There may be instances in which consumers behave in an "irrational" manner by buying more as the price rises and less as the price falls because they associate price with quality. But in the economic analysis of demand, it is assumed buyers do not associate price with quality and will therefore follow the law of demand.

The law of demand can be observed in the curve shown in Figure 3.1, derived from the schedule of numbers in Table 3.1. Notice that the curve in this figure slopes

Table 3.1   Market Demand for Pizza

Price (per slice)	Q_D
$7.00	0
6.00	100
5.00	200
4.00	300
3.00	400
2.00	500
1.00	600
0	700

downward and to the right, indicating that the quantity of pizza demanded increases as the price falls and vice versa.

A change in the demand for pizza or any other product is indicated by a change in the entire schedule of quantities demanded at a list of prices, or a shift in the demand curve either to the left or to the right. We see these changes in Table 3.2 and Figure 3.2.

To summarize, we can say the following:

Changes in price result in **changes in the quantity demanded** (i.e., movements *along* the demand curve).

Changes in the nonprice determinants result in **changes in demand** (i.e., *shifts* in the demand curve).

This difference can be seen in Table 3.2 in the following manner. At the price of $5 the quantity demanded in the first list of responses (Q_{D1}) is 200. If the price drops to $4, then the *quantity demanded* increases to 300. However, if the *demand* increases

Figure 3.1   Market Demand Curve for Pizza

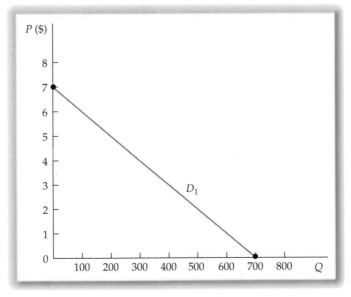

Table 3.2 Different Levels of Market Demand for Pizza

Price (per slice)	Q_{D1}	Q_{D2}	Q_{D3}
$7.00	0	100	0
6.00	100	200	0
5.00	200	300	100
4.00	300	400	200
3.00	400	500	300
2.00	500	600	400
1.00	600	700	500
0	700	800	600

to Q_{D2}, then at the price of $5 the quantity increases to 300 and in fact increases by 100 units at each price being offered.

Factors that can cause demand to change are called **nonprice determinants of demand**. Following is a list of these determinants and a brief elaboration of their impact on demand:

1. ***Tastes and preferences.*** Why do people buy things? Marketing professors, corporate market researchers, and advertising executives spend their careers trying to answer this question. Economists use a general-purpose category in their list of nonprice determinants called *tastes and preferences* to account for the personal likes and dislikes of consumers for various goods and services. These tastes and preferences may themselves be affected by other factors. Advertising, promotions, and even government reports can have profound effects on demand via their impacts on people's tastes and preferences for a particular good or service.

2. ***Income.*** As people's incomes rise, it is reasonable to expect their demand for a product to increase and vice versa. In the next chapter, the possibility of demand moving in the *opposite direction* to changes in income is discussed.

Figure 3.2 Shifts in the Market Demand for Pizza

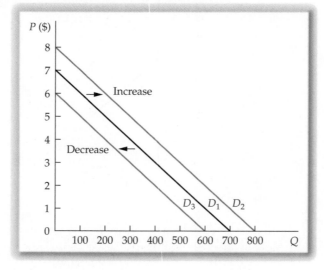

3. ***Prices of related products.***   A good or service can be related to another by being a sub-stitute or by being a complement. If the price of a substitute product changes, we expect the demand for the good under consideration to change in the *same direction* as the change in the substitute's price. Consider, for example, what would happen to the demand for software if the price of computer hardware falls, or to the demand for music downloads (from legitimate sites!) if the price of MP3 players falls. It is reasonable to expect that the demand for the two items would *rise* as a result of a *fall* in the price of their respective *complementary* products.

4. ***Future expectations.***   If enough buyers expect the price of a good or service to rise (fall) in the future, it may cause the current demand to increase (decrease). In markets for various financial instruments (e.g., stocks, bonds, negotiable certificates of deposit, U.S. Treasury bills), as well as for agricultural commodities and precious metals, expec-tations of future price changes among both buyers and sellers play an important part in determining the market demand. In most of these types of markets, speculation among buyers and sellers is an important factor to consider. Buyers and sellers act on a current price of a product not for its immediate consumption but because of the possibility of gaining from some future transaction. (Recall the old adage "buy low and sell high.") In fact, for most of these products, a sizable and growing *futures* market has emerged, in which buyers and sellers conduct transactions for these products at some agreed-upon future date. Naturally, expectations of future price movements have an impact on the supply and demand for the future delivery of a commodity. In turn, movements of futures prices could have an impact on the current (also called "spot") supply and demand for the commodity.

    This factor can also affect the demand for consumer and commercial products. For example, the demand for DVD recorders, digital cameras, home entertainment systems, laptop computers, and personal digital assistants was probably not as high as sellers expected when these products were first introduced, because buyers were waiting for their prices to come down at a later time.

5. ***Number of buyers.***   The impact of the number of buyers on demand should be appar-ent; as far as sellers are concerned, the more the merrier. What is interesting, nonethe-less, is how changing demographics and tastes and preferences within demographic groups can affect the pool of potential buyers for a particular good or service. In other words, sheer numbers (i.e., population) may not be as important as differences within the population. For example, the tracking of the baby boom generation from childhood to adulthood and eventually to retirement age has proven to be a fascinating study for market researchers. One can plainly see the impact on the demand for such items as children's apparel, furniture, and toys during the 1950s and 1960s, when this group was growing up.

    As the baby boomers grew into their teen years, the demand for such items as records, stereos, certain types of cars, and admissions to movie theaters went up accord-ingly. Market researchers are now busy contemplating the impact on the demand for an assortment of goods and services—from health care to retirement condominiums—that will stem from the "graying" of this segment of the population. On the other hand, there may very well be the start of a new generation of boomers. In 2006, a number of news sources reported that births in the United States hit a 45-year high.[2] We can well imagine how happy the sellers of products and services for infants and children are to learn about this statistic.

We discuss further how changes in these factors change demand and market price. But first we introduce the concept of supply. By combining supply with demand, we can conduct a complete analysis of the market, both in the short run and in the long run.

---

[2]There are many sources reporting this. For example, see the Digital Journal site: http://www.digitaljournal.com/article/249008/U_S_Births_Highest_in_45_Years.

MARKET SUPPLY

The **supply** of a good or service is defined as

> *Quantities* of a good or service that people are ready to *sell* at various *prices* within some given *time period, other factors* besides price held constant.

Notice that the only difference between this definition and that of demand is that in this case the word *sell* is used instead of *buy.* Just as in the case of demand, supply is based on an assumed length of time within which price and the other factors can affect the **quantity supplied.**

Recall that the law of demand states that the quantity demanded is related inversely to price, other factors held constant. In contrast, the law of supply states that quantity supplied is related *directly* to price, other factors held constant. Thus, any schedule of numbers representing a relationship between price and quantity supplied would show a *decrease* in the quantity supplied as price falls.

Table 3.3 shows a hypothetical supply schedule. Also shown are two additional supply schedules, one indicating a greater supply and the other showing a reduced supply. These schedules are shown as supply curves in Figure 3.3. The supply curve has a positive slope, reflecting the direct relationship between price and quantity supplied.

In analyzing the supply side of the market, it is important to make the distinction between *quantity supplied* and *supply.* The distinction between these two terms is the same as that used for the demand side of the market:

> Changes in *price* result in **changes in the quantity supplied** (i.e., movements along the supply curve).
>
> Changes in *nonprice determinants* result in **changes in the supply** (i.e., shifts of the supply curve).

Just as there are nonprice determinants of demand, there are **nonprice determinants of supply.** A change in any one or a combination of these factors will change market supply (i.e., cause the supply line to shift to the right or the left). We briefly discuss each factor to understand why this is expected to occur:

1. ***Costs and technology.***   The two factors of costs and technology can be treated as one because they are so closely related. *Costs* refer to the usual costs of production, such as labor costs, costs of materials, rent, interest payments, depreciation charges, and general and administrative expenses—in other words, all items usually found in a firm's income statement. *Technology* refers to technological innovations or improvements introduced to

Table 3.3   Market Supply for Pizza

P	Q_{S1}	Q_{S2}	Q_{S3}
$7	600	700	500
6	500	600	400
5	400	500	300
4	300	400	200
3	200	300	100
2	100	200	0
1	0	100	0
0	0	0	0

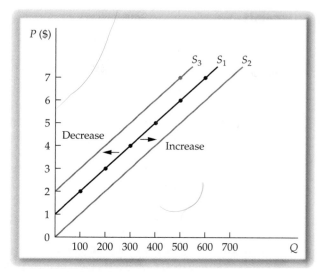

Figure 3.3   Supply Curves for Pizza

reduce the unit cost of production (e.g., automation, robotics, and computer hardware and software utilization). Technological changes that result in entirely new products for final consumption are not considered part of this category. These new products would have to be considered in an entirely different market analysis. In any event, unit cost reductions, whether from technological innovations or simply management decisions, will result in an increase in market supply. Increases in the unit cost of production will have the opposite effect.

2. ***Prices of other goods or services offered by the seller.***   From the consumer's stand-point, any good or service has other goods or services related to it either as substitutes or as complements. From the producer's standpoint, there can also be substitutes or complements for a particular good or service offered in the market. For example, sup-pose the sellers of pizza notice that the price of hot dogs increases substantially. In the extreme case, they may drop their line of pizza and substitute hot dogs. Or they may at least reduce the amount of resources (e.g., labor and store space) devoted to the sell-ing of pizza in favor of hot dogs. In either case, the market supply of pizza would decrease. If the sellers were already selling two (or more) products, the change in mar-ket conditions would prompt them to reallocate their resources toward the more prof-itable products. (Given this possibility, it may be more appropriate to say that the sell-ers consider pizza and hot dogs as "competing" products rather than as "substitute" products.)

3. ***Future expectations.***   This factor has a similar impact on sellers as on buyers; the only difference is the direction of the change. For example, if sellers anticipate a rise in price, they may choose to hold back the current supply to take advantage of the higher future price, thus decreasing market supply. As we discuss in the "Market Demand" section, an expected rise in price will increase the current demand for a product.

4. ***Number of sellers.***   Clearly, the number of sellers has a direct impact on supply. The more sellers, the greater the market supply.

5. ***Weather conditions.***   Bad weather (e.g., floods, droughts, unusual seasonal tempera-tures) will reduce the supply of an agricultural commodity. Good weather will have the opposite impact.

With this discussion of supply, we are now able to combine supply with demand into a complete analysis of the market.

MARKET EQUILIBRIUM

Now that we have reviewed the definitions and mechanics of demand and supply, we are ready to examine their interaction in the market. Market demand and supply are compared in Table 3.4 and Figure 3.4.

You can see in both the table and the graph that at the price of $4, the market is cleared in the sense that the quantity demanded (300) is equal to the quantity supplied (300). Thus, $4 is called the **equilibrium price**, and 300 is referred to as the **equilibrium quantity**. Another way to view this market situation is to imagine what would happen if the price were not at the equilibrium level. For example, suppose the price were at a higher level, say $5. At this price, as you can see in Table 3.4, the quantity supplied would exceed the quantity demanded, a condition called a **surplus**. At a lower price, say $3, the situation is reversed: the quantity demanded exceeds the quantity supplied. This situation is called a **shortage**. Both the surplus and the shortage conditions are indicated in Figure 3.4.

In the event of a surplus or a shortage, various competitive pressures cause the price to change (decrease in the case of a surplus, and increase in the event of a shortage). The price thus serves to clear the market of the imbalance. The clearing process continues until equilibrium (i.e., quantity demanded equals quantity supplied) is achieved. In the case of a surplus, sellers wanting to rid themselves of the extra items offer the product at a lower price to induce people to buy more. At the same time, as the price falls, suppliers are discouraged from offering as much as before. In the case of a market shortage, as the price rises toward the equilibrium level, the market is cleared because the quantity demanded decreases while the quantity supplied increases. In the event of a shortage, sellers try to take advantage of the situation by raising their prices, and people are thus discouraged from buying as much as before. Also, sellers are induced to offer a greater number of items in the market. Both actions serve to clear the market of a shortage.

To summarize the material in this section, remember the following definitions:

Equilibrium price: The price that equates the quantity demanded with the quantity supplied (i.e., the price that clears the market of a surplus or shortage).

Equilibrium quantity: The amount that people are willing to buy and sellers are willing to offer at the equilibrium price level.

Shortage: A market situation in which the quantity demanded exceeds the quantity supplied, *at a price below the equilibrium level.*

Surplus: A market situation in which the quantity supplied exceeds the quantity demanded, *at a price above the equilibrium level.*

Table 3.4   Supply and Demand for Pizza

P	Q_D	Q_S
$7	0	600
6	100	500
5	200	400
→4	300	300
3	400	200
2	500	100
1	600	0
0	700	0

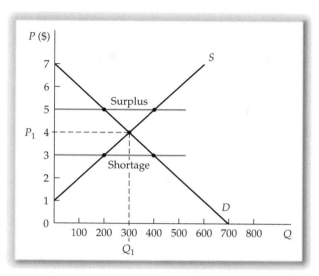

Figure 3.4   Supply and Demand Curves for Pizza, Indicating Market Equilibrium

COMPARATIVE STATICS ANALYSIS

The model of market demand, supply, and equilibrium price and quantity developed in the preceding sections can now be used to analyze the market. The particular method of analysis we use is called *comparative statics analysis*. This is a commonly used method in economic analysis and is used throughout the text. In general, this method of analysis proceeds as follows:

1. State the assumptions needed to construct the model.
2. Begin by assuming the model is in equilibrium.
3. Introduce a change in the model. In so doing, a condition of disequilibrium is created.
4. Find the new point at which equilibrium is restored.
5. Compare the new equilibrium point with the original one.

In effect, comparative statics analysis is a form of sensitivity analysis, or what business people often refer to as *what-if* analysis. For example, if we were doing a what-if analysis of a company's cash flow, we would start with a given pro forma income statement adjusted to provide the cash flow for a given period of time. We would then conduct sensitivity analysis by supposing certain factors changed, such as revenue, cost, or the rate of depreciation. We would then inspect how changes in these factors would change the cash flow of the firm over time. In the same manner, economists conduct a what-if analysis of their models.

The term *statics* alludes to the theoretically stable point of equilibrium, and *comparative* refers to the comparison of the various points of equilibrium. The ensuing sections explain exactly how comparative statics analysis is used in the analysis of the market.

Module 3A   ### Short-Run Market Changes: The "Rationing Function" of Price

Let us continue with our analysis of pizza. Following the steps involved in comparative statics analysis, we start by assuming all factors except the price of pizza are held constant, and the various patterns of response to price among buyers and sellers are represented by the supply and demand lines in Figure 3.4. We make a fresh start by

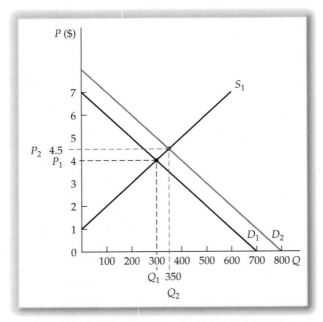

Figure 3.5   Increase in Demand for Pizza and Resulting Impact on Market Equilibrium

redrawing this graph in Figure 3.5. It would also be useful to recall all nonprice determinants that could affect the demand or supply for a product. They are listed for you in Table 3.5.

As noted in step 2 in the previous section, we begin this analysis in the condition of equilibrium. This is denoted in Figure 3.5 as the point where the supply line intersects with the D_1 demand line (i.e., the price level where quantity supplied is equal to quantity demanded).

Based on step 3, we introduce a change in one or more of the assumptions made when the model was constructed. Any one or more of the factors shown in Table 3.5 can cause this change. Let us assume a new government study shows pizza to be the most nutritious of all fast foods and that consumers substantially increase their demand for pizza as a result of this study. In Figure 3.5, this increase is represented by a shift in the demand curve from D_1 to D_2. As you can see, this shift results in a new, higher equilibrium price of $4.50. Notice also that the new equilibrium quantity is greater than the original equilibrium quantity.

Table 3.5   Nonprice Determinants of Demand and Supply

Demand	Supply
1. Tastes and preferences	1. Costs and technology
2. Income	2. Prices of other products offered
3. Prices of related products	3. Future expectations among sellers
4. Future expectations among buyers	4. Number of sellers
5. Number of buyers	5. Weather conditions (particularly for agricultural products)

The comparison of the new equilibrium point with the original one (step 5 in comparative statics analysis) leads us to conclude that, as a result of a change in tastes and preferences, the price of pizza rises, and so does the quantity bought and sold.

This analysis can be repeated using other possible changes in market conditions (e.g., the price of cheese rises, the price of soft drinks falls). Each time, the same procedure should be followed. If we consider only one possible change at a time, the effects on equilibrium price and quantity can be illustrated as in Figure 3.6. Instead of using specific numbers, we have designated the prices and quantities with the symbols P and Q along with appropriate subscripts. We can summarize the effects shown in the graphs as follows:

> An increase in demand causes equilibrium price and quantity to rise. (See Figure 3.6*a*.)
>
> A decrease in demand causes equilibrium price and quantity to fall. (See Figure 3.6*b*.)

Figure 3.6   Changes in Supply and Demand and Their Short-Run Impact on Market Equilibrium (the Rationing Function of Price)

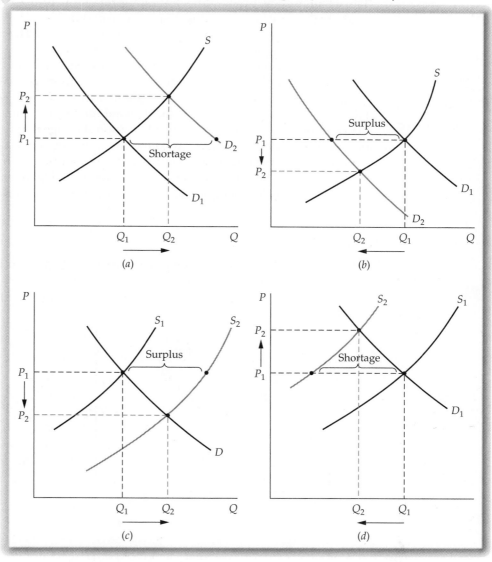

An increase in supply causes equilibrium price to fall and quantity to rise. (See Figure 3.6c.)

A decrease in supply causes equilibrium price to rise and quantity to fall. (See Figure 3.6d.)

In Figure 3.6, we observe that the shift in demand or supply has in effect created either a shortage or a surplus at the original price P_1. Thus, the equilibrium price has to rise or fall to clear the market. When the market price changes to eliminate the imbalance between quantities supplied and demanded, it is serving what economists call the **rationing function of price**. The term *rationing* is often associated with shortages, but we define it to also include a surplus situation.

Long-Run Market Analysis: The "Guiding" or "Allocating" Function" of Price

The comparative statics analysis presented earlier required only that you consider the response of equilibrium price and quantity to a given change in supply or demand. This response was dubbed the "rationing function" of price. Let us consider what might happen as a result of this change in market price. To illustrate this, we examine the market for hot dogs, a presumed substitute for pizza. The two markets are represented by the supply and demand diagrams in Figure 3.7.

Now let us assume that at the same time people's tastes and preferences change in favor of pizza, their tastes and preferences become more adverse to hot dogs (e.g., for health reasons). The changes in the demand for the two products are shown in Figure 3.7 by a downward shift in the demand for hot dogs and an upward shift in the demand for pizza (D_1 to D_2). This would cause a shortage in the pizza market and a surplus in the hot dog market. As we know, the rationing function of price will immediately start to correct these market imbalances. As the price of hot dogs falls, the surplus is eliminated; as the price of pizza rises, the shortage is eliminated. (For the purpose of the analysis, it really does not matter where the price of pizza stands in relation to the

Figure 3.7   Short-Run and Long-Run Changes in Supply (in Response to an Initial Change in Demand)

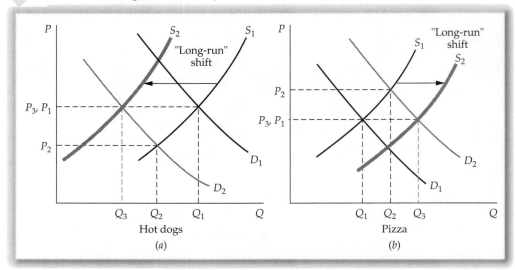

price of hot dogs. To simplify matters, we have assumed the two prices were about equal before the change in tastes and preferences occurred. The point is that after price performs its rationing function, the equilibrium price of pizza will be higher than the equilibrium price of hot dogs in relative terms.)

Now suppose the prices have indeed changed, and the two markets are once again in equilibrium. What do you suppose will happen next? As you might imagine, the depressed price of hot dogs will cause the sellers to begin allocating less of their resources to this market. Some may even go out of the business of making or selling hot dogs. In contrast, the higher price of pizza will induce the allocation of more resources into this market. New pizza stands and restaurants may be opened. Food companies may build new plants to produce frozen pizza for distribution through supermarkets. The effect of these follow-on adjustments to the initial change in equilibrium prices can be seen in the figure as a rightward shift in the supply of pizza and a leftward shift in the supply of hot dogs.

After this "long-run" adjustment is made, equilibrium price and quantity may return to the levels at which they were before the initial changes in demand took place (i.e., P_3 in each market may be close to or equal to P_1). But the main point is that Q_3 is considerably less than Q_1 in the hot dog market and considerably more than Q_1 in the pizza market. These differences represent the shifting of resources out of the hot dog market and into the pizza market. Several centuries ago, Adam Smith referred to this shifting of resources into and out of markets in response to price changes as the "invisible hand."[3] Another way to express these shifts in supply is that they represent a response to "price signals" sent to the owners of the factors of production. In any event, when resources have been shifted out of the market for hot dogs and into the market for pizza, price is fulfilling its **guiding** or **allocating function**. Defined in a more formal manner, the guiding or allocating function of price is the movement of resources into or out of markets in response to a change in the equilibrium price of a good or service.

The preceding example illustrates a basic distinction made in economic analysis between the "short run" and the "long run." This distinction has nothing to do directly with a specific calendar time. Instead, it refers to the amount of time it takes for sellers and buyers to react to changes in the market equilibrium price. The following descriptions of the short run and the long run helps readers distinguish the two time periods:

1. **Short run**
   a. Period of time in which sellers already in the market respond to a change in equilibrium price by adjusting the amount of certain resources, which economists call *variable inputs*. Examples of such inputs are labor hours and raw materials. A short-run adjustment by sellers can be envisioned as a movement along a particular supply curve.
   b. Period of time in which buyers already in the market respond to changes in equilibrium price by adjusting the quantity demanded for a particular good or service. A short-run adjustment by buyers can be envisioned as a movement along a particular demand curve.

2. **Long run**
   a. Period of time in which new sellers may enter a market or the original sellers may exit from a market. This period is long enough for existing sellers to either increase or decrease their *fixed factors* of production. Examples of fixed factors include property,

---

[3]For Smith, the "visible" hand was that of the government, which might try to dictate the allocation of resources among different markets by the command process rather than by the market process.

plant, and equipment. A long-run adjustment by sellers can be seen graphically as a shift in a given supply curve.

b. Period of time in which buyers may react to a change in equilibrium price by changing their tastes and preferences or buying patterns. (The *Wall Street Journal* and other sources of business news may refer to this as a "structural change" in demand.) A long-run adjustment by buyers can be seen graphically as a shift in a given demand curve.

Another good way of distinguishing the short run from the long run is to note that the rationing function of price is a short-run phenomenon, whereas the guiding function is a long-run phenomenon.

Let us summarize the short-run "rationing function" and the long-run "guiding function" of price in terms of our example involving pizza and hot dogs:

1. Changing tastes and preferences cause the demand for pizza to increase and the demand for hot dogs to decrease.

2. The changing demand for the two products causes a shortage in the pizza market and a surplus in the hot dog market.

3. In response to the surplus and shortage in the two markets, price serves as a *rationing* agent by decreasing in the hot dog market and increasing in the pizza market. That is, the short-run response by suppliers of the two products is to change their variable inputs (i.e., movement downward along the supply line in the market for hot dogs, and movement upward along the supply line in the market for pizza).

4. In the *long run,* price fulfills its *guiding* function by causing sellers and potential sellers to respond by increasing capacity or entering the market for pizza and by decreasing capacity or leaving the market for hot dogs (i.e., rightward shift in the supply line for pizza and leftward shift in the supply line for hot dogs).

5. As a result of the shifts in supply, new equilibrium levels of price and quantity are established. The new quantities bought and sold represent shifts in resources out of one market and into the other.

The distinction between short- and long-run changes in the market can also be made in cases that begin with changes in supply rather than in demand. A classic example is the case of the Organization of Petroleum Exporting Countries (OPEC) and the world oil market. In the early 1970s, OPEC conspired to raise the price of oil by limiting production to an amount that would support a price above the current level. The supply-and-demand diagram shown in Figure 3.8 illustrates this action. As we can see, limiting the production of oil can be envisioned as a leftward shift in the supply line to the level where it intersects the demand curve for oil at some designated point above the current market price (i.e., P_2 rather than P_1). The short-run response by consumers to the increase in oil prices was to reduce their consumption of oil. However, in the terms specific to our analysis, this reduction can be seen as a decrease in the *quantity demanded* for oil. In other words, the decrease in the supply of oil (i.e., the shift of the supply line to the left) prompted a *movement back along the demand curve* for oil.

Over time, U.S. consumers began to change their pattern of oil consumption as a result of the high price. They formed car pools, bought more fuel-efficient cars, lowered their thermostats in their homes, and even tried to follow the new 55-mph speed limit established on highways throughout the country. Industrial users of oil responded by substituting more fuel-efficient machinery as soon as it became cost efficient to make these changes. The effect of this *long-run* change in the pattern of oil usage caused the demand for oil to gradually fall. Graphically, this is presented by a leftward shift of the demand curve for oil from D_1 to D_2. Notice that as a result of this long-run shift in demand, the equilibrium price and quantity fell. As seen in Figure 3.8, the long-run

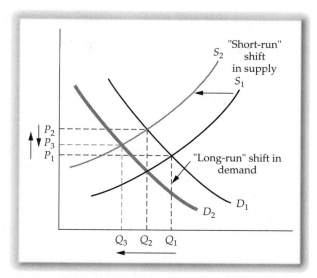

Figure 3.8   Short-Run and Long-Run Changes in Demand (in Response to an Initial Change in Supply)

quantity that is bought and sold (i.e., Q_3) was now even less than it was before this decrease in demand took place. This indicates a further shift of resources out of this market.

The previous events occurred more than 35 years ago. After a series of ups and downs associated with such world events as the U.S. problem with Iran in the late 1970s and the 1990 Gulf War, the price of oil settled at around $20 per barrel throughout the second half of the 1990s. Sometimes, the average price even fell into the teens. In mid-2003, the price of oil began to climb to about $50 per barrel. At first, American consumers appeared to continue with "business as usual." An article in the *New York Times* at that time quoted an oncologist from Wisconsin as saying, "I don't like gas being this expensive. My driving is integral to my job. It's integral to my pleasure in life. I won't cut back on that. I might cut back on other things." (He drove an SUV that got 18 miles to the gallon.) Another SUV owner, a nurse from Massachusetts, was also quoted. "I have to have a car," she explained. "I have a little girl I have to drive everywhere. In the suburbs you have to drive."[4]

When we came across this article, we agreed with the basic premise that driving is essential, particularly in the suburbs. But at the same time, is it necessary for people to drive gas-guzzling SUVs? The interesting thing about the long run in economic theory is that there is no specified time period. At the time this current edition is being prepared, the price of oil is more than double the level it was when the individuals cited above were quoted and experts anticipate a possible tripling or even *quadrupling* of the $50 a barrel price that existed in 2003. At this price level, the long-run forces appear to have affected people's choice of cars. In 2007, the press reported that the U.S. sales of the hybrid Toyota Prius exceeded the level of sales of the Ford Explorer.[5]

---

[4]"Laissez-Faire My Gas Guzzler, Already: Never Mind the Price, Just Fill 'er Up," *New York Times,* September 7, 2004.
[5]Bernard Simon, "Toyota Prius Sales Pass Ford Explorer in the U.S.," *Financial Times,* January 11, 2008.

Using Supply and Demand in Forecasting

Chapter 5 is devoted to the subject of demand estimation and forecasting. But we should point out here that a fundamental part of economic forecasting is to understand the nature of the determinants of supply and demand. Forecasting supply is somewhat easier than forecasting demand, particularly if factors such as natural disasters (e.g., droughts or floods in the market for food products), international conflicts, or political crises (e.g., Iraq War and turmoil in Venezuela and the market for oil) are not involved. For example, in the market for manufactured goods, one essentially needs to assess the current and future capacity of the producers. This could be done by counting the number of factories in operation and their utilization rates, or by looking at the overall level of inventories in the industry.

The more difficult challenge is to estimate demand. As you see in chapter 5, economists try to understand and forecast demand by using the statistical analysis of data collected either from historical records or from a cross section of economic entities (e.g., consumers, households, companies, states, regions, or countries). Much effort is made to understand the quantitative relationship between changes in the determinants of demand and the amount of demand of a particular good or service. Sometimes, a more qualitative assessment of the impact of changes in these determinants in demand can be quite useful in the making of management decisions. Consider the following examples:

1. ***The "Low-Carb" Trend in America:*** In 2002, many Americans began to adopt low-carbohydrate diets (e.g., "Atkins Diet," "South Beach Diet"). Is this just a fad, or does it represent a longer-term trend in the way Americans eat? The answer to this question is important to the food manufacturers who began to offer special products to meet this increased demand for "low-carb" food. Certainly, the sellers of Krispy Kreme doughnuts would want to know more about this change in the tastes and preferences of consumers. Until early 2004, Krispy Kreme was considered one of the fastest growing and most successful fast-food chains in the United States. But apparently, this change in eating habits has had an impact on the demand.[6]

Table 3.6   Short-Run and Long-Run Changes in the Market

Initial Change (Short-Run Time Period)	Follow-on Change (Long-Run Time Period)
Increase in demand causes *price to rise*	*Supply increases* as new sellers enter the market and original sellers increase production capacity
Decrease in demand causes *price to fall*	*Supply decreases* as less profitable firms or those experiencing losses exit the market or decrease production capacity
Increase in supply causes *price to fall*	*Demand increases* as tastes and preferences of consumers eventually change in favor of the product relative to substitutes
Decrease in supply causes *price to rise*	*Demand decreases* as tastes and preferences of consumers eventually change away from the product and toward the substitutes

---

[6]Audra Burch, "Krispy Kreme Blames Drop in Shares on Low-Carb Craze," *Knight Ridder/Tribune Business News,* May 8, 2004.

2. ***The World Market for Flat-Screen Television Sets:***   Flat-screen TVs have rejuvenated what many considered to be a mature market. There are two types of screens: plasma and liquid crystal display (LCD). Plasma screens are available in larger sizes and are relatively less expensive. However, LCDs tend to last longer and have certain viewing advantages. They are not produced in sizes as large as plasma screens, but each new generation of flat-panel displays brings them closer in size and price to the plasma ones. But in a surprise move in the industry, one of the leading manufacturers of LCDs, Chi Mei Optoelectronics of Taiwan, announced in late summer 2004 that it was suspending construction of the seventh-generation plant (which was scheduled to come on line in 2006). In doing so, the company was in fact "questioning the viability of the industry's race to build bigger television screens."[7] Until then, Chi Mei had followed a strategy typical of any other manufacturer in the consumer electronics or high-tech industry: keep developing bigger and better products at a lower cost. The sixth-generation LCD screen, scheduled for mass production in 2005, would range in size from 32 to 37 inches. The seventh generation would result in 40-inch screens. The director of finance for Chi Mei stated that investment in the seventh-generation "fab" was being suspended because of the uncertainty of what demand would be in 2006. In his words, "So we will continue reviewing this and if we come to the conclusion that smaller sizes are to remain the mainstream, a sixth-generation fab will be enough." An analyst with Merrill Lynch in Taipei believed that "thirty-two inch LCD panel prices will have to come down from the current [production cost of] US$1,000 to US$700 next year to bring the retail price down to the magic US$1,500 level at which consumers start buying."

SUPPLY, DEMAND, AND PRICE: THE MANAGERIAL CHALLENGE

A critical factor that managers must consider when making decisions such as the pricing of products and the allocation of a company's scarce resource is the market environment in which their company is competing. This chapter focuses on the mechanics of supply and demand in a highly competitive market. In the extreme case, the forces of supply and demand are the sole determinants of market price. This type of market is called "perfect competition." (For complete details about this market, see chapter 8.) Managers operating in perfectly competitive markets are simply "price takers" trying to earn a profit by making decisions about the allocation of resources based on their short- and long-run assessment of the movements of supply, demand, and prices.

There are other types of competitive markets in which firms act as "price makers" by exercising varying degrees of control over the price of their product. We refer to this type of market as "imperfectly competitive" and the control of market price as **market power**. This power to strongly influence market price may stem from these firms' ability to differentiate their product through advertising, brand name, or special features or add-on services. Also, many oligopolistic firms hold extremely large shares of the market, and their sheer size enables them to dictate prices. (Microsoft and its products for the PC immediately come to mind as an example.) Nonetheless, supply and demand do establish the overall framework in which prices are set. For example, regardless of how strong the market power of a firm, it would be extremely difficult for it to raise prices in the face of falling or sluggish market demand. To dramatize the difference between price-taking and price-making management situations, we look at the market for coffee in contrast to the market for air travel during the first half of this decade.

---

[7]This section is from "Chi Mei Halts Flat-Panel Project," *Financial Times*, September 9, 2004.

Case 3.1 *Coffee:* "Buy Low and Sell High"

In 2000, overproduction in the international coffee market caused the price of coffee to drop below production costs. In December 2001, coffee prices reached a low of 41.5 cents per pound, the lowest price in more than 30 years. Farmers in countries such as Angola, Honduras, Sri Lanka, and Zimbabwe even stopped tending their coffee trees in an effort to save on spending for fertilizer and maintenance. Part of the problem was the usual cyclical swings in price caused by the movements of supply and demand. Recall our discussion of the short- and long-run movements in price. In response to a high price, supply increases. There is often a tendency for supply to overshift to the right, causing prices to plummet. The "long-run adjustment" of supply with demand is rarely, if ever, as smooth as depicted in textbook diagrams.[8]

With coffee prices so low, it is believed that consumers would benefit with a lower price for a cup of coffee. However, as readers well know, not all cups of coffee are created equal. While coffee prices kept falling, specialty coffee retailers such as Starbucks were charging its customers $3.50 for a "tall skinny latte." Despite the fact that Starbucks is usually located in high-rent areas, we can imagine that the markup on these specialty drinks, given the wholesale price of coffee, definitely helps pay the rent and more.[9] This shows that, although the wholesale market for coffee may be subject to the vagaries of shifting supply and demand, the retail market provides a better opportunity for sellers to exert market power by catering to the tastes and preferences of those who prefer a higher-quality product and are willing to pay for it. Starbucks is a company that until now has played with the forces of supply, demand, and market power like a virtuoso: It buys low in the depressed wholesale market and sells high in the differentiated specialty retail market.

In mid-2004, wholesale prices started to move upward, increasing by about 30 percent between May and June. The effects of the farmers who had stopped or reduced production due to low prices had started to make an impact on the market. (Imagine a leftward "long-run" shift in the supply curve.) There was also a drought and unusually low temperatures in Brazil, the world's largest coffee producer.[10] (Imagine a leftward "short-run" shift in the supply curve.) Big coffee sellers, unlike Starbucks and other specialty retailers, had not been able to raise prices during the past 4 or 5 years because of the overall depressed market for coffee beans. Now the cost pressures from the higher price of wholesale beans have finally enabled them to justify the raising of their prices to restaurants and other away-from-home customers.

What will consumers do in the face of rising prices for nonspecialty coffee? As is explained in great detail in chapter 4, the demand for coffee is considered to be relative inelastic. Therefore, industry analysts expect coffee drinkers to consume about the same amount as they always have. As a 10-cup-per-day consumer interviewed by a newspaper reporter stated, "I hate that the price might go up, but I got to have my coffee."[11]

Interestingly enough, Starbucks actually welcomes the higher wholesale price of coffee. As explained by its CEO, Rin Smith, "We are paying higher prices for coffee, which we think is a good thing. One of the consequences of the low prices is that a lot of farmers have gone out of business and that threatens our *long-run* [emphasis added] supply." This statement shows that sometimes continuity of supply can be as important as the purchase price. If higher coffee prices help keep coffee farmers in business, then buyers like Starbucks are willing to pay the higher price. Moreover, as stated earlier, differentiated sellers such as Starbucks are in even better positions to raise the price than the processors who sell coffee to restaurants. In fact, in September 2004, Starbucks announced that it was raising the average price of its beverages by 11 cents, citing "increases in the cost of coffee and sugar."[12] ∎

---

[8]"Coffee Bean Prices Perk Up 30 Percent in Last Month as Supply Trickles Down," *Chicago Tribune*, June 5, 2004.
[9]"Where Coffee Is the New Wine," *Financial Times*, February 1, 2002.

[10]For additional discussion on Brazil and the coffee market, see Appendix 4A.
[11]"Coffee Bean Prices Perk Up. . . " *op. cit.*
[12]"Starbucks to Boost Coffee Prices in U.S.," *USA Today*, September 28, 2004.

Case 3.2 *Air Travel:* "Buy High and Sell Low"

Ever since the U.S. airline industry was deregulated in the late 1970s, the major air carriers have been struggling to overcome the resulting competition that beset them. In the booming 1990s, the major airlines had finally started to earn respectable profits. But the technology bust, short recession, and post-9/11 downturn in air travel dissolved any hopes of their establishing a long-term record of profitability. When this edition was being prepared, their losses continued to mount. United Airlines and USAirways were in protected bankruptcy under Chapter 11. Delta Airlines seemed to be headed for the same fate. American Airlines was threatened with bankruptcy in 2003. Its purchase of TWA several years earlier apparently made it no more secure than the other "legacy" carriers.

Yet, the "low-cost carriers" have survived and even thrived in the deregulated environment. Southwest Airlines was one of the pioneers in introducing low-cost, no-frills airline service, offering flights of relatively short distances (usually less than 500 miles).[13] In doing so, it believed its competition to be more the automobile than the major airlines. Its financial success in using a different type of business model soon led to the start of JetBlue and AirTran (formerly ValueJet).

The success of the low-cost airlines can be seen in their very nomenclature. In markets where fierce competition leads to price reductions, only those with a low-cost structure can survive. An alternative would be to take the "Starbucks approach" and offer premium services at a higher price. To a large extent, this is what the major airlines have tried to do by catering to business travelers who have typically been more sensitive to the scheduling of flights rather than the price. However, when the entire market demand slumps, it becomes much more difficult to rely on those segments of the market that are willing to pay more for premium service. Furthermore, to reduce cost many companies have been restricting the travel of their employees or requiring them to substitute this travel with more Web-based or video conferences. If travel is required, employees are being required to find the lowest fares.

In an effort to compete with the low-cost carriers, the legacy airlines have been continuing to pare down their workforce and negotiating with the unions to reduce wages. Prior to September 11, 2001, United Airlines had more than 100,000 employees. In 2004, this number had fallen to less than 55,000. On September 8, 2004, Delta Airlines announced a layoff of 7,000 workers. In January 2005, Delta announced a sweeping reduction in its air fare structure. The company is hoping that its lower structure will enable it to survice these price cuts.

What has made the situation even worse for the legacy airlines is the rising price of oil. In the fall of 2004, the price of oil was almost $50 per barrel. This caused American Airlines to project its fuel bill in 2004 to be about $1 billion more than planned. If the legacy airlines were unable to sustain their higher prices in the face of mounting competition from the low-cost airlines, they have certainly not been able to pass on higher fuel costs by increasing airfares. However, some of the major airlines made a feeble attempt to do so by charging a ticketing fee. In September 2004, Northwest Airlines announced that it would begin charging passengers $5 per ticket for trips booked through its reservations agents and $10 for those purchased at airports. American Airlines quickly followed suit. American Airlines reported that this fee was expected to bring in additional revenue of about $25 million per year.[14]

In conclusion, market forces have caught the management of the major airlines in a cost trap with hardly a means of getting out. Supply and demand conditions for oil have drastically raised fuel prices, and at the same time supply and demand conditions for air travel have made it difficult, if not impossible, to increase air fares. Contrast this to the situation facing the managers of the sellers of coffee. Specialty coffee retailers such as Starbucks enjoyed huge profits by being able to mark up the price of their coffee while paying relatively little for the beans. As supply and demand

---

[13]For more on the Southwest Airlines low-cost model, see chapter 7.

[14]"Laissez-Faire My Gas Guzzler, Already," *op. cit.*

conditions push up the price of the beans, large coffee suppliers have been able to raise the price of their product. Not only *can* these large sellers raise the price, but they also *want* to make these increases because they believe that coffee drinkers will not reduce the amount demanded. A complete discussion of the responsiveness of buyers to changes in price is presented in chapter 4. ∎

GLOBAL APPLICATION: THE MARKET FOR COBALT

The markets for commodities such as food, oil, and minerals offer some of the best examples of supply and demand at work. The price of oil and its underlying supply and demand conditions are always making headline news. But at the time this edition was being prepared, the rising price of a little-known but important commodity, cobalt, was also sharing some of the spotlight with the $100+ barrel of oil. Rather than elaborate further on the often discussed market for oil, let us take a closer look at how the forces of supply and demand play a direct part in determining the market price and output of cobalt. Because cobalt is such an important part of the world economy, a discussion of its market dynamics can also serve as our "Global Application" section, which we include at the end of each chapter.

The Current Market Situation

Cobalt is a rare metal produced mainly as a by-product from the mining of copper and nickel.[15] Table 3.7 shows the production for the first part of this decade. As you can see in this table, world production is relatively small. In the first half of this decade, world production ranged from 37,900 to 52,400 metric tons per year. Furthermore, output in recent years has not increased very much above the level produced in 2004. In recent years, world production averaged about 60,000 tons annually.[16]

According to industry expert Kim B. Shedd, cobalt is a "strategic and critical metal used in many diverse industrial and military applications." It is also used to make magnets, catalysts for petroleum and chemical industries, drying agents for paints, steel-belted radial tires, lithium ion batteries, and numerous other industrial and consumer products.[17] Lithium ion batteries are used to power such important products as mobile phones, laptop computers, and hybrid cars. After a number of years of relative stability, the price of cobalt has increased by almost 60% to $40.25 per pound, the highest since a modern market for cobalt began in the early 1970s.[18]

A major source of the recent rise in the world price of cobalt is the reduction in the world supply because the government of the Democratic Republic of the Congo (DRC) imposed a ban on the exporting of cobalt in October 2007. (Notice in Table 3.7 that the DRC was the top producer of cobalt in 2004 and continues to be among the top producers in the world.) The entire country (formerly called Zaire) continues to be plagued by ongoing political, social, and economic upheaval and armed conflict. So it is difficult to say if and when the government plans to remove this export ban.

---

[15]Numerous easily accessible Web sites provide excellent general information about cobalt. One concise and informative source for non-geologists is provided by the Mineral Information Institute. See http://www.mü.org/Minerals/photocobalt.html.

[16]Chris Flood, "Battery Demand Galvanises Price of Cobalt," *Financial Times,* January 1, 2008.

[17]Kim B. Shedd is an industry expert whose work is found in numerous government publications. This general information comes from one of Shedd's studies found on the Internet at www.minerals.usgs.gov/minerals/pubs/commodity/cobalt/210798.pdf. The original source and the publication date were not identified in the PDF document. But further references checks revealed that Shedd is a well-established authority on the subject of strategically important minerals.

[18]The idea for this section came from the article by Chris Flood cited in footnote 16.

Table 3.7 Cobalt: World Mine Production, by Country (Metric tons, cobalt content)

Country	2000	2001	2002	2003	2004
Australia	5,600	6,300	6,700	6,900	6,700
Botswana	308	325	269	294	223
Brazil	900	1,100	1,200	1,300	1,400
Canada	5,298	5,326	5,148	4,327	5,197
China	90	150	1,000	700	800
Congo	11,000	15,000	14,500	12,000	16,000
Cuba	2,852	3,417	3,384	3,465	3,580
Kazakhstan	300	300	300	300	300
Morocco	967	1,242	1,453	1,391	1,600
New Caledonia	1,200	1,400	1,400	1,400	1,400
Norway	100	100	100	–	–
Russia	4,000	4,600	4,600	4,800	4,700
South Africa	580	560	520	400	460
Zambia	4,600	8,000	10,000	11,300	10,000
Zimbabwe	79	95	87	79	59
Total	37,900	47,900	50,700	48,700	52,400

Source: United States Geological Survey Mineral Resources Program as found in http://www.indexmundi.com/en/commodities/minerals/cobalt/cobalt_t8.html. (This table's many explanatory footnotes were not included for purposes of simplification.)

But this reduction in supply, combined with the growing demand for cobalt for making batteries for consumer electronics products such as cell phones, laptop computers, and hybrid cars, has resulted in the sharp price increases. (As noted earlier, in 2007 the Toyota Prius surpassed the Ford Explorer in U.S. auto sales.)[19]

A Brief History of the Market for Cobalt

An analysis of the movement of cobalt prices over the past few decades provides further examples of the forces of supply and demand at work. Figure 3.9 shows price movements of cobalt between 1959 and 1998. Industry expert Kim Shedd has provided explanatory notes to accompany this figure to help explain some more pronounced movements in price. This figure and the accompanying notes provide excellent illustrations of the kinds of "nonprice determinants" of supply and demand that we discussed throughout this chapter.[20]

Implications for Managers

The rising demand and the relatively fixed supply of cobalt means that managers of companies that require this mineral in their products must build higher costs of production into their business planning and forecasts. As you have learned in this chapter, over the economic long run, managers would try to see if they can find substitutes for this product. According to the Mineral Information Institute,

> There are some replacements for cobalt, but they don't always work as well as cobalt. For example, nickel-iron or neodymium-iron-boron alloys can be

---

[19]Bernard Simon, *op. cit.*
[20]Kim B. Shedd, "Significant Events Affecting Cobalt Prices Since 1958," www.minerals.usgs.gov/minerals/pubs/commodity/cobalt/210798.pdf.

used to make strong magnets. Nickel and special ceramics can be used to make cutting and wear-resistant materials. Nickel-base alloys containing little or no cobalt can be used in jet engines. Manganese, iron, cerium, or zirconium can be used in paint driers.[21]

Until new technology innovations occur or perhaps new major sources of cobalt are discovered, we suppose that consumers can be expected to pay more for those products containing cobalt.

Figure 3.9   Annual Average Cobalt Price (Dollars per pound)

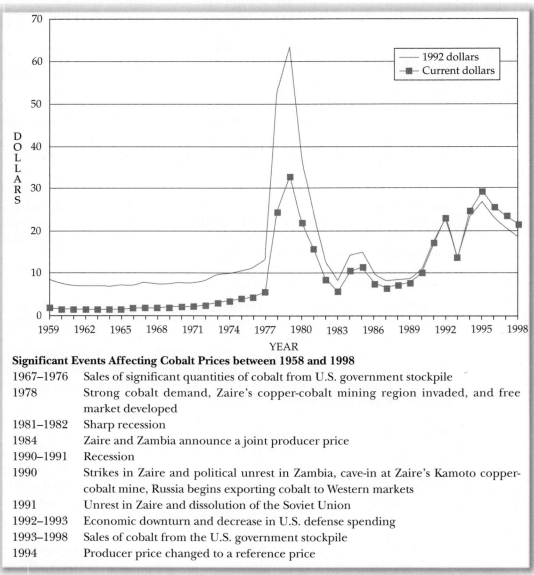

Significant Events Affecting Cobalt Prices between 1958 and 1998

1967–1976	Sales of significant quantities of cobalt from U.S. government stockpile
1978	Strong cobalt demand, Zaire's copper-cobalt mining region invaded, and free market developed
1981–1982	Sharp recession
1984	Zaire and Zambia announce a joint producer price
1990–1991	Recession
1990	Strikes in Zaire and political unrest in Zambia, cave-in at Zaire's Kamoto copper-cobalt mine, Russia begins exporting cobalt to Western markets
1991	Unrest in Zaire and dissolution of the Soviet Union
1992–1993	Economic downturn and decrease in U.S. defense spending
1993–1998	Sales of cobalt from the U.S. government stockpile
1994	Producer price changed to a reference price

---

[21]Mineral Information Institute, *op. cit.*

The Solution

Rather than present her findings in a formal report using overhead slides, Nicole believed she would be more effective by simply providing her boss with an informal briefing. In fact, Nicole noticed a backlash among senior executives regarding the excessive use of huge "decks" of slides. They actually seemed to detract from the presenter's message. She knew she could send Bob all the details in a complete deck after she made her key points to him in this informal discussion.

"Bob, my staff has carefully gone over all available information about the potential market for tea. Right now the supply of the standard tea in a bag that the majority of Americans continue to drink is provided by three dominant players: Lipton (owned by our archrival, Unilever), Bigelow (with its leading brand, Constant Comment), and Twinings (with its British teatime image). But the real growth of this market is in the hundreds of varieties of green teas, exotic black teas, and even white and red teas. And right now, the supply for these varieties is being met by hundreds of specialty companies, many of whom distribute their product online and through retail stores. More important, these suppliers of 'designer teas' are able to charge a higher price than the standard teas sold by the large incumbents because of the strength and nature of the demand for this product. And it's not just the successful startups such as The Republic of Tea and Adagio Teas that are making an impact in this market. In 1999, Starbucks began offering Tazo, a brand that was started 10 years before by a small company in Portland, Oregon. Once Starbucks began selling this brand, tea sales per store tripled. In fact, there is a company based in Atlanta called Teavana that has started a chain of tea houses.

"I believe that the explosive demand for the new teas can be explained simply by using the traditional economic factors that drive the demand for any product. Let me summarize these factors:

1. ***The Impact of Income on Demand:*** The new designer teas appeal to consumers with higher incomes. (After all, who would be more willing to pay a premium price for a cup of tea?) One way that we got an insight into this aspect of demand for expensive teas is by looking at the phenomenal growth of the retail food chain Whole Foods. Whole Foods (sometimes called jokingly 'Whole Paycheck') caters to exactly the same type of consumer that would buy designer teas. Indeed, next time you visit this store, check out its display of tea and coffee. You'll be amazed at the variety (and prices) of their stock. One of the key reasons for the success of Whole Foods is an increase in the proportion of U.S. households earning $100,000 or more from 18 percent 10 years ago to 22 percent in 2004. This increase in the income segment that desires and can afford this product has clearly helped boost the overall market demand for designer teas, exotic coffees, and most of the other products sold at Whole Foods.[22]

2. ***The Impact of Tastes and Preferences on Demand:*** Our preliminary marketing studies indicate that the people who buy this product actually consider it a 'necessary' part of their life. In other words, designer tea is not simply a product, but part of a tea drinker's lifestyle. Moreover, many people in our survey tell us that the preparation and the drinking of tea counteracts the day-to-day stresses of the high-tech, 24/7 work life that we all now seem to lead. Tea is perceived to have a more calming effect than any other beverage, particularly coffee, and even the process of brewing tea becomes a soothing ritual that breaks up the hectic pace of the work day.

3. ***Prices of Related Products:*** We do not know for certain, but we believe that coffee is considered a closer substitute for tea than either bottled water or carbonated beverages (particularly those without caffeine). Starbucks' great success with its Tazo brand of tea indicates that many of the same people who demand fancy coffee seem to desire designer teas. In fact, tea has even been dubbed 'the new coffee.'[23] We all know what has been happening to the price of coffee. No doubt the recent increase in coffee prices has helped increase the demand for its close substitute, tea."

"Okay, Nicole, I really like this idea. But I'm not fully convinced, and I also think we should see how our new initiatives in the bottled water business turn out before we try something else. Have your staff send me more details, and I would be particularly interested if you were able to provide me with a quantitative analysis of the impact of those factors you mentioned on the demand for designer teas. But to be honest, you have really got me thinking seriously about this product. In fact, I wonder how much we would have to pay for The Republic of Tea? But maybe that's jumping too far ahead. Let's see the analysis first."

---

[22]John Gapper, "Comment: Organic Foods Stores Are on a Natural High," *Financial Times*, September 16, 2004.
[23]Olsen, *op. cit.*

SUMMARY

This chapter presents the basic elements of supply and demand. We begin by introducing the *law of demand* and the *law of supply* and the nonprice factors that affect demand and supply. The law of demand states that, other factors held constant, the quantity demanded is inversely related to price. The law of supply states that, other factors held constant, the quantity supplied is directly related to price. Other factors that affect demand are (1) tastes and preferences, (2) income, (3) prices of related products, (4) number of buyers, and (5) future expectations. Other factors that affect supply are (1) costs, (2) technology, (3) prices of other products that sellers can supply, (4) number of sellers, (5) future expectations, and (6) weather conditions. Both numerical and graphical examples of supply and demand and how they interrelate to determine the equilibrium price and quantity were presented. Appendix 3A presents the same material in algebraic terms.

We study how price serves a short-run rationing function and a long-run guiding function in the marketplace. Price serves a rationing function when it increases or decreases to clear the market of a shortage or surplus caused by a change in market conditions (i.e., a shifting of the supply or demand curve). Price changes serve as a guiding function signaling producers or consumers to put more or less of their resources in the affected markets.

In explaining the rationing and guiding functions of price, we note the particular way in which economists define the short run and the long run. We also discuss how comparative statics analysis is used to explain the rationing and guiding functions of the price. This technique, involving the comparison of equilibrium points before and after changes in the market have occurred, is a standard way of analyzing problems and is used throughout this text.

IMPORTANT CONCEPTS

Change in demand: The result of a change in one or more of the nonprice determinants of demand, graphically represented by a *shift* in the demand curve (rightward for an increase in demand and leftward for a decrease in demand). (p. 47)

Change in supply: The result of a change in one or more of the nonprice determinants of supply, graphically represented by a *shift* in the supply curve (rightward for an increase and leftward for a decrease). (p. 50)

Change in the quantity demanded: The result of a change in the price of a good or service, graphically represented by a *movement along* a particular demand curve. (p. 47)

Change in the quantity supplied: The result of a change in the price of a good or service, graphically represented by a *movement along* a particular supply curve. (p. 50)

Demand: Quantities of a good or service that people are ready to buy at various prices, other factors besides the price held constant. Demand can be expressed as a numerical schedule, as a demand curve on a graph, or as an algebraic equation. (p. 46)

Equilibrium price: The price that equates the quantity demanded with the quantity supplied; the price that clears the market of any shortage or surplus. (p. 52)

Equilibrium quantity: The amount that people are ready to buy and sell at the equilibrium price level. (p. 52)

Guiding function of price: Also referred to as the *allocating function of price*, the movement of resources into or out of markets as a result of changes in the equilibrium market price. This is considered to be a long-run function. On the supply side of the market, sellers may enter or leave the market or may vary all their factors of production. On the demand side, consumers may change their tastes or preferences or find long-lasting alternatives to a particular good or service. (p. 57)

Law of demand: The quantity demanded depends *inversely* on price. (p. 46)

Long run: A time period in which new sellers may enter a market or sellers already in a market may leave. This time period is sufficient for both old and new sellers to vary *all* their factors of production. From the standpoint of consumers, the long run provides time enough to respond to price changes by actually changing their tastes or preferences or their use of alternative goods and services. For example, suppose bad weather in Brazil results in an increase in the price of coffee. In the short run, people are expected to buy less coffee because of the higher price. However, in the long run, they may buy even less coffee because the higher price will have prompted them to drink more tea on a regular basis. (p. 57)

Market demand: The sum of all individual demands for a good or service. (p. 46)

Market power: The power to set the market price. (p. 61)

Nonprice determinants of demand: (1) Tastes and preferences, (2) income, (3) prices of related products (i.e., substitutes or complements), (4) future expectations, (5) number of buyers. (p. 48)

Nonprice determinants of supply: (1) Costs, (2) technology, (3) prices of other products that may be produced by a firm, (4) future expectations, (5) number of sellers, (6) weather conditions. (p. 50)

Quantity demanded: The amount that people are ready to buy at a given price. (p. 46)

Quantity supplied: The amount that people are ready to sell at a given price. (p. 50)

Rationing function of price: The increase or decrease in price to clear the market of any shortage or surplus. This is considered to be a short-run function because both buyers and sellers are expected to respond only to price changes. (p. 53)

Shortage: A condition that exists in the market when the quantity demanded exceeds the quantity supplied at a price *below* the equilibrium or market-clearing price. (p. 52)

Short run: A time period in which only those sellers already in the market may respond to a change in market price by using more or less of their variable resources. From the standpoint of consumers, the short run is a period in which they respond only to price changes. As a result of a change in price, consumers may change their tastes or preferences or their use of alternative goods or services. However, in economic analysis, these related changes are considered long-run phenomena. (p. 53)

Supply: Quantities of a good or service that people are ready to *sell* at various prices, other factors besides price held constant. Supply can be expressed as a numerical schedule, as a supply curve on a graph, or as an algebraic equation. (p. 50)

Surplus: A condition that exists in the market when the quantity supplied exceeds the quantity demanded at a price that lies *above* the equilibrium or market-clearing price. (p. 52)

QUESTIONS

1. Define *demand.* Define *supply.* In your answers, explain the difference between *demand* and *quantity demanded* and between *supply* and *quantity supplied.*
2. List the key nonprice factors that influence demand and supply.
3. In defining demand and supply, why do you think economists focus on price while holding constant other factors that might have an impact on the behavior of buyers and sellers?
4. Define comparative statics analysis. How does it compare with sensitivity analysis or what-if analysis used in finance, accounting, and statistics?
5. Define the *rationing function* of price. Why is it necessary for price to serve this function in the market economy?
6. Define the *guiding* or *allocating function* of price.
7. Discuss the differences between the short run and the long run from the perspective of producers and from the perspective of consumers.
8. Explain the difference between shortages and scarcity. In answering this question, you should consider the difference between the short run and the long run in economic analysis.
9. Why do you think it is important for managers to understand the mechanics of supply and demand both in the short run and in the long run? Give examples of companies whose

business was either helped or hurt by changes in supply or demand in the markets in which they were competing.

10. "If Congress levies an additional tax on luxury items, the prices of these items will rise. However, this will cause demand to decrease, and as a result the prices will fall back down, perhaps even to their original levels." Do you agree with this statement? Explain.

11. Overheard at the water cooler in the corporate headquarters of a large manufacturing concern: "The competition is really threatening us with their new product line. I think we should consider offering discounts on our current line in order to stimulate demand." In this statement, is the term *demand* being used in a manner consistent with economic theory? Explain. Illustrate your answer using a line drawn to represent the demand for this firm's product line.

12. Briefly list and elaborate on the factors that will be affecting the demand for the following products in the next several years. Do you think these factors will cause the demand to increase or decrease?
    a. Convenience foods (sold in food shops and supermarkets)
    b. Products purchased on the Internet
    c. Fax machines
    d. Film and cameras
    e. Videos rented from retail outlets
    f. Pay-per-view television programing
    g. Airline travel within the United States; airline travel within Europe
    h. Gasoline

13. Briefly list and elaborate on the factors that will be affecting the supply of the following products in the next several years. Do you think these factors will cause the supply to increase or decrease?
    a. Crude oil
    b. Beef
    c. Computer memory chips
    d. Hotel rooms
    e. Fast food outlets in emerging markets
    f. Credit cards issued by financial institutions
    g. Laptop computers
    h. PC servers

PROBLEMS

1. The following function describes the demand condition for a company that makes caps featuring names of college and professional teams in a variety of sports.

$$Q = 2,000 - 100\,P$$

where Q is cap sales and P is price.
    a. How many caps could be sold at $12 each?
    b. What should the price be in order for the company to sell 1,000 caps?
    c. At what price would cap sales equal zero?

2. Consider the following supply and demand curves for a certain product.

$$Q_S = 25,000\,P$$
$$Q_D = 50,000 - 10,000\,P$$

    a. Plot the demand and supply curves.
    b. What are the equilibrium price and equilibrium quantity for the industry? Determine the answer both algebraically and graphically. (Round to the nearest cent.)

3. The following relations describe the supply and demand for posters.

$$Q_D = 65{,}000 - 10{,}000\,P$$
$$Q_S = -35{,}000 + 15{,}000\,P$$

where Q is the quantity and P is the price of a poster, in dollars.

a. Complete the following table.

Price	Q_S	Q_D	Surplus or Shortage
$6.00			
5.00			
4.00			
3.00			
2.00			
1.00			

b. What is the equilibrium price?

4. The following relations describe monthly demand and supply for a computer support service catering to small businesses.

$$Q_D = 3{,}000 - 10\,P$$
$$Q_S = -1{,}000 + 10\,P$$

where Q is the number of businesses that need services and P is the monthly fee, in dollars.

a. At what average monthly fee would demand equal zero?
b. At what average monthly fee would supply equal zero?
c. Plot the supply and demand curves.
d. What is the equilibrium price/output level?
e. Suppose demand increases and leads to a new demand curve:

$$Q_D = 3{,}500 - 10\,P$$

What is the effect on supply? What are the new equilibrium P and Q?

f. Suppose new suppliers enter the market due to the increase in demand so the new supply curve is $Q = -500 + 10\,P$. What are the new equilibrium price and equilibrium quantity?

g. Show these changes on the graph.

5. The ABC marketing consulting firm found that a particular brand of portable stereo has the following demand curve for a certain region:

$$Q = 10{,}000 - 200\,P + 0.03\,\text{Pop} + 0.6\,I + 0.2\,A$$

where Q is the quantity per month, P is price ($), Pop is population, I is disposable income per household (S), and A is advertising expenditure ($).

a. Determine the demand curve for the company in a market in which $P = 300$, Pop $= 1{,}000{,}000$, $I = 30{,}000$, and $A = 15{,}000$.
b. Calculate the quantity demanded at prices of $200, $175, $150, and $125.
c. Calculate the price necessary to sell 45,000 units.

6. Joy's Frozen Yogurt shops have enjoyed rapid growth in northeastern states in recent years. From the analysis of Joy's various outlets, it was found that the demand curve follows this pattern:

$$Q = 200 - 300\,P + 120\,I + 65\,T - 250\,A_c + 400\,A_j$$

where Q = Number of cups served per week
P = Average price paid for each cup
I = Per capita income in the given market (thousands)

T = Average outdoor temperature

A_c = Competition's monthly advertising expenditures (thousands)

A_j = Joy's own monthly advertising expenditures (thousands)

One of the outlets has the following conditions: $P = 1.50$, $I = 10$, $T = 60$, $A_c = 15$, $A_j = 10$.

   a. Estimate the number of cups served per week by this outlet. Also determine the outlet's demand curve.

   b. What would be the effect of a $5,000 increase in the competitor's advertising expenditure? Illustrate the effect on the outlet's demand curve.

   c. What would Joy's advertising expenditure have to be to counteract this effect?

7. Illustrate the example of the world sugar market with supply and demand diagrams. Be sure to show how the relative shifts in supply and demand have led to the reduction in the world price of sugar.

8. Over the past decade, the demand for CDs has dramatically increased. What are some of the causes of this increase in demand? According to supply-and-demand theory, price should rise when demand increases. However, in recent years the average price of a CD has actually fallen. Explain this apparent contradiction between the theory and fact.

9. Suppose a firm has the following demand equation:

$$Q = 1,000 - 3,000\,P + 10\,A$$

where Q = quantity demanded

     P = product price (in dollars)

     A = advertising expenditure (in dollars)

Assume for the following questions that $P = \$3$ and $A = \$2,000$.

   a. Suppose the firm dropped the price to $2.50. Would this be beneficial? Explain. Illustrate your answer with the use of a demand schedule and demand curve.

   b. Suppose the firm raised the price to $4.00 while increasing its advertising expenditure by $100. Would this be beneficial? Explain. Illustrate your answer with the use of a demand schedule and a demand curve. (Hint: First construct the schedule and the curve assuming $A = \$2,000$. Then construct the new schedule and curve assuming $A = \$2,100$.)

10. A travel company has hired a management consulting company to analyze demand in 26 regional markets for one of its major products: a guided tour to a particular country. The consultant uses data to estimate the following equation (the estimation technique is discussed in detail in chapter 5):

$$Q = 1,500 - 4P + 5A + 10I + 3PX$$

where Q = amount of the product demanded

     P = price of the product in dollars

     A = advertising expenditures in *thousands* of dollars

     I = income in *thousands* of dollars

    PX = price of some other travel products offered by a competing travel company

   a. Calculate the amount demanded for this product using the following data:

$$P = \$400$$
$$A = \$20,000$$
$$I = \$15,000$$
$$PX = \$500$$

   b. Suppose the competitor reduced the price of its travel product to $400 to match the price of this firm's product. How much would this firm have to increase its advertising in order to counteract the drop in its competitor's price? Would it be worth it for them to do so? Explain.

c. What other variables might be important in helping estimate the demand for this travel product?

11. Following are three sample equations. Plot them on a graph in which Q is on the vertical axis and P is on the horizontal axis. Then transform these equations so P is expressed in terms of Q and plot these transformed equations on a graph in which P is on the vertical axis and Q is on the horizontal axis.

   a. $Q = 250 - 10\,P$
   b. $Q = 1{,}300 - 140\,P$
   c. $Q = 45 - 0.5\,P$

12. Use the following equation to derive a demand schedule and a demand curve. What types of products might exhibit this type of nonlinear demand curve? Explain.

$$Q = 100P^{-0.3}$$

The Mathematics of Supply and Demand

This appendix presents the short-run analysis of supply and demand using algebraic equations and graphs. As you will see, the mechanics of supply and demand can be very concisely expressed in algebraic equations. Furthermore, viewing the demand function in terms of an equation will better prepare you for the next two chapters on demand elasticity and estimation.

The demand function for a good or service can be expressed mathematically as:

$$Q_D = f(P, X_1, \ldots, X_n)$$

where Q_D = Quantity demanded
  P = Price
$X_1, \ldots, X_n$ = Other factors believed to affect the quantity demanded

Using pizza once again as our example, let us assume that price and the nonprice factors affect the demand for pizza in the following way:

$$Q_D = -100\,P + 1.5\,P_{hd} - 5\,P_{sd} + 20\,A + 15\,\text{Pop} \tag{3A.1}$$

where Q_D = Quantity demanded for pizza (pies)
  P_{hd} = Price of hot dogs (cents)
  P_{sd} = Price of soft drinks (cents)
  A = Advertising expenditures (thousands of dollars)
Pop = Percentage of the population aged 10 to 35

Suppose we hold constant all factors affecting the quantity demanded for pizza except price by assuming the values of these nonprice factors to be

$P_{hd} = 100$ ($1.00 or 100 cents)
$P_{sd} = 75$ ($.75 or 75 cents)
$A = 20$ ($20,000)
Pop = 35 (35 percent)

Substituting these values into Equation (3A.1) gives us

$$Q_D = -100\,P + 1.5\,(100) - 5\,(75) + 20\,(20) + 15\,(35) = 700 - 100\,P \tag{3A.2}$$

All the values of the nonprice variables are now included in the constant term, 700. Plotting this equation gives us the demand curve shown in Figure 3A.1.

Those familiar with the graphical presentation of algebraic equations may be puzzled about the way in which economists present the supply and demand equations in graphical form. As a rule, the dependent variable is placed on the vertical or Y axis, and the independent variable is placed on the horizontal or X axis. Given this format, one would expect Q, the dependent variable, to be placed on the vertical axis and P, the independent variable, to be placed on the horizontal axis. However, in this chapter, as well as in chapter 4, Q is placed on the horizontal axis, and P on the vertical axis. It seems that the originator of these diagrams, Professor Alfred Marshall, first presented them in this manner.[24]

Figure 3A.1 Demand Curve

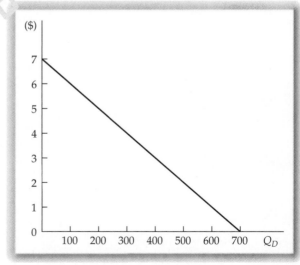

---

[24]Alfred Marshall, *Principles of Economics*, 8th ed., Philadelphia: Porcupine Press, 1920, reprinted 1982, p. 288.

74

Regardless of Marshall's original reasons for reversing the axes, let us simply state that in the analysis of cost, revenue, and profit, the quantity of output is the independent variable. Thus, placing Q on the horizontal axis in the analysis of supply and demand simply prepares us for its subsequent designation as an independent variable.

In the meantime, an adjustment must be made in linking the supply and demand equations to their graphs in order to conform to mathematical convention. In supply-and-demand analysis, whenever an equation such as $Q_D = 700 - 100\,P$ is plotted on a graph, we must do one of two things. If we want to be consistent with mathematical convention, we must place Q_D on the vertical axis and the P on the horizontal axis. This is shown in Figure 3A.2a. If we want to follow the usual format in economics, we must rearrange the terms in the equation so P is expressed in terms of Q_D.

$$Q_D = 700 - 100P$$
$$100\,P = 700 - Q_D$$
$$P = \frac{700 - Q_D}{100}$$
$$P = 7 - 0.01\,Q_D$$

As such, P is now the dependent variable and can be plotted on the vertical axis. Q_D is now the independent variable and can be plotted on the horizontal axis. This is illustrated in Figure 3A.2b.

Let us review this point by assuming one of the nonprice factors affecting the quantity demanded for pizza has changed. In particular, suppose the price of hot dogs increases to $1.20. In Equation (3A.2), this would increase the constant or "Y intercept" term from 700 to 730. This, in effect, would cause the demand curve to shift from its original position to the new one shown in Figure 3A.2a. Figure 3A.2b shows the effect of an increase in the price of hot dogs on the transformed demand equation. In this case, the constant term or "Y intercept" increases from 7 to 7.3 and is also shown by a rightward shift in the demand curve.

We now focus on the supply by assuming the supply equation is the same as the curve used in Table 3.4 and Figure 3.3. This equation can be expressed as

$$Q_S = -100 + 100\,P \qquad \text{(3A.3)}$$

Once the supply and demand equations are given, there are several ways to find the equilibrium price and quantity. One way is to solve for the supply and demand equations simultaneously. This is done by first setting up the two equations in the following way:

$$Q_D = 700 - 100\,P$$
$$Q_S = -100 + 100\,P$$

Figure 3A.2   Transforming the Demand Curve

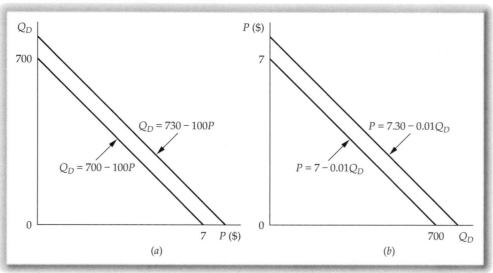

(a)   (b)

We can then eliminate P by adding the equations together. This gives us

$$2 Q = 700 - 100$$
$$= 600 \qquad \textbf{(3A.4)}$$
$$Q^* = 300$$

To find the equilibrium price (P^*), we simply return to either the demand or the supply equation, insert the value for the equilibrium quantity, (300), and solve for P. Using Equation (3A.2), this would give us

$$300 = 700 - 100\, P$$
$$100\, P = 700 - 300$$
$$P^* = 4$$

Notice that when we added the supply and demand equations, we no longer made the distinction between Q_S and Q_D, because in equilibrium $Q_S = Q_D$. In fact, this brings us to the other way in which the supply and demand equations can be used to determine the equilibrium price and quantity. By definition, market equilibrium occurs when the quantity supplied is equal to the quantity demanded. Thus, we can set Equation (3A.2) equal to Equation (3A.3) and solve for the unknown P. That is,

$$700 - 100\, P = -100 + 100\, P$$
$$200P = 800$$
$$P^* = 4$$

By inserting the value of 4 into either equation, we obtain the equilibrium quantity, 300.

You now have three ways to view the basic elements of supply and demand. First, there are supply and demand schedules, as shown in Tables 3.1, 3.2, 3.3, and 3.4, in which the equilibrium price is found by matching the quantity supplied with the quantity demanded. Second, there are supply and demand diagrams, as presented in most of the figures in this chapter, in which price and quantity are determined by the intersection of the supply and demand curves. Finally, there are supply and demand equations that enable one to find equilibrium price and quantity by solving for the unknowns in the two equations. For teaching purposes, the use of graphs is favored. But regardless of the manner in which the concepts of supply and demand are presented, there remains the challenge for business decision makers to ascertain the actual supply and demand data for their particular industries and organizations.

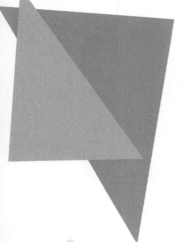

Demand Elasticity

Learning Objectives

Upon completion of this chapter, readers should be able to:

- Define and measure elasticity.
- Apply the concepts of price elasticity, cross-elasticity, and income elasticity.
- Understand the determinants of elasticity.
- Show how elasticity affects revenue.

The Situation

Henry Caulfield is the owner-operator of a local Gas 'n Go gas station and convenience store. Henry chose to locate his store in an area at least 10 minutes away by car from the nearest supermarket or grocery store. For the most part, Henry's business has been quite successful.

Then one day he noticed that a new grocery store was opening just one block away. A month later he noticed that a new convenience store had opened for business less than a 3-minute drive away. Henry realized that to maintain the status quo in the face of this new competition, he would have to make some tough decisions about his pricing and promotion policies and the mix of items carried in his store.

The items that he carried were typical of those found in retail establishments of this type, with beer, cigarettes, hot coffee, and soft drinks accounting for about 75 percent of total sales. Soft drinks were by far the best-selling item in his store. Essentially, the retail price of soft drinks was based on the wholesale price plus a markup of about 400 percent. Henry recognized that this markup was considerably higher than the one used by a supermarket, but he believed that people were willing to pay more for the convenience.

On certain occasions, Henry would offer a particular brand of soft drink at a substantial discount. Regardless of whether he lost or made money on soft drinks by this action, he found that it helped to attract additional customers into his store, and gasoline sales actually increased. Several people from an adjacent town told him that they waited until they were in the vicinity of his station to fill their tanks because of his discount on soda. Given the public's responsiveness to special discounts on soft drinks and the ability of this product to promote other products, Henry decided to use the pricing of soft drinks as his main weapon against his new competition. Instead of offering a temporary discount, he decided to reduce the price of soft drinks permanently. However, after a month, despite the lower soft drink prices, there was a noticeable decline in his revenue from soft drinks. Henry realized that he would have to reassess his competitive tactic.

THE ECONOMIC CONCEPT OF ELASTICITY

In chapter 3, we study the idea of demand and discuss the movement along a demand curve (i.e., change in quantity demanded). The demand curve sloped downward to the right; this means, of course, that the lower the price, the greater the quantity of the product consumed. We are now going to discuss the question of how sensitive the change in quantity demanded is to a change in price. The measurement of this sensitivity in percentage terms is called the **price elasticity of demand**. Henry Caulfield made implicit use of this concept when he decided to lower his soft drink prices to compete with the new stores in his area. But this is only one of the elasticity measures with which we concern ourselves in this chapter. We also cover the concepts of income elasticity, cross-elasticity, and supply elasticity.

In most general terms, we can define **elasticity** as a percentage relationship between two variables, that is, the percentage change in one variable relative to a percentage change in another. In different terms, we divide one percentage by the other:

$$\text{Coefficient of elasticity} = \frac{\text{Percent charge in A}}{\text{Percent change in B}}$$

The result of this division is the **coefficient of elasticity.** It is then our task to interpret the coefficient and determine the effects of the change. The meaning of the size and the sign of the coefficient (the coefficient may be negative or positive) is the focus of our inquiry for the remainder of this chapter. Let us first turn to the most frequently encountered elasticity concept, the price elasticity of demand.

THE PRICE ELASTICITY OF DEMAND

When Henry Caulfield contemplated lowering his price to counteract his new competition, he was dealing with price elasticity of demand. He was determining whether by lowering his prices he would raise his unit sales sufficiently to increase his total revenue.[1]

When we speak of the price elasticity of demand, we are dealing with the sensitivity of quantities bought to a change in the producer's price. Thus, this concept describes an action that is within the producer's (or, in this case, the dealer's) control. Other elasticities discussed later are outside the producer's control and may evoke other actions on the producer's part to counteract them.

Demand price elasticity is defined as a percentage change in quantity demanded caused by a 1 percent change in price. Let us develop this concept mathematically. We can write the expression, "percentage change in quantity demanded" as

$$\frac{\Delta\text{Quantity demanded}}{\text{Initial quantity demanded}}$$

where Δ (delta) signifies an absolute change. The second part of this relationship, "percentage change in price," can be written as

$$\frac{\Delta\text{Price}}{\text{Initial price}}$$

---

[1]More important, he was wondering whether he would actually increase his profits with this action. However, we are not yet in a position to deal with this question.

Dividing the first expression by the second, we arrive at the expression for the price elasticity of demand:

$$\frac{\Delta \text{Quantity}}{\text{Quantity}} \div \frac{\Delta \text{Price}}{\text{Price}} = \frac{\% \Delta \text{Quantity}}{\% \Delta \text{Price}}$$

This is the general expression. We turn now to the actual computation of elasticities, and we describe two methods of obtaining the price elasticity of demand.

 Module 4A

Measurement of Price Elasticity

Let us begin with **arc elasticity**, the method most commonly used in economics textbooks. The formula for this indicator is

$$E_p = \frac{Q_2 - Q_1}{(Q_1 + Q_2)/2} \div \frac{P_2 - P_1}{(P_1 + P_2)/2}$$

where E_p = Coefficient of arc price elasticity
Q_1 = Original quantity demanded
Q_2 = New quantity demanded
P_1 = Original price
P_2 = New price

The numerator of this coefficient, $(Q_2 - Q_1)/(Q_1 + Q_2)/2]$, indicates the percentage change in the quantity demanded. The denominator, $(P_2 - P_1)/(P_1 + P_2)/2)$, indicates the percentage change in the price.

Notice that the change in each variable is divided by the *average* of its beginning and ending values. For example, if the price of a product rises from \$11 to \$12, causing a fall in the quantity demanded from 7 to 6, the formula gives the following price elasticity coefficient:

$$E_p = \frac{6 - 7}{(7 + 6)/2} \div \frac{12 - 11}{(11 + 12)/2}$$
$$= \frac{-1}{6.5} \div \frac{1}{11.5}$$
$$= \frac{-1}{6.5} \times \frac{11.5}{1}$$
$$= \frac{-11.5}{6.5}$$
$$= -1.77$$

The reason the arc elasticity formula employs the average of the beginning and ending values can be clearly seen. If we had used the beginning values, the coefficient would be

$$E_p = \frac{6 - 7}{7} \div \frac{12 - 11}{11}$$
$$= \frac{-1}{7} \div \frac{1}{11}$$
$$= \frac{-1}{7} \times \frac{11}{1}$$
$$= \frac{-11}{7}$$
$$= -1.57$$

However, suppose the price fell from $12 to $11, causing the quantity demanded to rise from 6 to 7 units. Using the beginning values would result in a coefficient of -2 (readers can make this calculation themselves to obtain the answer). Thus, the *same* unit change in price and quantity gives *different* values of elasticity, depending on whether the price increases or decreases.[2] By using the average of the beginning and ending values, we avoid this ambiguity. The price elasticity coefficient is the same whether price increases or decreases.

An additional source of ambiguity arises in the computation of elasticity when we consider changes over different ranges of price and quantity. For example, suppose the values of price and quantity provided in the preceding analysis are part of the hypothetical demand schedule shown in Table 4.1.

The numbers in this schedule indicate a linear relationship between quantity demanded and price, with a unit change in price resulting in a unit change in quantity over the entire range of the schedule.[3] Suppose we compute the arc elasticity for a price change from $12 to $10 rather than between $12 and $11. Using the arc elasticity formula gives

$$E_p = \frac{6-8}{(8+6)/2} \div \frac{12-10}{(10+12)/2}$$
$$= \frac{-2}{7} \div \frac{2}{11}$$
$$= \frac{-2}{7} \times \frac{11}{2}$$
$$= \frac{-22}{14}$$
$$= -1.57$$

Table 4.1   Hypothetical Demand Schedule

Price	Quantity
$18	0
17	1
16	2
15	3
14	4
13	5
12	6
11	7
10	8
9	9
8	10
7	11
6	12
5	13

---

[2]The reason for this ambiguity is simply that the base number differs between a percentage increase and a decrease between two numbers. A good example of this can be found in the retail trade. Suppose a company buys a dress wholesale for $100 and marks it up 100 percent, thereby establishing the retail price at $200. Suppose in a clearance sale the company decides to sell it at cost. This would represent a 50 percent markdown (i.e., from $200 down to $100).

[3]The algebraic expression of this demand equation is $P = 18 - Q$, or $Q = 18 - P$.

Notice that the coefficient is different from the previously computed value. In fact, for any given value of price, the arc elasticity coefficient will vary depending on the new price's distance from the original price.[4]

To adjust for the ambiguity inherent in the use of the arc formula, economists recommend the use of **point elasticity**, the second of the two ways to compute the elasticity coefficient. This method of computation is expressed as follows (we use the Greek letter ϵ when we are referring specifically to point elasticity):

$$\epsilon_p = \frac{dQ}{dP} \times \frac{P_1}{Q_1}$$

To compute point elasticity, we employ one of the economist's favorite mathematical devices, the derivative. Students familiar with elementary calculus, or who learned about it in the mathematical appendix that can be found on our Web site, will have no difficulty with this expression. The key is that by assuming very small changes (actually, in calculus the change is "infinitesimally small") in price and quantity around some given level, we avoid the problem of the measure of elasticity differing based on the amount of change.

To find the derivative of Q with respect to P (i.e., dQ/dP), we need the algebraic expression of the demand equation. The equation implied in Table 4.1 is $Q = 18 - P$. The derivative of Q with respect to P is -1. Thus, the point elasticity coefficient at $12 and 6 units is:

$$\epsilon_p = -1 \times \frac{12}{6}$$
$$= -2$$

Actually, whenever the demand equation is linear, the point elasticity formula appears almost too simple because the first derivative of this equation with respect to P is a constant. From a practical standpoint, there is really no need to use calculus for finding the point elasticity of a linear demand function. The first derivative dQ/dP is the same as the (constant) slope of the demand line, $\Delta Q/\Delta P$. Thus, the point elasticity of a linear demand function can be expressed as:

$$\epsilon_p = \frac{\Delta Q}{\Delta P} \times \frac{P_1}{Q_1}$$

Of course, in cases where the demand curve is nonlinear, calculus must be employed to compute point elasticity. For example, consider the following demand curve.

$$Q = 100 - P^2$$

Assuming $P_1 = 5$, then $Q = 75$. Then the point elasticity is

$$\epsilon_p = -2P \times \frac{5}{75}$$
$$= -2(5) \times \frac{5}{75}$$
$$= \frac{-50}{75}$$
$$= -0.67$$

---

[4]Interested readers should try computing the arc elasticity for changes between $12 and $9, between $12 and $8, and so on. They will find that the arc elasticity decreases as the change in price increases.

Although it is very convenient to use linear demand curves, in reality the shape of the demand curve may be different. In the preceding illustration, price decreases will bring forth smaller increases in quantity. Such a demand curve would take on a concave shape. In contrast, the demand curve may be convex. (The equation for such a curve would be, for instance, $Q = 10/p^2$.) An example of such a demand curve would occur when, for instance, some quantities would be purchased even at a very high price; in such a case, the demand curve would become almost vertical near the price axis.

So far we have discussed both linear and nonlinear demand curves whose elasticity changes as we move along the curve. However, we could encounter a demand curve whose elasticity is constant over its relevant range. Such a curve would be described by the following equation:

$$Q = aP^{-b}$$

a being a constant, and $-b$ representing the elasticity coefficient. This nonlinear equation can be converted to linear by expressing it in logarithms:

$$\log Q = \log a - b(\log P)$$

Such a demand curve would plot as a straight line on double log (or log-log) graph paper, and its elasticity $(-b)$ would be the same at any point on the curve. For example, let the demand equation be $Q = 100P^{-1.7}$. From this equation, we can generate the following demand schedule:

Quantity	10	12.5	15	17.5	20	22.5	25	27.5	30
Price	3.875	3.398	3.052	2.788	2.577	2.405	2.260	2.137	2.030

The two graphs in Figure 4.1 illustrate this demand curve. Figure 4.1a shows the curve using the normal arithmetic scales. In Figure 4.1b the scales are transformed into logarithms, and the demand curve plots as a straight line, signifying that the elasticity is constant throughout.[5]

Figure 4.1   Constant Elasticity

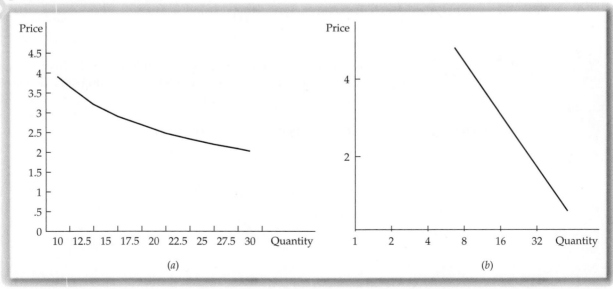

(a)   (b)

---

[5]We encounter constant elasticity again in chapter 6 when we discuss the Cobb-Douglas production function.

The concept of point elasticity, as well as the use of calculus, is found to be of particular importance in chapter 5, when the estimation of demand equations is discussed. However, for now, using discrete changes and the arc elasticity coefficient would appear to be the more realistic thing for Henry Caulfield (and most other practical businesspeople) to do. He may not be familiar with calculus, but this certainly does not detract from his business acumen. He is dealing with a concrete problem: how much he will sell if he lowers his price by a discrete quantity (i.e., a certain number of cents). Arc elasticity is perfectly suitable for this problem.

We must realize, however, that in actual business situations, the effects of elasticity may be calculated in simple percentage terms, using the starting price and quantity as base numbers. For instance, a businessperson may state that it is expected that a 10 percent decrease in price will result in a 20 percent increase in quantity, implying that elasticity is -2; as an example, a decrease in price from $10 to $9 will increase quantity sold from 1,000 to 1,200 units. Of course, this would suggest that raising the price from $9 to $10 (an 11.1 percent increase) would decrease quantity from 1,200 to 1,000 units (a decrease of 16.7 percent). The elasticity in this case is -1.5. This asymmetry creates the same problem discussed earlier, which was solved by employing arc elasticity. In actual situations, however, we must be realistic and understand that a movement down along the demand curve may not bring about the same results as a movement up along the demand curve. Even more important, we should remember that mathematical refinement may not be the most essential thing. What is critical to the businessperson faced with a decision is whether a decrease in price will create sufficiently more quantity to improve profits.

Economists, in their neat way, have created categories of elasticity:

1. *Relative elasticity of demand:*

$$E_p > 1 \text{ (in absolute terms)}^6$$

This occurs when a 1 percent change in price causes a change in quantity demanded greater than 1 percent. The coefficient calculated earlier, 1.77, is a case of relatively elastic demand.

2. *Relative inelasticity of demand:*

$$0 < E_p < 1 \text{ (in absolute terms)}$$

Here the percentage change in price is greater than the corresponding change in quantity. For example, in Table 4.1 as price is lowered from 8 to 7, quantity rises from 10 to 11, giving a coefficient of 0.71.

3. *Unitary elasticity of demand:*

$$E_p = 1 \text{ (in absolute terms)}$$

A 1 percent change in price results in a 1 percent change in quantity in the opposite direction.

These are three common measures of elasticity. But there are also two limiting cases at the extremes of the elasticity scale:

1. *Perfect elasticity:*

$$E_p = \infty \text{ (in absolute terms)}$$

In this case, there is only one possible price, and at that price an unlimited quantity can be sold. The demand curve for $E_p = \infty$ is a horizontal line. We encounter a demand curve with this shape later, when we discuss perfect competition.

---

[6]Because a demand curve has a negative slope, the coefficient of price elasticity will be negative. However, it is often more efficient to ignore the minus sign and to discuss the elasticity coefficient in absolute terms. Later in this chapter, we discuss cross-price elasticity and income elasticity. Here absolute terms cannot be used because the existence of a negative or positive sign gives the result a significantly different meaning.

2. *Perfect inelasticity:*

$$E_p = 0$$

Under this condition, the quantity demanded remains the same regardless of price. Such a demand curve may exist for certain products within a particular price range. An example may be the case of salt. Today's price of salt is about 44 cents per pound. If this price were to rise to 54 cents (a significant percentage increase), or fall to 34 cents (a significant percentage decrease), it is very doubtful that the consumption of salt would change.

Both of these extreme cases, although possible under certain conditions, will seldom be observed in real life. Still, the two limits should be well understood by every student of economics.

The Determinants of Elasticity

Now that we have described what elasticity is, let us look into the reasons that the demand for some goods and services is elastic, whereas for others it is inelastic. In other words, what determines elasticity? As we look into this question, we must remember that the elasticity for a particular product may differ at different prices. Thus, although the demand elasticity for salt is very low—possibly zero—in the vicinity of its current price, it may not be so inelastic at $5 or $10 per pound.

It is often said—and many use this as a rule of thumb—that demand is inelastic for goods considered to be necessities, and it is elastic for luxury products. For example, the demand for furs, gems, and expensive automobiles is probably more elastic than the demand for milk, shoes, and electricity.

Unfortunately, the luxury/necessity dichotomy is ambiguous. Demand for expensive automobiles may be elastic, but if we consider the demand for Mercedes autos, we will probably find that within the prevailing price range, a movement up or down of several thousand dollars would make relatively little difference to those people who are in the market for this particular kind of car. The probable reason for such inconsistencies is relatively simple: one person's luxury is another person's necessity.

Several important factors that influence demand elasticity are outlined in Figure 4.2 and discussed in the next few pages.

Probably the most important determinant of elasticity is ease of substitution. This argument cuts both ways: if there are many good substitutes for the product in question, elasticity will be high; conversely, if this commodity is a good substitute for others, its demand elasticity will also be high. The broader the definition of a commodity, the lower its price elasticity will tend to be because there is less opportunity for substitution. For instance, the demand elasticity for beer or bread will tend to be less than that for a particular brand of beer or for white bread. There are fewer substitutes for bread in general (particularly if we include in this definition other baked products, such as rolls and bagels) than there are for white bread or, even further, a specific brand of white bread. If the price of bread rises (relative to other products), we may consume

- Ease of substitution
- Proportion of total expenditures
- Durability of product
  - Possibility of postponing purchase
  - Possibility of repair
  - Used product market
- Length of time period

Figure 4.2 Factors Affecting Demand Elasticity

somewhat less bread than before. However, if the price of brand A white bread rises while other white bread prices remain the same, then one would expect the quantity of brand A demanded to drop significantly as consumers switch to other brands.

Henry's convenience store was once the only game in town, so to speak. His nearest competitor was relatively distant. Now customers can substitute for Henry's merchandise by walking one block to the grocery store. Because Henry was most likely selling the same soft drink brands as his close competitor, the substitution effect is extremely strong.

Another major determinant of demand elasticity is the proportion of total expenditures spent on a product. Here we can go back to our salt example. The reason for the low elasticity of demand for salt is that the proportion of a consumer unit's (e.g., an individual, a family, and so on) income spent on salt is extremely small. A hefty price increase (e.g., from 44 cents to 54 cents per pound) would probably cause a shrug of the shoulder and would affect consumption of salt very little.

The spending on soft drinks by a typical individual or a family constitutes a larger portion of income than spending on salt. However, in most circumstances, spending on soda still represents a relatively small percentage of a family's income. Thus, we would not expect a change in price to affect the quantity demanded significantly. Still, in households where large quantities of soft drinks are consumed, a price change could have some effect on quantities sold, although it would probably require a substantial change in price to affect purchases significantly.

However, for a product such as a large appliance, the situation may be entirely different. To most families, a clothes washer represents more than a trivial expense, and a price change could have an important impact on purchases. Thus, we expect the demand elasticity for a clothes washer to be considerably greater than that for salt or soft drinks. There is another possible reason for the relatively high demand elasticity of a clothes washer. An appliance purchase may be postponable because there is commonly a choice between buying and repairing. Faced with a higher purchase price, a consumer may choose to repair the old appliance.[7]

Despite the entry of new firms into Henry's market, the geographic size of the market is limited to a relatively small local area. As markets broaden, more and more product substitution becomes possible. Advances in modes of transportation and communication and decreases in their cost have increased the size of markets over time. Thus, the number of substitutes competing for consumers' dollars has increased. Markets have not only widened within national borders, they have more frequently crossed borders, increasing the importance of international trade. Although advances in transportation and communications have been instrumental, an extremely important trend toward freer trade through international trade agreements has undermined artificial barriers (tariffs and quotas). This has increased competition globally and, thus, has increased demand elasticities facing firms. The consumer is the ultimate beneficiary of such trends.

The Effect of Elasticity on Price and Quantity

The response to a change in supply is determined, to a great extent, by the price elasticity of demand. This is of great importance to a businessperson who must be able to adjust its production and prices to a change in economic conditions. Except in

---

[7]The choice between buying and maintaining becomes even more pronounced for the purchase of an automobile. Here, of course, the price and the proportion of a person's income are considerably higher. In this case, there is a third possibility for the consumer: the purchase of a used car. Thus, recalling what we said about substitutability, we can say that the elasticity of demand for cars in general is lower than the demand elasticity for new cars. Of course, it is also possible to purchase a used washing machine, but there is no organized market for these as there is for cars.

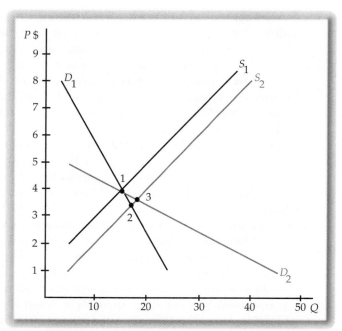

Figure 4.3   Effect of Elasticity on Price and Quantity

the case of perfectly elastic or perfectly inelastic demand, both price and quantity produced will be affected. The extent of the change of each is determined by the price elasticity of demand.

In Figure 4.3, we have charted a demand curve D_1 whose equation is $Q = 27 - 3P$. The equation for the supply curve S_1 is $Q = -5 + 5P$. The resulting equilibrium price is \$4 and quantity is 15 units (point 1).[8] If we chart another, considerably more elastic, demand curve, D_2, of the form $Q = 55 - 10P$, with the same supply curve, the equilibrium point will be the same, $Q = 15$, and $P = 4$. Now, let us say that supply increases, and the supply curve S_2 is of the form $S = 0 + 5P$. With the new supply curve, the equilibrium points for the two demand curves will no longer be the same. With D_1 the price will be \$3.375 and quantity 16.875 units (point 2). However, with D_2 the result will be $P = 3.667$ and $Q = 18.333$ (point 3). The more elastic demand curve, D_2, has resulted in a smaller price decrease but a larger quantity increase than D_1, the less elastic curve. The reader should try this exercise with the same demand curves, but with a decrease in supply to, say, $Q = -10 + P$. In this case, the more elastic demand curve will result in a larger decrease quantity and a smaller increase in price. Thus, we can see that it is extremely important for a manager to have a good idea regarding the sensitivity of demand to price changes. Making the wrong decision in raising or lowering price in response to changing supply conditions could be disastrous to the manager's company.

The Elasticity of Derived Demand

This section of the elasticity discussion represents a small digression, albeit an important one. So far we have discussed demand elasticity for a final product, that is, a product purchased for consumption, such as soft drinks, a clothes washer, salt, white bread, or beer.

---

[8]The reader can use Excel Module 3A, which can be accessed on the Companion Website, to calculate the equilibrium point and draw a graph.

We are now going to look briefly at the demand for items that go into the production of a final commodity, such as materials, machinery, and labor. The demand for such components of a final product is called **derived demand.** In other words, these components are not demanded for their own sake but because there is a demand for the final product requiring them.

The great British economist Alfred Marshall, about whom previous references are made, described four principles governing the elasticity of the derived demand curve.[9] According to Marshall, the derived demand curve will be more inelastic:

1. The more essential is the component in question
2. The more inelastic is the demand curve for the final product
3. The smaller is the fraction of total cost going to this component
4. The more inelastic is the supply curve of cooperating factors

An example illustrates this concept. Let us consider demand for residential housing (the final product) and the derived demand for one class of labor employed in construction, electricians. After all, the demand for electricians does not exist for its own sake but is due to the demand for housing. Probably all of Marshall's principles apply in this case, but two of them are particularly important. The first is essentiality: you just cannot build a house without employing electricians. Second, the cost of electrical work is probably a relatively small percentage of the entire cost of the house.

Suppose the electricians demand and obtain a substantial wage increase. A contractor may try to cut a few corners with regard to electrical work, but most of it must still be done. Thus, the employment of electricians will not decrease much. The implication here is that the elasticity of demand for electricians is low. Assume the work of electricians involves 10 percent of the total cost of construction (this cost is probably overstated). A 10 percent wage increase for electricians represents a 1 percent increase in the total cost of construction. This small addition to the total cost will most likely not trigger a price increase and thus will not affect the employment of electricians to any significant extent. If we also consider the probability that the demand for housing is somewhat inelastic and that the supply elasticity of cooperating factors (i.e., other crafts employed on the project) is rather low, we can conclude that the demand elasticity for electricians is relatively low.

These conclusions tend to hold in the short run much more than in the long run. Over a short period of time, employment of electricians will not drop very much. However, given a longer adjustment period, elasticity of demand will rise as people find ways to substitute for the expensive factor, both on the production side and on the consumption side.[10]

Elasticity in the Short Run and in the Long Run

A long-run demand curve will generally be more elastic than a short-run curve. Here "short run" is defined as an amount of time that does not permit a full adjustment by consumers to a price change. In the shortest of runs, no adjustment may be possible, and the demand curve over the relevant range may be almost perfectly inelastic. As the time period lengthens, consumers will find ways to adjust to the price change by using substitutes (if the price has risen), by substituting the good in question for another (if the price has fallen), or by shifting consumption to or from this particular product (i.e., by consuming more or less of other commodities).

---

[9]Alfred Marshall, *Principles of Economics*, 8th ed., Philadelphia: Porcupine Press, reprinted 1982, pp. 319–20.
[10]A very interesting analysis of short- and long-run elasticity effects on the economic power of labor unions can be found in Milton Friedman, *Price Theory: A Provisional Text*, Hawthorne, NY: Aldine, 1962, pp. 155–59.

A good example is the case of energy costs. When heating oil prices shot up in the 1970s, the immediate response by consumers was not great. As time passed, however, consumers adjusted their oil consumption. They became used to lower temperatures around the house and at work. They began to dress more warmly indoors. (Would this result in a higher demand for sweaters? We look at this particular idea, known as cross-elasticity, later in this chapter.) Over a still longer period, consumers (including one of the authors) converted their homes from oil heat to gas heat. Not only was there conversion, but more newly built homes were equipped with gas heat. In addition, homes up for resale would advertise gas heating to attract potential buyers, and gas-heated homes commanded a premium price. How can we demonstrate this phenomenon graphically?

We can represent this relationship between the short run and the long run using a series of short-run demand curves intersected by the long-run demand curve, as illustrated in Figure 4.4. Each of the short-run demand curves (D_{S1} to D_{S5}) is rather inelastic. Assume the original position is point a, which represents a price of P_1 and a quantity of Q_1. If the price rises to P_2, consumers will, in the short run, decrease the quantity demanded to point b, at quantity Q_2, a relatively small difference in quantity. As time passes, during which consumers adjust to using substitutes, a new short-run demand curve, D_2, will result, and demand will take place at point c, at Q_3, which represents a much larger decrease in quantity. Thus, we can connect points a and c to illustrate the change in quantity demanded in the long run. Then, for constantly increasing prices, we can generate new short-run demand curves, D_{S3}, D_{S4}, and D_{S5}, and connect points d, e, and f to create a long-run demand curve.

In other words, in the short run, price changes increase or decrease the quantity demanded very little, up or down each short-run curve. However, over time, adjustment permits movement to another short-run curve, and a long-run demand curve is created. The long-run demand curve formed from a point on each short-run curve is obviously far more elastic.

The lengths of the short run and the long run depend on how quickly an adjustment can be made. In the case of heating oil, the long run represented several years. But let us return to the case of Henry Caulfield. Once Henry cuts his price (if he decides to do so), the news will probably spread quite quickly around the community. The adjustment from the short run to the long run will probably be a matter of days, or weeks at most.

Figure 4.4   Short-Run versus Long-Run Elasticity

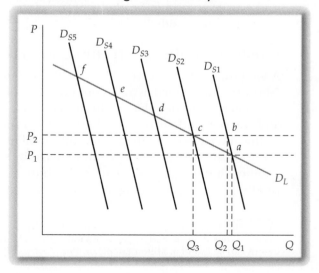

Demand Elasticity and Revenue

Demand elasticity in itself is a rather interesting concept. However, if all it meant was the responsiveness of quantity to price change, it could be easily dismissed. But there is an aspect of demand elasticity that is terribly important to Henry Caulfield or any other businessperson in the throes of a pricing decision (in either direction).

There is a relationship between the price elasticity of demand and revenue received. A decrease in price would decrease revenue if nothing else were to happen. But because demand curves tend to be downward sloping, a decrease in price will increase the quantity purchased, and this will increase receipts. Which of the two tendencies is stronger? Remember that elasticity is defined as the percentage change in quantity divided by the percentage change in price. If the former is larger (and, therefore, the coefficient will be greater than 1 in absolute terms), then the quantity effect is stronger and will more than offset the opposite price effect.

What does that entail for revenue? If price decreases and, in percentage terms, quantity rises more than price has dropped, then total revenue will increase. We summarize the rules describing the relationship between elasticity and total revenue (TR) in Table 4.2.

Let us return to the example of a straight-line demand curve and see what happens to revenue. You will remember that elasticity on such a curve decreases as we move down and to the right. Total revenue and arc elasticity at each price interval are calculated in Table 4.3. Figures 4.5 and 4.6 show graphically the relationship between elasticity and revenue. It is obvious that as price decreases, revenue rises when demand is elastic, falls when it is inelastic, and reaches its peak (i.e., is level) when elasticity of demand equals 1.

At this point, we can formally introduce a term we use a great deal throughout this book: **marginal revenue**. This concept can be defined as the change in total revenue as quantity changes by one unit.[11]

$$\Delta \text{TR} \div \Delta Q$$

Now we can add to the previous table a *marginal revenue* column. This is shown in Table 4.4.[12] Marginal revenue is positive as total revenue rises (and the demand curve is elastic). When total revenue reaches its peak (elasticity equals 1), marginal revenue reaches zero.[13]

Table 4.2　The Relationship between Price Elasticity and Total Revenue (TR)

	Demand		
	Elastic	Unitary Elastic	Inelastic
Price increase	TR↓	$\overline{\text{TR}}$	TR↑
Price decrease	TR↑	$\overline{\text{TR}}$	TR↓

---

[11]Readers with knowledge of calculus will see that we are dealing again with a derivative, $d\text{TR}/dQ$, the derivative of total revenue with respect to quantity.

[12]In this table, only a subset of the prices and quantities is shown. This should be sufficient for an understanding of the concept of marginal revenue.

[13]Again, elementary calculus will be of help. As was shown in the online appendix, where the mathematics of managerial elasticity was explained, if $d\text{TR}/dQ$ equals zero, we can solve for the maximum revenue.

Table 4.3   Demand Schedule Showing Total Revenue and Elasticity Values

Price	Quantity	Arc Elasticity	Revenue
$18	0		0
17	1	−35.0	17
16	2	−11.0	32
15	3	−6.2	45
14	4	−4.1	56
13	5	−3.0	65
12	6	−2.3	72
11	7	−1.8	77
10	8	−1.4	80
9	9	−1.1	81
8	10	−0.9	80
7	11	−0.7	77
6	12	−0.6	72
5	13	−0.4	65
4	14	−0.3	56
3	15	−0.2	45
2	16	−0.2	32
1	17	−0.1	17
0	18	0	0

Figure 4.7 shows the mathematical and graphical relationship between the demand curve and marginal revenue (MR). It turns out that when the demand curve is described by a straight line, the marginal revenue curve is twice as steep as the demand curve. Under these circumstances, the marginal revenue curve can be drawn by bisecting the distance between the *Y*-axis (vertical axis) and the demand curve. Of course, at the point where marginal revenue crosses the *X*-axis

Figure 4.5   The Elasticity–Demand Relationship

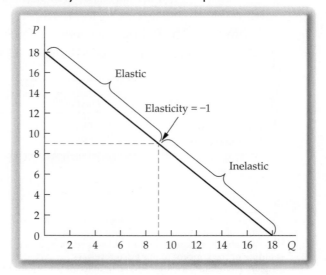

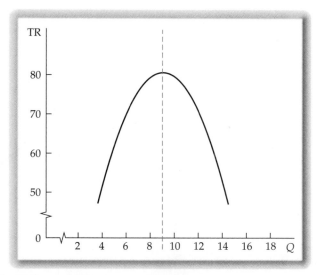

Figure 4.6   The Effect of Elasticity on Total Revenue

(horizontal axis), the demand curve is unitarily elastic (and total revenue reaches its maximum).[14]

All of this is going through Henry's mind as he is deciding how to counteract his competition. For him to benefit from decreasing his price, the demand curve for soft drinks from his store must be elastic. A price cut leading to a decrease in revenue would be self-defeating (or even disastrous). But this is not his only concern. If Henry is a profit maximizer, then it is profit, not revenue, that concerns him. If the demand

Table 4.4   Demand Schedule with Marginal Revenue Added

Price	Quantity	Total Revenue	Marginal Revenue	Arc Elasticity
$13	5	65	9	−3.0
12	6	72	7	−2.3
11	7	77	5	−1.8
10	8	80	3	−1.4
9	9	81	1	−1.1
8	10	80	−1	−0.9
7	11	77	−3	−0.7

---

[14]In mathematical terms, the path from the demand curve to the marginal revenue curve can be traced as follows:

$$\text{Demand curve:} \qquad P = a - bQ$$
$$\text{Total revenue:} \qquad PQ = aQ - bQ^2$$
$$\text{Marginal revenue:} \qquad d\text{TR}/dQ = a - 2bQ$$

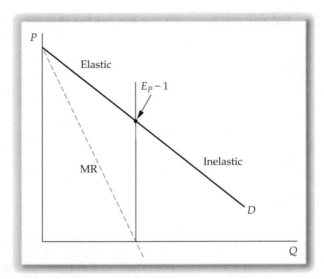

Figure 4.7   The Relationship between Demand and Marginal Revenue

for his product is elastic, revenue will increase. But as he sells more units, his total cost will, of course, rise. Will the increase in revenue more than offset the additional cost? That is the question uppermost in Henry's mind. Unfortunately, we are not ready to answer at this point. We first have to study production functions and cost functions, and then link demand and cost in chapters 8 and 9.

The Mathematics of Elasticity

It is now time to apply some of the calculus you have learned. Point elasticity was mentioned earlier in this chapter and was said to require the use of differential calculus. The formula for point elasticity was given as

$$dQ/dP \times P/Q$$

For this formula to be employed, the demand curve has to be stated in the form of an equation. The equation for the demand curve represented in Table 4.1 is

$$Q = 18 - P$$

Therefore, dQ/dP equals -1. This is the slope of the straight-line demand curve.

As stated in the discussion of arc elasticity, elasticity changes along the demand curve (except in the case of constant elasticity discussed previously). So does point elasticity, of course. Thus, the point at which elasticity is measured must be specified. For example, the point elasticity at $Q = 5$ and $P = 13$ is

$$-1 \times 13 \div 5 = -2.6$$

In Table 4.3, the arc elasticity was shown to be -3 in the interval between $P = 13$ and $P = 14$ and between $Q = 4$ and $Q = 5$, and -2.3 in the next interval. Point elasticity, as should be expected, is somewhere between the two arc elasticities. At $Q = 10$ and $P = 8$, the result is

$$-1 \times 8 \div 10 = -0.8$$

We are now in the inelastic section of the demand curve.

We also mentioned the use of calculus in reference to marginal revenue, which was defined as $d\text{TR}/dQ$. For this purpose, we reverse our demand function so that quantity becomes the independent variable.

Demand:	$P = 18 - Q$
Total revenue:	$\text{TR} = PQ = 18Q - Q^2$
Marginal revenue:	$d\text{TR}/dQ = 18 - 2Q$

At $Q = 5$ and TR $= 65$, marginal revenue is

$$18 - (2 \times 5) = 8$$

Again, because we are measuring TR at a point rather than over an interval, the result (MR $= 8$) will be somewhat different from the marginal revenue obtained in Table 4.4, where discrete differences were used in the calculation.

At $Q = 10$, MR $= 18 - (2 \times 10) = -2$. We are now in the area of negative marginal revenue (relative inelasticity on the demand curve), or at a quantity higher than the one that produces maximum revenue.

If we want to find the point where revenue is maximized, we look for the point at which MR $= 0$. Thus,

$$18 - 2Q = 0$$
$$18 = 2Q$$
$$9 = Q$$

This result, again, is not the same but is very similar to the number found in Table 4.4, where discrete intervals rather than infinitely small differences were used.

Empirical Elasticities

In chapter 5, we explain how economists estimate demand curves and elasticities from industry and product data. However, it may be of interest at this point to reinforce the meaning of price elasticity by mentioning briefly the results of some studies published in recent years:

A study of the demand for coffee estimated the price elasticity to be -0.2 in the short run and -0.33 in the long run.

A study of the demand for kitchen and other household appliances stated that the elasticity was -0.63.

Meals (excluding alcoholic beverages) purchased at restaurants have a high demand elasticity of -2.27.

A study of air travel demand over the North Atlantic found price elasticity to be -1.2. Furthermore, the elasticity for first-class travel was, as one would expect, considerably lower than that for economy travel, -0.4 and -1.8, respectively. A recent study estimates the price elasticity of passenger travel for the U.S. airline industry to be a high -1.98.

The price elasticity of beer has been estimated at -0.84 and of wine at -0.55.

The price elasticity of white pan bread in Chicago appeared to be -0.69, while for premium white pan bread elasticity was measured at 1.01. This is consistent with the idea that there are more substitutes for premium white pan bread brands than for all white pan bread.

In the short run, demand elasticity for cigarettes in the United States appeared to be -0.4, but it was higher, although still quite low, in the long run at -0.6. A study of the effect of tax increases on the consumption of cigarettes in Canada found price elasticity to be between -0.45 and -0.47. This would indicate that the taxing authority would be able to increase its revenue when taxes are increased. Another study looked at the price elasticity of cigarettes in China and Russia and obtained extremely low elasticities, between 0 and -0.15.

A study of wine imports into the United States estimated the price elasticity of Chilean wines to be about -1.6, while the elasticity of French and Italian wines was less than -0.3.

The price elasticity of crude oil was calculated for 23 countries for the period of 1979 to 2000. In the short run, oil demand appears to be very price inelastic. The estimate for the United States was $-.06$. Long-run elasticities were found to be higher; for the United States, it was -0.45. The averages for all 23 countries were -0.05 in the short run and -0.18 in the long run.

A survey of many studies dealing with gasoline demand found that in the short run elasticity is about -0.3, while in the long run it ranges from -0.6 to -0.8. Thus demand is price inelastic in both cases but much more so in the short run.

A recent study of elasticities for Internet services found the price elasticity for subscribers to be between -0.6 and -0.7. These results were based on data from countries that are members of the Organization for Economic Cooperation and Development (OECD).

A study of gasoline demand for four low-income developing Asian countries estimated short-run price elasticities to be between -0.12 and -0.17 and long-run elasticities to be -1.18. For seven middle-income countries the numbers were about -0.3 in the short run and -0.58 in the long run.

The price elasticity of demand for private care in nursing facilities in Texas was estimated to be -0.69.[15]

THE CROSS-ELASTICITY OF DEMAND

The previous discussion dealt with the influence of a price change on the quantity demanded of the product subject to the price change. **Cross-elasticity** (or cross-price elasticity) deals with the impact (again, in percentage terms) on the quantity demanded of a particular product created by a price change in a related product

[15]A. A. Okunade, "Functional Forms and Habit Effects in the U.S. Demand for Coffee," *Applied Economics,* 24, (1992), pp. 1203–12; H. S. Houthakker and L. D. Taylor, *Consumer Demand in the United States: Analysis and Projections,* 2nd ed., Cambridge, MA: Harvard University Press, 1970, pp. 63, 81; J. M. Cigliano, "Price and Income Elasticities for Airline Travel," *Business Economics,* September 1980, pp. 17–21; D. Heien and G. Pompelli, "The Demand for Alcoholic Beverages: Economic and Demographic Effects," *Southern Economic Journal,* January 1989, pp. 759–69; Bahram Adrangi and Kambiz Raffiee, "New Evidence on Fare and Income Elasticity of the U.S. Airline Industry," *Atlantic Economic Journal,* Vol. 28, Issue 4, December 2000, p. 493; Gregory J. Werden, "Expert Report in United States v. Interstate Bakeries Cop. and Continental Baking Co.," *International Journal of the Economics of Business,* July 2000, pp. 139–48; Ping Zhan, Corinne Husten, and Gary Giovino, "Effect of the Tobacco Price Support Program on Cigarette Consumption in the United States: An Updated Model," *American Journal of Public Health,* Vol. 90, Issue 5, May 2000, pp. 746–800; Jonathan Gruber, Anindya Sen, and Mark Stabile, "Estimating Price Elasticites When There Is Smuggling," *Journal of Health Economics,* Vol. 22, Issue 5, September 1, 2003, pp. 821ff; Peter M. Lance, John S. Akin, William H. Dow, and Chung-Ping Loh, "Is Cigarette Smoking Sensitive to Price? Evidence from Russia and China," *Journal of Health Economics,* Vol. 23, Issue 1, January 1, 2004, pp. 137ff; James R. Seale Jr., Mary A. Merchant, and Alberto Basso, "Imports versus Domestic Production: A Demand System Analysis of the U.S. Red Wine Market," *Review of Agricultural Economics,* Vol. 25, Issue 1, Spring–Summer 2003, pp. 1870–2002 ; John C. B. Cooper, *Price Elasticity of Demand for Crude Oil: Estimates for 23 Countries,* OPEC Review, March 2003; Daniel J. Graham and Stephen Glaister, "The Demand for Automobile Fuel," *Journal of Transport Economics and Policy,* Vol. 36, Part 1, January 2002, pp. 1–26; Rajeev K. Goel, Edward T. Hsieh, Michael A. Nelson and Rati Ram, "Demand Elasticities for Internet Services," *Applied Economics,* Vol. 38, Issue 9, May 20, 2006, pp. 75–80; Robert McRae, "Gasoline Demand in Developing Asian Countries," *Energy Journal,* 1994, Vol. 15, Issue 1, pp. 143–155; Kris Joseph Knox, Eric C. Blankmeyer and J. R. Stutzman, "Private-Pay Demand for Nursing Facilities in a Market with Excess Capacity," *Atlantic Economic Journal,* 2006, 34, pp. 75–83.

(while everything else remains constant). What is the meaning of "related" products? In economics, we talk of two types of relationships: **substitute good** and **complementary good.**

In Henry Caulfield's case, we are dealing with substitutes. The sodas sold by the new grocery store are substitutes for those sold by Henry. They probably are the same products (same brands) but are sold by different suppliers, and one supplier can be considered a substitute for the other. Of course, there are also substitutes on Henry's own shelves—he stocks different brands of cola, for example.

Much of the time when we consider cross-elasticity we are dealing with similar products (not just different brands of the same product) in a more general sense. Thus, chicken and beef can be considered to be substitutes; a change in the price of chicken will have an effect on the consumption of beef. Other instances of substitutes come to mind easily: coffee and tea, butter and oleomargarine, aluminum and steel, and glass and plastic.

Complements are products that are consumed or used together. Henry sells potato chips, pretzels, and other "munchies" that are consumed together with soft drinks. Other cases of complementary products are peanut butter and jam, stereo sets and CDs, tennis rackets and tennis balls, and personal computers and disks.

The definition of cross-elasticity is a measure of the percentage change in quantity demanded of product A resulting from a 1 percent change in the price of product B. The general equation can be written as

$$E_X = \frac{\Delta Q_A}{Q_A} \div \frac{\Delta P_B}{P_B}$$

Again, we run into a little problem regarding the denominator in this expression, and arc elasticity comes to the rescue:[16]

$$E_X = \frac{(Q_{2A} - Q_{1A})}{(Q_{2A} + Q_{1A})/2} \div \frac{(P_{2B} - P_{1B})}{(P_{2B} + P_{1B})/2}$$

What about cross-elasticity coefficients? First, let us look at the sign. A decrease in the price of the supermarket's soft drinks will cause the quantity of soft drinks sold by Caulfield to decrease. Of course, if the supermarket raises prices, Caulfield's sales will rise. Thus, the sign of cross-elasticity for substitutes is positive. In contrast, the coefficient sign for cross-elasticity of complements is negative. For instance, a decrease in the price of CDs could lead to increased purchases of stereo systems.

To measure the strength of the elasticity coefficient, we employ a more arbitrary definition than for demand elasticity. As a rule of thumb in business, two products are considered good substitutes or complements when the coefficient is larger than 0.5 (in absolute terms, because the coefficient for complements is negative).

---

[16]The following equation, obtained by arithmetic manipulation, may be easier for some readers:

$$E_X = \frac{(Q_{2A} - Q_{1A})}{(P_{2B} - P_{1B})} \times \frac{(P_{2B} + P_{1B})/2}{(Q_{2A} + Q_{1A})/2}$$

Or, if point elasticity is of interest, the use of calculus gives

$$\frac{dQ_A}{dP_B} \times \frac{P_B}{Q_A}$$

The calculations would proceed similarly to those for demand elasticity.

Empirical Elasticities

Again, it should be useful to briefly mention some study results:

A study of the residential demand for electric energy found the cross-elasticity with respect to prices of gas energy to be low, about +0.13.

Aluminum's cross-elasticity of demand with respect to prices of steel was estimated at about +2.0, and even somewhat higher with respect to copper.

The cross-elasticity of demand for beef with respect to pork prices was calculated to be about +0.25. With respect to prices of chicken, it was about +0.12. Both numbers indicate that the products are substitutes, but in this study, the elasticity coefficients were relatively low.

The cross-elasticity for domestic and imported cigarettes in Taiwan is a positive 2.78, indicating that they are substitutes.

A study of demand elasticity of kerosene in Indonesia estimated its cross-elasticity with electricity was only 0.097 in the short run and 0.261 in the long run. The authors ascribe the low value (during the study period 1957–1992) to the lack of access to electricity in a majority of households.

A study of red wine production in the United States and imports from other countries estimated several cross-price elasticities. Price increases in several of the imported wines have a positive effect on the quantity demanded of U.S. red wines. Red wines from Chile appeared to have a significant effect; a 1 percent price rise increased the quantity demanded for U.S. wines by 1.2 percent. Wines from other countries also had a positive, but smaller, effect: the cross-price elasticity for Australian wines was 0.4, while it was 0.3 for French wines and only 0.04 for wines from Spain.

A study of the impact of used books on new books at Amazon.com showed that used books are not a particularly good substitute for new books. The cross-price elasticity was only 0.088.

Another recent study estimates cross-price elasticities for various types of meats in Jordan. It concluded that beef and poultry are substitutes for mutton, with coefficients of 0.66 and 1.88, respectively. However, the cross-price elasticity for fish was only 0.33.[17]

INCOME ELASTICITY

Before the arrival of his competitors, Henry Caulfield saw his sales grow, not only as the number of households in the area increased, but also as the household income level in the area rose. This represents quantity of sales as a function of (i.e., influenced by) consumers' income. As a measure of the sensitivity of this relationship, economists use the term **income elasticity** of demand. The general expression for this elasticity is

$$E_Y = \%\Delta Q \div \%\Delta Y$$

[17]R. Halvorsen, "Residential Demand for Electric Energy," *Review of Economics and Statistics*, 57 (February 1975), pp. 12–18; Merton J. Peck, *Market Control in the Aluminum Industry*, Cambridge, MA: Harvard University Press, 1961, pp. 31–34; Daniel B. Suits, "Agriculture," in Walter Adams, *The Structure of American Industry*, 8th ed., New York: Macmillan, 1990, p. 11; Chee-Ruey Hsieh, Teh Wei Hu, and Chien-Fue Jeff Lin, "The Demand for Cigarettes in Taiwan: Domestic Versus Imported Cigarettes," *Contemporary Economic Policy*, Vol. 17, No. 2, April 1999, pp. 223–234; Rajindar K. Koshal and Manjulika Koshal, "Demand for Kerosene in Developing Countries: A Case of Indonesia," *Journal of Asian Economics*, Vol. 10, Issue 2, Summer 1999, pp. 329–336; James S. Seale Jr., Mary A. Marchant, and Alberto Basso, "Imported versus Domestic Production: A Demand System Analysis of the U.S. Red Wine Market," *Review of Agricultural Economics*, Vol. 25, Issue 1, Spring–Summer 2003, pp. 187–202, Anindya Ghose, Michael D. Smith, and Rahul Telang, "Internet Exchanges for Used Books, and Empirical Analysis of Product Cannibalization and Welfare Impact," *Information Systems Research*, Vol. 17, No. 1, March 2006, pp. 3–19; Amer S. Jabarin, "Estimation of Meat Demand System in Jordan," *International Journal of Consumer Studies*, Vol. 29, No. 3, May 2006, pp. 232–238.

where Y represents income.[18] The definition of income elasticity is a measure of the percentage change in quantity consumed resulting from a 1 percent change in income.

As before, we turn to arc elasticity for the actual calculation of income elasticity:[19]

$$E_Y = \frac{(Q_2 - Q_1)}{(Q_2 + Q_1)/2} \div \frac{(Y_2 - Y_1)}{(Y_2 + Y_1)/2}$$

In the case of income elasticity, the coefficient can be either positive or negative. For most products, one would expect income elasticity to be positive. After all, given a rise in income, a person will spend more. Thus, when the coefficient is positive, we refer to the income elasticity as normal. (Later, this definition is refined in relation to elasticities for "superior" commodities.)

The coefficient of $+1$ represents another dividing line. As income rises, people can increase consumption of products (and services) proportionally, less than proportionally, or more than proportionally to the income rise. If the expenditure on product A goes up by 10 percent when income goes up by 10 percent, then the income elasticity coefficient equals 1. That is, the proportion of the consumer's income spent on this commodity remains the same before and after the change in income.[20] Suppose a consumer's annual income is $30,000 and spending on clothing is $2,700 per year. If this person's annual income rises by 10 percent to $33,000, and he or she then spends $2,970 annually on clothing—also a 10 percent increase—the proportion of total income spent on clothing remains at 9 percent.

If the income elasticity coefficient is greater or less than 1, the fraction of income spent on the product in question changes more or less than proportionally with income. Products whose income elasticities exceed $+1$, taking larger portions of consumers' income as incomes increase, are often referred to as "superior" commodities.

Again, a brief review of empirical studies that have estimated income elasticities illustrates this concept:

> Short-run income elasticity for food expenditure has been estimated to be about 0.5 and the elasticity of restaurant meals 1.6. The results show that as incomes rise, spending for food eaten at home increases at a slower rate than income and, thus, takes up a smaller portion of income. In contrast, the expenditure on restaurant meals rises substantially more rapidly as incomes rise, thus becoming a higher proportion of income.

> The short-run income elasticity for jewelry and watches appeared to be 1.0; however, the elasticity in the long run was estimated at 1.6. Apparently, consumers take some time to adjust their demand.

> The income elasticity for air travel between the United States and Europe was a relatively high 1.9. Recently, the income elasticity for passenger travel with the U.S. airline industry has been estimated at unity.

---

[18]Again, in terms of calculus, this expression could be written as

$$\epsilon_y = \partial Q/\partial Y \times Y \div Q$$

This, of course, expresses the point elasticity. Also, as the reader can see partial derivatives have been used. As in all other cases of elasticity, the assumption is that only the effect of income on quantity is being measured, with all other possible variables in the demand relationship, (e.g., price, price of related products, interest rates, advertising) held constant.

[19]As in the case of the other elasticities, the equation can be rewritten in several different forms. The student can select the equation that is most convenient:

$$E_Y = [(Q_2 - Q_1) \div (Q_2 + Q_1)] \div [(Y_2 - Y_1) \div (Y_2 + Y_1)]$$
$$E_Y = [(Q_2 - Q_1) \div (Q_2 + Q_1)] \times [(Y_2 + Y_1) \div (Y_2 - Y_1)]$$
$$E_Y = [(Q_2 - Q_1) \div (Y_2 - Y_1)] \times [(Y_2 + Y_1) \div (Q_2 + Q_1)]$$

[20]Remember that, by definition, the price of the product remains the same. Thus it does not matter whether we measure an increase in quantity of the product or in expenditures on the product.

A study of food demand in Spain, which divided food into six categories, found that only meat had an income elasticity of greater than one, 1.54, thus classifying it as a superior good. The elasticity of fish was 0.81, while fats and oils were the lowest at 0.35.

A survey of studies of demand for gasoline found that short-run income elasticity tends to range between 0.35 and 0.55, while in the long run demand is more elastic, in the range between 1.1 and 1.3.

Income elasticities of food expenditures of the Hispanic population in the United States were estimated for three categories: total food, food eaten at home, and food eaten away from home. The results all showed elasticities of less than 1—the proportion of income spent on food decreases as income increases. For the three categories, income elasticities were 0.29, 0.21, and 0.49, respectively. As expected, food eaten away from home had the highest elasticity.

The coefficients of income elasticity for passenger railway transportation in Slovenia turned out to be less than 1, in the range from 0.43 to 0.93.

The income elasticity for subscribers to the Internet was estimated to be in excess of 1, thus making it a superior commodity. This study was based on data from OECD countries.

Another study examined the income elasticities for gasoline demand in 11 Asian countries. Separate elasticities were calculated for 7 middle-income countries and 4 low-income countries. In the middle-income countries, short-run elasticities were found to be between 0.57 and 0.67, and long run elasticities were 1.7. For low-income countries the results were 0.74 to 0.79 and 1.18, respectively.

The income elasticity for housing in Spain was estimated to be between 0.7 and 0.95. This was lower than the results of some previous studies.[21]

It is possible that the income elasticity coefficient will be less than zero. This would occur if the quantity bought of (or the expenditure on) a product were to decrease absolutely as the result of an increase in income. Although such a result may at first seem implausible, a little reflection shows that such a condition may very well exist. Some products will be demanded by consumers whose incomes are low: but as incomes rise, and consumers feel "better off," they will shift consumption to goods more commensurate with their new economic status. What types of products would be disfavored? The usual examples that economists use are potatoes, pork and beans, and canned luncheon meat. Commodities of this type are usually referred to as **inferior goods.**

So, let us now recapitulate the concept of income elasticity by specifying three categories:

Income elasticity >1: superior goods

Income elasticity ≥ 0, and ≤ 1: normal goods

Income elasticity <0: inferior goods

We can depict these situations graphically as shown in Figure 4.8.

---

[21]Houthakker and Taylor, *Consumer Demand in the United States*, pp. 62–63, 72. Actually, this study measured the relationship between spending on food and total expenditures, rather than income. Because the proportion of total expenses to income is relatively stable, this substitution does not significantly change results. J. M. Cigliano, "Price and Income Elasticities for Airline Travel," *Business Economics,* September 1980, pp. 17–21; Bahram Adrangi and Kambiz Raffiee, "New Evidence on Fare and Income Elasticity of the U.S. Airline Industry," *Atlantic Economic Journal,* Vol. 28, Issue 4, December 2000, p. 493; A. Garcia and J. M. Gil, "Spanish Food Demand: A Dynamic Approach," *Applied Economics,* Vol. 30, Issue 10, October 1998, pp. 1399–1405; Daniel J. Graham and Stephen Glaister, "The Demand for Automobile Fuel," *Journal of Transport Economics and Policy,* Vol. 36, Part 1, January 2002, pp. 1–26; Bruno A. Lanfranco, Glen C. W. Ames, and Chung I. Huang, "Food Expenditure Patterns of the Hispanic Population in the United States," *Agribusiness,* Vol. 18, Issue 2, 2002, pp. 197–211; Jani Bekö, "Some Evidence on Elasticities of Demand for Services of Public Railway Passenger Transportation in Slovenia," *Eastern European Economics,* Vol. 42, No. 2, March–April 2004, pp. 63–85; Rajeev K. Hsieh, Edward T. Nelson, and Michael A. Ram, "Demand Elasticities for Internet Services," *Applied Economics,* Volume 38, Issue 9; Robert McRae, "Gasoline Demand in Developing Asian Countries, *Energy Journal,* 1994, Vol. 15, issue 1, pp. 143–55; Daniel Fernández-Kranz and Mark T. Hon, "A Cross-Section Analysis of the Income Elasticity of Housing Demand in Spain," *Journal of Real Estate Finance and Economics,* 2006, 32, pp. 449–470.

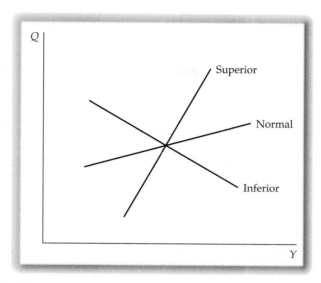

Figure 4.8 Categories of Income Elasticity

OTHER ELASTICITY MEASURES

We have covered the three most common elasticity measures, but there are others. Elasticity is encountered every time a change in some variable affects quantities. For instance, one thing that Henry could do to counteract his competition is to advertise his products. He might speculate how an increase in advertising expenses would affect his total sales. Thus, **advertising elasticity** can be defined as the percentage change in quantity relative to a 1 percent change in advertising expenses. Advertising elasticity has been studied in economic literature. A few years ago, an investigation was conducted into the effects of advertising for beef, poultry, and pork. The results of both generic and brand advertising were measured. Generic advertising did not appear to have any statistically significant results. In contrast, brand advertising had significant, although rather small effects on the consumption of these meats. Thus, a 10 percent increase in advertising increased the consumption of beef by 0.07 percent, the consumption of pork by 0.33 percent, and of poultry by 0.5 percent.

Another study was conducted to examine the effect of advertising on milk consumption in five cities in New York State. The elasticities ranged from 0.014 to 0.088; again, this effect appeared to be small but positive.[22]

Another variable that could have a significant impact on demand—particularly for durable goods—is the interest rate. No one would deny that shifts in mortgage interest rates can cause significant changes in the demand for residential (or nonresidential) construction. Also, the special loan rates offered by automobile manufacturers to customers beginning in the 1980s appear to stimulate car sales, and sales tend to sag when the low rates are terminated.

Elasticity could also be calculated in relation to population size. What is the effect on sales of changes in population? For instance, we could calculate the elasticity

---

[22]Gary W. Brewster and Ted C. Schroeder, "The Impacts of Brand and Generic Advertising on Meat Demand," *American Journal of Agricultural Economics,* Vol. 77, November 1995, pp. 969–79; John Lenz, Harry A. Kaiser, and Chanjin Chung, "Economic Analysis of Generic Milk Advertising Impacts on Markets in New York State," *Agribusiness,* Vol. 14, No. 1, January/February 1998, pp. 73–83.

of demand for baby carriages as a result of population increases due to the baby boom (and the children of the baby boomers). Or we could investigate the effect of a change in the number of adults (population older than the age of 18) on the annual purchases of automobiles (again, as always, holding all other variables constant). Of course, in Henry Caulfield's case, changes in his community's population will affect his sales. The degree to which sales will be affected is measured by elasticity.

These are just a few examples of possible elasticity calculations. In chapter 5, when we discuss demand estimation, we see that economists use many variables to explain changes in demand. Although price elasticity, cross-elasticity, and income elasticity are the ones most frequently measured, elasticities can be obtained for a large variety of variables.

ELASTICITY OF SUPPLY

Before we close this chapter, it is useful to devote a little space to the **price elasticity of supply**. The price elasticity of supply measures the percentage change in quantity supplied as a result of a 1 percent change in price. In other words, this elasticity is a measure of the responsiveness of quantities produced by suppliers to a change in price. In chapter 3, a supply schedule and a supply curve are developed, and the curve slopes upward and to the right. Thus, the arc coefficient of supply elasticity,

$$E_S = \frac{(Q_2 - Q_1)}{(Q_2 + Q_1)/2} \div \frac{(P_2 - P_1)}{(P_2 + P_1)/2}$$

is a positive number: quantity and price move in the same direction.

The interpretation of the coefficient is the same as for the case of demand elasticity. The higher the coefficient, the more quantity supplied will change (in percentage terms) in response to a change in price.

Again, as in the case of demand elasticity, it is important for a manager to know how supply elasticity affects price and quantity when demand changes. When the supply curve is more elastic, the effect of a change in demand will be greater on quantity than on price of the product. In contrast, with a supply curve of low elasticity, a change in demand will have a greater effect on price than quantity.

GLOBAL APPLICATION: PRICE ELASTICITIES IN ASIA

In our examples of price elasticity studies we mentioned several that were done in countries other than the United States. Here we describe briefly a group of studies spanning a large number of consumer products conducted by ACNielsen in Asia during 2001–2002.

The study looked at elasticities in various product categories, by brands and among countries. The numbers we quote below are in absolute terms. When overall categories were studied, price elasticities were relatively low, with 70 percent being less than 2.0 and 35 percent below 1.0. The average was 1.5. However, when individual brands were examined, price elasticities were considerably higher. The average for Asian countries was 2.3. For example, food and beverage brands had price elasticity of 3.0 and household and personal care items' elasticity was 2.2. These findings conform to our previous discussion of determinants of elasticity: the broader the definition of a commodity, the lower will be the price elasticity.

There appear to be substantial differences in price elasticities among the different countries of Asia. For instance, consumers in Malaysia and Hong Kong were considerably more responsive to price changes—well above the Asian average of 2.3—while the Philippines and Korea exhibited elasticities of less than 1.5.[23]

Another study examined price and income elasticities for imports and exports in five Asian countries—India, Japan, Philippines, Sri Lanka, and Thailand. The author used long-term time series to make his estimates. (You will learn more about time series regressions in chapter 5.) He found the following elasticities:

	Import		Export	
	Price	Income	Price	Income
India	−0.51	−0.11	−0.55	0.45
Japan	−0.91	0.84	−0.80	2.84
Philippines	−0.17	0.57	−1.06	0.89
Sri Lanka	−0.48	−0.39	0.48	0.90
Thailand	−0.20	0.90	−3.76	0.82

The implications of these findings are as follows:

1. If imports are price inelastic (as they are in almost all cases), a rise in import prices will lead to an increase in the import bill.
2. If imports are income elastic, an increase in incomes will entail a more than proportionate increase in imports.
3. If exports are price inelastic, export earnings will rise as prices increase.
4. If exports are income elastic, an increase in world incomes will lead to a greater than proportionate increase in exports.[24]

The Solution

Henry Caulfield is no stranger to the economic concept of price elasticity. He has a bachelor's degree in business administration and was doing well as the regional manager of a large supermarket chain when he decided to leave his job and open his own business. Indeed, it was his understanding of price elasticity that prompted him to reduce the soft drink prices as a way of competing against the two new stores in his area. When he had offered special discounts on soft drinks in the past, he noticed that people were very responsive. In fact, Henry had kept a record of the relationship between price and sales, a part of which is shown in Table 4.5. The "special" price was offered as part of the store's "Fourth of July Celebration" sale.

The data indicate an elastic demand for soft drinks at Henry's store. When demand is price elastic, a reduction in price causes total revenue to increase. This was exactly what had happened when Henry had offered his "Fourth of July" celebration special. He was now puzzled because the permanent price reduction did not seem to be having the same positive effect on his total revenue.

Then, in a flash, it dawned on him. One of the most important aspects of demand elasticity—and, for that matter, of any aspect of economic analysis—is the assumption that certain factors are held constant in the examination of the impact of one variable on another. In this case, it was assumed that other factors besides price did not have an impact (or at least not much of an impact) on quantity when Henry had offered the special holiday price for his soft drink. What other factors besides price might now be taken into account?

(continued)

[23]*Pricing for Success,* www.2.acnielsen.com/pubs/2003_q3_ap_pricing.html.
[24]Dipendra Sinha, "A Note on Trade Elasticities in Asian Countries," *The International Trade Journal,* 15:2, pp. 221–237.

(continued)

Table 4.5   Sales Data for 2-Liter Bottles of Soft Drinks

Average Price	Average Weekly Sales	Total Revenue
Regular Price: $1.89	1,050	$1,985
Special Price: $.89	2,450	2,181

To begin with, last summer Henry did not have any close competitors. Therefore, when he offered his discount, there was no other store nearby to match this price reduction. Obviously, the two new stores were not going to stand by idly watching potential customers go to Henry because he had the lowest price for soft drinks. Therefore, the demand for soft drinks at Henry's store was much less elastic than he believed because he was unable to take away their business. To make matters worse, this "price war" among the three stores might have actually reduced their total soft drink revenues. This is because when all three stores dropped their price, they might well have brought the quantity demanded into the inelastic range of their combined demand curves. (We assume here that the three stores constitute the entire local market for soft drinks.)

Regardless of the reaction of his competitors and the possible impact that their price cuts might have had on the degree of price elasticity, there was one simple fact that Henry had completely overlooked. Last year's discount took place in summer, a time when the seasonal demand for this product increases anyway. Thus, when Henry cut the price, the demand for his product had already started to increase and his increased revenue may have been caused by the fact that during this time the demand curve was moving to the right.

One final factor had to be considered. In the past, his discounts on soft drinks were "specials" and, therefore, temporary in nature. Consumers knew that they had to take advantage of these specials during a designated period. Because they now realized that the price of soft drinks in Henry's store was permanently lowered, they were in no hurry to buy the product. In other words, Henry had failed to take "future expectations" into account.

Thus, to be able to measure elasticity, Henry would have to separate the effects on unit sales of price from all the other nonprice determinants of demand. Because he had not done this, he had overestimated the degree of responsiveness by his customers to his price reduction. As a result, unfortunately, the reduction in soft drink prices did not provide a solution for Henry. But at least he now understood why it did not.[25] In addition, this analysis reminded Henry never to take for granted that "other factors remain constant." In the real world, conditions are changing all the time, and it is important to factor these changes into the analysis. As a small consolation, Henry realized that the entry of additional suppliers into the market was all part of the economics of running a successful business. After all, if people did not think he was making any money, they would probably not be as willing to start a competing enterprise.

---

[25]Our example may help you understand an apparent paradox in the pricing of soft drinks in supermarkets. Very often, substantial discounts on soft drinks are offered at all supermarkets during the summer (i.e., "summer specials"). These discounts either may be offered by the soft drink companies to the supermarkets, which then pass them on to customers, or they may be initiated by the supermarkets themselves. Why should they do this at a time when demand is high? After all, economic theory states that an increase in demand causes prices to rise, other factors held constant. What probably happens is that one of the major soft drink companies decides to take market share away from the other major producers by cutting its price. The others quickly follow. The same is true among supermarkets. These price wars can and do occur at any time during the year. It is just that a "summer special" is a good reason to have a sale.

SUMMARY

This chapter deals with the important concept of elasticity. In the most general terms, elasticity is defined as the sensitivity of one variable to another or, more specifically, the percentage change in one variable caused by a 1 percent change in another. Several forms of elasticity connected with the demand curve were discussed.

The first was price elasticity of demand: the percentage change in the quantity demanded of a product caused by a percentage change in its own price. Because demand curves slope downward and to the right, the coefficient of price elasticity is negative. If the coefficient is less than -1 (or greater than 1 in absolute terms), demand is said to be elastic. In contrast, the elasticity coefficient can indicate inelasticity or unitary elasticity.

Elasticity is also tied to total revenue. When demand is elastic, revenue rises as quantity demanded increases; revenue reaches its peak at the point of unitary elasticity and descends as quantity rises on the demand curve's inelastic sector. From the concept of revenue, we develop marginal revenue as the change in revenue when quantity changes by one unit. Marginal revenue is positive at quantities where demand is elastic and becomes negative when the demand curve becomes inelastic.

Next, we explain cross-elasticity, the relationship between the demand for one product and the price of another. Products can be substitutes, and their cross-elasticity is then positive; cross-elasticity is negative for products that are complements.

The third major elasticity concept, income elasticity, measures the sensitivity of demand for a product to changes in the income of the population. Goods and services are defined as superior, normal, and inferior, depending on the responsiveness of spending on a product relative to percentage changes in income.

The examples calculated in the chapter use the method of arc elasticity, which measures changes in both variables over discrete intervals, rather than point elasticity, which deals with change over an infinitely small interval and consequently may require knowledge of elementary calculus.

Several other subtopics appear in this chapter:

Other elasticities, such as advertising and interest elasticity.

Derived demand, which is the demand for inputs to a final product, and the price elasticity of derived demand.

Supply elasticity, the measure of the sensitivity of quantities produced to the price charged by the producers.

In chapter 5, which discusses methods of estimating demand functions, elasticity concepts are employed again, and they reappear in various guises in many of the chapters that follow.

IMPORTANT CONCEPTS

Advertising elasticity: The percentage change in quantity demanded caused by a 1 percent change in advertising expenses. (p. 99)

Arc elasticity: Elasticity that is measured over a discrete interval of a demand (or a supply) curve. (p. 79)

Coefficient of elasticity: The percentage change in one variable divided by the percentage change in the other variable. (p. 78)

Complementary good: A product consumed in conjunction with another. Two goods are complementary if the quantity demanded of one increases when the price of the other decreases. (p. 95)

Cross-elasticity: The percentage change in the quantity consumed of one product as a result of a 1 percent change in the price of a related product. (p. 94)

Derived demand: The demand for products or factors that are not directly consumed but go into the production of a final product. The demand for such a product or factor exists because there is demand for the final product. (p. 87)

Elasticity: The sensitivity of one variable to another or, more precisely, the percentage change in one variable relative to a percentage change in another. (p. 78)

Income elasticity: The percentage change in quantity demanded caused by a 1 percent change in income. (p. 96)

Inferior good: A product whose consumption decreases as income increases (i.e., its income elasticity is negative). (p. 98)

Marginal revenue: The change in total revenue resulting from changing quantity by one unit. (p. 89)

Point elasticity: Elasticity measured at a given point of a demand (or a supply) curve. (p. 81)

Price elasticity of demand: The percentage change in quantity demanded caused by a 1 percent change in price. (p. 78)

Price elasticity of supply: The percentage change in quantity supplied as a result of a 1 percent change in price. (p. 100)

Substitute good: A product that is similar to another and can be consumed in place of it. Two goods are substitutes if the quantity consumed of one increases when the price of the other increases. (p. 95)

QUESTIONS

1. State the general meaning of *elasticity* as it applies to economics. Define the *price elasticity of demand.*

2. Explain the difference between *point elasticity* and *arc elasticity*. What problem can arise in the calculation of the latter, and how is it usually dealt with? In actual business situations, would you expect arc elasticity to be the more useful concept? Why or why not?

3. It has often been said that craft unions (electricians, carpenters, etc.) possess considerably greater power to raise wages than do industrial unions (automobile workers, steel workers, etc.). How would you explain this phenomenon in terms of demand elasticity?

4. Discuss the relative price elasticity of the following products:
   a. Mayonnaise
   b. A specific brand of mayonnaise
   c. Chevrolet automobiles
   d. Jaguar automobiles
   e. Washing machines
   f. Air travel (vacation)
   g. Beer
   h. Diamond rings

5. What would you expect to happen to spending on food at home and spending on food in restaurants during a decline in economic activity? How would income elasticity of demand help explain these changes?

6. Would you expect the cross-elasticity coefficients between each of the following pairs of products to be positive or negative? Why?
   a. Personal computers and software
   b. Electricity and natural gas
   c. Apples and oranges
   d. Bread and VCRs

7. Why is it unlikely that a firm would sell at a price and quantity where its demand curve is price inelastic?

8. Which products would exhibit a higher elasticity with respect to interest rates, automobiles or small appliances? Why?

9. The immediate effect of gasoline price increases in the aftermath of the Persian Gulf crisis in August 1990 on gasoline consumption was not very significant. Would you expect the consumption of gasoline to be more severely affected if these higher prices remained in effect for a year or more? Why or why not?

10. In December 1990, the federal tax on gasoline increased by 5 cents per gallon. Do you think that such an increase, reflected in the price of gasoline, would have a significant impact on gasoline consumption?

11. Why do you think that whenever governments (federal and state) want to increase revenues, they usually propose an increase in taxes on cigarettes and alcohol?

12. Could a straight-line demand curve ever have the same elasticity on all its points?

13. If a demand curve facing a firm is horizontal or nearly so, what does it say about this firm's competition?

14. A company faced by an elastic demand curve will always benefit by decreasing price. True or false? Explain.

15. Discuss the income elasticities of the following consumer products:
    a. Margarine
    b. Fine jewelry
    c. Living room furniture
    d. Whole lobsters

16. If the income elasticity of tomatoes is estimated to approximate +0.25, what would you expect to happen to the consumption of tomatoes as personal income rises?

17. (Read the "The Market for Used Automobiles" section in Appendix 4A before answering the question.) When prices of used cars dropped about 10 percent in October 2001, their sales increased by 4.5 percent. Does this mean that the demand elasticity for used cars is 0.45?

18. In 2002 the U.S. Postal Service increased first-class postage rates from 34¢ to 37¢. The service had been losing money. One of the reasons is increased competition from companies such as United Parcel Service and Federal Express. Another reason is the use of faxes and e-mail, as well as electronic bill payment. With this decrease in demand for postal services, why do you think that the Postal Service is seeking a rate increase?

19. A Canadian apparel company, Roots, agreed to provide the U.S. Olympic team at the 2002 Winter Olympics with various types of clothing, including berets, for free, and further, to turn over a portion of its profits on sales of this clothing to the U.S. Olympic Committee. The beret became an instant success, and Roots sold a large number of them. What type of elasticity does this arrangement represent?

PROBLEMS

1. The Acme Paper Company lowers its price of envelopes (1,000 count) from $6 to $5.40. If its sales increase by 20 percent following the price decrease, what is the elasticity coefficient?

2. The demand function for a cola-type soft drink in general is $Q = 20 - 2P$, where Q stands for quantity and P stands for price.
   a. Calculate point elasticities at prices of 5 and 9. Is the demand curve elastic or inelastic at these points?
   b. Calculate arc elasticity at the interval between $P = 5$ and $P = 6$.
   c. At which price would a change in price and quantity result in approximately no change in total revenue? Why?

3. ABC Sports, a store that sells various types of sports clothing and other sports items, is planning to introduce a new design of Arizona Diamondbacks' baseball caps. A consultant has estimated the demand curve to be

$$Q = 2,000 - 100P$$

where Q is cap sales and P is price.
   a. How many caps could ABC sell at $6 each?
   b. How much would the price have to be to sell 1,800 caps?
   c. Suppose ABC were to use the caps as a promotion. How many caps could ABC give away free?

   d. At what price would no caps be sold?
   e. Calculate the point price elasticity of demand at a price of $6.
4. The equation for a demand curve has been estimated to be $Q = 100 - 10P + 0.5Y$, where Q is quantity, P is price, and Y is income. Assume $P = 7$ and $Y = 50$.
   a. Interpret the equation.
   b. At a price of 7, what is price elasticity?
   c. At an income level of 50, what is income elasticity?
   d. Now assume income is 70. What is the price elasticity at $P = 8$?
5. Mr. Smith has the following demand equation for a certain product: $Q = 30 - 2P$.
   a. At a price of $7, what is the point elasticity?
   b. Between prices of $5 and $6, what is the arc elasticity?
   c. If the market is made up of 100 individuals with demand curves identical to Mr. Smith's, what will be the point and arc elasticity for the conditions specified in parts a and b?
6. The Teenager Company makes and sells skateboards at an average price of $70 each. During the past year, they sold 4,000 of these skateboards. The company believes that the price elasticity for this product is about -2.5. If it decreases the price to $63, what should be the quantity sold? Will revenue increase? Why?
7. The ABC Company manufactures AM/FM clock radios and sells on average 3,000 units monthly at $25 each to retail stores. Its closest competitor produces a similar type of radio that sells for $28.
   a. If the demand for ABC's product has an elasticity coefficient of -3, how many will it sell per month if the price is lowered to $22?
   b. The competitor decreases its price to $24. If cross-elasticity between the two radios is 0.3, what will ABC's monthly sales be?
8. The Mesa Redbirds football team plays in a stadium with a seating capacity of 80,000. However, during the past season, attendance averaged only 50,000. The average ticket price was $30. If price elasticity is -4, what price would the team have to charge in order to fill the stadium? If the price were to be decreased to $27 and the average attendance increased to 60,000, what is the price elasticity?
9. The Efficient Software Store had been selling a spreadsheet program at a rate of 100 per month and a graphics program at the rate of 50 per month. In September 2007, Efficient's supplier lowered the price for the spreadsheet program, and Efficient passed on the savings to customers by lowering its retail price from $400 to $350. The store manager then noticed that not only had sales of the spreadsheet program risen to 120, but also the sales of the graphics program increased to 56 per month. Explain what has happened. Use both arc price elasticity and arc cross-elasticity measures in your answer.
10. Given the demand equation $Q = 1,500 - 200P$, calculate all the numbers necessary to fill in the following table:

| | | Elasticity | | Total | Marginal |
P	Q	Point	Arc	Revenue	Revenue
$7.00					
6.50					
6.00					
5.50					
5.00					
4.50					
4.00					
3.50					
3.00					
2.50					

11. Would you expect cross-elasticity between the following pairs of products to be positive, negative, or zero?
    a. Television sets and VCRs
    b. Rye bread and whole wheat bread
    c. Construction of residential housing and furniture
    d. Breakfast cereal and men's shirts
    Explain the relationship between each pair of products.

12. In order to attract more customers on Mondays (a slow day), Alex's Pizza Shop in Austin decided to reduce the price of their pizza rolls from $3.50 to $2.50. As a result, Monday sales increased from 70 to 130. Also, Alex's sales of soft drinks rose from 40 to 90.
    a. Calculate the arc price elasticity of demand for the pizza rolls.
    b. Calculate the arc cross-price elasticity of demand between soft drink sales and pizza rolls prices.

13. According to a study, the price elasticity of shoes in the United States is 0.7, and the income elasticity is 0.9.
    a. Would you suggest that the Brown Shoe Company cut its prices to increase its revenue?
    b. What would be expected to happen to the total quantity of shoes sold in the United States if incomes rise by 10 percent?

14. A book store opens across the street from the University Book Store (UBS). The new store carries the same textbooks but offers a price 20 percent lower than UBS. If the cross-elasticity is estimated to be 1.5, and UBS does not respond to its competition, how much of its sales is it going to lose?

15. A local supermarket lowers the price of its vanilla ice cream from $3.50 per half gallon to $3. Vanilla ice cream (unit) sales increase by 20 percent. The store manager notices that the (unit) sales of chocolate syrup increase by 10 percent.
    a. What is the price elasticity coefficient of vanilla ice cream?
    b. Why have the sales of chocolate syrup increased, and how would you measure the effect?
    c. Overall, do you think that the new pricing policy was beneficial for the supermarket?

16. The Compute Company store has been selling its special word processing software, Aceword, during the last 10 months. Monthly sales and the price for Aceword are shown in the following table. Also shown are the prices for a competitive software, Goodwrite, and estimates of monthly family income. Calculate the appropriate elasticities, keeping in mind that you can calculate an elasticity measure only when all other factors do not change.

Month	Price Aceword	Quantity Aceword	Family Income	Price Goodwrite
1	$120	200	$4,000	$130
2	120	210	4,000	145
3	120	220	4,200	145
4	110	240	4,200	145
5	114	230	4,200	145
6	115	215	4,200	125
7	115	220	4,400	125
8	105	230	4,400	125
9	105	235	4,600	125
10	105	220	4,600	115

17. The demand curve for product X is given as $Q = 2000 - 20P$.
    a. How many units will be sold at $10?
    b. At what price would 2,000 units be sold? 0 units? 1,500?
    c. Write equations for total revenue and marginal revenue (in terms of Q).
    d. What will be the total revenue at a price of $70? What will be the marginal revenue?
    e. What is the point elasticity at a price of $70?

f. If price were to decrease to $60, what would total revenue, marginal revenue, and point elasticity be now?

g. At what price would elasticity be unitary?

18. The Transportation Authority in Anytown, USA, raised bus fares from $1 to $1.15 on January 1, 2006. The authority's statistics show that the number of passengers riding buses decreased from 672,000 in 2006 to 623,000 in 2007.

a. How much did revenue change?

b. What is the arc elasticity for bus travel in Anytown?

c. The answer to b would be correct if all conditions (except price) remained the same between 2006 and 2007. Can you think of any other changes that would have affected the result?

19. (Read the "Newspapers and Their Price Elasticity" section in Appendix 4A before answering the question.) What is the arc demand elasticity for the London *Times?* What happened to revenue as a result of the price decrease?

20. The Distinctive Fashions Company increased its advertising budget for its leading brand of ladies' dresses from $10,000 in 2006 to $15,000 in 2007. Its sales increased from 900 units to 1,050 units, while the price remained the same at $120 per dress. Calculate the advertising elasticity of these dresses. Was this a wise move by the company?

21. Manning Inc. is the leading manufacturer of garage doors. Demand for residential garage door sales depends, of course, on the rate of new house building activity, which in turn depends on changes in income per capita. During the past year, Manning sold 10,000 garage doors at an average price of $1,500 per door. In the coming year, disposable income per capita is expected to increase from $32,000 to $34,000. Without any price change, Manning expects current-year sales to rise to 12,000 units.

a. Calculate the arc income elasticity of demand.

b. The company economist estimates that if the price of doors is increased by $100, they could sell 11,500 doors. What is the arc price elasticity and what would be the company's revenue?

c. Should they raise the price even more?

Applications of Supply and Demand

Chapters 3 and 4 lay the foundation for the student's knowledge of supply and demand and elasticity. Knowing these elements is essential for further study of economics and is a prerequisite for all the chapters that follow.

Before we discuss the various building blocks that will complete the study of managerial economics, this appendix endeavors to reinforce the concepts of supply and demand and of elasticity in two ways:

1. Some specific applications of supply and demand are discussed, including the effects of price controls, and excise taxes.

2. Various actual situations as reported in the press are introduced and discussed, and it is shown that the materials we have just learned can be applied to analyze these situations.

Interference with the Price Mechanism

In chapter 3, we discuss the movement toward equilibrium in both the short and long run. A change in demand or supply will call forth actions that will cause equilibrium to occur at a new supply–demand intersection. It is shown that in the short run, price changes will eliminate shortages or surpluses. In the long run, resources in the economy shift from the production of one product to another in response to changes in demand. The shift away from one equilibrium and the move to a new equilibrium will proceed when these movements are permitted to occur freely and are not impeded by any outside interference. Thus, when the supply of corn decreased and price rose so the market cleared at this new price—that is, at the new intersection of supply and demand—there was nothing inhibiting this change from taking place.

However, with present economic institutions, free movement of prices is not always allowed. At least three times in the last 60 years,[26] price controls were

imposed in the United States. Prices on various products were set (or fixed at existing levels), and these products could not be sold at prices higher than those prescribed by government. Such a policy is usually referred to as setting a *price ceiling*. If the price ceiling for a product is set at the prevailing equilibrium level, then the ceiling will have no effect (until a change in circumstances dictated a higher price). But if the price were set below the equilibrium price,[27] then, as explained in chapter 3, a shortage would result. In Figure 4A.1, the equilibrium price is P_0 and the quantity sold (and clearing the market) at this price is Q_0. If for some reason the price winds up at P_1 under free-market conditions (i.e., no price controls), the price will rise until the equilibrium price (P_0) is again reached. But if the price is prescribed

Figure 4A.1 The Effect of a Price Ceiling on Supply and Demand

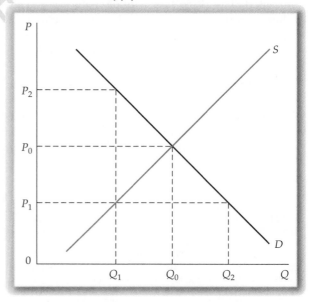

[26]During World War II, the Korean War, and again in 1971.

[27]It is obvious that a ceiling set above the equilibrium price would be meaningless.

109

to be no higher than P_1,[28] the movement toward equilibrium will not take place. Only Q_1 will be supplied while Q_2 is demanded at the lower price, so a shortage of magnitude $Q_1 - Q_2$ will be established. Thus, only the consumers in the interval $0 - Q_1$ will be able to buy this particular product. What will be the result of this forced disequilibrium? Possibly consumers will try to shift their demand to other products, causing a pressure on the other products' prices. If these products are also price controlled, shortages of these other goods will occur.

There is another possible result. Because only Q_1 units of the product will be supplied at price P_1, these units could be purchased at price P_2 along the demand curve. Consumers would be willing to pay P_2, a price higher than the equilibrium price, P_0, for the limited quantity Q_1. Thus, a strong pressure on the price will be exerted, and somewhere in this process the difference between P_1 and P_2 will be paid to the suppliers.

An example of such a case was the price of automobiles after World War II. A ceiling price below the price level that would have cleared the market was imposed on new cars. This low price caused automobile manufacturers to limit their production. However, consumers were paying high prices for these cars in the way of a dealer's premium. They may also have received lower trade-in prices on their old automobiles or may have bought their new car as a "used" one because second-hand cars were not price controlled. The price they actually paid was indeed higher than it could have been if the manufacturers had charged a higher list price.[29] Similarly, where rent ceilings have been imposed many people end up paying a bonus to the superintendent or to a rental agent.

Another example precedes those just discussed by more than 150 years. During the Revolutionary War, the legislature of Pennsylvania imposed limits on prices of goods sold to the military and was thus instrumental in creating extreme shortages of food for George Washington's army at Valley Forge.[30]

We can also present a very current example. The African country of Zimbabwe has been experiencing extreme hyperinflation, sometimes estimated at 10,000 percent per year. In the middle of 2007, Robert Mugabe, the country's president, issued an order slashing prices in half. In response to this order, "Zimbabwe's economy is at a halt." As reported by the *New York Times*, "meat is virtually nonexistent," "gasoline is nearly unobtainable," and "[hospital] patients are dying for lack of basic medical supplies." Manufacturing has slowed because businesses cannot produce goods for less than their government-imposed sales prices. "It appears . . . that not even an unchallenged autocrat can repeal the laws of supply and demand."[31]

On the other side of the price control coin are price floors. In such cases, a price is established below which the product or service may not be sold. An excellent example of a price floor is the legal minimum wage. Employers are not allowed to pay their workers less than the established minimum, so must, therefore, deal with the disturbance to a price equilibrium.[32]

If the equilibrium wage (e.g., per hour) for some unskilled work were to be at level W_0 as shown in Figure 4A.2, but the law stated that a wage lower

Figure 4A.2   The Effect of a Price Floor on Supply and Demand

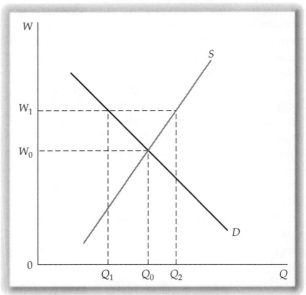

---

[28]Price ceilings can be enforced by the government imposing fines or even prison sentences on violators. Such punishment would have appeared rather lenient to some of our ancestors. During the times of price controls in ancient Egypt, Greece, and Rome, the death sentence was the penalty for breaking price control laws. The edict of Diocletian in A.D. 301 imposed the death sentence on those selling at prices higher than decreed, as well as on those buying at such prices (Robert L. Schuettinger and Eamonn F. Butler, *Forty Centuries of Wage and Price Controls*, Washington, DC: Heritage Foundation, 1979, p. 23).
[29]Milton Friedman, *Price Theory: A Provisional Text*, Hawthorne, NY: Aldine, 1962, p. 18.
[30]Schuettinger and Butler, *Forty Centuries*, p. 41.

[31]Michael Wines, "Caps on Prices Only Deepen Zimbabweans' Misery," *New York Times*, July 28, 2007.
[32]Wages are, of course, the price of labor, so it is quite correct to discuss minimum wages under the topic of price floors.

than W_1 is illegal, then a surplus of labor $Q_1 - Q_2$ would exist. In the absence of the minimum wage law, wages would drop to W_0, and the quantity supplied and demanded of labor would meet at Q_0. Thus all workers offering themselves for employment at that wage would be hired.

But if the wage cannot fall below W_1, what will happen? The unemployed will look for work elsewhere. If the minimum wage prevails in all types of employment, they would not be able to find work. However, there are still some forms of employment in the United States that are not covered by law. A person can also become self-employed, in which case minimum wages do not apply.[33]

The effect of increases in minimum wages on employment has been widely studied by economists for many years. In the past, most economists agreed that increases in minimum wages had a negative effect on employment, especially in the case of young and unskilled workers. Unemployment has generally been the highest among teenage workers, many of whom have dropped out of school and acquired few if any skills.[34] However, several recent studies have questioned the traditional findings, concluding that minimum wage increases have not necessarily led to decreased employment.[35] Although the new studies cast doubt on the traditional hypothesis, it is much too early to dismiss it. Much additional research is necessary to clarify the

effect that increases in minimum wages have on employment.[36]

Several additional points should be made regarding the impact of minimum wages. Even if an increase in the minimum does have a negative effect on employment, workers who remain employed at the higher wage will benefit. The workers can be found in the interval $0 - Q_1$.[37] Second, the short-run effects of an increased legal minimum are probably stronger than the long-run effects. As time passes, the wage levels in the economy will rise (either due to inflation or in real terms), and at some point the minimum wage may approach the free-market equilibrium wage. A third point also appears worth mentioning. Because an increase in the minimum wage must be passed by the legislature (the U.S. Congress in the case of a federal minimum), it is a part of the political process. Legislators may be reluctant to enact a minimum wage increase if it would increase unemployment. Thus, such legislation may be passed only if it would appear to have a minimal effect.

The Incidence of Taxes

From the viewpoint of the economics of the firm, one important example of applied analysis using supply and demand curves and elasticities is in the area of the incidence or effect of excise taxes on the prices and quantities of products.

An excise tax is a tax imposed as a specific amount per unit of product. It is also sometimes referred to as a specific tax, as compared with a sales tax, which is levied as a percent of the price of the product or service. The federal excise tax on gasoline as of this writing is 18.4 cents per gallon. The sales tax, which is usually collected by states and local communities, in the city of Phoenix, Arizona, for example, is 8.3 percent of the price of a product. Sales taxes are often referred to as ad valorem taxes. We could discuss the incidence of either ad valorem or specific taxes, but we choose the latter for our

---

[33]At the risk of sounding facetious, the extreme case of self-employment is unemployment.

[34]Among many studies, see, for instance, C. Brown, C. Gilroy, and A. Kohen, "The Effect of the Minimum Wage on Employment and Unemployment," *Journal of Economic Literature,* 20 (June 1982), pp. 487–528; B. S. Frey, W. Pommerehne, F. Schneider, and G. Gilbert, "Consensus and Dissension among Economists: An Empirical Inquiry," *American Economic Review,* 74 (December 1984), pp. 986–94; T. G. Moore, "The Effect of Minimum Wages on Teenage Unemployment Rates," *Journal of Political Economy,* July/August 1971, pp. 897–902. A more recent study that finds negative effects on employment is D. Deere, K. M. Murphy, and F. Welch, "Employment and the 1990–1991 Minimum Wage Hike," *American Economic Review Papers and Proceedings,* 85 (May 1995), pp. 232–37.

[35]See, for instance, D. Card and A. B. Krueger, "Minimum Wages and Employment: A Case Study of the Fast-Food Industry in New Jersey and Pennsylvania," *American Economic Review,* 84 (September 1994), pp. 772–84; D. Card, "Do Minimum Wages Reduce Employment? A Case Study of California, 1987–89," *Industrial and Labor Relations Review,* 46 (October 1992), pp. 38–54; L. F. Katz and A. B. Krueger, "The Effect of the Minimum Wage on the Fast-Food Industry," *Industrial and Labor Relations Review,* 46 (October 1992), pp. 6–21; *State Minimum Wages and Employment in Small Businesses,* Fiscal Policy Institute, April 21, 2004.

[36]A good summary of the recent research and an analysis of various hypotheses regarding the effect of minimum wages on employment is M. Zavodny, "Why Minimum Wage Hikes May Not Reduce Employment," *Economic Review,* Federal Reserve Bank of Atlanta, 83, 2 (second quarter 1998), pp. 18–28.

[37]It is an interesting decision, implicitly made by the U.S. Congress when it passes a law increasing the minimum wage, whether the overall welfare of the country will be increased if some part of the labor force has its wages improved while another part has its income lowered.

Table 4A.1   Demand and Supply and Tax Incidence

		Quantity Supplied	
Unit Price	Quantity Demanded	Without Tax	With Tax
$6	5	25	20
5	10	20	15
4	15	15	10
3	20	10	5
2	25	5	0
1	30	0	

analysis. The principles and applications are similar, but a specific tax provides a simpler and more straightforward illustration.

A numerical example aids in this exposition. Table 4A.1 shows the demand and supply schedules for a particular product. The equilibrium price is $4. At this price, 15 units will be demanded, and 15 units will be supplied, thus clearing the market.[38] The demand and supply curves are shown in Figure 4A.3a, where an equilibrium at $P = 4$ and $Q = 15$ can be observed.

Now suppose the government imposes an excise tax of $1 per unit, which it will collect from the sellers. The effect is to shift the supply curve up by the unit tax. The shift can be thought of in the following way: before the enactment of the tax, suppliers offered to sell 20 units at $5. But now, for the producers to obtain $5 per unit, these products will have to be sold at $6 apiece (of which $1 will be remitted to the government).[39] In effect, the production cost for this good has risen by $1 per unit. The last column in Table 4A.1 shows the new supply schedule.

Figure 4A.3   The Influence of an Excise Tax on Supply and Demand

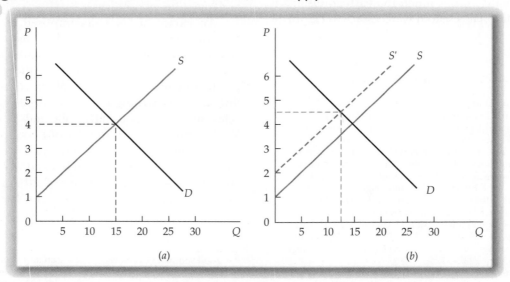

(a)   (b)

---

[38]An arithmetic solution can be obtained as follows: the equation of the demand curve for the schedule shown in Table 4A.1 is $Q_D = 35 - 5P$, and the equation for the supply curve is $Q_S = -5 + 5P$. Solving for $Q_D = Q_S$, we obtain

$$35 - 5P = -5 + 5P$$
$$40 = 10P$$
$$4 = P$$

[39]The equation of this new supply curve is $Q_S = -10 + 5P$.

The important question to be asked is what will be the market-clearing price and quantity after the imposition of the new excise tax. An easy answer would be $1 more than before, or $5. Certainly, the suppliers would prefer not to receive less per unit than they had been getting before the tax. But this is not the correct answer, except in very rare cases.[40] The new intersection will be at $4.50, and the quantity will be 12.5 units.[41]

Thus, sellers will receive only $3.50 per unit after the imposition of the tax, and consumers will be paying 50 cents more than before. In economic jargon, 50 cents of the tax has been shifted forward to consumers, and 50 cents has been shifted back to the producers. This new equilibrium is shown in Figure 4A.3b.

How the incidence of the tax is distributed between the two parties to the transaction depends on the elasticity of the supply and demand curves. The more elastic the demand curve, the larger will be the portion of the tax that the supplier has to bear. In Figure 4A.4a, we repeat the demand and supply curves previously shown and add a second demand curve, which (before the tax) also intersects the supply curve at $4 and 15 units but at all other points is flatter (more elastic) than the original demand function. In Figure 4A.4b, the tax is added on to the supply curve. With the new demand curve, the equilibrium price is $4.42, and the quantity demanded is just above 12 units.[42]

The effect of the tax on the equilibrium quantity is of significance to the government unit levying the tax. It is obvious that a government setting a new (or increasing an old) excise tax is taking such action to increase its revenue. However, if the demand curve for the particular product is very elastic, the erosion of the revenue base will cut short the amount of revenue the government expects to collect. In the present case, the government would have collected $12.50 in revenue with the original demand curve and only $12.08 for the more elastic demand curve. Had the demand curve been perfectly inelastic (vertical), then not only would the entire tax have been shifted to the consumer, but government

Figure 4A.4   Effect of Demand Elasticity on Equilibrium

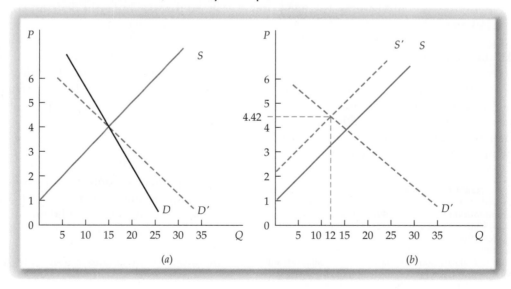

(a)

(b)

---

[40]This will occur where the demand curve is perfectly inelastic.
[41]Using our equations,

$$35 - 5P = -10 + 5P$$
$$45 = 10P$$
$$4.5 = P$$

[42]The equation for the more elastic demand curve is $Q_D = 43 - 7P$ and the equilibrium price is

$$43 - 7P = -10 + 5P$$
$$53 = 12P$$
$$4.4167 = P$$

revenue would have been $15 because the number of units sold would have remained at 15. Thus, a government would prefer to enact an excise tax on a product with low demand elasticity.[43]

Some of the more familiar excise taxes are those on tobacco and alcohol. Because the consumption of these products is not considered desirable by today's standards, tobacco and alcohol are frequently among the first to be selected when additional taxes are contemplated. All states, as well as the federal government, impose an excise tax on these two products. In some cases, the amount of the tax on each unit is greater than 50 percent of the total price of the product. Because of the low esteem in which these products are held by a large segment of the population, opposition to the imposition of a tax (or an additional tax) is generally not great (except by the two industries involved). These taxes are often referred to as "sin" taxes. But would it have been attractive to levy such high excise taxes on these two products had the demand curve for them been very elastic?[44] Probably not, because the tax base would have eroded significantly. Therefore, the government unit that wants to achieve what is popularly known as a "revenue enhancement" will find it considerably more favorable to enact an excise tax on products whose demand elasticity in the range of the tax increase is relatively low. Tobacco and alcohol seem to fit this category well. Thus, a government unit can claim to be taxing "undesirable" commodities and at the same time help to maximize its revenue.

Among the many proposals to fight the large federal deficits of the late 1980s was the imposition of a very large tax (as much as 30 to 50 cents per gallon) on gasoline. The popular estimate has been that each cent of tax would decrease the deficit by

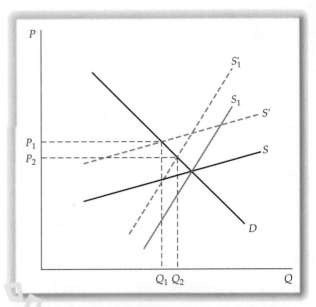

Figure 4A.5   Supply Elasticity and Tax Incidence

about $1 billion. However, such calculations may not consider what would happen to the consumption of gasoline over time. The experience with OPEC's price increases in the 1970s and early 1980s shows that the long-run demand curve for gasoline is by no means inelastic.

The elasticity of supply is also important from the viewpoint of tax incidence. From Figure 4A.5, we can see that the effect on the price and quantity is greater the higher the elasticity of supply. If supply elasticity is relatively low, the producer will bear the greater burden of the tax.[45]

Actual Situations

We now turn to some actual events, reported in newspapers and journals, that can easily be explained using supply-and-demand analysis. Some of these items describe events that took place a number of years ago. These older examples are included because they teach us lessons regarding

---

[43]You have certainly been subjected to a tax increase in some product you consume, whether it was tobacco, gasoline, or alcohol, to mention just three products on which excise taxes are levied by both federal and local governments. You will probably recall that on the day the tax was increased, the price of say, gasoline, rose by the precise amount of the tax. This is because, first of all, the increase may have been relatively small in comparison to the total price, so the demand curve may be quite inelastic in this relatively narrow price range. Second, as we have already learned, demand elasticity tends to be lowest in the very short run, so the tax may be completely (or almost completely) shifted to the consumer at first. But as time passes, there may be a series of small price decreases, or—and this is the more likely scenario in an inflationary environment—prices may not rise as quickly as they otherwise would have.

[44]In chapter 4, we point out that price elasticity for alcohol and cigarettes is considerably less than 1 (in absolute terms).

[45]Again, as in the case of demand, chances are that in the very short run, supply curves will be rather inelastic because suppliers cannot immediately remove resources from this industry to another pursuit. As time progresses, however, and resources shift out of the affected industry, the supply curve will become more elastic, and both price and production will be affected to a more significant degree.

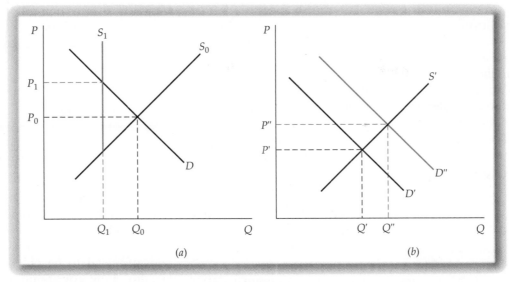

Figure 4A.6 Imposition of Voluntary Export Restraints

supply–demand analysis that are really timeless. Together with these, a number of recent examples illustrate how the subjects discussed in chapters 3 and 4 have current applications.

Voluntary Export Restraints

In 1981, the United States and Japan agreed that Japan would limit its exports of cars to the United States to 1,680,000 annually. The limit was later increased but was still considerably below the number that would have been sold in the United States in the absence of this quota. What was the result? The price of Japanese vehicles rose. The effect of such a limitation can be seen in Figure 4A.6a. The original quantity and price of Japanese cars sold in the United States are shown as Q_0 and P_0. The imposition of the "voluntary" export quota on Japan at a limit less than the equilibrium quantity changed the shape of the supply curve. At the level of exports, Q_1, the supply curve becomes vertical, and the demand curve now intersects the supply curve at P_1—a new, higher price.

Given the restriction, the Japanese began to ship their higher-priced models to the United States to satisfy the upper portion of the market. Because the demand for Japanese cars now could not be satisfied, American consumers sought to purchase domestic or other imported automobiles. Such

action shifted the demand curve for the rest of the automobile market to the right, as illustrated in Figure 4A.6b, thus increasing the number and the price of vehicles purchased. It was estimated by one economist that new car prices in 1984 were $1,500 higher than they would have been had quotas not been in effect. The additional cost to American consumers was $13 billion. The beneficiaries of this increased cost were the big three automobile manufacturers (to the tune of about $6 billion in higher profits), the autoworkers (about $3 billion in overtime payments), and the American dealers of Japanese cars and the Japanese manufacturers themselves (about $4 billion).[46] Subsequently, Japanese automobile manufacturers began to produce their cars in the United States. In 1985 and thereafter, the U.S. dollar weakened considerably against the Japanese yen. The prices of Japanese cars in the United States rose significantly, permitting U.S. manufacturers to continue to increase their prices and enjoy higher profits.[47] But in 1998, with the Japanese yen displaying substantial weakness, it was Japanese cars that appeared to have a price advantage.

---

[46]Yoshi Tsurumi, "They're Merely a Subsidy for Detroit," *New York Times,* December 16, 1984.
[47]"Schools Brief," *Economist,* October 25, 1986, pp. 84–85.

Economic Consequences of Other Import Restrictions

A 1973 study calculated that the loss to American consumers due to import restrictions on sugar was $586 million per year. Ilse Mintz estimated that the restrictions raised the price of sugar by 2.57 cents per pound and decreased consumption from 23.2 to 22.4 billion pounds per year. Figure 4A.7 shows this situation. The shaded area representing consumer loss can be calculated as follows:

0.0257×22.4 billion	$575.7 million
$0.0257 \times (23.2 - 22.4$ bill.$) \times 0.5$	10.3 million
	$586.0 million

A similar type of study performed in 1977 looked at the consequences of the imposition of import quotas on steel. The study showed that a price increase of $11 per ton of steel and a resulting decrease in steel consumption of 0.9 million tons per year would have cost the consumer more than $1 billion per year and would have created a gain of about $870 million for U.S. steel producers. Thus, consumers lose more than U.S. producers gain. Part of the difference would accrue to foreign producers. Another part is due to the decrease in steel consumption, and another results due to the substitution of high-cost U.S. steel for cheaper foreign steel.[48]

Figure 4A.7 Effect of Import Restrictions on Sugar Demand

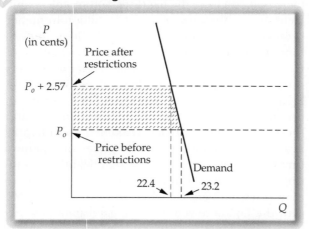

Table 4A.2 U.S. Consumption per Capita, in Pounds

	1975	1987
Beef	88.0	73.4
Chicken	39.9	62.7
Fish	12.2	15.4

Source: Reprinted by permission of *Wall Street Journal*, © 1989 Dow Jones and Company, Inc. All rights reserved worldwide.

The Demand for Beef

In the 1980s, there was a shift away from beef demand. The result was an increase in the consumption of seafood, but the main beneficiary of this shift in demand appeared to be chicken. Table 4A.2 shows data for these consumption changes over 12 years.

Demand for beef was very high into the early 1970s, and prices kept rising. However, the concern raised about the link between red meat and cholesterol levels was instrumental in putting a check on beef demand. Also, around this same time, chicken producers developed new and convenient chicken products that appealed to the public. Table 4A.2 shows that beef consumption per capita dropped 16 percent from 1975 to 1987, while chicken consumption rose 57 percent. Fish consumption also rose significantly, 26 percent, but considerably less than chicken.

During this period, the U.S. cattle population decreased substantially. As discussed previously, a change in supply is a long-run reaction to changes in demand.[49] More recently, however, the beef industry has begun to take steps that appear to have stopped the demand slide. Actually, there has been some increase in the demand for beef, as the industry has had some limited success with advertising campaigns. In 1987, cattle growers voted to establish a $1-per-animal fund for product and nutritional research and a national advertising campaign. One possible way to combat the demand for chicken is to offer branded merchandise, a method chicken producers have been using for years. The beef industry appears to be rather slow in emulating some of the marketing techniques of

---

[48]Ilse Mintz, *U.S. Import Quotas: Costs and Consequences*, Washington, DC: American Enterprise Institute, 1973; Federal Trade Commission, *Staff Report on the United States Steel Industry and Its International Rivals*, November 1977. Both of these studies are discussed in Edwin Mansfield, *Microeconomics*, 5th ed., New York: W. W. Norton, 1985, pp. 100–103, 509–12.

[49]The discussion in this section is based on the following articles: Marj Charlier, "Beef's Drop in Appeal Pushes Some Packers to Try New Products," *Wall Street Journal*, August 8, 1985; Marj Charlier, "The U.S. Beef Industry Just Can't Seem to Get the Hang of Marketing," *Wall Street Journal*, January 4, 1989.

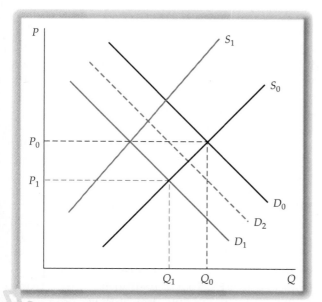

Figure 4A.8   The Downward Shift in Beef Demand

demand curve to the right, from D_1 and D_2. Whether the new demand curve will be between D_1 and D_0 or even to the right of D_0 cannot be foreseen. The danger lurking in this effort to increase beef demand was that, given the low level of beef herds,[54] beef prices could soar, thus discouraging consumers. If the supply curve for beef in the short run is rather inelastic, this is what could happen.

What we describe was the situation prevailing during the 1980s and early 1990s. Despite some efforts by the beef industry, the demand for beef has declined by some 41 percent over the past 25 years. But more recently, the beef industry appears to have learned some lessons from the chicken producers. Now, the industry is spending hundreds of millions of dollars to "reverse a decades-long decline in red meat consumption." Some of the large firms in the industry, such as Hormel Foods, Inc., and IBP, Inc., (now a unit of Tyson Foods, Inc.), are branding their products. One thrust in this effort is to shorten the cooking process by selling branded precooked packaged beef that can then be finished in microwave ovens in a matter of minutes. This is primarily intended to attract families with working couples that do not have the time to spend several hours preparing dinners. Although these meats tend to sell at prices considerably higher than raw meat, the two companies expected to sell about $100 million of their product in 2002. "Within a decade, say some industry officials, microwavable red meats could easily generate $1 billion in sales." These companies are also producing high-quality steak and chops using their own brand labels for consumers who are not interested in microwaving their meat. In addition, some supermarket chains prefer to sell meats under their own labels, such as Kroger Company's Cattleman's Collection.[55]

In 2003, it appeared that beef had made a real comeback. Demand for beef surged and prices hit records, increasing 38 percent over the prior year. These price increases were also helped by a tighter supply resulting from a ban on Canadian beef, which had accounted for 8 percent of U.S. beef consumption, due to the discovery of mad cow disease in Canada.[56]

the chicken producers, but, according to the research director of the beef council, "there is a sense of emergency that we have to become marketers."[50] These trends are graphically depicted in Figure 4A.8. The original equilibrium of beef prices and production was at the intersection of P_0 and Q_0. As consumer preferences shifted from beef to chicken and fish, the demand curve for beef moved to the left, from D_0 to D_1. Quantities produced were less, and prices declined relatively.[51]

Over time, resources shifted out of beef production. According to the National Cattlemen's Association, the number of beef cattle decreased from 130 million in 1975 to about 110 million in 1985.[52] The shift of resources is shown on Figure 4A.8 as a movement of the supply curve from S_0 to S_1. This action tended to stabilize beef prices during the period.[53] In the last few years, as just described, beef producers have begun to fight back, if not always effectively. The various campaigns mounted by the industry to convince consumers of beef's beneficial qualities are intended to move the

---

[50]Charlier, "U.S. Beef Industry."
[51]Absolute prices of both chicken and beef may have risen due to inflationary factors, which were very strong in the 1970s and early 1980s.
[52]Charlier, "Beef's Drop in Appeal."
[53]Similarly, increases in chicken-producing resources dampened the price effect of the increased chicken demand.

[54]Beef supplies were further depleted in 1988 because of the severe drought.
[55]Scott Kilman, "A Roast Is a Roast? Not in the New Game of Marketing Meat," *Wall Street Journal*, February 20, 2002.
[56]Scott Kilman, "U.S. Beef Enjoys a Bull Market, Enriching Ranchers and Packers," *Wall Street Journal*, September 26, 2003.

Demand for Various Consumer Products

It is a well-known fact that women have significantly increased their participation in the labor force since the end of World War II. After the war, men returned from the armed services, and women, who had taken the men's place in the work force, returned to their traditional pursuits. In 1947, women made up about 28 percent of total employment. Women then began to enter the labor force again, and the proportion of female employment rose to 35 percent by 1965 and to 45 percent by 1987. With the change in women's functions, a change in U.S. living patterns and consumption habits followed. According to a *Wall Street Journal* article, homes in the United States are not quite as clean as they were in the past.[57] Whereas women once spent much of their time as housewives, their acceptance into the labor force has changed this traditional role. "Sales of scouring powder, mildew removers, floor wax and dishwashing liquid slipped again last year, continuing a 10-year trend," according to Selling Areas Marketing, Inc., a New York–based research company.[58] In contrast, sales of paper plates and aluminum baking pans have risen significantly. In addition, new time-saving household products have come to the market, and a new service business—maid services—has sprung up.

In the late 1990s, U.S. supermarkets and packaged goods manufacturers faced another shift in consumer demand. With the economy thriving and a significant number of households with working couples, there has been a vast increase in spending on restaurant and take-away meals at the expense of at-home eating. In 1997, it was estimated that away-from-home eating accounted for about 45 percent of total spending on food. The profits of packaged goods manufacturers slipped in 1998. Supermarkets were actually being hit not only by increased restaurant eating but also by competition from discount stores such as Wal-Mart. Many supermarket chains are now trying to compete by having special sections that prepare both hot and cold meals packaged for consumers who do not want to cook meals at home. Usually the profit margin on such meals is greater than on the usual items on grocery shelves, which offsets the decreases in sales of supermarkets' regular merchandise.[59]

A shift in demand patterns also occurred after the events of September 11, 2001. It appears that American consumers turned to "mundane and homey activities and purchases." Among the beneficiaries of the change in the public's mood were stores dealing with old-fashioned crafts like quilting and knitting, and fast foods like pizza and ice cream. In contrast, there was a decline of business at fancy restaurants. Sales of DVDs and television sets as well as kitchen appliances, such as cooking ranges, were going well.[60]

Newspapers and Their Price Elasticity

In July 1994, the French daily newspaper *Le Quotidien* suspended publication. To boost its revenue in the face of increasing competition and France's recession, *Le Quotidien* slashed its price from FF6 to FF4. Its circulation increased from 30,000 units to 40,000. But this resulted in a decrease of its revenue from FF180,000 per day to FF160,000. The demand curve turned out to have an arc elasticity of −0.71. A similar action involved a decrease in the price of the London *Times* in September 1993. The price was dropped from 45 to 30 pence, while the daily prices of its competitors remained unchanged. Between August 1993 and May 1994, the *Times'* daily circulation rose from 355,000 to only 518,000, resulting in a decrease in revenue. Again, the demand curve appears to have been inelastic.[61] More recent examples, with similar results, can be found in the United States. In 2000, the *New York Post* decreased the price of its daily paper from 50 cents to 25 cents—a 50 percent decrease—resulting in a 29 percent increase in circulation. In 2001, the *Los Angeles Times* increased its price from 25 cents to 50 cents (having dropped it in 1996) and circulation fell only 5 percent.[62]

---

[57]Betsy Morris, "Homes Get Dirtier as Women Seek Jobs and Men Volunteer for the Easy Chores," *Wall Street Journal,* February 12, 1985.

[58]Morris, "Homes Get Dirtier."

[59]Richard Tomkins, "Home Truths for U.S. Grocers," *Financial Times,* August 11, 1998.

---

[60]Leslie Kaufman and Julian E. Barnes, "Craving a Comfort Zone," *New York Times,* October 10, 2001; Christopher Bowe, "Consumers Turn to the Kitchen in Times of Strife," *Financial Times,* October 16, 2001; and Elliot Spagat, "Retailers Pin Hope on 'Cocooning' TV Buyers," *Wall Street Journal,* October 18, 2001.

[61]Alice Rawsthorn, "Crisis in French Press May See More Casualties," *Financial Times,* July 6, 1994; R. W. Stevenson, "A Cheaper Times of London Wins Readers," *New York Times,* June 13, 1994.

[62]Patricia Callahan, "Four Knight Ridder Papers Cut Prices," *Wall Street Journal,* June 11, 2002. The relatively small response to a price decrease, may not lead to a decrease in profitability. When newspapers' circulations increase, newspapers may increase their rates for advertising, thus making up for the loss.

Controlling Traffic in City Centers

In 1998, Singapore began a new system of controlling traffic in its city center. Motorists must purchase prepaid cash cards and tolls are deducted electronically from this card (which is placed on the car's dashboard). The tolls differ depending on the time of the day a car enters the city. If a car enters the central area without this card, its registration plate will be photographed and a violation notice mailed. The program appears to have been successful. Traffic has decreased by 17 percent during the enforcement period, and the speed at which cars pass through the city center has increased. Singapore is not the only city using this procedure; among others, several Norwegian cities use such cards.[63] A different method to decrease traffic is used in Minneapolis. Here, one of the largest employers, American Express Financial Advisors, is subsidizing the area's bus systems in return for greatly reduced monthly bus tickets for its employees.[64]

Although actions in both Singapore and Minneapolis aim at decreasing rush hour traffic, the two methods have very different effects on the demand for the use of automobiles. In the case of Singapore, the action has increased the cost of travel into the city center, and has caused a movement up along the demand curve, a decrease in the quantity demanded. In contrast, in Minneapolis, the result is to lower the cost of bus travel, a substitute for car commuting. The demand curve for auto travel will now shift to the left, a decrease in demand.

The effect of these two actions can be illustrated by simple graphs. Assume that the demand for automobile traffic in Singapore is as shown on Figure 4A.9a. If the quantity demanded before the imposition of the toll is at P_0 and Q_0, then after the toll is implemented, the new equilibrium will be at the intersection of P_1 and Q_1. This, of course, as we saw in chapter 3, is a decrease in quantity demanded. Now, let us take a look at the Minneapolis situation. In this case, Figure 4A.9a represents the demand for bus travel. The decrease in bus fares resulting from the financial aid given to the bus systems, will cause a move on the demand curve from P_0 (the price of fares before the decrease) to P_2; this is an increase in quantity demanded from Q_0 to Q_2. Figure 4A.9b depicts the demand for automobile traffic into downtown. Demand curve D_0 represented the demand before the bus fare cuts went into effect. With the decrease in bus fares, the substitution effect will result in a new demand curve D_1, and

Figure 4A.9   The Effect of Two Different Policies on Automobile Travel

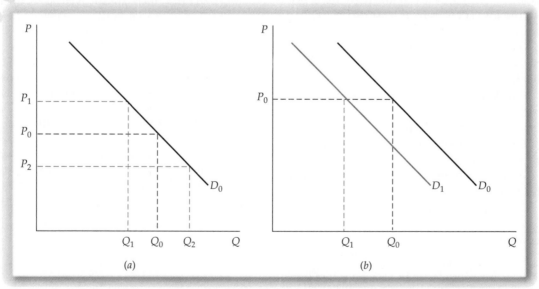

[63]Sheila McNulty and John Parker, "How to Stop Traffic Jams," *Financial Times,* May 9, 1998.
[64]*Wall Street Journal,* August 27, 1998.

the demand for automobile travel will decrease from point Q_0 to Q_1.

The city of London adopted a system very similar to that of Singapore in February 2003. A charge of £5 was levied on automobiles entering the center of London on weekdays from 7 A.M. to 6:30 P.M. Six months later, it was reported that the scheme had decreased London traffic by 16 percent[65] and in 2005 it was reported that congestion in London was reduced by 30 percent. Also in 2005, the congestion charge was increased to £8 and discounts were introduced for monthly or annual payments.[66] Stockholm conducted a trial of the congestion tax in 2006 and implemented it on a permanent basis on August 1, 2007. It is in effect from 6:30 A.M. to 6:30 P.M. on weekdays. The charge varies during the time of day.[67] And finally, in April 2007, the mayor of New York City proposed an $8 tax for cars entering the lower portions of Manhattan.[68] However, the New York State legislature voted not to enact the mayor's proposal.

The Market for Used Automobiles

In 2005, in order to improve sales, American automobile manufactures initiated "employee pricing," giving to all buyers discounts previously granted only to employees. Consequently, many buyers who would otherwise buy used cars were now purchasing new ones. The result was a significant increase in the sales of new cars, and a corresponding increase in trade-ins. The glut of used cars drove their prices down to the lowest levels in at least two years. In the two months from May to July 2005, prices fell at least 5 percent and were expected to decline further. Dealers throughout the United States had 120,000 more used cars on their lots than they would have had if there had been no increase in new-car sales.[69]

A similar situation occurred in 2001, when car dealers began to offer 0 percent financing on new cars in the aftermath of the attacks on the World Trade Center and Pentagon. In October 2001 new car sales rose by 35 percent. In addition, because of the expected decrease in travel, many car rental companies reduced their fleets by 20 to 30 percent. As a result the inventory of used cars increased sharply and resulted in price decreases of 10 percent and even as much as 20 percent.[70] (Try to draw demand and supply curves for new cars and used cars to illustrate this situation.)

The French Wine Industry

Over the past several years, the French wine industry has been suffering. From 1999 to 2000 alone, exports of French wines dropped 5.4 percent, and millions of liters of unsold wine were accumulating in French cellars. France's market share in the United States has dropped from 7 percent to 5 percent in 3 years. During this period, sales of producers in California, Australia, and Chile have been rising sharply in the world's important markets of North America, Northern Europe, and Asia. What are the major reasons for this shift in demand from the world's leading wine producers to a group of upstarts in the rest of the world? According to a recent article there are several:[71]

1. French vintners are restricted by the government as to the types of grapes that can be produced in a particular region, and how they are cultivated.
2. They are paid by the amount of grapes they deliver, thus impairing careful growing, and resulting in inconsistent quality.
3. Predominantly, French producers are small, scattered firms (there are about 20,000 of them) that are finding it difficult to compete efficiently with large, new-world companies. Only one French company is among the world's ten largest producers.
4. The many different regional and local labels of French wines make it difficult for consumers (except for connoisseurs) to understand what they are buying, compared with the simple labeling by the new world's large wine-producing companies.
5. The dispersed nature of the French wine industry is no match for its large foreign rivals when it comes to marketing and promotion programs. For example, U.S. company E. & J. Gallo, the world's largest producer, spent $2.5 million on marketing in England alone, while the entire Bordeaux wine-producing region spent less than half of that amount in 2000.

[65]"Smooth Start to London Traffic Tax," www.cnn.com/World, February 17, 2003; "London's Traffic Tax Paying Off," www.news24.com, August 17, 2003.
[66]"Congestion Charge Increases to £8," *BBC News,* April 1, 2005.
[67]"Stockholm Congestion Tax," *Wikipedia,* August 26, 2007.
[68]Maria Newman, "Mayor Proposes a Fee for Driving to Manhattan," *New York Times,* April 22, 2007.
[69]Jennifer Saranow, "Where the Real Deals Are: Luxury Used Cars," *Wall Street Journal,* August 11, 2005.

[70]Sholem Freeman and Karen Lundegaard, "New-Car Deals Shake Up Market for Used Vehicles," *Wall Street Journal,* November 16, 2001.
[71]William Echikson and others, "Wine War," *BusinessWeek,* September 3, 2001, pp. 54–60.

The problems of the French wine industry are not going away. The crisis appears to continue. Exports continue to fall, and the French population is consuming less wine. Recently, wine growers have met with government ministers to try to find a solution. One of the suggestions was to reclassify wine as a "natural food" rather than an alcoholic drink under French law. Such a change would permit wine makers more freedom to advertise. Advertising is now restricted due to a law passed in 1991 to decrease alcohol consumption in France. In a way, this presents the French government with a paradox. It has undertaken a program to reduce alcohol consumption and there has been some success in decreasing the per capita consumption of wine and also decreasing the number of deaths due to automobile accidents. "Overproduction, competition from New World wines and falling domestic consumption have led to steep price cuts for French wine."[72]

On the other hand, the problem that French champagne makers face is just the opposite. The industry continues to prosper. The global sales of champagne have been rising (some 54 percent between 1990 and 2004). However, the champagne grape growing area is limited to 84,000 acres due to a 1927 law that set the boundaries. There is a great deal of competition for any acreage that becomes available. A two-and-a-half-acre tract producing high-quality champagne may sell for $1.2 million. There has been a push to increase the size of the champagne region, but it is not expected that this will happen in the next several years.[73]

The Woes of the U.S. Furniture Industry

Historically, rising home sales have led to healthy sales of furniture. In 2002, record sales of new and used homes were forecasted. However, the U.S. furniture industry did not benefit from this growth. The reason for this state of affairs is intense competition, mainly from China and also from Canada. Furniture imports to the United States are reported to have risen some 71 percent since 1999, and it is estimated that imports now comprise more than 40 percent of the U.S. market. The growth has been particularly significant in metal and wood furniture—less so in upholstered furniture.

Although cheaper imports benefit the consumer, they have had a devastating effect on the U.S. furniture industry. "To compete, some U.S. companies are joining the competition." One example is Furniture Brands International, Inc. After closing down several of its domestic plants, it began to import products for its Lane division from Asia.[74]

A Price Action That Misfired

In October 2003, the Universal Music Group, a unit of Vivendi Universal SA and the world's largest music company, cut its CD prices by up to 30 percent. This action, which Universal named "JumpStart," was taken to improve the suffering music business. The CD wholesale price was lowered to $9.09 from $12.98, and it was expected that retail shops would lower their prices to $12.98, the price suggested by Universal. Universal expected that this retail price decrease would make it possible for the smaller stores to compete with mass merchants. Given the illegal downloading of music, this lower price did not appeal to consumers as much as was expected. Moreover, many music retailers did not implement the price cut or were otherwise slow to put it into effect. The smaller retailers believed that they could not afford to cut their prices, unlike some of their big rivals—such as Wal-Mart—that can afford to cut their margins and make up the decrease with sales of other, higher-price products. Another problem created by Universal was that it ceased making "co-op advertising" payments to retail stores. These payments actually represented a subsidy to help retailers from sustaining losses. Universal had calculated that, given the price cuts, it needed a 21 percent increase in volume to break even. However, increases amounted to only 8 percent to 13 percent in most weeks. As a result, Universal's revenue decreased by 11 percent during the first quarter of 2004. In April 2004, Universal partially backtracked and raised its wholesale prices; however, they remained lower than before JumpStart.[75]

Verizon and Demand Elasticity

In 2005 the federal government announced that it would discontinue a surcharge, called the Universal

[72]Jo Johnson, "Winemakers Call Crisis Talks with Ministers as French Exports Fall," *Financial Times,* July 22, 2004.
[73]Sarah Nassauer, "Champagne's Land Lock," *Wall Street Journal,* August 12, 2005.
[74]Jon E. Hilsenrath and Peter Wonacott, "Imports Hammer Furniture Makers," *Wall Street Journal,* September 20, 2002.
[75]Ethan Smith, "Why a Grand Plan to Cut CD Prices Went Off the Track," *Wall Street Journal,* June 4, 2004.

Service Fund fee, that it had levied on Verizon's DSL service. Verizon could have passed on this price break to its customers and possibly attracted more customers at the lower price. Instead, Verizon decided to replace the government fee with a supplier surcharge of about the same amount. How could this be explained? The answer is price elasticity of demand. Apparently Verizon assumed that the increase in number of customers would not bring in as much revenue as raising the price. In other words, the assumption was that at the current price the demand was price inelastic. Of course, this could be a short-run occurrence. In the long run, customers may find alternative services to be a better deal.[76]

Tobacco Production Is on the Rise

Tobacco production had been subsidized by the U.S. government since 1938. The law guaranteed a minimum price and at the same time allotted quotas to tobacco farmers. In 2004 subsidies were discontinued. As a consequence, the acreage devoted to tobacco growing in the United States dropped from 408 thousand acres to 297 thousand acres, a decrease of 27 percent. But since 2005, acreage has risen some 20 percent to 355 thousand acres. The unsubsidized tobacco is now cheaper (about $1.60 per pound compared to $1.98 before subsidies were ended), and production in the United States has become competitive as an export. China, Russia, and Mexico have become major importers as demand for cigarettes is still growing in those countries. Tobacco companies are recruiting new tobacco farmers and are offering them financial assistance. Tobacco is now being produced in areas such as southern Illinois where it had not been produced in any significant quantities since World War I. In Pennsylvania, production has more than doubled since 2004. A farmer in Illinois has estimated that, even at this lower price, he is netting about $1,800 per acre of tobacco compared to $250 from his corn crop, even though corn is now selling at record prices due to the increased demand for ethanol. Thus, in the words of Professor David Orden of Virginia Tech, "we are finding out that farming can be done without subsidies."[77]

The Demand for Corn

The ethanol boom pushed corn prices to over $4 per bushel in early 2007. At the end of March, the U.S. Department of Agriculture reported that farmers were expected to plant some 90.5 million acres of corn in 2007, a 15 percent increase over 2006 and the highest acreage since 1944. As a result, the acreage for other products, particularly soybeans and cotton, would be impacted by 11 percent and 20 percent, respectively. On that day, corn's future prices dropped by 5 percent. By September 2007 the price of corn had decreased to $3.65 per bushel and was expected to drop further to $3.20 by the end of the year as the demand for ethanol was lower than previously predicted. In the same month the Department of Agriculture raised its forecast of corn production to 13.3 billion bushels, 26 percent over the prior year, and expected that stocks of corn will be double those in 2006.[78]

The Coffee Glut in Brazil

A very large crop of coffee in Brazil, the world's leading coffee bean grower, as well as in other countries, caused a steep decline in the price of coffee in 2001.

Brazil attempted to decrease the supply of coffee by using a "global retention scheme." Brazil was going to keep more than 2 million bags (at 60 kilograms per bag) off the market. However, this plan collapsed in September 2001 when other coffee-producing countries refused to cooperate. In November, Brazil's policy makers planned to introduce another program, under which the government would finance 70 percent of the value of coffee that producers would hold back for a year.

One of the problems that producers in Brazil face is the rather low productivity and thus high cost of coffee production. According to one authority,

---

[76]Andrew Cassel, "The Economy, Verizon's Lesson about Elasticity of Demand," *Philadelphia Inquirer,* August 23, 2006.
[77]Lauren Etter, "U.S. Farmers Rediscover the Allure of Tobacco," *Wall Street Journal,* September 18, 2007.

[78]Lauren Etter, "Hot Commodity on Wall Street: USDA's Crop-Production Report," *Wall Street Journal,* March 24–25, 2007; Andrew Martin "Farmers to Plant Largest Amount of Cotton Since '44," *New York Times,* March 31, 2007; Prasenjit Bhattacharya, "*S Corn Prices Forecast Down to $3.20 Per Bushel by End '07," *Dow Jones Commodities Service,* September 4, 2007; Bill Thompson, "USDA Sees Higher US Corn Production; Weaker Ethanol Demand," *Dow Jones Commodities Service,* September 12, 2007. However, contrary to these forecasts, the price of corn stood at approximately $8.00 per bushel in June 2008.

"at current prices, the break-even point is at 45 bags per hectare (2.471 acres). But in the past year, productivity has averaged 17 bags around here." Many coffee producers have had to seek alternative products, such as soybeans, passion fruit, and grains. It has also been estimated that 10 percent of the coffee-growing area has been abandoned since the end of the year 2000, and it is expected that additional land will be left idle by 2002 harvest time.[79]

---

[79]Thierry Ogier, "There's an Awful Lot of Coffee in Brazil," *Financial Times*, November 9, 2001.

SUMMARY

As the preceding examples show, it is extremely important that a manager or entrepreneur understand such cause-and-effect relationships. Demand and supply curves move continually in an economic society. It is management's task to identify such movements, understand their consequences, and design strategies and tactics to minimize adverse results and take advantage of new opportunities. Knowledge of economic interrelationships is a tool that will assist decision makers in taking these important actions.

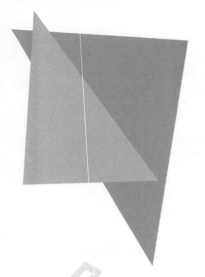

Demand Estimation and Forecasting

Learning Objectives

Upon completion of this chapter, readers should be able to:

- Specify the components of a regression model that can be used to estimate a demand equation.

- Interpret the regression results (i.e., explain the quantitative impact that changes in the determinants have on the quantity demanded).

- Explain the meaning of R^2.

- Evaluate the statistical significance of the regression coefficients using the t-test and the statistical significance of R^2 using the F-test.

- Recognize the challenges of obtaining reliable cross-sectional and time series data on consumer behavior that can be used in regression models of demand.

- Understand the importance of forecasting in business.

- Describe six different forecasting techniques.

- Show how to carry out least squares projections, and decompose them into trends, seasonal, cyclical, and irregular movements.

- Explain basic smoothing methods of forecasting, such as the moving average and exponential smoothing.

The Situation

Frank Robinson, recently brought into Global Foods, Inc., to build a forecasting department, finds his new position to be very challenging and quite interesting. However, he also knows that forecasting, even in the relatively stable soft drink industry, can be a thankless task. From various forecast requests on his desk, he pulls out the one for the company's lemon-lime soda, Citronade, a brand recently purchased from an older, established company. He has been asked to estimate sales for the next year, and the deadline for his report is nearing. He has annual sales data for the last 11 years, and he also has sales data by quarter. In an industry where sales show considerable increases during the summer months, a forecast that estimates sales for the seasons of the year is very important.[1]

(continued)

---

[1]Sales forecasts for a real company are usually made on a monthly, not a quarterly, basis. But for the purposes of this text, quarterly data are used. This is done to economize on the quantity of data used. The methods employed in the analysis of the data are identical whether quarterly or monthly figures are employed. In fact, in the appendix of this chapter, we provide an expanded example using weekly data.

(continued)

Frank first looks at the annual data, and he quickly computes year-to-year changes. These numbers are shown in Table 5.1. He notices that, although sales were up in each of the years, the percentage growth from year to year appears to have a declining trend. He will have to consider this phenomenon when he makes his forecast.

Quarterly data are shown in Table 5.2. As he looks over these numbers, Frank realizes that he has several busy days ahead of him.

Table 5.1   Sales of Citronade (in Thousands of Cases)

Year	Annual Sales	Change	Percent Change
1997	3,892		
1998	4,203	311	8.0
1999	4,477	274	6.5
2000	4,810	333	7.4
2001	5,132	322	6.7
2002	5,407	275	5.4
2003	5,726	319	5.9
2004	6,023	297	5.2
2005	6,360	337	5.6
2006	6,641	281	4.4
2007	6,954	313	4.7

Table 5.2   Quarterly Sales of Citronade, 1997–2007 (in Thousands of Cases)

Year	1st Qtr	2nd Qtr	3rd Qtr	4th Qtr	Total
1997	842	939	1,236	875	3,892
1998	907	1,017	1,331	948	4,203
1999	953	1,103	1,406	1,015	4,477
2000	1,047	1,180	1,505	1,078	4,810
2001	1,124	1,267	1,576	1,165	5,132
2002	1,167	1,340	1,670	1,230	5,407
2003	1,255	1,403	1,766	1,302	5,726
2004	1,311	1,495	1,837	1,380	6,023
2005	1,390	1,565	1,940	1,465	6,360
2006	1,455	1,649	2,026	1,511	6,641
2007	1,536	1,714	2,103	1,601	6,954

DEMAND ESTIMATION

INTRODUCTION

Key Chapter Objectives

In the previous chapters, we analyze the demand function from a theoretical stand-point. We show how each of the determinants of demand—price and nonprice factors, such as tastes and preferences and income—affects the amount people are willing to purchase of a particular good or service. Hypothetical numerical examples were devised to illustrate the concept of elasticity, a key way in which we measure the sensitivity of quantity demanded to changes in price and the nonprice determinants of demand. It is vital for managers to use whatever tools and data are available to explain and forecast demand. Think about how much better off the managers of Krispy Kreme donuts would have been if they had been able to forecast the impact that change in dietary habits of American consumers would have on donut consumption. Also consider the advantage the managers of the manufacturers of LCD screens would have if they could forecast the sales of sixth- and seventh-generation screens. They would then be able to optimally invest in plant capacity and operations.

This chapter presents two important statistical approaches to estimating and forecasting the demand for a product. We recognize that both topics are covered extensively in other courses offered in a typical business curriculum. Moreover, the power and ease of use of various software packages make it relatively easy for managers to generate quantitative studies of demand using regression and forecasting techniques. Therefore, this chapter is intended to be an overview of how the techniques of analysis are used in various types of studies. But these advances do not diminish the importance of obtaining good data, correctly interpreting and evaluating the analytical results, and using the results to make good management decisions. These factors are the essence of our chapter's coverage of this topic. Let us begin with a statement about the importance of obtaining good data for use in whatever type of statistical analysis managers can use.

The Critical Importance of Good Data

When computers began to be used for business operations and analysis, there was a frequently used acronym, "GIGO," which stood for "garbage in, garbage out." Readers may not recall this somewhat dated expression, but recounting it helps make an important point: Statistical analyses are only as good as the accuracy and appropriateness of the sample of information that is used.

Readily available and reliable data for use in economic studies pertaining to countries, regions, or industries (e.g., analysis and forecasting of the gross domestic product, interest rates, foreign exchange rates, industry output) are provided by official sources such as the U.S. Department of Commerce, the U.S. Department of Labor, the Organization of Economic Development, the World Bank, and the United Nations. However, data that can be used for the analysis of specific product categories (e.g., demand for pizza or cell phones) may be more difficult and costly to obtain.

The leading providers of market research services in the United States and for much of the developed countries of the world are ACNielsen and Information Resources, Inc. (IRI). A visit to either company's Web site will provide readers with a good idea of the kinds of products and services offered to market research clients, most of whom are large food and beverage and other types of fast-moving packaged consumer goods companies. No doubt if our "Global Foods," were a real company, it would be using the services of one of them, as do actual companies such as Kraft

Foods, Coca-Cola and PepsiCo, Nestlé and Unilever. In the appendix to this chapter, we utilize actual historical data on the demand for wine that was obtained by IRI.[2]

There are numerous ways in which market researchers seek out the "truth" of consumer behavior. They might use the direct approach of a **consumer survey**, either face to face (e.g., stopping people in shopping centers) or by telephone. Another direct approach is the focus group. Typically, this method involves market researchers observing behind a two-way mirror the answers and body language of selected groups of consumers who are asked specific questions about a company and its competitors. Perhaps some of you have been involved in this type of data gathering.[3]

Another way that ACNielsen measures the behavior of consumers is by having people participate in consumer panel surveys. Volunteers in this activity are provided with a scanner that enables them to record their store purchases by reading the bar codes of every item they bought. The survey participants then transmit the scanned data to the market research firm on a regular basis via a special modem attached to their home phones.

Technology is making it possible for retail stores to accumulate, store, and process large amounts of data about consumer behavior. The data are primarily collected with the aid of scanning technology such as bar code readers and point-of-sale terminals. More recently, RFID technology (radio frequency capability encoded into computer chips) will make it even easier for stores to track their inventory and sales. Wal-Mart, the largest company in the world, has mandated that a number of its major suppliers attach these devices to their products. Already Wal-Mart has built a data warehouse of information about what every single customer purchases in every one of its stores every day of the year. The amount of data stored in its warehouse is allegedly second only to that stored by the U.S. government.

The procedure commonly used by economists to estimate consumer demand with whatever data are made available is **regression analysis**. In addition to its application in demand estimation, it is used to estimate production and cost functions (see chapters 6 and 7). It is also used in macroeconomic studies of consumption, investment, international trade, and interest rates. In the ensuing section on regression analysis, we briefly explain regression analysis, how to interpret its results, and how to apply the results to management decisions. A much more comprehensive discussion of this topic, including the theoretical foundation for regression analysis, can be obtained in a statistics or econometrics text. Hence, we consider this presentation on regression analysis as more of a "management briefing" than an academic presentation.

REGRESSION ANALYSIS: A MANAGEMENT BRIEFING

Specifying the Regression Equation and Obtaining the Data

In estimating the demand for a particular good or service, first determine all the factors that might influence this demand. Suppose we wanted to estimate the demand for pizza by college students in the United States. What variables would most likely affect their demand for pizza? We could start to answer this question by using price and all the nonprice determinants listed in chapter 3 (i.e., tastes and preferences,

---

[2]Go to www.acnielsen.com and www.us.infores.com. For market research on Internet advertising and shopping, DoubleClick (www.doubleclick.com) is a major company in the field.
[3]One of the authors actually likes to participate in telephone consumer surveys because it gives him a good idea of what companies are looking for in their market research. He has also recently participated in a focus group session initiated by a major airline. The purpose of the session was to find out what the participants thought about one of the leading low-cost airlines and what the company could do to fight back against this type of competition. In exchange for his time, he was given 10,000 frequent flier points.

income, prices of related goods, future expectations, number of buyers). But it is not always possible or appropriate to include all these variables in a particular demand analysis. As an example of this, in the demand for pizza, one would not think that "future expectations" would play an important role. In addition, there may be sudden shifts in tastes and preferences that may not be measured easily. For example, the "low carb" diet craze may well have an impact on the demand for pizza but it would be somewhat challenging to measure this change.[4]

Ideally, all variables that are believed to have an impact on demand should be included in the regression analysis. In reality, the variables used in regression analysis are based on the availability of data and the cost of generating new data. The two types of data used in regression analysis are **cross-sectional** and **time series.** Cross-sectional data provide information on variables for a given period of time. Time series data give information about the variables over a number of periods of time. For the purpose of illustration, let us assume we have obtained cross-sectional data on college students by conducting a survey of thirty randomly selected college campuses in the United States during a particular month.

Suppose we have gathered the following information for each campus from this survey: (1) average number of slices consumed per month by students, (2) average price of a slice of pizza in places selling pizza in and around the campus, (3) annual tuition cost, (4) average price of a soft drink sold in the pizza places, and (5) location of the campus (urban versus suburban or rural). The data obtained from our hypothetical survey are presented in Table 5.3.

The reasons for selecting these variables are based on the economic theory of demand. Therefore, it should be clear why the price of pizza and the price of its complementary product, a soft drink, were selected for this study. But sometimes a researcher may have to use some creativity in coming up with variables that represent such factors as income and tastes and preferences. Because of the difficulty of finding out the average income of the students (or their families) who attend a particular college, tuition was used as a proxy variable. The location dummy variable is included to determine whether the demand for pizza is affected by the number of available substitutes for pizza. The assumption behind this is that colleges in urban areas may have more eating establishments from which to choose, and this might adversely affect the students' demand for pizza.

Using these data, we then express the regression equation to be estimated in the following linear, additive fashion:

$$Y = a + b_1X_1 + b_2X_2 + b_3X_3 + b_4X_4$$

where Y = Quantity of pizza demanded (average number of slices per capita per month)

a = Constant value or Y intercept

X_1 = Average price of a slice of pizza (in cents)

X_2 = Annual tuition (in thousands of dollars)

X_3 = Average price of a 12-ounce can of soft drink (in cents)

X_4 = Location of campus (1 if located in a concentrated urban area, 0 if otherwise)

b_1, b_2, b_3, b_4 = Coefficients of the X variables measuring the impact of the variables on the demand for pizza

---

[4]However, this may be just a short-run effect. The popularity of the low carb and other diets usually tends to have a limited life. But pizza has been a favorite food for a long time.

Table 5.3   Sample Data: The Demand for Pizza

COLLEGE	Y	X_1	X_2	X_3	X_4
1	10	100	14	100	1
2	12	100	16	95	1
3	13	90	8	110	1
4	14	95	7	90	1
5	9	110	11	100	0
6	8	125	5	100	0
7	4	125	12	125	1
8	3	150	10	150	0
9	15	80	18	100	1
10	12	80	12	90	1
11	13	90	6	80	1
12	14	100	5	75	1
13	12	100	12	100	1
14	10	110	10	125	0
15	10	125	14	130	0
16	12	110	15	80	1
17	11	150	16	90	0
18	12	100	12	95	1
19	10	150	12	100	0
20	8	150	10	90	0
21	9	150	13	95	0
22	10	125	15	100	1
23	11	125	16	95	1
24	12	100	17	100	0
25	13	75	10	100	1
26	10	100	12	110	1
27	9	110	6	125	0
28	8	125	10	90	0
29	8	150	8	80	0
30	5	150	10	95	0

Y = Quantity
X_1 = Price of pizza (in cents)
X_2 = Tuition (in $000)
X_3 = Price of soft drinks (in cents)
X_4 = Location

Y, or the quantity demanded, is called the dependent variable. The X variables are referred to as the independent or explanatory variables. It is important to note the unit of measurement used for each variable. The researcher may choose how to record the data for use in regression analysis. Here we are measuring the prices of pizza and soft drinks in cents and tuition in thousands of dollars. Notice, too, that the unit of measurement for the location variable is quite different from the others. It takes the value of "1" if the campus is located in an urban area and "0" otherwise. By measuring location in this way, the location variable is considered to be a *binary* or *dummy variable.* Given this particular setup of the regression equation and measurement scheme for the variables, we can now estimate the values of the b coefficients of the independent variables, as well as the a intercept term, by using any one of the many available software packages containing regression analysis.

Estimating and Interpreting the Regression Coefficients

Among the software packages used by economists to conduct a regression analysis of the demand for a good or service are SPSS, SAS, and Micro TSP. To estimate the demand for pizza, we employed the regression function contained in Excel. Although it only contains the basic elements of regression (e.g., it does not provide a Durbin-Watson test), we believe it is perfectly suitable for many types of regression analysis that would be conducted in business research. Besides, Excel is more available in both businesses and colleges and universities than are statistical software packages.

Using the regression function in Excel, we obtained the following estimates for our pizza-demand regression equation:

$$Y = 26.67 - 0.088X_1 + 0.138X_2 - 0.076X_3 - 0.544X_4$$
$$\quad\quad\quad (0.018)\quad\ (0.087)\quad\ (0.020)\quad\ (0.884)$$

$R^2 = 0.717$ Standard error of Y estimate $= 1.64$
$\overline{R}^2 = 0.67$ $F = 15.8$

(Standard errors of the coefficients are listed in parentheses.)

Before interpreting these results, we should first think about what direction of impact changes in the explanatory variables are expected to have on the demand for pizza as evidenced by the signs of the estimated regression coefficients. To put it more formally, we can state the following hypotheses about the anticipated relationship between each of the explanatory variables and the demand for pizza:

Hypothesis 1:   The price of pizza (X_1) is an inverse determinant of the quantity of pizza demanded (i.e., the sign of the coefficient is expected to be negative).

Hypothesis 2:   Assuming tuition to be a proxy for income, pizza could be either a "normal" or an "inferior." Therefore, we hypothesize that tuition (X_2) is a determinant of the demand for pizza, but we cannot say beforehand whether it is an inverse or a direct determinant (i.e., the sign of the coefficient could be either positive or negative).

Hypothesis 3:   The price of a soft drink (X_3) is an inverse determinant of the demand for pizza (i.e., the sign of the coefficient is expected to be negative).

Hypothesis 4:   Location in an urban setting (X_4) is expected to be an inverse determinant of the demand for pizza.

Turning now to the regression results, we observe that the X_1 coefficient has a negative sign, and this is exactly what we would expect because of the law of demand. As the price of pizza (X_1) changes, the quantity demanded for pizza will change in the opposite direction. This is what a negative coefficient tells us. The positive sign of the tuition coefficient tells us that tuition costs and quantity of pizza demanded are directly related to each other. Higher tuition costs are associated with a greater demand for pizza, and vice versa. Thus, pizza appears to be a "normal" product. The negative sign of the soft drink price confirms the complementarity between soft drinks and pizza. As the price of a soft drink goes up, college students tend to buy less pizza. The opposite would hold true for a reduction in the price of a soft drink. Finally, the negative sign of the dummy location variable tells us that those students who attend colleges in urban areas will buy about half a slice of pizza per month (i.e., 0.544) less than their counterparts in the suburbs or rural areas.

An interpretation of the magnitudes of the estimated regression coefficients is a bit more involved. Each estimated coefficient tells us how much the demand for pizza will change relative to a unit change in each of the explanatory variables. For example, a b_1 of −0.088 indicates that a unit change in price will result in a change in the demand for pizza of 0.088 in the opposite direction. Price, as you will recall, was measured in cents. Therefore, according to our regression estimates, a 100-cent (or $1.00) increase will result in a decrease in the quantity demanded for pizza of 8.8 (100 × 0.088). A tuition increase of one unit (in this case $1,000) results in an increase in the quantity demanded for pizza of 0.138. Are these changes and those associated with changes in the price of soft drinks and the location of the college campus substantial or inconsequential?

Researchers who are constantly estimating the demand for a particular good or service will have a fairly accurate idea whether the magnitudes of the coefficients estimated in a particular study are high or low relative to their other work. But if there are no other studies available for comparison, then researchers can at least use the elasticities of demand to gauge the relative impact that the explanatory variables have on the quantity demanded.

From our discussion of elasticity in chapter 4, you can see that regression analysis results are ideal for point-elasticity estimation. Recall that the formula for computing point elasticity is

$$\in_X = \frac{dQ}{dX} \cdot \frac{X}{Q}$$

where Q = quantity demanded and X = any variable that affects Q (e.g., price or income). In the case of our estimated demand for pizza, let us assume the explanatory variables have the following values:

Price of pizza (X_1) = 100 (i.e., $1.00)
Annual college tuition (X_2) = 14 (i.e., $14,000)
Price of a soft drink (X_3) = 110 (i.e., $1.10)
Location of campus (X_4) = Urban area (i.e., X_4 = 1)

Therefore, inserting these values into the estimated equation gives us

$$Y = 26.67 - 0.088\,(100) + 0.138\,(14) - 0.076\,(110) - 0.544\,(1)$$
$$= 10.898 \text{ or } 11 \text{ (rounded to the nearest slice)}$$

To compute the point elasticities for each variable assuming the preceding values, we simply plug in the appropriate numbers into the point-elasticity formula. The partial derivative of Y with respect to changes in each variable (i.e., $\delta Y/\delta X$) is simply the estimated coefficient of each variable.

$$\text{Price elasticity: } -0.088 \times \frac{100}{10.898} = -0.807$$

$$\text{Tution elasticity: } 0.138 \times \frac{14}{10.898} = 0.177$$

$$\text{Cross-price elasticity: } -0.076 \times \frac{110}{10.898} = -0.767$$

With these estimates, we can say that the demand for pizza is somewhat price inelastic and that there is some degree of cross-price elasticity between soft drinks and pizza. Judging from the rather low elasticity coefficient of 0.177, tuition does not appear to have that great an impact on the demand for pizza.

Statistical Evaluation of the Regression Results

Our regression results are based on a *sample* of colleges across the country. How confident are we that these results are truly reflective of the *population* of college students? The basic test of the statistical significance of each estimated regression coefficient is called the *t*-**test**. Essentially, this test is conducted by computing a *t*-value or *t*-statistic for each estimated coefficient. This is done by dividing the estimated coefficient by its **standard error**.[5] That is:

$$t = \frac{\hat{b}}{\text{standard error of } \hat{b}}$$

As is the common practice in presentations of regression results, the standard errors in our pizza regression are presented in parentheses under the estimated coefficients. To interpret the value of *t*, we use the *t*-**table**. The convention in economic research is to select the .05 level of significance. This means you can be 95 percent confident that the results obtained from the sample are representative of the population. We also need to know the number of **degrees of freedom** involved in the estimate. The term, degrees of freedom, is defined as *n-k*-1, where "*n*" represents the sample size and "*k*" the number of independent variables. The "1" represents the constant or intercept term. Therefore, in our pizza example, we have 30-4-1 or 25 degrees of freedom.

Turning to the *t*-table shown in Table A.4 in Appendix A, we see that the critical *t*-value at the .05 level of significance is 1.708 using a **one-tail test** and 2.060 using a **two-tail test**.[6] If the *t*-value computed for a particular estimated coefficient is greater than 1.708, we can say that the estimate is "significant at the .05 level" using a one-tail test. If it is greater than 2.060, then the same can be said, but with a two-tail test. A simple and useful way to handle the critical level is to use the **rule of 2**. This means that if the absolute value of *t* is greater than 2, we can conclude that the estimated coefficient is significant at the .05 level.

It is evident from the preceding regression equation that X_1 (price of pizza) and X_3 (price of soft drinks) are statistically significant because the absolute values of their *t*-statistics are 4.89 and 3.80, respectively. The other two variables, X_2 (tuition) and X_4 (location), are not statistically significant because the absolute values of their *t*-statistics are less than 2.

If the estimated coefficient of a variable passes the *t*-test, we can be confident that the variable truly has an impact on demand. If it does not pass the *t*-test, then in all likelihood, the variable does not truly have an impact for the whole population of college students. In other words, the regression coefficients are nonzero numbers simply because of a fluke in the sample of students that we took from the population.

In statistical analysis, the best we can hope for is to be confident that our sample results are truly reflective of the population that they represent. However, we can never be absolutely sure. Therefore, statistical analysts set up degrees of uncertainty. As explained in greater detail later in this chapter, using the rule of 2 generally implies

[5]In the following equation, the little "hat" (circumflex) over the *b* is a commonly used notation in statistical analysis to denote a value estimated from sample data.
[6]Please refer to a statistics text for a complete explanation of the one-tail and two-tail tests. We provide a brief explanation of these terms in the "Important Concepts" section at the end of this chapter.

a 5 percent level of significance. In other words, by declaring a coefficient that passes the rule-of-2 version of the *t*-test to be statistically significant, we leave ourselves open to a 5 percent chance that we may be mistaken.

Another important statistical indicator used to evaluate the regression results is the **coefficient of determination** or R^2. This measure shows the percentage of the variation in a dependent variable accounted for by the variation in all the explanatory variables in the regression equation. This measure can be as low as 0 (indicating that the variations in the dependent variable are not accounted for by the variation in the explanatory variables) and as high as 1.0 (indicating that all the variation in the dependent variable can be accounted for by the explanatory variables). For statistical analysts, the closer R^2 is to 1.0, the greater the explanatory power of the regression equation.

In our pizza regression, $R^2 = 0.717$. This means that about 72 percent of the variation in the demand for pizza by college students can be accounted for by the variation in the price of pizza, the cost of tuition, the price of a soft drink, and the location of the college. As explained later in this chapter, R^2 increases as more independent variables are added to a regression equation. Therefore, most analysts prefer to use a measure that adjusts for the number of independent variables used so equations with different numbers of independent variables can be more fairly compared. This alternative measure is called the adjusted R^2. As it turns out, the adjusted R^2 for this equation is 0.67.

Another test, called the **F-test**, is often used in conjunction with R^2. This test measures the statistical significance of the entire regression equation rather than of each individual coefficient (as the *t*-test is designed to do). In effect, the *F*-test is a measure of the statistical significance of R^2. The procedure for conducting the *F*-test is similar to the *t*-test. A critical value for *F* is first established, depending on the degree of statistical significance that the researcher wants to set (typically at the .05 or .01 level). The critical "*F*-values" corresponding to these acceptance levels are shown in Table A.3 in Appendix A. As can be seen, there are two "degrees of freedom" values that must be incorporated in the selection of the critical *F*-value. These values essentially relate to the sample size and number of independent variables in the equation, and the sample size minus the number of independent variables plus the intercept of the equation. Therefore, because the pizza example has a sample size of 30 and four independent variables, the degrees of freedom are 4 and 25 (30 minus 4 minus 1). Table A.3 shows that at the .05 level, the critical *F*-value with those degrees of freedom is 2.76. At the .01 level, the critical value is 4.18. Because the regression results for the demand for pizza indicates an *F*-value of 15.8, we can conclude that our entire equation is "statistically significant" at the .01 level.

Review of Key Steps for Analyzing Regression Results

We now review all the key steps discussed so far in the regression analysis of a demand equation using the following equation:

$$Q = 70 - 10P + 4P_x + 50I$$
$$(3) \quad (2) \quad (30) \text{ (standard errors of the estimated coefficients are noted in parentheses)}$$

$n = 56$
$R^2 = 0.47$

where Q = Quantity of a product demanded
P = Price of the product (in cents)
P_X = Price of a related product (in cents)
I = Per capita income (in dollars)
n = Sample size
R^2 = Adjusted multiple coefficient of determination

Step 1: *Check Signs and Magnitudes*

The negative sign for the P variable indicates an inverse relationship between price and the quantity demanded for the product. A unit *increase* in price (i.e., 1 cent) will cause the quantity to *decrease* by ten units. A unit *decrease* in price will cause the quantity to *increase* by ten units. So, for example, if price was decreased by $1.00, quantity would increase by 1,000 units.

The positive sign for the P_X variable indicates a direct relationship between the price of a related product and the quantity demanded. This indicates that the related product is a *substitute* for the product in question. For example, if the price of the related product changes by one unit (i.e., 1 cent), then the quantity demanded of the product in question will change by four units in the *same direction*.

The positive sign for the I variable indicates that the product is *normal* or perhaps *superior,* depending on the magnitude of the income elasticity coefficient. A unit change in per capita income (i.e., $1,000) will cause the quantity to change by fifty units in the *same direction*.

Step 2: *Compute Elasticity Coefficients*

To compute elasticity coefficients, we need to assume certain levels of the independent variables P, P_X, and I. Let us say they are as follows:

$P = 100$ (remember, this is 100 cents or $1.00)
$P_X = 120$ (also in cents)
$I = 25$ (this represents $25,000)

Inserting these values into the previous equation gives us

$$Q = 70 - 10(100) + 4(120) + 50(25)$$
$$Q = 800$$

We now use the formula for point elasticity to obtain the elasticity coefficients. Recall that

$$\epsilon_X = \frac{dQ}{dX} \cdot \frac{X}{Q}$$

Using this formula, we obtain

$$\epsilon_p = -10 \cdot \frac{100}{800}$$
$$= -1.25$$
$$\epsilon_{p_x} = 4 \cdot \frac{120}{800}$$
$$= .6$$
$$\epsilon_I = 50 \cdot \frac{25}{800}$$
$$= 1.56$$

Step 3: *Determine Statistical Significance*

Using the "rule of 2" as an approximation for the .05 level of significance, we can say that P and P_X are statistically significant because their t values are both greater than 2 (e.g., 3.3 and 2, respectively). I is not statistically significant at the .05 level because its t value is only 1.67.

As an added consideration, we note that the R^2 of 0.47 indicates that 47 percent of the variation in quantity can be accounted for by variations in the three independent variables P, P_X, and I. Although this is not actually an indication of statistical significance, it does show the explanatory power of the regression equation. For cross-section data, this R^2 level can be interpreted as being moderately high.

Implications of the Regression Analysis for Management Decisions

In our experience, the "bottom line" in the business world of any statistical analysis, including regression analysis, is the extent to which the results can help managers make good decisions. In our pizza example, the results indicate that the price of pizza and the price of its complementary product, the soft drink, are key factors influencing the demand for pizza. Their elasticity coefficients are both less than 1 and both variables' coefficients passed the *t*-test. What does this mean for those in the pizza business? First, it means that they can expect price decreases to lead to decreases in revenue, other factors remaining constant. Therefore, they would probably not want to try lowering price in an effort to increase sales. But they could try lowering the price of soft drinks, with the anticipation that the lower price of the soft drink will attract people to buy the pizza.

In statistical analysis, it is often as important to find out what does *not* pass the *t*-test as much as it is to find out what passes. In our example, we learned that tuition and location do not have statistically significant impacts on pizza demand. Moreover, the magnitudes of their coefficients were relatively small. For managers of national chains such as Pizza Hut or Domino's, this would indicate that they would not have to be very concerned about the type of college (private or public) or its location (urban or rural) in deciding where to open pizza franchises.

It is hoped that this summary is sufficient for those instructors and readers who simply want a general idea of how regression analysis can be used in business analysis and decision making. For a more detailed discussion, continue with the rest of this chapter.

PROBLEMS IN THE USE OF REGRESSION ANALYSIS

Sometimes, even the best data and most powerful computer software cannot compensate for certain statistical problems arising from the efforts to measure the quantitative relationship between the amount demanded and the determinants of demand. We briefly address three of the most important problems.

The Identification Problem

The identification problem presents perhaps the greatest challenge to those using regression analysis to estimate the demand for a particular good or service. To explain this problem, let us return to our pizza example. Suppose we had time series data relating the per capita consumption of pizza with the price of pizza over a 20-year period. The scatter plot of this information is shown in Figure 5.1*a*. Notice that the scatter tends to slope upward and that a least squares regression estimate would reflect this pattern of relationship. Does this mean that the consumers of pizza behave irrationally and demand more pizza at higher prices? Common sense would balk at such a conclusion, but then why the positive coefficient of the price variable in the demand equation? The alert reader will state that what we have identified as a demand equation is probably some sort of supply equation or perhaps the result of the movement in *both* supply and demand for pizza over the past 20 years. As can be seen in Figure 5.1*b,* if the supply remained constant over the past 20 years while demand shifted upward (because of changes in such factors as income, number of buyers, and tastes and preferences over this time period), the regression equation would really be a reflection of the supply curve S_1. If the supply increased but demand increased more than the supply, then the regression estimate would really be a reflection of the

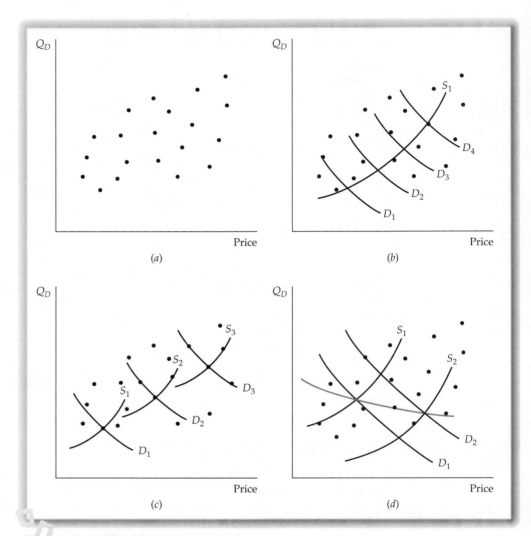

Figure 5.1   The Identification Problem

intersection of the various *S* and *D* curves in Figure 5.1*c*. Figure 5.1*d* shows still another possibility. In this case, supply shifts more than demand so the estimated regression line is downward sloping and more like what we would expect of a demand curve. Nonetheless, this estimated demand curve is flatter than the true demand curves, which have gradually shifted to the right over the years. Thus, the regression estimate of the relationship between price and quantity demanded would be biased in the sense that it would indicate a much greater price elasticity than actually exists in the population of pizza consumers.

There are advanced estimation techniques, such as the methods of *two-stage least squares* and *indirect least squares*, that can help the researcher deal with samples in which the simultaneous shifting of demand and supply takes place. Essentially, these techniques involve the simultaneous consideration of the supply and demand equations with the use of a single regression equation. A discussion of these techniques lies outside the scope of this text. But the principal point to remember is that if the identification problem is not recognized and dealt with by the researcher, the method of ordinary least squares will result in biased estimates of the regression coefficients.

Multicollinearity

One of the key assumptions made in the construction of the multiple regression equation is that the independent variables are not related to each other in any systematic way. If this assumption is incorrect, then each estimated coefficient may give a distorted view of the impact of the change in each independent variable. For example, suppose a regression model states that the demand for luxury foreign-made automobiles depends on price, income, and education. The latter variable is included because education is a proxy for tastes and preferences, and those with higher levels of education are hypothesized to have a greater preference for luxury foreign cars. But, as you would expect, education and income are closely associated. If their values tend to move up and down together, the least squares method may arbitrarily assign a high value to the coefficient of one variable and a low coefficient value to the other. In effect, if two variables are closely associated, it becomes difficult to separate out the effect that each has on the dependent variable. The existence of such a condition in regression analysis is called *multicollinearity*.

If the regression results pass the *F*-test (the measure of the overall statistical significance of the regression equation) but fail the *t*-test for each regression coefficient, it is usually a sign that multicollinearity is present in the sample data. Multicollinearity can also be detected by examining the correlation coefficient between two variables suspected of being closely related.[7] As a rule of thumb, correlation coefficients of 0.7 or more provide a basis for researchers to suspect the existence of multicollinearity.

If multicollinearity is a serious problem in the regression analysis, it will tend to introduce an upward bias to the standard errors of the coefficients. This will tend to reduce the *t*-values (which, you will recall, are computed using the standard errors of the coefficients). This makes it harder to reject the null hypothesis and, of course, to identify statistically significant independent variables in the regression model.

It should be pointed out, however, that if the researcher simply wants to use the estimated regression coefficients as a basis for forecasting future values of the dependent variable, multicollinearity does not pose a serious problem. It is only when the researcher wants to understand more about the underlying structure of the demand function (i.e., what are the key determinants of demand) that this particular statistical problem should be resolved. Most software packages automatically produce a correlation coefficient matrix for the entire set of independent variables used in the regression equation. A standard remedy for multicollinearity is to drop one of the variables that is closely associated with another variable in the regression equation.

Autocorrelation

Autocorrelation is a problem that is usually encountered when time series data are used. For this reason, it is often referred to as *serial correlation*. Let us use the case of simple regression, involving only the dependent variable *Y* and one independent variable, *X*. Essentially, autocorrelation occurs when the *Y* variable relates to the *X* variable according to a certain pattern. For example, in Figure 5.2*a*, the scatter plot reveals that as *X* increases (presumably over time), the *Y* value deviates from the regression line in a very systematic way. In other words, the *residual term,* or the difference between the observed value of *Y* and the estimated value of *Y* given $X(\hat{Y})$, alternates between a positive and a negative value of approximately the same magnitude

---

[7]The correlation coefficient is a measure of the degree of association between two variables. This measure, denoted *r*, ranges from a value of -1 (perfect negative correlation) to 1 (perfect positive correlation).

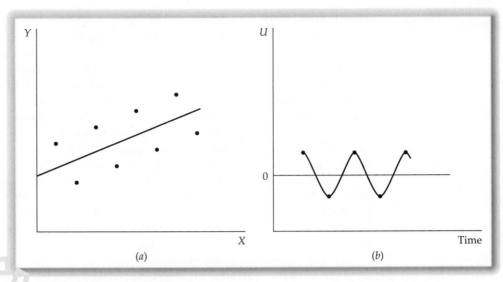

Figure 5.2   Autocorrelation

throughout the range of X values. In fact, if we were to plot these residuals on a separate graph, they would have the pattern shown in Figure 5.2b.

One possible cause of autocorrelation is that there are effects on Y not accounted for by the variables included in the regression equation. It might also be that the true relationship between Y and the independent variable(s) is nonlinear. But regardless of the reason, if autocorrelation is present in the regression analysis, it creates a problem for the validity of the t-test. Simply stated, autocorrelation tends to increase the likelihood that the null hypothesis will be rejected. This is because autocorrelation gives a downward bias to the standard error of the estimated regression coefficient ($SE_{\hat{b}}$). Recalling that the t-value is defined as $\hat{b}/SE_{\hat{b}}$, we can see that a smaller $SE_{\hat{b}}$ would tend to increase the magnitude of the t-value, other factors held constant. Thus, in the presence of autocorrelation, researchers may well declare that certain independent variables have a statistically significant impact on the dependent variable when in fact they do not. From a policy standpoint, suppose the estimated coefficient of the advertising variable in a regression model of demand passed the t-test when it really should not have. A firm might then be led to increase its advertising expenditures when in fact it should be looking at other ways to expand demand (e.g., through promotions, alternative channels of distribution, or price actions).

It may be difficult to identify autocorrelation simply by observing the pattern of the residuals of a regression equation. A standard test for identifying the presence of this problem is the *Durbin-Watson test*. The Durbin-Watson statistic (i.e., DW) is now routinely calculated in regression software packages and is presented automatically in the computer printout. As in the case of the t-test and the F-test, there is a Durbin-Watson table listing the critical values of this statistic for a given level of significance (usually the .05 level). We have included such a table in the appendix at the back of this text (see Table A.5 in Appendix A). As a rule of thumb, if the DW statistic is around 2, there is in all probability no autocorrelation present in the data. If the DW statistic indicates the presence of autocorrelation, there are certain things a researcher can do to correct the problem. These include transforming the data into a different order of magnitude or introducing leading or lagging data in the time series.

EXAMPLES OF REGRESSION ANALYSIS IN ECONOMIC RESEARCH

Probably the most practical application of regression analysis in economic research is in the estimation of consumer demand.[8] Much of the data on consumer buying behavior, collected by such companies as ACNielsen and IRI, are proprietary. Sometimes these data are made available to researchers. Professor Stephen Erfle was able to obtain information on the consumer demand for wine collected by IRI and received permission to use this for his research. The results of his study using IRI data are presented in this chapter's appendix. In addition, we offer two short examples of the use of regression analysis used in other types of studies besides the estimation of consumer demand. Material quoted below are from abstracts of these studies provided by www.ingentaconnect.com.

Brief Summary of Two Recent Examples of Economic Studies Using Regression Analysis

Quoted materials are from abstracts of these articles provided by www.ingentaconnect.com.

Short Example #1:

"Value-Based Management, EVA and Stock Price Performance in Canada"[9]

Purpose: "The purpose of this paper is to determine the extent to which Canadian companies have embraced value-based management (VBM) methods, identify the characteristics of these companies and of the executives responsible for the introduction of VBM in their organizations and assess the stock price performance of the companies that use VMB vs. those that do not."

Data Sources: The study is based on a survey of CEOs of a large sample of Canadian companies.

Example of Dependent Variable Used: Stock price performance.

Example of Independent Variable: Whether or not the company used VBM in its management systems (=1 if used VBM, =0 otherwise).

Main Regression Findings: "The statistical analysis . . . results indicates companies that used EVA had a better stock price performance than those not using EVA. Moreover, our logit regression analysis shows that companies with better stock market performance exhibited higher likelihood of using EVA."

Practical Implications: "The study implies that the lower usage of EVA in Canada, especially at the corporate level, provides some explanation for the stock market underperformance of the Canada market vs. the USA in the 1990s."

Short Example #2:

"Religious Market Competition and Clergy Salary: Evidence from SBC Congregations in the South"[10]

Purpose: To test the impact of religious market competition, or pluralism, on clergy salary.

Data Source: "We utilize a rich and unique data source covering 13,825 Southern Baptist Convention churches in seven Southern states."

Dependent Variable: Clergy salaries.

---

[8]We also provide examples of academic studies of cost using regression analysis in chapter 7.
[9]George Athanassakos, *Management Decision*, Vol. 45, no. 9, 2007, pp. 1397–1411.
[10]Micelle Trawick and Stephen E. Lile, *The American Journal of Economics and Sociology*, Vol. 66, no. 4, October 2007, pp. 747–763.

Independent Variables: Measure of concentration among Southern Baptist churches and concentration among other Judeo-Christian demominations.

Description of Study and Main Findings: "We link county-level religious market and socio-economic data to the county in which each church is located. Two measures of religious output market are used. One is a narrow output market definition calculated using only SBC churches. The other is a more broadly defined measure calculated using 132 Judeo-Christian denominations. Using regression analysis, we conclude that greater concentration among Southern Baptist churches' members within a given county area has a positive, and statistically significant, impact on Southern Baptist clergy salaries, while greater concentration among other denominations has no impact on Southern Baptist clergy salaries. Most importantly, we show that Southern Baptist churches exhibit predictable economic behavior despite the ethereal nature of the product they provide."

GLOBAL APPLICATION: FOOD IN SPAIN, CIGARETTES IN TAIWAN

Example 1: Regression Analysis of Basic Foods in Spain

A time series study of the demand for six classes of food for the period 1964 to 1991 in Spain was performed. The six different classifications were

1. Bread and cereals
2. Meat
3. Fish
4. Milk, dairy products, and eggs
5. Fruits, vegetables, and potatoes
6. Fats and oils

The results show that changes in food demand (in terms of calories consumed) do not depend only on current income and prices, but also on lagged values of these variables. Consumers of food in Spain do not immediately adjust their expenditures when incomes or prices change. Rather they appear to show a certain level of inertia. Of the above six categories, only meat is shown to be a "superior" good, with an income elasticity of 1.54. Among the other five groups, only fruits and vegetables have income elasticity close to unity (.9), while the elasticity of fats and oils is the lowest, at 0.35. In terms of own price elasticities, meat shows the highest coefficient of -0.8. All the others are also negative; all have t-test results that are significantly different from zero. Most cross-elasticities are quite low and not statistically significant, showing that there is no great substitutability among these products. There are a few exceptions, the largest one being fish and meat, whose t-test result is significant. The R^2 for the equation is a relatively high 0.63.[11]

Example 2: Regression Analysis of the Demand for Cigarettes in Taiwan

A recent time series study investigated the demand for cigarettes in Taiwan, not only as a function of income and price, but also looked into the influence of antismoking campaigns and the impact of the opening of Taiwan's market to imported cigarettes. Data for 30 years (1966–1995) were used. The basic estimating equation was written as follows:

$$C_t = a_0 + a_1 P_t + a_2 Y_t + a_3 H_t + a_4 X_t + e_t$$

where C_t = Annual cigarette consumption per capita,
P_t = Average retail price of cigarettes per pack,

---

[11]A. Gracia, J. M. Gil, and A. M. Angulo, "Spanish Food Demand: A Dynamic Approach," *Applied Economics*, October 1998, 30(10), pp. 1399–1405.

Y_t = Disposable income per capita, in 1991 New Taiwan dollars,
H_t = Measure of smoke-related health information,
X_t = Other determinants,
e_t = Random error term, and
a_{0-4} = Regression coefficients

In addition, separate demand functions were estimated for domestic and imported cigarettes. The equations used in these calculations were similar to the previous one, except that one term was added to each equation. In the domestic cigarette demand equation, the price of imported cigarettes was included to measure cross-price elasticity. In the equation for imported cigarettes, the price of domestic cigarettes was included. Two measures of health information were used:

1. Market share of low-tar cigarettes
2. Strongly worded warning labels adopted in 1992. A dummy variable of 0 up to 1991 and 1 thereafter was employed.

Some of the other explanatory variables included lagged consumption, market share of imported cigarettes, and female labor force participation.

The results for the overall model were as follows:

Price elasticity −0.5 to −0.6
Income elasticity 0.14 to 0.22
Low-tar impact −0.04

All three of these had statistically significant coefficients at the 1 percent or 5 percent level. The effect of warning labels was also negative but not statistically significant, and the impact of imported cigarettes was positive but only significant at the 10 percent level in some of the models.

When domestic and imported cigarettes were considered separately, the results were similar. The cross-price elasticities in both equations were positive, indicating that domestic and imported cigarettes are substitutes. The coefficients of determination for the various models were quite satisfactory. They were approximately 0.91 for the overall equations and 0.71 to 0.88 for the equations in which domestic and imported cigarettes were studied separately.[12]

FORECASTING

INTRODUCTION

One of the authors remembers a poster he saw, many years ago, on the wall of the office of the director of market research of a large manufacturing corporation. It said: "Forecasting is very difficult, especially into the future." One could add: "Accurate forecasting is even more difficult." Certainly, there is a great deal of truth in this statement. But despite the difficulty of forecasting, and forecasting accurately, it is an integral part of our lives. Many of us eagerly watch television weather forecasts or pay heed to the predictions of a favorite stock market guru, knowing only too well how inaccurate they may be. In an even less formal sense we make forecasts when we buy a lottery ticket, bet on a horse, or decide whether to carry an umbrella when we leave the house.

---

[12]Chee-Ruey Hsieh, Teh-Wei Hu, and Chien-Fu Jeff Lin, "The Demand for Cigarettes in Taiwan: Domestic vs. Imported Cigarettes," *Contemporary Economic Policy*, April 1999, pp. 223–234.

In the worlds of business, government, or even nonprofit institutions, forecasting becomes even more important. In a world where organizations and their environments are continually becoming more complex and changes occur more rapidly, decision makers need help in weighing many factors and understanding constantly changing relationships to arrive at decisions whose results have ever-increasing impacts.[13] Using existing resources and acquiring additional resources appropriately requires maximum information about the company's future.

All organizations conduct their activities in an uncertain environment, and probably the major role of forecasting is to reduce this uncertainty. But no forecast, however extensive and expensive, can remove it completely. Managers who use forecasts in their work "need to develop realistic expectations as to what forecasting can and cannot do."[14] "Forecasting is not a substitute for management judgment in decision making; it is simply an aid to that process."[15]

SUBJECTS OF FORECASTS

Business uses forecasting to obtain information about many subjects. In the final analysis, firms are interested in future sales and profits—the bottom line. But to get there, a large number of forecasts may be necessary. In this section of the chapter, we outline the various categories of forecasts—from the most macro forecasts to individual series.

➤ Forecasts of gross domestic product—which describe the total production of goods and services in a country.
➤ Forecasts of the components of GDP—for example, consumption expenditure, producer durable equipment expenditure, and residential construction.
➤ Industry forecasts—for Global Foods, this would represent forecasts of sales of soft drinks, bottled water, and its other products.
➤ Forecasts of sales for a specific product—for instance, diet cola.

Demand Estimating and Demand Forecasting

In the first part of this chapter, regression analysis and demand estimation are discussed. There is a great deal of similarity between demand forecasting and demand estimating. The difference between the two lies largely in the ultimate purpose of the analysis.

The demand estimating technique will be used by a manager interested in probing the effect on the demand (or quantity demanded) of a change in one or more of the independent variables. Thus, a pricing manager may want to know the impact on the sales of the company's club soda as a result of a price change, of a competitor's price changes, or, for example, of a change in the company's advertising expenses.

In contrast, forecasting puts less emphasis on explaining the specific causes of demand changes and more on obtaining information regarding future levels of sales activity, given the most likely assumptions about the independent variables. Indeed, in some cases, to be discussed later in this chapter, forecasting is achieved without the introduction of any causal factors; future sales are predicted solely by projecting the past into the future.

---

[13]The introductory sections of this chapter draw heavily on Steven C. Wheelwright and Spyros Makridakis, *Forecasting Methods for Management,* 5th ed., New York: John Wiley & Sons, 1989.
[14]Ibid., p. 44.
[15]Ibid., p. 30.

PREREQUISITES OF A GOOD FORECAST

Certain conditions should be met by any good forecast:

➤ A forecast must be consistent with other parts of the business. For instance, a sales forecast of 10 percent growth must ensure there are sufficient manufacturing facilities and labor force to produce this increase.

➤ A forecast should be based on knowledge of the relevant past. However, when underlying conditions have changed significantly, past experience may be of no help in making a forecast. Moreover, sometimes there is no past on which to rely. This is the case when we are dealing with a new product or technology. Under these circumstances, analysts' judgments must be injected into the forecasting process. In some cases, "forecasts based purely on the opinion of 'experts' are used to formulate the forecast or scenario for the future."[16]

➤ A forecast must consider the economic and political environment, as well as any potential changes.

➤ A forecast must be timely. An accurate forecast that is too late to be acted on may be worthless.

FORECASTING TECHNIQUES

There are many different forecasting methods. One of the challenges facing a forecaster is choosing the right technique. The appropriate method depends on the subject matter to be forecast and on the forecaster, but we can discuss some of the factors that enter into consideration.[17]

1. The item to be forecast. Is one trying to predict the continuance of a historical pattern, the continuance of a basic relationship, or a turning point?
2. The interaction of the situation with the characteristics of available forecasting methods. The manager must judge the relation between value and cost. If a less expensive method can be used to achieve the desired results, it certainly should be.
3. The amount of historical data available.
4. The time allowed to prepare the forecast. Selection of a specific method may depend on the urgency of the situation.

One other point about forecasting cost and accuracy should be added here. Generally, when the requirements for forecast accuracy are high, more sophisticated and more complex methods may be used. Such methods are, as a rule, more costly. Thus, a manager will authorize greater expenditures when relatively high accuracy is warranted. However, "Empirical studies have shown that simplicity in forecasting methods is not necessarily a negative characteristic or a detriment with regard to forecasting accuracy. Therefore, the authors would advise against discarding simple methods and moving too quickly to replace them with more complex ones."[18]

---

[16]John E. Hanke, Dean W. Wichern, and Arthur G. Reitsch, *Business Forecasting*, 7th ed., Upper Saddle River, NJ: Prentice Hall, 2001, p. 421. This is another text we recommend for students who are interested in exploring the subject of forecasting in more detail.

[17]This section relies heavily on Wheelwright and Makridakis, *Forecasting Methods*, pp. 30–31.

[18]Ibid., p. 309. This quote deals with the merits of relatively simple time series methods versus more complex explanatory techniques. "Thus, the evidence suggests that explanatory models do not provide significantly more accurate forecasts than time series methods, even though the former are much more complex and expensive than the latter" (p. 297).

Forecasting techniques can be categorized in many ways. We use the following six categories:

1. Expert opinion
2. Opinion polls and market research
3. Surveys of spending plans
4. Economic indicators
5. Projections
6. Econometric models

As we see in the following pages, some of the methods can be classified as qualitative, others as quantitative. **Qualitative forecasting** is based on judgments of individuals or groups. The results of qualitative forecasts may be in numerical form but generally are not based on a series of historical data.

Quantitative forecasting, in contrast, generally uses significant amounts of prior data as a basis for prediction. Quantitative techniques can be naive or causal (explanatory). **Naive forecasting** projects past data into the future without explaining future trends. **Causal** or **explanatory forecasting** attempts to explain the functional relationships between the variable to be estimated (the dependent variable) and the variable or variables that account for the changes (the independent variables).

Although judgmental (qualitative) forecasting is used frequently, the use of quantitative methods has been growing rapidly. A recent survey by the Institute of Business Forecasting reported that time series models that extrapolate past data into the future were used by 72 percent of the companies surveyed. Simple models (such as averages and simple trend) accounted for 60 percent of those using times series, and exponential smoothing (which we will discuss later in this chapter) accounted for 30 percent. "The reason why time series models are used most in businesses is because they are easier to understand and easier to use. Plus, they generally work well for short-term forecasting." Causal forecasting methods were used by 17 percent and qualitative methods were used in 11 percent of the cases. Surveys were the most popular in the latter category. However, this survey also found that in many cases members of various functions (marketing, production, finance, and sales) of the companies met periodically to review the quantitative forecasts (often called baseline forecasts). "Where necessary, they collectively overlay judgment on the baseline forecast." This was actually done by 83 percent of the companies surveyed. However, a somewhat earlier study of manufacturing companies concluded that judgmental methods are still prevalent in many business organizations.[19]

Expert Opinion

Various types of techniques fit into the category of expert opinion. Only two are discussed here.

> **Jury of executive opinion:** Forecasts are generated by a group of corporate executives assembled together. The members of the panel may represent different functions within the corporation (intraorganizational) or different corporations (interorganizational). This has been a rather successful technique. However, there is a danger that a panel member who is persuasive but not necessarily knowledgeable may have undue influence

[19]Chaman L. Jain, "Benchmarking Forecasting Practices in America," *Journal of Business Forecasting*, Vol. 25, Issue 4, Winter 2006–07, pp. 9–13; Chaman L. Jain, "Benchmarking Forecasting Models," *Journal of Business Forecasting*, Vol. 25, Issue 4, Winter 2006–07, pp. 14–17. Curiously, however, Hanke, Wichern, and Reitsch, *Business Forecasting*, p. 421, state that "research has shown that, when historical data are available, the judgment modification of the forecasts produced by analytical methods tends to reduce the accuracy of the forecasts." Nada R. Sanders, "The Status of Forecasting in Manufacturing Firms," *Production and Inventory Management Journal*, 38, 2, 1997, pp. 32–37.

on the results. A similar method is to solicit the views of individual salespeople. However, "[o]ften sales people are either overly optimistic or pessimistic. At other times they are unaware of the broad economic patterns that may affect demand."[20]

The Delphi Method: This method, developed by the Rand Corporation in the 1950s, is used primarily in predicting technological trends and changes. Delphi also uses a panel of experts. However, they do not meet. The process is carried out by a sequential series of written questions and answers. Although in the past such iterative procedure could have been quite time consuming, computers and e-mail have shortened the process significantly. The iterations are conducted until the range of answers is narrowed. Finally, a consensus (or convergence of opinions) is obtained. An early example of this method was a study that asked to forecast five subjects as far as 50 years into the future: scientific breakthroughs, population growth, automation, space programs, and future weapon systems.[21]

Although the Delphi method has often been successful, it has drawbacks: "insufficient reliability, oversensitivity of results to ambiguity of questions, different results when different experts are used, difficulty in assessing the degree of expertise, and the impossibility of predicting the unexpected."[22] Given the long-term nature of Delphi predictions, these criticisms do not appear to differ greatly from those leveled against forecasts in general.

Opinion Polls and Market Research

You are probably familiar with opinion polling because most of us have at one time or another been subjected to telephone calls or written questionnaires asking us to assess a product or sometimes a political issue. Rather than soliciting experts, opinion polls survey a population whose activity may determine future trends. **Opinion polls** can be very useful because they may identify changes in trends, which, as we see later in this chapter, may escape detection when quantitative (both naive and explanatory) methods are used.

Choice of the sample population is of utmost importance because the use of an unrepresentative sample may give completely misleading results. Further, the questions must be stated simply and clearly. Often a question is repeated in a somewhat different form so the replies can be cross-checked.

Market research is closely related to opinion polling. Thorough descriptions of this method can be found in marketing texts. Market research will indicate "not only why the consumer is or is not buying (or is or is not likely to buy), but also who the consumer is, how he or she is using the product, and what characteristics the consumer thinks are most important in the purchasing decision."[23] This information can then be used to estimate the market potential and possibly the market share.

Surveys of Spending Plans

The use of **surveys of spending plans** is quite similar to opinion polling and market research, and the methods of data collection are also quite alike. However, although opinion polling and market research usually deal with specific products and are often conducted by individual firms, the surveys discussed briefly here seek information about "macro-type" data relating to the economy.

1. **Consumer intentions.**   Because consumer expenditure is the largest component of the gross domestic product, changes in consumer attitudes and their effect on subsequent spending are a crucial variable in the forecasts and plans made by businesses. Two well-known surveys are reviewed here.

---

[20]Wheelwright and Makridakis, *Forecasting Methods*, p. 242.
[21]T. J. Gordon and O. Helmer, *Report on a Long-Range Forecasting Study*, Rand Corporation, P-2982, September 1964. (Described in Harold Sackman, *Delphi Critique*, Lexington, MA: Lexington Books, 1975, pp. 37–39, 104.)
[22]Wheelwright and Makridakis, *Forecasting Methods*, p. 326
[23]Ibid., p. 245.

a. ***Survey of Consumers, Survey Research Center, University of Michigan.*** This is probably the best known among the consumer surveys conducted. Initiated in 1946, it is conducted monthly. It contains questions regarding personal finances, general business conditions, and buying conditions. The answers to these questions are summarized into an overall index of consumer sentiment and a large number of indexes covering replies to the more detailed questions.

b. ***Consumer Confidence Survey, The Conference Board.*** A questionnaire is mailed monthly to a nationwide sample of 5,000 households. Each month a different panel of households is selected. The resulting indexes are based on responses to questions regarding business conditions (current and 6 months hence), employment conditions (current and 6 months hence), and expectations regarding family income 6 months hence. The replies are then summarized monthly into three indexes: the Consumer Confidence Index, the Present Situation Index, and the Expectations Index. This survey has been published since 1967.

2. ***Inventories and sales expectations.*** A monthly survey published by the National Association of Purchasing Agents is based on a large sample of purchasing executives.

Economic Indicators

The difficult task of predicting changes in the direction of activity is discussed previously. Some of the qualitative techniques discussed in the preceding sections are aimed at identifying such turns. The barometric technique of **economic indicators** is specifically designed to alert business to changes in economic conditions.

The success of the indicator approach to forecasting depends on the ability to identify one or more historical economic series whose direction not only correlates with, but also precedes that of the series to be predicted. Such indicators are used widely in forecasting general economic activity. Any one indicator series may not be very reliable; however, a composite of leading indicators can be used to predict. Such a series should exhibit a slowing (and an actual decrease) before overall economic activity turns down, and it should start to rise while the economy is still experiencing low activity.

Forecasting on the basis of indicators has been practiced in an informal fashion for many years. It is said that Andrew Carnegie used to assess the future of steel demand by counting the number of chimneys emitting smoke in Pittsburgh. Much of the work of establishing economic indicators was done at the National Bureau of Economic Research, a private organization. Today, economic indicator data are published monthly by The Conference Board in *Business Cycle Indicators*. These monthly data are reported in the press and are widely followed.[24]

There are three major series: leading, coincident, and lagging indicators. As their names imply, the first tells us where we are going, the second where we are, and the third where we have been. Although the leading indicator series is probably the most important, the other two are also meaningful. The coincident indicators identify peaks and troughs, and the lagging series confirms upturns and downturns in economic activity.

Many individual series are tracked monthly in the *Business Cycle Indicators*, but only a limited number are used in the construction of the three major indexes. The leading indicator index contains ten series, and the coincident and lagging indicators are made up of four and seven components, respectively. All the series making up the indexes are listed in Table 5.4.

It is rather evident why some of the indicators qualify as leading. They represent not present expenditures, but commitments indicating that economic activity will take place in the future. Among these are manufacturers' new orders and building permits.

[24]The data can also be accessed on the World Wide Web at www.tcb-indicators.org.

Table 5.4   Economic Indicators

Leading indicators

1. Average weekly hours, manufacturing
2. Average weekly initial claims for unemployment insurance
3. Manufacturers' new orders, consumer goods and materials
4. Vendor performance, slower deliveries diffusion index
5. Manufacturers' new orders, nondefense capital goods
6. Building permits, new private housing units
7. Stock prices, 500 common stocks
8. Money supply, M2
9. Interest rate spread, 10-year Treasury bonds less federal funds
10. Index of consumer expectations

Coincident indicators

1. Employees on nonagricultural payrolls
2. Personal income less transfer payments
3. Industrial production
4. Manufacturing and trade sales

Lagging indicators

1. Average duration of unemployment
2. Inventories to sales ratio, manufacturing and trade
3. Labor cost per unit of output, manufacturing
4. Average prime rate
5. Commercial and industrial loans
6. Consumer installment credit outstanding to personal income ratio
7. Consumer price index for services

Others are not quite as obvious. But one would expect employers to increase the hours of their work force as they increase production before committing themselves to new hiring. Stock market prices and money supply are usually believed to precede cycles.

The month-to-month changes in each component of the series are computed and standardized to avoid undue influence of the more volatile components. The individual series are then combined to create the index. The index has a base period 1996 = 100.[25] The Conference Board also computes a diffusion index that tends to indicate the breadth of the indicator index movement.

How good a forecaster are the leading indicators? To answer this question, we must establish some criteria. First, how many months of change in the direction of the index are necessary before a turn in economic activity is expected? A general rule of thumb is that if, after a period of increases, the leading indicator index sustains three consecutive declines, a recession (or at least a slowing) will follow. On this basis, the leading indicators have predicted each recession since 1948. Second, how much warning do the indicators give (i.e., by how many months do they lead) of the onset of a recession?

The following chart shows the lead times in number of months at both peaks and troughs of the business cycle since World War II.[26]

---

[25]An explanation of the methods to compute, update, and standardize the indexes is available on the Web site cited in footnote 24. An excellent source of information on the entire subject of economic indicators is *Business Cycle Indicators Handbook,* The Conference Board, 2001.
[26]See any recent issue of *Business Cycle Indicators* for this information.

Cycle	Peak	Trough
1948–49	−4	−4
1953–54	−6	−6
1957–58	−23	−2
1960–61	−11	−3
1969–70	−8	−7
1973–75	−9	−2
1980–80	−15	−3
1981–82	−3	−8
1990–91	−6	−2
2001–01	−14	−8

It is obvious that the lead times vary considerably and that the lead times at peaks tend to be longer than those at troughs. So we can sum up by observing that leading indicators do warn us about changes in the direction of economic activity, but they really do not forecast lead times reliably. In addition, we must be aware of several other drawbacks:

1. In some instances, the leading indicator index has forecast a recession when none ensued.
2. A decline (or a rebound after a decline) in the index, even if it forecasts correctly, does not indicate the precise size of the decline (or rise) in economic activity.
3. The data are frequently subject to revision in the ensuing months. Thus, the final data may signal a different future from the one suggested by the orginally published data.

The preceding criticisms of this forecasting method are certainly significant, but they indicate that this technique should be improved rather than discarded. The existing indicators are reevaluated periodically, and new ones are developed. As the structure of the economy changes, some of the indicators lose their relevance. For instance, in 1996, shortly after the Conference Board took over the publication of the indexes, two components of the leading indicator index were removed, while one series was added. The present index may still be overly weighted toward manufacturing activities and neglect service industries, which make up a continuously increasing portion of our economy. The growing importance of international trade and capital flows suggests the inclusion in the index of a series reflecting these activities. In the meantime, the use of leading indicators has spread to a large number of foreign countries.

In short, despite its drawbacks, the index of leading indicators (and the other two indexes as well) is a useful tool for businesspeople and will continue to be closely watched. As always, reliance on this method must be tempered by the knowledge of its imperfections.

Projections

We now turn to **trend projections**, which we previously identified as a naive form of forecasting. Several different methods are discussed, but they all have a common denominator: past data are projected into the future without taking into consideration reasons for the change. It is simply assumed that past trends will continue. Three projection techniques are examined here:

1. Compound growth rate
2. Visual time series projection
3. Time series projection using the least squares method

If annual data are to be forecast, any of these three methods can be used. However, more frequent data, such as monthly or quarterly, may be necessary. If there appear to be significant seasonal patterns in the data, a smoothing method must be applied. The moving-average method of smoothing is discussed, along with the least squares time series projection.

Module 5A   Constant Compound Growth Rate

The constant **compound growth rate** technique is extremely simple and is widely used in business situations. When quick estimates of the future are needed, this method has some merit. And, as we will find out, it can be quite appropriate when the variable to be predicted increases at a constant percentage (as opposed to constant absolute changes). But care must be exercised not to apply this technique when it is not warranted.

The most rudimentary application of this method is to take the first and last years of past data, and to calculate the constant growth rate necessary to go from the amount in the first period to the amount in the last. This problem is solved in the same way as if we were to calculate how much a specific sum deposited in an interest-bearing account grows in a certain number of years at a constant rate of interest that is compounded annually. This calculation can be made by using any handheld calculator or by using Table A.1 in Appendix A.

Frank Robinson will make the projection for Citronade using Table A.1 from Appendix A. The first and last period amounts are known, and the missing number is the growth rate. To solve for the growth rate, the formula is as follows:

$$(1 + i)^n = E/B$$

where E = Last year's amount
$\quad B$ = First year's amount
$\quad\ \ i$ = Growth rate
$\quad\ n$ = Number of years

Applying this formula to the 1997 and 2007 sales of Citronade from Table 5.1,

$$6,954/3,892 = 1.7867$$

Because there are 10 years intervening between the two sales periods, the growth rate can be found by entering the table at ten periods and moving to the right until a number close to 1.7867 is found. At 6 percent, the factor is 1.7908. Thus, the growth rate of Citronade over the last 10 years is just under 6 percent.

Can, therefore, next year's sales be estimated at 7,371,000 cases, a 6 percent annual increase? Looking at the year-to-year increases in Table 5.1, Robinson noticed that the growth rate achieved in the early years (through 2001) has not been approached since. Whereas during the first 4 years of the available data, growth ranged between 6.5 and 8 percent, the second 4 years registered increases between 5 and 6 percent, and the rise in the last 2 years was less than 5 percent. Growth has been declining over the 10-year period.

This illustrates a major problem that is frequently encountered when the compound growth rate method of projection is employed. The only two numbers considered in determining the growth rate were the first and the last; any trends or fluctuations between the original and terminal dates are disregarded. Thus, when year-to-year percentage growth is not stable, any estimates based on this result can be misleading.

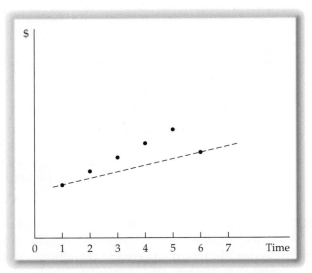

Figure 5.3   An Example in Which the Constant Compound Growth Rate Approach Would Be Misleading

Figure 5.3 illustrates what may happen. The data plotted in the graph show a strong increase in each year except for the last value, which may have been caused by an exceptional occurrence such as a severe recession or a strike. If the compound growth rate approach is used, any forecast based only on the first and last observations may be quite misleading.

Visual Time Series Projections

A series of numbers is often difficult to interpret. Plotting the observations on a sheet of graph paper (or entering paired data into a computer plotting program) can be very helpful because the shape of a complicated series is more easily discerned from a picture.

Frank Robinson did just that. He had two types of graph paper available to him. One was the familiar kind, with arithmetic scales on both axes, which he used to plot the annual data of Citronade sales, as shown in Figure 5.4. The observations appear to form a relatively straight line. As a matter of fact, one could easily draw a straight line just by putting a ruler through the observations, so some points fall above and some below the line. Projecting the line to 2008 would give us a fairly good prediction—if the growth, in absolute number of cases, reflects past increases. The reason that a straight line is such a good fit is that the absolute annual increases in sales fluctuate around their mean of 306,000 cases without exhibiting any kind of trend.

There is another type of graph paper often used to observe trends—semilogarithmic. This graph has an arithmetic scale along the horizontal axis, but the vertical axis transforms numbers into a logarithmic format. Equal distances between numbers on the vertical scale represent a doubling. Thus, the distance between 1 and 2 is the same as that between 2 and 4, between 4 and 8, and so on.[27] In

---

[27]Incidentally, the point of origin on the vertical axis is 1, not 0.

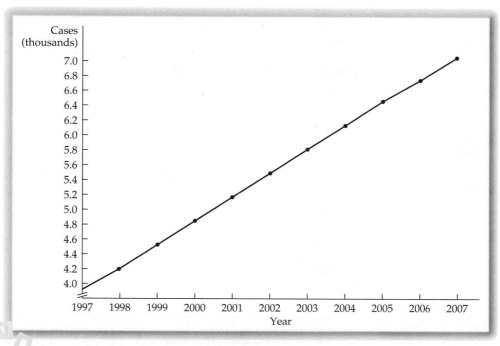

Figure 5.4   Annual Sales of Citronade (1997–2007)

the semilogarithmic format, if observations that exhibit a constant growth rate are plotted, they will fall on a straight line.[28] The data for Citronade, as can be seen in Figure 5.5 where the annual observations are plotted, indicate growth at a decreasing rate. Thus, if Frank Robinson were to base his projections on this line, he would have to continue the curve on its decreasing slope.

Frank found that the compound growth rate for Citronade sales from 1997 to 2007 was 6 percent. A line representing an annual growth rate of 6 percent in Figure 5.5 is a straight line because constant growth is assumed. But a projection of the straight line would result in a higher sales estimate for 2008 than if the decreasing year-to-year percentage of growth were taken into consideration.

---

[28]A simple example will explain why a constant percentage growth rate shows up as a straight line on a logarithmic scale. Assume the first period's quantity is 100 and it grows by 20 percent each year. Then translate each number into a common logarithm, and calculate the differences for each series:

Raw Data	Absolute Difference	Logarithm	Difference in Logarithms
100		2.0	
120	20	2.0792	0.0792
144	24	2.1584	0.0792
172.8	28.8	2.2375	0.0791
207.36	34.56	2.3167	0.0792

Although the absolute differences increase, the differences between logarithms remain constant. Thus, if the vertical scale of a graph is shown in terms of logarithms, constant percentage differences will plot as a straight line.

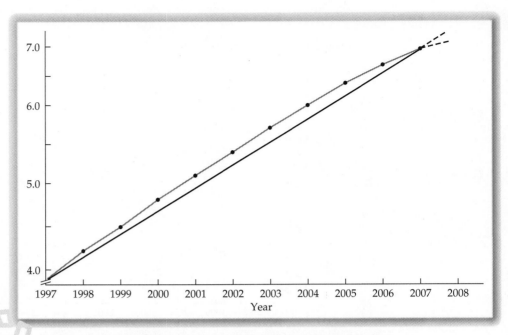

Figure 5.5   Semilogarithmic Graph of Changes in Citronade Sales

If we projected 2008 sales along the 6 percent growth line, our estimate would be 7,371,000 cases. Projecting sales by using the 10-year absolute average growth of 306,000 cases we would arrive at 7,260,000 cases, a 4.4 percent increase, a quantity that would closely correspond to the value that would be indicated by projecting the line showing actual observations. The latter would appear to be the more reasonable estimate.

Although under some circumstances this type of forecast may be sufficiently accurate, most forecasters would believe that a more detailed estimate—particularly given the seasonal nature of soft drink demand—is essential. Thus, Frank will move on to perform a time series analysis using a least squares equation, and also to identify the seasonal pattern of Citronade sales.

Time Series Analysis

In this section, we continue to explore **time series forecasting**. However, instead of visual estimation, a more precise statistical technique will be employed: the method of least squares. This method was introduced earlier in this chapter and was used to estimate demand. Whereas demand estimation requires the use of one or more independent variables, and the interactive relationship between these variables is of great importance, in the context of time series analysis there is only one independent variable: time. Thus, this system of forecasting is "naive" because it does not explain the reason for the changes; it merely says that the series of numbers to be projected changes as a function of time.

Despite the mechanical nature of this type of forecast, time series analysis has much to recommend it:

1. It is easy to calculate. A large number of software packages is available.
2. It does not require much judgment or analytical skill by the analyst.

3. It describes the line with the best possible fit, and provides information regarding statistical errors and statistical significance.

4. It is usually reasonably reliable in the short run, unless an absolute turn in the series occurs.

The fact that time series analysis does not take into consideration causative factors does not mean that an analyst using this method should not consider additional information about changes in the underlying forces. Any analyst using this naive method of prediction should try to fine tune the conclusions based on information that could alter the results.[29]

When data are collected over a number of periods in the past, they usually exhibit four different characteristics:

1. *Trend.*   This is the direction of movement of the data over a relatively long period of time, either upward or downward.

2. *Cyclical fluctuations.*   These are deviations from the trend due to general economic conditions. For instance, if one were to observe data for the GDP over time, a long-run upward trend would be evident. Also evident in this series would be movement around that trend as the economy rises more quickly or less quickly (or actually declines).

3. *Seasonal fluctuations.*   A pattern that repeats annually is characteristic of many products. Toy sales tend to rise briefly before Christmas. Fashions have spring and fall seasons. In the soft drink industry, the expectation is for higher sales during the warmer periods of the year (i.e., June through September). Thus, time series in which data are collected more frequently than annually (monthly, quarterly) can exhibit seasonal variations.

4. *Irregular.*   Departures from norm may be caused by special events or may just represent "noise" in the series. They occur randomly and thus cannot be predicted.

Thus, time series data can be represented by the following mathematical expression:

$$Y_t = f(T_t, C_t, S_t, R_t)$$

where Y_t = Actual value of the data in the time series at time t
T_t = Trend component at t
C_t = Cyclical component at t
S_t = Seasonal component at t
R_t = Random component at t

The specific form of this equation could be additive:

$$Y_t = T_t + C_t + S_t + R_t$$

Other forms could also exist. The specification most commonly used is the multiplicative form:

$$Y_t = (T_t)(C_t)(S_t)(R_t)$$

Thus, the changes in the actual values (Y_t) are determined by four factors. The task of the analyst is to "decompose" the time series of Y into its four components.

We can now return to Frank Robinson's problem of forecasting Citronade sales not only for the entire year of 2008, but for each quarter. This entire procedure is summarized in Table 5.5.

---

[29]It is essential that all changes and alterations are well documented by the analyst so a trail to her or his reasoning can be established.

Table 5.5   Citronade Quarterly Sales Analysis

(1) Quarter	(2) Actual	(3) Moving Average	(4) Centered Moving Average	(5) Ratio Actual/ CMA	(6) Adjusted Seasonal Factors	(7) Data Deseason- alized	(8) Trend	(9) Cycle and Irregular	(10) Cycle
1	842				0.889	946.7	940.1	100.70	
2	939				0.991	947.2	959.4	98.73	100.74
3	1,236	973.0	981.1	1.260	1.229	1,006.0	978.7	102.79	99.99
4	875	989.3	999.0	0.876	0.891	982.5	998.0	98.45	100.50
5	907	1,008.8	1,020.6	0.889	0.889	1,019.8	1,017.3	100.25	99.22
6	1,017	1,032.5	1,041.6	0.976	0.991	1,025.8	1,036.5	98.97	100.61
7	1,331	1,050.8	1,056.5	1.260	1.229	1,083.3	1,055.8	102.60	100.19
8	948	1,062.3	1,073.0	0.884	0.891	1,064.4	1,075.1	99.00	99.84
9	953	1,083.8	1,093.1	0.872	0.889	1,071.5	1,094.4	97.91	98.94
10	1,103	1,102.5	1,110.9	0.993	0.991	1,112.6	1,113.7	99.90	99.60
11	1,406	1,119.3	1,131.0	1.243	1.229	1,144.4	1,133.0	101.01	99.94
12	1,015	1,142.8	1,152.4	0.881	0.891	1,139.6	1,152.3	98.90	100.13
13	1,047	1,162.0	1,174.4	0.892	0.889	1,177.2	1,171.6	100.48	99.78
14	1,180	1,186.8	1,194.6	0.988	0.991	1,190.3	1,190.9	99.95	100.55
15	1,505	1,202.5	1,212.1	1.242	1.229	1,225.0	1,210.1	101.22	99.88
16	1,078	1,221.8	1,232.6	0.875	0.891	1,210.4	1,229.4	98.45	100.29
17	1,124	1,243.5	1,252.4	0.897	0.889	1,263.8	1,248.7	101.21	100.15
18	1,267	1,261.3	1,272.1	0.996	0.991	1,278.0	1,268.0	100.79	100.55
19	1,576	1,283.0	1,288.4	1.223	1.229	1,282.7	1,287.3	99.65	100.18
20	1,165	1,293.8	1,302.9	0.894	0.891	1,308.1	1,306.6	100.11	99.57
21	1,167	1,312.0	1,323.8	0.882	0.889	1,312.1	1,325.9	98.96	99.85
22	1,340	1,335.5	1,343.6	0.997	0.991	1,351.7	1,345.2	100.48	99.69
23	1,670	1,351.8	1,362.8	1.225	1.229	1,359.3	1,364.4	99.62	99.97
24	1,230	1,373.8	1,381.6	0.890	0.891	1,381.1	1,383.7	99.81	100.00
25	1,255	1,389.5	1,401.5	0.895	0.889	1,411.1	1,403.0	100.57	99.96
26	1,403	1,413.5	1,422.5	0.986	0.991	1,415.2	1,422.3	99.50	99.93
27	1,766	1,431.5	1,438.5	1.228	1.229	1,437.4	1,441.6	99.71	99.76
28	1,302	1,445.5	1,457.0	0.894	0.891	1,461.9	1,460.9	100.07	99.79
29	1,311	1,468.5	1,477.4	0.887	0.889	1,474.0	1,480.2	99.59	100.07
30	1,495	1,486.3	1,496.0	0.999	0.991	1,508.0	1,499.5	100.57	99.53
31	1,837	1,505.8	1,515.6	1.212	1.229	1,495.2	1,518.8	98.45	99.92
32	1,380	1,525.5	1,534.3	0.899	0.891	1,549.5	1,538.0	100.74	99.85
33	1,390	1,543.0	1,555.9	0.893	0.889	1,562.9	1,557.3	100.36	100.41
34	1,565	1,568.8	1,579.4	0.991	0.991	1,578.6	1,576.6	100.13	99.81
35	1,940	1,590.0	1,598.1	1.214	1.229	1,579.0	1,595.9	98.94	100.30
36	1,465	1,606.3	1,616.8	0.906	0.891	1,644.9	1,615.2	101.84	100.29
37	1,455	1,627.3	1,638.0	0.888	0.889	1,636.0	1,634.5	100.09	100.84
38	1,649	1,648.8	1,654.5	0.997	0.991	1,663.3	1,653.8	100.58	99.74
39	2,026	1,660.3	1,670.4	1.213	1.229	1,649.0	1,673.1	98.56	99.80
40	1,511	1,680.5	1,688.6	0.895	0.891	1,696.6	1,692.3	100.25	99.90
41	1,536	1,696.8	1,706.4	0.900	0.889	1,727.0	1,711.6	100.90	100.34
42	1,714	1,716.0	1,727.3	0.992	0.991	1,728.9	1,730.9	99.88	99.53
43	2,103	1,738.5			1.229	1,711.7	1,750.2	97.80	99.76
44	1,601				0.891	1,797.6	1,769.5	101.59	66.46

Seasonality   The process of decomposition starts with identifying and removing the seasonal factor from our series of numbers in order to calculate the trend. We use the method of **moving averages** to isolate seasonal fluctuations.

Column 1: This column simply represents all the quarters of the 11 years, 1997 through 2007, numbered sequentially.

Column 2: All the quarterly data, originally shown in Table 5.2, are listed here.

Column 3: The first step in the deseasonalizing process is to calculate a quarterly average for the first year (i.e., the first four quarters). The result is 973.0, so this number is placed next to quarter 3 in this column. The next number is obtained by moving down one quarter: the first quarter is dropped; the fifth quarter is added; and the average of quarters 2, 3, 4, and 5 is calculated to be 989.3. This number is placed next to quarter 4. The same procedure is then followed for the rest of the quarters. Because of the averaging, the data for the first two quarters and the last quarter are lost.

   The first moving average was placed next to the third quarter. It could also have been placed next to the second quarter. Actually, the average of four quarters belongs between the second and third quarters. This computation is made in column 4.

Column 4: An average of two adjacent numbers in column 3 is calculated and placed at the third quarter. Because 973.0 in column 3 should have appeared between quarters 2 and 3, and 989.3 should have been between quarters 3 and 4, the average of these two, 981.1, is correctly placed at quarter 3. All centered moving averages are placed in column 4. With this procedure, the next to the last number is now lost.

Column 5: We now obtain the seasonal factors. They are the ratios obtained by dividing the actual numbers in column 2 by the centered moving averages of column 4. Observing the numbers in column 5, it can be seen that every fourth quarter, starting with quarter 3 (i.e., quarter 3, 7, 11, and so on), has a factor greater than 1. These quarters represent the summer months (July to September), when soda consumption is at its peak. It can also be seen that data for the second calendar quarters (i.e., quarters 6, 10, 14, and so on) are rather close to 1, whereas the quarters representing fall and winter are generally below 0.9.

Column 6: To obtain a quarterly seasonal index, we must average the ratios obtained by quarter in column 5. This is done in Table 5.6. The quarterly patterns are quite obvious.[30]

   The four averages should add to 4; they do not because of rounding. A minor adjustment must now be made. The results are then transferred to column 6 of Table 5.5.

Column 7: When the actual data of column 2 are divided by the seasonal factors of column 6, the deseasonalized series of numbers in column 7 is obtained. Both the actual and the deseasonalized data have been plotted in Figure 5.6. The latter series, as should be expected, is much smoother than the former.

The first step of the decomposition procedure has now been completed:

$$(T \times C \times S \times R)/S = T \times C \times R$$

The new series has eliminated the seasonality. The next step is to calculate the trend.

---

[30]There appears to be minor downward trend in the third-quarter data. This is discussed later.

Table 5.6   Averaging of Seasonal Factors

Year	First Quarter	Second Quarter	Third Quarter	Fourth Quarter	Total
1997			1.260	0.876	
1998	0.889	0.976	1.260	0.884	
1999	0.872	0.993	1.243	0.881	
2000	0.892	0.988	1.242	0.875	
2001	0.897	0.996	1.223	0.894	
2002	0.882	0.997	1.225	0.890	
2003	0.895	0.986	1.228	0.894	
2004	0.887	0.999	1.212	0.899	
2005	0.893	0.991	1.214	0.906	
2006	0.888	0.997	1.213	0.895	
2007	0.900	0.992			
Average	0.890	0.992	1.229	0.891	4.002
Adjusted Average	0.889	0.991	1.229	0.891	4.000

The Trend Line   Computation of the trend uses the least squares method. The dependent variable is the deseasonalized series in column 7 of Table 5.5. The independent variable is time. Each quarter is numbered consecutively; although the initial number usually does not matter, it is easiest and most logical to start with 1. Thus, the consecutive numbers in column 1 of Table 5.5 represent the independent variable.

The form of the equation depends on the shape of the deseasonalized series. A casual observation of the deseasonalized series appears to indicate that a

Figure 5.6   Citronade Sales Deseasonalized

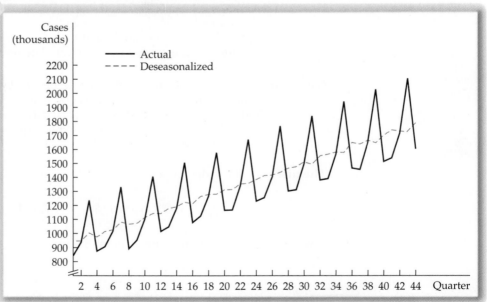

straight line would be most appropriate, but we actually tried three different possibilities:

$$\text{Straight line: } Y = a + b(t)$$
$$\text{Exponential line:}^{31} \ Y = ab^t$$
$$\text{Quadratic line:}^{32} \ Y = a + b(t) + c(t)^2$$

Although all three calculations gave acceptable results, the simplest—the straight line—gave the best statistical answers. Its coefficient of determination (R^2) was .996, and the t-statistic for the independent variable was 103.6—highly significant.

The exponential and quadratic equations also had very high R^2s, but their t-statistics were considerably lower (and the squared term in the latter was actually not statistically significant).

The straight-line trend equation was

$$Y = 920.8 + 19.2882t$$

Column 8:   Using this equation, we arrive at the trend numbers in column 8.

Column 9:   Then, by dividing the data in column 7 by those in column 8, we eliminate the trend from the deseasonalized series. In terms of the fraction used previously,

$$(T \times C \times R)/T = C \times R$$

Thus, only the cycle and random elements remain in column 9, which is in percentage form.

Cycle and Random Elements   At this point we could stop the analysis and do a forecast. The data in column 9 fluctuate rather irregularly within a range of about 5 percentage points. Part of this variation is due to random factors, which cannot be predicted and therefore should be ignored. However, there could be some longer business cycle wave in the data. To isolate the cycle, another smoothing operation can be performed with a moving average.

Column 10:   The preferred length of the moving-average period cannot be determined, except in each individual case. In our illustration, we used three periods. If the moving average correctly eliminates the random variations remaining in column 9, then the swings that appear in column 10 should represent a cyclical index.

When the index rises above 100 percent, the indication is that economic activity is strong; the opposite holds for index numbers below 100 percent. The data in column 10 fluctuate very little—less than 2 percentage points. Therefore, no great adjustment is needed here. However, if the indication is that the economy is in a down-turn, which may be expected to have some influence on soft drink sales, then a minor forecast adjustment can be made. Such an adjustment can be based on current general forecasts for the economy as a whole or on the latest published leading economic indicators.

---

[31]This is the equation that would best fit a straight line on a semilogarithmic chart, representing constant percentage growth from period to period.
[32]This equation would fit a curve on a graph with arithmetic scales.

Forecasting with Smoothing Techniques

Before we leave the section on projections, one other naive method should be mentioned. This method involves using an average of past observations to predict the future. If the forecaster believes that the future is a reflection of some average of past results, one of two forecasting methods can be applied: simple moving average or exponential smoothing.

The smoothing techniques, either moving average or exponential smoothing, work best when there is no strong trend in the series, when there are infrequent changes in the direction of the series, and when fluctuations are random rather than seasonal or cyclical. Obviously, these are very limiting conditions. However, if a large number of forecasts is needed quickly and if the estimates involve only one period into the future, then one of these two techniques can be employed.

Moving Average　　The average of actual past results is used to forecast one period ahead. The equation for this construction is simply

$$E_{t+1} = (X_t + X_{t-1} + \ldots + X_{t-N+1})/N$$

where E_{t+1} = Forecast for the next period ($t + 1$)
X_t, X_{t-1} = Actual values at their respective times
N = Number of observations included in the average

The forecasts for Citronade, with their strong trend and seasonal patterns, would certainly not lend themselves well to this simple projection method. Instead, a hypothetical example is used. Twelve observations are shown in the second column of Table 5.7.

Table 5.7　　Moving-Average Forecasting

Period	Actual	3-Month Moving Average			4-Month Moving Average			5-Month Moving Average		
		Forecast	Absolute Error	Squared Error	Forecast	Absolute Error	Squared Error	Forecast	Absolute Error	Squared Error
1	1,100									
2	800									
3	1,000									
4	1,050	967	83	6,944						
5	1,500	950	550	302,500	988	513	262,656			
6	750	1,183	433	187,778	1,088	338	113,906	1,090	340	115,600
7	700	1,100	400	160,000	1,075	375	140,625	1,020	320	102,400
8	650	983	333	111,111	1,000	350	122,500	1,000	350	122,500
9	1,400	700	700	490,000	900	500	250,000	930	470	220,900
10	1,200	917	283	80,278	875	325	105,625	1,000	200	40,000
11	900	1,083	183	33,611	988	88	7,656	940	40	1,600
12	1,000	1,167	167	27,778	1,038	38	1,406	970	30	900
13		1,033			1,125			1,030		
Total			3,133	1,400,000		2,525	1,004,375		1,750	603,900
Mean			348	155,556		316	125,547		250	86,271

Note: Some of the squared errors appear to be incorrect; this is so because decimals have been omitted.

The forecaster must decide how many observations to use in the moving average. The larger the number of observations in the average, the greater the smoothing effect. If the past data appear to contain significant randomness while the underlying pattern remains the same, then a larger number of observations is indicated. In Table 5.7, three moving averages have been computed—3, 4, and 5 months. The resulting estimates are shown in the forecast columns. For example, the forecast of 967 units in period 4 of the 3-month moving average was obtained as follows:

$$E_4 = (X_1 + X_2 + X_3)/N$$
$$= (1{,}100 + 800 + 1{,}000)/3$$
$$= 2{,}900/3 = 967$$

The three forecast columns diverge widely. These variations are shown graphically in Figure 5.7. As more observations are included in the moving average, the forecast line becomes smoother.

Which moving average should be used? One selection method is to calculate the mean error and the mean squared error of the differences between the actual data and the forecast.[33] The series with the smallest squared error would be preferred. In the example of Table 5.7, the 5-month moving average minimizes the deviations.

Figure 5.7   Forecasting with Moving Averages

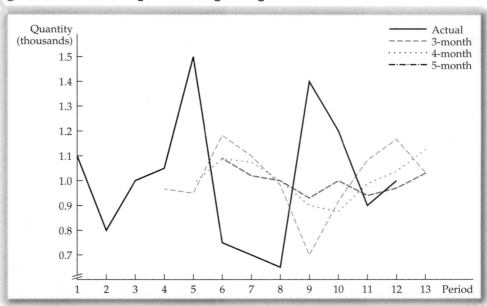

---

[33]The formula for the mean squared error is

$$\dfrac{\sum_{n=1}^{N}(E_n - X_n)^2}{N}$$

Instead of the mean squared error, we could calculate the root mean squared error by taking the square root of the previous equation.

Exponential Smoothing　The moving-average method awards equal importance to each of the observations included in the average, and gives no weight to observations preceding the oldest data included. However, the analyst may believe that the most recent observation is more relevant to the estimate of the next period than previous observations. In that case, it is more appropriate to employ the **exponential smoothing** method, which allows for the decreasing importance of information in the more distant past. This is accomplished by the mathematical technique of geometric progression. Older data are assigned increasingly smaller weights; the sum of the weights, if we approached an infinitely large number of observations, would equal 1. All the complex formulations of the geometric series can be simplified into the following expression:

$$E_{t+1} = wX_t + (1 - w)E_t$$

where w is the weight assigned to an actual observation at period t.

Thus, to make a forecast for one period into the future, all that is needed is the previous period's actual observation and the previous period's forecast. The analyst does not need the extensive historical data required for the moving-average method. The most crucial decision the analyst must make is the choice of the weighting factor. The larger the w (i.e., the closer to 1), the greater will be the importance of the most recent observation. Therefore, when the series is rather volatile and when w is large, the smoothing effect may be minimal. When w is small, the smoothing effect will be considerably more pronounced. This result can be seen in Table 5.8 and Figure 5.8 where ws of 0.2, 0.4, and 0.8 have been used.[34] Which weights should be used? We can again calculate the mean squared error, as was done in Table 5.8. Using $w = 0.2$ minimizes the error, so this is the best weight for this set of data.

Table 5.8　Exponential Smoothing Forecasting

Period	Actual	Smoothing Factor = 0.2			Smoothing Factor = 0.4			Smoothing Factor = 0.8		
		Forecast	Absolute Error	Squared Error	Forecast	Absolute Error	Squared Error	Forecast	Absolute Error	Squared Error
1	1,100									
2	800	1,100	300	90,000	1,100	300	90,000	1,100	300	90,000
3	1,000	1,040	40	1,600	980	20	400	860	140	19,600
4	1,050	1,032	18	324	988	62	3,844	972	78	6,084
5	1,500	1,036	464	215,667	1,013	487	237,364	1,034	466	216,783
6	750	1,128	378	143,247	1,208	458	209,471	1,407	657	431,491
7	700	1,053	353	124,457	1,025	325	105,370	881	181	32,897
8	650	982	332	110,375	895	245	59,910	736	86	7,443
9	1,400	916	484	234,467	797	603	363,779	667	733	536,915
10	1,200	1,013	187	35,109	1,038	162	26,207	1,253	53	2,857
11	900	1,050	150	22,530	1,103	203	41,156	1,211	311	96,528
12	1,000	1,020	20	403	1,022	22	472	962	38	1,434
13		1,016			1,013			992		
Total			2,728	978,180		2,886	1,137,973		3,043	1,442,033
Mean			248	88,925		262	103,452		277	131,094

Note: Some of the squared errors appear to be incorrect; this is so because decimals have been omitted.

[34]Note that the forecast for period 2 in each case is the actual observation of period 1. Because there is no forecast for period 1, a forecast must be made up. Any number could have been used, but the actual observation is probably the most logical choice.

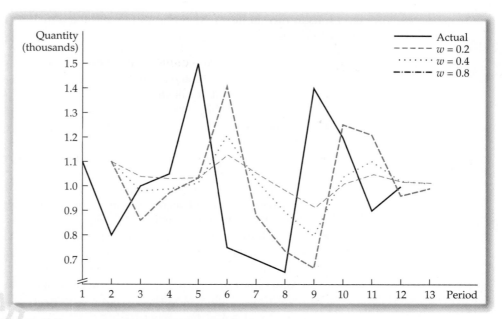

Figure 5.8   Exponential Smoothing Forecasting

Both of these naive forecasting techniques have their advantages and disadvantages. The simplicity of the methods is certainly an advantage. However, their usefulness is limited to cases where there is an underlying stability (i.e., no trend) with period-to-period random fluctuations. When a trend or a repeating pattern of fluctuations is present, the time series method with deseasonalization is a much better technique to use. In any case, the two methods just discussed should be employed only for extremely short-term estimates—preferably just one period into the future.

Box-Jenkins Forecasting Method   Only a brief mention of this sophisticated and fairly complex model is made here. Readers interested in greater detail should consult a business forecasting book.[35]

The Box-Jenkins model, as do time series analysis and smoothing models, relies on prior observations, rather than exogenous independent variables, to arrive at a forecast. However, it does not assume a specific pattern of prior data. Rather, it permits the choice among a large number of models. Through an iterative procedure, it arrives at the best result (i.e., the one that produces the smallest errors).

Two Recent Forecasting Methods

A Sales Forecasting Survey[36]   An article published in 2005 presents the results of a survey that was conducted to discover whether forecasting practices have changed over the previous 20 years and whether forecasting results have improved. It compares

---

[35]For instance, Hanke, Wichern, and Reitsch, *Business Forecasting*, chapter 9, or J. Holton Wilson and Barry Keating, *Business Forecasting*, 3d ed., Irwin McGraw-Hill, 1998, chapter 7.

[36]Teresa M. McCarthy, Donna F. Davis, Susan L. Golicic, and John T. Menzer, "The Evolution of Sales Forecasting Management: A 20-Year Longitudinal Study of Forecasting Practices," *Journal of Forecasting*, Vol. 25, Issue 5, August 2005, pp. 303–324.

its results to two similar surveys that were conducted in 1995 and 1984.[37] Some of the major findings of this survey were as follows:

➤ The most familiar forecasting techniques were moving averages followed by exponential smoothing, regression and straight-line projection.

➤ The familiarity with qualitative methods (such as jury of executive opinion) decreased from the previous surveys.

➤ Exponential smoothing appeared to be the most satisfactory method, followed by trend-line analysis.

➤ The satisfaction level with the various techniques appears to be declining from previous surveys.

➤ Despite the great improvement in tools such as software that are now available to forecasters, the overall degree of accuracy of the forecasts is substantially lower than that of the previous two studies.

➤ The authors conclude that the major reasons for the decline in accuracy are:
  • Lack of familiarity by users with techniques, and lack of satisfaction with forecasting systems.
  • Most forecasting personnel are not held accountable for performance.
  • Sales forecasting performance does not affect compensation of forecasting personnel.

➤ The authors state that "sales forecasting will not improve until companies commit the resources . . . with personnel trained in the use of sales forecasting techniques . . . properly measured and rewarded for performance."

Forecasting the Demand for New Drugs   A very recent article reported on a method used by pharmaceutical companies to forecast the demand for newly introduced drugs. The firms use marketing research called "new drug acceptance and new drug adoption studies to estimate the percentage of the target market" that will use the new drug immediately and later over its life cycle. The method utilizes the Gompertz curve, which is an S-shaped curve that describes the new drug use. Please refer to Figure 5.9 to see a typical Gompertz curve. To develop this curve three variables must be entered: the intercept or minimum value, the asymptote or maximum value, and the slope or rate of change. To obtain these values the forecasters will estimate their values from "an analog or a previously launched drug of the same kind in the same market." But because this is an innovative drug, such information may not always be available. Then researchers will have to look for information elsewhere. Thus, in the instance of a new drug for Attention Deficit Hyperactivity Disorder (ADHD), cited in the article, the marketing research was conducted among physicians two years before the launch of the product to ascertain the percentage growth of this drug over its life cycle. From this survey the forecasters were able to estimate the three variables to obtain the forecast over several years.[38]

Econometric Models

Up to this point, all the quantitative forecasting techniques discussed can be classified as naive. In this section of the chapter, our brief discussion concentrates on models

---

[37]John T. Menzer and James E. Cox, Jr., "Familiarity, Application, and Performance of Sales Forecasting Techniques," *Journal of Forecasting*, Vol. 3, Issue 5, January–March 1984, pp. 27–36; John T. Menzer and Kenneth B. Kahn, "Forecasting Technique Familiarity, Satisfaction, Usage and Application," *Journal of Forecasting*, Vol. 14, Issue 5, September 1995, pp. 465–476.

[38]Michael Latta, "How to Forecast the Demand of a New Drug in the Pharmaceutical Industry," *The Journal of Business Forecasting*, Vol. 25, Issue 3, Fall 2007, pp. 21–23, 28.

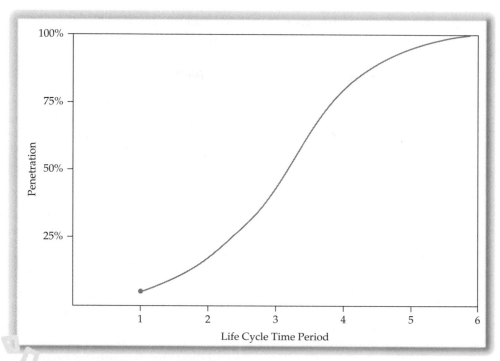

Figure 5.9   The Gompertz Curve

that are termed *causal* or *explanatory*. These **econometric forecasting models** were described in detail earlier in this chapter.

Regression analysis is an explanatory technique. Unlike the case of a naive projection, which relies on past patterns to predict the future, the analyst performing regression analysis must select those independent (or explanatory) variables that are influential in determining the dependent variable. Although simple projection models often give adequate results, the use of explanatory variables in the analysis can enhance the accuracy and the credibility of the estimates. Of course, no regression equation will explain the entire variation of the dependent variable because in most economic relationships there are numerous explanatory variables with complex interrelationships. As already explained, the person performing the analysis will have to settle for the inclusion of a limited number of variables, an equation that approximates the functional relationships, and results that explain a significant portion of, but not the entire variation in, the dependent variable.

The regression methods previously described employ a single equation to make estimates. Here we discuss a few studies of single-equation regression models of demand in which many of the variables are in the form of time series.

Among the many studies of automobile demand, the one written by Daniel Suits[39] is quite interesting. He combined the demand equations for new cars and used cars into one, as follows:

$$\Delta R = a_0 + a_1 \Delta Y + a_2 \Delta P/M + a_3 \Delta S + a_4 \Delta X$$

where R = Retail sales, in millions of new cars

$\quad\quad Y$ = Real disposable income

[39]Daniel B. Suits, "The Demand for New Automobiles in the United States, 1929–1956," *Review of Economics and Statistics,* August 1958, pp. 273–80.

P = Real retail price of new cars

M = Average credit terms (number of months of the average installment contract)

S = Existing stock, in millions of cars

X = Dummy variable

All the variables are in terms of first differences; thus, the equation estimates year-to-year changes. The years 1942 through 1948 have been excluded from the time series because of the war years, when no automobiles were produced, and the immediate postwar period, when significant distortions existed in the automobile market.

The dummy variable X takes into account the fact that not all the remaining years in the series can be treated equally. The years 1941, 1952, and 1953 were considered exceptional. The first two were assigned a value of $+1$, the third a value of -1, and all the other years a value of 0.

Having specified the equation, Suits calculated the coefficients (the as) and tested the results by predicting 1958 new auto sales. "The demand equation predicts a level of sales of slightly less than 6.0 million. This compares favorably with a preliminary estimate of 6.1 million actual sales for the year and stands in sharp contrast with sales forecasts of 6.5 million and over, which were common in the industry at the start of the year."[40]

Another economist studied the demand for computers.[41] He specified the following equation in terms of logarithms:

$$\log(y_t/y_{t-1}) = a_0 - a_1\log p_t - a_2\log y_{t-1}$$

where y_t = Stock of computers in year t

y_{t-1} = Stock of computers in year $t - 1$

p = Real price of computers

The demand in this equation is measured as the percentage change in the stock of computers from one year to the next.

A further example is given for coffee demand in the United States.[42] Coffee demand was estimated with the following equation:

$$Q = b_0 + b_1 P_0 + b_2 Y + b_3 P + \sum_{i=1}^{3} b_4 D_i + b_5 T$$

where Q = Per capita (population over age 16) quantity of coffee

P_0 = Real retail price of coffee, per pound

Y = Real per capita disposable income

P = Real retail price of tea, per quarter pound

D_i = Binary (dummy) variable for quarters of the year

T = Time trend

---

[40]Ibid., p. 273.

[41]Gregory Chow, "Technological Change and the Demand for Computers," *American Economic Review,* December 1967, pp. 1117–30.

[42]Cliff J. Huang, John J. Siegfried, and Farangis Zardoshty, "The Demand for Coffee in the United States, 1963–1977," *Quarterly Review of Economics and Business,* 20, 2 (summer 1980), pp. 36–50.

The authors found that coffee consumption is sensitive to its own price, that there had been a long-term decline in coffee consumption, and that significantly less coffee was consumed during the spring and summer months. The other coefficients did not turn out to be statistically significant. Thus, the consumption of coffee could be estimated from the time trend, the quarterly changes, and an assumption made regarding coffee prices.

A last example is a more recent one, and represents a demand forecast prepared for a specific product for a specific company. Columbia Gas of Ohio forecasts daily demand by using both time series and regression analysis. Two years of historical data are used to obtain the regression. The time series serves to forecast growth. The forecast is then based on a combination of the regression analysis and the growth rate:

$$Q = (1 + G) \times (a + b_1 T + b_2 P + b_3 W)$$

where Q = Daily demand in MDTH (thousand dekatherms)
G = Growth rate
T = Forecasted temperature
P = Prior day temperature
W = Forecasted wind speed
a = Intercept
b_1, b_2, b_3 = Coefficients

The R^2 of the regression equation is .983.

This forecast "is used mainly to ensure that scheduled supplies are in balance with forecasted demands over the next five-day period." The company receives a 5-day weather forecast twice daily.[43]

In each study, the numerical coefficients (the as and the bs) were obtained by regression analysis. To forecast using these equations, it is necessary, of course, to make estimates of each independent variable for the period indicated.[44] Alternative forecasts can be created by assuming different values for each independent variable.

An important warning is in order regarding the use of regression equations for forecasting. All the parameters (coefficients) in a regression equation are estimated using past data (whether time series or cross-sectional analysis has been employed). The forecast based on such estimates will be valid only if the relationships between the dependent variable and the independent variables do not change from the past into the future. Literally, a regression equation is valid only within the limits of the data used in it. When we venture outside these limits (i.e., forecast with independent variables outside the range of the past), we are treading on dangerous ground. Still, forecasting with the least squares method is a much-used technique, often employed quite successfully. But its limitations must not be forgotten by the analyst.

Although many forecasting problems can be solved with the use of single-equation regression models, there are instances when one equation is not sufficient. In such cases, economists often turn to multiple-equation systems. Extremely large models used by economists to predict the GDP and its component parts are examples of such models, which may include hundreds of variables and equations.

---

[43]H. Alan Catron, "Daily Demand Forecasting at Columbia Gas," *Journal of Business Forecasting,* Summer 2000, pp. 10–15.
[44]In the case of lagged variables, actual data may be available. See, for instance, y_{t-1}, the stock of computers at the end of the previous year in the equation used in Chow, "Technological Change."

A single-equation model can be used when the dependent variable can be estimated using independent variables that are determined by events not part of the equation. But what happens when the determining variables are determined by other variables within the model? Then a single equation is insufficient.

In a multiple-equation system, variables are referred to as *endogenous* and *exogenous*. Endogenous variables are comparable to the dependent variable of the single-equation model; they are determined by the model. However, they can also influence other endogenous variables, so they may appear as "independent" (i.e., on the right side of the equation) variables in one or more of the equations. Exogenous variables are from outside the system and are not determined within it; they are truly independent variables.

The following is an example of an extremely simple two-equation model of the private economy:

$$C = a_0 + a_1 Y$$
$$Y = C + I$$

where C = Consumption
Y = National income
I = Investment

Here C and Y are endogenous variables. I is assumed (rather unrealistically) to be exogenous, or determined by forces outside the system of equations.

Another simple multiequation model represents the interrelationships of activities within a firm:

$$\text{Sales} = f(\text{GDP, Prices})$$
$$\text{Cost} = f(\text{Quantity of product, Factor prices})$$
$$\text{Expenses} = f(\text{Sales, Factor prices})$$
$$\text{Product price} = f(\text{Cost, Expenses, Profit})$$
$$\text{Profit} = \text{Sales} - \text{Cost} - \text{Expenses}$$

Here there are five endogenous variables. The exogenous variables are GDP, Quantity of product, and Factor prices. These equations are given in functional form only. The specific forms of the equations would, of course, have to be specified.

Such systems of equations would then be solved to obtain all of the coefficients. The statistical methods used to solve for all the numerical values are beyond the scope of this textbook.

GLOBAL APPLICATION: FORECASTING EXCHANGE RATES

In chapter 2, the additional challenges facing a multinational corporation are discussed. Such a corporation must forecast sales, expenses, and cash flows for its operations in different countries. The results from these transactions generated in the home country will depend on the exchange rate between the foreign and domestic currency. Often a company makes substantial investments in foreign operating facilities from which it expects to obtain cash flows. Thus, multinational corporations (MNCs) are vitally interested in forecasting exchange rates in both the short and long run.

A frequently used method to forecast exchange rates for relatively short periods into the future is through the forward rate. To understand this, two types of exchange rates must be defined:

1. Spot exchange rate—the price of one currency against another for transactions being completed immediately

2. Forward exchange rate—the price of one currency against another for a transaction that will occur at some point in the future

An extremely active exchange market exists, and financial officers can easily ascertain both spot and forward rates for the ten major currencies, which represent a predominant portion of all transactions. One view of the forward rate is that it represents the market's consensus on what the future spot rate should be. Thus, if today's spot rate is $1.998 for 1 British pound sterling and the 90-day forward rate is $1.989, then one can argue that the market consensus is that the pound will decrease in value by $0.009 relative to the U.S. dollar 90 days hence.

Is the forward rate a good predictor of the spot exchange rate for major currencies? On the average, the forward rate will be equal to the future spot rate; in other words, negative and positive errors in the forecasts will be offset. It can, therefore, be said that the forward rate is an unbiased forecaster of the spot rate. It makes for a best-guess forecast. However, this does not make it an accurate forecast at any one time. Still, for the short run, it is probably as good an estimator as we have. In addition to its lack of accuracy, other shortcomings must be considered:

1. The present exchange rate system does not permit currencies to float freely. Governments interfere in the exchange rate markets when they consider it to be of benefit to their country's economy.

2. Although forward rates can be established for relatively long periods into the future (in some cases, they can go out as far as 10 years), by far the largest volume of forward contracts is for 180 days or less.

3. Reliable forward markets exist only for currencies of the leading industrial economies of the world.

Longer-term exchange rate forecasts often use econometric models. A major problem in constructing these multiple regression models is in finding appropriate reliable independent variables. In most cases, the independent variables are stated in terms of differentials between the domestic and foreign measures, such as:

1. Growth rates of GDP
2. Real interest rates
3. Nominal interest rates
4. Inflation rates
5. Balance of payments

A significant number of complex models is in use today. Here we use a simple hypothetical model to illustrate the estimate of a relationship between the domestic currency and a foreign currency:

$$E_t = a + bI_t + cR_t + dG_t$$

where E = Exchange rate of a foreign currency in terms of the domestic currency
I = Domestic inflation rate minus foreign inflation rate
R = Domestic nominal interest rate minus foreign nominal interest rate
G = Domestic growth rate of GDP minus the growth rate of foreign GDP
t = Time period
a, b, c, d = Regression coefficients

Such forecasts have all the advantages and disadvantages usually found in the application of regression analysis to economic problems:

1. Which variables should be included?
2. What form should the regression equation adopt?
3. Are accurate measurements of independent variables available? Data may be inadequate for other than the major industrial countries.

4. To forecast exchange rates, it may be necessary to forecast the independent variables. It is not surprising that it may be as difficult to forecast independent variables accurately as it is to forecast the exchange rates themselves.

By now the reader has probably concluded that forecasting exchange rates is not an easy task. But then, no forecasts are easy. The accuracy of exchange rate forecasts has been inconsistent at best. However, this should not deter business people from attempting to make such forecasts. Even if inaccurate, they enhance a manager's knowledge of her environment and provide a manager with insights into the economic variables that affect international decision making.

The discussion of this subject has been limited to its bare essentials. Students interested in studying this topic further can do so by reading one of several textbooks dealing with international financial management.[45]

The Solution

Frank Robinson is now ready to make his forecast for 2008. He will do it in three steps:

1. He will project the trend for the four quarters of 2008.
2. He will apply the seasonal factors.
3. He may then make an adjustment for cyclical influences.

Because the trend equation is $Y = 920.8 + 19.2882(t)$, his trend forecasts will be as follows:

$$1\text{st qtr}: 920.8 + 19.2882(45) = 1,788.8$$
$$2\text{nd qtr}: 920.8 + 19.2882(46) = 1,808.1$$
$$3\text{rd qtr}: 920.8 + 19.2882(47) = 1,827.3$$
$$4\text{th qtr}: 920.8 + 19.2882(48) = 1,846.6$$

Next, each result must be multiplied by the seasonal factors:

$$1\text{st qtr}: 1,788.8 \times 0.889 = 1,590.2$$
$$2\text{nd qtr}: 1,808.1 \times 0.991 = 1,791.8$$
$$3\text{rd qtr}: 1,827.3 \times 1.231 = 2,245.8$$
$$4\text{th qtr}: 1,846.6 \times 0.891 = 1,645.4$$

Frank noticed, however, that the seasonal factors in Table 5.6 exhibit some trends over the 11 years. The third-quarter factor has been decreasing and the first- and fourth-quarter factors appear to be rising. To see the effect of these changes, Frank decides to use the average of the last three observations for each quarter (and adjust to a total of 4, as was done previously). When he applies his new factors to the trend numbers, he obtains the following results:

$$1\text{st qtr}: 1,788.8 \times 0.894 = 1,599.2$$
$$2\text{nd qtr}: 1,808.1 \times 0.993 = 1,795.3$$
$$3\text{rd qtr}: 1,827.3 \times 1.213 = 2,216.6$$
$$4\text{th qtr}: 1,846.6 \times 0.900 = 1,662.0$$

He decides that this last computation is more valid. The last step in his procedure is to evaluate the effect of cycles and random factors. He decides that the cycle's influence on soft drink sales will be neutral in the coming year. Although an estimate of random factors cannot be made, Frank knows that the company has plans to implement a strong advertising campaign on behalf of Citronade during the second quarter of 2008. At this point, however, he does

(continued)

---

[45]For example, Dennis J. O'Connor and Alberto T. Bueso, *International Dimensions of Financial Management*, New York: Macmillan, 1990. The preceding discussion has drawn on material contained in this book.

(continued)

not have sufficient information regarding the effect of advertising on sales. He makes a note to mention that in his report as a possible plus and to try to make some quantitative estimates later.

An additional point deserves attention. We have assumed the product whose sales Frank is forecasting has been in existence for at least 11 years. Had this been a new flavor, not previously produced, the forecast would have been much more difficult. If competing companies had been selling a similar product in the past, market information would be available in terms of very detailed statistics published by the beverage industry. Frank could then base his forecast on these data and assume some pattern of market penetration for the new brand. If, however, this is a completely new flavor not previously produced in the industry, it may be necessary to conduct market research to establish a base for a forecast. Another method would be to study the sales patterns of other soft drink products from point of introduction and to base the new product forecast on their histories.

SUMMARY

The aim of this chapter is to present an introduction to regression analysis and forecasting, with a primary emphasis on how the techniques of these disciplines are applied to management problems.

We focused the application of regression analysis on the estimation of demand. This particular application can be summarized as follows:

1. Specification of the regression model of demand
2. Collection of the relevant data
3. Estimation of the regression equation
4. Analysis and evaluation of the regression results (e.g., t-test, F-test, R^2), and adjustment or correction for any statistical problems (e.g., multicollinearity, autocorrelation, incorrect functional form)
5. Assessment of regression findings for use in making policy decisions

In a formal econometrics course, most of the emphasis is placed on steps 1, 3, and 4 (i.e., the more technical aspects of this type of statistical analysis). In business, the most important steps are 2 and 5. Powerful computers and sophisticated software packages are available to everyone today at such a reasonable cost that it has become elementary to apply regression analysis to the estimation of demand or any other aspect of business research. The real challenge is to obtain *good* data and to apply judiciously the results of the regression analysis to the managerial decision-making process. In these two areas of regression analysis, no textbook or course can take the place of actual hands-on experience.

Forecasting is an important activity in many organizations. In business, forecasting is a necessity.

This chapter summarizes and discusses a number of forecasting techniques. Six categories of forecasts are included:

1. *Expert opinion* is a qualitative technique of forecasting based on the judgment of knowledgeable people. The Delphi method is another type of expert opinion forecast that is generally applicable in forecasting technological advances.
2. *Opinion polls and market research* are conducted among survey populations, not experts, to establish future trends or consumer responses.
3. *Surveys of spending plans* are concerned with such important economic data as consumer sentiment. The forecasts are based on replies to questionnaires or interviews.
4. *Economic indicators* are indexes of a number of economic series intended to forecast the short-run movements of the economy, including changes in direction.

5. *Projections,* a quantitative method, employ historical data to project future trends. Usually, no causes for trends are identified.

6. *Econometric models* are explanatory or causal models in which independent variables that influence the statistic to be forecast are identified.

The chapter also examines the decomposition of least squares projections into trends, seasonal and cyclical fluctuations, and irregular movements.

One other naive forecasting method was mentioned: forecasting with smoothing techniques. Smoothing techniques fall into two major categories, moving averages and exponential smoothing, and are useful when there are no pronounced trends in the data and when fluctuations from period to period are random.

IMPORTANT CONCEPTS

Demand Estimation

Coefficient of determination (R^2): A measure indicating the percentage of the variation in the dependent variable accounted for by variations in some designated independent variable. Its value ranges from 0 to 1. Zero indicates that variations in the independent variable account for none of the variation in the dependent variable. One indicates that 100 percent of the variation in the dependent variable can be accounted for by the variations in the independent variable. In multiple regression analysis, this measure is referred to as the *multiple coefficient of determination.* (p. 133)

Consumer survey: The attempt to obtain data about demand directly by asking consumers about their purchasing habits through such means as face-to-face interviews, focus groups, telephone surveys, and mailed questionnaires. (p. 127)

Cross-sectional data: Data on a particular set of variables for a given point in time for a cross-section of individual entities (e.g., persons, households, cities, states, countries). (p. 128)

Degrees of freedom: An adjustment factor that is required in conducting the *t*-test. This number is found by subtracting the number of independent variables plus 1 from the number of observations in the sample; that is, d.f. $= n - (k + 1) = n - k - 1$. (p. 132)

F-test: A test for the statistical significance of the R^2 value. If this test is passed, a researcher can be quite confident that all the estimated coefficients of a regression model together are not zero for the population under study. (p. 133)

One-tail test: This refers to the nature of the alternative hypothesis in the *t*-test. If the alternative hypothesis states that the population coefficient is positive, then the upper tail of the *t*-distribution is used. If the alternative hypothesis states that

the population coefficient is negative, then the lower tail is used. In either case, only one tail is used. (p. 132)

Regression analysis: A statistical technique for finding the best relationship between a dependent variable and selected independent variables. If one independent variable is used, this technique is referred to as *simple regression.* If more than one independent variable is used, it is called *multiple regression.* (p. 127)

Rule of 2: A general rule of thumb employed by economists in conducting the *t*-test. Essentially, it states that any *t*-ratio of 2 or more indicates that the estimated coefficient is statistically significant at the 0.05 level. (p. 132)

Standard error ($\text{SE}_{\hat{b}}$): A measure of the deviation of an estimated regression coefficient from the hypothesized value of the true (but unknown) population coefficient. In the *t*-test, the standard error of a particular estimated coefficient is divided into this coefficient, thereby indicating the *t*-value. (p. 132)

t-table: A numerical table indicating the different values of the *t*-ratio and the frequency of their occurrence in a *t*-distribution whose mean value is zero. (p. 132)

t-test: A test for the statistical significance of the estimated regression coefficients. If a coefficient passes this test, then a researcher can be quite confident that the value of the true population coefficient is not zero. (p. 132)

Time series data: Data for a particular set of variables that track their values over a particular period of time at regular intervals (e.g., monthly, quarterly, annually). (p. 128)

Two-tail test: A *t*-test in which the alternative hypothesis states that the population coefficient may be either positive or negative (i.e., it is not zero); that is, either the upper or the lower tail of the *t*-distribution may be used. (p. 132)

Forecasting

Causal (explanatory) forecasting: A quantitative forecasting method that attempts to uncover functional relationships between independent variables and the dependent variable. (p. 144)

Compound growth rate projection: Forecasting by projecting the average growth rate of the past into the future. (p. 149)

Delphi method: A form of expert opinion forecasting that uses a series of written questions and answers to obtain a consensual forecast, most commonly employed in forecasting technological trends. (p. 145)

Econometric forecasting model: A quantitative, causal method that uses a number of independent variables to explain the dependent variable to be forecast. Econometric forecasting employs both single- and multiple-equation models. (p. 163)

Economic indicators: A barometric method of forecasting in which economic data are formed into indexes to reflect the state of the economy. Indexes of leading, coincident, and lagging indicators are used to forecast changes in economic activity. (p. 146)

Exponential smoothing: A smoothing method of forecasting that assigns greater importance to more recent data than to those in the more distant past. (p. 160)

Jury of executive opinion: A forecast generated by experts (e.g., corporate executives) in meetings.

A similar method is to ask the opinion of sales representatives who are exposed to the market on a daily basis. (p. 144)

Moving average method: A smoothing technique that compensates for seasonal fluctuations. (p. 155)

Naive forecasting: Quantitative forecasting that projects past data without explaining the reasons for future trends. (p. 144)

Opinion polls: A forecasting method in which sample populations are surveyed to determine consumption trends. (p. 145)

Qualitative forecasting: Forecasting based on the judgment of individuals or groups. Also called *judgmental forecasting*. (p. 144)

Quantitative forecasting: Forecasting that examines historical data as a basis for future trends. (p. 144)

Surveys of spending plans: Examinations of economic trends such as consumer sentiment and inventory. (p. 145)

Time series forecasting: A method of forecasting from past data by using least squares statistical methods. A time series analysis usually examines trends, cyclical fluctuations, seasonal fluctuations, and irregular movements. (p. 152)

Trend projections: A form of naive forecasting that projects trends from past data. Trend projections usually employ compound growth rates, visual time series, or least squares time series methods. (p. 148)

QUESTIONS

Demand Estimation

1. Explain the difference between time series data and cross-sectional data. Provide examples of each type of data.
2. Would there be any differences in the set of variables used in a regression model of the demand for consumer durable goods (e.g., automobiles, appliances, furniture) and a regression model of the demand for "fast-moving consumer goods" (e.g., food, beverages, personal care products)? Explain.
3. Briefly explain the meaning of R^2. A time series analysis of demand tends to result in a higher R^2 than one using cross-sectional data. Why do you think this is the case?
4. Summarize the steps involved in conducting the t-test. What is the basis for using the "rule of 2" as a convenient method of evaluating t-ratios?
5. Briefly explain the meaning of the F-test. Why do you think this test is considered to be more important in multiple regression analysis than it is in simple regression analysis?
6. What is *multicollinearity*? How can researchers detect this problem? What is the impact of this problem on the regression estimates? What steps can be taken to deal with this problem?
7. What is the identification problem? What effect will this problem have on the regression estimates of a demand function? Explain.

Forecasting

1. "The best forecasting method is the one that gives the highest proportion of correct predictions." Comment.

2. Enumerate methods of qualitative and quantitative forecasting. What are the major differences between the two?

3. Discuss the benefits and drawbacks of the following methods of forecasting:
   a. Jury of executive opinion
   b. The Delphi method
   c. Opinion polls
   Each method has its uses. What are they?

4. a. Why are manufacturers' new orders, nondefense capital goods, an appropriate leading indicator?
   b. Why is the index of industrial production an appropriate coincident indicator?
   c. Why is the average prime rate charged by banks an appropriate lagging indicator?

5. Discuss some of the important criticisms of the forecasting ability of the leading economic indicators.

6. Manhattan was allegedly purchased from Native Americans in 1626 for $24. If the sellers had invested this sum at a 6 percent interest rate compounded semiannually, how much would it amount to today?

7. The compound growth rate is frequently used to forecast various quantities (sales, profits, and so on). Do you believe this is a good method? Should any cautions be exercised in making such projections?

8. Describe projections that use either moving averages or exponential smoothing. Under what conditions can these techniques be used? Which of the two appears to be the more useful?

9. How do econometric models differ from "naive" projection methods? Is it always advisable to use the former in forecasting?

10. You have been asked to produce a forecast for your company's new product, bottled water. Discuss the kind of information you would look for in order to make this forecast.

11. The following are the monthly changes in the index of leading economic indicators during 2001 and January 2002:

January	+.1	August	0
February	+.1	September	−.6
March	−.3	October	+.1
April	−.1	November	+.8
May	+.6	December	+1.3
June	+.2	January 2002	+.6
July	+.3		

What would be your prediction for the U.S. economy in 2002?

PROBLEMS

Demand Estimation

1. One of the most difficult tasks in regression analysis is to obtain the data suitable for quantitative studies of this kind. Suppose you are trying to estimate the demand for home furniture. Suggest the kinds of variables that could be used to represent the following factors, which are believed to affect the demand for any product. Be as specific as possible about how the variables are going to be measured. Do you anticipate any difficulty in securing such data? Explain.

Determinants of Demand for Furniture	Suggested Variables to Use in Regression Analysis
Price	
Tastes and preferences	
Price of related products	
Income	
Cost or availability of credit	
Number of buyers	
Future expectations	
Other possible factors	

2. You are the manager of a large automobile dealership who wants to learn more about the effectiveness of various discounts offered to customers over the past 14 months. Following are the average negotiated prices for each month and the quantities sold of a basic model (adjusted for various options) over this period of time.
   a. Graph this information on a scatter plot. Estimate the demand equation. What do the regression results indicate about the desirability of discounting the price? Explain.

Month	Price	Quantity
Jan.	12,500	15
Feb.	12,200	17
Mar.	11,900	16
Apr.	12,000	18
May	11,800	20
June	12,500	18
July	11,700	22
Aug.	12,100	15
Sept.	11,400	22
Oct.	11,400	25
Nov.	11,200	24
Dec.	11,000	30
Jan.	10,800	25
Feb.	10,000	28

   b. What other factors besides price might be included in this equation? Do you foresee any difficulty in obtaining these additional data or incorporating them in the regression analysis?

3. The maker of a leading brand of low-calorie microwavable food estimated the following demand equation for its product using data from 26 supermarkets around the country for the month of April:

$$Q = -5,200 - 42P + 20P_X + 5.2I + 0.20A + 0.25M$$
$$(2.002) \quad (17.5) \quad (6.2) \quad (2.5) \quad (0.09) \quad (0.21)$$
$$R^2 = 0.55 \qquad n = 26 \qquad F = 4.88$$

Assume the following values for the independent variables:

Q = Quantity sold per month

P (in cents) = Price of the product = 500

P_X (in cents) = Price of leading competitor's product = 600

I (in dollars) = Per capita income of the standard metropolitan statistical area (SMSA) in which the supermarket is located = 5,500

A (in dollars) = Monthly advertising expenditure = 10,000

M = Number of microwave ovens sold in the SMSA in which the supermarket is located = 5,000

Using this information, answer the following questions:

a. Compute elasticities for each variable.
b. How concerned do you think this company would be about the impact of a recession on its sales? Explain.
c. Do you think that this firm should cut its price to increase its market share? Explain.
d. What proportion of the variation in sales is explained by the independent variables in the equations? How confident are you about this answer? Explain.

4. A manufacturer of computer workstations gathered average monthly sales figures from its 56 branch offices and dealerships across the country and estimated the following demand for its product:

$$Q = +\,15{,}000 - 2.80P + 150A + 0.3P_{pc} + 0.35P_m + 0.2P_c$$
$$(5{,}234)\quad(1.29)\quad(175)\quad(0.12)\quad(0.17)\quad(0.13)$$
$$R^2 = 0.68 \qquad\qquad \text{SEE} = 786 \qquad\qquad F = 21.25$$

The variables and their assumed values are

Q = Quantity
P = Price of basic model = 7,000
A = Advertising expenditures (in thousands) = 52
P_{pc} = Average price of a personal computer = 4,000
P_m = Average price of a minicomputer = 15,000
P_c = Average price of a leading competitor's workstation = 8,000

a. Compute the elasticities for each variable. On this basis, discuss the relative impact that each variable has on the demand. What implications do these results have for the firm's marketing and pricing policies?
b. Conduct a *t*-test for the statistical significance of each variable. In each case, state whether a one-tail or two-tail test is required. What difference, if any, does it make to use a one-tail versus a two-tail test on the results? Discuss the results of the *t*-tests in light of the policy implications mentioned.
c. Suppose a manager evaluating these results suggests that interest rates and the performance of the computer (typically measured in millions of instructions per second, or MIPS) are important determinants of the demand for workstations and must therefore be included in the study. How would you respond to this suggestion? Elaborate.

5. You are given the following demand for European luxury automobiles:

$$Q = 1{,}000P^{-0.93}P_a^{0.75}P_j^{1.2}I^{1.6}$$

where P = Price of European luxury cars
P_a = Price of American luxury cars
P_j = Price of Japanese luxury cars
I = Annual income of car buyers

Assume that each of the coefficients is statistically significant (i.e., that they passed the t-test). On the basis of the information given, answer the following questions:

a. Comment on the degree of substitutability between European and American luxury cars and between European and Japanese luxury cars. Explain some possible reasons for the results in the equation.
b. Comment on the coefficient for the income variable. Is this result what you would expect? Explain.
c. Comment on the coefficient of the European car price variable. Is that what you would expect? Explain.

Forecasting

1. If the sales of your company have grown from $500,000 five years ago to $1,050,150 this year, what is the compound growth rate? If you expect your sales to grow at a rate of 10 percent for the next five years, what should they be five years from now?

2. The sales data for the Lonestar Sports Apparel Company for the last 12 years are as follows:

1996	$400,000	2002	$617,000
1997	440,000	2003	654,000
1998	480,000	2004	700,000
1999	518,000	2005	756,000
2000	554,000	2006	824,000
2001	587,000	2007	906,000

   a. What is the 1996–2007 compound growth grate?
   b. Using the result obtained in part a, what is your 2008 projection?
   c. If you were to make your own projection, what would you forecast?

3. Based on past data, Mack's Pool Supply has constructed the following equation for the sales of its house brand of chlorine tablets:

$$Q = 1,000 + 100t$$

where Q is quantity and t is time (in years), with 2003 = 0.
   a. What is the sales projection for 2008?
   b. The tablet sales are seasonal, with the following quarterly indexes:

Quarter 1	80%
Quarter 2	100%
Quarter 3	125%
Quarter 4	95%

What is the quarterly sales projection for 2008?

4. The sales data over the last 10 years for the Acme Hardware Store are as follows:

1998	$230,000	2003	$526,000
1999	276,000	2004	605,000
2000	328,000	2005	690,000
2001	388,000	2006	779,000
2002	453,000	2007	873,000

   a. Calculate the compound growth rate for the period of 1998 to 2007.
   b. Based on your answer to part a, forecast sales for both 2008 and 2009.
   c. Now calculate the compound growth rate for the period of 2002 to 2007.
   d. Based on your answer to part c, forecast sales for both 2008 and 2009.
   e. What is the major reason for the differences in your answers to parts b and d? If you were to make your own projections, what would you forecast? (Drawing a graph is very helpful.)

5. The Miracle Corporation had the following sales during the past 10 years (in thousands of dollars):

1998	200	2003	302
1999	215	2004	320
2000	237	2005	345
2001	260	2006	360
2002	278	2007	382

   a. Calculate a trend line, and forecast sales for 2008. How confident are you of this forecast?
   b. Use exponential smoothing with a smoothing factor $w = 0.7$. What is your 2008 forecast? How confident are you of this forecast?

6. You have the following data for the last 12 months' sales for the PRQ Corporation (in thousands of dollars):

January	500	July	610
February	520	August	620
March	520	September	580
April	510	October	550
May	530	November	510
June	580	December	480

a. Calculate a 3-month centered moving average.
b. Use this moving average to forecast sales for January of next year.
c. If you were asked to forecast January and February sales for next year, would you be confident of your forecast using the preceding moving averages? Why or why not?

7. Office Enterprises (OE) produces a line of metal office file cabinets. The company's economist, having investigated a large number of past data, has established the following equation of demand for these cabinets:

$$Q = 10,000 + 60B - 100P + 50C$$

where Q = Annual number of cabinets sold
B = Index of nonresidential construction
P = Average price per cabinet charged by OE
C = Average price per cabinet charged by OE's closest competitor

It is expected that next year's nonresidential construction index will stand at 160, OE's average price will be \$40, and the competitor's average price will be \$35.
a. Forecast next year's sales.
b. What will be the effect if the competitor lowers its price to \$32? If it raises its price to \$36?
c. What will happen if OE reacts to the decrease mentioned in part *b* by lowering its price to \$37?
d. If the index forecast was wrong, and it turns out to be only 140 next year, what will be the effect on OE's sales?

8. The GDP of the United States, both in current and real dollars, from 1987 to 2004 was as follows:

	Current	Real (2000 chain)
	($ in billions)	
1987	4,740	6,475
1988	5,104	6,743
1989	5,484	6,981
1990	5,803	7,113
1991	5,996	7,101
1992	6,338	7,337
1993	6,657	7,533
1994	7,072	7,836
1995	7,398	8,032
1996	7,817	8,329
1997	8,304	8,704
1998	8,747	9,067
1999	9,268	9,470
2000	9,817	9,817
2001	10,128	9,891
2002	10,470	10,049
2003	10,961	10,301
2004	11,686	10,676

   a. Fit a linear (straight-line) trend to each of the data sets.
   b. Now fit an exponential trend to these data.
   c. Based on both the linear and exponential trend lines, what would have been your GDP (both current and real) forecast for the years 2005 and 2006?
   d. Would any of these trend lines be good predictors of GDP? Why or why not?

9. An economist has estimated the sales trend line for the Sun Belt Toy Company as follows:

$$S_t = 43.6 + 0.8t$$

S_t represents Sun Belt's monthly sales (in millions of dollars), and $t = 1$ in January 2003. The monthly seasonal indexes are as follows:

January	60	April	110	July	90	October	110
February	70	May	110	August	80	November	140
March	85	June	100	September	95	December	150

Forecast monthly sales for the year 2008.

10. The MNO Corporation is preparing for its stockholder meeting on May 15, 2008. It sent out proxies to its stockholders on March 15 and asked stockholders who plan to attend the meeting to respond. To plan for a sufficient number of information packages to be distributed at the meeting, as well as for refreshments to be served, the company has asked you to forecast the number of attending stockholders. By April 15, 378 stockholders have expressed their intention to attend. You have available the following data for the last 6 years for total attendance at the stockholder meeting and the number of positive responses as of April 15:

Year	Positive Responses	Attendance
2002	322	520
2003	301	550
2004	398	570
2005	421	600
2006	357	570
2007	452	650

   a. What is your attendance forecast for the 2008 stockholder meeting?
   b. Are there any other factors that could affect attendance, and thus make your forecast inaccurate?

11. In the Columbia Gas of Ohio study that forecasted the demand for gas (see p. 165), the company developed the following coefficients for their equation:

Growth rate	.015
Intercept	1376.0
Forecasted temperature	−17.1
Prior day temperature	−3.7
Forecasted wind speed	4.2

Forecast the demand for gas for a day, when the expected average temperature will be 40 degrees, the prior day's average temperature was 37, and the average wind speed is predicted to be 8 miles per hour.

The Demand for White Zinfandel in Los Angeles

Stephen Erfle, Dickinson College[46]

This appendix provides a demand analysis using actual data on consumer purchases for specific types of wine. The appendix has three parts. First, the analysis and results are discussed without specific reference to how those results were obtained. Next, we show how the analysis is performed in Excel. Finally, extensions to the analysis are suggested using the data provided.

An Analysis of the Demand for White Zinfandel

As noted in chapter 5, the data obtained from companies like ACNielsen and Information Resources, Inc. (IRI) are highly proprietary in nature. Fortunately, the author of this section was given permission by IRI to use selected historical data on the wine industry extracted from its InfoScan Reviews. InfoScan data is provided using 4-week time periods (13 periods per year). For this analysis, we shall track sales in five wine categories (or types) over 52 time periods from 1996 to 1999 in the Los Angeles food market. Five statistics are given for each observation: dollar sales; volume sales; unit sales; average price per unit; and all commodity value (ACV) weighted distribution. Unit sales counts the number of bottles sold, regardless of bottle size. Volume sales is equivalized on 9-liter cases. Readers can download the data from this textbook's Web site.

Ideally, we would like to calculate demand for a specific wine, for example, Mumm Cuvee Napa, Brut Prestige. Such an analysis would include information regarding Mumm's substitutes such as Domaine Chandon and Piper Sonoma. We could easily accomplish this task with the more detailed data that is available (for a fee) from IRI (indeed,

the author has done exactly that analysis for Seagram). The data used in this appendix are more aggregated—information is provided on grape varieties, not specific brands of those varieties. Given aggregated data, the most effective demand analysis will occur for the variety that is most homogeneous. White zinfandel fits the bill. Simply put, there is not much price or perceived quality dispersion between various brands of white zinfandel. Producers of white zinfandel may dispute this but greater quality and price dispersion exists for the other three grape varieties. White zinfandel is most like a commodity.

As can be seen in Figure 5A.1, unit sales of white zinfandel, Q, are flat across the four-year sample provided by IRI. Each year has a noticeable peak during the Thanksgiving and Christmas holidays (the 12th and 13th time periods) each year. The four price series in Figure 5A.2 depict an interesting pattern. All four price series exhibit an upward trend but the prices for three of the varietals (chardonnay, cabernet sauvignon, and merlot) peak during the holidays. The same is *not* true of white zinfandel, where there is actually a noticeable dip in price during the holidays.

The scatterplot in Figure 5A.3 depicts an inverse relation between price and quantity for white zinfandel. The data "cloud" has a central core with peak observations to the right. As noted in chapter 4, two functional forms are readily available: linear and constant elasticity. Both forms produce reasonable estimates, but the fit is better and coefficient interpretation is easier for the constant elasticity demand (CED) form. (This superior fit is not surprising if you consider the CED function depicted in figure 4.1a of the previous chapter. This curve fits the data depicted in figure 5A.3 nicely.)

A line fit plot from a preliminary regression is provided in order to emphasize the point described in Figure 4.1. The CED *curve* in (Q,P) space in Figure 4.1a is *linear* in (Ln(Q), Ln(P)) space in

---

[46]The authors are grateful to Professor Erfle for writing this appendix for this edition.

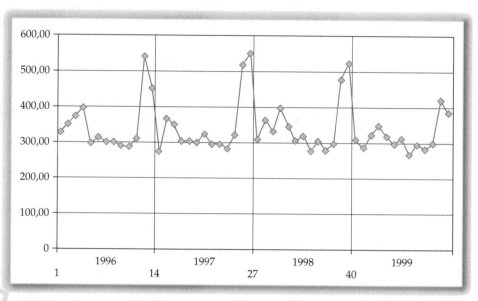

Figure 5A.1   Unit Sales of White Zinfandel in Los Angeles

4-weekly observations, 1996–1999, 52 observations total. Time = 1 to 52.

Figure 5A.2   Price of White Zinfandel, Chardonnay, Cabernet Sauvignon, and Merlot

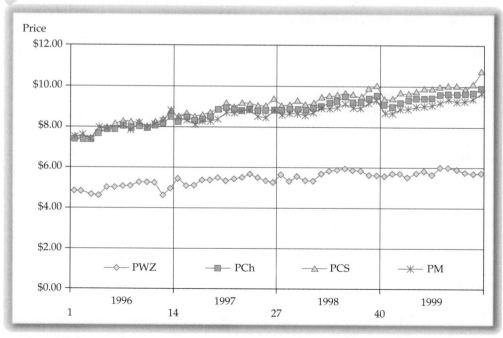

4-weekly observations, 1996–1999, 52 observations total. Time = 1 to 52.

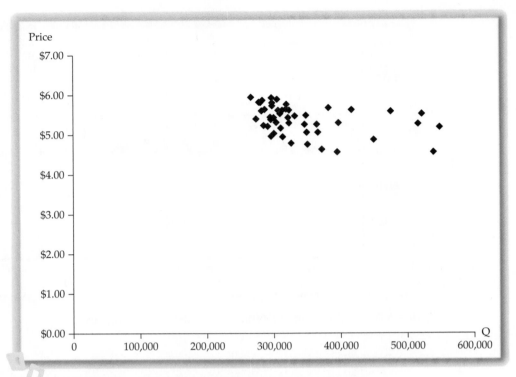

Figure 5A.3 Unit Sales of White Zinfandel in Los Angeles

Figure 4.1*b*. This linearity allows for estimation using regression analysis. This preliminary regression is:

$$\text{Ln}(Q_{WZ}) = 14.038 - 0.819 \cdot \text{Ln}(P_{WZ}) + 0.409 \cdot \text{Peak}$$
$$R^2 = 0.797, \text{SEE} = 0.084$$

Peak is a dummy variable that equals 1 during the 12th and 13th time periods each year, otherwise it equals zero. Each coefficient is significantly different from zero, and this regression explains nearly 80 percent of the variance in white zinfandel sales over this period. The line fit plot from this regression is shown in Figure 5A.4. This shows two lines of Predicted $\text{Ln}(Q_{WZ})$ squares in $(\text{Ln}(Q), \text{Ln}(P))$ space—as expected, given that a dummy variable has been added to a univariate equation. Peak sales are approximately 50 percent higher than off-peak sales, all else held constant.[47] The inner line is predicted off-peak sales and the outer line is predicted peak

sales. This simplified model is *not* the preferred model but is provided to help explain the linearity inherent in CED functions in the log-log format. Line fit plots for the preferred models are also linear but this linearity is obscured in two-dimensional diagrams.

Various equations are estimated based on the presence of various cross-price series in the model. Each has the form:

$$\text{Ln}(Q_{WZ}) = a + b \cdot \text{Ln}(P_{WZ}) + c \cdot \text{Ln}(P_{\text{OtherWine}})$$
$$+ d \cdot \text{Time} + e \cdot \text{Peak}$$

Time takes on values from 1 to 52. Each regression includes the price of white zinfandel because the good's own price must be included in any demand analysis. Coefficients and t statistics for each of the eight models are provided together with adjusted R^2 and standard error of estimates in Table 5A.1. Each price coefficient in the log-log demand equation is a price elasticity of demand. The coefficient b is the own-price elasticity of demand and the c coefficients are cross-price elasticities. The regressions are grouped according to how many cross-price independent variables are included in the model. Before

---

[47]This can be seen in Figure 5A.1, where off-peak sales are on the order of 300K units per period and peak sales are about 450K units per period. The factor of proportionality is given by $e^{\text{Peak coefficient}} - 1$. In this regression, that factor of proportionality is $50.6\% = e^{0.409} - 1$.

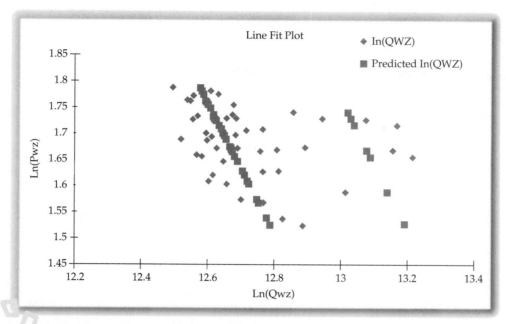

Figure 5A.4 Preliminary CED Line Fit Plot

discussing the cross-price effects, it is worth noting the consistency of results provided by the independent variables common to all of the models.

Model A expands on the preliminary regression discussed above by including a time counter to test for trend. The coefficient of time, $d = 0.0051$, implies an annual growth rate of 6.8 percent per year, all else held constant.[48] The other models imply annual growth between 1.7 percent and 6.2 percent. The t statistic for the coefficient of time in each model suggests that sales of white zinfandel are flat—the trend that is apparent in Model A is due to the lack of cross-price information in that model. In all specifications, demand for white zinfandel is elastic with own-price elasticity (coefficient b) ranging from -1.82 to -2.36. The 95 percent confidence interval on a coefficient represents that range of values over which that individual coefficient is likely to occur. The 95 percent confidence interval on b represents the range of likely values of own-price

elasticity. In each model, this 95 percent confidence interval does not include -1, so we are confident in our belief that demand for white zinfandel is elastic.[49] Peak demand is approximately 40 percent higher than off-peak demand in each specification (coefficient e). The range of proportional increases is 38 percent to 43 percent (38 percent $= e^{0.32} - 1$ and 43 percent $= e^{0.36} - 1$).

Models B–D include a single cross-price independent variable. All three have positive coefficients for c, meaning that all are substitutes for white zinfandel. Model B is the best of the group because of the highest t statistic on the cross-price variable, highest adjusted R^2, and lowest standard error of estimate. This result is also reasonable from a market perspective—chardonnay is a white wine, and it is reasonable to assume that it would be a closer substitute for white zinfandel than either cabernet sauvignon or merlot, which are both red wines.

---

[48]If Y is time series data with n time periods per year, you can find the annual growth rate of Y using a regression model with ln(Y) as the dependent variable and time as an independent variable. The annual growth rate in this instance is g = $(e^{\text{coefficient of time}})^n - 1$. In this instance, 6.8% = $(e^{0.0051})^{13} - 1$. The coefficient of time is often called the *periodic growth rate*.

[49]Were we to have brand-based demand for white zinfandel data (for example, the demand for Sutter Home white zinfandel as a function of both Sutter Home's price and Beringer's white zinfandel price), the resulting demand elasticity would be even more elastic. The 95 percent confidence interval on b is in cells **F18:G18** on each regression worksheet in Excel.

Table 5A.1 Constant Elasticity Demand Functions: Unit Sales of White Zinfandel in Los Angeles

i Model		Intercept a	Ln(P_{WZ}) b	Ln(P_{Ch}) c_{Ch}	Ln(P_{CS}) c_{CS}	Ln(P_M) c_M	Time[ii] d	Peak e	Adj. R^2	SEE
A	Coef.	15.60	−1.82				0.0051	0.36	0.823	0.077
	t Stat	28.13	−5.21				3.22	10.64		
B	Coef.	14.10	−2.36	1.16			0.0016	0.32	0.833	0.075
	t Stat	15.34	−5.44	2.00			0.71	8.52		
C	Coef.	14.78	−2.10		0.62		0.0029	0.33	0.824	0.077
	t Stat	16.58	−4.94		1.17		1.19	7.75		
D	Coef.	15.31	−1.89			0.20	0.0046	0.35	0.819	0.078
	t Stat	15.08	−4.57			0.34	2.30	8.33		
E	Coef.	14.19	−2.34	2.06	−0.95		0.0023	0.34	0.833	0.075
	t Stat	15.35	−5.40	1.87	−0.97		0.95	8.13		
F	Coef.	14.80	−2.36	2.42		−1.60	0.0013	0.35	0.842	0.073
	t Stat	15.29	−5.58	2.77		−1.89	0.58	8.84		
G	Coef.	15.22	−2.07		1.26	−0.88	0.0025	0.33	0.824	0.077
	t Stat	15.13	−4.85		1.46	−0.94	1.03	7.80		
H	Coef.	14.78	−2.35	2.60	−0.26	−1.51	0.0015	0.35	0.838	0.074
	t Stat	15.07	−5.51	2.29	−0.25	−1.61	0.63	8.42		

i. The dependent variable in each model is Ln(unit sales of white zinfandel in L.A.).

ii. 4-weekly observations, 1996–1999, 52 observations total. Time = 1 to 52. Peak is the 12th and 13th time period each year (i.e., Thanksgiving and Christmas).

Models E–G include two cross-price independent variables. In this instance, one acts as a substitute and the other acts as a complement to white zinfandel, but only in model F are both statistically significant (merlot is significant at the 10 percent level). Model F is the best specification in Table 5A.1; it has the highest adjusted R^2 and lowest standard error of estimate of all regressions in the table. Chardonnay is a substitute and merlot is a complement to white zinfandel in this specification.

The final specification, model H, includes three cross-prices as well as the price of white zinfandel. Comparing models F and G with H provides a nice example of the multicollinearity problem. As is visually clear from Figure 5A.2, chardonnay, cabernet sauvignon, and merlot prices track one another quite closely. This is especially apparent during peak periods as noted above. This is confirmed by the correlations provided in Table 5A.2. Chardonnay, cabernet sauvignon, and merlot are all highly collinear with correlation coefficients between 0.975 and 0.988. These prices are also correlated with white zinfandel prices, but the correlation is not as high. Putting highly correlated

independent variables in a regression model produces the multicollinearity problem discussed in chapter 5. Estimated coefficients vary in magnitude and lose significance relative to models where fewer collinear variables are included. Notice, for instance, that cabernet sauvignon's coefficient changes sign between G and H due to the addition of pricing information on chardonnay. Put another way, the introduction of cabernet pricing in moving from F to H involves both chardonnay and merlot coefficients becoming less significant (reduced t statistics). Even though H uses more explanatory variables, it does a less accurate job of prediction as signified by the lower adjusted R^2 and higher SEE of H relative to F. In conclusion, F is the preferred model of demand for white zinfandel given the data available to us from IRI.

Using Excel to Perform the Regression Analysis

A number of available statistical software packages such as SPSS and SAS can be used to perform regression analysis. In this section, we demonstrate

Table 5A.2   Correlation Matrix of Wine Prices in Los Angeles

	P_{WZ}	P_{Ch}	P_{CS}	P_M
$P_{\text{white zinfandel}}$	1			
$P_{\text{chardonnay}}$	0.891	1		
$P_{\text{cabernet sauvignon}}$	0.862	0.988	1	
P_{merlot}	0.841	0.975	0.981	1

how the most readily available generic software package, Excel, can also be used for this same task. The data used to perform this analysis are located in the **Data** worksheet to the **Appendix5.xls** file on this textbook's Web site. Five columns of data are provided for each of the five wine types—table wine, cabernet sauvignon (CS), chardonnay (Ch), merlot (M), and white zinfandel (WZ). As noted above, we focus on a comparison of unit sales and price. When performing regression analyses, it is convenient to create a separate worksheet that contains the regression data. This worksheet is called **DataReg.** (In this section of the appendix, **boldfaced** characters refer to Excel names or commands and *italic* characters refer to information (labels, numbers, or equations) you will need to type into cells. *Italics* are also used when *clicking* or *dragging* is required.)

If you want to try doing this analysis yourself, open your own blank document (by *clicking* the **New Blank Document** icon on the **Standard** toolbar), then try to create a file that looks like **Appendix5.xls.** Copy the entire **Data** worksheet to the new workbook by opening a new file, then going back to **Appendix5.xls** to the **Data** worksheet. Highlight the entire worksheet by *clicking* above the **1** and to the left of the **A** in the upper left corner of the spreadsheet. Once this is highlighted, *click* the **Copy** icon on the **Standard** toolbar. Move to the new worksheet, *click* on cell **A1,** and then *click* **Paste.**[50] Copy individual series using the same strategy: Highlight individual columns on the **Data** worksheet by *clicking* the column label (i.e., the **A** or **B**), then paste to columns on the **DataReg**

worksheet. The five IRI series used to produce the above analysis are copied from columns **L, R, X, AC,** and **AD** of the **Data** worksheet to columns **L:P** on **DataReg.** (Note: A group of rows, columns or cells is denoted using a colon.) The order of columns (variables) has been reorganized so that quantity is first (unit sales of WZ) in column **L,** followed by the prices of WZ, Ch, CS, and M.

Figures are easy to create in Excel using the **Chart Wizard** found on the **Standard** toolbar. (Note that copies of Figures 5A.1–3 are in **A2:AP67** on the **DataReg** worksheet.) For example, to create Figure 5A.1, highlight cells **L1:L53,** then *click* **Chart Wizard.** The **Chart Wizard popup menu** appears on the screen. Choose **Line Chart type** and maintain the **Chart sub-type** suggested (this is the **Line with markers displayed for each data value** subtype). *Click* **Press and Hold to View Sample** at the bottom of the popup menu to see a file that looks similar to Figure 5A.1. (When creating any figure in Excel, it is easy to check to see what you are getting by using this view sample feature.) *Click* **Finish** to obtain a copy that can be further formatted as required. (We will not focus on formatting issues in this appendix.) A similar process produces Figure 5A.2 simply by highlighting **M1:P53** prior to using the **Chart Wizard.** Figure 5A.3 is produced by highlighting **L1:M53,** then using the **XY (Scatter) Chart type.** When creating scatterplots, the order of the series matters. Note that column **L** contains Q_{WZ} and **M** contains P_{WZ}, therefore the resulting scatterplot has the standard (Q, P) orientation used to describe demand.

The regressions that form the core of this analysis require a time counter as well as a dummy variable that is turned on during the 12th and 13th periods each year (recall that IRI uses 4-week time periods rather than months for each observation— the exact timing of these observations is given in column **A** of the **Data** worksheet). The CED regressions also use logarithms of price and quantity rather than P and Q. Each of these variables is easily created in Excel.

---

[50]In some versions of Excel, you may see ###### in some cells after copying. This simply means that columns have not been formatted with sufficient width. To reformat column widths (or row heights) move the mouse to the right column boundary that you wish to change at the column icon (for example, if you wish to widen **A** move to the **A/B** boundary between the letters **A** and **B**) until you see a **double arrow with bar,** *click,* and move to adjust the width as necessary.

To create a time counter (like the one in column **E**), type *Time* in **E1,** then type *1* in **E2** and *2* in **E3.** Then highlight **E2:E3** by *clicking* on **E2** and holding down the mouse and moving to **E3** (with the open white + sign showing). Lift the mouse and move to the lower right corner of cell **E3.** Once a black + sign without arrows appears, *click* and *drag* to **E53.** All *dragging* in Excel uses the black + sign. By contrast, if the + sign has arrows, then *dragging* will move the cell (or group of cells) rather than replicate the pattern.

The Peak dummy variable in column **F** is created by doing one year's worth of the series, then simply replicating what was done. Type *Peak* in **F1** and *0* in **F2.** *Drag* the zero down to cell **F12** (next to the 11 in **E12**). Type *1* in **F13** and **F14.** This is a full year of the dummy variable, Peak. From here, *click* on cell **F15,** type = *F2,* and press *Enter* to replicate the pattern. Notice that a 0 appears in cell **F15** even though it is based on an equation rather than a number entered from the keyboard. *Click* on cell **F15** and *drag* it to **F53.** Once you release the mouse, you will have a variable that takes on the value 0 in periods 1–11 and 1 in periods 12 and 13 for all four years.

The dependent variable, $Ln(Q_{WZ})$, is the natural logarithm of unit sales of white zinfandel. Type the label in **A1,** then in cell **A2** type the equation = *ln(L2)* and press *Enter. Click* on **A2** and *drag* to **A53** to create this series. Do the same to create logarithmic versions of each of the price series.

You are now ready to run a regression. Excel requires that all independent variables be contiguous, therefore you will have to move series each time you wish to run a different regression. Each regression shown uses the same dependent variable, $Ln(Q_{WZ})$, but the independent variables vary from model to model. The **DataReg** worksheet is set up ready to run the preferred model, F. This model is shown on worksheet **CED F.** To create this regression yourself, start from the **DataReg** worksheet and *click* on the **Tools** dropdown menu, then *click* **Data Analysis.**[51] Once you click **Data Analysis,** the **Data Analysis popup menu** appears. Scroll down to **Regression** and *click* **Regression,** then *click* **OK.** The **Regression popup menu** appears. This menu allows you to describe what you want in the regression.

Regression requires you to identify the dependent and independent variables. The dependent variable is what you are trying to explain, and the independent variables are what you are using to explain the dependent variable. Unfortunately, Excel calls these concepts **Y range** and **X range** rather than dependent and independent variables. In "Excel speak," **Y range** is the dependent variable and **X range** is the independent variable(s).[52] If you are wondering why this matters, it is because economists are exactly backwards with respect to the most basic geometric models. Demand is quantity as a function of price—quantity is the dependent variable but it is on the X axis (and price is the independent variable despite being on the Y axis). With that said, *click* on the **Input Y range** area and highlight **A1:A53.** Next, *click* on the **Input X range** area and highlight **B1:F53.** *Click* **Labels.** (Always use **Labels,** otherwise the regression will be difficult to decipher because it will call the independent variables X variable 1, X variable 2, etc.) I have also clicked **Residuals, Residual Plots,** and **Line Fit Plots** but that is not necessarily required.[53] *Click* **OK** and the regression is provided in a new worksheet.

All of the regressions in Table 5A.1 as well as the preliminary regression are obtained by simply adjusting the independent variables that are included in the **Input X range** of the regression model. Each time you adjust the independent variables to create a new model you must follow one rule—the independent variables must be contiguous. You cannot reference series one at a time that you wish to include in the set of independent variables. For example, suppose you want to run the model that includes all three "other" prices (model H) and you wish to have them in the order shown in Table 5A.1. In this instance, you must insert $Ln(P_{CS})$ between the prices of chardonnay and merlot (in columns **C** and **D**). To accomplish this you can simply move columns **D:F** over one column by highlighting all three columns (*click* on the

---

[51]If **Data Analysis** is not available, *click* **Add-Ins,** then *click* **Analysis ToolPak** and **Analysis ToolPak—VBA,** then *click* **OK. Data Analysis** should now be available from the **Tools** dropdown menu. (If it is not, **Save** the file you have been working on Quit Excel, then open Excel. **Data Analysis** will now be available.)

[52]Only one dependent variable is allowed in regression analysis (the **Input Y Range** must be univariate) but multiple independent variables are allowed (the **Input X Range** may be multivariate) in regression analysis.

[53]**Residuals** is useful to *click* even if you do not plan to use residuals because it is one of the few places on Excel's regression output where the dependent variable is listed. In this instance this is not much of an issue because there is only one dependent variable for all of the regressions, but often this will not be the case. To see where Excel "hides" this important information, see, for example, cell **B28** on worksheet **CED F.** The other place where this information is available is on the **Line Fit Plots.**

D at the top of the spreadsheet, then hold the mouse down until it runs over **E** and **F** as well). Once all three columns are highlighted, they can be moved by moving the mouse to the right edge of column **G** until you see a large open diagonal white arrow pointing at a black + with arrows. *Click* and hold down the mouse, then *drag* all three columns one to the right (so that column **D** is now empty). Next *click* on column **J** and move it into column **D** using the same technique you just used on the other columns. When you run this regression, you need not redo the entire **Regression popup menu**— you need only change the *F* to a *G* in the **Input X range,** then *click* **OK.** This strategy streamlines running multiple regression models.

The nine regressions described above are shown on separate worksheets labeled **CEDPreliminary** and **CED A—CED H.** (To change a worksheet name—from **Sheet #**—simply *double click* on the tab and type the new name.) Figure 5A.4 is a **Line Fit Plot** from the **CEDPreliminary** worksheet, but it is worth noting that the axes have been reversed (by changing some of the **Source Data** within the **Chart Wizard**) so that it has the standard orientation expected of a demand curve in (Q,P) space rather than (P,Q) space.[54] Of course, the Ps and Qs are actually Ln(P)s and Ln(Q)s. All of the **Line Fit Plots** on other worksheets have not been reversed—in each, the vertical axis is the dependent variable: $Ln(Q_{WZ})$.

---

[54]To do this, **RIGHT** click on a chart you wish to change and a series of options emerge. The one used in this instance is **Source Data.** The X and Y values for both series must be switched on the **Series** tab.

Table 5A.1 is created by copying **Coefficient** and *t* **Statistic** information from each of the regression worksheets (starting in **B16** and **D16**) onto a new worksheet. This is accomplished in **B1:R8** of the **Table 5A.1** worksheet. Note that each regression has different cross-price information. As a result, take care to line up the data. For example, cells **C6:H6** are blank because the price of merlot is not included in models A–C. The regressions in **B1:R8** are oriented vertically (with two columns per regression) but Table 5A.1 depicts the regressions horizontally. To switch rows and columns, use **Copy, Paste Special** (from the **Edit** pulldown menu), **Transpose.** From here the completed table is easily obtained by adding further labels and formatting and by copying adjusted R^2 and SEE information from **B6:B7** of each worksheet to **J13:K27.**

The coefficient of Time and the Peak coefficient are interpreted in the text based on the information provided in Table 5A.1. That interpretation uses calculations described in the text and performed in cells **L13:M27.** It is worth noting that only two equations need to be entered into Excel (in **L13:M13**). *Drag* these equations to **L27:M27.** In the process, the even-numbered rows are nonsense (since they are based on exponentiated *t* statistics), but these rows can be quickly deleted, leaving calculations of relevant statistics for each regression in odd-numbered rows.

The final part of the analysis is the correlation matrix provided as Table 5A.2. This is easily obtained from the **DataReg** worksheet. Once on this worksheet, *click* **Tools, Data Analysis, Correlation.** *Click* on the **Input Range** area. Highlight **M1:P53** and *click* **Labels in First Row** and **OK.** The correlation matrix will appear on a new worksheet. This is easily formatted to look like Table 5A.2.

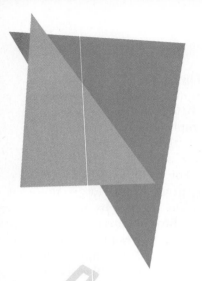

The Theory
and Estimation
of Production

Learning Objectives

Upon completion of this chapter, readers should be able to:

- Define the production function and explain the difference between a short-run and a long-run production function.

- Explain the "law of diminishing returns" and how it relates to the Three Stages of Production.

- Define the Three Stages of Production and explain why a rational firm always tries to operate in Stage II.

- Provide examples of types of inputs that might go into a production function for a manufacturing company and for a service company.

- Describe the various forms of a production function that are used in the statistical estimation of these functions.

- Briefly describe the Cobb-Douglas function and cite a few statistical studies that used this particular functional form in their analysis.

- (Appendix 6A) Discuss the key differences between productivity in the production of goods vs. productivity in the production of services, and list important factors that can help to improve productivity in services.

- (Appendix 6B) Describe isoquant and isocost curves and explain how the tangency of these curves help to determine the optimal combination of inputs for a firm to utilize.

- (Appendix 6C) Use the tools of calculus to determine a firm's optimal combination inputs.

The Situation

The meeting of Global Foods' top production managers must have been important because it was attended by CEO Bob Burns as well as by Jim Hartwell, vice president of manufacturing. Its purpose was to go over the plans for rolling out the company's new bottled water product, "Waterpure." Christopher Lim, manager of the company's largest bottling plant, in St. Louis, Missouri, knew that this product was considered to be the hope of the sagging beverage division. He also suspected that there was going to be more than the usual plans for the bottling operation because of the additional presence of Nicole Goodman, senior VP of marketing.

(continued)

(continued)

The meeting began with a few opening remarks by the CEO about the phenomenal growth of the bottled water industry and how and why Global Foods hoped to get into this market. Chris noticed that all but a few of the 15 people at the meeting had their own bottle of water in front of them and thought that this more than any other statistic made the point. Then came the surprise. The opening presentation was given by the senior VP of marketing, not manufacturing.

Nicole Goodman began to make a compelling case for a radical change in the packaging of this product. "You all have seen how Coca-Cola has spent millions of dollars in advertising and packaging in order to focus on the shape of its original glass bottle and how Pepsi-Cola recently changed the look of its label and logo. But packaging can be considered even more important in the market for bottled water, because after all what are we selling?

"What I propose is that we combine the tradition of Coca-Cola with the design innovation of Pepsi-Cola and a French company that makes another beverage called Orangina to create our own distinct packaging. We propose to sell our water in a green glass bottle shaped like a bottle of champagne. To go along with this packaging, we intend to advertise our product as the 'champagne of bottled water.'"

"How original," thought Chris. "I seem to recall that some time ago a beer company used a similar tag line in their advertising. But forget the advertising, doesn't she realize how expensive it is to use glass rather than plastic? There has to be a reason why both Coke and Pepsi don't use glass for most of their bottling, particularly here in the States."

As if in anticipation of Chris's negative thoughts, Nicole continued by saying, "I know some of you might be thinking that this champagne idea is not very original. But our market research indicates that people between the ages of 15 and 35 are the key consumers of bottled water, and so most of our potential customers will be too young to remember that Miller beer commercial. We in marketing realize that it will be you in manufacturing that will actually implement our 'creative' ideas. We know that this will present some interesting production challenges in terms of the setup of the fill lines, the stacking of the cases for shipment and delivery, and so on. But I know you're up to the challenge. We want to begin a pilot program in one of our bottling plants. In consulting with both Bob and Jim, they both recommended strongly that we begin with our bottling plant in St. Louis. Chris, we want you to put together a plan for rolling out our new product in the next quarter."

THE PRODUCTION FUNCTION

Christopher Lim's concerns are certainly justified. No matter how much revenue is generated by the marketing plan, if the cost of production cannot be contained, the company will not be able to earn an acceptable level of profit. In economics, the analysis of cost begins with the study of the production function. The **production function** is a statement of the relationship between a firm's scarce resources (i.e., its **inputs**) and the output that results from the use of these resources. Economic cost analysis can then be seen as the application of a monetary unit such as dollars to measure the value of this input usage in the production process. Therefore, both this chapter on production and the following chapter on cost really deal with the same general topic of economic cost analysis. Because of the length and complexity of this topic, we have divided its presentation into two separate chapters.

In mathematical terms, the production function can be expressed as:

$$Q = f(X_1, X_2 \ldots \ldots X_k)$$

where Q = Output
$X_1 \ldots \ldots X_k$ = Inputs used in the production process

Note that we assume this relationship between inputs and output exists for a specific period of time. In other words, Q is *not* a measure of accumulated output over time. There are two other key assumptions that you should be aware of. First, we are assuming some given "state of the art" in the production technology. Any innovation in production (e.g., the use of robotics in manufacturing or a more efficient software package for financial analysis) would cause the relationship between given inputs and their output to change. Second, we are assuming whatever input or input combinations are included in a particular function, the output resulting from their utilization is at the maximum level. With this in mind, we can offer a more complete definition of a production function:

> A production function defines the relationship between inputs and the maximum amount that can be produced within a given period of time with a given level of technology.

For Christopher's company, the Xs could represent raw materials, such as carbonated water, sweeteners, and flavorings; labor, such as assembly line workers, support staff, and supervisory personnel; and fixed assets, such as plant and equipment.

For purposes of analysis, let us reduce the whole array of inputs in the production function to two, X and Y. Restating Equation (6.1) gives us

$$Q = f(X, Y)$$

where Q = Output
X = Labor
Y = Capital

Notice that although we have designated one variable as labor and the other as capital, we have elected to keep the all-purpose symbols X and Y as a reminder that any two inputs could have been selected to represent the array.

As stated earlier, in economic analysis the distinction between the short run and the long run is not related to any particular measurement of time (e.g., days, months, or years). Instead it refers to the extent to which a firm can vary the amounts of the inputs in its production process. Thus, a **short-run production function** shows the maximum quantity of a good or service that can be produced by a set of inputs, assuming the amount of at least one of the inputs used remains unchanged. A **long-run production function** shows the maximum quantity of a good or service that can be produced by a set of inputs, assuming the firm is free to vary the amount of *all* the inputs being used.

A hypothetical production function with two inputs is displayed in Table 6.1. The numbers in the matrix indicate the amount of output that would result from various combinations of X and Y. For example, the use of 2 units of X and 2 units of Y yields 18 units of output. Adding one more unit of X while holding constant the

Table 6.1 Representative Production Table

Units of Y Employed	Output Quantity (Q)							
8	37	60	83	96	107	117	127	128
7	42	64	78	90	101	110	119	120
6	37	52	64	73	82	90	97	104
5	31	47	58	67	75	82	89	95
4	24	39	52	60	67	73	79	85
3	17	29	41	52	58	64	69	73
2	8	18	29	39	47	52	56	52
1	4	8	14	20	27	24	21	17
	1	2	3	4	5	6	7	8
				Units of X Employed				

amount of Y yields an additional 11 units of output ($Q = 29$). Increasing both X and Y by 1 unit yields 41 units of output. The additional 1 unit of X with Y unchanged is considered to be a "short-run" change. An increase in both inputs by 1 unit is a "long-run" change.

A SHORT-RUN ANALYSIS OF TOTAL, AVERAGE, AND MARGINAL PRODUCT

Before we go on to a more detailed analysis of the production function, certain key terms employed throughout this chapter should be clarified. First, economists use a number of alternative terms in reference to inputs and output:

Inputs	Output
Factors	Quantity (Q)
Factors of production	Total product (TP)
Resources	Product

Second, in the short-run analysis of the production function, two other terms besides the quantity of output are important measures of the outcome. They are **marginal product (MP)** and **average product (AP)**. If we assume X to be the variable input, then

$$\text{Marginal product of } X = MP_X = \frac{\Delta Q}{\Delta X}, \text{ holding } Y \text{ constant}$$

$$\text{Average product of } X = AP_X = \frac{Q}{X}, \text{ holding } Y \text{ constant}$$

In other words, the marginal product can be defined as the change in output or **total product** resulting from a unit change in a variable input, and the average product can be defined as the total product (TP) per unit of input used.

The data in Table 6.2 shows a short-run production function. Here we see what happens to output when increasing amounts of input X are added to a fixed amount of input Y ($Y = 2$). Table 6.3 restates this information by focusing on the impact on TP, MP, and AP resulting from increases in X, while holding Y constant at 2 units.

Table 6.2 Short-Run Changes in Production Showing Factor Productivity

Units of Y Employed	Output Quantity (Q)							
8	37	60	83	96	107	117	127	128
7	42	64	78	90	101	110	119	120
6	37	52	64	73	82	90	97	104
5	31	47	58	67	75	82	89	95
4	24	39	52	60	67	73	79	85
3	17	29	41	52	58	64	69	73
2	(8)	(18)	(29)	(39)	(47)	(52)	(56)	(52)
1	4	8	14	20	27	24	21	17
	1	2	3	4	5	6	7	8
	Units of X Employed							

Table 6.3   Short-Run Production Functions, Q, MP, AP

Variable Input (X)	Total Product (Q or TP)	Marginal Product (MP)	Average Product (AP)
0	0		
1	8	8	8
2	18	10	9
3	29	11	9.67
4	39	10	9.75
5	47	8	9.4
6	52	5	8.67
7	56	4	8
8	52	−4	6.5

The impact is also illustrated in the graphs in Figure 6.1. These tables and the figure indicate that the total product is 8 when 1 unit of X is used, it increases to a maximum of 56 when 7 units of X are used, and it decreases to 52 units when unit 8 of the X input is added. Also notice in Table 6.3 that MP begins at 8 units, increases to a maximum of 11, and falls off to an ultimate value of −4. Average product also begins at 8,

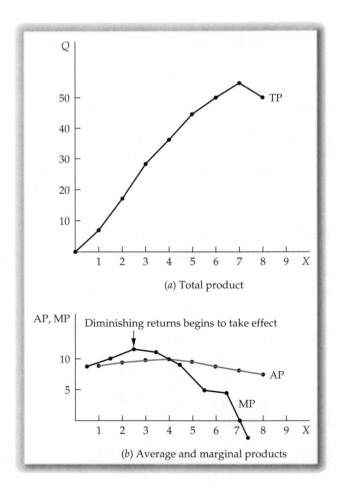

(a) Total product

(b) Average and marginal products

Figure 6.1   Short-Run Production with $Y = 2$

increases to a maximum of 9.75, and then drops to 6.5 units when 8 units of X are combined with the fixed amount of Y. The pattern of these changes can be seen in Figure 6.1. The total product is plotted in Figure 6.1a, and the average and marginal products are plotted in Figure 6.1b.

We can observe that when Q, the quantity of the total product, reaches its maximum, MP = 0. We see also that initially (as more units of X are added to the production process), MP is greater than AP, and it then becomes less than AP. Furthermore, MP = AP at AP's highest point. Because we are dealing with incremental unit changes in the input, it is difficult to see these points in Table 6.3, but they can be seen clearly in Figure 6.1. In the next section, we have more to say about the pattern of change in Q, AP, and MP and, more important, the reasons for the pattern of change.

The Law of Diminishing Returns

The key to understanding the pattern of change in Q, AP, and MP is the phenomenon known as the **law of diminishing returns**. This law states:

> As additional units of a variable input are combined with a fixed input, at some point the additional output (i.e., marginal product) starts to diminish.

Diminishing returns are illustrated in both the numerical example in Table 6.3 and the graph of these same numbers in Figure 6.1. As you examine this information, think "change" as you see the word "marginal." Therefore, the "marginal product" of an input such as labor is the change in output resulting from an additional unit of input. Notice in Table 6.3 that we have placed the marginal product *between* each interval of input and the resulting output. For example, the marginal product of the first unit of input, 8, is placed between 0 and 1 input or between 0 and 8 units of output. Continuing on, we see that marginal product reaches its maximum of 11 between the second and third units of input. It is precisely at this point, 2.5 units of input, that we can say the law of diminishing returns will begin to take effect.[1]

In situations in which it would not be possible to consider intervals of less than one unit, it is necessary to approximate the point at which diminishing returns occurs. Suppose you were a manager who could actually measure and track your employees' marginal product. The first person's MP would be 8, the second one would be 10, and the third person's would be 11. It would be only on the addition of the fourth person that you would realize that the law of diminishing returns had occurred because this person's MP would be less than that of the previous worker. In summary we can say that, given the numbers in Table 6.3, the law of diminishing returns occurs in theory precisely at 2.5 units of input. In practice, a manager would have to add a fourth unit of labor in order to observe the law in action.

There are two key concerns of a practical nature that we advise readers to keep in mind when considering the impact of the law of diminishing returns in actual business situations. First, there is nothing in the law that states *when* diminishing returns will start to take effect. The law merely says that if additional units of a variable input are combined with a fixed input, *at some point*, the marginal product of the input will start to diminish. Therefore, it is reasonable to assume a manager will only discover the point of diminishing returns by experience and trial and error. Hindsight will be

---

[1]The idea that diminishing returns will occur at this point is based on an analysis using calculus, in which the first derivative of the total product function, marginal product, is set to zero. The amount of input that fulfills this condition is then considered the exact point at which marginal product is maximized and the law of diminishing returns will begin to take effect. See Appendix C at the end of this chapter for a complete explanation of this approach.

more valuable than foresight. Second, when economists first stated this law, they made some very restrictive assumptions about the nature of the variable inputs being used. Essentially, they assumed all inputs added to the production process were exactly the same in individual productivity. The only reason why a particular unit of an input's marginal product would be higher or lower than the others used was because of the order in which it was added to the production process.

Let us examine more closely the possible reasons for the occurrence of diminishing returns. Essentially, these reasons have to do with the physical limitations of the fixed input and the variable inputs that are added to this fixed input. Suppose we assume the numbers in Table 6.3 represent a simple manufacturing situation where the variable input is labor and the fixed input is the factory and its machinery. Suppose more labor is added to this fixed capital. Clearly when no workers are employed, TP or output is zero. The first worker produces 8 units. Thus, his MP is equal to 8 and his AP is also equal to 8. When two workers are used, their combined efforts yield a TP of 18. This implies that two people working together can produce more than the sum of their efforts working as separate individuals. (AP of one worker = 8 and AP of the two workers = 9.) Moreover, we see that the MP of the second worker is greater than that of the first (MP of second worker = 10, > MP of first worker = 8).

Because it is assumed in economic theory that each worker is equally productive, this must mean that the effect of teamwork and specialization enables additional workers to contribute more than those added previously to the production process, a phenomenon that we can refer to as "increasing returns." But as still more workers are added, there are fewer and fewer opportunities for increasing returns through specialization and teamwork and at some point additional workers result in diminishing returns. Eventually, there may be so many workers relative to the fixed capacity that they may start to interfere with each other's activities. In this case, the additional workers lead to negative marginal returns, causing the total product to decrease. We see this occurring in Table 6.3 when the eighth person is added to the production process. In this case, the old adage "too many cooks spoil the soup" seems to have been realized.

Economists who first thought about the law of diminishing returns relied primarily on deductive reasoning rather than empirical verification to explain the law's existence. It was critical for them to establish this law because it then helped explain the "Three Stages of Production" and the phenomenon of increasing marginal cost (explained in detail in chapter 7). Furthermore, when this law was established in the nineteenth century, the primary examples used to illustrate its impact on production involved agriculture, with land being the fixed factor of production, and farmers being the variable factors. At some point, it was reasoned, with a fixed amount of land, additional farm workers would result in diminishing amounts of additional harvested output.

To illustrate this law with more contemporary examples, we offer an example based on an actual situation involving a soft drink bottling facility. In addition, we provide two examples related to information technology.

The Sorting of Refillable Glass Bottles

In the early days of the soft drink industry, most drinks were packaged in returnable, refillable glass bottles. Now most drinks are packaged in plastic bottles or aluminum cans. But in some parts of the United States (particularly in Michigan) and in many parts of the rest of the world, returnable, refillable bottles are still used extensively.

There are three basic ways to sort and clean the returned bottles: (1) a totally automatic sorting system, (2) a totally manual sorting system, and (3) a hybrid system. The choice of system depends primarily on the anticipated volume of returned bottles. A typical manual sorting area is about 30 feet long, and there is usually no room in a plant for expansion. Each sorter requires about 3 feet of space in which to work. A conveyor carrying the returned empties runs along a wall and sorters work from one side of this conveyor.

The standard productivity measure used in a plant is "cases sorted per person-hour." If only one person is sorting bottles, he or she will not be able to keep up with the flow. The bottles tend to back up, and the system has to stop while the sorter tries to catch up.[2] In an interview with a bottling plant manager, the authors learned that typically two sorters per flavor are used.[3] Thus, if five flavors need to be sorted, ten people work at the conveyor belt. These ten sorters take up the maximum length of the sorting area (30 feet) if the recommended amount of 3 feet per person is allocated. The plant manager explained that if more than ten sorters are used, productivity tends to decrease because the workers start to get in each other's way. Although no quantitative detail was provided, we think that readers can well imagine that at this point, the law of diminishing returns would be starting to take effect, with each additional worker beyond ten sorting fewer returned bottles than the previously added worker.

> *Fixed input:* Machinery and working area square footage
>
> *Variable input:* People working as sorters

Development of Applications Software

Suppose you are the manager of a team of software engineers that is helping your company develop a new billing system. Suppose your project management plan calls for writing approximately 500 lines of program code every day to reach the objective. You have a team of five programmers each writing about 100 lines of code a day. To speed things up (as the deadline rapidly approaches), you decide to add more programmers to your team. You notice that the first additional person you add (the sixth member of the team) adds only 90 lines of code and the next person hired after that adds only 80 lines. Assuming the two additional programmers are equally skilled and work well as team members with the established group, you conclude that the law of diminishing returns must be at work.

> *Fixed input:* The programming language and the hardware used to develop the applications program
>
> *Variable input:* Software programmers

Response Time on a Data Network

You are a manager of a data communications network that is responsible for issuing approval codes for a credit card operation. After a credit card is swiped, the data are sent from the merchant's bank to the bank that issued the cardholder the card via the data communications network. The approval code comes back to the merchant within an average of 3 seconds. The merchants complain that this is too long. Software programmers are put to work to make the adjustments in software that will reduce the average to 2 seconds. Ten programmers working 10 hours a week for 2 weeks reduce the response time down to 2 seconds. Merchants continue to complain and want the average reduced further to 1 second. As the network manager, you try again with another ten programmers working the same amount of time as the previous

---

[2]Readers can imagine that this is very much what might happen in Stage I of the production process. (See next section for stages of production.)

[3]Interview with a former student of one of the authors, who used to work as a bottling plant manager for Pepsi-Cola.

addition of programmers. You find that the same additional time and effort does not yield the desired 1-second reduction in response time. You conclude that the law of diminishing returns is at work.

Fixed input: The technological infrastructure (i.e., the hardware and bandwidth of the transmission facilities of the physical network and the limits and capabilities of the software)

Variable input: Software programmers

In summary, these examples illustrate how diminishing returns can be caused by the physical limitations of fixed capital such as machinery and workspace, the technological limitations of computer hardware and software, and the personnel and management problems caused by increasing numbers of people working with a fixed capacity.

The Three Stages of Production in the Short Run

The short-run production function can be divided into three distinct **stages of production**. To illustrate this phenomenon, let us return to the data in Table 6.3 and Figure 6.1. For your convenience, Figure 6.1 has been reproduced as Figure 6.2. As the figure indicates, Stage I runs from zero to four units of the variable input X (i.e., to the point at which average product reaches its maximum). Stage II begins from this point

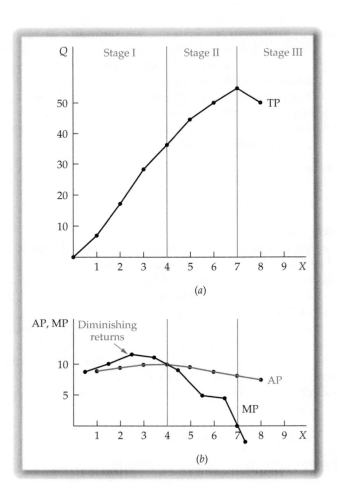

Figure 6.2 The Three Stages of Production

and proceeds to seven units of input X (i.e., to the point at which total product is maximized). Stage III continues on from that point. According to economic theory, in the short run, "rational" firms should only be operating in Stage II. It is clear why Stage III is irrational: The firm would be using more of its variable input to produce less output! However, it may not be as apparent why Stage I is also considered irrational. The reason is that if a firm were operating in stage I, it would be grossly underusing its fixed capacity. That is, it would have so much fixed capacity relative to its usage of variable inputs that it could increase the output per unit of variable input (i.e., average product) simply by adding more variable inputs to this capacity. Figure 6.3a summarizes the three stages of production and the reasons that the rational firm operates in Stage II of the short-run production function.

If you are still not clear about the irrational nature of Stage I, there is an alternative explanation. In Figure 6.3b, we have designated two levels of variable input usage: X_1 and X_2. Here we see that the average product is the same whether X_1 or X_2

Figure 6.3   Explanation of Production Stages

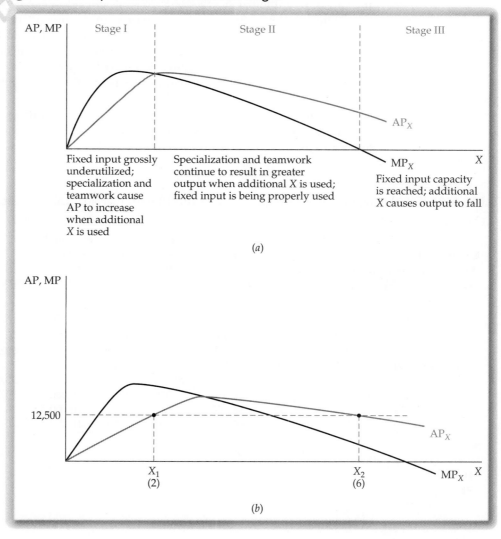

(a)

(b)

units of the variable input are used. If output per variable input is the same regardless of which input level is used, the firm should employ X_2 because the total product will be higher.

Module 6A
Module 6B
Module 6C

Derived Demand and the Optimal Level of Variable Input Usage

Given that a firm's short-run production has only one "rational" stage of production (i.e., Stage II), we must still determine the level of input usage within Stage II that is best for the rational, profit-maximizing firm. To demonstrate how we determine the optimal level of input usage within Stage II, we have created another numerical illustration, shown in Table 6.4. In this table, we observe that Stage II occurs from 60,000 to 80,000 units of total product. In terms of labor input, this Stage II ranges from four to eight units of input. But which level of output (or input) usage should we consider to be optimal? In answering this question, note that this table resembles the setup of a spreadsheet program, because MP is placed at the *same* level of output that results from an additional unit of input rather than *between* the two levels of output as shown in Table 6.3. In fact, we have provided you with an Excel exercise so you can experiment with your own variations of the example shown in Table 6.4.

The answer to this question is based on a concept introduced in chapter 4, derived demand. Recall that the demand for inputs is derived from the demand for their output. In other words, it would do no good for the firm to decide how many units of variable input to use without knowing how many units of output it could sell, the price of the product, and the monetary costs of employing various amounts of the X input.

To see exactly how this works, assume a firm is operating in a perfectly competitive market for its input and its output. That is, it can sell as many units of the product as it wants as long as it does so at the going market price. Moreover, it can hire as many

Table 6.4   Combining Marginal Revenue Product (MRP) with Marginal Labor Cost (MLC)

Labor Unit (X)	Total Product (Q or TP)	Average Product (AP)	Marginal Product (MP)	Total Revenue Product (TRP)	Marginal Revenue Product (MRP)	Total Labor Cost (TLC)	Marginal Labor Cost (MLC)	TRP – TLC	MRP – MLC
0	0		0	0		0		0	0
1	10,000	10,000	10,000	$ 20,000	$20,000	$10,000	$10,000	$10,000	$10,000
2	25,000	12,500	15,000	50,000	30,000	20,000	10,000	30,000	20,000
3	45,000	15,000	20,000	90,000	40,000	30,000	10,000	60,000	30,000
4	60,000	15,000	15,000	120,000	30,000	40,000	10,000	80,000	20,000
5	70,000	14,000	10,000	140,000	20,000	50,000	10,000	90,000	10,000
6	75,000	12,500	5,000	150,000	10,000	60,000	10,000	90,000	0
7	78,000	11,143	3,000	156,000	6,000	70,000	10,000	86,000	−4,000
8	80,000	10,000	2,000	160,000	4,000	80,000	10,000	80,000	−6,000

Note: P = Product price = $2
   W = Cost per unit of labor = $10,000
MRP = MP × P
TLC = X × W
MLC = ΔTLC/ΔX

X inputs as it desires as long as it pays these inputs the going market price (i.e., the competitive wage rate). Note that four new measures are added to Table 6.4:

Total revenue product (TRP): The market value of the firm's output, computed by multiplying the total product by the market price ($Q \times P$).

Marginal revenue product (MRP): The change in the firm's total revenue product resulting from a unit change in the number of inputs used ($\Delta TRP/\Delta X$). It can also be computed by multiplying the marginal product by the product price ($MP \times P$).

Total labor cost (TLC): The total cost of using the variable input, labor, computed by multiplying the wage rate (which we assume to be some given and constant dollar amount) by the number of variable inputs employed (Wage rate $\times X$).

Marginal labor cost (MLC): The change in total labor cost resulting from a unit change in the number of variable inputs used. Because the wage rate is assumed to be constant regardless of the number of inputs used, the MLC is the same as the wage rate.[4]

In deriving the figures for these measures in Table 6.4, we have assumed a product price of $2 and a wage rate of $10,000 per unit. Given these figures, you can see that a rational firm would want to hire 6 units of labor. Up to that point it pays for the firm to add more labor because the additional **marginal labor cost (MLC)** to the firm to do so is more than made up for by the additional **marginal revenue product (MRP)** brought in by the sale of the increased output. Beyond that point the firm would pay more in additional labor cost than it would receive in additional revenue.

Can you discern how the demand for the output is incorporated into this analysis, that is, how the demand for the input *X* is actually derived from the demand for the output? Suppose the market demand increased and drove the market price up to $4. This would increase the market value of the labor input's efforts. In other words, the market value of each additional labor unit's contribution to the total product would double. This increase in the labor input's MRP would then justify the firm's use of a seventh unit of labor. Thus, an increase in the market demand for the output leads to an increase in the demand by the firm for labor input, all other factors held constant. The original figures from Table 6.4, as well as the case in which market price is assumed to increase to $4, are illustrated in Figure 6.4.

We can summarize this relationship between the demand for the output and the demand for the input in terms of the following optimal decision rule:

A profit-maximizing firm operating in perfectly competitive output and input markets will be using the optimal amount of an input at the point at which the monetary value of the input's marginal product is equal to the additional cost of using that input—in other words, when **MRP = MLC**.

The Case of Multiple Inputs (Abridged Version)

This section presents a relatively nonquantitative explanation of optimal input decisions involving two or more inputs. For a complete treatment of multiple inputs using numerical tables, graphs, and algebraic equations, refer to Appendix 6B at the end of this chapter.

---

[4]This term is also referred to as *marginal resource cost* (MRC) and *marginal factor cost* (MFC). By assuming the firm hires workers in a perfectly competitive labor market, we also assume it can hire as many workers as it chooses at some going market wage rate determined by the supply and demand for this particular type of worker. This would not be the case if the firm were operating in an imperfectly competitive labor market. We do not consider the imperfectly competitive case in this text. Interested readers should consult any economics principles or intermediate microeconomics text for a full discussion on this type of labor market and its impact on the input decisions of the firm.

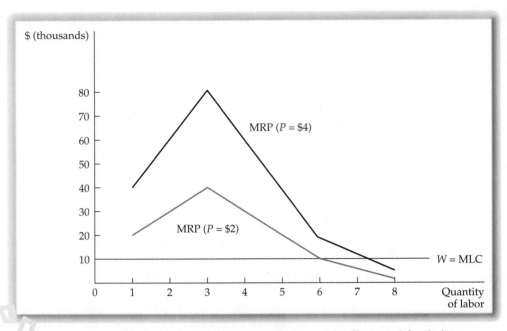

Figure 6.4   The Effect of Increased Market Price on the Demand for Labor

In the example illustrated in Table 6.4, we show how a firm could use the concept of equalizing at the margin to determine the optimal usage level of a single variable input. This same equalizing concept applies to a situation in which two or more inputs are being considered. In the multiple input case, we must consider the relationship between the *ratio* of the marginal product of one input and its cost to the *ratio* of the marginal product of the other input (inputs) and its (their) cost. Expressed mathematically for "*k*" inputs:

$$\frac{\text{MP}_1}{W_1} = \frac{\text{MP}_2}{W_2} = \frac{\text{M}_K}{W_K}$$

Let us consider the case of a global manufacturing company that has manufacturing facilities in two different countries: a high-wage country and a low-wage country. We can analyze this problem by treating labor in the high-wage country as one input and labor in the other country as another input. At first glance, it might seem obvious that a country seeking to minimize its costs and hence maximize its profits should try to manufacture as much as possible in the low-wage country. This would mean using mostly the low-wage labor input. But production theory suggests that the firm should not only look at input costs, but also the marginal products of each input *relative* to their respective costs.

Suppose you are the production manager of a company that makes computer parts and peripherals in Malaysia and Costa Rica. At the current levels of production and input utilization in the two countries, you find that:

Marginal product of labor in Malaysia (MP_{Mal}) = 18
Marginal product of labor in Costa Rica (MP_{CR}) = 6
Wage rate in Malaysia (W_{Mal}) = \$6/hr.
Wage rate in Costa Rica (W_{CR}) = \$3/hr.

How much would you produce in each manufacturing facility? Because labor is cheaper in Costa Rica, you might be tempted to produce most of your output in that country. However, a closer look at the MP:wage ratios reveals the opposite conclusion. That is,

$$\frac{\text{MP}_{\text{Mal}}}{W_{\text{Mal}}} > \frac{MP_{\text{CR}}}{W_{\text{CR}}} \text{ or } \frac{18}{\$6} > \frac{6}{\$3}$$

This means that at the margin, the last dollar spent on a unit of labor in Costa Rica would yield 2 units of output (6/$3), while in Malaysia the last dollar spent would result in 3 additional units of output (18/$6). This inequality implies that the firm should begin to shift more of its production away from Costa Rica to Malaysia, until the two ratios are equalized. In theory, this optimal or equilibrium point would occur because, as more labor is used in Malaysia, the law of diminishing returns would start to reduce the MP of labor in this country. With less labor being used in Costa Rica, the law of diminishing returns would work in reverse, causing the marginal product of labor in this country to rise. Of course, this assumes a short-run condition whereby the complementary fixed inputs used along with labor remain constant.[5]

Once the implication of the basic model is understood, other factors can be brought in. If these factors outweigh the MP-input cost criteria, a company may well modify its decision. For example, despite Malaysia's higher MP/wage ratio, there may be political and economic risk factors to consider. (This was indeed the case when the Malaysian government imposed foreign exchange controls in 1998 by requiring foreign investors to keep their profits in Malaysia for at least 1 year before they could be repatriated.) In contrast, Costa Rica is a fairly stable economy with leaders who do not seem to want to impose any such trade and finance restrictions. Its proximity to U.S. markets would also reduce transportation costs. Furthermore, it has a democratic government (with no standing army) and a highly skilled work force with strong English language skills.

THE LONG-RUN PRODUCTION FUNCTION

In the long run, a firm has time enough to change the amount of all its inputs. Thus, there is really no difference between fixed and variable inputs. Table 6.5 uses the data first presented in Table 6.1 and illustrates what happens to total output as both inputs X and Y increase 1 unit at a time. The resulting increase in the total output as the two inputs increase is called **returns to scale**.

Looking more closely at Table 6.5, we see for example that if the firm uses 1 unit of X and 1 unit of Y, it will produce 4 units of output. If it doubles its inputs (i.e., 2 units of X and 2 units of Y), it will produce 18 units of output. Thus, a doubling of inputs has produced more than a fourfold increase in output. Proceeding further, we notice that an additional doubling of inputs (i.e., 4 units of X and 4 units of Y) results in more than a threefold increase in output, from 18 to 60. What we are observing in this table is *increasing returns to scale*.

---

[5]Over time, there might be another factor causing the two ratios to begin to equalize. If there are enough companies that see this inequality, their combined increase in demand for labor in Malaysia may start to drive up the wage rate in this country, while a decrease in demand for labor in Costa Rica may slow the rate in increase in wage rates or even cause them to fall. Thus equalizing at the margin could take place because of changes in the values of the denominators of the ratios as well as the value of their numerators.

Table 6.5   Returns to Scale

Units of Y Employed	Output Quantity							
8	37	60	83	96	107	117	127	⦸128
7	42	64	78	90	101	110	⦸119	120
6	37	52	64	73	82	⦸90	97	104
5	31	47	58	67	⦸75	82	89	95
4	24	39	52	⦸60	67	73	79	85
3	17	29	⦸41	52	58	64	69	73
2	8	⦸18	29	39	47	52	56	52
1	⦸4	8	14	20	27	24	21	17
	1	2	3	4	5	6	7	8

Units of X Employed

According to economic theory, if an increase in a firm's inputs by some proportion results in an increase in output by a greater proportion, the firm experiences *increasing returns to scale*. If output increases by the same proportion as the inputs increase, the firm experiences *constant returns to scale*. A less than proportional increase in output is called *decreasing returns to scale*.

You might simply assume firms generally experience constant returns to scale. For example, if a firm has a factory of a particular size, then doubling its size along with a doubling of workers and machinery should lead to a doubling of output. Why should it result in a greater than proportional or, for that matter, a smaller than proportional increase? For one thing, a larger scale of production might enable a firm to divide tasks into more specialized activities, thereby increasing labor productivity. Also, a larger scale of operation might enable a company to justify the purchase of more sophisticated (hence, more productive) machinery. These factors help explain why a firm can experience increasing returns to scale. In contrast, operating on a larger scale might create certain managerial inefficiencies (e.g., communications problems, bureaucratic red tape) and hence cause decreasing returns to scale. More will be said about the factors that can cause increasing or decreasing returns to scale in chapter 7, when we discuss the related concepts of economies and diseconomies of scale.

One way to measure returns to scale is to use a coefficient of output elasticity:

$$E_Q = \frac{\text{Percentage change in } Q}{\text{Percentage change in all inputs}}$$

Thus,

If $E_Q > 1$, we have increasing returns to scale (IRTS).
If $E_Q = 1$, we have constant returns to scale (CRTS).
If $E_Q < 1$, we have decreasing returns to scale (DRTS).

Another way of looking at the concept of returns to scale is based on an equation that was first presented at the outset of this chapter:

$$Q = f(X, Y)$$

Recall in the original specification of this equation that it may include as many input variables as necessary to describe the production process (i.e., *i* variables). For ease of discussion, we limit this number to two: X and Y. Now suppose we increase the amount of each input by some proportion k. For example, if we increase the inputs by 10 percent, $k = 1.10$. If we double the inputs, $k = 2.0$. Of course, Q is expected to increase by some proportion as a result of the increase in the inputs. Let h represent the magnitude of this increase. Expressed in terms of Equation (6.3),

$$hQ = f(kX, kY)$$

Using this notation, we can summarize returns to scale in the following way:

If $h > k$, the firm experiences increasing returns to scale ($E_Q > 1$).
If $h = k$, the firm experiences constant returns to scale ($E_Q = 1$).
If $h < k$, the firm experiences decreasing returns to scale ($E_Q < 1$).

We illustrate returns to scale with a numerical example. Suppose we have the following production function:

$$Q_1 = 5X + 7Y$$

If we use 10 units of each input, the output will be

$$Q_1 = 5(10) + 7(10)$$
$$= 50 + 70 = 120 \text{ units}$$

Now let us increase each input by 25 percent (i.e., $k = 1.25$). This will give us

$$Q_2 = 5(12.5) + 7(12.5)$$
$$= 62.5 + 87.5 = 150$$

The 25 percent increase in X and Y has led to a proportional increase in output (i.e., 150 is 25 percent more than 120).

We can also illustrate the concept of returns to scale graphically. Figure 6.5 shows the three possible types of returns to scale. In each case, we assume the inputs (X and Y) are increased by the same proportion; thus, they are both included on the horizontal axis. Obviously, these graphs are idealized representations of returns to scale. In reality, we would not expect the changes in output relative to the changes in inputs to behave in such a smooth and orderly fashion.

Figure 6.5   Graphic Representations of Returns to Scale

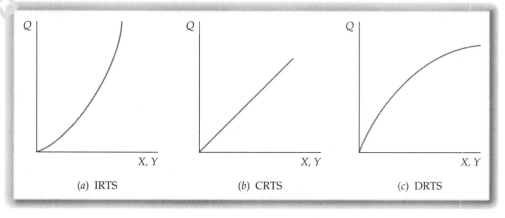

(a) IRTS   (b) CRTS   (c) DRTS

THE ESTIMATION OF PRODUCTION FUNCTIONS

Following our examination of demand theory, we turned to the subject of demand estimation. Now it is time to examine another of a managerial economist's important tasks, the estimation of production functions. This section deals with three major topics. First, we discuss the possible shapes of production functions. Second, we discuss the Cobb-Douglas production function, a form that has been commonly used by economists since its introduction in the 1920s. Last, we look at the data needed for estimation and some of the production function studies published by economists.

The Various Forms of a Production Function

Earlier in this chapter, the short-run production function was introduced. As you remember, the short run is characterized by the existence of a fixed factor to which we add a variable factor. Thus, the simple function, containing just one variable factor and one fixed factor, can be written as follows:

$$Q = f(L)_K$$

where output Q is determined by the quantity of the variable factor L (labor) with the fixed factor K (capital) given.[6]

The theoretical part of this chapter assumed the production function starts with increasing marginal returns followed by decreasing marginal returns. In other words, all three stages of production are present. This situation is represented by a cubic function:

$$Q = a + bL + cL^2 - dL^3$$

where a is the constant and b, c, and d are coefficients. Figure 6.6a shows the total product line,[7] and Figure 6.6b shows the average and marginal product curves. All three stages of production are present.

It is possible, however, that the data employed in the estimate will exhibit diminishing marginal returns but no stage I. Such an estimate is represented by the quadratic function:

$$Q = a + bL - cL^2$$

Figures 6.7a and 6.7b depict total and unit product curves, respectively. Both graphs show diminishing marginal returns, but increasing marginal returns and thus stage I are absent.[8]

In performing empirical research, it may be possible to identify a linear production function, $Q = a + bL$. This function exhibits no diminishing returns; the total product will be a straight line with slope b, and both the MP and AP lines will be horizontal and equal.[9] Of course, a straight-line production function may hold in some

---

[6]In the prior discussion, the letters X and Y designated inputs. This emphasized the production function's generality. Here we use L (for labor) and K (for capital) because these are the letters that are frequently employed to indicate variable and fixed factors. In long-run analysis, of course, both L and K are variable.

[7]Total product curves should, in theory, be drawn from the origin because it is most likely that no production would occur in the absence of any variable factor. However, when production functions are estimated using regression analysis, it is probable that the fitted line will have a positive or negative y-intercept. Thus, in the equations that follow we include the intercept a. It should be noted that this value probably has no economic significance.

[8]If the intercept is present, average product is equal to $a/L + b - cL$. However, if the intercept is omitted, the average product will be a straight line, as shown in Figure 6.7b.

[9]Again, if the intercept is present, the average product will show a decline. If, however, the intercept is omitted, the average product will be horizontal and equal to marginal product.

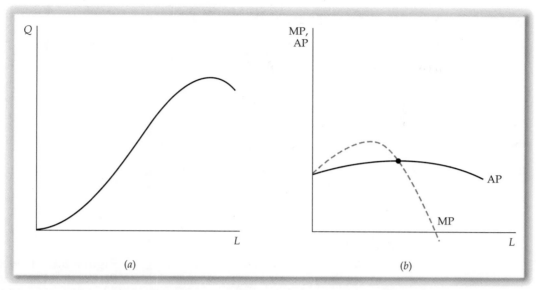

(a)   (b)

Figure 6.6   Cubic Production Function

real situations, but given the existence of a fixed factor, constant marginal product should not be expected to prevail over a wide range of quantities produced.

Another form of the production function is the **power function**, which takes the following form:

$$Q = aL^b$$

The shape of this production function depends on the exponent b, as is shown in Figure 6.8.

Figure 6.7   Quadratic Production Function

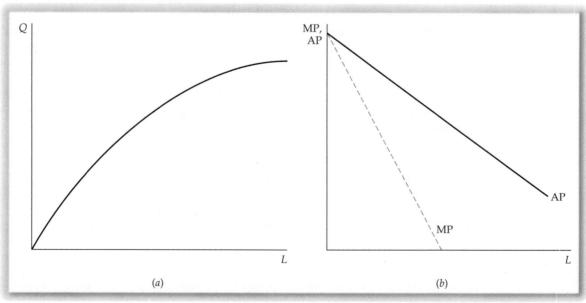

(a)   (b)

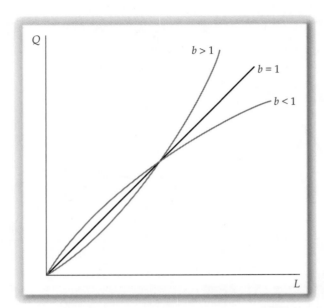

Figure 6.8 Power Production Function

A major advantage of the power function is that it can be transformed into a linear function when it is expressed in logarithmic terms, making it amenable to linear regression analysis:

$$\log Q = \log a + b \log L$$

The direction of marginal product depends on the size of the exponent b. If $b > 1$, marginal product is increasing; if $b = 1$, it is constant; and if $b < 1$, it is decreasing. It cannot, however, exhibit two directions for marginal product on the same function, as was possible with the cubic equation form. This function is used frequently in empirical work. One reason for its popularity is that it can be readily transformed into a function with two or more independent variables:

$$Q = a X_1^b X_2^c \ldots \ldots X_n^m$$

Using more than one independent variable in a production function is certainly more realistic than limiting the analysis to only one, and when it is assumed all inputs are variable, we have then moved from short-run analysis to the long run. Indeed, this function can be employed in both analyses. In a simple two-variable model (e.g., labor and capital), the power function permits the estimation of marginal product (e.g., when labor changes and capital remains the same) and of returns to scale (when both variables change).

The Cobb-Douglas Production Function

The **Cobb-Douglas production function** was introduced in 1928,[10] and it is still a common functional form in economic studies today. It has been used extensively to estimate both individual firm and aggregate production functions. It has undergone significant criticism but has endured. "It is now customary practice in economics to

---

[10]C. W. Cobb and P. H. Douglas, "A Theory of Production," *American Economic Review*, 8, 1 (March 1928, suppl.), pp. 139–65. Charles W. Cobb was a mathematician; Paul H. Douglas was an economist, and later a U.S. senator from Illinois.

deny its validity and then to use it as an excellent approximation."[11] It was originally constructed for all the manufacturing output (Q) in the United States for the years 1899 to 1922. The two inputs used by the authors were number of manual workers (L) and fixed capital (K). The formula for the production function, which was suggested by Cobb, was of the following form:

$$Q = aL^bK^{1-b}$$

What are the important properties of this function that have kept it popular for more than 70 years?

1. To make this equation useful, both inputs must exist for Q to be a positive number. This makes sense because total product is a result of combining two or more factors.[12]
2. The function can exhibit increasing, decreasing, or constant returns. Originally, Cobb and Douglas assumed returns to scale are constant. The function was constructed in such a way that the exponents summed to $b + 1 - b = 1$. (A brief description of the mathematics of the Cobb-Douglas function can be found in Appendix 6C.) However, in later studies, they (as well as other researchers) relaxed this requirement and rewrote the equation as follows:

$$Q = aL^bK^c$$

Under this construction, if $b + c > 1$, returns to scale are increasing and if $b + c < 1$, returns are decreasing.[13] Constant returns exist when $b + c = 1$.
3. The function permits us to investigate the marginal product for any factor while holding all others constant. Thus it is also useful in the analysis of short-run production functions. In the two-factor model discussed here, the marginal product of labor turns out to be $MP_L = bQ/L$, and the marginal product of capital is $MP_K = cQ/K$. (The mathematics of this result are shown in Appendix 6C.) Each coefficient will usually be less than 1, and this will mean that they each exhibit diminishing marginal returns. Thus, production takes place in Stage II, which is the relevant area of production.
4. The elasticity of production is an important concept as discussed in Appendix 6C. In the Cobb-Douglas function, the elasticities of the factors are equal to their exponents, in this case b and c. Thus, the elasticities of labor and capital are constants.
5. Because a power function can be converted to a linear function by using logarithms, it can be estimated by linear regression analysis, which makes for a relatively easy calculation with any software package.
6. Although we limit our discussion to just two input variables (L and K), Cobb-Douglas can accommodate any number of independent variables, as follows:

$$Q = aX_1^b X_2^c X_3^d \ldots \ldots X_n^m$$

7. A theoretical production function assumes technology is constant. However, the data fitted by the researcher may span a period over which technology has progressed. One of the independent variables in the previous equation could represent technological change (a time series) and thus adjust the function to take technology into consideration.

The Cobb-Douglas function has the following shortcomings:

1. The Cobb-Douglas cannot show the marginal product going through all three stages of production in one specification. (A cubic function would be necessary to achieve this.)

---

[11]George J. Stigler, *The Theory of Price*, 4th ed., New York: Macmillan, 1987, p. 153.
[12]If an additive function (e.g., $Q = a + bL + cK$) were employed, output would still be positive even if one of the two inputs were zero.
[13]Of course, if the function contained more than two factors, the exponents would still have to equal more than one for increasing returns, less than one for decreasing, and one for constant.

2. Similarly, it cannot show a firm or industry passing through increasing, constant, and decreasing returns to scale.

3. There are also important problems with specification of data to be used in empirical estimates. These problems are discussed next.

Statistical Estimation of Production Functions

Let us turn now to a description of the data that would be used in empirical estimates of production functions. Later, we also review some published studies. When the statistical estimate concerns a plant, or group of plants, the data will come from company records—accounting, employment, purchasing, manufacturing, and others.

If only one product is produced in a plant, Q is specified in physical units (e.g., number, tons, gallons). However, if a plant produces a number of different products, and it is not possible to segregate properly the inputs and outputs of the products, estimation becomes considerably more difficult. In such a case, the investigator probably must settle for some measure of value, assigning weights to products depending on the value (in terms of cost or selling price) produced. There are some obvious problems with this procedure. First, over time the data will have to be deflated to account for price or cost changes. Second, the price or cost of a product may not be an exact reflection of the inputs combined in the total value. However, until better measurement methods are found, such valuing methods will have to suffice.

Measuring inputs also can vary in the level of difficulty. Inputs should be measured as "flow" rather than "stock" variables, and this is not always possible.[14]

Usually, the most important input is labor. Hours of labor input are probably the best measure for our purposes. Data for direct labor hours are ordinarily available from company records. If they are not, then number of direct workers is the next best choice. However, it must be remembered that number of workers is a stock variable and does not necessarily represent the amount of labor expended in production. For materials, a physical measure is again best. In some cases, such data are readily available (weight of materials consumed, for instance). Of course, because we do not want to proliferate the number of independent variables, choosing only the most important raw material may be indicated. Alternatively, a combination (by weight or value) may prove to be a viable option. Utilities (electricity, gas, etc.) may also be included; in this case, physical quantities should be fairly easily obtained.

The most difficult input variable is the all-important capital input. How can one measure the use of plant, machinery, and equipment in production? Because different components of plant and equipment are of varying durability and different input intensity, usage per period is hard to establish. In some cases, periodic depreciation may be an indicator of capital use. However, depreciation as recorded in the company's books is often based on accounting convention or legal requirement. Further, the projected depreciation life of a piece of equipment tends to depend on tax rules because the firm wants to take advantage of the fastest write-off permitted for tax purposes. Some capital items, such as land, are not depreciated. Unless some rather consistent measurement of capital usage can be designed by the researcher (and this is certainly a formidable task), the common method of measuring capital by the use of a stock variable (e.g., fixed assets) is probably indicated. Obviously, this is not a perfect solution because the price of these assets depends on when the assets were acquired. Thus, the asset figure must be adjusted by a price index. Should gross fixed assets

---

[14]Flows measure the usage of services consumed in producing a product, whereas stocks represent the amounts of factors present and available for productive use.

(i.e., the original cost of all plant and equipment) be used, or net fixed assets (gross assets minus accumulated depreciation)? Again, this is a difficult question. There is no specific answer. The method used must be determined by the investigator as that which is most reasonable (and available) for each specific case.

If the production function estimate is to be accomplished using regression analysis, then we must choose between time series and cross-sectional analysis. The former would be preferable if data have been collected over a period of time in a given plant. However, it would be necessary to make adjustments for inflation if the variables are in monetary (rather than physical) terms. Also, a time variable (or a dummy variable) may have to be employed to account for changes in technology.

Cross-sectional analysis is favored when the data collected cover a number of plants in a given time period. But here again, problems may arise. The various plants may not employ the same level of technology. If the data are in monetary terms, an adjustment for differential price or wage levels at different geographic locations would be necessary.

Although a theoretical production function assumes output is produced at the most efficient input combinations, in reality such an ideal situation is certainly not assured whichever estimating method is used. Ultimately, there is no perfect way to measure and analyze the data. The researcher must choose the most appropriate method.

A Numerical Example of a Cobb-Douglas Production Function

A cross-sectional sample of twenty soft drink bottling plants has been selected. The data are given for a specific month in 1998. Only two independent variables are used: (1) number of direct workers and (2) plant size. Plants range from 1 to 1.75, based on a size and capacity measure developed by engineers.

Production, the dependent variable, is stated in terms of gallons of product shipped during the period. Table 6.6 contains the data and the results of the analysis.

The Cobb-Douglas function of the form $Q = aL^bK^c$ was applied to the numbers. The regression output in the table shows the results.[15] The regression equation is as follows:

$$Q = 15.14L^{0.66}K^{0.32}$$

R^2 (the coefficient of determination) is quite high, showing that 98 percent of the deviations are explained. The two coefficients are significantly different from zero because they both pass the t-test.[16] The sum of the two coefficients is 0.985. Because this result is so close to 1, it can be assumed the plants exhibit constant returns to scale. Each input indicates decreasing marginal returns.

Three Studies of Individual Production Functions

In 1967, a study of the production function of the Pacific halibut industry was published. A Cobb-Douglas function appeared to give good results and showed that constant returns are probably the rule in this industry. A "good captain" variable was added—a confidential rating of the management abilities of the captains of the thirty-two boats in the sample. It was found that good captains made a difference.[17]

---

[15]The results were calculated using the Excel regression analysis program. The raw data were transformed into logarithms, and a straight-line regression in logarithms was computed. The constant of 1.18 is a logarithm, and 15.14 is its antilog.
[16]Labor's t-test is significant at the 1 percent level, and capital's is significant at the 5 percent level.
[17]Salvatore Comitimi and David S. Huang, "A Study of Production and Factor Shares in the Halibut Fishing Industry," *Journal of Political Economy*, August 1967, pp. 366–72.

Table 6.6   Production Function: Soft Drink Bottling

Total Product	Labor	Capital
97	15	1.00
98	17	1.00
104	20	1.00
120	22	1.00
136	22	1.25
129	25	1.25
145	30	1.25
170	32	1.25
181	35	1.25
166	30	1.50
175	35	1.50
190	38	1.50
212	42	1.50
220	44	1.50
207	45	1.50
228	44	1.75
226	47	1.75
240	52	1.75
270	55	1.75
280	58	1.75

Summary Output

Regression Statistics

R Square	0.980965846
Adjusted R Square	0.978726534
Standard Error	0.020818585
Observations	20

	Coefficients	Standard Error	t Stat
Intercept	1.1800154	0.096022924	12.288892
X Variable 1	0.6643702	0.075371367	8.8146228
X Variable 2	0.3214714	0.147006777	2.1867796

Another study included management in the production function equation. This study dealt with a sample of plants of a multinational consumer goods manufacturer. Time series and cross-sectional data were combined to obtain 127 observations over 8 years (1975–1982). Management was measured as a performance ranking of each plant in terms of three criteria—output goal attainment, cost over- or underfulfillment, and quality level of output. The results showed that the management variable was statistically significant. Another feature of this study was the conclusion that increasing returns existed up to a certain plant size and that decreasing returns resulted at larger sizes.[18]

A 2005 study used the Cobb-Douglas function as a base and then added several management policies to determine whether these policies contributed to increases in productivity. The study examined three relatively small companies over a period of

---

[18]Robert N. Mefford, "Introducing Management into the Production Function," *Review of Economics and Statistics*, February 1986, pp. 96–104.

four to five years. The three companies were in a sophisticated printing business, the manufacture of air filtration systems, and furniture production, respectively. The results suggest "that a substantial portion of productivity improvements are indeed under the control of management." Of the six management policies examined, two had a positive and mostly statistically significant effect on productivity. These two were:

1. Dollars spent for asset maintenance and technology improvements
2. Benefits derived from job specialization and reorganization[19]

Aggregate Production Functions

A large proportion of the studies performed using the Cobb-Douglas function did not deal with data for individual firms, but rather with aggregations of industries or even the economy as a whole. Although much of this work has proved to be quite fruitful in describing production functions, the interpretation of the results may not be quite as meaningful as for individual production functions. When data for the economy as a whole are used, the model must accommodate different technologies and different processes, and thus does not represent a specific technological process of a given firm. When the aggregation is done at the level of an industry rather than the overall economy, the assumption of similar technology is more appropriate, but even in such a case many dissimilarities may occur.

Gathering data for such aggregate functions can be difficult. For the economy as a whole, gross national or domestic product—in real terms—could be used to measure output. For specific industries, data from the Census of Manufactures or the production index published by the Federal Reserve Board can be employed. Data for investment and depreciation by industry are also available for the construction of appropriate indexes for the capital variable. The Bureau of Labor Statistics publishes a great deal of data on employment and work hours.

Cobb and Douglas performed their earliest study on U.S. manufacturing in the form of a time series regression for the years 1899 to 1922. Using the original version of their formula, they obtained the following result:

$$Q = 1.01 L^{0.75} K^{0.25}$$

Other studies used the same technique with similar results.

In 1937, David Durand suggested that the equation should not necessarily limit the results to constant returns to scale.[20] After Durand's article, it was accepted that the exponents in the equation no longer had to equal 1. Douglas corrected the original study and found that the coefficient of labor was reduced to about two-thirds, whereas capital's exponent rose to about one-third. But the sum of the two exponents still summed to about 1, and thus constant returns to scale appeared to prevail.[21]

At about the same time, cross-sectional analysis, rather than time series, came into use, and most of the studies done since then have used this technique. The observations were now individual industries in a particular year. Many other studies were conducted on data from the United States, Australia, Canada, and New Zealand. In a majority of these investigations, the sum of the exponents turned out to be very close to 1.

[19]Craig S. Galbraith and Emmanuel Nkwenti-Zamcho, "The Effect of Management Policies on Plant-Level Productivity: A Longitudinal Study of Three U.S. and Mexican Small Businesses," *Journal of Small Business Management*, Vol. 43, Issue 4, October 2005, pp. 418–431.

[20]David Durand, "Some Thoughts on Marginal Productivity with Special Reference to Professor Douglas," *Journal of Political Economy*, 45, 6 (December 1937), pp. 740–58.

[21]The history of the Cobb-Douglas function and the major studies were summarized by Douglas himself in his article, "The Cobb-Douglas Production Function Once Again: Its History, Its Testing, and Some New Empirical Values," *Journal of Political Economy*, 84, 5 (October 1976), pp. 903–15.

In another study, the author performed a cross-sectional study of eighteen industries using data from the Census of Manufactures.[22] The observation units were individual states. Three independent variables were used:

1. Production worker hours
2. Nonproduction worker years
3. Gross book value of depreciable and depletable assets

The dependent variable, Q, was represented by the value added in each industry.

The results showed that the sums of the three exponents in the eighteen industries ranged from about 0.95 to 1.11, indicating a span from decreasing to increasing returns. Tests of significance showed that in only five of the eighteen industries was the sum of the coefficients significantly different from 1. Thus, again, in the majority of cases, constant returns to scale appeared to dominate.

A more recent time series study estimated China's economic growth during the period 1952 to 1998 and attempted to predict its growth through 2010. It uses the traditional Cobb-Douglas function with GDP as the dependent variable. Labor and capital are the independent variables, and a third variable is also added. This is a trend variable that represents technical progress. The computed coefficients are 0.6136 for capital and 0.4118 for labor, and the trend coefficient equals 0.0263. Actually, the trend variable is fixed at zero through 1978 and shows the above increase after 1979. The results shows returns that are very close to constant.[23]

Another recent study investigated the impact of computer-related input on firm productivity for a sample of 399 enterprises in Shanghai, China. It found that, in the heavy industry sector, the number of computer-using workers had a much more positive effect on output than the number of workers not using computers. This effect was much less for state-operated enterprises than non–state-operated enterprises. Also interesting was the conclusion that the contribution of labor to output was less than capital's contribution.[24]

A rather interesting application of the cross-sectional Cobb-Douglas function is represented by a study of the importance of various baseball statistics to the success of a baseball team. The dependent variable was a team's win/loss percentage relative to the league average. The independent variables were slugging percentage, on base percentage, number of stolen bases, unearned runs allowed, and earned run average. Surprisingly, the offensive statistics proved to be more important than the defensive statistics. All coefficients were statistically significant, and the equation exhibited increasing returns to scale.[25]

THE IMPORTANCE OF PRODUCTION FUNCTIONS IN MANAGERIAL DECISION MAKING

As stated in the introductory section of this chapter, the production function is an important part of the economic analysis of the firm because it serves as the foundation for the analysis of cost. This is shown in chapter 7. But for managers, an understanding

[22]John R. Moroney, "Cobb-Douglas Production Functions and Returns to Scale in U.S. Manufacturing," *Western Economic Journal,* 6, 1 (December 1967), pp. 39–51.
[23]Gregory C. Chow and Kui-Wai Li, "China's Economic Growth: 1952–2010," *Economic Development and Cultural Change,* 51, 1 (October 2002), pp. 247–56.
[24]Y. C. Ng and M. K. Chang, "Impact of Computerization on Firm Performance, a Case of Shanghai Manufacturing Enterprises," *Journal of the Operational Research Society,* 54, 10 (October 2003), pp. 1029–37.
[25]Mark D. Woolway, "Using an Empirically Estimated Production Function for Major League Baseball to Examine Worker Disincentives Associated with Multi-Year Contracts," *The American Economist,* 41, 2 (Fall 1997), pp. 77–83.

of the basic concepts discussed in this chapter also provides a solid conceptual frame-work for decisions involving the allocation of a firm's resources both in the short run and in the long run. Another key management principle illustrated in the economic theory of production is planning, discussed in the following subsection.

Careful Planning Can Help a Firm to Use Its Resources in a Rational Manner

In our discussion of the short run, we state that a firm is expected to have three stages of production. Stage I represents the underutilization of a firm's fixed inputs relative to its variable ones. Stage III represents an overutilization of its fixed inputs relative to its variable ones. Indeed, firms operating in this stage would find their total output *decreasing* as they increased their variable input. The only stage for a rational firm to be in is Stage II. Assuming this information is well known to managers, why would a firm find itself in Stage I or III? The answer is, of course, that production levels do not depend on how much a company wants to produce, but on *how much its customers want to buy.*

Suppose we consider the short-run production function shown in Figure 6.9. As we can see, Stage II applies to production levels between $Q_1 = 200$ and $Q_2 = 275$. If people want to buy less than 200 units or more than 275 units, for example, then in the short run the firm would be forced to operate in either Stage I or Stage III.

The information in Figure 6.9 implies that for a firm to avoid having to operate in either Stage I or Stage III, there must be careful planning regarding the amount of fixed inputs that will be used along with the variable ones. In business, this is often referred to as *capacity planning.* For example, if the firm anticipated that the demand for its product would be in the range of 200 to 275, then the capacity implied in Figure 6.9 is perfect for its needs. However, if a firm forecasts the demand to be greater than 275, it would have to consider increasing its capacity so Stage II would include the higher level of output. By the same token, if the firm forecasts a demand less than 200, it would have to consider decreasing its capacity. These alternative capacity levels are illustrated in Figure 6.10.

Figure 6.9   Production Stages and Capacity Planning

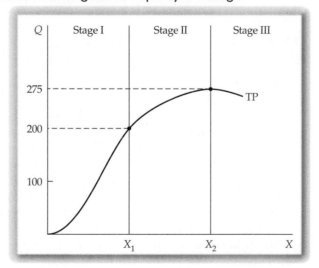

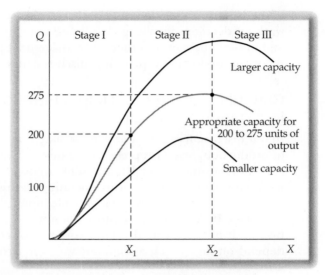

Figure 6.10   Adjusting Capacity Based on Demand

Good capacity planning requires two basic elements: (1) accurate forecasts of demand, and (2) effective communication between the production and marketing functions (particularly in large organizations where these functions are often handled by separate work groups). The first element is rather obvious but, as you have seen in chapter 5, not easy to achieve. The second element may not be so obvious, especially for those who have not had work experience in large organizations. It is not uncommon for manufacturing people to proceed merrily with their production plans on a purely technical basis (i.e., from a strictly engineering point of view) without fully incorporating the marketing plans of those whose main responsibility is to sell the products. It is also quite possible for marketing people to try to sell as many units of the product as possible (as marketing people are supposed to do) without consulting the production people as to whether the firm has the capacity to meet the increase in demand. A full discussion of these problems of management and organization is beyond the scope of this book. However, they are mentioned to underscore the importance for managers of understanding production theory.

GOING "BEYOND THE CURVES": CURRENT PRODUCTION ISSUES AND CHALLENGES FOR TODAY'S MANAGERS

The heart of the economic theory of production can be expressed as production curves showing the relationship between inputs and output. But the intensity of current global competition often requires managers to go beyond these curves. Being competitive in production today mandates that today's managers also understand the importance of speed, flexibility, and what is commonly called "lean manufacturing."

Speed of production is required because rapidly changing technology renders products on the market obsolete very quickly and because today's consumers often change their tastes and preferences at the same fast pace. These "supply side" and "demand side" changes are quite evident in the world of consumer electronics, in particular the cellular phone market. For example, it is not uncommon for consumers in South Korea and other parts of Asia to want new-model cell phones every six months or so. And cell phone manufacturers and service providers are constantly trying to offer new third-generation (3G) products such as streaming music, video games, and connections to popular sites such as iTunes and YouTube. Indeed, as soon as 3G services were finally rolling out, the industry was already talking about 4G.

For cell phone manufacturers such as Nokia, Samsung, and SonyEricsson, the relationship between inputs and output is important, but the speed at which new products can be brought to market as well as the flexibility of response to changing consumer tastes is equally as important. Over the last decade and the first part of this one, the Finnish company Nokia had established itself as the world's leading manufacturer of cell phones. But around 2003–2004, Motorola launched its sleek Razr phone with a clamshell shape. Samsung and LG, the two biggest Korean competitors, also had their own version of this type of phone. The interesting question is why Nokia did not respond as quickly to this change and begin producing more of these types of phones (also referred to as "flip phones"), rather than its "chocolate bar"–shaped phones. As an industry professional explained to one of the authors, one factor was that Nokia realized that it would have to reconfigure all its factory setups in order to start making these types of phones. The capital investment required for this change was deemed uneconomical at that time in terms of the time and money involved in plant reconfiguration. Meanwhile, Motorola was able to gain market share and earn considerable profit at the expense of its competitors, particularly Nokia. Eventually, Nokia began to adjust its production capabilities to the changing tastes and preferences of the market.[26]

One of the best examples of the importance of speed and flexibility in production is the phenomenal growth of the Spanish retail store Zara. Numerous case studies have been written about the amazing rise of this trendy clothing chain. In Spain, Zara's home base, the company has its own manufacturing facilities located relatively close to its stores. Zara does contract out some of its production to offshore operations in Asia, but reserves these facilities for the production of less trendy, classic fashions. Its company-owned local factories are in constant communication with its stores in order to get feedback on the latest consumer whims and fancies. Its factories are able to respond to suggestions from its stores within 2 to 4 weeks. Competitors' normal response time could be between 4 to 12 months. Zara produces each fashion item in small quantities, thereby creating a type of scarcity. Shoppers in a Zara store are often told by salespeople that they should buy the item when they want it because they might not find it when they return to the store.[27] Zara also produces a lot more styles, thereby giving its customers more choices while at the same time increasing its chances of finding "hit" fashion items.[28]

"Lean manufacturing" has become quite a popular buzzword among consultants and manufacturing executives. In reality, we believe that this term refers to the production approach that goes into much greater detail about what it really means for a company to lower its unit costs. This is not to detract from its importance. According

---

[26]This was explained to Philip Young by a manager in one of his corporate education programs whose company was a prime contractor for Nokia. Interestingly enough, there is "no rest for the weary." Motorola subsequently lost its lead in the clamshell phones because it began to discount its price too quickly. This helped the company to gain further market share but eroded its profit margin prematurely. And as was to be expected, Razr began to fade in popularity. As this edition is being written, Nokia has regained its strength as the number 1 cell phone manufacturer, and companies such as Samsung and LG have increased their share over Motorola.

[27]Salespeople in Costco, the successful warehouse store chain based in the United States, are known to tell this to their customers as well.

[28]Devangshu Dutta, "Retail@the Speed of Fashion," reference article taken from www.3isite.com. See also K. Ferdows, M. Lewis, and J. Macluca, "Rapid Fire Fulfillment," *Harvard Business Review*, Vol. 11, no. 11, November 2004. On a recent trip to Madrid, one of the authors was told by a salesperson at one of Zara's busiest stores near the Plaza Mayor that it was not unusual for new items to arrive several times in the same day.

to a popular Web site on this subject, lean manufacturing involves avoiding or eliminating "seven types of deadly waste."[29] They are:

1. Overproduction (inventory ties up cash and inventory carrying costs increase expenses)
2. Waiting (underutilization of assets affects downstream production)
3. Unnecessary movement of materials (wastes time and increases chances of handling damage)
4. Extra processing (extra operations such as rework, reprocessing, handling, or storage)
5. Inventory
6. Motion (unnecessary motion)
7. Defects

CALL CENTERS: APPLYING THE PRODUCTION FUNCTION TO A SERVICE

Most production function examples involve manufacturing or agriculture. To illustrate how the concepts in this chapter can be used for a service activity, let us consider the example of a call center represented by the following production function:

$$Q = f(X, Y)$$

where Q = number of calls
X = variable input (this includes call center representatives and the complementary hardware such as PCs, desks, and software if site licenses are sold on a per-user basis)
Y = fixed input (this includes the call center building, hardware such as servers and telecommunications equipment, and software site licenses up to the designated maximum number of users)

Using this basic production function, it is possible to consider a number of applications of concepts. The following are offered as examples.

Three Stages of Production: Stage I could be a situation in which there is so much fixed capacity relative to number of variable inputs that many representatives sit around idle, waiting for calls to come in. Stage II could be a situation in which representatives are constantly occupied and callers are connected to representatives immediately after the call is answered or are kept waiting no more than a certain amount of time (e.g., 3 minutes). If callers are kept waiting for longer than 3 minutes, the call center manager might consider adding more call center representatives. Stage III could be a situation in which callers begin to experience a busy signal on a more frequent basis or call representatives may begin to experience a slower computer response or more frequent computer "down times." These are all technical manifestations of overloaded computer processing power or transmission capacity (i.e., insufficient bandwidth).

Input Combinations: A number of input combinations could be considered in the operation of a call center. To begin with, there is the location trade-off in which the productivity of call center representatives in two or more locations might be considered relative to the cost of each representative (including wages, training costs, costs associated with turnover rates, etc.).

Numerous cities in the United States have established themselves as attractive locations for call centers because of their large pools of qualified labor available at wage rates relatively lower than the national average. High on the list of these are Sioux Falls,

---

[29]See www.leaninnovations.ca/seven_types.html.

South Dakota; Jacksonville, Florida; St. Louis, Missouri; and Salt Lake City, Utah. Early on, Salt Lake City was identified as being a desirable location for call centers because of its large concentration of people with foreign language skills.[30] At the beginning of this decade, call center operations in the United States and the United Kingdom started to shift to India and the Philippines, where there are large pools of English-speaking workers.[31]

The main reason companies relocate their call centers to other countries is to reduce costs by utilizing lower paid workers. However, a recent development in the U.S. fast-food industry indicates that call centers are also being used to increase service productivity. Readers may well be familiar with this phenomenon, but when the authors found out about this development in call center operations, they were astounded. Consider what was reported in the *New York Times* several years ago:

> Like many American teenagers, Julissa Vargas, 17, has a minimum-wage job in the fast-food industry—but hers has an unusual geographic reach. "Would you like your Coke and orange juice medium or large?" Ms. Vargas said into her headset to an unseen woman who was ordering breakfast from a drive-through line. She did not neglect the small details—"You Must Ask for Condiments," a sign next to her computer terminal instructs—and wished the woman a wonderful day. What made the $12.08 transaction remarkable was that the customer was not just outside Ms. Vargas's workplace here on California's central coast. She was at a McDonald's in Honolulu. And within a two-minute span Ms. Vargas had also taken orders from drive-through windows in Gulfport, Miss., and Gillette, Wyo.
>
> Ms. Vargas works not in a restaurant but in a busy call center in this town, 150 miles from Los Angeles. She and as many as 35 others take orders remotely from 40 McDonald's outlets around the country. The orders are then sent back to the restaurants by Internet, to be filled a few yards from where they were placed.
>
> The people behind this setup expect it to save just a few seconds on each order. But that can add up to extra sales over the course of a busy day at the drive-through.[32]

A complete discussion about increasing productivity in the service sector through such means as the outsourcing of certain components of a service function is presented in Appendix 6A.

Another trade-off involves capital and labor. The cost of upgrading the hardware and software used by each call center representative could be measured against the number of representatives used in the call center. For example, the installation of an automated call distribution system or a voice recognition software package could result in the reduction in the number of call representatives working at any time in the center.

Returns to Scale: One can well imagine that a call center would be amenable to increasing returns to scale. This is evidenced by the number of smaller companies who outsource their operations to companies that specialize in call center operations. These "third-party" vendors are able to provide call center services at a lower cost to the company mainly because their size enables them to take advantage of increasing returns to scale.

---

[30]Alan Crane, "Telephone Contact with Customers Is Ripe for Outsourcing," *Financial Times,* September 13, 1996.

[31]"U.S. Dials 1–800 Bangalore: Toll-Free Inquiries Are Increasingly Answered in India," *Washington Post,* August 5, 2001. It is interesting to note that in France, call center operations have been set up in the French-speaking countries in North and Central Africa.

[32]Matt Richtel, "The Long-Distance Journey of a Fast-Food Order," *New York Times,* April 11, 2006. Reprinted by permission of *New York Times* and PARS International.

INTERNATIONAL APPLICATION: IS CHINA RUNNING OUT OF WORKERS?[33]

In the never-ending search for lower-cost labor, manufacturers from the United States and other high-wage, industrialized countries have been shifting their production facilities to China over the past decade. The industrial economic boom in China has directly affected and benefited roughly 300 million of its people, most of whom reside in the coastal cities. Companies from the high-wage countries have assumed manufacturing wages in China will remain low in the face of rising demand for labor because there remains a potential labor supply of 900 million rural workers to keep supply even with demand. However, as pointed out in an article in *BusinessWeek,* this may not be the case in certain instances. The article points to the specific case of Taiwanese businessman Hayes Lou. Lou moved his bicycle and motorcycle factory from Superior, Montana, to Dongguan, in Guangdong Province, China, in 1989. The plentiful "dirt cheap" labor enabled Lou's business to grow rapidly, with an expansion of several new factories over the course of this time. But 15 years later, in 2004, Lou suddenly found himself with a labor shortage problem. One of his factories is running well below capacity because he has been unable to find 170 of the 300 workers that he needs. His increase in wages of about 30 percent (to about $85 per month) has still not helped remedy this situation. Moreover, Lou claims that many of his fellow factory owners are in similar straits.

It appears that what Lou has been experiencing is classic microeconomic theory at work. Recall our discussion of multiple inputs and also see Appendix 6A. Among the factors contributing to the lagging of supply relative to the demand for labor in China are (1) the opening of factories in the interior of China, thereby offering options to rural workers beyond the coastal areas such as Dongguan; (2) the effect that China's one-child policy has had on the number of women available for work in the factories (most factory workers are women); (3) improving living conditions in the rural areas (making it easier for families to keep their young people "down on the farm"); and (4) government tax incentives and subsidies to the agricultural sector.

Nevertheless, this situation is still relative to the situation in the rest of the world. For example, despite rising wages in China, they are still at about one-third the level of those in Malaysia. Most of these wage increases have affected companies in China owned by businesspeople from Taiwan and Hong Kong, who tend to pay the lowest wages. Multinational corporations, particularly those based in the United States, were already paying among the highest wages and therefore have not had as much of a labor shortage problem as their counterparts from Taiwan and Hong Kong.

The Solution

To: Robert Burns, CEO
           Nicole Goodman, SVP of Marketing
           Jim Hartwell, SVP of Manufacturing
From: Christopher Lim, Production Manager
Re: The Economic Feasibility of Packaging in Glass Bottles and Key Related Issues

Before beginning plans to bottle and distribute Waterpure, I feel that I must bring up certain production issues that I was not able to cover at our meeting last week. I have had considerable experience in glass packaging from my previous job as head of bottling for our Latin American beverage division. Glass is a more expensive material than

(continued)

---

[33]This section is based on Dexler Roberts and Frederik Balfour, "Is China Running Out of Workers?" *BusinessWeek,* October 25, 2004.

(continued)

either plastic or aluminum. With the latest slump in aluminum prices and technology developments in plastic, the price differential is widening even further. The reason why glass is so expensive is that it is much heavier and more fragile than these other materials. This causes higher production costs because (1) there are more back injuries to employees (thereby increasing our medical insurance premiums), (2) there is a need for special handling care (e.g., bottle carriers, protective cardboard), (3) breakage occurs, and (4) the greater weight increases the cost of fuel used in transportation.

We use a considerable number of glass bottles in emerging market countries because the total cost differential between glass and aluminum or plastic is not as great in these countries. For example, because of lower labor costs in South America, we can better afford to use the more labor-intensive process of handling the heavy glass bottles. The machinery to blow out the plastic pellets into 1- and 2-liter bottles is a lot more expensive in these countries than here in the United States. Furthermore, people in emerging market countries seem to like the idea of receiving their deposit back when returning glass bottles, however small the amount might seem to you to be.

However, a real issue that I think we should address even before devising a packaging, production, and distribution plan is the source of our bottled water. As you know, to be considered "spring water," bottled water must actually come from a spring. The industry has grown so rapidly over the past few years that companies are having a harder time finding good sources of spring water. I have heard of bottled water companies hiring geologists to look for water just as oil companies hire them to look for new sources of oil. Therefore, we should consider the cost of "manufacturing" the product itself—water—before even considering the cost of packaging. I eagerly await your response to the issues raised in this memo.

SUMMARY

The topics in this chapter represent the foundation for the economic analysis of supply. After all, people may be willing to purchase a firm's product at a certain price, but will the firm be willing to supply the product at this price? The answer to this question begins with the relationship between the firm's inputs and the resulting output, that is, the firm's production function. In the short run, where at least one of the firm's inputs is fixed, we have learned that the firm is subject to the law of diminishing returns and the three stages of production. This means that as additional inputs are added to the fixed input, at some point the additional output (i.e., marginal product) resulting from the additional input will start to diminish. Once this level of production is exceeded, the output per unit of variable input (i.e., average product) will reach a maximum and then start to diminish. The point of maximum average product marks the end of Stage I and the beginning of Stage II, the stage in which the rational firm should be operating. The use of still more units of variable inputs will eventually cause the total output to decline (i.e., cause MP to assume negative values). By assigning monetary values to both the variable input and the output along with the use of marginal analysis, we were able to determine precisely where in Stage II the firm should be operating. A similar analysis can be used to derive the conditions for the optimal use of more than one input. (See Appendix 6C.)

The long-run function, in which a firm is able to vary all its inputs, was also considered in this chapter. When a firm is able to vary its entire scale of production, it may experience varying returns to scale. That is, the increase in output may be proportional, less than proportional, or greater than proportional to the increase in all its inputs.

Most studies of production functions have used an exponential expression that results in a monotonically increasing output as inputs are added. This model was introduced by Cobb and Douglas in the 1920s. The original studies used the time series method of analysis, but researchers soon switched to cross-sectional regression, which they found more useful. The Cobb-Douglas function permits the investigation of both marginal product in short-run situations (with the presence of a fixed factor) and returns to scale in the long run. It is difficult to summarize the large number of studies conducted over the years, but the results generally indicate that constant returns to scale are the rule in manufacturing industries in the United States and in other countries.

In chapter 7, we present an analysis of a firm's cost function. We then see how a solid background in the economic analysis of production will provide a better understanding of the cost structure of a firm, in both the short and the long run.

IMPORTANT CONCEPTS (Items with * are discussed in Appendix 6B or 6C)

Average product (AP): The total product divided by the number of units of a particular input employed by the firm. (p. 189)

Cobb-Douglas production function: A power function in which total quantity produced is the result of the product of inputs raised to some power (e.g., $Q = aL^bK^c$). (p. 204)

Inputs: The resources used in the production process. Examples in economic analysis generally involve the inputs *capital* (representing the fixed input) and *labor* (representing the variable input). Other terms used in reference to these resources are *factors* and *factors of production*. (p. 187)

*__Isocost:__ A line representing different combinations of two inputs that a firm can purchase with the same amount of money. In production analysis, the isocost indicates a firm's budget constraint. (p. 242)

*__Isoquant:__ A curve representing different combinations of two inputs that produce the same level of output. (p. 237)

Law of diminishing returns: A law stating that as additional units of a variable input are added to a fixed input, at some point the additional output (i.e., the marginal product) will start to diminish. Because at least one input is required to be fixed for this law to take effect, this law is considered a short-run phenomenon. (p. 191)

Long-run production function: The maximum quantity of a good or service that can be produced by a set of inputs, assuming the firm is free to vary the amount of *all* inputs being used. (p. 199)

Marginal labor cost (MLC): The additional cost to the firm of using an additional unit of labor. This is also referred to as *marginal factor cost* (MFC) or *marginal resource cost* (MRC). Labor is used in this term because it is the most commonly used variable input in the economic analysis of production. (p. 197)

Marginal product (MP): The change in output resulting from a unit change in one of the firm's variable inputs. (p. 189)

*__Marginal rate of technical substitution (MRTS):__ Given two inputs X and Y, the marginal rate of technical substitution of X for Y represents the reduction in Y relative to the amount of X that a firm must add to replace Y to maintain the same amount of output. Mathematically speaking, it is represented by the slope of some given isoquant or $\Delta Y/\Delta X$ ($\delta y/\delta x$ for continuous isoquants). (p. 239)

Marginal revenue product (MRP): The additional amount of revenue resulting from the use of an additional unit of a variable input. It can be calculated by taking an input's marginal product and multiplying it by the market price of the product. For example, given some input i, that $\text{MRP}_i = \text{MP}_i \times P$. (p. 197)

MRP = MLC rule: A rule that guides a firm in its decision about how many units of a variable input it should use relative to its fixed input. The rule states that the firm should employ a particular input up to the point at which the revenue contribution of the additional input is equal to the cost incurred by the firm to employ this particular input. In the case of more than one input, this condition applies separately for every input used by the firm. (p. 197)

Power function: A mathematical function of the form $Y = X^n$, where n is a fixed number and X takes positive values continuously. (p. 203)

Production function: The maximum quantity of a good or service that can be produced by a set of inputs. Production functions are divided into two types: short run and long run. (p. 187)

Returns to scale: The increase in output that results from an increase in all of a firm's inputs by some proportion. If the output increases by a *greater* proportion than the increase in inputs, the firm is experiencing increasing returns to scale. If the output increases by the *same* proportion as the inputs, the firm is experiencing constant returns to scale. Finally, if the output increases by a *smaller* proportion than the increase in inputs, the firm is experiencing decreasing returns to scale. (p. 199)

Short-run production function: The maximum quantity of a good or service that can be produced by a set of inputs, assuming the amount of *at least one* of the inputs used remains unchanged as output varies. (p. 188)

Stages of production: In a short-run production function, there are three stages of production. Stage I starts at zero and ends at the point where the firm has reached the maximum level of *average* product. Stage II continues from this point on to the point at which the firm has reached the maximum level of *total* product. Stage III continues from this point on. Economic theory suggests that the rational firm will try to produce in the short run in Stage II. In Stage I the firm would be underutilizing its fixed inputs, and in Stage III it would be overutilizing its fixed inputs. (p. 194)

Total product (TP):   The firm's output for a given level of input usage, also referred to as *quantity*, or simply *Q*. (p. 189)

QUESTIONS

1. Explain the difference between a short-run and long-run production function. Cite one example of this difference in a business situation.

2. Define the *law of diminishing returns*. Why is this law considered a short-run phenomenon?

3. What are the key points in a short-run production function that delineate the three stages of production? Explain the relationship between the law of diminishing returns and the three stages of production.

4. Explain why a firm's adherence to the MRP = MLC rule enables it to find the optimal number of units of a variable input to use in the short-run production process.

5. Define returns to scale. Why is this considered a long-run phenomenon?

6. According to the rule for optimal input usage, a firm should hire a person as long as her marginal revenue product is greater than her marginal cost to the company. It is well known that many companies have management training programs in which new trainees are paid relatively high starting salaries and are not expected to make substantial contributions to the company until after the program is over (programs may run between 6 to 18 months). In offering such training programs, is a company violating the optimality rule? Explain.

7. Explain the relationship between marginal product and average product. Why can we expect marginal product to equal average product at average product's maximum point?

8. Cite and discuss possible reasons a firm may actually find itself operating in Stage I or Stage III of the short-run production function.

9. Discuss the problems of measuring productivity in actual work situations. How might productivity be measured for each of the following industries?
   a. Education (e.g., elementary and secondary education, higher education—undergraduate and graduate)
   b. Government (e.g., the Social Security Office, the Internal Revenue Service)
   c. Manufacturing (e.g., soap and toothpaste, computers, heavy machinery)
   d. Finance and insurance (e.g., banks, insurance companies, brokerage houses)

10. For those of you with current or previous work experience, how is (was) productivity measured in your organization?

11. What are the two statistical methods most frequently used to estimate production functions? What are the advantages and disadvantages of each method?

12. Design a study of a production function for a steel mill and another one for a call center. Which variables would you use, and what statistical method would you select for each function? In general, compare and contrast the production function for a product and one for a service.

Refer to Appendix 6B and 6C to help you answer questions 13–16.

13. What are the properties of the Cobb-Douglas function $Q = aL^bK^{1-b}$. What conceptual change occurs when the equation is changed to $Q = aL^bK^c$?

14. In a power function $Q = aV^b$, how can you tell whether diminishing marginal returns are present?

15. When a Cobb-Douglas function with at least two inputs shows the existence of constant returns to scale, it implies that the marginal product of each input is diminishing. True or false? Explain.

16. Write a production function equation that expresses the existence of diminishing marginal returns. How will this equation differ from one that shows both increasing and decreasing marginal returns?

PROBLEMS

1. Indicate whether each of the following statements is true or false. Explain why.
   a. When the law of diminishing returns takes effect, a firm's average product will start to decrease.
   b. Decreasing returns to scale occurs when a firm has to increase all its inputs at an increasing rate to maintain a constant rate of increase in its output.
   c. A linear short-run production function implies that the law of diminishing returns does not take effect over the range of output being considered.
   d. Stage I of the production process ends at the point where the law of diminishing returns occurs.

2. The Oceanic Pacific fleet has just decided to use a pole-and-line method of fishing instead of gill netting to catch tuna. The latter method involves the use of miles of nets strung out across the ocean and therefore entraps other sea creatures besides tuna (e.g., porpoises, sea turtles). Concern for endangered species was one reason for this decision, but perhaps more important was the fact that the major tuna canneries in the United States will no longer accept tuna caught by gill netting.

   Oceanic Pacific decided to conduct a series of experiments to determine the amount of tuna that could be caught with different crew sizes. The results of these experiments follow.

Number of Fishermen	Daily Tuna Catch (lb)
0	0
1	50
2	110
3	300
4	450
5	590
6	665
7	700
8	725
9	710

   a. Determine the point at which diminishing returns occurs.
   b. Indicate the points that delineate the three stages of production.
   c. Suppose the market price of tuna is $3.50/pound. How many fishermen should the company use if the daily wage rate is $100?
   d. Suppose a glut in the market for tuna causes the price to fall to $2.75/pound. What effect would this have on the number of fishermen used per boat?
   Suppose the price rose to $5.00/pound. What effect would this have on its hiring decision?

   e. Suppose the firm realizes that to keep up with the demand for tuna caught by the more humane pole-and-line method of fishing, each of its boats must catch at least 1,000 pounds of fish per day. Given the preceding data, what should it consider doing? Explain.

3. A firm has the following short-run production function:

$$Q = 50L + 6L^2 - 0.5L^3$$

where Q = Quantity of output per week
      L = Labor (number of workers)

   a. When does the law of diminishing returns take effect?
   b. Calculate the range of values for labor over which Stages I, II, and III occur.
   c. Assume each worker is paid $10 per hour and works a 40-hour week. How many workers should the firm hire if the price of the output is $10? Suppose the price of the output falls to $7.50. What do you think would be the short-run impact on the firm's production? The long-run impact?

4. The owner of a small car rental service is trying to decide on the appropriate numbers of vehicles and mechanics to use in the business for the current level of operations. He recognizes that his choice represents a trade-off between the two resources. His past experience indicates that this trade-off is as follows (**see Appendix 6B for help in answering this question**):

Vehicles	Mechanics
100	2.5 (includes one part-timer)
70	5
50	10
40	15
35	25
32	35

   a. Assume the annual (leasing) cost per vehicle is $6,000 and the annual salary per mechanic is $25,000. What combination of vehicles and mechanics should he employ?
   b. Illustrate this problem with the use of an isoquant/isocost diagram. Indicate graphically the optimal combination of resources.

5. An American company that sells consumer electronics products has manufacturing facilities in Mexico, Taiwan, and Canada. The average hourly wage, output, and annual overhead cost for each site are as follows:

	Mexico	Taiwan	Canada
Hourly wage rate	$1.50	$3.00	$6.00
Output per person	10	18	20
Fixed overhead cost	$150,000	$90,000	$110,000

   a. Given these figures, is the firm currently allocating its production resources optimally? If not, what should it do? (Consider output per person as a proxy for marginal product.)
   b. Suppose the firm wants to consolidate all its manufacturing into one facility. Where should it locate? Explain.

6. The owner of a car wash is trying to decide on the number of people to employ based on the following short-run production function:

$$Q = 6L - 0.5L^2$$

where Q = Number of car washes per hour
L = Number of workers

a. Generate a schedule showing total product, average product, and marginal product. Plot this schedule on a graph.
b. Suppose the price of a basic car wash (no undercoating, no wax treatment, etc.) in his area of business is $5. How many people should he hire if he pays each worker $6/hour?
c. Suppose he considers hiring students on a part-time basis for $4/hour. Do you think he should hire more workers at this lower rate? Explain.

7. The Noble Widget Corporation produces just one product, widgets. The company's new economist has calculated a short-run production function as follows:

$$Q = 7V + 0.6V^2 - 0.1V^3$$

where Q is the number of widgets produced per day and V is the number of production workers working an 8-hour day.
a. Develop a production schedule with V equaling 1 to 10.
b. Calculate average and marginal products.
c. Draw a graph.

8. Suppose Noble's production function (see problem 7) is as follows:

$$Q = 7V - 0.5V^2$$

where Q is the number of widgets produced per day and V is the number of production workers working an 8-hour day.
a. Develop a production schedule with V equaling 1 to 10.
b. Calculate average and marginal products.
c. Draw a graph.
d. Discuss the difference between the form of the production function in this problem and the form in problem 7. Discuss, among other things, the implications for the three stages of production.

9. The International Calculator Company of China produces handheld calculators in its plant. It tries to keep the number of workers in the plant constant so the only variable factor that can be measured is materials. Over the last seven monthly periods, the data for materials and quantity produced were the following:

Materials	Quantity
70	450
60	430
80	460
95	490
77	465
100	550
85	490

a. Calculate a Cobb-Douglas production function of the form $Q = aM^b$.
b. Discuss the important properties of your results.
c. What is the marginal product of materials?

10. The Brady Corporation has eleven plants located around the world. In a recent year, the data for each plant gave the number of labor hours (in thousands), capital (total net plant assets, in millions), and total quantity produced:

Capital	Labor	Quantity
30	250	245
34	270	240
44	300	300
50	320	320
70	350	390
76	400	440
84	440	520
86	440	520
104	450	580
110	460	600
116	460	600

The plants all operate at a similar level of technology so a production function can be derived from the data.

a. Use a Cobb-Douglas production function to calculate a regression, and discuss the important characteristics of your results, such as the form of the equation, R^2, and the statistical significance of the coefficients.

b. Calculate the estimated production for each plant.

c. Does the result indicate constant, decreasing, or increasing returns to scale?

d. What are the elasticities of production of labor and of capital? What is the meaning of the elasticities?

e. Is the marginal product of labor decreasing? (See Appendix 6C to answer this question.)

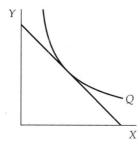

Refer to Appendix 6B and 6C for help in answering problems 11–15.

11. Show what will happen to the diagram above as a result of the changes listed.

a. The firm's budget increases.

b. The price of Y decreases.

c. The price of X decreases.

d. Y becomes more expensive, and X becomes less expensive.

e. Technology makes the Y input more productive.

f. Technology increases the productivity of both inputs by the same proportion.

12. Suppose you are given the following production function:

$$Q = 100K^{0.5}L^{0.5}$$

a. Use this function to generate the data for the following table:

K									
8									
7									
6									
5									
4									
3									
2									
1									
0	1	2	3	4	5	6	7	8	L

b. Identify as many isoquants as you can.
c. Comment on the returns to scale exhibited in this figure. (*Suggestion:* Start by assuming one unit of L and one unit of K are used. Then systematically increase both inputs by some given proportion.)

13. Following are different algebraic expressions of the production function. Decide whether each one has constant, increasing, or decreasing returns to scale.
    a. $Q = 75L^{0.25}K^{0.75}$
    b. $Q = 75A^{0.15}B^{0.40}C^{0.45}$
    c. $Q = 75L^{0.60}K^{0.70}$
    d. $Q = 100 + 50L + 50K$
    e. $Q = 50L + 50K + 50LK$
    f. $Q = 50L^2 + 50K^2$
    g. Based on the answers for the preceding equations, can you make any generalizations about the functional form of a production equation, the relative magnitudes of the coefficients, and the nature of the returns to scale? Explain.

14. Use the production matrix presented to answer the following questions.

Y	8	31	67	101	133	161	184	202	213	
	7	30	62	93	122	147	168	184	193	
	6	27	54	82	108	130	149	168	163	
	5	23	45	69	91	108	126	137	142	
	4	17	34	54	72	89	101	108	111	
	3	12	25	38	54	65	74	79	79	
	2	6	14	24	33	44	54	47	43	
	1	3	7	11	17	27	19	16	8	
		1	2	3	4	5	6	7	8	X

a. Determine the returns to scale for this matrix. (Start with one unit of X and one unit of Y.)
b. Suppose the firm has a budget of $100, and the price of Y is $20 and the price of X is $10. What is the optimal combination of inputs X and Y for this firm?
c. Suppose the prices of Y and X are now $10 and $20, respectively. What effect will this have on the firm's optimal input combination?
d. Illustrate the answers to the preceding questions with the use of an isoquant/isocost diagram.

15. The economist for the ABC Truck Manufacturing Corporation has calculated a production function for the manufacture of their medium-size trucks as follows:

$$Q = 1.3L^{0.75}K^{0.3}$$

where Q is number of trucks produced per week, L is number of labor hours per day, and K is the daily usage of capital investment.

a. Does the equation exhibit increasing, constant, or decreasing returns to scale? Why?
b. How many trucks will be produced per week with the following amounts of labor and capital?

Labor	Capital
100	50
120	60
150	75
200	100
300	150

c. If capital and labor both are increased by 10 percent, what will be the percentage increase in quantity produced?
d. Assume only labor increases by 10 percent. What will be the percentage increase in production? What does this result imply about marginal product?
e. Assume only capital increases by 10 percent. What will be the percentage increase in production?
f. How would your answers change if the production function were $Q = 1.3L^{0.7}K^{0.3}$ instead? What are the implications of this production function?

Productivity in Services[34]

The vital importance of service activities to the world economy needs no introduction. The service sector is the fastest growing in the global economy as measured by GDP, employment, and exports. According to the WTO (World Trade Organization), it accounts for roughly two-thirds of global output, one-third of global employment (over two-thirds in the more developed economies), and almost 20 percent of global trade. The ability to innovate and drive productivity growth in service activities is essential for the success of firms and nations, and for raising living standards worldwide.

When economists first developed their theories of production in the first half of the last century, manufacturing was the key sector in the developed countries of North America and Europe, and agriculture still made up a large portion of a country's labor force and output. In the rest of the world, agriculture was the biggest sector. But regardless of which part of the world or which sector, it would be safe to assume that the output Q of the production function would be a tangible good. Now that the service sector is such an important part of the global economy, we believe that it is important to look at some of the special challenges that arise in the measurement and improvement of production when the output Q is a service rather than a good.

Of course in the production function for goods, the output Q is considered at a very high level of abstraction, because there are all types of tangible product outputs. By the same token, the production of services is equally diverse, with different components displaying vast differences in capital intensity, innovation, and prospects for growth. So in measuring and studying service productivity, it is very important to capture these differences and to understand how and why they change over time, across firms or industries, and across locations.

Productivity as a Measure of Health

The concept of productivity is very simple: how much output can be produced from a given set of inputs. The output can be as straightforward as a single product or service that a firm sells, or it can be a weighted average of products and services aggregated over a firm or other institution, industry, country, or set of countries. Naturally, there are many kinds of inputs, but they are normally grouped into the broad categories of labor, capital, and intermediate inputs.[35] Most generally, therefore, productivity can be expressed as:

$$\text{Productivity} = \frac{\text{Output index}}{\substack{\text{Combined index for labor,} \\ \text{capital, and intermediate inputs}}} \quad \text{(6A.1)}$$

Three types of productivity are commonly studied:

1. ***Labor productivity (LP):*** Calculated by ignoring the capital and intermediate inputs in Equation (6A.1). The labor input can be measured in units of time or people and is often aggregated using weights to differentiate between different skill levels. LP is perhaps the most commonly discussed measure of productivity, and in fact many authors refer to it simply as *productivity*. LP is closely watched as a critical measure of economic health, because its growth is strongly linked to the standard of living.

2. ***Partial productivity measures (PPMs):*** Calculated by selecting some subcomponent of the output and a corresponding subcomponent of the input. Examples would include meals/server (restaurant); calls/person/hour (call center); computer servers managed/full-time employee (IT outsourcing). These kinds of productivity measures tend to be most helpful in targeted analyses of a business activity, or to compare one's execution of a business activity against industry benchmarks.

3. ***Multifactor (or total factor) productivity (MFP or TFP):*** Calculated by including all relevant outputs and inputs. This is the most complete, all-encompassing productivity measure.

---

[34]This appendix was reprinted by permission of Matthew Denesuk, Ph.D., IBM Global Technology Services.
[35]Intermediate inputs refer to a combination of energy, materials, and enabling services needed to produce the output. If the value of intermediate inputs is removed from the gross output measure, one is left with "value-added." If value-added is used as an output measure, then the intermediate inputs can be ignored.

Because it includes all the relevant inputs and outputs, MFP is the productivity measure that should correlate most closely with a firm's (or other economic system's) profitability and competitive advantage. In practice, however, LP and/or PPMs, which are easier to measure, are found to be good indicators of advantage if they are targeted at the most important elements of the economic activity in question. Because labor is such an important input in many businesses (especially in many services businesses), LP and/or PPMs based on labor inputs are often strategic measures to track and improve.

It is important, nevertheless, to distinguish productivity from cost efficiency. Because productivity measures typically look at input and output *quantities* (rather than *costs* or *prices*), variations in costs and prices (e.g., with activities operating in different countries) can result, at least temporarily, in lower productivity economic activity operating at higher profitability. For example, assuming the cost of inputs remains constant, output prices could rise proportionately more than input productivity falls, thereby causing a net increase in profitability.

How one analyzes productivity depends specifically on the kind of economic system being analyzed, the goals of the analysis, and the kinds of data available. A macroeconomist might be interested in the sustainability of economic growth in a national economy and will employ broad measures of the labor force, capital equipment, and aggregate business outputs to evaluate LP and MFP measures. Partial productivity measures are more relevant in managerial economic decision analysis. For example, in this chapter, we saw how economic theory states that increases in a particular input, holding other inputs constant, result in output changes that follow the three stages of production.

Improving Productivity

In principle, what is needed to improve productivity in service systems (economic systems with a high component of service activities) is the same as in manufacturing: to increase the level of assets (or capital) per worker, where "asset" needs to be understood in its broader sense to include intellectual assets and other "nonrival"[36] assets. In some cases, the path may be a straightforward extension of existing strategies. For example, an airline may improve labor productivity by flying larger planes. But in other cases, a more radical rethinking of the service process may be required to make the service amenable to an increase in assets.

A basic mechanism for productivity improvement, understood at least since the time of Adam Smith, is rooted in the concept of *specialization*. As a worker is able to focus on a relatively narrow task, he or she tends to get progressively better at it (provided job satisfaction does not diminish appreciably). The intensity of time devoted to this task tends to result both in accumulating skill, as well as to the development of better means (assets) for performing the task.

Effective specialization, however, requires that the work be broken into a set of components, each of which can separately support some amount of specialization. This in turn requires that the overall work process be substantially standardized, so that the same components, interacting in essentially the same ways, are employed in most deliveries of the service. Investment in technology (new processes, tools, machinery, etc.) for improving the performance of each component can be justified on the basis of its extent of repeated usage. Scale economies and other efficiencies that correspond to growing productivity inevitably result (see Figure 6A.1). Thus a level of standardization ultimately enables effective increases in assets (in the broad sense) to drive growth in an economic system.

The Challenges of Improving Productivity in Services: "Baumol's Disease"

One cannot really talk about the challenges associated with productivity in service systems without referring to William Baumol. In a famous paper in the latter half of the 1960s,[37] he posited that there

---

[36]Nonrival assets can be described roughly as assets that are not depleted as they are used (for example, a business process, a manufacturing process, deep industry knowledge, software for which one has full rights).

[37]W. J. Baumol, "Macroeconomics of Unbalanced Growth: The Anatomy of an Urban Crisis," *American Economic Review*, 57, no. 3 (June 1967): 415–426. Also see: Barry P. Bosworth and Jack E Triplett (2003), *Productivity Measurement Issues in Services Industries: "Baumol's Disease" Has Been Cured.* The Brookings Institution and James Heilbrun (2003), *Baumol's Cost Disease* (PDF), originally in Edward Elgar, *A Handbook of Cultural Economics,* 2003.

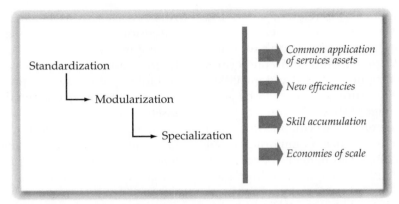

Figure 6A.1   Following a process of standardization → modularization → specialization enables a service activity to consistently leverage various types of assets that enable improving productivity and scalability.

were basically two types of economic activities, distinguished by their "technological structure":

1. "Technologically progressive" activities, in which capital investment and the potential for economies of scale enable continuing increases in labor productivity

2. Other activities that, while they might experience occasional spurts in labor productivity, fundamentally resist sustained productivity growth

Naturally, one can always divide things into two buckets based on the value of a particular variable, but Baumol created a stir by arguing that to a large extent, *service industries tend to fall into the growth-resisting category.* He and others have articulated arguments for this and their nuances over the years, and they can be understood as emanating from the fact that with most service industries, *the labor input, and its interaction with the customer, is an integral part of the output.*

Several growth-inhibiting factors are associated with this intimate labor-output linkage:

1. ***Direct linkage between labor quantity and output quality:*** Reducing the labor quantity very often reduces—in fact or perception—the quality of the output, and thereby the effective level of the output. This contrasts with manufacturing, where labor activities are largely shielded from the customer, and where the manufacturer therefore has more latitude in changing the production system in ways that reduce labor.[38] For example, most people probably have no

idea—and don't really care—how many people it took to make their refrigerator. But parents do focus on the teacher/pupil ratio at a school; people notice or get annoyed when it seems as if no one is available to help them at the department store; and a business customer will be unhappy if only one junior associate shows up for the kick-off meeting of a consulting engagement.

2. ***Customer as input:*** The customer's labor (and sometimes other customer assets) is often an important input, and a firm normally has much less control over this input than over its own labor, making it more difficult to standardize and manage the process effectively.

3. ***Customization:*** Service offerings are often customized to some extent for each customer (which is typically seen as value-adding), and this limits the extent to which standardization and its efficiency and scale benefits can be leveraged.[39]

4. ***Intangibility of the output:*** Because the output of many services activities can be difficult to define consistently (which is in part due to the three points above), it can be very difficult to measure. And, as a general principle, one cannot improve what one cannot measure. This is addressed in more detail in the next section.

Other factors include the fact that services cannot generally be stored (so they cannot be pre-made), and that their production often requires being located physically near the client.

---

[38]In a recent book (*Service Is Front Stage: Positioning Services for Value Advantage,* Insead Business Press, 2006), James Teboul distinguishes services from manufacturing by the relative amount of these "front stage" activities, in which there is direct interaction with the customer.

[39]It should be noted that made-to-order or just-in-time manufacturing processes (e.g., as pioneered in the personal computer industry by Dell Computer) effectively incorporate a large service aspect into what had been seen as more of a manufacturing business, and this brings some of the challenges in improving production productivity.

Measurement of Services Productivity

Output intangibility, customization and other sources of output heterogeneity, accounting for the customer's inputs, and difficulty in adjusting output measures to include quality factors all contribute to difficulties in measuring service productivity. Although there are also challenges in productivity measurement for more manufacturing-oriented activities, the fact that these latter activities produce a more tangible product, for which the quality factors can generally be well defined and measured in-house before the product is sold, makes these challenges much more manageable.

Consider the commercial airline industry. Because of the substantial degrees of standardization, relatively little customer input quantity, and a high level of technology leverage, this might be considered one of the service industries more amenable to measurement. Conceptually, the purpose of their services is to move people and their luggage from one place to another. Thus, a straightforward measure for output could be revenue passenger–miles (i.e., the number of miles flown by paying customers), perhaps with revenue weightings for international vs. domestic and first class vs. business class vs. coach. In addition, one might want to segment further to account for the major economic differences between shorter and longer flights.

But even with such a refined output definition, investments that result in higher quality service—and thus greater output—will not be reflected in the output measure (except insofar as this quality creates additional demand, which available capacity can fulfill). For example, investment in more flight attendants, gate agents, and/or better meal service can improve the customer experience and benefits substantially. The same can be said for investments that reduce travel delays, such as in-process management and technology, or redundant staff and equipment. At the firm level, a given airline might be able to generate such measures, but it is clearly quite difficult for industry analysts or government agencies to create measures that capture all these components of output and track them accurately over long time periods.

Output measurement is even more challenging in businesses such as consulting, where (1) the customer and his or her organization is a substantial participant (i.e., input) in the value creation process; and (2) each unit of output the service provider sells can be virtually unique, described by a customized, co-written contract. So how does a $50K strategy consulting engagement three years ago compare to a $60K engagement today? Do they correspond to essentially the same level of output, with the difference due to simple inflation-type forces? Or have new technologies improved the ability to execute such engagements, such that twice the level of effective output can now be delivered with modest additional labor input? Or have there been variations in the inputs (data, person-hours, equipment, etc.) that the customer provided in their participation in the process?

In principle, one can simply take revenue as a proxy for output, and this is commonly done in industries for which the government has published "deflators" that correct for inflation and other sources of changes in output level per dollar (e.g., in computer hardware, real output per dollar has grown enormously over the last few decades, and the deflator must account for this). Clearly, however, this just passes the output measurement problem along to the government agency or other group that will publish the deflator.

Although deflators exist for some services industries, there is not sufficient history in many of them, and the relatively coarse granularity is difficult to apply at the firm or market level. On the other hand, analysis of service industries that do not prodigiously employ technology should not be as sensitive to the specific deflator used. Gronroos and Ojasalo[40] have described many of the difficulties in measurement of service productivity and proposed a simple, easy to calculate measure equal to the total revenue divided by the total cost. Note that this can be seen as closely aligned with an MFP measure (where dollar amounts are used to combine the inputs and outputs), and contains the same information as the profit margin.[41]

Why Service Productivity Matters

With service activities being such a large fraction of developed economies (and growing rapidly in the developing world), an intrinsic resistance to productivity growth is troubling. But in his work referred to

---

[40]Gronroos and Ojasalo, "Service Productivity: Towards a Conceptualization of the Transformation of Inputs into Economic Results in Services," *Journal of Business Research*, 57 (2004), pp. 414–423.
[41]Mathematically, this measure = $1/(1 - margin)$.

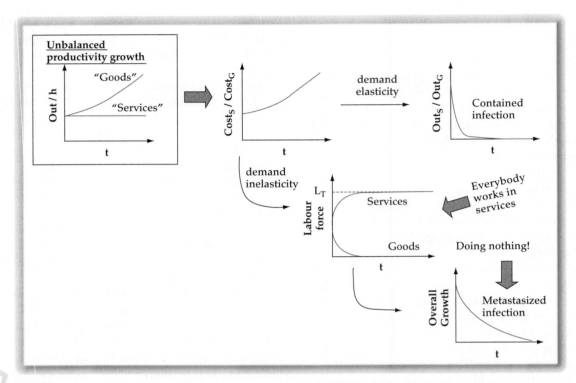

Figure 6A.2 Schematic depiction of "Baumol's Disease," in which many services are posited to be intrinsically low-growth, and whereby under certain economic conditions, such low-growth activities can depress an entire economic system.

earlier, Baumol went still further. Based on the price elasticity of demand for a given service, he posited two scenarios (see Figure 6A.2):

1. *Elastic demand:*   Because productivity stagnation in an underperforming activity will raise its relative costs, if the price elasticity of demand is large (such as for many nonessential goods), then these rising costs should cause demand for the activity to continually diminish. In this case, it reduces the productivity of the overall economy in proportion to its size (a "contained infection," if you will).

2. *Inelastic demand:*   If the price elasticity of demand is small (such as for health care, many foodstuffs), the rising costs will cause the activity to continually absorb more and more of the available labor resources. This will deprive the more productive activities of needed inputs and concentrate resources in the less productive activities, thus producing a "double whammy" effect that can sharply diminish overall economic growth (a "metastasized infection").

Because services are such a large part of most economic systems, either scenario bodes ill for overall economic growth, but if the inelastic case applies to a substantial fraction of these underperforming services, the deleterious effects are effectively amplified.

Thus a focus on large, relatively inelastic areas (such as health care) is doubly important.

Service Productivity: The Data

Overall productivity growth in the goods sector has traditionally been higher than that in the services sector, and this continues to be true as of this writing. However, the size of the gap between them, which is what spurred the deep concerns associated with Baumol's Disease, has been narrowing sharply, leading some to claim that "Baumol's Disease has been cured."[42] In fact, recent studies demonstrate that increases in labor productivity growth (i.e., productivity acceleration) has been associated *mostly* with the services sector in the latter part of the 1990s, and due *entirely* to services in the first half of the 2000s—when goods productivity actually declined (see Figure 6A.3).

To understand the drivers of this growth, one can use a technique known as *growth accounting,* using

---

[42]For example, see Jack E. Triplett and Barry P. Bosworth in *The New Economy and Beyond: Past, Present and Future,* pp. 34–71, ed. Dennis W. Jansen (2007, Edward Elgar Publishing, UK).

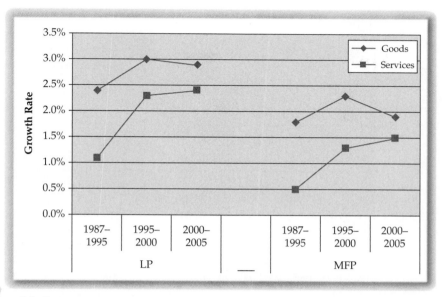

Figure 6A.3   Productivity (LP and MFP) growth rates for the goods sector and the services sector over three time periods between 1987 and 2005. Goods still exhibit stronger productivity growth, but acceleration has been much stronger in services. Data from Barry P. Bosworth, and Jack E. Triplett, "The Early 21st Century U.S. Productivity Expansion Is Still in Services," *International Productivity Monitor,* 14 (2007), pp. 3–19.

data describing labor, capital investment, and prices (wages, effective rental prices) to estimate how much of the observed growth is coming from various types of capital deepening and from MFP. A commonly used approach demonstrates that MFP changes can be estimated by subtracting weighted changes in capital intensity from changes in the LP.[43] The interpretation is that MFP is the "unexplained" portion of the changes in LP and is thus associated with whatever important production factors the analyst has not included. Traditionally, these are grouped under the label "technological changes" and can include, for example, different kinds of intangible capital, improvement in processes, or methods available broadly.[44] For the study referred to in Figure 6A.3, the estimated relative contributions of capital and labor tell an interesting story (see Figure 6A.4). In the goods sector, despite the recent downtrend, MFP plays a dominant role in overall productivity growth. In services, MFP and capital are much more comparable, but the growth in MFP has clearly been outpacing that of the capital contribution. Whether and to what extent this trend continues, it may be an

important indicator of the sustainability of services productivity growth.

Although the services sector overall is exhibiting promising productivity growth, there is a considerable amount of heterogeneity—the sector is made up of many industries that exhibit widely varying productivity characteristics. For example, in the same study referred to in Figure 6A.3, it was found that, despite a jump in the 1995–2000 period, the "food services and drinking places" industry has displayed low and shrinking LP (see Figure 6A.5). Both capital investment and MFP have dropped off, and one can wonder whether the jump observed was a one-time event associated with a unique opportunity to deploy new technology. The critical question in a case like this is whether the decline in investment was due to a lack of opportunities for improving productivity—which would bode ill for the future—or due to some other constraint on investment (such as a temporary decline in demand).

For a quite different example, the "professional and business services industry" has shown rapid growth in measured LP, exceeding the sector average by about 0.7 percentage points in the latest period. This was apparently driven by accelerating investments in capital (mostly information technology) as well as steadily increasing MFP, and there are no obvious indications that this growth cannot be sustained.

---

[43]For example, see Robert J. Barro and Xavier Sala-i-Martin, *Economic Growth,* 2nd ed., MIT Press (2004), pp. 434–460.
[44]Note that, defined this way, MFP estimates also include whatever measurement errors may have been made in calculating LP, traditional capital, or the weighting factors.

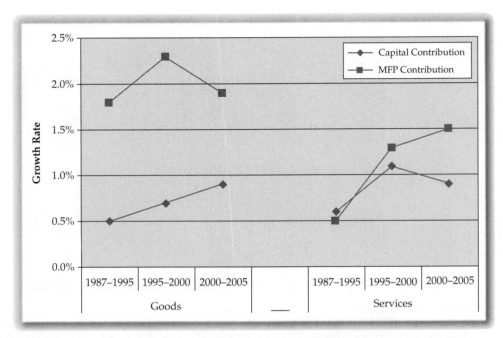

Figure 6A.4   Contributions of MFP and of capital to the observed growth rate in labor productivity over three time periods between 1987 and 2005. Despite a recent decline in capital contribution, the services sector is exhibiting increasing MFP. The data are taken from the same study referred to in Figure 6A.3.

Figure 6A.5   Two examples of labor productivity growth and the contributions of capital and MFP. "Food services & drinking places" shows overall poor productivity performance, despite what appears to have been a short-term boost in the 1995–2000 period. "Professional & business services" has exhibited very strong productivity growth, with no indication that continued growth is not sustainable. The data are taken from the same study referred to in Figure 6A.3.

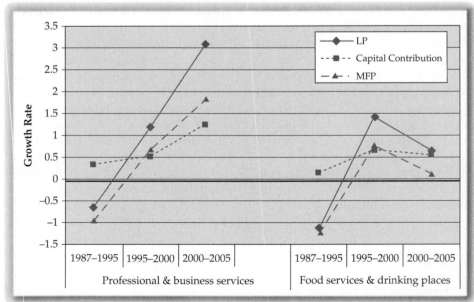

Service Productivity: The Opportunities

General Principles

As stated earlier, productivity in service systems can be increased by increasing the level of asset uptake (where "asset" is to be understood in its broad sense, to include new processes, methods, tools, IT software/hardware, as well as more conventional equipment), and/or by increasing the intrinsic skill level of the people involved (e.g., through training, good HR practices). The assets can be targeted to either replace or enhance labor, or to make labor fundamentally more efficient.

Replace or Enhance Labor.   In situations where service activities are highly customized, labor can be replaced, for example, with predeveloped output components. These output components may be mass-produced or be nonrival in nature, so that their use increases labor productivity by providing incremental output with essentially no incremental labor. For example, consider the IT services industry. From a firm's experience-based understanding of difficulties with fraud detection in the insurance industry, it may develop a set of detection algorithms, committed to software code, that it can employ in a nonrival manner to multiple future customers.[45] Similarly, such a firm may use its experience gathering customer requirements to develop a simplified template to quickly gather the requirements of a new customer. Going further, such a template can lead to the creation of a standard "menu" of service offerings from which the customer may pick and choose.[46] Such a reduction in scope permits additional opportunities for service firms to predevelop content, tools, and processes and, through specialization effects, to more rapidly improve execution skills. And because the customer's role in co-creating value in service activities is one of the factors that makes it difficult to increase (and even measure) productivity, the use of menus and related constructs serves to more tightly define the customer's role and permits a more industrialized service. With such "productized" services, the customer may have less choice, but in return may receive higher value through better time-to-value, lower cost, and/or higher quality.

Another example relates to self-service, whereby some amount of the customer's interaction with a person is replaced by interaction with assets. ATMs used for self-service banking are a common example, as are the many self-help kiosks that are increasingly seen in retail environments. Even in IT services, a customer can be provided with detailed instructions for performing an initial assessment of the current state of their IT infrastructure and for gathering requirements for the desired end-state. From the perspective of the service provider, self-service can increase labor productivity substantially, because less provider labor is needed, and because any additional labor provided by the customer is generally not counted as a formal input.

As discussed earlier, a service often needs to be substantially standardized for tools or predeveloped output components to have a sufficient utilization rate to be effective. Without this standardization, the assets cannot generally apply across enough instances of the provided service offerings for there to be a substantial impact on the overall productivity. There are, however, exceptions. For example, providing consultants with general-purpose tools (such as information access tools, collaboration tools, expense reporting tools, or travel planning tools) can improve labor productivity without having to standardize the way these consultants do their core work. Or providing improved excavation equipment or nail guns in the construction industry can improve productivity without reducing the level of customization associated with the work. Often, however, such an approach is limited in terms of the extent to which it can provide sustained productivity growth, or in its ability to fundamentally improve the scalability characteristics (i.e., how output scales with the number of consultants) of the business.

Make Labor Fundamentally More Efficient.   It has been argued (for example, by Levitt[47]) that the apparent resistance of service activities to productivity growth is due more to social factors—such as people's perception of what a given type of service should look like—as well as by a lack of imagination in applying technology and "industrial thinking" to service systems. The fundamentals of labor efficiency can be

---

[45]If there is enough demand for such a software asset, it can be made into a conventional product and be governed by traditional product economics (substantial up-front development and hardening, documentation, support infrastructure, etc.). The services software asset must typically be governed by a model in between a product and a service.

[46]Menu-oriented approaches have been successfully applied in many areas, e.g., automotive service, financial services, insurance, and (obviously) restaurants.

[47]Theodore Levitt, "The Industrialization of Service," *Harvard Business Review* (September–October 1976), pp. 63–71.

improved, it is argued, by undertaking a dramatic redesign of the entire service system and/or selecting a narrow market selection in which such redesign is more feasible. Examples include fast-food restaurants (like McDonald's)[48] and specialized automotive repair/maintenance facilities (like Jiffy Lube), which generally provide reduced menus of service offerings, but are able to provide a level of convenience, speed, reliability, and/or other value attributes that enable them to grow productivity while pleasing their customers. Such industrialized service firms are generally not arrived at through a gradual adoption of new assets, but through a radical redesign requiring substantial up-front investment and a greatly changed (and often untested) value proposition—not for the faint of heart.

In summary, labor productivity in service systems can be improved by enhancing or replacing labor, or by radically changing the structure of the service to use labor more efficiently. These approaches, which require up-front investment, can leverage predeveloped output components, new

tools, and rapid skills accumulation through specialization to drive productivity growth.

Real-World Example: IT and Business Services

The ratio of a firm's revenue (suitably deflated) to its headcount is easy to measure and can be taken as a rough proxy for labor productivity. Figure 6A.6 shows panel data for three categories of service firms over the time period from 1999 to 2006. The labor-based group comprises a set of firms that provide service offerings including IT and business process outsourcing, systems and applications management, and consulting—but on a predominantly custom and labor-based basis. Their flat labor productivity (R/HC) behavior indicates that they can grow only by hiring and training large numbers of people.

The standardized, asset-based group includes companies that have generally narrowed their focus and standardized and specialized on a set of asset-based offerings, including payroll and benefits management services, credit and risk management, insurance process services, and financial transaction services. These service activities include substantial labor components, but focus and standardization enable the firms to become more asset-based and to attain continuing productivity increases. These

---

[48]McDonald's and other fast-food chains have even started outsourcing the order-taking function in their drive-through operations.

Figure 6A.6 The behavior of deflated revenue per person—a rough proxy for labor productivity— for labor-based services firms and for asset-based services firms. Asset-based firms are able to increase their labor productivity through technology leverage.

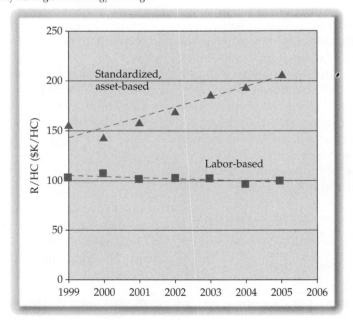

businesses, with growing labor productivity, are fundamentally more scalable because they are not as dependent on large volumes of net new labor acquisition (which involves added costs of hiring, training, retaining) for growth.

The asset-based firms display a growing labor productivity proxy and the apparent ability to grow by making better use of technology. Labor-based firms exhibit a slightly decreasing labor productivity proxy, suggesting that growth requires substantial increases in labor contribution.

Interestingly, further analysis reveals that the labor-based firms invest more in traditional capital assets (which would include computers and other equipment), while the asset-based firms focus more on intellectual and intangible assets, which arise from such activities as R&D and such organizational support activities as sales, marketing, and general administration.[49]

A Hypothetical Example

A simple, if frivolous, example can be used to demonstrate important concepts related to assets and services productivity growth. Consider a business with a snow removal service offering, where the main asset workers employ is a simple snow shovel. Assume that on average about three hours are required to remove the snow from a customer property using this asset. Such a business could employ

relatively low-wage workers to achieve labor productivity of about three properties per day per person, and would be flexible enough to handle almost any type of job if sufficient labor is available.

If a snowblower appliance is acquired and employed, a worker will require higher skill (and salary), but might be able to complete on average about 10 properties per day per person, provided that the property characteristics were amenable to snow clearing with a snowblower. This improvement, however, requires higher capital investment, a higher-skill/higher-wage employee base, and maintenance expenses (e.g., repairs, gas). Thus although labor productivity will clearly improve, the behavior of MFP (and profitability) will depend on the price of snowblowers and the cost of capital, maintenance costs, and the utilization of the assets, that is, the quantity of services engagements to which the asset can be applied. This latter factor in turn depends on the marketing/sales function's ability to find and secure enough customers whose properties are amenable to snow removal using a snowblower, and on the quantity of snow days.

If a snowplow is used, still higher skill levels may be needed, but a single worker might be able to complete about 40 properties, provided the property characteristics (e.g., shape, ground contours) permitted the snowplow to be effective. Again, however, to estimate the impact on MFP (and profit), one must evaluate the impact of the other factors of production and the extent to which they will be applied to instances of the firm's services. Two scenarios corresponding to different utilization rates are depicted in Table 6A.1 and Figure 6A.7.

---

[49]Matthew Denesuk, "Modelling Productivity and Performance Growth in Labor-Based, Custom Services Firms" paper presented at the Frontiers in Service Conference, San Francisco, CA, October 4–7, 2007.

Table 6A.1   How Service Technology Assets Would Affect a Snow Removal Business

	Unit price	Labor cost/day	10 days / year Equip. cost/day	40 days / year Equip. cost/day	Labor productivity (properties/ day)	10 days / year Gronroos productivity (MFP)	40 days / year Gronroos productivity (MFP)
Use shovel	$30	$75	$0.00	$0.00	3.3	1.3	1.3
Use snowblower	$30	$150	$20.30	$8.82	10	1.8	1.9
Use truck	$30	$200	$840.00	$266.00	40	1.2	2.6

Assumptions: unit price constant at $30; labor markup = 25%; cost of capital = 10%; snowblower cost = $600 + $5/day; plow cost = $30,000 + $75/day; asset intensity = (asset value) / (revenue).

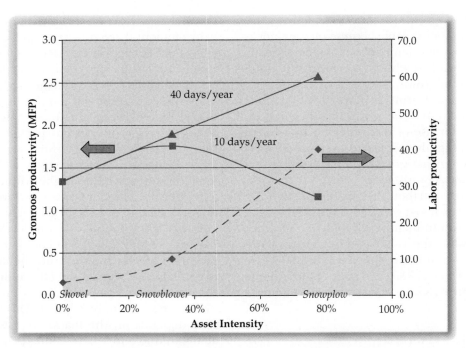

Figure 6A.7 The variation of labor productivity and a specific MFP proxy as a function of asset intensity for a hypothetical snow removal service offering. Although labor productivity increases monotonically with asset intensity, the behavior of the MFP proxy depends on the asset utilization rate.

In this particular example, although labor productivity increases continuously with asset intensity—and dramatically so at higher levels—the MFP proxy, which should relate more closely to overall business performance, exhibits behavior that is very sensitive to the asset utilization rate. In either scenario, the snowblower improves the MFP proxy, but the snowplow only does so at the higher asset utilization rate. Naturally, the actual behavior exhibited depends on the interplay of numerous economic factors, such as the different wage rates, the cost of capital, maintenance costs, and demand for the different service activities. Clearly, in making business decisions, one must take a holistic view of productivity and its relation to business performance. Although this is a rather mundane example, the principles demonstrated apply more broadly to examples based on intellectual assets, where offering standardization is needed to achieve high asset utilization rates.

Appendix 6 B

The Multiple-Input Case

In this appendix, we examine in greater detail the more general case in which a firm seeks the optimal combination of inputs, rather than simply the optimal level of one particular input. For explanatory purposes, we address the problem of determining the optimal combination of inputs using the two-input case. Mathematically, there is no problem in considering any number of inputs, but we use two inputs for ease of graphical illustration. Nonetheless, it should be noted that the decision rule for determining the optimal combination of inputs is the same whether two inputs or more than two are used in the production process.

From the standpoint of economic theory, the two-input case can be considered either a short-run or a long-run analysis, depending on what assumption is made about the nature of the firm's inputs. If we assume the firm has only two inputs (or, more realistically, that all its inputs can be divided into two basic categories), then the two-input case must be considered a long-run analysis because, in effect, all the firm's inputs are allowed to vary. However, if the firm is assumed to have other inputs that are being held constant while the two inputs are being evaluated, then the analysis must be considered short run. Readers should be able to discern from

the context of our discussion which case applies for our examples.

To illustrate the two-input case, we use the data in Table 6.1, reproduced as Table 6B.1. Suppose the firm produces 52 units of output ($Q = 52$). According to the table, the firm can employ the following combinations of inputs Y and X, respectively: 6 and 2, 4 and 3, 3 and 4, 2 and 6, and 2 and 8. Together, they form the isoquant shown in Table 6B.1. An **isoquant** is a curve representing the various combinations of two inputs that produce the same amount of output. Notice that isoquants for $Q = 29$ and $Q = 73$ are also shown in Table 6B.1. The isoquant for $Q = 52$ is plotted in Figure 6B.1.

A continuous production function, in which inputs are assumed to be perfectly divisible, is illustrated in Figure 6B.2. Here the isoquant appears as a smoothed-out version of that depicted in Figure 6B.1. Notice that both the discrete and continuous isoquants are downward sloping and convex to the origin.

The latter characteristic means that the slope of the isoquant becomes less steep as one moves downward and to the right. These characteristics pertain to the degree to which the two inputs can be substituted for one another.

Table 6B.1   Representative Production Table Illustrating Isoquants

Units of Y Employed				Output Quantity (Q)				
8	37	60	83	96	107	117	127	128
7	42	64	78	90	101	110	119	120
6	37	(52)	64	(73)	82	90	97	104
5	31	47	58	67	75	82	89	95
4	24	39	(52)	60	67	(73)	79	85
3	17	(29)	41	(52)	58	64	69	(73)
2	8	18	(29)	39	47	(52)	56	(52)
1	4	8	14	20	27	24	21	17
	1	2	3	4	5	6	7	8
				Units of X Employed				

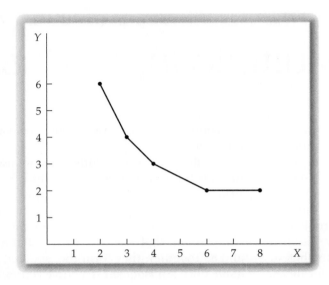

Figure 6B.1 Graph of Isoquant $Q = 52$

Substituting Input Factors

The degree of substitutability of two inputs is a measure of the ease with which one input can be used in place of the other in producing a given amount of output. To explain this further, let us use the example of the making of soft drinks. Consider the ingredients listed on the label of a typical soft drink:

> Carbonated water, sugar and/or corn syrup, citric acid, natural flavoring, sodium benzoate as a preservative, and caramel coloring.

Notice that the sweetening component of the recipe is listed as "sugar and/or corn syrup." This implies that the two ingredients are *perfect substitutes* for each other. The linear isoquant shown in Figure 6B.3a depicts the perfect substitutability between the two ingredients. The hypothetical numbers on the X- and Y-axes serve to caution you not to assume perfect substitutability means the two inputs must be substitutable at a ratio of 1 to 1. In this illustration, the substitution ratio is 2 to 1. That is, 2 grams of sugar can always be substituted for 1 gram of corn syrup, no matter how much sugar or corn syrup is used.

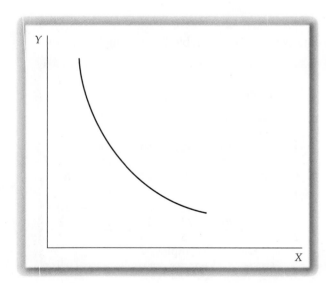

Figure 6B.2 Isoquant for Continuous Production Function

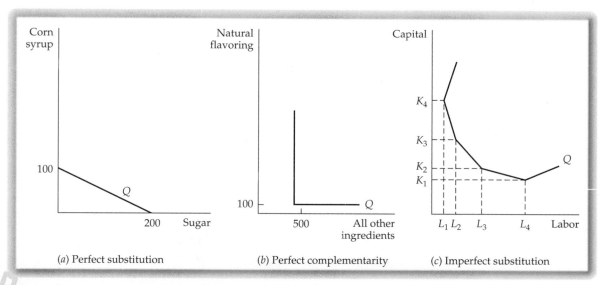

Figure 6B.3   Substitutability of Two Inputs in a Production Function

If we divide a soft drink into two components, "natural flavoring" and "all other ingredients," we can illustrate the relationship between these two inputs with the isoquant shown in Figure 6B.3b. Presumably, what gives the soft drink its special flavor is the unique ratio of the flavoring to the rest of the components. The hypothetical numbers in Figure 6B.3b indicate that adding one more part of flavoring without increasing the other contents by five parts will not yield more output. Thus, we see that natural flavoring and the other ingredients are what economists term *perfect complements* to each other because they must always be used together in some fixed proportion (i.e., one part of flavoring and five parts of the other ingredients).

Between the extremes of perfect substitutability and perfect complementarity lies the case illustrated in Figure 6B.3c. Here labor and capital are *imperfect substitutes* for each other. That is, one can be substituted for the other, but only up to a limit. (As shown in the figure, any addition of labor beyond L_4 units requires more capital rather than less to maintain the level of output at Q.) Furthermore, as more of one input is used in place of the other, it becomes increasingly difficult to substitute. As can be seen in Figure 6B.3c, when the firm is employing L_1 units of labor and K_4 units of capital, it can substitute a relatively small amount of labor for capital and still maintain the same level of output. However, when it is using L_2 units of labor and K_3 units of capital, it must substitute a larger amount of labor to maintain

the same level of output. More will be said about imperfect substitution in the next section.

In terms of selecting the optimal combination of inputs, it is clear that the case of imperfect substitutability represents the greatest challenge to the firm. Perfectly complementary inputs must be used together in some fixed proportion. The case of perfectly substitutable inputs is equally trivial. If one input can always be substituted in some fixed amount for another (no matter how much of each input is being used), the only determinant of the optimal combination is input price.

In the case of imperfectly substitutable inputs, the optimal combination depends both on the degree of substitutability and on their relative prices. For example, suppose labor costs much less than capital. Does this automatically mean that the firm should use more labor relative to capital (i.e., a labor-intensive production process)? No, because the relative productivities of the two inputs also have to be considered. If capital is much more productive than labor, it will benefit a firm to use more capital relative to labor if the difference in productivity more than compensates for the difference in cost.

Before we explain how economists determine the optimal combination of two inputs that are imperfect substitutes, we should explain how the degree of imperfection is measured. The measurement itself is called the **marginal rate of technical substitution** (**MRTS**). We consider an example in which we gradually substitute more of the X input for the Y input.

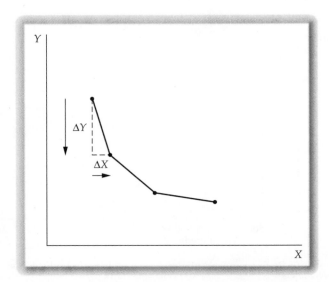

Figure 6B.4   MRTS (X for Y)

Algebraically, the marginal rate of technical substitution of X for Y can be expressed as:

$$\text{MRTS } (X \text{ for } Y) = \frac{\Delta Y}{\Delta X}$$

Notice that the numerator shows the amount of Y that is removed from the production process, and the denominator indicates the amount of X needed to substitute for Y to maintain the same amount of output. Graphically, the MRTS can be represented by moving downward and to the right along any isoquant (Figure 6B.4). Indeed, if we look back at the algebraic expression of MRTS (X for Y), we see that it is the measure of the slope of the isoquant.

To see exactly how MRTS is measured along the isoquant, let us use the discrete case illustrated in Table 6B.1. The different input combinations that can be used to produce 52 units of output are summarized in Table 6B.2. The changes in Y and X as one moves from combination A to E are shown in Figure 6B.5. Moving from combination A to E, we measure the marginal rate of technical substitution of X for Y as follows:

Notice that because the isoquant is downward sloping, $\Delta Y/\Delta X$, or the MRTS, will always have a negative value. However, in discussing the economic significance of MRTS, it is easier to treat it as a positive value. Therefore, let us for the moment simply drop the negative sign. Thus, for example, the MRTS between A and B becomes: MRTS = 2/1. Between B and C and between C and D, the MRTS values are 1 and 1/2, respectively. Expressed as an absolute value, MRTS can be clearly seen to diminish as we move from combination A to combination E. Economists refer to this phenomenon as the *law of diminishing marginal rate of technical substitution*. As you might expect, this relates to the law of diminishing returns.

When we move from A to B, we substitute one unit of X for two units of Y. In other words, the loss in output resulting from the use of two fewer units of Y can be made up for by adding one unit of X. When we move from B to C, the loss in output

Movement	MRTS $(X \text{ for } Y) = \dfrac{\Delta Y}{\Delta X}$
A to B	$\dfrac{-2}{1}$
B to C	$\dfrac{-1}{1}$
C to D	$\dfrac{-1}{2}$
D to E	$\dfrac{0}{2}$

Table 6B.2   Input Combinations for Isoquant $Q = 52$

Combination	Y	X
A	6	2
B	4	3
C	3	4
D	2	6
E	2	8

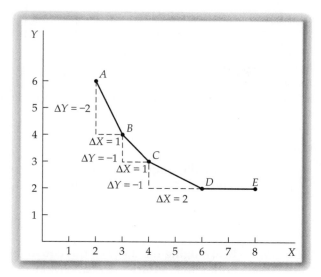

Figure 6B.5   Measuring MRTS along an Isoquant

resulting from the use of one fewer unit of Y must be made up for by adding one unit of X. From C to D we see that the loss in output resulting from the use of one fewer unit of Y must be made up for by adding two units of X. Finally, when we move from D to E, we find that rather than substituting X for Y, we must add more units of X to maintain the output level at 52.

Apparently, as we move from A to D, increasingly more X must be added relative to the amount of Y taken out of the production process to maintain the same amount of output. We started out by having to add only 1 unit of X to replace 2 units of Y and ended up having to add 2 units of X to replace 1 unit of Y. In other words, as more X is used relative to Y in the production process, the productivity of

X diminishes relative to Y. This is a result of none other than the law of diminishing returns. Recall that this law states that as additional units of a variable factor are added to a fixed factor, at some point the additional output starts to diminish. If this holds true when one of the inputs is fixed, it must certainly hold when this same input is reduced.

To understand fully why increasingly more of input X is needed to compensate for the loss of a given amount of input Y to maintain the same output, we need to incorporate the concept of marginal product into our analysis. Looking back at Table 6.1 (reproduced as Table 6B.3 for your convenience), we observe that the movement from A to B actually involves two distinct steps. First, input Y is reduced by 2 units (from 6 to 4), resulting in a reduction in

Table 6B.3   Representative Production Table

Units of Y Employed	Output Quantity (Q)							
8	37	60	83	96	107	117	127	128
7	42	64	78	90	101	110	119	120
6	37	52	64	73	82	90	97	104
5	31	47	58	67	75	82	89	95
4	24	39	52	60	67	73	79	85
3	17	29	41	52	58	64	69	73
2	8	18	29	39	47	52	56	52
1	4	8	14	20	27	24	21	17
	1	2	3	4	5	6	7	8
				Units of X Employed				

output by 13 units (from 52 to 39). This is indicated by the downward-pointing arrow in Table 6B.3. Next input X is added to the production process to compensate for the reduction in Y. As can be seen in the table, an additional unit of X is required to restore the output to its original level of 52. This is indicated by the right-pointing arrow in the table.

Recall from an earlier discussion that the marginal product is defined as the change in output relative to the change in some given input. In this case, the movement from A to B in two separate steps reveals that the marginal product of input Y is

$$\frac{\Delta Q}{\Delta Y} = \frac{-13}{-2} = 6.5$$

The marginal product of input X is

$$\frac{\Delta Q}{\Delta X} = \frac{13}{1} = 13$$

Proceeding next to combination C and then on to D using the same two-step process gives us the following ratios of the marginal products of X and Y: between B and C, $MP_X/MP_Y = 1$; between C and D, $MP_X/MP_Y = 1/2$.

In reviewing the ratios of the marginal products of X and Y along the isoquant $Q = 52$, you probably have spotted an important link between the MRTS, the slope of the isoquant, and these ratios. Indeed, they are all equal. More specifically,

$$MRTS = \frac{\Delta Y}{\Delta X} = -\frac{MP_X}{MP_Y} \qquad (6B.1)$$

This equation is illustrated in Table 6B.4.

Because Equation (6B.1) plays an important part in a later section of this appendix, let us briefly explain its derivation. Consider once again the movement along an isoquant between two given points. As illustrated using specific numbers in the previous pages, this movement involves two distinct steps: the reduction in one input (e.g., input Y) and

the increase in the other input (e.g., input X). The decrease in the output resulting from a decrease in input Y can be stated as

$$-MP_Y \times \Delta Y$$

The increase in output resulting from an increase in input X can be stated as

$$MP_X \times \Delta X$$

Along the isoquant, the output level must be maintained at a constant level. Thus,

$$-\frac{MP_Y}{\Delta X} = \frac{MP_X}{\Delta Y}$$

Rearranging the terms in this equation and remembering that $MRTS = \Delta Y/\Delta X$ gives us

$$MRTS = \frac{\Delta Y}{\Delta X} = -\frac{MP_X}{MP_Y}$$

The Optimal Combination of Multiple Inputs

Earlier we state that the determination of the optimal combination of imperfectly substitutable inputs depends on both their relative prices and on the degree to which they can be substituted for one another. In the previous section, you learn that the degree to which one input can be substituted for another is actually a reflection of the relationship between their marginal products. Therefore, the optimal combination of inputs depends on the relationship between the inputs' relative marginal products and their relative prices. In the case of two inputs, we can state this relationship mathematically as

$$\frac{MP_X}{MP_Y} = \frac{P_X}{P_Y} \qquad (6B.2)$$

To demonstrate this relationship, we use **isocost** curves and combine them with the isoquant curves

Table 6B.4 MP_X/MP_Y in Relation to MRTS (X for Y)

Combination	Q	Y	MP$_X$	X	MP$_Y$	MRTS (X for Y)	MP$_X$/MP$_Y$
A	52	6		2			
B	52	4	13	3	6.5	2	2
C	52	3	11	4	11	1	1
D	52	2	6.5	6	13	1/2	1/2

developed in the previous section. First, we rearrange Equation (6B.2) in the following way:

$$\frac{MP_X}{P_X} = \frac{MP_Y}{P_Y} \qquad \text{(6B.3)}$$

In other words, two inputs are combined in the best possible way when the marginal product of the last unit of one input in relation to its price is just equal to the marginal product of the last unit of the other input in relation to its price.

Let us now return to the more formal economic analysis of optimal input combinations by explaining the optimality rule with the use of isoquants and isocost curves. Suppose $P_X = \$100$ and $P_Y = \$200$. Suppose further that a firm has a budget of $1,000 to spend on inputs X and Y. At these prices and this expenditure limit, any of the combinations of X and Y in Table 6B.5 could be purchased.

Algebraically, the budget can be expressed as follows:

$$E = P_X \times X + P_Y \times Y \qquad \text{(6B.4)}$$

where E = Total budget allotment for inputs X and Y
P_X = Price of X
P_Y = Price of Y
X = Quantity of input X
Y = Quantity of input Y

In other words, the amount spent for X and Y is equal to the number of units of X multiplied by its price plus the number of units of Y multiplied by its price. In this case,

$$\$1,000 = \$100X + \$200Y \qquad \text{(6B.5)}$$

Using this equation to plot the numbers in Table 6B.5, we obtain the isocost curve shown in Figure 6B.6.

Note that the isocost curve is linear because the prices of the inputs are constant. A few algebraic manipulations of Equation (6B.4) indicate that the prices of the inputs in relation to each other (i.e., P_X/P_Y) are represented by the slope of the isocost line:

$$E = P_X \times X + P_Y \times Y$$
$$P_Y \times Y = E - P_X \times X$$
$$Y = \frac{E}{P_Y} - \frac{P_X}{P_Y} \times X \qquad \text{(6B.6)}$$

Figure 6B.7 combines the isocost curve shown in Figure 6B.6 and the isoquant shown in Figure 6B.5. Note that the isocost line and the isoquant are

Table 6B.5   Input Combinations for $1,000 Budget

Combination	X	Y
A	0	5
B	2	4
C	4	3
D	6	2
E	8	1
F	10	0

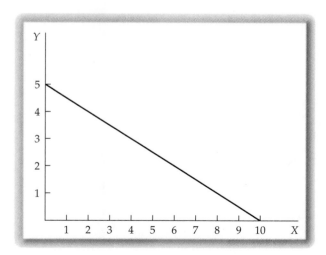

Figure 6B.6   Isocost Curve for Inputs X and Y

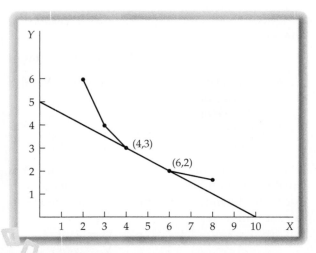

Figure 6B.7   Optimal Combinations of Inputs X and Y

tangent to each other between points (4,3) and (6,2). This means that between these two points the slopes of the two curves are identical. Therefore, if the slope of the isocost line is $-P_X/P_Y$ and the slope of the isoquant is $-MP_X/MP_Y$, then between these two points

$$\frac{MP_X}{MP_Y} = \frac{P_X}{P_Y}$$

If we cancel the negative signs on both sides of the equation, we arrive at the optimality rule first stated in Equation (6B.2). Given a budget of $1,000 and

the input combinations represented by the isoquant in Figure 6B.7, the firm would employ the optimal combination of inputs if it used either four units of X and three of Y or six units of X and two of Y.

We are not able to find a unique combination of inputs because we have used a discrete set of input combinations. Graphically, we can show quite easily how the use of a continuous production function enables us to find one optimal input combination. In Figure 6B.8, we have combined the isocost curve with a series of smoothed or continuous production isoquants. Point B represents the firm's optimal combination of inputs. Let us explain why.

To begin with, point D must be ruled out because at that point the firm would not be spending the full amount of its budget allotment. In contrast, point E represents a combination beyond the limits set by the budget. This leaves points A, B, and C, each representing a combination that can be purchased with the budget allotment. Of these three points, point B represents the best combination because the firm would be producing the maximum amount given its budget limitation.

In terms of the marginal analysis developed previously, we can see that point B is the only one that fulfills the optimality condition expressed in Equations (6B.2) and (6B.3). That is, at point B, the slope of the isocost curve and the slope of the isoquant are identical. (Recall that the slope of a continuous isoquant is measured by the slope of the

Figure 6B.8   Selecting the Optimal Input Combination for a Continuous Production Function

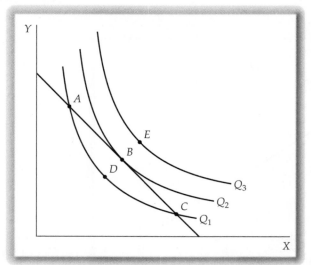

line tangent to the curve at a particular point.) Therefore, at point B, $MP_X/MP_Y = P_X/P_Y$.

The Optimal Levels of Multiple Inputs

By following the optimality condition first presented in Equations (6B.2) and (6B.3), a firm ensures it will be producing in the least costly way, regardless of the level of output. Therefore, Equation (6B.2) could be more specifically called the condition for cost minimization. But how much output should the firm be producing? The answer to the question, as was the case for a single input, depends on the demand for the product.

As you recall, the decision regarding the number of units of a single input to use was based on the condition $P_X = MCL = MRP_X$. That is, the firm should use the X input up to the point at which its cost (i.e., P_X) just equals the market price of the additional input's efforts (i.e., MRP_X). By the same token, the decision rule for two or more inputs requires that the firm use each input up to the point

$$P_i = MRP_i \qquad \text{(6B.7)}$$

where P_i = Price of input i
    MRP_i = Marginal revenue product of input i

If the firm is using two inputs (X and Y), its optimality condition is

$$P_X = MRP_X \text{ and } P_Y = MRP_Y \qquad \text{(6B.8)}$$

We can explain the rationale for the optimality condition with two or more inputs simply by saying that what applies in the case of one input must apply to more than one input. However, there is a more formal explanation in microeconomic theory using several terms and concepts that are not presented in detail until chapter 8. Nonetheless, following is a brief version of this theoretical explanation.

According to economic theory, the firm that wants to maximize its profit will always try to operate at the point where the extra revenue received from the sale of the last unit of output produced is just equal to the additional cost of producing this output. In other words, its optimal level of production is at the point where marginal revenue (MR) is equal to marginal cost (MC). In chapter 9, you learn in much greater detail about the rationale and application of the MR = MC rule. For now, let us simply explain the justification for the rule governing the optimal use of more than one input.

Marginal cost, or MC, is the cost of producing an additional unit of output. Using the terms developed in previous examples in this chapter,

$$MC = \frac{P_i}{MP_i} \qquad \text{(6B.9)}$$

where MC = Marginal cost of production
    P_i = Price of the input i (i.e., the cost to the firm of using an additional unit of the input i)
    MP_i = Marginal product of the input i

For example, suppose the input used is labor (measured in hourly units), and the price of labor is the wage rate given to the firm under perfectly competitive labor market conditions. Assume a wage rate of $10 per hour. Also assume a particular hour of labor has a marginal product of 20 units of output. On a per-unit basis, these additional 20 units will cost the firm $0.50 (i.e., $10/20) to produce. In other words, at this point the marginal cost is $0.50.

Let us assume the firm is operating at the profit-maximizing level of output—in other words, at the point where

$$MR = MC \qquad \text{(6B.10)}$$

Let us also assume the firm employs two inputs, X and Y. Substituting Equation (6B.9) into (6B.10) gives

$$MR = \frac{P_X}{MP_X} \text{ for the } X \text{ input} \qquad \text{(6B.11)}$$

$$MR = \frac{P_Y}{MP_Y} \text{ for the } Y \text{ input} \qquad \text{(6B.11)}$$

Rearranging terms gives us

$$P_X = MR \times MP_X \text{ and } P_Y = MR \times MP_Y \qquad \text{(6B.12)}$$

Because $MR \times MP_i = MRP_i$, the firm will be satisfying the optimality condition with that combination of X and Y at which

$$P_X = MRP_X \text{ and } P_Y = MRP_Y \qquad \text{(6B.13)}$$

In short, the optimal level of multiple inputs occurs when the additional revenue that each input accounts for is just equal to the additional cost to the firm of using each input. Another way to view this optimality condition is to remember that it is actually derived from the assumption that the firm is already producing at the profit-maximizing level

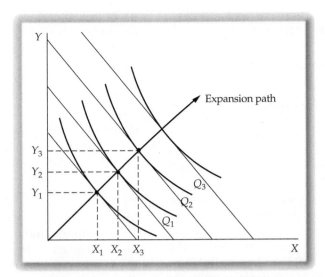

Figure 6B.9 Cost-Minimizing and Profit-Maximizing Input Combinations

of output (i.e., where MR = MC). This, in turn, implies that the firm is combining its inputs in an optimal fashion. If not, then it could not possibly be maximizing its profit.

Figure 6B.9 illustrates the difference between the cost-minimizing and the profit-maximizing combinations of inputs. You can see that any one of the points along the "expansion path" represents the cost-minimizing combination of inputs X and Y. However, suppose the MR = MC rule for

profit maximization dictates that a firm produce Q_2 units for sale in the competitive marketplace. As you can see, this implies that only one combination of inputs (X_3 and Y_3) should be used. All the other combinations of inputs will be cost efficient but will not enable the firm to maximize its profits.

Incidentally, when returns to scale are measured, economists always assume the firm is operating with the optimal combination of inputs. In Figure 6B.10,

Figure 6B.10 Optimal Input Combinations and Returns to Scale

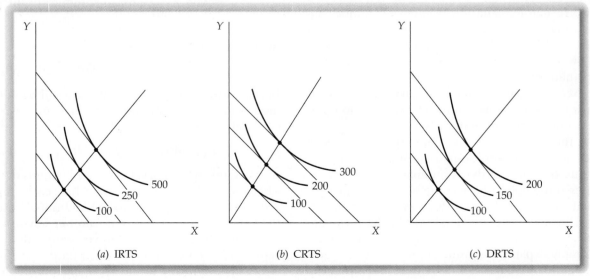

we view returns to scale "from above" rather than "from the side" as we did back in Figure 6.5. In this figure, the different levels of output resulting from increases in input are found on a ray from the origin. (This ray is actually the locus of points indicating the optimal combination of inputs for different levels of

budgetary constraint.) As implied by the hypothetical numbers assigned to the isoquants, the values of these isoquants in relation to the values of the optimal input combinations indicate whether the firm is experiencing increasing, constant, or decreasing returns to scale.

Expressing the Production Function with the Use of Calculus

In this chapter, we rely primarily on tables and graphs to illustrate our analysis of the production function. This appendix shows you how calculus can be used in the analysis.

A Brief Review of the Production Function

The production function expresses the relationship between the output and one or more inputs. The output is referred to either as *total product* (TP) or Q (quantity). We began our analysis of the production function by presenting the relationship between different combinations of two inputs (i.e., labor and capital) and output in a numerical table (see Table 6C.1). As already explained, the production function takes the general form:

$$Q = f(L, K) \qquad \textbf{(6C.1)}$$

where Q = Quantity of output
L = Labor (i.e., the variable input)
K = Capital (i.e., the fixed input)

By stating this general functional form in more specific terms, we have an equation that can be used to generate a tabular model of the production function.

One popular form is the *Cobb-Douglas* production function. It can be stated as follows:

$$Q = AL^a K^b \qquad \textbf{(6C.2)}$$

Q, L, and K have the same definitions as in Equation (6C.1). The values for A, a, and b determine the actual values in the production table. For example, suppose $A = 100$, $a = 0.5$, and $b = 0.5$. The production function would be

$$Q = 100L^{0.5}K^{0.5} \qquad \textbf{(6C.3)}$$

This equation can be used to generate the numbers in Table 6C.1.

Marginal Product: The First Derivative of the Total Product Function

As we show in the discussion of isoquants, the marginal product expressed in terms of calculus is the partial derivative of the total product function. We can use the Cobb-Douglas form of the production function shown in Equation (6C.3) to illustrate

Table 6C.1   Cobb-Douglas Production Function

K	Output Quantity							
8	282	400	488	564	628	688	744	800
7	264	373	456	528	588	644	700	744
6	244	345	422	488	544	600	644	688
5	223	315	385	446	500	544	588	628
4	200	282	346	400	446	488	528	564
3	173	244	300	346	385	422	456	488
2	141	200	244	282	315	345	373	400
1	100	141	173	200	223	244	264	282
	1	2	3	4	5	6	7	8

how the derivative is used to find this marginal product.

Suppose we want to find the marginal product of the fourth unit of labor added to the production process, assuming we are currently using four units of capital. We simply take the partial derivative of the equation with respect to L, set $L = 4$ and $K = 4$, and find the resulting value of total product:

$$\frac{\delta Q}{\delta L} = 100(0.5)L^{-0.5}K^{0.5}$$
$$= 100(0.5)4^{-0.5}4^{0.5}$$
$$= 50$$

In Table 6C.1 we note that the marginal product of the fourth unit of labor assuming 4 units of capital is 54 (i.e., $400 - 346$). The two values differ because the use of calculus actually enables us to compute marginal product right at the point at which four units of labor are being used, rather than that amount of output resulting from the addition of the fourth unit.

Converting the Cobb-Douglas Function into a Linear Form

1. The Cobb-Douglas function is nonlinear; it is an exponential function. However, it can be converted into a linear function in terms of logarithms:

$$Q = aL^bK^c$$
$$\log Q = \log a + b\log L + c\log K$$

2. The original form of the function was

$$Q = aL^bK^{1-b}$$

This model assumes constant returns to scale. In other words, if both labor and capital inputs are changed by a certain proportion s, Q will also change by s:

$$Q = a(sL)^b(sK)^{1-b}$$
$$= a(s^bL^b)(s^{1-b}K^{1-b})$$
$$= (s^{b+1-b})(Q)$$
$$= s^1Q$$

Thus, the new quantity, Q, will equal the old quantity times s—the proportion by which both L and K changed.

The later version of the function relaxed the requirement of constant returns because it permitted $b + c$ to be less than, equal to, or greater than 1. In this case, the results would be as follows:

$$Q = a(sL)^b(sK)^c$$
$$= a(s^bL^b)(s^cK^c)$$
$$= a(s^{b+c})(L^bK^c)$$
$$= (s^{b+c})(Q)$$

If $b + c > 1$, then for an input change s, Q will increase by more than s (i.e., increasing returns). If $b + c < 1$, the increase in Q will be less than s (i.e., decreasing returns).

3. The marginal product of a factor is the partial derivative of quantity of output with respect to the factor:

$$MP_L = \delta Q/\delta L$$
$$= abL^{b-1}K^{1-b}$$
$$= abL^bL^{-1}K^{1-b}$$
$$= bL^{-1}Q$$
$$= bQ/L$$

Similarly, the marginal product of capital, MP_K, equals cQ/K or $(1 - b)$ Q/K.

4. The elasticity of production measures the sensitivity of total product to a change in an input in percentage terms:

$$E_Q = \frac{\text{Change in } Q\,(\%)}{\text{Change in } input\,(\%)}$$

or, in the case of labor,

$$\Delta Q/Q \div \Delta L/L = \Delta Q/Q \times L/\Delta L = \Delta Q/\Delta L \times L/Q$$
$$= \Delta Q/\Delta L \div Q/L$$

$\Delta Q/\Delta L$ is, of course, the marginal product of labor; Q/L is the average product of labor (with capital held constant). Thus, the elasticity of production is equal to the marginal product divided by the average product. It was shown that the marginal product of labor is bQ/L and, as we have just pointed out, the average product of labor is Q/L. Dividing MP_L by AP_L,

$$MP_L/AP_L = bQ/L \div Q/L = bQ/L \times L/Q = b$$

Thus, the elasticity of production for labor is b (and for capital, it is c). These are the original constant exponents of the Cobb-Douglas function. For any percentage increase (or decrease) in the quantity of a factor, holding quantity of the other factor or factors the same, the increase (or decrease) in total product will be a constant percentage. Because the exponents are less than 1, the percent increase in total product is less than the increase in the quantity of the factor.

The Optimal Combination of Two Inputs

In the main body of this chapter, we show that if a firm is producing a level of output that maximizes its profit, then it must be using its inputs in such a way that the marginal revenue product of every input used is equal to its price (or cost). In other words, if a firm uses k inputs, then

$$MRP_1 = \text{Cost of input 1}$$
$$MRP_2 = \text{Cost of input 2}$$
$$\vdots$$
$$MRP_K = \text{Cost of input } K$$

Earlier we show why a rational firm would be using its inputs in the most cost-efficient manner if it combined them in such a way that the ratio of each input's marginal product relative to its price is equal for all inputs used:

$$\frac{MP_1}{P_1} = \frac{MP_2}{P_2} = \cdots = \frac{MP_K}{P_K}$$

In this section, we employ calculus to demonstrate mathematically why this is so.

We begin by stating the profit function in the following manner:

$$\pi = TR - TC \qquad \text{(6C.4)}$$

where π = Total profit
TR = Total revenue
TC = Total cost

By definition, total revenue is equal to price times quantity:

$$TR = P \times Q \qquad \text{(6C.5)}$$

where P = Price of the output
Q = Quantity of output sold

Total cost is equal to the amounts of the inputs used multiplied by their respective prices. Let us assume the firm is using two inputs, labor and capital, and their prices are the wage rate and some rental cost of using the capital. Thus, we can say that

$$TC = wL + rK \qquad \text{(6C.6)}$$

where L = Labor
K = Capital
w = Wage rate of labor
r = Rental cost of using capital

Substituting Equations (6C.6) and (6C.5) into Equation (6C.4) gives us

$$\pi = PQ - (wL + rK) \qquad \text{(6C.7)}$$

As you know, the production function can be stated in general terms as

$$Q = f(L, K) \qquad \text{(6C.8)}$$

Substituting this equation into Equation (6C.8) gives us

$$\pi = Pf(L, K) - wL - rK \qquad \text{(6C.9)}$$

To find the level of input that will maximize the firm's profit, we can take the partial derivative of the profit function with respect to each input, L and K, while holding the other one constant and set each equal to zero:

$$\frac{\delta \pi}{\delta L} = Pf_L - W = 0 \qquad \text{(6C.10)}$$

$$\frac{\delta \pi}{\delta K} = Pf_K - r = 0 \qquad \text{(6C.11)}$$

If we express Equations (6C.10) and (6C.11) in terms of the prices of the inputs, we obtain

$$w = Pf_L \qquad \text{(6C.12)}$$
$$r = Pf_K \qquad \text{(6C.13)}$$

Recall that the definition of the marginal product of a particular input is the change in output with respect to a change in that input. In other words,

$$MP_L = f_L \qquad \text{(6C.14)}$$
$$MP_K = f_K \qquad \text{(6C.15)}$$

Recall further that the definition of the marginal revenue product (MRP) is the MP of a particular input multiplied by product price. Thus, Equations (6C.12) and (6C.13) are nothing more than a restatement of the conditions necessary for the optimal use of inputs discussed earlier in the main body of this chapter. That is,

$$Pf_L = MRP_L = w \qquad \text{(6C.16)}$$
$$Pf_K = MRP_K = r \qquad \text{(6C.17)}$$

Now that we have established the relationship, we can easily use the same equations and notations to show how the condition necessary for the most cost-efficient combination of inputs is derived. If we divide Equation (6C.12) by Equation (6C.13), we obtain

$$\frac{W}{r} = \frac{Pf_L}{Pf_K}$$

The P's in the denominator and the numerator on the right-hand side cancel out, giving

$$\frac{W}{r} = \frac{f_L}{f_K}$$

Using the definitions of marginal product stated in Equations (6C.14) and (6C.15) and rearranging the terms gives the condition for the most efficient combination of input usage:

$$\frac{MP_L}{W} = \frac{MP_K}{r} \qquad\qquad \textbf{(6C.18)}$$

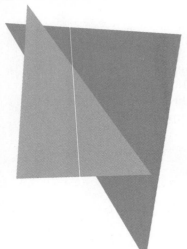

The Theory and Estimation of Cost

Learning Objectives

Upon completion of this chapter, readers should be able to:

- Define the cost function and explain the difference between a short-run and a long-run cost function.
- Explain the linkages between the production function and the cost function.
- Distinguish between economic cost and accounting cost.
- Explain how the concept of relevant cost is used in the economic analysis of cost.
- Define short-run total cost, short-run total variable cost, and total fixed cost and explain their relationship to each other.
- Define average cost, average variable cost, and average fixed cost and explain their relationship to each other in the short run. Do the same for average cost and average variable cost in the long run.
- Compare and contrast the short-run cost function and the long-run cost function and explain why economies of scale is considered to be a long-run phenomenon.
- Provide at least four reasons for the existence of economies of scale.
- (Appendix 7A) Use the tools of calculus to derive the short-run average cost and average variable cost functions from the total cost function.
- (Appendix 7B) Cite several studies that have estimated the cost functions in actual market situations.
- (Appendix 7B) Explain how empirical cost studies and cite several studies.

The Situation

Adam Michaels, the plant manager at Shayna Soda Company, was going through his daily routine of opening his mail on Monday morning when he came across a marketing flyer from Lawrence Aluminum Products, a company he had never heard of. The company was in New Jersey, about 400 miles away from his plant in upstate New York. At first he didn't pay too much attention to it, but then he saw that the base cost of soda cans was almost 30 percent lower than what he was now paying. He read on about the company and was impressed with its offer. The company offered an even higher discount if you integrated with their technology and took advantage of electronic purchase orders. Shayna Soda Company required technological upgrades, so maybe this would be a perfect opportunity to switch both suppliers and

(continued)

(continued)

computer systems. Adam was always under pressure from Corporate to increase the profitability of its soda production so his excitement on the potential of this change was high.

Adam called in Terry Roberts, the product availability manager, and told her of his discovery. "Terry, this sounds like a great opportunity for us and I want you to investigate this company a little more and let me know what we need to do to get supply from them." Terry did not look excited about the project.

"But, Adam," she replied, "what about Kayla Containers? We are their main customer and this could put them out of business."

"Terry, this is a business decision and although I like Kayla Containers, we need to stay in business, too. Please get on it, and give me a report by Friday."

Terry went back to her office and picked up the phone to call Lawrence Aluminum Products. She was directed to Joseph Matthews, the director of sales. Terry told Joseph who Shayna Soda was and the type of cans that it would need. Lawrence had the right specifications on the can and actually had a little higher grade of quality in the aluminum. She continued to tell him their needs and asked how it would work to get Shayna's logo and artwork on the cans. Joseph explained that they could do the logo and artwork with no problem, but Shayna would need to pay a one-time fee to set up the specifications. Moreover, the base price of the cans would go up 10 percent due to the extra coloring and production time. Terry quickly figured that even with the increase, the cost would be lower than Kayla Containers' product.

"OK," Terry continued. "What about delivery?"

"Delivery is no problem," Joseph responded. "We have trucks that deliver in your area once a week. We would get your order in and put it on the next truck going out. And by the way, if you need to change the delivery date and request it in time, we can do it for you but we charge a bit more. If you want our base delivery fee, you must take delivery when we schedule it."

"Is it a flat fee or by the mile?" Terry asked.

"It's by the mile."

Terry began to be concerned with the delivery aspect of the offer. "What about lead time? What do you require?"

"We have a pretty good turnaround time, so we only need five days," Joseph replied.

"Five days!" Terry shot back. "That's not great."

"Well, to be honest, most of the time we can give that, but sometimes we may be able to meet your needs sooner, if we know your general plans in advance," Joseph continued. "Ideally, we like to have a monthly forecast. In fact, we can offer you a discount if you integrate with our current technology for submitting forecasts and purchase orders and you make payment through the automated clearinghouse."

What Joseph was saying now really began to pique Terry's interest because the company was planning on improving its supply chain management anyway, particularly the procurement link of the chain.

"What would be the cost of that?" Terry asked.

"Well, you would need to purchase the software and the necessary support to set it up and integrate it with ours," Joseph stated nonchalantly.

"You don't help with any of the costs?" Terry asked.

"No. That would be your responsibility. But we can refer you to the contractors that helped us and offer any advice along the way. It would be of benefit to you in the long run, though. Just think of the efficiencies you could have."

Joseph concluded the conversation by giving Terry all the numbers to do the necessary calculations. Terry spent the next couple of days figuring out all the aspects of the calculations.

THE IMPORTANCE OF COST IN MANAGERIAL DECISIONS

In the decade of the 1990s, the most commonly used way to contain or to cut costs was to reduce the number of people on a company's payroll. *Restructuring, downsizing, right sizing, redundancy,* and *force management* are all terms used in reference to this action. Over this past decade, these terms have taken on an additional dimension with the concept referred to as *shared services*. This typically refers to the consolidation of such "back office" and support functions as finance and accounting (e.g., purchasing and accounts payable), information technology (IT), and human resources (HR). This is not a new concept. However, what is relatively new is where such consolidations or close tie-ins take place between the different "Centers of Excellence" (as shared service centers are often called) and the rest of the company. This is largely because of the proliferation and falling cost of broadband communications. Now a company can have its support function relating to headquarters as well as to all its other locations in the world where it operates.

Depending on the location, terms such as "onshore," "near-shore," and "offshore" are used to describe the situation. Companies recognize that they still require people to run their operations. So the idea is not to reduce labor as much it is to optimize labor by reconfiguring where the labor being used is located and how it is organized. In addition to this particular trend in cost reduction, we have also noticed more companies trying to cut costs by reducing their assets (often referred to in the popular press as an "asset-light" strategy). We will provide examples of all these current efforts to reduce cost in the latter part of this chapter, after we discuss the economic theory of cost. (See pp. 280–286.)

An additional way in which companies have tried to cut costs to remain competitive is to merge, consolidate, and then reduce headcount. It is no surprise that megamergers making the news in recent years primarily involve companies that have been experiencing considerable changes in the economics of their business. Over the past decade, a number of big companies have merged to become even bigger ones in such industries as financial services, telecommunications, airlines, and pharmaceuticals. In financial services, the merger of Citicorp and Travelers Insurance was considered a "blockbuster" in the 1990s. Another major consolidation in the financial services industry, in particular in the credit card business, came when Bank of America bought MBNA in 2005 for $35 billion. (Only a year before Bank of America had bought Fleet Bank for $48 billion.) At that time, MBNA was considered to be the largest "monoline" bank, which is a bank that focuses primarily on the issuing of credit cards such as MasterCard and Visa. When Bank of America's decision was announced, this is what the press had to say:

> With the acquisition, Bank of America, the nation's third-largest bank, becomes its largest credit-card issuer, with $143 billion in managed outstanding balances and 40 million active accounts. Bank of America said it will add more than 20 million new customer accounts as well as affinity relationships with more than 5,000 partner organizations and financial institutions.
>
> *Bank of America said it expects to eliminate 6,000 jobs from the merged companies.*[1] [Emphasis added]

In 2004, the merger of Bank One and JP Morgan Chase made the headlines. In the pharmaceutical industry, Pfizer purchased Pharmacia (a company which only a few years before was the result of a merger between Upjohn and Pharmacia). Another example of a merger of companies which themselves were the result of previous mergers is Glaxo Welcome and SmithKline Beecham. This company operates under the simplified name GSK. In telecommunications, there were some key mergers among the "Baby Bells" (the original seven operating companies resulting from the breakup of AT&T in 1984). Verizon is a result of the merger of Nynex and Bell Atlantic and GTE (the only major telecom company not part of the original AT&T). SBC is a result of the merger of SBC, Ameritech, and Pacific Telesis. In 2005, SBC acquired

---

[1]www.consumeraffairs.com/news04/2005/bofa_mbna.htm.

AT&T and took on the name AT&T. In that same year, Verizon acquired MCI. In 2006, AT&T acquired Bell South, thereby also consolidating the Cingular Wireless brand that the two companies had owned jointly. Soon afterwards, Cingular was rebranded AT&T Wireless.

As explained earlier, the economic analysis of cost begins with the production function. We therefore begin the analysis of cost by showing the links between production and cost functions. But before doing so, we review briefly the particular way in which cost is defined and used in economic analysis.

THE DEFINITION AND USE OF COST IN ECONOMIC ANALYSIS

In a typical business organization, cost is generally considered the domain of the accounting department. Its presentation to the outside world (e.g., to bankers, bond holders, investors, and suppliers) is based on generally accepted accounting principles (GAAP). For purposes of internal analysis and decision making, the definition of cost is based on the concept of relevancy. By definition, a cost is considered to be relevant if it is affected by a management decision. Any cost not affected by a decision is considered irrelevant. Both economists and managerial or cost accountants (as opposed to financial accountants) use the concept of **relevant cost** when analyzing business problems and recommending solutions. Following are some important ways to distinguish between relevant and irrelevant cost.

Historical versus Replacement Cost

Suppose a manufacturer of a video game system has an inventory of $750,000 worth of 16-bit chips left over from a discontinued system. Strong protectionist measures by Congress have created a shortage of these chips, driving their market value up to $1,000,000. Meanwhile, the firm decides to reenter the video game market. (This time, it will manufacture the product in Thailand and will begin production with the leftover inventory of chips.) How much will it cost the firm to use this inventory? Although the **historical cost** is $750,000, the replacement value is $1,000,000. According to the principle of relevant cost, the firm should use the latter figure in computing its cost of reentering the video game market.[2] Let us see why this is so.

If the firm were to decide not to proceed with the project but instead to sell its inventory of chips in the open market, it could receive the full market value of $1,000,000. Therefore, by using the chips, it is forgoing the opportunity to receive $1,000,000 for their sale. Moreover, if it decided to buy chips rather than use its inventory, it would have to pay $1,000,000 for the same quantity that it holds in inventory. The $1,000,000 is the relevant sum because it is the amount that has an impact on the alternatives being considered.

Opportunity Cost versus Out-of-Pocket Cost

Previous discussions pointed out that **opportunity cost** is one of the most important and useful concepts in economic analysis because it highlights the consequences of making choices under conditions of scarcity. We can now use this term in a more

---

[2]The recording of the cost of an asset for purposes of financial reporting is subject to GAAP, which state that assets and liabilities should be recorded in financial statements at historical cost. Inventories may be reported at historical cost or current market value, whichever is lower. But regardless of the rule set for external reporting, economists and cost accountants (as opposed to financial accountants) recommend that a firm use current market value for internal management decisions.

specific way to help explain the concept of relevant cost. Opportunity cost, as you recall, is the amount or subjective value that is forgone in choosing one activity over the next best alternative. This type of cost can be contrasted with "out-of-pocket cost." On occasion, economists refer to opportunity cost as *indirect cost* or *implicit cost,* and refer to out-of-pocket cost as *direct cost* or *explicit cost.*

In the case of the company with the inventory of computer chips, we can clearly see that the opportunity cost of using the inventory in its second attempt to penetrate the video game market involves the cost of not being able to resell the inventory for $1,000,000. Seen in this way, this sum is the firm's "relevant opportunity cost." The $750,000 is not relevant because it is not the opportunity cost of going ahead with the project. Incidentally, the firm's out-of-pocket cost of using chips would be the cost of buying additional chips for the production process. For example, if the firm decides that it needs $1,500,000 worth of chips (at current market prices) in the first year of the project's operation, we can infer that this figure consists of $1,000,000 in opportunity cost and $500,000 in additional out-of-pocket cost.

Sunk versus Incremental Cost

Let us evaluate the cost to the firm of using its inventory of chips with a reversal in market conditions. Instead of the firm's inventory increasing in value, suppose something happens to cause its value to fall to $550,000. For example, the introduction of a 32-bit video game system would drastically reduce the demand for and price of the 16-bit system. Under these circumstances, how much will it cost the firm to use the inventory for which it originally paid $750,000? To answer this question, we employ the distinction that economists make between *incremental* and *sunk* costs. **Incremental cost** is the cost that varies with the range of options available in a decision. **Sunk cost** is the cost that does not vary in accordance with the decision alternatives. Our computer manufacturer has already paid $750,000 for the chips and can really do nothing about the fact that changes in market conditions have driven the value of the chips down to $550,000. If the firm decides to sell the inventory, it will receive at the most only $550,000. If it decides to go ahead with the project, the incremental cost (i.e., the part of its cost that is affected by the decision) of using the inventory of chips will be $550,000 and not $750,000. And, as you have probably already concluded, the $200,000 difference between these two sums must be considered a sunk cost to the firm. As it turns out, the $550,000 can also be considered the opportunity cost of using the chips instead of selling them. Therefore, in summary, the firm should consider $550,000 to be the relevant cost of using its inventory of chips because it is an *incremental opportunity cost.*

A dramatic example of the use of incremental and opportunity costs to determine relevant cost is the case of a new technology suddenly rendering the entire inventory of chips obsolete. For example, the introduction of a 64-bit game system would virtually destroy the market for 16-bit games. In this event, no one would want to buy the chips at any price, and the value of this inventory would be reduced to zero. The entire $750,000 investment in inventory would be considered a sunk cost to the firm. Furthermore, because the resale value of the inventory is zero, the firm's use of the chips in its project would not incur an opportunity cost.[3] In economic terms, the chips

---

[3] We avoid using the term *indirect cost* in reference to opportunity cost because some readers may confuse it with another definition. In manufacturing, *indirect cost* usually refers to the cost of using labor not directly involved in the making of a product (e.g., finance, personnel, research and development, and other support or staff functions).

would represent a "free resource" because there would be no amount forgone with their use in the project. Would the firm be tempted to use the chips simply because of this? Would you want to build a new video game system with obsolete chips? If people will not buy the product, there would indeed be a high opportunity cost in terms of forgone sales.

THE RELATIONSHIP BETWEEN PRODUCTION AND COST

The economic analysis of cost is tightly bound to the economic analysis of production discussed in chapter 6. As a matter of fact, one can say that the cost function used in economic analysis is simply the production function expressed in monetary rather than physical units. Furthermore, all the limiting assumptions used in specifying the short-run production function apply to the short-run cost function. The only additional assumption needed to determine the short-run economic cost function pertains to the prices of the inputs used in the production process. Here we assume the firm acts as a "price taker" in the input market; that is, it can hire or use as many or as few inputs as it desires, as long as it pays the going market price for them.

Table 7.1 presents an example of the numerical relationship between production and cost in the short run. The cost of using the variable input is determined by multiplying the number of units by the unit price. In this case, each unit of labor is assumed to be the equivalent of a 40-hour work week. The weekly wage rate is $500. As indicated in the table, when the total product (Q) increases at an *increasing rate,* **total variable cost (TVC)** increases at a *decreasing* rate. When Q increases at a *decreasing* rate, TVC increases at an *increasing* rate. Plotting these numbers on a graph makes it quite apparent that total variable cost is a "mirror image" of total product (Figure 7.1).

In chapter 6, the marginal product was defined as the change in total product divided by the change in the amount of the variable input used in the production process. Similarly, the rate of change in total variable cost is called **marginal cost**. Expressed in symbols,

$$\text{MC} = \Delta\text{TVC}/\Delta Q \text{ or } \text{MC} = \Delta\text{TC}/\Delta Q$$

Table 7.1   Relationship between Production and Cost, Short Run

Total Input (L)	Q	TVC (L × $500)	MC (ΔTVC/ΔQ)	Reference Point in Figure 7.1
0	0	$ 0		
1	1,000	500	$ 0.50	
2	3,000	1,000	0.25	A(A′)
3	6,000	1,500	0.16	B(B′)
4	8,000	2,000	0.25	C(C′)
5	9,000	2,500	0.50	D(D′)
6	9,500	3,000	1.00	E(E′)
7	9,850	3,500	1.42	F(F′)
8	10,000	4,000	3.33	G(G′)
9	9,850	4,500	−3.33	H(H′)

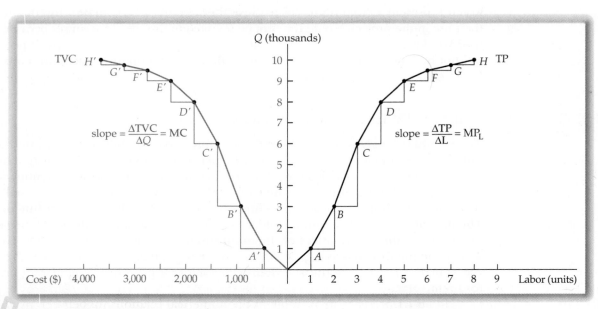

Figure 7.1   Short-Run Production and Cost

Note that marginal cost is either the change in total variable cost or the change in total cost with respect to the change in output. This is because the **total fixed cost** component of **total cost** never changes as output increases. Using marginal cost and marginal product, we can restate the relationship shown in Figure 7.1 in this way: When the firm's marginal product is increasing, its marginal cost of production is decreasing; when its marginal product is decreasing (i.e., *when the law of diminishing returns takes effect*), its marginal cost is increasing.

The relationship between diminishing returns and increasing marginal cost can also be illustrated algebraically. First, assume the variable input is labor (L), and its unit cost is some given wage rate (W). Now let us start by defining marginal cost as:

$$MC = \frac{\Delta TVC}{\Delta Q} \qquad (7.1)$$

Because TVC = $L \times W$, we can say that

$$\Delta TVC = \Delta L \times W \qquad (7.2)$$

Substituting Equation (7.2) into Equation (7.1) gives us

$$MC = \frac{\Delta L \times W}{\Delta Q} = \frac{\Delta L}{\Delta Q} \times W \qquad (7.3)$$

Recalling the definition of MP, we know that $MP_L = \Delta Q/\Delta L$. Incorporating this observation into Equation (7.3) gives us

$$MC = \frac{1}{MP} \times W = \frac{W}{MP} \qquad (7.4)$$

Clearly, Equation (7.4) tells us that, assuming a constant wage rate, MC will decrease when MP increases and will increase when MP decreases (i.e., when the law of diminishing returns takes effect).

In economic theory, the relationship between diminishing returns and marginal cost represents a key link between a firm's short-run production function and its short-run cost function because it is the law of diminishing returns that gives the short-run cost function its distinctive nonlinear form. Consequently, as seen in ensuing sections of this chapter, the firm's total cost, total variable cost, average cost, average variable cost, and marginal cost functions are all constructed in accordance with this nonlinearity.

THE SHORT-RUN COST FUNCTION

This section deals with the focal point of this chapter: the firm's short-run cost function. A numerical model of the behavior of the firm's short-run cost is shown in Table 7.2. Before commenting on each column in the table, let us review all the assumptions that economists make in specifying a model of this kind:

1. The firm employs two inputs, labor and capital.
2. The firm operates in a short-run production period. Labor is its variable input, and capital is its fixed input.
3. The firm uses the inputs to make a single product.
4. In producing the output, the firm operates at a given level of technology. (Recall that in our discussion of the short-run production function, we assumed the firm uses state-of-the-art technology in the production process. The same holds when we talk about short-run cost.)
5. The firm operates at every level of output in the most efficient way.
6. The firm operates in perfectly competitive input markets and must therefore pay for its inputs at some given market rate. In other words, it is a price taker in the input markets.
7. The firm's underlying short-run production function is affected by the law of diminishing returns.

Table 7.2   Total and Per-Unit Short-Run Cost

Quantity (Q)	Total Fixed Cost (TFC)	Total Variable Cost (TVC)	Total Cost (TC)	Average Fixed Cost (AFC)	Average Variable Cost (AVC)	Average Total Cost (AC)	Marginal Cost (MC)
0	$100	$ 0.00	$ 100.00				
1	100	55.70	155.70	$100.00	$ 55.70	$155.70	$ 55.70
2	100	105.60	205.60	50.00	52.80	102.80	49.90
3	100	153.90	253.90	33.33	51.30	84.63	48.30
4	100	204.80	304.80	25.00	51.20	76.20	50.90
5	100	262.50	362.50	20.00	52.50	72.50	57.70
6	100	331.20	431.20	16.67	55.20	71.87	68.70
7	100	415.10	515.10	14.29	59.30	73.59	83.90
8	100	518.40	618.40	12.50	64.80	77.30	103.30
9	100	645.30	745.30	11.11	71.70	82.81	126.90
10	100	800.00	900.00	10.00	80.00	90.00	154.70
11	100	986.70	1,086.70	9.09	89.70	98.79	186.70
12	100	1,209.60	1,309.60	8.33	100.80	109.13	222.90

As we proceed in this chapter, you will see why these assumptions are crucial to the understanding of the short-run cost function.

The variables listed in Table 7.2 are defined as follows:

Quantity (Q): The amount of output that a firm can produce in the short run. (*Total product* is also used in reference to this amount.)

Total fixed cost (**TFC**): The total cost of using the fixed input K.

Total variable cost (**TVC**): The total cost of using the variable input L.

Total cost (**TC**): The total cost of using all the firm's inputs (in this case, L and K).

Average fixed cost (**AFC**): The average or per-unit cost of using the fixed input K.

Average variable cost (**AVC**): The average or per-unit cost of using the variable input L.

Average total cost (**AC**): The average or per-unit cost of using all the firm's inputs.

Marginal cost (**MC**): The change in a firm's total cost (or, for that matter, its total variable cost) resulting from a unit change in output.

The important relationships among these various measures of cost can be summarized as follows:

$$TC = TFC + TVC$$
$$AC = AFC + AVC \ (or \ TC/Q)$$
$$MC = \Delta TC/\Delta Q \ (or = \Delta TVC/\Delta Q)$$
$$AFC = TFC/Q$$
$$AVC = TVC/Q$$

In evaluating the schedule of numbers in Table 7.2, note that as a matter of convenience, we have considered unit changes in output over the range of production being considered. Because ΔQ will always be equal to 1, we can quickly figure the marginal cost as output increases. For example, the marginal cost of the second unit of output is simply the change in the firm's total cost (or total variable cost) between 1 unit and 2 units of production. In Table 7.2, we observe that this amount is $49.90.

As output increases from 0 to 12, observe what happens to the various measures of cost. Total fixed cost, as expected, remains constant at $100 over the range of output. Total variable cost increases at a decreasing rate, but when the fourth unit of output is produced, it starts to increase at an increasing rate. The same is true for total cost. When the numbers are plotted on a graph (see Figure 7.2a), the rate of change in total cost can be seen as the slope of the TC curve. The constancy of fixed cost is depicted by the horizontal line emanating from the corresponding point on the Y-axis.

As for the per-unit cost measures, we see that **average fixed cost (AFC)** declines steadily over the range of production. This is to be expected, because a constant sum of $100 is being divided by the larger amounts of output. **Average variable cost (AVC)** declines, reaches a minimum at 4 units of output, and then starts to increase. **Average total cost (ATC or AC)** behaves in a similar fashion but reaches its minimum point at 6 units of output. Marginal cost declines and then starts to increase once the third unit of output is produced.

Notice in Table 7.2 that the values for marginal cost are placed between the output intervals, indicating that this measure of cost shows how total cost changes as a result of a unit change in quantity. For this same reason, marginal cost data are also plotted on a diagram between the output intervals. This particular way of showing marginal cost graphically can be seen in Figure 7.2b, along with the average total cost and average variable cost curves.

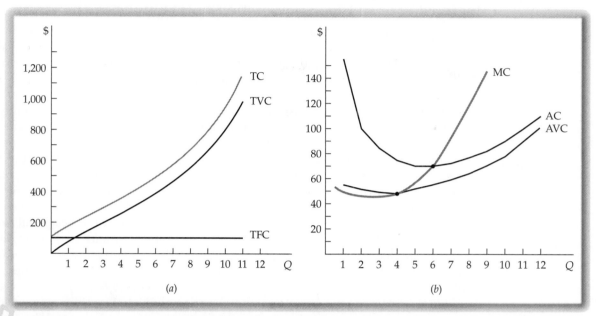

Figure 7.2   Total Cost, Total Variable Cost, Total Fixed Cost, Average Cost, Average Variable Cost, and Marginal Cost

Figure 7.2*b* shows a particular relationship between marginal cost and the two other per-unit cost measures that is not as evident in Table 7.2. Notice that when marginal cost is equal to average variable cost, the latter measure is at its minimum point. (This occurs at 4 units of output.) When marginal cost is equal to average cost, average cost is at its minimum point. (This occurs at 6 units of output.) Another way to describe these relationships is to state that as long as marginal cost is below average variable cost, average variable cost declines as output increases. However, when marginal cost exceeds average variable cost, average variable cost starts to increase. The same relationship holds between marginal cost and average total cost. The economic significance of these relationships is explained in chapter 9. But for now, it is important at least to note these relationships among the different per-unit measures of cost. Summarizing these relationships in abbreviated form:

When MC < AVC, AVC is falling.
When MC > AVC, AVC is rising.
When MC = AVC, AVC is at its minimum point.

To summarize the relationship between marginal cost and average cost, simply substitute AC for AVC.

It is important to understand how the concept of relevant cost can be incorporated into the analysis of short-run cost. Suppose a firm is currently producing 6 units of output per period and is considering increasing this amount to 7. In deciding whether to produce the seventh unit of output, the relevant cost is the marginal cost. In other words, it is the *change* in total cost and not the total cost itself that must be considered. This is because whether the firm produces 6 or 7 units of output per time period, it still must pay the same amount of fixed cost. By evaluating the change in total cost, the firm automatically excludes fixed cost from consideration.

Increasing Cost Efficiency in the Short Run

As is seen in chapters 8 through 10, the short-run cost function plays a central part in the economic analysis of production and pricing. For now, we can appreciate the value of this model by considering the ways in which a company might attempt to become more economically efficient. The assumptions listed when the model was specified provide a convenient guide.

To start with, the model assumes the firm is already operating as efficiently as possible. If we assume the firm is in fact operating as best it can with state-of-the-art technology, then the only possibility to reduce cost in the short run is for the inputs to decrease in price. If this were to happen, there would be a downward shift in the firm's short-run cost curves. This effect is shown in Figure 7.3a and b. Notice that a reduction in the firm's fixed cost (e.g., a reduction in rental payments) would simply cause the average cost line to shift downward, whereas a reduction in the firm's variable cost (e.g., a reduction in wage rates or raw materials costs) would cause all three cost lines—AC, AVC, and MC—to shift. MC actually shifts downward and to the right.

The purchase of capital equipment was not considered in the discussion because we assumed it to be our model's fixed input. Actually, the addition of capital equipment could be considered a short-run change *if we assume labor to be the fixed input*. For example, a workforce of a certain size might be given additional machinery with which to work. The point is that in the short-run analysis of cost, at least one of the inputs must be held constant.

 Module 8A

Alternative Specifications of the Total Cost Function

In economic analysis, the most common form of the short-run cost function is the one that has been used thus far in this chapter. That is, the **total cost function** is specified as a cubic relationship between total cost and output. As output increases, total cost first

Figure 7.3   Effects on Short-Run Cost Structure of Price Changes in Variable and Fixed Inputs

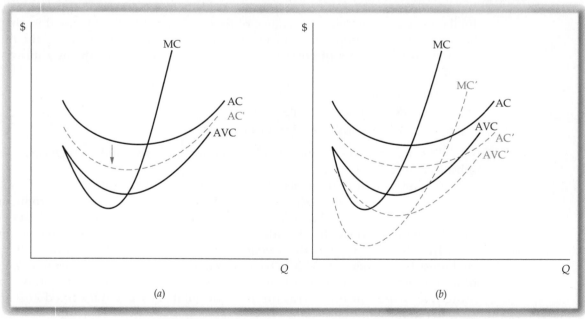

increases at a decreasing rate, and then at some point it increases at an increasing rate. By now you should be well aware that this is due to the underlying relationship between the firm's variable input and the resulting output. Total cost increases at a decreasing rate because the firm is experiencing increasing returns to its variable input. When the law of diminishing returns takes effect, the firm begins to experience decreasing returns to its variable factor, thereby causing its total cost to begin increasing at an increasing rate.

In addition to this cubic form of the cost function, two other important functional relationships between total cost and output are considered in economic analysis. One is a quadratic relationship, and the other is a linear one. These relationships along with the cubic cost function are shown in Figure 7.4. This figure also shows the general algebraic expressions for the three forms of total cost. These variations can be explained once again by the underlying relationship between the firm's variable input and the resulting output. In Figure 7.4c, we can see that the quadratic total cost function increases at an increasing rate from the outset of production. This implies that the law of diminishing returns takes effect as soon as the firm starts to produce. In contrast, the linear cost function, shown in Figure 7.4e, indicates that total cost increases at a constant rate. Think about this for a moment. What does this mean in terms of the underlying relationship between the firm's variable input and its output? It means that the firm is experiencing neither increasing nor diminishing returns as its

Figure 7.4   Alternative Representations of Total, Average, and Marginal Costs

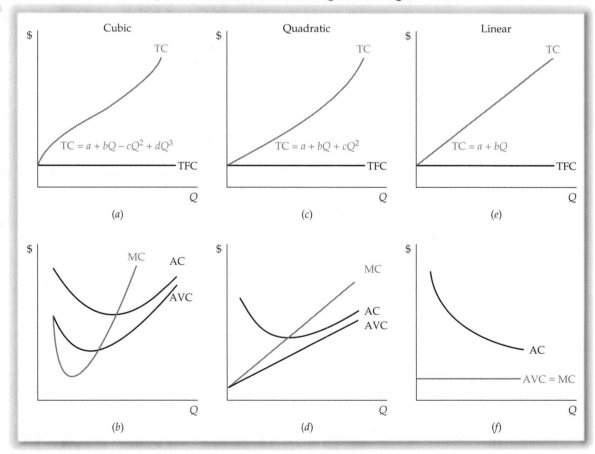

variable input is added to its fixed input. Each additional unit of variable input adds the *same* amount of additional output (marginal product) throughout the short-run range of production. Therefore, the change in the total cost relative to the change in output (which, as you recall, is indicated by the slope of the total cost line) is the same throughout the range of output considered.

Rather than discuss the different specifications of the firm's short-run cost function in terms of total cost, it might be easier and more meaningful to discuss the alternative forms in terms of unit costs, both average and marginal. Thus, instead of referring to total cost "increasing at an increasing rate," we can simply say that the firm's marginal cost is increasing. An increase in total cost at a constant rate means a constant marginal cost. We can also use Figure 7.4 to illustrate this point.

In Figure 7.4*b*, we see the familiar set of short-run cost curves depicted earlier. As output increases, marginal cost falls, reaches a minimum, and then starts to increase (as the law of diminishing returns takes effect). As it increases, marginal cost intersects with average variable cost and average total cost at their respective minimum points, for reasons explained earlier. In Figure 7.4*d*, we see that marginal cost increases as soon as production begins, just as we noted when evaluating the slope of the total cost function. As in the case of Figure 7.4*b*, marginal cost intersects average variable cost and average cost at their minimum points.

In the case of the linear cost function, shown in Figure 7.4*f*, the horizontal marginal cost line denotes that marginal cost remains constant as output increases. But also witness that marginal cost is equal to average variable cost, unlike the cases in Figures 7.4*b* and 7.4*d*. To illustrate this relationship, consider the following numerical example. Suppose you are given the following cost function:

$$\text{TC} = 100 + 0.50 \, Q \qquad\qquad (7.5)$$

Assuming the intercept and slope coefficients represent dollar units, this function tells us that the firm's total fixed cost is $100 and its marginal cost is $0.50. That is, each additional unit of production adds $0.50 to the firm's total cost. Omitting the fixed cost component of the equation gives us

$$\text{TVC} = 0.50 \, Q \qquad\qquad (7.6)$$

Recall by definition that AVC = TVC/Q. Dividing Equation (7.6) by Q gives an AVC of $0.50, which is the same as the marginal cost.

The mathematics of this example may seem rather trivial. Nonetheless, it is important to elaborate on this relationship between average variable cost and marginal cost because these two measures of cost are often used interchangeably in the business world. For example, when cost accountants use the term *standard variable cost*, they are usually referring to *both* marginal cost and average variable cost. In so doing, they are assuming the total cost function is linear, that the firm experiences neither increasing nor diminishing returns in the short run. The importance of these assumptions, as well as the role of the linear total cost function in economic analysis, are discussed further in appendices 7B and 8B.

THE LONG-RUN COST FUNCTION

The Relationship between Long-Run Production and Long-Run Cost

In the long run, all inputs to a firm's production function may be changed. Because there are no fixed inputs, there are no fixed costs. Consequently, all costs of production are variable in the long run. In most work situations, managers of firms make decisions

Table 7.3   Long-Run Cost Function

Scale of Production (Capacity Level)	Total Product (Output/Mo)	Long-Run Total Cost (LRTC)	Long-Run Marginal Cost (LRMC)	Long-Run Average Cost (LRAC)
A	10,000	$ 50,000	$5.00	$5.00
B	20,000	90,000	4.00	4.50
C	30,000	120,000	3.00	4.00
D	40,000	150,000	3.00	3.75
E	50,000	200,000	5.00	4.00
F	60,000	260,000	6.00	4.33

about production and cost that economic theory would consider short run in nature. For example, they might have to decide how many labor hours are required for a particular project or whether the existing work force requires more machinery to meet increased demand.[4] But from time to time, managers must make long-run production decisions. That is, they must consider possible changes in *all* the firm's inputs and, hence, changes in all the firm's cost of operation. Decisions of this kind are considered by economists to be part of a manager's planning horizon.

In explaining the nature of the long-run cost function, we begin with a schedule of numbers showing a firm's long-run cost function in relation to its long-run production function. Unlike the case of short-run cost presented in Table 7.2, the hypothetical numbers in Table 7.3 are based on the assumption that greater amounts of output are the result of increases in *all* the firm's inputs. Consistent with this assumption, this table implies that the firm would incur no cost if it chose not to produce any output, because in the long run there is no fixed cost.

As output increases, observe that total cost increases, but not at a constant rate. As with the short-run function, the rate of change of the long-run total cost function is called the marginal cost (long-run marginal cost, to be more precise). In looking at the long-run marginal cost column in Table 7.3, we see that this measure at first decreases, then is constant, and finally increases over the range of the output. The numbers in Table 7.3 are plotted on a graph in Figure 7.5. The rate of change in the long-run total cost can be seen by observing the slope of this curve, as well as by observing the behavior of the long-run marginal cost curve.

The reason for this particular behavior of the firm's long-run marginal cost (or the rate of change in its long-run total cost) pertains to returns to scale. As explained in chapter 6, economists hypothesize that a firm's long-run production function may at first exhibit increasing returns, then constant returns, and finally decreasing returns to scale. This being the case, we would expect a firm's long-run cost to change in a reciprocal fashion.

When a firm experiences increasing returns to scale, an increase in all its inputs by some proportion results in an increase in its output by some *greater* proportion. Assuming constant input prices over time, this means that if the firm's output

---

[4]Recall that we stated earlier that the "short run" in economic theory requires only that at least one of the inputs in the production function be held constant. Thus, we can treat the addition of capital equipment as a short-run change if the amount of factory space or the amount of labor, for example, remains unchanged.

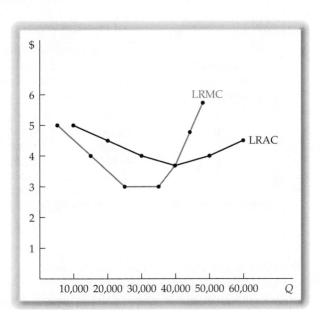

Figure 7.5 Long-Run Average and Marginal Cost

increases by some percentage, its total cost of production increases by some *lesser* percentage. The graphs in Figure 7.6 illustrate the reciprocal behavior of long-run cost and long-run production.

It is important to stress that although the long-run cost function appears to exhibit the same pattern of behavior as the short-run cost function, the reasons for their respective patterns are entirely unrelated. The short-run cost function is affected by increasing and diminishing returns, a phenomenon that is assumed to take effect when at least one of the inputs is held constant, and the long-run function is affected by increasing and decreasing returns to scale, a phenomenon assumed to take effect when all the firm's inputs are allowed to vary. Figure 7.7 serves as a reminder of this distinction.

Economies of Scale

One of the measures of cost in Table 7.3 has yet to be discussed: long-run average cost. This variable is the key indicator of a phenomenon called **economies of scale**. If a firm's long-run average cost declines as output increases, the firm is said to be experiencing economies of scale. If long-run average cost increases as output increases, economists consider this to be a sign of **diseconomies of scale**. There is no special term to describe the situation in which a firm's long-run average cost remains constant as output increases or decreases. We simply say that such a firm experiences neither economies nor diseconomies of scale. Figure 7.8 illustrates a typical U-shaped average cost curve reflecting the different types of scale economies that a firm might experience in the long run.

The primary reason for long-run scale economies is the underlying pattern of returns to scale in the firm's long-run production function. Further evaluation of Table 7.3 indicates that as long as marginal cost is falling, it is less than long-run average cost and in effect pulls the average down—a sure sign of economies of scale. However, once the firm starts to experience decreasing returns to scale, its long-run

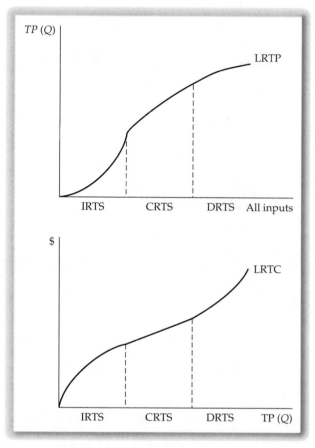

Figure 7.6   Returns to Scale for Long-Run Total Cost and Long-Run Total Production

Figure 7.7   Long-Run versus Short-Run Cost Function

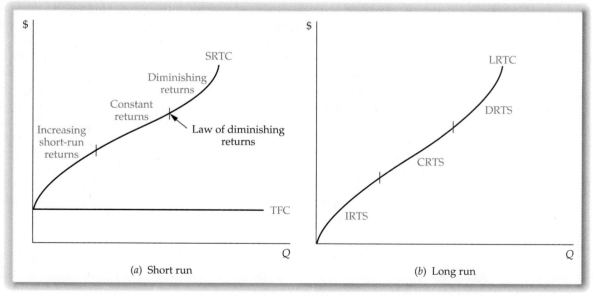

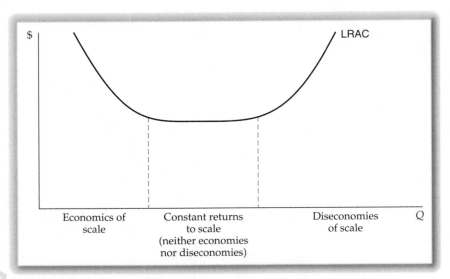

Figure 7.8   Long-Run Average Cost

marginal cost begins to rise. Eventually it becomes greater than long-run average cost, causing LRAC to rise and signifying diseconomies of scale.[5]

Scale economies and diseconomies may result from factors besides those relating to returns to scale. These other factors pertain primarily to the prices of the firm's inputs. For example, as the firm's scale of production increases, it may be able to exert some market power over its suppliers and thus receive volume discounts for bulk purchases of raw materials and component parts. Another example involves a firm's use of capital equipment with better *price–performance ratios.* As the firm increases its scale of production, it may be worthwhile to buy more cost-effective machinery whose price and capacity could not be justified at smaller scales of production. Only a few years ago, a typical illustration cited by economists of this type of scale economy was the computer. But with the advent of personal and midsize computers, there are now machines with prices and levels of computing power that are appropriate for firms of all sizes. Furthermore, with the tremendous advances in technology and software, the prices of the machines relative to their computing power (i.e., their price–performance ratios) do not differ much among the various sizes of computers.

We should briefly mention two other factors contributing to economies of scale. First, larger firms may be able to raise funds in capital markets at a lower cost than smaller ones. For instance, a large company may be able to secure short-term funds in the commercial paper market and long-term funds in the corporate bond market, whereas a small company may be able to secure borrowed funds only from a bank. Generally, the interest rates that firms must pay for funds in money and capital markets are less than for bank loans with comparable maturities. Second, a large firm may be able to take advantage of economies resulting from the spreading out of promotional costs. If a firm expands its scale of production, it may not have to expand its advertising budget by the same proportion, if at all. The same can be said about research and development expenditures.

---

[5]You should recognize the relationship between LRMC and LRAC to be the same mathematically as the relationship between SRMC and SRAC. That is, regardless of whether a short- or a long-run time period is assumed, when the marginal is below the average, it brings the average down. When the marginal is above the average, it pulls the average up.

As far as diseconomies of scale are concerned, if the firm's scale of production becomes so large that it begins to substantially affect the total market demand for its inputs, it may start to increase the price of these inputs. A typical case is the expansion of a major employer in a local area with a relatively fixed supply of labor. If the firm's higher scale of production sufficiently increases its demand for labor, it could begin to drive up local wage rates.

Another factor not related to the long-run production function that could cause diseconomies of scale is a firm's transportation costs. As a firm increases the production capacity of a particular manufacturing facility, per-unit transportation cost tends to rise rather than to fall. This is largely because transportation costs involve more than just the delivery of goods from one point to another. In addition, there are handling expenses, insurance and security expenses, and inventory costs (as goods await shipment). Increases in these types of expenses help to increase the total transportation cost to the extent that average transportation cost also increases. Furthermore, basic delivery expenses may rise at a faster rate than other kinds of cost if the firm has to ship the additional output to farther destinations. Economists hypothesize that eventually the increase in unit transportation cost will more than offset the fall in unit cost due to economies of scale. If this happens, then diseconomies of scale (i.e., rising average total cost) will result. Table 7.4 summarizes the key reasons for economies and diseconomies of scale. Factors that primarily relate to returns to scale are noted with an asterisk.

The Long-Run Average Cost Curve as the Envelope of Short-Run Average Cost

Up to now, we have been discussing long-run average cost as part of the firm's planning horizon. That is, the firm is assumed to be free to choose any level of capacity that it wants, because in our theoretical long-run time period, all inputs may vary. However, once a firm commits itself to a certain level of capacity, it must consider at least one of the inputs fixed as it varies the rest. In terms of production cost, this means that once a capacity level is decided on, the firm must work with a short-run cost function. We can illustrate this by returning to the example in Table 7.3.

Table 7.4   Factors Affecting Economies and Diseconomies of Scale

Possible Reasons for Economies of Scale
Specialization in the use of labor and capital*
Indivisible nature of many types of capital equipment*
Productive capacity of capital equipment rises faster than purchase price
Economies in maintaining inventory of replacement parts and maintenance personnel*
Discounts from bulk purchases
Lower cost of raising capital funds
Spreading of promotional and research and development costs
Management efficiencies (line and staff)*
Possible Reasons for Diseconomies of Scale
Disproportionate rise in transportation costs
Input market imperfections (e.g., wage rates driven up)
Management coordination and control problems*
Disproportionate rise in staff and indirect labor*

*Indicates reason directly related to economies or diseconomies of scale in the long-run production function.

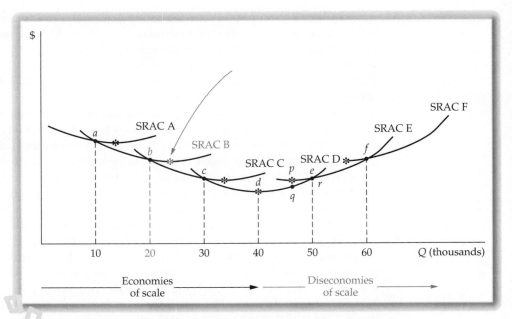

Figure 7.9 Capacity Level and Short-Run Average Cost

Suppose the capacity levels shown in the table represent plants of increasing size. Figure 7.9 shows these capacity levels in relation to each plant's short-run average cost curve. The points labeled *a* through *f* represent the levels of output and average cost shown in Table 7.3. The lines passing through the points indicate the short-run average cost curves that we imagine to exist once the firm has locked into one of the plant sizes represented by the labeled points.

As expected, short-run average cost (SRAC) curves for the larger plants are positioned to the right of the curves for smaller ones, indicating greater production capacity. For example, SRAC B is to the right of SRAC A because plant B is larger than plant A. But, as noted in Figure 7.9, plants with larger capacities are greatly influenced by economies and diseconomies of scale. Because of the impact of economies of scale, plant B's SRAC curve is positioned below and to the right of plant A's, so the minimum point of B's SRAC curve is *lower* than that for A. The same can be said for plant C's minimum SRAC in relation to plant B's and for D's in relation to C's. However, because of the impact of diseconomies of scale, plant E's SRAC curve is positioned above and to the right of D's, and plant F's is above and to the right of E's. That is, the SRAC curves of plants larger than plant D have progressively higher minimum average cost points. For reference, the minimum SRAC points for all the plants are marked in Figure 7.9 with asterisks.

Another important aspect of Figure 7.9 is that none of the labeled dots is at the lowest point of its respective short-run average cost curve *except for the dot representing plant D*. For example, the asterisk marking plant B's minimum short-run average cost depicts a level above the average cost that would be incurred by plant C in the short run for a comparable level of production (see arrow in Figure 7.9). A logical extension of this illustration is the observation that if a firm wants to produce between 20,000 and 30,000 units of output per month, it would be better off using the manufacturing capacity provided by plant C than to try to increase the usage of the smaller plant B. To understand the full economic implication of this observation, it is necessary to take a slight detour in our discussion to explain the particular way in which economists represent plant capacity with the use of short-run average cost curves.

You will recall that the typical short-run average cost curve (based on a cubic total cost function) declines, reaches a minimum point, and then rises as the firm produces more with some fixed amount of input. By definition, economists consider the lowest point of the short-run average cost curve to represent the firm's maximum capacity. Although "maximum capacity" usually denotes the physical limit of production (i.e., a plant simply cannot produce any more output), Figure 7.9 shows that a firm is clearly capable of producing beyond the output level at which average cost is at its lowest point. Rather than try to figure out the reason for this particular use of the term, just remember that for economists, "maximum plant capacity" coincides with a level of output that costs a firm the least amount per unit to produce in the short run.[6]

Thus, Figure 7.9 shows that over certain ranges of output, a firm is better off operating a larger plant at less than maximum capacity than a smaller plant at maximum capacity. The average cost of production in the larger plant is lower than the lowest possible average cost of production in the smaller plant. What causes this to happen? Economies of scale, of course. Because of this phenomenon, we can expect that over certain ranges of output, the reduction in average cost resulting from the economies of using a larger plant will be greater than the reduction in average cost resulting from operating a smaller plant at its most efficient (the economic "maximum") level of capacity!

As a cautionary note, we should add that once diseconomies of scale take effect, it is better for a firm to operate a plant of a given size beyond its "maximum capacity" than to build a plant of a larger size. We leave it to you to work through a detailed explanation of this observation. Suffice it to say that the reasoning is very similar to the explanation regarding the impact of economies of scale. (If you need help, refer to Figure 7.9, points *p*, *q*, and *r*.)

Looking at Figure 7.9 from another perspective, we can see that the firm's long-run average cost curve is actually the envelope of the various short-run average cost curves. As such, the long-run curve outlines the lowest per-unit costs that the firm will incur over the range of output considered, given the possibility of using plant sizes A through F. Figure 7.10*a* illustrates this point. As the number of choices of plant size approaches infinity, the envelope becomes a continuous version of the graph; this version is shown in Figure 7.10*b*. You should recognize it as the long-run average cost curve first shown in Figure 7.8.

Using Long-Run Average Cost as a Decision-Making Tool: The Importance of Coordinating Production Plans with Market Forecasts

In planning for its long-run capacity, which plant size should a firm choose? Using the schedule of numbers in Table 7.3, we can see that if a firm decides to build plant A, then the lowest per-unit cost of production it can expect is $5. But if it decides to build a plant with greater capacity—for instance, plant C—the potential for reducing per-unit cost is considerable because of economies of scale. Using plant C, the firm could produce its output for as little as $4 per unit. Indeed, this is where accurate forecasts of product demand are needed to help the firm plan for the best plant size. There would be no sense in investing in plant C, for example, if monthly

---

[6]Economists sometimes refer to this point as "minimum efficiency scale," or MES. This term is generally used in industrial organization textbooks.

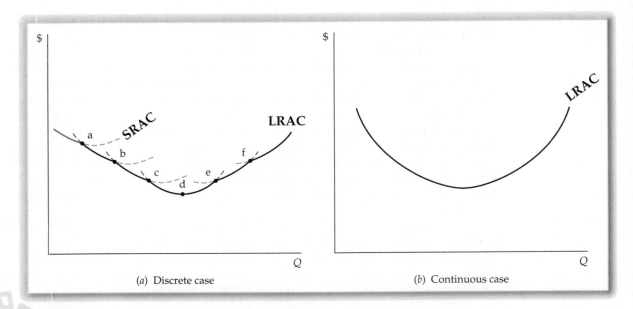

Figure 7.10　Forming LRAC Curve from SRAC Curves

demand is only 20,000. In this case, the smaller plant B would be more suitable. Actually, given the plant size options shown in Table 7.3 and Figure 7.9, we see that it is not necessary for a firm to forecast a specific amount of demand, but it should at least have a good idea of what the range of demand will be in the future. Table 7.5 presents a schedule showing the most appropriate plant size for different ranges of demand and production.

You should recognize that because diseconomies of scale take effect when plant E is used, plant D is appropriate for a wider range of production than the other plants. The penalty for selecting the inappropriate level of capacity is the incurrence of unnecessary cost, whether the actual demand turns out to be above or below the range used as a basis for the firm's decision on long-run production capacity. In Figure 7.11, we can see that if the firm had decided to build plant B and the demand turned out to be 25,000, it would lose on a per-unit basis the amount depicted by the arrow. If demand were such that it required the firm to produce only 5,000 units per month, the firm would suffer a similar type of loss.

Table 7.5　Optimal Plant Size According to Expected Demand

Units of Output Produced Based on Expected Demand	Appropriate Plant Size
0 to 10,000　　　A	
10,000 to 20,000	B
20,000 to 30,000	C
30,000 to 50,000	D
50,000 to 60,000	E
60,000 to 70,000 (not shown on graph)	F

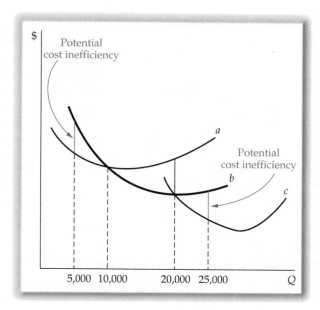

Figure 7.11   Unnecessary Costs Due to Inappropriate Plant Size

As a final comment on long-run cost, it is easy to put the onus for picking the best level of long-run capacity on the market forecasters. After all, their estimates of future demand should be the main guide for the decision makers who plan production capacity. Nevertheless, the production people in a business could become carried away with considerations of production capacity and efficiency for their own sake (e.g., "let us build a plant of the size that will enable us to benefit substantially from economies of scale") and convince the management to overbuild the company's long-run capacity. Certainly, optimal long-run production decisions require a balanced contribution from both the engineers and the marketing people.

THE LEARNING CURVE

The **learning curve** is a line showing the relationship between labor cost and additional units of output. Its downward slope indicates that this additional cost per unit declines as the level of output increases because workers improve with practice. The reduction in cost from this particular source of improvement is often referred to as the *learning curve effect*.

Specifically, a learning curve is measured in terms of the percentage decrease in additional labor cost each time output doubles. Table 7.6 presents data for an "80 percent" learning curve. Each time the output doubles, the cost of producing the next increment of output decreases to 80 percent of the previous level (i.e., declines by 20 percent). As you can see in this table, the first unit costs $100,000; the second unit costs 80 percent of this amount, or $80,000; the fourth unit costs 80 percent of this amount, or $64,000; and so on. Notice that the percentage reduction is actually with respect to labor hours. However, given some wage rate (in this case, $10/hour), the labor cost decreases by the same percentage. The data in Table 7.6 are plotted in Figure 7.12.

Table 7.6   Numerical Example of the Learning Curve

Unit Number	Unit Labor Hours	Cumulative Labor Hours	Cumulative Average Labor Hours	Unit Labor Cost	Cumulative Average Labor Cost
1	10,000	10,000.0	10,000	$100,000	$100,000
2	8,000	18,000.0	9,000	80,000	90,000
4	6,400	31,421.0	7,855.3	64,000	78,553
8	5,120	53,459.1	6,682.4	51,200	66,824
16	4,096	89,201.4	5,575.1	40,960	55,751
32	3,276.8	146,786.2	4,587.1	32,768	45,871
64	2,621.4	239,245.3	3,738.2	26,214	37,382
128	2,097.2	387,439.5	3,026.9	20,972	30,269
256	1,677.7	624,731.8	2,404.6	16,777	24,046

Wage rate = $10/hr.

There is a mathematical formula for determining the pattern of reduction in labor cost based on a selected percentage decline. This formula is

$$Y_x = Kx^n$$

where Y_x = Units of factor (labor hours) or cost to produce xth unit
K = Factor units or cost to produce kth (usually first) unit
x = Product unit (the xth unit)
n = $\log S/\log 2$
S = Slope parameter

Figure 7.12   An 80 Percent Learning Curve

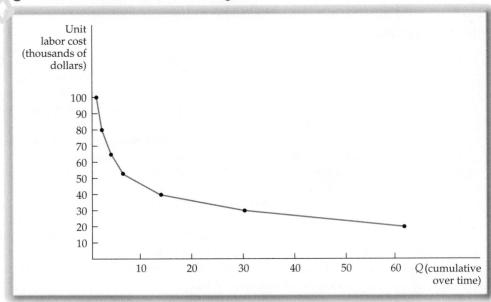

For an 80 percent learning curve, the number of direct labor hours required to produce the eighth unit of output is

$$S = .8$$
$$Y_8 = 100{,}000(8)^{\log.8/\log2}$$
$$= 100{,}000(8)^{-.322}$$
$$= \frac{100{,}000}{8^{.322}}$$
$$= \frac{100{,}000}{1.9535} = 51{,}200$$

This answer conforms to Table 7.6 and Figure 7.12. You may want to try constructing other learning curves based on different percentages, or refer to learning curve tables in an engineering textbook.

Although the learning curve is expressed in terms of the marginal cost of production, the impact of improving with practice can also be seen in terms of the decline in average cost. Table 7.6 also shows the cumulative labor cost and the cumulative average labor cost of producing various levels of output. As can be seen, the average labor cost also decreases, although not as sharply as the marginal labor cost. In any case, the learning curve effect clearly has an impact on the short-run cost presented earlier. In particular, the learning curve effect causes the short-run average cost curve to shift downward. This is shown in Figure 7.13.

The Japanese have been frequently cited in academic studies and in the popular press for their use of the learning curve in driving down costs. This is most dramatically shown in their production of computer chips and consumer electronics. Their particular use of the learning curve involves accelerating production experience through aggressive price-cutting measures. The price cuts enhance sales and give them production experience more rapidly. This in turn helps to drive down costs of production faster. The tactic of learning curve pricing is illustrated in Figure 7.14.

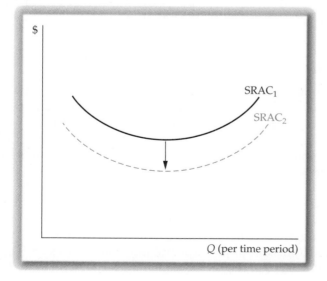

Figure 7.13   Impact of Learning Curve Effect on Short-Run Average Cost per Time Period

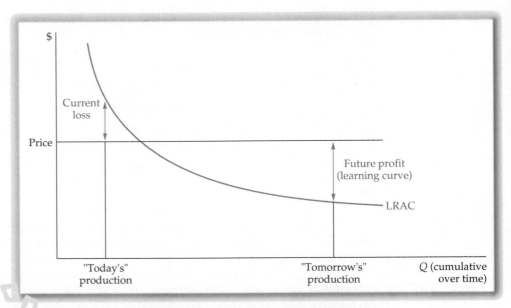

Figure 7.14 Pricing Based on Learning or Experience Curve

In concluding this section on the learning curve effect, we should note that this phenomenon was first observed in the production of aircraft more than 50 years ago. The reason cited for the learning curve effect was the repetition of tasks performed by workers actually manufacturing the product (e.g., direct labor). Later, the experience gained from repetition by those indirectly related to the production process (e.g., engineers, researchers) was also included in this phenomenon. Thus, such factors as the development of new process and engineering methods, the substitution of lower-cost materials or processes, and product redesign were also considered as factors causing unit costs to decrease as production levels increased. *The recognition* of these additional factors prompted the use of the broader term **experience curve**. Today, *experience curve* and *learning curve* are generally used interchangeably. However, some business managers and consultants still prefer to make a distinction between the two terms.

ECONOMIES OF SCOPE

Before summarizing this chapter, we should introduce briefly a concept often used in business but that does not quite fit into the conventional economic theory of cost, namely, **economies of scope**. This term can be defined as

> the reduction of a firm's unit cost by producing two or more goods or services jointly rather than separately.

The effort by our hypothetical firm Global Foods, Inc., to increase its profits by expanding into the soft drink industry offers a good example of a company seeking to take advantage of economies of scope. The company already has the knowledge, experience, and skills to produce and distribute processed food items and hopes to use these attributes in the production and distribution of soft drinks.

In a sense, the concept of economies of scope is closely related to economies of scale. Engaging in more than one line of business may require a firm to have a certain minimum scale of operation. Another way to view this relationship between scale and scope is to consider that a company's expansion into different lines of business naturally increases its scale of operation.

A good example of economies of scope is the case of Pepsi-Co's beverage and snack business relative to its distribution channels. Potentially, negotiations with wholesalers on pricing, with retailers on shelf space and product placement, and with bottlers and distributors on truck routing and delivery schedules could all be done with both types of products at the same time and by people of similar skills. Another example of economies of scope occurs in the area of mass advertising. Consider the millions of dollars that advertisers such as beer, auto, and soft drink beverage companies spend for a 30-second commercial during the Super Bowl. Now consider two hypothetical beer companies, one that has 20 million regular customers and the other that has only 5 million. Each company must spend the same amount of money but the bigger one is able to remind 4 times as many customers to remain loyal to its brand or brands.

ECONOMIES OF SCALE: THE SHORT RUN VERSUS THE LONG RUN

Economies of scale essentially means that a company's average cost decreases at higher levels of output. In microeconomic theory, *scale* implies a long-run time period. Recall that the economic meaning of *long run* implies that firms have time to adjust their fixed factors of production. In terms of cost, this means in effect that a firm's "fixed" cost is really "variable" in the long run. Another possible action that a firm could take in the long run is to merge with or acquire another firm or be acquired by another firm. When potential mergers are announced, the CEOs often tell the analysts that one of the benefits is "economies of scale."

From time to time, we have observed that the term *economies of scale* is used in the context of a "short-run" time period. In other words, authors of articles might say that a firm tries to take advantage of economies of scale by operating its plant at or near full capacity. This type of scale economies occurs because in so doing, a firm is spreading out its fixed or overhead costs. This was not the original intention of economic theorists, but we cannot prevent writers from using the term in this way. Therefore, a useful distinction can be made between "short-run economies of scale" and "long-run economies of scale." The reason for the first type of economies is the spreading of fixed cost. The reasons for the second type are listed in Table 7.4.

SUPPLY CHAIN MANAGEMENT

Supply chain management (SCM) has become an important way for companies to reduce their costs. Readers will undoubtedly study SCM in great detail in an operations research or production course in an undergraduate or MBA curriculum. Certain elements of SCM pertain either directly or indirectly to managerial economics. As you can see, SCM played a part in the "The Situation" vignette presented at the beginning of this chapter. Therefore, we now present a brief introduction to the subject.

Supply chain management can be defined as "efforts by a firm to improve efficiencies through each link of a firm's supply chain from supplier to customer." This is done primarily by fostering better communication and cooperation within each link by all parties involved. The goal of SCM is to increase profits primarily by reducing costs. But SCM can also help increase profits indirectly because a more efficiently operating supply chain can increase customer satisfaction. This in turn may

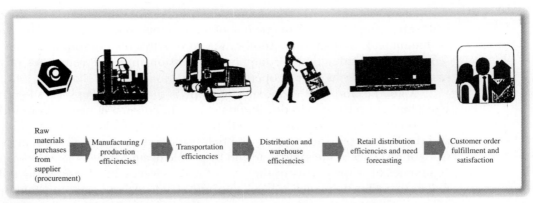

Figure 7.15   Supply Chain Management

enable firms to charge a premium price or at least help them retain their customers. Figure 7.15 shows a supply chain for a typical manufacturing company and the efficiencies that SCM wants to accomplish at each linkage point.

In the most general sense of the term, supply chain management includes all the firm's internal and external activities required to fulfill its customer's demand. Historically a typical firm, particularly in manufacturing, was a completely vertically integrated entity. U.S. Steel had its own coal mines that eventually fired up its mills. IBM made its own chips (and still does) that go into its computers. But in recent years, much more of a company's activities have been outsourced to other companies.[7] Does Folgers have its own coffee plantations? Does General Motors manufacture antilock brakes or catalytic converters? Have you ever heard of a company called Arima?[8] Herein lies the reason for the increasing importance of SCM among practioners, as well as the increasing attention given to it by academic economists. Presumably, a firm outsources certain activities to reduce costs. But once the activity is outside the direct control of the firm, there may be certain other costs that may in fact outweigh the cost savings of outsourcing. Let us continue with this discussion by focusing on just one particular aspect of the complete supply chain: the linkage between a raw material and parts supplier (henceforth referred to as the "outside supplier" or "vendor") and a manufacturing company that is purchasing these inputs (henceforth referred to as the "firm" or the "company"). In the context of this particular link, our topic is essentially the "make versus buy" decision that is also discussed in accounting and finance texts, as well as economics texts.[9]

From the perspective of managerial economics, the "make versus buy" decision or the trade-off between cost savings by going outside the firm versus costs incurred by

---

[7]For example, as described in chapter 15, semiconductor companies have significantly increased the outsourcing of the production of wafers and the packaging of chips. Another example is the fact that automobile companies have long been engaged in the outsourcing of many parts of a typical car. (The serious, lengthy, and combative strike of GM workers in 2000 was primarily about workers trying to stop GM's outsourcing of brake production.)

[8]Arima is a Taiwan-based, global company with $1.8 billion in annual sales that makes everything from wafers to battery packs to computer game software for its OEM clients. See *www.arima.com.tw.*

[9]Potentially any or all links of a supply chain could be outsourced in any type of industry. Therefore, supply chain management costs discussed in this section have much broader implications. Think about the supply chain problems that occur when a bank issuing credit cards outsources its direct mail advertising or its billing or even its call centers. Think about what eBay is. Some might consider it the ultimate outsourced retail company.

staying inside raises the most fundamental of all questions: What is a firm? Recall our discussion of this question at the outset of chapter 2, "The Firm and Its Goals." You may also recall that the seminal work on this subject was done by Professor Ronald Coase, who received a Nobel Prize in Economics for this work. Essentially, Coase postulated that a company compares the costs of organizing an activity internally with the cost of using the market system for its transactions. The cost incurred by using resources outside was what he called "transaction costs." These costs include the original investigation to find the outside firm, followed by the cost of negotiating a contract, and later, enforcing the contract.

Following Coase's path-breaking work, two other categories of costs of going outside the firm have been identified in addition to transactions costs: coordination costs and information costs.[10] Coordination costs arise because of the uncertainty and complexity of such tasks as timing the deliveries, meeting customer specifications, making alternative payments arrangements, and forecasting needs. Uncertainty exists because it simply may be impossible to plan for or insert in a contractual agreement what to do for every possible case in which an outside supplier is not able to completely satisfy the firm's requirements. Information costs arise because information is essential to the proper coordination of activities between the firm and its suppliers. For example, to meet the firm's exact specifications, a supplier might require timely and detailed information about a firm's sales. This may mean that a firm has to provide its suppliers with proprietary information. Short of sharing this type of information, the firm must be prepared to sacrifice some efficiency in the supplier's delivery obligations. If this information is shared, there is a certain amount of cost associated with setting up and maintaining the necessary technology platform (e.g., data communications network, logistics software, etc.). As is the case with coordination problems, the need for information flows complicates the relationship between a firm and its outside supplier that also cannot be easily addressed with a contract, no matter how detailed are the terms and conditions.

In the linkage between the firm purchasing the input and the firm supplying the input, one critical indicator of supply chain efficiency is the level of inventory. Ideally, the firm purchasing the input wants to hold no inventory in excess of what it needs to fulfill what its customers demand. Some years ago, Japanese automobile manufacturers became well known for their "just in time" (JIT) inventory control system. What we are talking about is very similar, except we consider JIT to be a part of a bigger picture (i.e., SCM). If anything goes wrong in this linkage, firms purchasing the input will find themselves with more or less inventory than desired. Firms selling the inputs will find themselves with an inventory problem that is a mirror image of the one experienced by firms purchasing its product. As a result, the vendor may be faced with either too much or too little capacity in its production facilities relative to the purchasing firm's mismatch of inventory levels and needs. In all cases, added costs are involved. How should this link of the supply chain be managed in such a way that neither party experiences these problems and added costs?

There are numerous consultants and software products out in the marketplace that promise firms an answer to this question not only for purchasing but for the entire supply chain. This is supposedly what a consultant implies when he or she uses the term *supply chain management* as a buzzword. Indeed, we can venture to say that all or most major consulting firms have their own supply chain management practice. Moreover, software companies such as Oracle and SAP offer software packages that

---

[10]One could argue that these costs are all part of transactions costs. However, supply chain management experts prefer to use these additional categories. See, for example, Ian Stuart and David McCutcheon, "The Manager's Guide to Supply Chain Management," *Business Horizons*, March/April 2000, pp. 35–44. Some of this section's comments on contracts and supplier relationships were taken from this article.

help companies to become more efficient in some or all aspects of their supply chain. Of course, there is a further symbiotic relationship between consultants and software companies. Ideally, they can both do business with a firm wanting to improve its supply chain management. How? The consultants (e.g., IBM Global Services, EDS, Accenture) are hired by the firm to implement the software!

If it were easy enough to hire a consultant and implement the right software package, then few firms would even have problems in the procurement linkage of the supply chain, or for that matter any other linkage in the chain. Yet it is safe to say that many still do. A key reason for this was cited earlier and has to do with a contract. As previously pointed out, no contract between a firm and its vendor can provide contingencies for every possible thing that could go wrong in the business relationship. Moreover, the more money and time involved, the more difficult it is to cover everything. Another reason is the difficulty of forecasting demand. This is exactly what happens in the case of the semiconductor industry supplying chips to hardware manufacturers.

To offset the inherent limitations of a contract, experts suggest that firms develop good working relationships with their suppliers. There are essentially two types of relationships. One type involves the firm and the outside supplier joining together in some sharing of resources. This is often termed a *strategic alliance*. The other type is a less involved relationship that involves the firm using two or more suppliers. This produces *competitive tension* among the suppliers, thereby helping the firm keep its purchase prices under control.

In our view, the type of relationship that a firm cultivates with its supplier depends on the characteristics of the inputs and the output. Competitive tension relationships are usually more appropriate when standardized inputs and output are involved. For example, a soft drink manufacturer buys high-fructose corn syrup, aluminum cans, or plastic bottles from outside suppliers. Strategic alliances are more useful in cases that involve highly differentiated products. A good example of this is the case of ST Microelectronics, a European integrated circuit (IC) manufacturer, and Nokia, the world's leading producer of cell phones. ST Microelectronics has always been a major supplier to Nokia since the early days of the cell phone industry. In mid-2007, this relationship was brought even closer when Nokia announced that it was going to transfer part of its IC operations to ST. Expected to be completed by the end of 2007, this move involved about 200 Nokia employees in Finland and the United Kingdom and "strengthens their collaboration on the licensing and supply of integrated circuit (IC) design and modem technologies for 3G and further generations.[11]

EXAMPLES OF WAYS COMPANIES HAVE CUT COSTS TO REMAIN COMPETITIVE

The consideration of cost in business decisions often evokes mixed feelings among managers. This is because efforts to reduce costs may involve the downsizing of staff, the layoff of workers, reductions in discretionary expenses for such things as training and travel, or the elimination of executive perquisites such as corporate jets. In contrast, efforts to increase revenues involve growth and all the activities that accompany it (e.g., new hires, better equipment, new offices, increases in discretionary spending and perquisites). Yet, from an objective standpoint, it is clear that a dollar saved, given some level of output and revenue, adds as much to the bottom line as an additional dollar of revenue, given some level of output and

---

[11]Anne-Francoise Pele, "Nokia to Move Chipset Technology, Workers to ST," *EETimes Europe*, August 8, 2007 (www.eetimes.eu/industrial/201303109).

cost. Following are examples of cost-cutting methods or procedures that firms have implemented to remain competitive.

1. ***The Strategic Use of Cost.***[12]   As we explain in chapter 9, a firm may choose to use cost leadership as the core of its strategy for competing in the marketplace. In the retail industry, the example that immediately comes to mind is Wal-Mart. In the airline industry, it is Southwest Airlines. Let us look closer at how this airline used cost leadership as an integral part of its strategy.

   Southwest Airlines began in 1967 as a small operation aimed at improving air service between Houston, Dallas–Fort Worth, and San Antonio, Texas. Today it is a formidable competitor in the short-haul (500 miles or less) air transportation market. Indeed, there are now certain routes (e.g., Burbank, California, to Las Vegas, Nevada) that the major airlines such as American Airlines have withdrawn from since Southwest's entry into the market. Southwest Airlines has achieved this success by being the low-cost provider of short-haul service. Its everyday fares can be as low as one-third of the standard fares charged by the major airlines on short-haul routes.

   Among the key cost items that gives Southwest a cost advantage over American and the other major airlines is payroll (it employs nonunion personnel), food (no food is served on short-haul flights), and depreciation (Southwest's fleet is not as new as American's).

   It is more meaningful to look at Southwest's cost advantage not as a series of ad hoc cost-cutting measures, but as the consequence of its overall market strategy. When the founders of Southwest Airlines devised their strategy of providing low-priced air transportation in the short-haul market, they anticipated being able to keep costs down by virtue of the very strategy that they selected. By flying only on short-haul routes, Southwest needed only one type of aircraft (the Boeing 737). This meant less training costs for flying and maintenance, as well as a lower inventory of replacement parts. Furthermore, short hauls require no in-flight meals. In addition, because it has positioned itself in the minds of its customers as a low-cost provider of air transportation, it can save more money by cutting out services or conveniences that customers generally expect from the major airlines. For example, Southwest does not take reservations, thereby saving money on staff and computer services. Whenever possible, it also uses secondary or alternative airports, thereby avoiding the higher landing fees charged by the major-hub airports.[13]

   The cost leadership model proved to be very resilient in the economic downturn following September 11, 2001. Although the major airlines were announcing huge losses for 2001, Southwest continued to earn a profit. Furthermore, Southwest's success has prompted other companies to copy this approach in Europe and in the United States. EasyJet in the United Kingdom and Ryan Air in Ireland have both become successful short-haul European carriers using the same "point-to-point" routing and low fares to attract leisure travels.

   At the time this edition is being prepared, the low-cost business model is not only proving that it can survive tough times, but it may also be the only way an airline can survive and perhaps be profitable in the future. In 2004, Southwest Airlines took the top spot in total number of passengers in the United States. Furthermore it continues to be profitable, while three of the top ten airlines in the United States are in bankruptcy. The article about this phenomenon in the *New York Times* quotes Professor Jagdish Sheth of Emory University as saying, "The traditional structure of being a one-stop shop for all the travel needs of your customers is not going to be the future at all."[14] Of course, rising fuel prices have hurt the big airlines even further. (See chapter 3 for additional discussion on the supply and demand for air travel.)

---

[12]For a good historical review of Southwest Airlines' start-up and operations, see Christopher H. Lovelock, "Southwest Airlines," Harvard Business School Case Study #575–060, 1975.
[13]Most of the material in this section was taken from Gene Walden and Edmund O. Lawler, *Marketing Masters: Secrets of America's Best Companies,* New York: HarperCollins, 1993, pp. 17–22.
[14]Micheline Maynard, "Survival of Fittest and Leanest Becomes Strategy for the Airlines," *New York Times,* October 30, 2004.

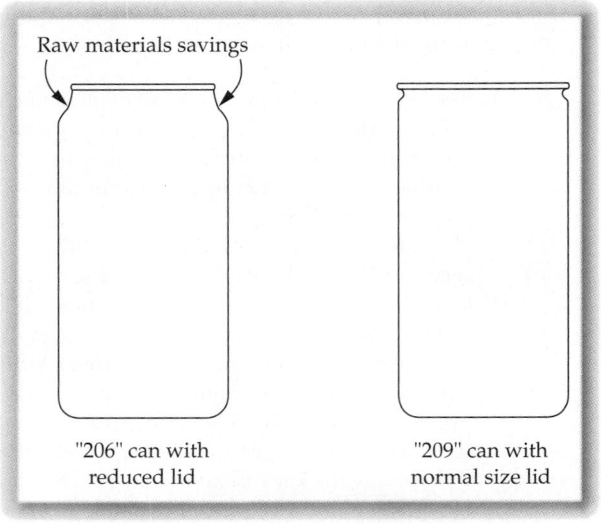

Raw materials savings

"206" can with
reduced lid

"209" can with
normal size lid

Figure 7.16   Using Reduced-Lid Can to Achieve Raw Materials Savings

2. *Reduction in Cost of Materials.*   Manufacturers are constantly seeking to cut costs by materials substitution or modification. In the beverage industry, one noticeable example of this is the reduction in the size of the lid of a 12-ounce aluminum can. Toward the end of the bottling process, each can on the conveyor belt passes a measuring device called a "fill height detector" that checks if there are at least 12 ounces of liquid in the container. Those with less are discarded. This measuring device shoots a gamma beam about one-quarter inch below the top of the can's lid. Because it is not necessary for the product to be filled to the very top of the can, the lid can be made slightly smaller by crimping the top portion of the can. The savings from the reduction in the aluminum content are considerable, given the millions of cans that are produced each year (Figure 7.16).

3. *Using Information Technology (IT) to Reduce Costs.*   From its early beginnings as a tool for the mechanization of routine business tasks such as accounting, IT has played an increasingly greater role in the efforts by companies to reduce costs. The real breakthrough in using IT to reduce costs began in the early 1990s with *enterprise resource planning* (ERP). SAP, a German company, was one of the first companies to offer services for this tool and continues today to be a leader in the industry. Another company offering similar products is Oracle.

   ERP is the industry term for software that enables companies to integrate their planning, scheduling, synchronization, and tracking of the entire chain of their production process. The use of ERP has helped companies cut costs and increase revenues by getting the right products into the hands of their customers in the most timely and efficient way. SAP's Web site (www.sap.com) provides examples of how companies have saved money by using its products and services. For example, Larry Bergner, vice president of technology for the Earthgrains Company (owner and operator of 39 bakeries and dough plants in the United States, and 8 bakeries and 1 dough plant in Europe), said that the use of SAP's products "has allowed us to control our disbursements from one central location, giving us better management of our working capital. It's [also] enabled us to streamline our procurement cycle, with an immediate savings of millions of dollars per year."[15] No doubt similar savings have also been achieved by using other companies' ERP products and services.[16]

---

[15]Retrieved February 12, 1999, from the World Wide Web: www.sap.com/products/industry/consum/media/earthgr.htm.

[16]Readers interested in all these special IT topics can obtain current information by reading industry trade journals or specialized periodicals on the subject. We believe *CIO* magazine is one of the best sources for the nontechnical manager.

4. ***Reduction of Process Costs.***   Cost savings stemming from the use of ERP has been getting most of the attention in the popular press and the literature on business studies. However, there are also more specific but equally important ways that appropriate software can help cut costs. More companies are starting to require that their employees use software packages to file travel and expense reports electronically. Studies by American Express found that U.S. companies spent about $175 billion on travel and expenses in 1998 and that the use of electronic filing can cut the cost of processing expense reports from $36.46 per paper report to as low as $7.91.[17]

5. ***Relocation to Lower-Wage Countries or Regions.***   We have already noted how a number of American companies have decided to relocate to regions or countries where wages are lower to reduce the cost of production. American companies are not the only ones to take this cost-reducing measure. Japanese companies have been relocating to all parts of Southeast Asia. German companies have been moving to Central European countries such as Poland, where wages are less than one-tenth of the average rate in Germany. There are other examples, such as an Austrian company moving to Slovakia and a French company partnering with a German company to manufacture products in Hungary. Furthermore, manufacturing companies are not the only ones who can benefit from the move to lower-wage countries. A thriving software development industry has emerged in India, where American and European companies find that the average wage rate of an Indian programmer is about one-fourth of a comparable person in the United States.[18]

6. ***Mergers, Consolidations, and Subsequent Downsizing.***   This particular approach to cost cutting was cited earlier in this chapter. We also discuss it briefly in chapter 14.

7. ***Layoffs and Plant Closings.***   Sometimes companies find it necessary to resort to simply laying off workers and closing down certain operations. The recession that began in the spring of 2001 triggered numerous layoffs by many companies. Ford and Kodak were among the more prominent companies that had to lay off thousands of their workers.

    Although downsizing and restructuring have become practically a way of life for corporate America, they have become much more common in many other parts of the world. Japan, in particular, has been hit hard by this management effort to cut costs. For the Japanese worker, long used to "lifetime employment," this has been difficult to handle.[19] However, it is gradually becoming more acceptable as an inevitable management tool. The recent success of Renault senior management in the turnaround of Nissan Motors, the company in which it holds a significant equity, is cited as an example of how layoffs can play an important role in the revival of an ailing Japanese company.[20]

8. ***Reduction in Fixed Assets.***   Fixed assets are long term investments in tangible resources (e.g. property, plant, and equipment) and intangible resources (goodwill, intellectual property, and software). Finance and accounting courses cover the use, measurement, and management of assets in great detail. In managerial economics, a firm's cost of buying and managing fixed assets tends to be covered at a rather high level of abstraction. We simply treat it as part of the fixed cost of doing business. More specifically, this fixed cost includes depreciation as an accrued expense on a company's income statement and a cash outlay

---

[17]"Software Is Easing Expense-Form Headaches," *Wall Street Journal*, December 28, 1998.
[18]See Peter Gumbel, "Western Europe Finds That It's Pricing Itself Out of the Job Market," *Wall Street Journal*, December 9, 1993; "Europe: The Push East," *Business Week*, November 2, 1994, pp. 48–49. Information about wage rates for Indian software programmers was acquired in an interview in November 1998, with a representative from Tata, India's largest manufacturing, service, and information technology conglomerate.
[19]In "Sign of Changed Times: Japan's Jobless Rate Rises to the U.S. Level," *Wall Street Journal*, December 28, 1998, the author of the article ported that Hoya Corporation, a Tokyo optical glass maker, laid off about one-third of its workforce through an early retirement program. Those who did not take the program would have faced pay cuts of 30 percent. One unnamed company supposedly ordered its older office workers to chop wood to persuade them to opt for retirement.
[20]"Nissan Returns to Profit," BBC News Service, May 17, 2001.

on its statement of cash flows. The addition of new capital investment in assets plus existing assets minus accumulated depreciation of the existing investments would rest on a company's balance sheet as net assets. Interestingly, economic theory, financial accounting and corporate finance all converge in their coverage of capital budgeting, which we cover in chapter 12.[21]

Regardless of how each discipline covers the topic, many of today's firms have sought to reduce their need for investment in assets in order to be more cost competitive. It helps to reduce their depreciation expenses as well as their cash outlays. This approach, which has been branded an "asset-light" strategy by the popular press, can be seen in some of the above-mentioned ways that companies seek to reduce costs. However, it has become such an important subject that it deserves mentioning in its own right.

It stands to reason that companies that are the most fixed asset intensive have the most to gain by pursuing an asset-light approach. Some years ago, the airlines and hotels saw the possibility of leasing their planes and hotels from the owners of these assets (who could well be leasing companies or partnerships of wealthy physicians). For airlines and hotels, the assets are owned by other parties while they concentrate on doing what they know best: providing travel and hospitality services. This same idea was taken up by manufacturers. A big breakthrough in the manufacturing of electronics products was made when companies such as Flextronics, an EMS (electronics manufacturing services) company based in Singapore, were contracted to make various finished products (not just the components) for global companies such as Sony and Ericsson. These global companies would then put their brand or trademark on the finished products supplied to them by the EMS. An important attraction of this move by the asset-light company was the reduction in inventory, which is a current asset, but an asset nonetheless.[22] Further back in the value chain of electronics manufacturing is the making of computer chips. If one were to build a brand-new fabrication facility to make the wafers that are then cut into the computer chips (called "fabs" in the industry), it could cost between $3 and $4 billion. Most companies would have to think very carefully before committing this amount of capital.

In the late 1980s, Taiwanese entrepreneurs came up with the idea that a company could devote itself to "carrying the load" of assets for the semiconductor industry. Today, the largest of these companies is Taiwan Semiconductor (TSMC). Founded in 1987, it had sales of close to $10 billion in 2006 and about 20,000 employees worldwide. So today, global "integrated chip manufacturers" such as Texas Instruments (those who design, manufacture, and test their chips) as well as "design houses" (those who focus only on designing the chips) use foundries such as TSMC in part or entirely in pursuit of their asset-light strategy.

At the time of the writing of this edition, we encountered still another example of an asset-light approach. According to the *New York Times*, "In a collaboration of a sort that would be *unthinkable in most industries* [emphasis added], T-Mobile UK and 3 UK, two British mobile phone operators, are combining their third-generation networks in a effort to save each of them 1 billion pounds over the next decade."[23] The

---

[21]We make no attempt to explain in any detail the relationship between the economic theory vs. financial accounting in the treatment of assets. Another chapter would probably have to be written for this. But we remind readers that you must always look for connections between the different courses that you take in your business curriculum.

[22]The sale of IBM's PC business to Lenovo might have created somewhat of a stir for certain people, because of the implications for manufacturing in the United States. Much of the IBM PC, as well as all other globally branded PCs was being made by contract manufacturers outside the United States well before this sale.

[23]Eric Sylvers, "Two British Mobile Phone Operators Share Networks," *New York Times*, December 31, 2007, p. C6.

article also talks about the two other U.K. companies (which also happen to be the largest), Vodafone and Orange, also considering a similar deal. Those familiar with the telecommunications industry, both wireline and wireless, will know that this industry is one of the most asset-intensive of any sector. But it seems to us that the sharing of assets would have interesting ramifications concerning maintenance and repair. If you happen to be a subscriber to one company and its service goes down, whom do you call or blame—your company or the one with whom it is sharing its assets?[24]

CAUTIONARY NOTE TO MANAGERS ABOUT THE USE OF COST-CUTTING AS A STRATEGY

In a later chapter of this book, we introduce the ideas on strategy developed by Professor Michael Porter.[25] One of the main ideas introduced in an early chapter of his book was about a company seeking a "differentiated" vs. a "cost leadership" approach to strategy.[26] We clearly saw an example of this in the case of Southwest Airlines discussed in the previous section. But in a later monograph, Porter warned about the long-run sustainability of such a strategy when a company focuses primarily on "operational excellence."[27] In the end, he believed that cost leadership strategies are more easily duplicated by rivals. Therefore, companies that want to attain a sustained competitive advantage should focus on a differentiated strategy. In other words, increasing profit by growing revenue and profit margin is more effective in the long term than increasing profit by only cutting cost.

We agree with Professor Porter about this. However, in times of crisis, companies cannot help but turn to cost-cutting to stay competitive. Moreover, the tremendous global competition today makes it imperative that all companies stay focused on being cost efficient, regardless of the level of demand for their products. But perhaps another disadvantage of focusing too much on the cost leadership approach, besides being easily copied, is the danger that this will distract senior management from closely watching and adjusting to consumer demand. Still worse, it could lead to developing a sense of complacency or what consultants might refer to as a "competitive blind spot." We believe such was the case at Dell Computer in recent times.

Over the years, Dell has become a textbook case of how a company can successfully compete using the low-cost approach. Its model of direct selling, primarily to businesses, combined with the outsourcing of much of the manufacture of its PCs (in the early days rivals would scoff at Dell by calling it a "bag and tag" shop), resulted in a true powerhouse in this market. But then, suddenly, the market started to shift. Businesses were starting to buy PCs more as replacements than as incremental acquisitions. Furthermore, the big boost in demand in the market was coming from people who wanted to buy laptops, not desktops for their home use, because of lower cost broadband services and the general desire to be more mobile. Purchasing agents of

---

[24]See the section at the end of this chapter on Global Applications for a discussion of the asset-light strategy in the chemical industry in China.
[25]Porter's ideas on strategy are probably the most quoted in the business world today. His first book on this subject is highly recommended and remains a classic text on strategy. It is in its 60th printing and has been translated into 19 languages. See Michael Porter, *Competitive Strategy: Techniques for Analyzing Industries and Competitors*,
[26]See chapter 9, pp. 375–377.
[27]Michael Porter, "What Is Strategy?" HBR OnPoint Enhanced Edition, February 1, 2000.

companies may feel comfortable buying laptops as well as desktops on the Internet, but not so with consumers. They would much prefer to go to a store and try out a laptop for themselves. Furthermore, Dell's models and designs were geared more toward the office than the family room. When Dell's profits began to dive partly because of this, an industry analyst, Sam Bhavasi, was quoted as saying, "Dell was not paying attention to the competitive landscape."[28]

GLOBAL APPLICATION: TOLL MANUFACTURING OF CHEMICALS IN CHINA

In our previous edition, the global application for this chapter dealt with the use of low-cost labor in the apparel industry.[29] This industry is well suited for using low-cost labor because the labor input is relatively high and the skill level is relatively low compared to other industries. But how amenable to outsourcing are industries that are less labor intensive and that require relatively more fixed capital investment? Take, for example, the chemical industry. The labor content in this industry is relatively low compared to the utilization of plant, equipment, and the amount of raw material content. The latter's cost has become even more prominent because of the increase in global oil prices.[30] Nonetheless, there are good reasons besides lower costs for a chemical company to consider outsourcing certain production activities.

A popular Web site for chemical processing has this to say about why a chemical company in any part of the world might want to outsource certain production activities:

> The outsourcing of business support functions such as information technology and human resources is as common in the chemical industry as any other . . . outsourced operations should allow the company to get on with doing what it knows best—producing chemicals. However, there are times when it might be better to outsource even that core activity of producing chemicals. For instance, your plant might not have *sufficient capacity* at the right time, your operators and engineers may lack the *necessary expertise* to execute a particular chemistry, or you may not even have all the *regulatory permits* (emphases added) required—any or all of these might persuade you to consider taking your production out of house to a *toll processor or contract manufacturer.*[31]

In addition to these important "noncost" reasons for outsourcing manufacturing, there is the fundamental economic motivation of cost savings. And it is primarily for this reason that global chemical companies engage in toll manufacturing in

---

[28]Quoted in Crayton Harrison, "Dell Shares Drop 10% on Warning: Computer Maker Loses $5 BIL. in Value on Profit Slowdown," *Dallas Morning News,* July 22, 2006.

[29]"Will All Our Clothes Be Made in China?" Paul Keat and Philip Young, *Managerial Economics*, 5th ed., Upper Saddle River, NJ: Prentice-Hall, 2006, pp. 266–267.

[30]Many of the chemicals that we use in the production of industrial and consumer goods are petrochemical derivatives. The "feedstock" from oil and natural gas go into such intermediate products as polyvinyl chloride and polystyrene. These in turn go into the making of everyday consumables that we take for granted, such as items made of plastic, paint coatings, and tire and rubber products. Chemical companies focus on using the feedstock to make the intermediates.

[31]Mike Spear, "Tap into Tollers," www.chemicalprocessing/com/articles/2005/514.

China. A major reason for the cost competitiveness of local Chinese manufacturers is because they are relatively small. Consequently, the type of technology that they use to produce chemicals is *relatively* more labor intensive than the kind of technology used by the large, global firms. Technology that utilizes more capital relative to labor requires a much higher level of output than the level produced by a typical Chinese firm in order to justify the heavy initial investment in capital.[32] China's lower wage rates combined with this higher rate of labor utilization give local companies a considerable cost advantage over their foreign counterparts. Therefore, the global giants are able to reduce their overall cost of production by supplementing their production with that of the lower cost toll manufacturers. In addition, the global companies do not have to invest as much in building new plants and equipment in China. This reduction in their capital spending is very much in line with the "asset-light" strategy that is currently being pursued in asset-intensive industries.[33]

But there is a negative side to this type of outsourcing: operational risk. This type of risk involves questions concerning reliability, continuity of supply, quality, and perhaps most important, security of intellectual property (IP). Large global chemical companies such as Dow Chemical and BASF have developed their own proprietary production methods and formulas. To ensure the quality of the output, the global outsourcers would need to share this IP with their toll manufacturers. But the toll manufacturers might use this IP without permission strictly for their own benefit and not as part of the contractual toll manufacturing agreement. Therefore, chemical companies in China (as well as everywhere else in the world) would have to be very sure that their toll manufacturers have a serious respect for intellectual property agreements as well as the know-how and capacity to meet contractual obligations.

Finally, let us look briefly at outsourcing from the point of view of the Chinese toll manufacturers. Currently, as already noted, they are relatively small firms. But like every business in a market economy, they all want to expand. Doing business with a global company helps them to do so. In addition, their business is also growing because of the booming Chinese economy. And as they grow, they feel that tolling for a well-known global company would give them added respectability and brand recognition throughout the entire Chinese market and perhaps even outside China. So they offer their tolling services to the global companies at very competitive prices in order to build up their reputation as well as their volume of business.

But as is the case for the global chemical manufacturers, there is also a negative side for local Chinese toll manufacturers. In exchange for more business and the "halo effect" of doing business with well-known global firms, the local companies face the prospects of increased capital investment (as they reach higher levels of production) and the added costs of compliance with the global companies' standards of quality of

---

[32]Refer back to Figure 6.10 of this chapter regarding the appropriate level of capital relative to demand. Also see Table 7.4. One of the reasons for economies of scale is the indivisible nature of many types of capital equipment. Also see Appendix A.

[33]These and other insights about the costs and benefits of toll manufacturing in China were obtained by one of the authors while working in corporate education programs in China. Another good example of the "asset-light" approach is found in the semiconductor industry. To build a new wafer fabrication plant today could cost up to $4 billion. Semiconductor companies who wish to pursue an asset-light production strategy can outsource the making of the silicon wafers to foundries such as Taiwan Semiconductor.

output, plant safety, and environmental protection. These additional costs involve such things as training, new software, implementation of new safety procedures, and increased wages of skilled labor (in order to reduce the high churn rate that is common among all Chinese manufacturing companies). As is the case in all economic decisions, there is a cost as well as a benefit to the toll manufacturing of chemicals in China from both the seller's and the buyer's perspective.

The Solution

Terry now needed to put all the pieces together to figure out if Lawrence Aluminum was really the right way to go. Even before crunching the numbers, she knew she had a somewhat delicate situation to consider. Her company had been doing business with Kayla Containers for many years, and the two companies had developed a close relationship (as well as friendly rivalry in the local softball league). If Shayna Soda stopped ordering from Kayla, Kayla could very easily go out of business. Lawrence was just a start-up, eager to grab new business by "low-balling" its prices. But what if Lawrence went out of business or decided not to source to upstate New York bottlers? Then what would her company do?

With this in mind, she turned to the facts. There was no denying that Kayla Containers had a higher base fee on soda cans, but that included the artwork. Furthermore, Kayla was always willing to change the artwork at no extra cost. Lawrence Aluminum's cans would be more than 20 percent cheaper in the base fee, but the artwork required an extra one-time fee. Terry took that fee and divided it out for the year to figure what the impact would be on the average cost of the cans for the first year. This fee increased the base cost of the cans another 2 percent. The cans were still considerably cheaper.

Next Terry considered the delivery charge. Kayla Containers was only 20 miles from Shayna's production plant. The delivery fee for Kayla was basically the same as Lawrence's base fee. But Kayla's fee was for only 20 miles delivery and Lawrence was for 400 miles delivery. In addition, Lawrence charged extra for specific time delivery and could even require the company to take inventory earlier than it wanted. Terry calculated the average cost of delivery annually using Kayla, and then for Lawrence. She also had to determine what the warehouse carrying costs would be for the inventory that would have to be held on early delivery. For each day that the cans were early, Shayna would incur extra costs for having that inventory on the floor. If the inventory needed to be moved for any reason, than there was a labor-hour issue involved. Now the costs really changed. Taking into consideration all these additional costs, Lawrence's base cost now jumped to 8% higher than Kayla.

Terry wanted to immediately run into Adam's office to tell him that Kayla was the better choice, but she first had to make sure that she covered all angles. She admitted that Lawrence Aluminum had a better quality aluminum, but Kayla's quality was perfectly acceptable and in fact better than Shayna's corporate minimum requirements. As far as technology was concerned, Terry knew that her company's computer systems needed to be upgraded in order for them to use a sophisticated supply chain management process regardless of which supplier they used.

The technology issue actually proved to be a critical factor in helping Terry to make her decision. She figured that if her company went with Lawrence Aluminum, then it would have to set up its systems according to this new vendor's specifications. Kayla, in contrast, did not have a sophisticated system in place and in fact was also thinking that it needed to upgrade its system. If Shayna stuck with Kayla, then Kayla would have to set up its system in a way that would integrate with Shayna's. It would be the other way around for Shayna if Lawrence Aluminum became the supplier. Terry e-mailed her friend Ryan over at Kayla to see if this would be a good move from Kayla's point of view. As soon as Ryan got her e-mail, he picked up the phone to talk to her in person. Given the possibility of losing a major customer and the fact that his company had to improve its systems anyway, there was no question in Ryan's mind that Kayla would work in every way possible to keep Shayna as its customer.

Now Terry was ready. It was Friday and she had all the answers to bring to Adam Michaels. As soon as she walked in, Adam asked, "When are we switching?"

Terry replied confidently, "We're not, we're sticking with Kayla."

◆ SUMMARY

This chapter is devoted to the analysis of the cost structure of the firm, both in the short run and the long run. In the short-run analysis, it is important to keep in mind that "behind the scenes," the law of diminishing returns causes the firm's marginal cost to increase, and that this increase in turn affects the pattern of behavior of the firm's average variable cost and average total cost. In the long-run analysis, it is important to recognize that certain factors may cause the firm's unit costs to decrease as its scale of operation increases. However, certain other factors may actually cause the unit cost to increase if the scale of operations becomes too large. In addition, other factors such as the learning curve effect and economies of scope must be taken into account in the long-run analysis of cost.

The material that is covered in this chapter may seem rather mundane because of the great emphasis placed on defining the various cost terms used in economic analysis. However, your patience and thoroughness in reading this chapter will be rewarded when you read the next four chapters. There you will find that the material in this chapter, together with the analysis of demand presented in chapters 3 and 4, forms the core of the economic analysis of the firm. As you will learn, all the decisions involving the production and pricing of goods or services—and, in a much broader sense, the very desirability for a firm to be in a particular line of business—depend on the demand for the particular product, the cost at which the firm is able to provide this product, and the competitive structure of the market in which it is operating.

◆ IMPORTANT CONCEPTS (Items with * are discussed in Appendix 7B.)

Average fixed cost (AFC): The fixed cost per unit of output. (p. 260)

Average total cost (AC or ATC): The total cost per unit of output. (p. 260)

Average variable cost (AVC): The variable cost per unit of output. (p. 260)

Diseconomies of scale: The increase in the unit cost of production as the firm increases its capacity. Like economies of scale, this is considered to be a long-run phenomenon. Among the more important reasons a firm may experience rising unit costs as its scale of production increases are (1) management coordination and control problems and (2) a disproportionate increase in staff in relation to indirect labor. (p. 266)

Economies of scale: The reduction in the unit cost of production as the firm increases its capacity (i.e., increases all its inputs). It is considered a long-run phenomenon. Among the reasons a firm experiences economies as its scale of production increases are (1) the ability to exact volume discounts from vendors, (2) the ability to use more fully specialization and division of labor, (3) the ability to justify the use of certain types of capital equipment or technology appropriate only for very large scales of production, and (4) management efficiencies resulting from an increased span of control at all levels of management. (p. 266)

Economies of scope: The reduction in cost resulting from the joint production of two or more goods or services. (p. 276)

***Engineering cost estimating:** A method of estimating long-run costs. Professionals familiar with production facilities calculate optimal combinations of inputs needed to produce given quantities of output. Monetary values are then assigned to obtain cost. (p. 306)

***Estimation of long-run cost functions:** Analysis that assumes all factors, especially capital, are variable. Cross-sectional regression analysis is customarily employed in the estimation. (p. 302)

***Estimation of short-run cost functions:** An analysis in which certain factors are assumed to be fixed during the period analyzed. Time series regression analysis is customarily employed in the estimation. (p. 299)

Experience curve: The relationship between the unit cost of labor and all inputs associated with the production process (i.e., both direct labor, such as factory workers, and indirect labor, such as design engineers). (p. 276)

Historical cost: The cost incurred in a past activity (e.g., the purchase price of an asset or the cost of a project incurred up to the point at which a decision is to be made). (p. 255)

Incremental cost: The total cost associated with a particular decision (e.g., the cost of building an additional wing to an office building, the cost of going into the soft drink business). If incremental cost is considered on a per-unit basis, it becomes marginal cost. For example, incremental cost can be considered the change in total variable cost, whereas marginal cost can be considered the change in total variable cost divided by the change in output. (p. 256)

Learning curve: The relationship between the unit cost of labor and the total amount of output produced by labor that is directly associated with the production process (i.e., "direct labor"). Essentially, this concept is based on the principle that one improves with practice. The resulting productivity gains lead to a reduction in the direct labor cost of producing a unit of output. (p. 273)

Marginal cost (MC):   The cost to a firm of producing an additional unit of an output. (p. 257)

Opportunity cost: The amount of subjective value forgone in choosing one activity over the next best alternative. (p. 255)

Relevant costs: Costs that are affected by a current decision alternative and that must therefore be taken into account in the decision. Variable costs and incremental costs are considered to be relevant costs. (p. 255)

Sunk cost: A cost incurred in the past that is not affected by a current decision. If a resource has no opportunity cost (i.e., it has no market value in an alternative use), it is considered to be sunk. (p. 256)

Supply chain management: Efforts by a firm to improve efficiencies through each link of a firm's supply chain from supplier to customer. (p. 277)

*Survivorship technique: A method for estimating long-run cost curves. The proportion of total industry output by firms of different sizes is observed over a period of time. That size segment of the industry that gains in proportion of industry output over time is deemed most efficient (lowest cost). (p. 307)

Total cost (TC):   The total cost of production, including both total variable and total fixed costs. (p. 258)

Total cost function: Economic analysis considers three basic functional forms of total cost: cubic, quadratic, and linear. The microeconomic theory of the firm relies almost entirely on the cubic function, and break-even analysis generally uses the linear form. (p. 262)

Total fixed cost (TFC):   A cost that remains constant as the level of output varies. In a short-run analysis, fixed cost is incurred even if the firm produces no output. (p. 260)

Total variable cost (TVC):   The total cost to a firm of using its variable inputs. (p. 260)

QUESTIONS

1. Define and compare the following types of cost:
   a. Sunk cost versus incremental cost
   b. Fixed cost versus variable cost
   c. Incremental cost versus marginal cost
   d. Opportunity cost versus out-of-pocket cost

2. Point out which costs in the preceding question are considered "relevant" and which are considered "irrelevant" to a business decision. Explain why.

3. Explain the relationship between a firm's short-run production function and its short-run cost function. Focus on the marginal product of an input and the marginal cost of production.

4. "If it were not for the law of diminishing returns, a firm's average cost and average variable cost would not increase in the short run." Do you agree with this statement? Explain.

5. Explain the distinction made in economic analysis between the short run and the long run.
6. Define *economies of scale*. How does this relate to returns to scale? Cite and briefly discuss the main determinants of economies of scale.
7. Define *diseconomies of scale*. Cite and briefly discuss the main determinants of this phenomenon.
8. Define *economies of scope*. Is this concept related to economies of scale? Explain.
9. Explain the relationship between the learning curve and a firm's cost function. Would economists consider the learning curve a short-run or a long-run phenomenon?
10. Define the *experience curve*. Compare its impact on a firm's cost function with that of the learning curve.
11. "Because of economies of scale, it is sometimes more cost effective for a firm to operate a large plant at less than maximum efficiency than a small plant at maximum efficiency." Do you agree with this statement? Explain.
12. When a company states its financial results in its annual report, it typically presents its income statement in the following way:

	Revenue
−	Cost of Goods Sold (including some depreciation)
	Gross Profit
−	Selling, General and Administrative Expenses
−	Research and Development
−	Depreciation
	Operating Profit
+/−	Net Interest (income and expense)
	Net Profit before Income Taxes
−	Taxes
	Net Profit after Income Taxes

"Cost of goods sold" includes all costs directly associated with making a product or providing a service. In retail merchandising this cost is essentially the wholesale cost of goods sold.

Discuss the differences between cost of goods sold and the concept of relevant cost used in this chapter. Are there any situations in which selling, general and administrative expenses, or research and development expenses might be considered as part of a firm's relevant costs? Explain.
13. Overheard at the water cooler: "I think our company should take advantage of economies of scale by increasing our output, thereby spreading out our overhead costs." Would you agree with this statement (assuming this person is not your boss)? Explain.

(Refer to Appendix 7B for help in answering questions 14 through 16.)

14. Discuss the estimation of short-run cost functions. Which regression method is most frequently used, and what are some of the problems a researcher will encounter? What adjustment factors may have to be employed?
15. Discuss the estimation of long-run cost functions. Which regression method is most frequently used, and what are some of the problems a researcher will encounter? What adjustment factors may have to be employed?
16. Comment briefly on the following methods of cost estimation:
    a. Engineering costs
    b. Survivorship principle
    Discuss the strengths and shortcomings of these methods and the circumstances under which each can be applied.

◻ PROBLEMS

1. Based on your knowledge of the definition of the various measures of short-run cost, complete this table.

Q	TC	TFC	TVC	AC	AFC	AVC	MC
0	120	—	—	x	x	x	x
1	—	—	—	265	—	—	—
2	—	—	264	—	—	—	—
3	—	—	—	161	—	—	—
4	—	—	—	—	—	—	85
5	—	—	525	—	—	—	—
6	—	—	—	120	—	—	—
7	—	—	—	—	—	97	—
8	—	—	768	—	—	—	—
9	—	—	—	—	—	97	—
10	—	—	—	—	—	—	127

2. Mr. Lee operates a greengrocery in a building he owns in one of the outer boroughs of New York City. Recently, a large chemical firm offered him a position as a senior engineer designing plants for its Asian operations. (Mr. Lee has a master's degree in chemical engineering.) His salary plus benefits would be $95,000 per year. A recent annual financial statement of his store's operations indicates the following:

Revenue	$625,000
Cost of goods sold	325,000
Wages of workers	75,000
Taxes, insurance, maintenance, and depreciation on building	30,000
Interest on business loan (10%)	5,000
Other miscellaneous expenses	15,000
Profit before taxes	$175,000

If Mr. Lee decides to take the job, he knows that he can sell the store for $350,000 because of the goodwill built with a steady clientele of neighborhood customers and the excellent location of the building. He would still hold on to the building, however, and he knows he could earn a rent of $50,000 on this asset. If he did sell the business, assume he would use some of the proceeds from the sale to pay off his business loan of $50,000. He could then invest the difference of $300,000 (i.e., $350,000 − $50,000) and expect to receive an annual return of 9 percent. Should Mr. Lee sell his business and go to work for the chemical company?

In answering this question, also consider the following information:
a. In his own business, Mr. Lee works between 16 and 18 hours a day, 6 days a week. He can expect to work between 10 and 12 hours a day, 5 days a week, in the chemical company.
b. Currently, Mr. Lee is assisted by his wife and his brother, both of whom receive no salary but share in the profits of the business.
c. Mr. Lee expects his salary and the profits of his business to increase at roughly the same rate over the next 5 years.

3. Joe enjoys fishing and goes out about 20 times per year. One day, his wife, Sarah, told him that fishing is simply too expensive a hobby. "I think that you should stop going fishing," she exclaimed. "I did a little calculation, and I figured that it costs us about $28.75 for every fish that you catch because you usually catch about 20 fish per trip. Besides, I always end up

having to clean them. We would be much better off buying ready-to-cook fish from the local fish market."

Comment on Sarah's remarks. Do you agree with her argument? Explain. (Following below are her cost estimates.)

Boat	$150
(cost = $30,000, usable for 10 years, 20 outings per year)	
Boat fuel	45
Dock fees and insurance for the boat (average per trip)	130
Travel expenses to and from the lake	25
(100 miles @ $0.25 per mile: gas, oil, and tires,	
$0.18, and depreciation and insurance, $0.07)	
New fishing equipment purchases this year (prorated over 20 trips)	25
Annual fishing license	35
Bait and miscellaneous expenses	50
Food	40
Beverages	35
Traffic fine received on the way to the lake	40
Total cost per trip	$575

4. You are given the following cost functions:

$$TC = 100 + 60Q - 3Q^2 + 0.1Q^3$$
$$TC = 100 + 60Q + 3Q^2$$
$$TC = 100 + 60Q$$

   a. Compute the average variable cost, average cost, and marginal cost for each function. Plot them on a graph.
   b. In each case, indicate the point at which diminishing returns occur. Also indicate the point of maximum cost efficiency (i.e., the point of minimum average cost).
   c. For each function, discuss the relationship between marginal cost and average variable cost and between marginal cost and average cost. Also discuss the relationship between average variable cost and average cost.

5. Decide whether the following statements are true or false and explain why.
   a. A decision maker must always use the historical cost of raw materials in making an economic decision.
   b. The marginal cost curve always intersects the average cost curve at the average cost's lowest point.
   c. The portion of the long-run cost curve that is horizontal indicates that the firm is experiencing neither economies nor diseconomies of scale.
   d. Marginal cost is relevant only in the short-run analysis of the firm.
   e. The rational firm will try to operate most efficiently by producing at the point where its average cost is minimized.

6. Indicate the effect that each of the following conditions will have on a firm's average variable cost curve and its average cost curve.
   a. The movement of a brokerage firm's administrative offices from New York City to New Jersey, where the average rental cost is lower
   b. The use of two shifts instead of three shifts in a manufacturing facility
   c. An agreement reached with the labor union in which wage increases are tied to productivity increases
   d. The elimination of sugar quotas (as it pertains to those firms that use a lot of sugar, such as bakeries and soft drink bottlers)
   e. Imposition of stricter environmental protection laws

7. You are given the following *long-run* cost function:

$$TC = 160Q - 20Q^2 + 1.2Q^3$$

a. Calculate the long-run average cost and marginal cost. Plot these costs on a graph.

b. Describe the nature of this function's scale economies. Over what range of output does economies of scale exist? Diseconomies of scale? Show this on the graph.

(Refer to Appendix 7B for help in answering the following problems.)

8. During the last 50 years or so, many studies of cost curves have been published. The results of two of these are summarized here. In each case, interpret the equation and discuss the shapes of the total cost curve, the marginal cost curve, and the average cost curve.

a. A study of a light plant over a 6-month period resulted in the following regression equation:

$$Y = 16.68 + 0.125X + 0.00439X^2$$

where Y = Total fuel cost
X = Output

b. An early study of the steel industry indicated the following results, based on annual data for 12 years.

$$Y = 182,100,000 + 55.73X$$

where Y = Total cost
X = Weighted output, in tons

A time series analysis usually indicates a short-run cost study. Do you believe that a 12-year period is too long? Explain.

9. You have been presented with the following cost data and asked to fit a statistical cost function:

Quantity	Total Cost
10	104.0
20	107.0
30	109.0
40	111.5
50	114.5
60	118.0
70	123.0
80	128.5
90	137.0
100	150.0

a. Plot the data on a graph, and draw a freehand curve that best fits the data.

b. Fit three possible statistical cost functions to the data. Use straight-line, quadratic, and cubic formulas. Do the results confirm the curve you drew in *a*?

c. Discuss the statistical results you obtained in *b*. Include in your discussion R^2, the coefficients, and the statistical significance of the coefficients.

d. If the data represent 10 months of production for one plant of a specific company, would you consider this to be a short-run analysis?

e. How would your answer to part *d* change if you were told that the data represent 10 different plants during a particular month of the year?

10. The economist for the Grand Corporation has estimated the company's cost function, using time series data, to be

$$TC = 50 + 16Q - 2Q^2 + 0.2Q^3$$

where TC = Total cost
  Q = Quantity produced per period

a. Plot this curve for quantities 1 to 10.
b. Calculate the average total cost, average variable cost, and marginal cost for these quantities, and plot them on another graph.
c. Discuss your results in terms of decreasing, constant, and increasing marginal costs. Does Grand's cost function illustrate all these?

11. Discuss the following three cost functions:

$$TC = 20 + 4Q$$
$$TC = 20 + 2Q + 0.5Q^2$$
$$TC = 20 + 4Q - 0.1Q^2$$

a. Calculate all cost curves:
   • Total cost
   • Total fixed cost
   • Total variable cost
   • Average total cost
   • Average fixed cost
   • Average variable cost
   • Marginal cost
b. Plot these curves on graphs.
c. Compare the shapes of these curves and discuss their characteristics. (Particularly interesting should be the last cost function, whose shape is often found in engineering cost studies.)

12. The Central Publishing Company is about to publish its first textbook in managerial economics. It is now in the process of estimating costs. It expects to produce 10,000 copies during its first year. The following costs have been estimated to correspond to the expected copies.

a. Paper stock	$8,000
b. Typesetting	$15,000
c. Printing	$50,000
d. Art (including graphs)	$9,000
e. Editing	$20,000
f. Reviews	$3,000
g. Promotion and advertising	$12,000
h. Binding	$22,000
i. Shipping	$10,000

In addition to the preceding costs, it expects to pay the authors a 13 percent royalty and its salespeople a 3 percent commission. These percentages will be based on the publisher's price of $48 per textbook.

Some of the preceding costs are fixed and others are variable. The average variable costs are expected to be constant. Although 10,000 copies is the projected volume, the book could sell anywhere between 0 and 20,000 copies.

Using the preceding data,
a. Write equations for total cost, average total cost, average variable cost, and marginal cost.
b. Draw the cost curves for quantities from 0 to 20,000 (in intervals of 2,000).

13. The Big Horn Corporation commissioned an economic consultant to estimate the company's cost function. The consultant collected a large amount of data for a number of years from the books of the corporation and came up with the following equation:

$$TC = 170 + 22Q + 1.5Q^2$$

where TC = Total cost (in thousands)
   Q = Quantity produced per period

a. Plot this curve for quantities 1 through 15.
b. Calculate the average total cost, average variable cost, and marginal cost, and plot them on another graph.
c. Discuss your results in terms of decreasing, constant, and increasing marginal costs. Does Big Horn's cost function illustrate all these?

A Mathematical Restatement of the Short-Run Cost Function

The general form of the short-run cost function is

$$TC = f(Q) \qquad \textbf{(7A.1)}$$

where TC = Total cost
Q = Output

As stated in this chapter, three specific forms of this function are used in economic analysis: the cubic, the quadratic, and the linear. Microeconomic theory relies primarily on the cubic equation because it encompasses the possibility of increasing returns to a factor as well as diminishing returns. The quadratic form of the total cost function implies that only the law of diminishing returns affects the short-run relationship between a firm's output and its variable input. The linear form indicates that neither increasing nor diminishing returns to a factor take place in the short run as the firm uses additional units of its variable input. In this appendix, we use calculus to state the cubic equation, the one most frequently used in economic theory.

Consider the following equation (which, incidentally, is the one used to generate the cost data in Table 7.2 and Figure 7.2):

$$TC = 100 + 60Q - 5Q^2 + 0.7Q^3 \qquad \textbf{(7A.2)}$$

The total fixed-cost component of this equation is simply the constant term, 100. The balance of the right-hand side gives us total variable cost. The average and marginal costs can be derived from Equation (7A.2) using the definitions provided in the chapter, which are restated in the following equations:

$$\text{Average fixed cost (AFC)} = \frac{TFC}{Q} = \frac{100}{Q} \qquad \textbf{(7A.3)}$$

$$\text{Average total cost (AC)} = \frac{TC}{Q} = \frac{100}{Q}$$
$$+ 60 - 5Q + 0.7Q^2 \qquad \textbf{(7A.4)}$$

$$\text{Average variable cost (AVC)} = \frac{TVC}{Q}$$
$$= 60 - 5Q + 0.7Q^2 \qquad \textbf{(7A.5)}$$

$$\text{Marginal cost (MC)} = dTC/dQ$$
$$= 60 - 10Q + 2.1Q^2 \qquad \textbf{(7A.6)}$$

Notice that to find marginal cost, we simply took the first derivative of the total cost function stated in Equation (7A.2).

The Estimation of Cost

Learning Objectives

Upon completion of this appendix, readers should be able to:

■ Describe the use of time series regression analysis in measuring short-run costs, evaluating its advantages and disadvantages.

■ Consider the question: are short-run marginal costs u-shaped or constant?

■ Describe the use of cross-section regression analysis in measuring long-run costs, and evaluate its advantages and disadvantages.

■ Consider the question: Are there economies of scale?

■ Show how long-run costs can also be estimated by using engineering cost estimates and the survivorship technique.

The study of cost curves has its origins with Joel Dean, who wrote the first textbook on managerial economics and conducted many of the studies, dating back to the 1930s.

As in the case of production functions, we are interested in estimating cost functions both in the short run and in the long run. The short-run function helps define short-run marginal costs and thus assists the manager in determining output and prices. In the long run, the decision that a firm faces involves building the most efficient size of plant. That determination will depend on the existence of scale economies and diseconomies.

Short-run cost functions (like short-run production functions) assume at least one factor is fixed. Thus, cost is influenced by the quantity produced as changes occur in the variable factor. To estimate such a short-run function, we must find data in which quantity and costs change while certain factors change and others remain fixed.

In investigating short-run cost functions using regression analysis, researchers have most frequently employed the time series technique with data for a specific plant or firm over time. It is important that when time series data are collected, the period over which observations are taken is limited to a relatively short span because the size of the plant or firm, as well as technology, should not change significantly during the time interval used in a short-run cost function. To conduct a meaningful analysis, there

must be a sufficient number of observations, and there must be variations in production from observation period to observation period.[34] Thus, each observation period, where possible, should be limited to a month, and sometimes even a shorter period (1 week or 2 weeks).

Long-run cost functions—the planning functions—allow for changes in all factors, including plant size (or capital investment in general). Most studies of long-run cost functions have employed cross-sectional analysis. Observations are recorded in a specific time period (e.g., 1 year) for a number of different plants of different sizes with different amounts of inputs and outputs. We discuss short-term and long-term analyses separately.

The Estimation of Short-Run Cost Functions

Problems and Adjustments

Economic versus Accounting Costs   Most empirical studies of cost functions have used accounting data that record the actual costs and expenses on a historical basis. However, decision-making data—economic data—should also include opportunity

---

[34]Ideally, these changes in quantities produced should occur under relatively normal circumstances rather than due to some abnormal upheaval. Thus, production cuts because of plant damage or a strike, for instance, may not produce valid data.

costs. No amount of adjustment will ever completely reconcile these concepts, but certain corrections can be made.

➤ Changes in prices of labor, materials, and other inputs must be adjusted so current prices are used.[35]

➤ Costs that are not a function of output should be excluded. Because we are dealing with short-run cost functions, fixed costs should not have an influence on pricing or output decisions.

➤ Closely allied to the previous point is the question of depreciation. Accountants usually record depreciation on a time-related basis. Depreciation is often not related to actual usage but follows accounting convention as adapted to tax rules. If "use" depreciation can be isolated from the accounting data, only that portion should be included in costs. But it must be kept in mind that recorded depreciation is based on the original cost of the equipment, whereas economic depreciation should be based on replacement value.

The problems that arise in the **estimation of short-run cost functions** because of differences between accounting and economic costs are the most difficult to solve. In most cases, some type of compromise is necessary. No definitive advice can be given here to prospective researchers. We can only point out the significant issues and suggest some possible appropriate adjustments. What is done in the final analysis depends on the data available and the ability of the investigator to make the corrections.

Rate Changes   In addition to inflationary changes in the prices of various inputs, costs can also change due to variations in tax rates, Social Security contributions, labor insurance costs (unemployment insurance or worker's compensation rates), and various benefit coverages that affect costs. Because most of these rate changes are not based on quantity produced, they should be excluded.

Output Homogeneity   The problems encountered in cost estimation are similar to those discussed for the production function. The analysis is easiest when output is relatively homogeneous. If only one product is produced in the plant, the quantity produced (or shipped) can be handled in a rather uncomplicated manner. But if there are several products moving through the plant simultaneously, some weighting apparatus must be employed to obtain the quantity produced.[36]

Timing of Costs   In many cases, costs and the service performed to create these costs do not occur at the same time. For instance, a machine that is in use continuously may be scheduled for maintenance periodically. In the airline industry, for example, major maintenance on engines is performed after a given number of flight hours. When such timing differences occur, care must be taken to spread the maintenance costs over the period of machine usage.

Accounting Changes   When a time series analysis using accounting data is performed, it is important that the researcher ascertain whether changes in accounting methods, such as depreciation methods and recording of development expenses, have occurred during the period included in the study. Such changes must be adjusted to reflect uniformity in the measurements over time.

Given all the warnings about the problems that can be encountered in empirical cost estimation, you may have been persuaded that no useful conclusions can be obtained from such studies. Actually, such difficulties have not turned away many economists. Starting with Dean in the 1930s and continuing today, economic journals contain many articles investigating statistical cost functions.

The Shapes of Short-Run Cost Functions

Earlier in this chapter, three different specifications of cost functions were shown. Each represents a possible shape of the cost curves. The economist, after collecting and adjusting the data, will use one of these specifications to measure the relationship between cost and output. Other statistical functions

---

[35]Because different inputs may incur different relative price changes, some factor substitution may result over time. It can only be hoped that such effects will not be significant, because they are extremely difficult, if not impossible, to remove.

[36]If a weighting scheme involving costs or direct inputs for each product is used, then, in a way, we are employing costs to determine output and then measuring costs as a function of this output. In other words, we are introducing a dependency into the relationship between costs and output, when we are really trying to determine the relationship between the two. This presents a serious problem. But again, as long as accounting and production records of a firm are employed, there is no easy way out of this dilemma.

could be employed (e.g., the Cobb-Douglas power function), but the three shapes are the ones most frequently encountered in statistical studies.

Figures 7.4*a* and *b* represent the normal theoretical function, which exhibits both decreasing and increasing marginal and average costs. The mathematical functions that describe the total, average, and marginal cost curves are the following[37]:

$$TC = a + bQ - cQ^2 + dQ^3$$
$$AC = a/Q + b - cQ + dQ^2$$
$$MC = b - 2cQ + 3dQ^2$$

The average cost curve is obtained by dividing TC by *Q*. To obtain the marginal cost curve, we used some elementary calculus; we took the first derivative of the total cost function.

If the data do not quite fit the previous cubic function, the quadratic function can be tested. The three equations in this case are as follows:

$$TC = a + bQ + cQ^2$$
$$AC = a/Q + b + cQ$$
$$MC = b + 2cQ$$

As can be seen in Figures 7.4*c* and *d*, the shapes of these functions differ substantially from the cubic function. The total cost curve consists of only that section that increases at an increasing rate. Thus, there are no decreasing marginal costs (increasing marginal product) in this construction. This can be seen in Figure 7.4*d*, where the MC curve is a straight line increasing at all points (i.e., not U-shaped).

A linear total cost function can also be fitted.[38] The three equations take the following form:

$$TC = a + bQ$$
$$AC = a/Q + b$$
$$MC = b$$

Figures 7.4*e* and *f* show the curves based on the linear form.[39] Note that the law of diminishing marginal returns has been eliminated. Each additional unit's cost is the constant, *b*. Thus, this specification of the cost curve exhibits strictly constant marginal costs. This type of analysis does not appeal intuitively to an economist, who knows that if units of a variable factor are continually added to a fixed factor (plant), somewhere at higher production levels unit costs must rise.

These three specifications can fit various types of cost data. But even when a really good set of data is available to the investigator, chances are that the range of observations will be rather limited and will tend to cluster around a midpoint. Very seldom will we have data corresponding to near-zero production, and very seldom will data be given for production equaling or exceeding theoretical capacity. Thus, the statistical results economists obtain may not reflect the behavior of costs at the two extremes of the curve. In the following discussion of some of the empirical work that has been performed in the past, we find that this is precisely the case.

A Sampling of Short-Run Cost Studies

There is a large number of cost studies from which we could choose for purposes of illustration. We have selected three studies covering different industries and different time periods. Although some of the estimating procedures have become somewhat more sophisticated over time, the studies all used time series regression analysis.

The Hosiery Mill One of several studies conducted by Joel Dean in the 1930s and 1940s focused on a mill of a large hosiery manufacturer.[40] Its equipment was highly mechanized and its labor skilled.

---

[37]If only variable costs are estimated, the total curve would be the variable cost curve. Theoretically, it should begin at the origin because there are no variable costs when production is zero. However, when the curves are statistically estimated, even if only variable costs are included, the line will most likely intercept the *Y*-axis at a point other than zero. From the investigator's viewpoint, this is not terribly important because most of the observations included in the statistical estimate will not be anywhere near zero production. The intercept thus turns out to be meaningless.

[38]In Appendix B of chapter 8, on break-even analysis, we use this function exclusively.

[39]The average total cost curve in this case declines continuously and approaches the marginal cost curve asymptotically. The reason for this, in the formula, is that the first term *a/Q*, decreases as *Q* increases and the second term, *b*, is a constant. If we were dealing exclusively with variable costs, where the *a* term does not exist (because costs are zero when production is zero), then AVC = *b* and the marginal and average variable costs equal each other. This, of course, must be true, because if each additional (marginal) unit costs the same, then the average variable cost of each unit does not change and must equal the marginal cost.

[40]Joel Dean, *Statistical Cost Functions of a Hosiery Mill,* Studies in Business Administration, 11, 4, Chicago: University of Chicago Press, 1941. This study and others have been reprinted in a volume of Dean's work, *Statistical Cost Estimation,* Bloomington: Indiana University Press, 1976.

Data for 54 months from 1935 to 1939 were employed. During this period, the size of the plant did not change, and the equipment remained approximately the same. Production during these months varied from zero to near physical capacity. Direct labor, indirect labor, and overhead costs were included. These costs were adjusted by factor price indexes. Output was a weighted index of individual products, and the weights were based on relative labor costs. The result, using a linear regression form, was

$$TC = 2,935.59 + 1,998Q$$

where TC = Total Cost
Q = Output, in pairs of hosiery

The results were statistically significant, and the correlation coefficient was 0.973 (and, therefore, the coefficient of determination, R^2, was 0.947).

Quadratic and cubic equations were also calculated but did not show a good fit to the data. Thus Dean's analysis points to the existence of a straight-line total cost curve, a decreasing average total cost curve, and constant marginal costs.

Road Passenger Transport   In the United Kingdom, J. Johnston collected data from one of the larger transportation companies, with a fleet of some 1,300 vehicles, that operated some 45 million car miles per year.[41] The data were grouped into 4-week periods over 3 years, 1949 to 1952. Production exhibited a marked seasonal pattern, so varying production amounts per period could be observed.

The costs included all the vehicle operations (wages, clothing, gasoline, oil, and tires), maintenance, depreciation (based on mileage), variable overhead, and a minor amount of fixed overhead. Output was measured in car miles during the period. The data were adjusted by individual price indexes where price changes had occurred.

Again, a straight-line total cost function provided the best fit:

$$TC = 0.65558 + 0.4433Q$$

where Q represents car miles, in millions. The correlation coefficient was 0.95. So, as in Dean's study, the total cost curve was a straight line with constant marginal costs.

Plastic Containers   In a study conducted for ten different products moving through a plant at the same time, twenty-one monthly observations were taken during the period of January 1966 to September 1967.[42] During this period plant capacity was fixed, and all input prices were also fixed by contract. Only direct costs of labor, machinery, and materials were included, so no allocation problems for overhead items had to be handled. The firm reported wide production fluctuations during the period, with several observations being somewhat above 90 percent of capacity level.

The straight-line function exhibited the best fit for each of the ten products. Tests to investigate cost interrelationships among the products showed no influence.

The authors also tested for the firm's aggregate cost–output relationship. The total physical output was obtained by weighting each product by its base period price. Again, the best results were given by a straight-line equation,

$$TC = 56,393 + 3.368Q$$

with the *t*-test significant at the 1 percent level and the R^2 a respectable 0.89.

Marginal Cost: U-Shaped or Constant?

Each of the three studies just cited concluded that in the short run, the total cost curve is a linear function of production and that the marginal cost is constant. In addition to the hosiery mill, Dean also studied a furniture factory and a leather belt shop. Johnston conducted investigations into a food processing firm and coal mining, among others. Studies of the steel industry, cement industry, and electric power were also done. Most of these came to conclusions similar to those of the three studies we described briefly. Actually, some of the researchers found decreasing marginal costs to be the rule.

Does that mean that economists should revise their thinking about U-shaped average and marginal cost curves? Although these findings should cause economists to pause and do some additional thinking, the results of these studies—even over the relatively long period of 50 or more years—can be reconciled with the traditional shapes of cost curves:

1. The data employed in most of the studies concentrated on output levels that were limited in range.

[41]J. Johnston, *Statistical Cost Analysis*, New York: McGraw-Hill 1960, pp. 74–86.

[42]Ronald S. Coot and David A. Walker, "Short-Run Cost Functions of a Multi-Product Firm," *Journal of Industrial Economics*, April 1970, pp. 118–28.

Thus, even though in some cases production may have taken place at about 90 percent of capacity, it is quite possible that plants are built and equipped in such a way that unit costs are relatively constant over a fairly long range of outputs. The cost curves that economists draw, as we have seen in this chapter, show very distinct minimum points to show their importance to students of elementary economics. However, the bottom of the curve may represent a fairly wide interval, and unit costs may rise (quite sharply) only when physical capacity is reached. Figure 7B.1 shows an average cost curve (A) that most students have seen drawn on blackboards. But curve B may be the one that is more true to life. The minimum point of this curve is not as low as that on curve A, but there is a relatively wide range of outputs on curve B where costs remain low—lower than for curve A. As production fluctuates from period to period, output is more likely to take place on the relatively constant unit cost segment on curve B than at curve A's narrowly defined minimum.

2. Many economists explain straight-line cost curves by pointing out that although theory requires capital inputs to be fixed in the short run, they really are not. For instance, when production increases, a firm can easily set up an additional assembly line to keep the fixed/variable input ratio constant. Thus, because the fixed factor is used in a fixed proportion with the variable factor, increasing marginal cost will not necessarily occur.

3. Regression analysis is not a perfect tool. If most of the observations fall into an intermediate output range, there may just not be a sufficient number of observations at the extremes to convert a linear fit to a curvilinear one.

Thus, although economists would certainly be more gratified if empirical work were to confirm their theories, the evidence of the studies is not so overwhelming that an immediate reevaluation of microeconomic theory is necessary. Further, real-life data seem to be consistent with the existence of upward-sloping marginal cost curves. We learned earlier that the upward-sloping short-run supply curve of a firm or industry is based on the existence of an upward-sloping marginal cost curve. The fact that rising demand for a product raises the price and causes an increase in quantity supplied in the short run is evidence of the existence of an upward-sloping supply curve that is theoretically explained by the existence of an upward-sloping marginal cost curve. Thus, despite some of the empirical findings, it appears that corporate managers act as if they were confronted by a marginal cost curve of the kind described by economic theory.

The Estimation of Long-Run Cost Functions

The **estimation of long-run cost functions** presents some new challenges. Remember, in the economic long run, all costs are variable. That means that capital (plant and equipment), which is ordinarily held fixed in the short run, is now permitted to change. As a matter of fact, it is precisely the goal of long-run cost analysis to trace unit costs for different sizes of plant and different amounts of equipment capacity. Our interest in long-run costs is to investigate the existence of returns to scale.

The question of costs in relation to size is important not only for planning decisions regarding plant or firm expansion. Firms must also consider costs when deciding on potential mergers. Will the synergy of the new units indicate a potential decrease in unit costs as a function of size?

Unlike the short-term cost function studies that use time series analysis, most long-run cost studies employ cross-sectional regression analysis. This method has several advantages:

1. Observations are recorded for different plants (or firms) at a given point of time. Because different plants generally come in different sizes, the independent variable, quantity of output, can vary over relatively large ranges.

Figure 7B.1   Theoretical versus Realistic Average Cost Curve

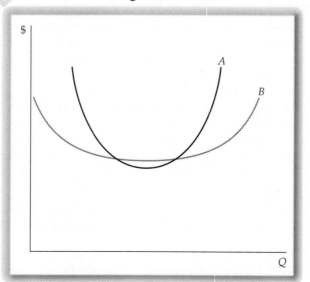

2. Because all observations are taken at a given point in time (e.g., 1 year), the technology is known and does not change. Under ideal circumstances, each plant will use that level of technology, within the known state of the art, that is most efficient for that specific plant. But this ideal is usually not reached, as is explained in the following discussion.

3. Adjusting the various costs for inflation or other price changes is not necessary under cross-sectional analysis. If annual observations are used for the sample of plants, an average figure for costs (e.g., per labor hour or ton of material) will be satisfactory. Only under conditions of very severe inflation—hyperinflation—would the averaging of annual costs become a significant problem, but any studies undertaken under such conditions would surely be of dubious quality in any case.

The use of the cross-sectional technique also creates some difficulties of which the researcher must be well aware. Just a few of these are the following:

1. Inflationary problems may be avoided by abandoning the time series method, but a new problem is introduced. Because the observations are taken from plants (or firms) in different geographic areas, we may encounter interregional cost differences in labor rates, utility bills, material costs, or transportation costs, for example. Adjustments to some common base must be made. But if relative prices of inputs differ, then the combination of inputs in a particular location may be a function of these relative differences. By adjusting prices to a specific benchmark, we may be obliterating the conscious choice made by management in a particular location based on relative prices of different inputs.

2. Although, as stated, the known state of the art for each firm is the same, it is not necessarily true that all plants are, at a given point of time, operating at the optimal level of technology. The assumption that each plant is operating most efficiently for its production level does not necessarily hold. This can be illustrated by drawing the familiar envelope curve. In Figure 7B.2 an envelope curve, *ABC*, is drawn. This long-run average cost curve represents all the optimal points of production. Point *B* is the minimum cost point, which represents the most efficient plant size. If, however, the plants in the sample do not operate at optimal points for any level of production, we may end up with observations along a curve such as *DF*, which will tend to be above the optimal curve, *ABC*, and which indicates not only a level, but also a slope quite different from the optimal cost curve. There really is no way to correct for this potential error completely.

3. If accounting data are used to make the estimates, it is important that the economist verify that there are

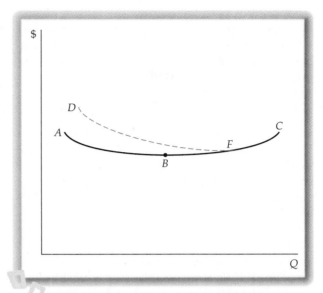

Figure 7B.2   Optimal and Suboptimal Cost Curves

no significant differences in the way costs are recorded on the firms' books of account. Different depreciation procedures, varying inventory valuation methods, and amortization of other expenses can lead to substantial distortions. The best possible adjustments must always be made.

4. Different companies may pay their factors differently. This is most important in the case of labor costs. Total labor costs can comprise varying fractions of wages and benefits (e.g., vacation time, holidays, and medical care). In some cases, employees may receive part of their income in stock, or stock may be sold to them at a discounted price. The estimator must be certain to include all relevant costs.

A Sampling of Long-Run Cost Studies

As in the case of short-run costs, a large number of inquiries into the properties of long-run costs have been conducted during the last 50 years or so. A small number of these are mentioned here to provide a flavor of method and results.

Shoe Store Chain   In one of the early studies conducted by Joel Dean, the sample comprised 55 metropolitan area shoe stores owned by one firm.[43] Pairs of shoes were the output. Costs were mainly

[43]Joel Dean and R. Warren James, *The Long-Run Behavior of Costs in a Chain of Shoe Stores: A Statistical Analysis,* Studies in Business Administration, 12, 3, University of Chicago Press, 1942, reprinted in Dean, *Statistical Cost Estimation,* pp. 324–60.

composed of selling expenses (including wages), handling expenses, and building expenses. Corporate allocations were omitted. The study was based on annual data for 1937 and 1938. Quadratic total cost curves gave the best fit for both years, indicating a U-shaped average cost curve and a rising marginal cost curve.

Building Societies   In the United Kingdom, building societies are roughly equivalent to savings and loan associations in the United States. Johnston studied 217 such enterprises in the year 1953.[44] The companies were grouped into six size categories based on total annual revenue.

Johnston found that a U-shaped long-run cost curve existed for these enterprises. Cost in this study was measured as a ratio of management expenses to revenue. Middle-size societies were found to have the lowest ratio. However, when Johnston segregated the 217 observations into 149 societies with no branches and 68 with branches, somewhat different results appeared. Most of the firms in the former group were concentrated in the four lower-size categories and most firms in the latter group were in the top four. When the nonbranch societies and the branch societies were analyzed separately, the former firms appeared to have a declining cost ratio, whereas the companies with branches had a constant ratio. Thus, the appearance of a U-shaped average cost curve, and therefore, economies of scale at the low end and diseconomies of scale at the high end, were the result of two separate underlying patterns.

Electric Utilities   The electric utility industry has been a frequent target of economists studying cost curves. Output is fairly easily defined (electricity produced), and the United States has a large number of independently owned utilities of many different sizes. Because these companies must regularly deal with state regulatory commissions in rate cases, they collect large volumes of data pertaining to costs and revenues. Utilities have also been observed to have constant productivity improvements and technological progress. The study summarized here was performed using 1971 data for 74 utilities.[45] Because the data are for 1971, this study rules out any effects of pollution control equipment on costs.

The major costs were best described by a quadratic function, which led to a U-shaped average cost curve. The cost coefficients were statistically highly significant. The authors identified the intervals for which economies of scale existed and the appropriate minimum cost point. They found that diseconomies of scale appeared beyond moderate firm size. Many earlier studies of utilities found economies of scale throughout the range of observations. This study, as well as another one for the year 1970,[46] found the possibility of scale diseconomies in firms of larger size.

A more recent study analyzed economies of scale for thirty-one regional private steam-electric utilities located in five Midwestern states in 1987. The author of this study found that significant economies of scale existed for twenty-one of the smaller utilities producing 32 percent of the total regional output. The larger firms showed no additional economies. The long-run cost curve for these firms was flat, and no diseconomies of scale were found.[47]

Financial Institutions   A more recent article reviewed some thirteen studies that attempted to estimate economies of scale and economies of scope for credit unions, savings and loan associations, and commercial banks.[48] Economies of scale are defined as those associated with firm size, whereas economies of scope relate to the joint production of two or more products. Economies of scale exist if per unit or average production costs decline as output rises. Economies of scope arise if two or more products can be jointly produced at a lower cost than is incurred in their independent production. Each study used a logarithmic function and employed similar measures of economies. The author summarized the results of these thirteen studies as follows:

➤   Overall economies of scale appear to exist only at low levels of output, with diseconomies at larger output levels.

➤   There is no consistent evidence of global economies of scope.

---

[44]Johnston, *Statistical Cost Analysis,* pp. 103–5.

[45]David A. Huettner and John H. Landon, "Electric Utilities: Scale Economies and Diseconomies," *Southern Economic Journal,* April 1978, pp. 883–912.

[46]L. R. Christensen and W. H. Greene, "Economies of Scale in U.S. Electric Power Generation," *Journal of Political Economy,* 84, 4 (August 1976), pp. 655–76.

[47]Albert A. Ocunade, "Economies of Scale in Steam-Electric Power Generation in East-North-Central U.S.," *Journal of Economics and Finance,* 17, 1, (Spring 1993), pp. 149–56.

[48]Jeffrey A. Clark, "Economies of Scale and Scope at Depository Financial Institutions: A Review of the Literature," *Economic Review,* Federal Reserve Bank of Kansas City, September/October 1988, pp. 16–33.

➤ There is some evidence of cost complementarities (product-specific economies of scope).

➤ The results appear to exist generally across the three types of institutions studied, as well as across different data sets and product and cost definitions.

Another study looked at the cost functions of the largest 100 commercial banks in the United States, ranging from \$2.5 to \$120.6 billion in assets in 1984. The authors found the minimum efficient scale to range between \$15 billion and \$37 billion in assets. The results appeared to contradict some of the earlier studies that found economies of scale in banking to disappear at much smaller sizes.[49]

Two Studies of Cost Curves in Switzerland
One study analyzed economies of scale in the Swiss electricity distribution industry using a cross-sectional sample of 39 publicly owned companies serving 130 cities over the period 1988–91. The results found economies of scale to be present for small, medium-sized, and large utilities. Using several models, the study estimated that the cost elasticity of output was less than one. The measure indicated that a 1 percent increase in the delivery of power increased variable costs by 0.86 percent. The author concludes that findings point to a possible decrease in costs of electricity distribution through a consolidation of local utilities.[50]

A second study measured the economies of scale in postal services in Switzerland. The sample consisted of 47 small local post offices in 2001. Data on total annual operating costs, hourly wages, and the price of capital (approximated by rental price per square meter) were obtained. The results showed that cost elasticities with respect to output were positive, implying economies of scale. A 1 percent increase in production (represented by number of collected mail items) increased total costs by 0.2 percent, while a 1 percent increase in distributed mail increased total costs by 0.6 percent. Most of the post offices in the sample were relatively small and did not reach the minimum efficiency scale. Thus, in this case again, the authors suggest that efficiency could be increased by combining post offices serving the same or adjacent areas.[51]

Bottling Plants Some years ago, the authors received access to some confidential cost and production data for more than thirty bottling plants of a large company. The plant sizes and their production varied widely; thus the data for a specific time period lent themselves to a cross-sectional regression analysis. It was our aim to investigate the potential existence of an optimum plant size.

A straight-line total cost function obtained fairly good results. The R^2 equaled 0.62 (quite high for a cross-sectional analysis) and the slope coefficient was statistically significant. Surprisingly, when a cubic function was fitted, the results improved considerably. With the equation $TC = a + bQ + cQ^2 + dQ^3$, we obtained the following answers:

$$R^2 = 0.70 \qquad F\text{-statistic} = 24.87$$

	A	B	C	D
Estimate	0.078	0.891	−0.096	0.004
t-test		3.653	−2.240	1.910

The t-tests for coefficients b and c are significant, for d, slightly low. The c coefficient is negative, indicating that the total cost curve would first increase at a decreasing rate and then at an increasing rate—resulting in a U-shaped unit cost curve.

Another piece of data was available—the percentages of canned and bottled sodas. Because the cost of cans was lower than the cost of bottles, we included the percent of canned soda production as another independent variable, with the following results:

$$R^2 = 0.83 \qquad F\text{-statistic} = 37.45$$

	A	B	C	D	E
Estimate	−0.177	1.316	−0.146	0.006	−1.575
t-test		6.358	−4.229	3.597	−4.823

All t-tests are now significant and coefficient e, the percentage of can production, has the correct (negative) sign, showing that production costs decrease as the proportion of cans increases.

[49]Sherrill Shaffer and Edmond David, "Economies of Superscale in Commercial Banking," *Applied Economics,* 23, 2 (February 1991), pp. 283–93.
[50]Massimo Filippini, "Economies of Scale and Utilization in the Swiss Electric Power Distribution Industry," *Applied Economics,* Vol. 28, Issue 5, May 1996, pp. 543–550.

[51]Massimo Filippini and Marika Zola, "Economies of Scale and Cost Efficiency in the Post Services: Empirical Evidence from Switzerland," *Applied Economic Letters,* Vol. 12, Issue 7, June 2005, pp. 437–441.

Granted that we used only data for one period and that we did not refine these data, we still obtained some good results indicating a U-shaped average cost curve and an optimal plant size.

Empirical Long-Run Cost Studies: Summary of Findings

Some of the studies just summarized show the possible existence of diseconomies of scale for larger firm and plant size. However, a majority of the empirically estimated functions suggest the existence of scale economies up to a point. As output increases to a substantial size, these economies rapidly disappear and are replaced by constant returns for long intervals of output. Most studies have not found the existence of declining average costs at very large quantities. Findings of diseconomies of scale for high rates of production are also rather rare.

Two Other Methods of Long-Run Cost Estimating

At the beginning of the discussion of cost estimating, we issued a warning that accounting magnitudes may not correspond to economic measures. However, all the regression analyses just reviewed employed accounting data and, through various adjustment procedures, attempted to make the numbers correspond more closely to the cost concepts meaningful to the economist. In addition, economists have tried to use methods that are not dependent on numbers drawn from companies' accounting records. Two techniques of analysis are discussed briefly: the engineering cost method and the survivorship technique.

Engineering Cost Estimates

Engineering costs are based on a thorough understanding of inputs and outputs and their relationships. Knowledgeable professionals will calculate the quantity of inputs needed to produce any quantity of outputs. These calculations are based on optimal assumptions (i.e., the largest output for a given combination of inputs). This is really a production function. From here it is a relatively easy step to apply monetary quantities to the inputs to arrive at costs.

The advantages of such a method are quite obvious. Technology is held constant. There are no problems of inflation. Problems of changing output mix are eliminated. As a matter of fact, such calculations are often made by corporations planning to introduce a new product. While the market research and product forecasting departments concentrate on preparing estimates of sales at different prices,

cost estimators in a corporation (engineers and others) prepare estimates of costs for different levels of output. Then members of the pricing department take all the available data and calculate profitability at different prices and levels of output. It is through this process that product prices are obtained.

Although the **engineering cost estimating** technique avoids some of the pitfalls of regression analysis, it suffers from some problems of its own. First, the estimates represent what engineers and cost estimators believe cost should be, not necessarily what they actually will be. Because they are really forecasts, calculations may omit certain components that contribute to costs. Further, most of the time, only direct output costs are estimated. Other costs that may be directly associated with the product (e.g., some portion of overhead and direct selling expenses) are not included, or if they are, it is through some rather arbitrary allocation. Often such estimates are made on the basis of pilot plant operations and do not consider actual production, which may be attended by bottlenecks and other problems, causing costs to differ from those estimated.

Generally, engineering cost estimates will show declining unit costs up to a point and substantially flat unit costs at higher production quantities. The possible existence of diseconomies of scale is usually ignored.

It is quite possible for a study to combine engineering cost estimates for some segments of costs with utilization of accounting data for others. Such an analysis was performed some years ago, when a group of economists at the Transportation Center at Northwestern University published a forecast of aircraft prices.[52] One important step in arriving at the forecast was the calculation of aircraft operating costs. These were computed for a large number of different types of aircraft and used both actual data and engineering estimates. Crew salaries were calculated from a number of union contracts and compared with historical data to arrive at an average. Maintenance costs were calculated from a formula supplied by the Air Transport Association. Fuel consumption was obtained from engineering curves produced by aircraft manufacturers and airlines, and reconciled with some actual published data. Other costs (employee benefits, landing fees, liability and property damage

---

[52]Stephen P. Sobotka, Paul G. Keat, Constance Schnabel, and Margaret Wiesenfelder, *Prices of Used Commercial Aircraft*, 1959–1965, Evanston, IL: Transportation Center at Northwestern University, 1959.

insurance) were estimated in similar ways. The resulting curves reflected direct operating costs per aircraft mile for a series of different stage length categories ranging from 0 to 200 miles to 2,500 miles and more. The resulting cost curves generally exhibited a downward slope up to the limit of the stage length that each aircraft could fly nonstop.

Survivorship Principle   A prominent American economist and Nobel Prize winner, George J. Stigler, developed an intriguing method for estimating long-run costs.[53] Stigler believed that the use of accounting data, with all their distortions and subsequent need for adjustments, made the validity of cost estimation based on such data questionable. His method was to observe an industry over time, categorize the firms in the industry by size (measured as a percent of total industry capacity or output), and then arrive at a conclusion regarding cost efficiency based on the relative growth or decline of these size categories. His results for the steel industry (using data for 1930, 1938, and 1951) showed that medium-size firms (defined as between 2.5 percent and 25 percent of industry capacity) appeared to have gained in share of total industry output over the 21-year period, from 35 percent to 46 percent of total, whereas small firms (less than 2.5 percent of capacity) and large firms (actually just one firm, with more than 25 percent of capacity) lost market share. Stigler concluded the existence of a U-shaped long-run average cost curve whose path first showed net economies of scale, then constant returns, and finally diseconomies of scale.

Economists have continued to use the **survivorship technique** to investigate economies of scale. For example, a later study by R. P. Rogers examined economies of scale in steel manufacturing in the United States. The author measured the distribution of production in conventional steel mills in 1976 and 1987. He classified steel mills into four size categories by their annual capacity (1–1.49 million tons, 1.5–4.5 million tons, 4.5–7.5 million tons, and more than 7.5 million tons). He then examined these four categories for the proportion of total capacity in the 2 years. He found that the 4.5 to 7.5 MT category increased its market share considerably. The results were consistent with a previous study by D. G. Tarr, who had used the engineering cost approach to estimate the mini-

mum optimal size (MOS) of a steel mill. Tarr had found the MOS plant to be of 6 MT capacity, which is the midpoint of Rogers' findings.[54]

A study of commercial health insurers found that the smallest-size firm category declined in numbers of firms, percentage of all firms, and percentage of total premium volume in the period 1958 to 1973. All but the smallest firms appeared to have held their own, and the largest did not appear to gain at the expense of their smaller rivals.[55]

A later study of the property-liability insurance industry appeared to show increases in the smallest and largest companies. The industry was divided into seven classes. All classes except the smallest and largest showed decreasing shares of output during the study period.[56]

Another study looked at the concentration in the trucking industry since deregulation. The industry was divided into six classes based on ton-miles hauled. The year 1975 was chosen as a benchmark to compare to the years 1981–1993, which followed deregulation. The results show that the two smallest classes and the largest class lost share of the business. The three middle-size classes gained about 23 percent of the trucking business. The author concludes that "the competition created by deregulation has to some extent disturbed the quiet life of monopoly carriers operating outside the efficient range."[57]

The survivorship principle is intuitively appealing due to its simplicity and avoidance of unreliable data. However, it also suffers some serious limitations. It is of no help in measuring costs for planning purposes. It merely tells us which company size appears to be more efficient; it says nothing about relative costs. Further, it implicitly assumes the industry is highly competitive so survival and

[53]George J. Stigler, "The Economies of Scale," *Journal of Law and Economics*, 1, 1 (October 1958), pp. 54–81.

[54]R. P. Rogers, "The Minimum Optimal Steel Plant and the Survivor Technique of Cost Estimation," *Atlantic Economic Journal*, 21 (September 1993), pp. 30–37; D. G. Tarr, "The Minimum Optimal Scale Steel Plant in the Mid-1970's," *FTC Working Paper, 3*, March 1997; D. G. Tarr, "The Minimum Optimal Scale Steel Plant," *Atlantic Economic Journal*, 12, 2 (1984), p. 122.
[55]Roger D. Blair and Ronald J. Vogel, "A Survivor Analysis of Commercial Health Insurers," *Journal of Business*, 51, 3 (July 1978), pp. 521–29.
[56]David Appel, John D. Worrall and Richard J. Butler, "Survivorship in the Property/Casualty Insurance Industry," *Journal of Risk and Insurance*, Vol. 52, no. 3, September 1985, pp. 424–440.
[57]James N. Giordano, "Returns to Scale and Market Concentration Among the Largest Survivors of Deregulation in the US Trucking Industry," *Applied Economics*, Vol. 29, Issue 1, January 1997, pp. 101–110.

prosperity are solely a function of efficient use of resources and not of market power or the erection of barriers to entry. Changing technology and inflation over a long span can also cause distortions. As time passes, the structure of an industry can change in such a way that firms of a certain size are favored over others.

Moreover, although Stigler's analysis of the steel industry showed a U-shaped cost curve, he could not obtain similar results for the automobile industry, where the survivor cost curve showed declining and constant portions, but there was no evidence of diseconomies of scale at high production quantities.

SUMMARY

Accounting data have generally been used to investigate short-run and long-run cost functions. These data present the researcher with a host of problems because the economic and accounting definitions of costs can differ substantially. Also, depending on how the data are collected, adjustments for price changes, geographic differentials, and other variations must be made.

Time series analysis has largely been used to estimate short-run costs, whereas the cross-sectional regression technique appears more suited for long-run cost estimation.

A large majority of these studies have concluded that marginal cost in the short run is relatively constant. In the long run, economies of scale predominate at the low end of production, and at higher output, constant returns to scale appear to exist.

The upward-sloping—U-shaped—average and marginal cost curves postulated by economic theory tend to be the exception in empirical findings. Although such results should make economists pause and reexamine some of their theoretical conclusions, the studies have generally been conducted in such a way that the possibility of eventually rising marginal costs and diseconomies of scale cannot be discounted.

Some economists prefer not to use accounting data in their inquiries. Thus, two other methods of cost estimation were briefly described in this appendix. Engineering cost analysis is based on the expert knowledge of the relationship between inputs and outputs and standard costs. It avoids the use of accounting information and does not run into the problem of adjusting for changing technology and inflation. The survivorship method bases its findings on the change in the proportion of total industry output produced by firms of different size categories. It concludes that the more efficient firms will gain share of production at the expense of less efficient ones.

Pricing and Output Decisions: Perfect Competition and Monopoly

Learning Objectives

Upon completion of this chapter, readers should be able to:

- Describe the key characteristics of the four basic market types used in economic analysis.

- Compare and contrast the degree of price competition among the four market types.

- Provide specific actual examples of the four types of markets.

- Explain why the $P = MC$ rule leads firms to the optimal level of production.

- Describe what happens in the long run in markets where firms that are either incurring economic losses or are making economic profits. Explain why this happens with particular attention to the key assumptions used in this analysis.

- Explain how and why the $MR = MC$ rule helps a monopoly to determine the optimal level of price and output.

- Explain the relationship between the $MR = MC$ rule and the $P = MC$ rule.

- (Appendix 8A) Use the tools of calculus to determine the optimal level of output for a firm in perfect competition and the optimal levels of price and output for a monopoly.

- (Appendix 8B) Explain how the fixed cost and variable cost help to determine a firm's break-even level of output.

- (Appendix 8B) Explain the concept of operating leverage and how it can be used to better understand the challenges faced by firms with a high fixed cost relative to their variable cost.

309

The Situation

For the job of product manager for the new beverage, Waterpure, Nicole Goodman, SVP of marketing, did not want a new MBA fresh out of the company's management training program. There was simply too much at stake to entrust the job to a rookie. She firmly believed that the job of bringing the new product to market should be given to a seasoned manager with a proven record of accomplishments. Finding a person with the necessary qualifications from within the company was not going to be easy because all successful product managers were rapidly promoted to higher management positions. Nicole could have used a "headhunter" firm to find an outside person, but she preferred to give someone within the company a chance to make the project work.

"I've got just the person for you," the executive vice president exclaimed at lunch one day. "There is a real sharp manager over in market research. I think he was the one who did the background study on the soft drink market. It would be nice to give him a chance to put his ideas into practice."

The person recommended for this critical job was none other than Frank Robinson, the head of the forecasting department. (See chapter 5.) In his first meeting with Nicole after being hired, Frank was briefed on the job. "Because this new product is so important to the growth strategy of our firm," Nicole said, "and because of your experience and accomplishments, we decided that we wanted you rather than one of the outside people who were considered for the job.

"One of the first tasks you should pursue is an analysis of the optimal price of this beverage. Tell us what price we should charge to maximize our profit in this new venture. The CEO told us the other day that the Wall Street analysts were questioning our judgment in getting into such a crowded and highly competitive market. We need to prove as fast as possible that we made the right decision, so we want to maximize our profit in this venture in as short a time as possible.

"As always, the management committee has the final say on the price of the new beverage, just as for all our products and services. But don't get discouraged. As I know from the other products that I've managed, pricing is a very useful exercise because it forces one to bring together all the different elements of the business. The market research that you have already done on this product will provide you with a quantitative estimate of the demand, as well as a general competitive analysis of the entire beverage industry. Our production people and cost accountants will give you the cost estimates. It will be up to you to put everything together to arrive at a suitable price for Waterpure."

INTRODUCTION

Readers who love to cook may well appreciate the fact that in Chinese cuisine one of the most difficult tasks is the preparation of the ingredients. Once the meats and vegetables are properly sliced and all the spices are secured, everything is thrown into the wok in a systematic and timely fashion, and usually within a minute or two the dish is ready. In a sense, we have been "slicing and dicing" over the past seven chapters and at last we are ready to cook. We have taken you through the definition of economics and managerial economics, the goals of the firm, the market forces of supply and demand, the various types of demand elasticity (own price, cross price, and income), the estimation and forecasting of demand, and the key factors underlying supply (production and cost). We now combine the relevant knowledge from these previous chapters to address one of the most important questions in managerial economics: How do firms establish their prices and output levels in order to achieve their business objective of profit maximization?

The pricing and output decision will actually be answered within the framework of four basic types of markets: perfect competition, monopoly, monopolistic competition, and oligopoly. The distinguishing characteristics of each of the four market types are presented in Figure 8.1A. This chapter deals with pricing and output decisions in perfect competition and monopoly. The pricing and output decisions of firms operating in monopolistic competition and oligopoly markets are analyzed in chapter 9. Perfect

Perfect Competition (no market power)
1. Large number of relatively small buyers and sellers
2. Standardized product
3. Very easy market entry and exit
4. Nonprice competition not possible

Monopoly (absolute market power subject to government regulation)
1. One firm, firm is the industry
2. Unique product or no close substitutes
3. Market entry and exit difficult or legally impossible
4. Nonprice competition not necessary

Monopolistic Competition (market power based on product differentiation)
1. Large number of relatively small firms acting independently
2. Differentiated product
3. Market entry and exit relatively easy
4. Nonprice competition very important

Oligopoly (market power based on product differentiation and/or the firm's dominance of the market)
1. Small number of relatively large firms that are mutually independent
2. Differentiated or standardized product
3. Market entry and exit difficult
4. Nonprice competition very important among firms selling differentiated products

Figure 8.1A   The Four Basic Market Types

competition and monopoly can be considered the two extreme market environments in which a firm competes in terms of **market power**. The concept of market power was introduced in chapter 3. But as a reminder, market power is simply the power of a firm to establish the price of its products. In **perfect competition**, there are so many sellers offering the same product that an individual firm has virtually no control over the price of its product. Moreover, there is no way for a particular firm to charge a higher price than its competitors because everyone sells a standardized product. Instead, the interaction of supply and demand decides the price for all participants in this type of **market structure**. A firm in this market has no market power and acts only as a **price taker**. All it can do is to decide whether to compete in the market and how much output to produce. In direct contrast to firms in perfect competition, the monopoly firm has a considerable amount of market power. Because it is the only seller in this type of market, it has the power to establish the price at whatever level it wants, subject to possible constraints such as government regulation. It is the consummate **price maker**.

In terms of market power, monopolistic competition and oligopoly are somewhere between the two extremes of perfect competition and monopoly. From a pedagogical standpoint, it is easier to understand and appreciate the particulars of monopolistic competition and oligopoly if there is first a thorough understanding of perfect competition and monopoly. This explains why we first cover perfect competition and monopoly in this chapter and the other two market types separately in the next one. Before proceeding to our first case of pricing and output decisions in perfect competition, let us elaborate further on market structure and the meaning of competition in economic analysis.

COMPETITION AND MARKET TYPES IN ECONOMIC ANALYSIS

The Meaning of Competition

In economic analysis, the most important indicator of the degree of competition is the ability of firms to control the price and use it as a competitive weapon. The extreme form of competition is "perfect" competition. In this market, the competition is so intense and the firms are so evenly divided that no one seller or group of sellers can exercise any control over the price. That is, they are all price takers. A second key measure of competition in economic analysis is the ability of a firm to earn an "above normal" or "economic" profit in the long run. This concept is described in greater detail in the next chapter. (Refer to chapter 3 for a definition of the "long run.")

Figure 8.1B is a reformatted version of Figure 8.1A. It shows the four market types according to the degree of competition as indicated by the extent of market power and the ability of firms to earn long-run economic profit. A firm in monopolistic competition may have some market power because its product can be differentiated from those sold by its competitors. A firm operating in an oligopoly derives its market power from its ability to differentiate its product, its relatively large size, or both.

Market entry and exit most directly affects the ability of a firm to earn economic profit in the long run. In perfect competition, entry into the market is easy. Therefore, if firms are observed to be earning economic profit, over time the entry of new firms eager to partake in these profits quickly reduces the ability of both incumbents and new entrants to earn economic profit. The same applies to monopolistic competition. This in fact helps us understand the basis for its name. This market is deemed to be *monopolistic* because product differentiation enables firms to exercise some market power (i.e., to act as price makers). In contrast, it is *competitive*

Figure 8.1B   Comparison of Four Market Types by Characteristics Affecting the Degree of Competition

Market Characteristics	Perfect Competition	Monopolistic Competition	Oligopoly	Monopoly
		Market Type		
Number and size of firms	Very large number of relatively small firms	Large number of relatively small firms	Small number of relatively large firms	One
Type of product	Standardized	Differentiated	Standardized or differentiated	Unique
Market entry and exit	Very easy	Easy	Difficult	Very difficult or impossible
Nonprice competition	Impossible	Possible	Possible or difficult	Not necessary
Key Indicators of Competition				
Market power	None	Low to high	Low to high	High
Long-run economic profit	None	None	Low to high, subject to mutual interdependence	High, subject to regulation

because over time the entry of new firms reduces and ultimately eliminates any economic profit.

In the case of oligopoly, the size and/or the ability to differentiate a product provide firms with considerable market power. Furthermore, because it is relatively difficult to enter this market, there is more opportunity to earn economic profit for an extended period of time. It should be quite obvious why a monopoly is not competitive from the standpoint of economic analysis. Being the only firm, it has the ultimate power to set its price, and its ability to earn economic profit is only constrained by government regulation or perhaps by the introduction of breakthrough technologies or substitute products from completely different industries.

Nonprice competition plays a secondary role in determining the degree of competition in economic analysis. However, we recognize that nonprice factors often come to mind first when people think about how firms compete with one another. Nonprice competition involves firms trying to gain an advantage over one another by differentiating their products using such means as advertising, promotion, the development of new products and product features, and customer service. For example, when we consider the competition between Coke and Pepsi, we may think about the amount of money each spends to have well-known entertainers endorse their products. When we consider the battle between IBM and Sun Microsystems in the computer hardware market, we might consider the speed and reliability of each company's line of servers.

The extent to which buyers and sellers have information about the price of the product and the product itself (e.g., product quality, reliability, and integrity) can also be a factor in determining a firm's market power or competitive advantage. For example, have you ever bought an item at a store only to find out the next day that you could have bought it for less at another store? Your first reaction might have been anger at the first store for charging you more. But a store can do this if there are people like you who do not have complete information about the selling prices of the item wherever it is available.[1] Moreover, incomplete information about the product itself may well lead to the exercise of market power among sellers. A general overview of this situation is presented at the end of this text. (See chapter 11.)

Examples of Market Types

Perfect Competition

The markets for agricultural products (e.g., corn, wheat, coffee, pork bellies), financial instruments (e.g., stocks, bonds, foreign exchange), precious metals (e.g., gold, silver, platinum), and the global petroleum industry provide good examples of this type of market. In each market, the products are standardized commodities, and supply and demand are clearly the primary determinants of their market price.[2] Of course, it is precisely because of this that sellers sometimes form cartels in order to raise the price or to keep it from falling. OPEC and the International Coffee Growers Association are good examples of this. As explained in chapter 3 and later in chapter 10, these sellers band together to control price by restricting the supply of their product.

---

[1]This is why economists believe that retail shopping on the Internet helps make markets more competitive because it makes it easier for potential buyers to compare prices among the sellers.
[2]For an excellent review of market conditions in commodities, see "Oversupply and Slackened Demand Vex Commodity Markets," *New York Times,* January 2, 2002.

Monopoly

Examples of a pure **monopoly** are not easy to find. Some years ago, good examples could be found among government-sanctioned and regulated monopolies in the telecommunications and gas and electric industries. But these markets have been deregulated and opened up to competition over the past several decades, not just in the United States, but all over the world (see chapter 14). Patent laws sometimes provide companies with temporary monopolies. The pharmaceutical industry can definitely be said to earn economic profit during the time in which its products are protected by patents. There are certain industries in which a company is so dominant that it might be said to exhibit monopolistic status. The dominance of Microsoft in PC operating systems has led to its antitrust problems. In certain situations, a firm may enjoy monopoly status because of its particular surroundings. Simple examples come to mind, such as the only Brazilian barbecue restaurant (*churrascaria*) in town or a "last chance" gas station at the edge of the Nevada desert.

Monopolistic Competition

Small businesses, particularly retail and service establishments, provide the best examples of this kind of market. Among them are boutiques, luggage stores, shoe stores, stationery shops, restaurants, repair shops, laundries, and beauty parlors. There are many of them in any given city or area of the city. The start-up capital is relatively low, so it is fairly easy to start these types of businesses. Each one tries its best to stand out among its many competitors by differentiating its product. A Chinese restaurant may attempt to differentiate itself by offering a cuisine from a relatively unknown region of China. A dry cleaner may try to distinguish itself by keeping longer store hours or by having its service clerks greet every regular customer by name as he or she enters. If customers perceive these kinds of differences to be important enough, these retail establishments may be able to charge a higher price than their competitors.

Oligopoly

The oligopoly market is generally considered to be the playing field of big businesses. In the United States, a large segment of the manufacturing sector competes in oligopoly markets. For example, in the manufacturing sector, oil refining, certain types of computer hardware and software, chemicals and plastics, processed foods, tobacco, steel, automobile, copper, and soft drinks can all be considered oligopoly markets. Parts of the service sector also contain good examples of oligopoly markets. For example, airline travel, long-distance telecommunications service, and Internet access are dominated by a relatively small number of large companies. The names of these oligopoly firms are a prominent part of any listing of large companies based on the size of total revenue such as the *Fortune* 500 (American companies) and the *BusinessWeek* Global 100.

Market Types and Competition in Theory and Reality

The four different market structures discussed previously are intended by economists to be a theoretical framework in which to analyze the pricing and output decisions of the firms in these markets. As is the case with all theoretical constructs, the relationship between these four distinct market types and the actual market conditions may vary. Certain markets fit well into these market types. Others may not exhibit all four characteristics of a particular market type. Still others may evolve over time from one type to another. These differences between theory and reality and the possible blurring of distinctions from one market type to another are discussed more thoroughly in chapter 9. So now we proceed to examine pricing and output decisions using the four idealized types of markets as a conceptual framework, starting with perfect competition.

PRICING AND OUTPUT DECISIONS IN PERFECT COMPETITION

The Basic Business Decision

Imagine a firm that is considering entry into a market that is perfectly competitive. If it decides to compete in this market, it will have no control over the price of the product. Therefore, the firm's managers must make a business case for entering this market on the basis of the following questions:

1. How much should we produce?
2. If we produce such an amount, how much profit will we earn?
3. If a loss rather than a profit is incurred, will it be worthwhile to continue in this market in the long run (in hopes that we will eventually earn a profit) or should we exit?

Perhaps even the output decision may seem superfluous. After all, is not the firm so small that it can sell as much as it wants without affecting the market price? Yes, but although the market price does not vary with an individual firm's level of output, the *unit cost* of production most certainly does. Think back to our discussion in chapter 7 about the cost of additional units of output. If we assume marginal cost rises as output increases (thanks to the law of diminishing returns), then it seems reasonable to expect that eventually the extra cost per unit will exceed the selling price of the product. At this point, it would no longer make sense for a profit-maximizing firm to produce because each additional unit sold would cost the firm more to produce than the price at which it could sell the product. Much more will be said about this shortly. But the point to emphasize here is that there is indeed a limit as to how much a perfectly competitive firm should produce in the short run. It is up to the firm to determine this limit.

Because the perfectly competitive firm must operate in a market in which it has no control over the selling price, there may be times when the price does not fully cover the unit cost of production (i.e., average cost). Thus, a firm must assess the extent of its losses in relation to the alternative of discontinuing production. In the long run, a firm that continues to incur losses must eventually leave the market. But in the short run, it may be economically justifiable to remain in the market, with the expectation of better times ahead. This is because in the short run certain costs must be borne regardless of whether the firm operates. These fixed costs must be weighed against the losses incurred by remaining in business. It is reasonable to expect that a firm will remain in business if its losses are less than its fixed costs—at least in the short run.

Key Assumptions of the Perfectly Competitive Market

As you are well aware, it is critical to know the assumptions made in the development of an economic model. Let us summarize the key assumptions made in analyzing the firm's output decision in perfect competition.

1. The firm operates in a perfectly competitive market and therefore is a price taker.
2. The firm makes the distinction between the short run and the long run.

3. The firm's objective is to maximize its profit in the short run. If it cannot earn a profit, then it seeks to minimize its loss. (See chapter 2 for a review of the goals of a firm.)

4. The firm includes its opportunity cost of operating in a particular market as part of its total cost of production.

All four assumptions have been discussed earlier, some in greater detail than others. But it might be useful to review certain aspects of these assumptions before proceeding to numerical and graphical examples.

For the economic analysis of a firm's output and pricing decisions to have a unique solution, the firm must establish a single, clear-cut objective. This objective is the maximization of profit in the short run. If the firm has other objectives, such as the maximization of revenue in the short run, the output that it would select would differ from the one based on this model. (See chapter 10 for a discussion of the Baumol revenue maximization model.)

The consideration of opportunity cost in the cost structure of the firm is vital to this decision-making model. The firm must check whether the going market price enables it to earn a revenue that covers not only its out-of-pocket costs, but also the costs incurred by forgoing alternative activities. A brief numerical example should help to convey this point.

Suppose the manager of a "stop and shop" convenience store wants to own and operate a store of her own. She knows she will have to leave her job and use $50,000 of her savings (currently invested and yielding a 10 percent return). A statement of the projected cost of operating in the first year follows.

Cost of goods sold	$300,000
General and administrative expenses	150,000
Total accounting cost	$450,000
Forgone salary for being a store manager	45,000
Forgone returns from investments (10% return)	5,000
Total opportunity cost	$50,000
Total economic cost (total accounting cost plus total opportunity cost)	$500,000

To keep this example as simple as possible, we did not include depreciation and taxes.

Suppose this budding entrepreneur forecasts revenue to be $500,000 in the first year of operation. From an accounting standpoint, her profit would be $50,000 ($500,000 − $450,000). But from an economic standpoint, her profit would be zero because the revenue would just equal her total **economic cost**. Certainly, there would be nothing wrong with "breaking even" in the economic sense of the term because this indicates that the firm's revenue is sufficient to cover both its out-of-pocket expense and its opportunity cost. Another way to view this situation is to note that when a firm "breaks even" in the economic sense, it is actually earning an accounting profit equal to its opportunity cost. In other words, if this entrepreneur's annual revenue is $500,000, she will earn an accounting profit that offsets the opportunity cost of going into business for herself. In economic terms, she would be earning a **normal profit**.

The reason for using the term "normal" can be seen in situations in which the entrepreneur's revenue is higher or lower than $500,000. Suppose her revenue is $550,000. In this case, she will earn a profit of $50,000 ($550,000 − $500,000). We refer to this sum as "above normal," "pure," or **economic profit** because it represents an amount in excess of the out-of-pocket cost plus the opportunity cost of running the business.

Table 8.1   Normal Profit, Economic Profit, and Economic Loss

	Normal Profit	Economic Profit	Economic Loss
Revenue	$500,000	$550,000	$480,000
Accounting cost	−450,000	−450,000	−450,000
Opportunity cost	−50,000	−50,000	−50,000
Profit	$0	$50,000	($20,000)
	Note: Accounting profit of $50,000 equals the opportunity cost of $50,000.	Accounting profit of $100,000 exceeds the opportunity cost of $50,000.	Accounting profit of $30,000 is less than the opportunity cost of $50,000.

In the case where revenue is less than economic cost, clearly a loss is incurred. However, this **economic loss** might well coincide with a firm earning an accounting profit. For example, suppose our entrepreneur's revenue is $480,000. The economic loss would be $20,000 ($480,000 − $500,000), but the accounting profit would be $30,000 ($480,000 − $450,000). Table 8.1 summarizes the three scenarios discussed previously.

With these assumptions in mind, we are now ready to discuss the decision-making process. Suppose that in determining whether to operate in a particular market at some level of output, the firm is faced with the short-run total cost structure presented in Table 8.2. (For convenience, the cost data are the same as those first presented in Table 7.2.)

Let us assume the market price is $110. Given this price, the firm is free to produce as much as or as little as it desires. The demand, total revenue, marginal revenue, and average revenue schedules for this firm are shown in Table 8.3. Notice that because the price to the firm remains unchanged regardless of its output level, the total, marginal, and average revenue schedules do not resemble the schedules

Table 8.2   Total and Per-Unit Short-Run Cost

Quantity (Q)	Total Fixed Cost (TFC)	Total Variable Cost (TVC)	Total Cost (TC)	Average Fixed Cost (AFC)	Average Variable Cost (AVC)	Average Total Cost (AC)	Marginal Cost (MC)
0	$100	$ 0.00	$ 100.00				
1	100	55.70	155.70	$100.00	$ 55.70	$155.70	$ 55.70
2	100	105.60	205.60	50.00	52.80	102.80	49.90
3	100	153.90	253.90	33.33	51.30	84.63	48.30
4	100	204.80	304.80	25.00	51.20	76.20	50.90
5	100	262.50	362.50	20.00	52.50	72.50	57.70
6	100	331.20	431.20	16.67	55.20	71.87	68.70
7	100	415.10	515.10	14.29	59.30	73.59	83.90
8	100	518.40	618.40	12.50	64.80	77.30	103.30
9	100	645.30	745.30	11.11	71.70	82.81	126.90
10	100	800.00	900.00	10.00	80.00	90.00	154.70
11	100	986.70	1,086.70	9.09	89.70	98.79	186.70
12	100	1,209.60	1,309.60	8.33	100.80	109.13	222.90

Table 8.3   Revenue Schedules

Quantity	Price (AR)	TR	MR
0	$110	$ 0	
1	110	110	$110
2	110	220	110
3	110	330	110
4	110	440	110
5	110	550	110
6	110	660	110
7	110	770	110
8	110	880	110
9	110	990	110
10	110	1,100	110
11	110	1,210	110
12	110	1,320	110

analyzed in chapter 4. As a price taker, the firm faces a demand curve that is "perfectly elastic." That is, customers are willing to buy as much as the firm is willing to sell *at the going market price*. This special type of demand curve can be seen in Figure 8.2. Moreover, the firm receives the same marginal revenue from the sale of each additional unit of product. This marginal revenue is simply the price of the product. Recall that the price is tantamount to average or per-unit revenue. Hence, a perfectly competitive firm's demand is also its marginal and its average revenue over the range of output being considered. Note in Figure 8.2 that the demand curve is also labeled "AR" and "MR."

Figure 8.3 compares the perfectly elastic demand curve with the typical downward-sloping linear demand curve used in chapter 4. It also shows the total revenue curves in relation to the two types of demand curves. As is the case with perfect elasticity, a downward-sloping demand curve is the same as the average revenue curve because *P* by definition is equal to AR. However, recall that a linear, downward-sloping demand curve

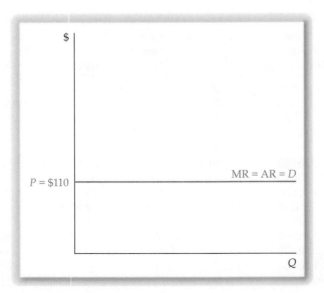

Figure 8.2   Perfectly Elastic Demand Curve

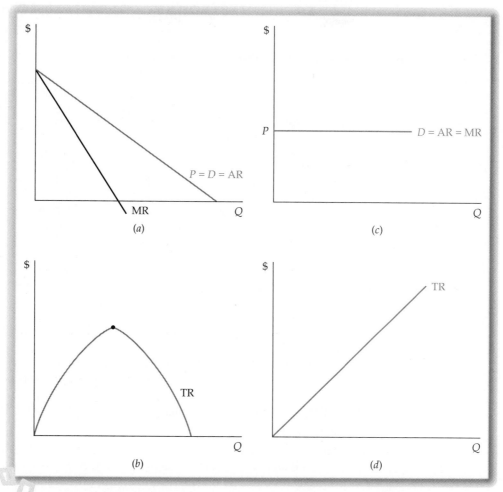

Figure 8.3   Different Types of Demand Curves and Associated Total Revenue Curves

is associated with a marginal revenue curve that is twice as steep. In addition, this type of demand results in a nonlinear total revenue curve that reaches a maximum at the point at which marginal revenue equals zero (see Figure 8.3*b*). In contrast, as shown in Figure 8.3*d*, there is no limit to the amount of total revenue that firms can garner in a perfectly competitive market. The more a firm produces, the more revenue it will obtain. The limit to its output is based on revenue in relation to the firm's cost of production, that is, the profit earned at various levels of output.

Armed with its cost and revenue schedules, all that a firm needs to do is to combine the sets of information to find the level of output that maximizes its profit (or minimizes its loss).

 Module 8A   ## The Total Revenue–Total Cost Approach to Selecting the Optimal Output Level

The most logical approach to selecting the optimal level of output is to compare the total revenue with the total cost schedules and find that level of output that either maximizes the firm's profit or minimizes its loss. This is shown in Table 8.4 and

Table 8.4   Cost and Revenue Schedules Used to Determine Optimal Level of Output

Quantity (Q)	Price (P)	Total Revenue (TR)	Total Fixed Cost (TFC)	Total Variable Cost (TVC)	Total Cost (TC)	Total Profit (π)
0	$110	$ 0	$100	$ 0.00	$ 100.00	$−100.00
1	110	110	100	55.70	155.70	−45.70
2	110	220	100	105.60	205.60	−14.40
3	110	330	100	153.90	253.90	76.10
4	110	440	100	204.80	304.80	135.20
5	110	550	100	262.50	362.50	187.50
6	110	660	100	331.20	431.20	228.80
7	110	770	100	415.10	515.10	254.90
8	110	880	100	518.40	618.40	261.60
9	110	990	100	645.30	745.30	244.70
10	110	1,100	100	800.00	900.00	200.00
11	110	1,210	100	986.70	1,086.70	123.30
12	110	1,320	100	1,209.60	1,309.60	10.40

Figure 8.4. As can be seen in the table and the figure, this output level is 8, at which the firm would be earning a maximum profit of $261.60. Graphically, this output level can be seen as the one that maximizes the distance between the total revenue curve and the total cost curve. By convention, this point has been labeled Q^*.

The Marginal Revenue–Marginal Cost Approach to Finding the Optimal Output Level

Marginal analysis is at the heart of the economic analysis of the firm. Once we explain how marginal analysis is used by the firm to determine its optimal level of output, we rely primarily on this type of analysis throughout the rest of this chapter.

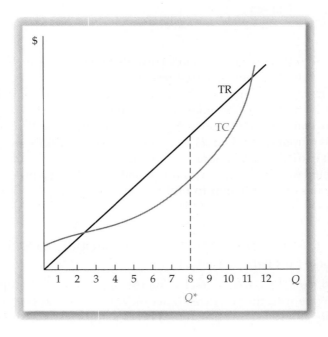

Figure 8.4   Determining Optimal Output from Cost and Revenue Curves— Perfect Competition

Table 8.5   Using Marginal Revenue (or Price) and Marginal Cost to Determine Optimal Output: *The Case of Economic Profit*

Quantity (Q)	Marginal Revenue (MR = P = AR)	Average Fixed Cost (AFC)	Average Variable Cost (AVC)	Average Total Cost (AC)	Marginal Cost (MC)	Marginal Profit (Mπ)
0	$100					
1	110	$100.00	$ 55.70	$155.70	$ 55.70	$ 54.30
2	110	50.00	52.80	102.80	49.90	60.10
3	110	33.33	51.30	84.63	48.30	61.70
4	110	25.00	51.20	76.20	50.90	59.10
5	110	20.00	52.50	72.50	57.70	52.30
6	110	16.67	55.20	71.87	68.70	41.30
7	110	14.29	59.30	73.59	83.90	26.10
8	110	12.50	64.80	77.30	103.30	6.70
9	110	11.11	71.70	82.81	126.90	−16.90
10	110	10.00	80.00	90.00	154.70	−44.70
11	110	9.09	89.70	98.79	186.70	−76.70
12	110	8.33	100.80	109.13	222.90	−112.90

Table 8.5 presents the cost and revenue data on a per-unit basis. The marginal revenue and marginal cost columns contain the key numbers the firm must use to decide on its optimal level of output. Let us examine the marginal revenue and the marginal cost associated with additional units of output, starting with zero units. As you can see in Table 8.5, the first unit would result in additional revenue of $110 and cost the firm an additional $55.70 to make. The second unit would add another $110 to revenue and another $49.90 to the firm's total cost. Continuing in this manner, we observe that it would be worthwhile for the firm to produce more as long as the added benefit of each unit produced and sold (i.e., the marginal revenue) exceeds the added cost (i.e., the marginal cost). Because the marginal revenue is equal to the existing market price, it does not change as output increases. However, because of the law of diminishing returns, the firm's marginal cost begins to increase with the fourth unit of output. From that point on, each additional unit of output costs *increasingly more* to produce. Between 0 and 8 units of output, we observe that marginal revenue exceeds marginal cost. However, production of the ninth unit of output will cost the firm more than the revenue that it would add (MC = $126.90 and MR = $110). In Table 8.5, MR = MC actually occurs between 8 and 9 units of output, but we use 8 as the approximate level of optimal output.

Using the relationship between marginal revenue and marginal cost to decide on the optimal level of output is referred to in economics as the **MR = MC rule**. The rule is stated as follows:

A firm that wants to maximize its profit (or minimize its loss) should produce a level of output at which the additional revenue received from the last unit is equal to the additional cost of producing that unit. In short, MR = MC.

The MR = MC rule applies to any firm that wants to maximize its profit, regardless of whether it has the power to set the price. However, in the particular case in which the firm has no power to set the price (i.e., it is a price taker), the MR = MC rule can be restated as the **P = MC rule**. This is simply because when a firm is a price taker, its marginal revenue is in fact the going market price. (Refer to Figure 8.3 for an illustration of this.)

Table 8.5 shows that by following the MR = MC rule and producing 8 units of output, the firm would earn a profit of $261.60 [8(AR − AC)], which is what we already learned by following the total revenue − total cost approach. Hence, the rule apparently works. Another way to think about MR and MC is in terms of marginal (i.e., additional) profit. If TR − TC is equal to total profit, then MR − MC must be equal to marginal profit. The last column in Table 8.5 indicates the amount of additional profit that would be earned by the firm in producing additional units of output. As you can see, this column is merely the difference between the MR column and the MC column. When MR is equal to MC, marginal profit must be zero. When marginal profit is equal to zero, it indicates that the firm can make no more *additional* profit and, therefore, should not produce at a higher level of output.

Of course, there is nothing to prevent the firm from producing more or less than 8 units of output. As you can see in the last column of Table 8.4, it would still earn a profit if it produced at any of the output levels 2 to 12, but none of these amounts except 8 is the *maximum* that it could earn. Remember that we are now referring to *total revenue* and *total cost*. If the firm were to produce at the level where these two measures are equal, then clearly all it would be doing is earning a "normal" profit.

Although the optimal output level can be found just as easily by using the TR − TC approach, economists rely much more on the MR − MC approach in analyzing the firm's output decision. Essentially, this approach is an extension of the basic analytical technique of "marginal analysis" first introduced in the chapters on demand, production, and cost. Furthermore, the practical implications of this approach are similar to those discussed in these earlier chapters. Often, firms do not have the benefit of complete columns of numbers depicting cost and revenue. Instead, they must rely on actual cost and revenue data at a particular level of output and then conduct sensitivity analysis involving relatively small incremental changes around that level. As is illustrated in the ensuing sections, "marginal analysis" is much better suited to this situation than "total analysis."

The MR − MC Approach in Graphs

A graphical analysis using the MR − MC approach employs the data in Table 8.5 and is shown in Figure 8.5. Also shown is the firm's demand curve, a horizontal line intersecting the vertical axis at the level of the given market price of $110. Thus, the demand curve of this price-taking firm is "perfectly elastic." The optimal output level is clearly seen as the level at which the firm's MC line and its MR line (demand line) intersect. The amount of profit earned is represented by the shaded rectangle *ABCD*. Because these graphs are used in this way throughout the rest of the chapter, it is crucial that you clearly understand their interpretation.

Points on each of the unit cost curves indicate the dollar value of the cost at different levels of output. Therefore, at output level Q^*, the average cost is represented by the distance between point C and the horizontal axis (i.e., CQ^*). It follows that because total cost is average cost multiplied by the quantity of output, it is shown as the area of the rectangle determined by OQ^* and CQ^* (rectangle $ODCQ^*$). In the same manner, we can show that total revenue can be displayed as the rectangle determined by OQ^* and BQ^* (rectangle $OABQ^*$). Therefore, profit (i.e., the shaded rectangle *ABCD*) can be represented by the difference between the larger rectangle, depicting total revenue, and the smaller one, showing total cost.

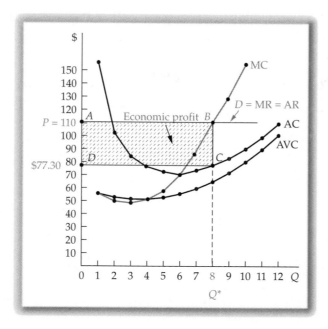

Figure 8.5 Graphical MR − MC Approach Indicating the Earning of Economic Profit

Economic Profit, Normal Profit, Loss, and Shutdown

The preceding example assumed the market price was high enough for the firm to earn an economic profit by following the MR = MC rule. But because the firm is just one of many price-taking sellers in this market, there is no reason to expect that market price will always be this beneficial for the firm. Given the vagaries of supply and demand, it is just as likely that a firm will be faced with prices that result in only normal profit—or worse, in operating losses. Tables 8.6 and 8.7 and Figure 8.6 demonstrate

Table 8.6 Using Marginal Revenue (or Price) and Marginal Cost to Determine Optimal Output: The Case of Normal Profit

Quantity (Q)	Marginal Revenue (MR = P = AR)	Average Fixed Cost (AFC)	Average Variable Cost (AVC)	Average Total Cost (AC)	Marginal Cost (MC)	Marginal Profit (Mπ)	Total Profit or Loss (Q[P − AC])
0	$71.87						$−100.00[a]
1	71.87	$100.00	$ 55.70	$155.70	$ 55.70	$ 16.17	−83.83
2	71.87	50.00	52.80	102.80	49.90	21.97	−61.86
3	71.87	33.33	51.30	84.63	48.30	23.57	−38.28
4	71.87	25.00	51.20	76.20	50.90	20.97	−17.32
5	71.87	20.00	52.50	72.50	57.70	14.17	−3.15
6	71.87	16.67	55.20	71.87	68.70	3.17	0
7	71.87	14.29	59.30	73.59	83.90	−12.03	−12.04
8	71.87	12.50	64.80	77.30	103.30	−31.43	−43.44
9	71.87	11.11	71.70	82.81	126.90	−55.03	−98.46
10	71.87	10.00	80.00	90.00	154.70	−82.83	−181.30
11	71.87	9.09	89.70	98.79	186.70	−114.83	−296.12
12	71.87	8.33	100.80	109.13	222.90	−151.03	−447.12

[a]If Q = 0, firm still incurs a total fixed cost of $100 in the short run.

Table 8.7   Using Marginal Revenue (or Price) and Marginal Cost to Determine Optimal Output: The Case of Economic Loss

Quantity (Q)	Marginal Revenue (MR = P = AR)	Average Fixed Cost (AFC)	Average Variable Cost (AVC)	Average Total Cost (AC)	Marginal Cost (MC)	Marginal Profit (Mπ)	Total Profit or Loss (Q[P − AC])
0	$58						$−100.00
1	58	$100.00	$ 55.70	$155.70	$ 55.70	$ 2.30	−97.70
2	58	50.00	52.80	102.80	49.90	8.10	−89.60
3	58	33.33	51.30	84.63	48.30	9.70	−79.89
4	58	25.00	51.20	76.20	50.90	7.10	−72.80
5	58	20.00	52.50	72.50	57.70	0.30	−72.50
6	58	16.67	55.20	71.87	68.70	−10.70	−83.22
7	58	14.29	59.30	73.59	83.90	−25.90	−109.13
8	58	12.50	64.80	77.30	103.30	−45.30	−154.44
9	58	11.11	71.70	82.81	126.90	−68.90	−223.29
10	58	10.00	80.00	90.00	154.70	−96.70	−320.00
11	58	9.09	89.70	98.79	186.70	−128.70	−448.69
12	58	8.33	100.80	109.13	222.90	−164.90	−613.56

these possibilities. To focus on the marginal revenue-marginal cost approach, we include only the per-unit cost data in the tables and figure.

The situation depicted in Table 8.7 and Figure 8.6*b* indicates a loss for the firm. Does this mean that the firm should not be in this market? As you know, in the short run, the firm must bear certain fixed costs regardless of the level of its output. Using the data in Table 8.7, if the firm were to shut down its operations (i.e., if $Q = 0$), it would still have a fixed cost of $100. Given the market price of $58, we know that the best that a firm can do is to follow the MR = MC rule, produce 5 units of output, and lose $72.50. But if the firm were to shut down, it would lose

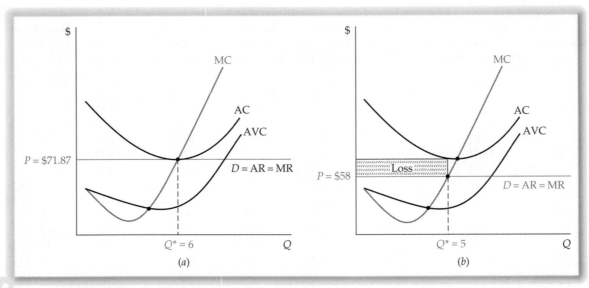

Figure 8.6   (*a*) Normal Profit and (*b*) Economic Loss

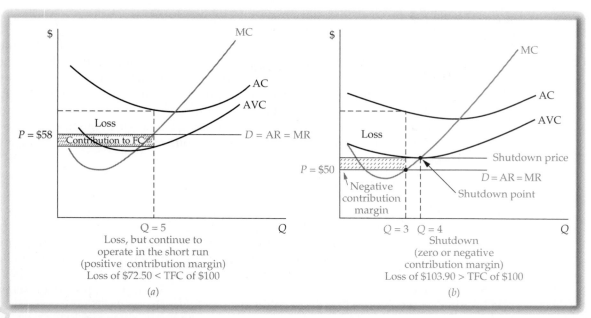

Figure 8.7   Contribution Margin

$100 because this is the amount of fixed cost that it would incur, whether or not it operates in the short run. Therefore, with a market price of $58, *it would be better for a firm to operate at a loss than to cease its activities in this market.* This is illustrated in Figure 8.7*a*.

Another way to understand this rationale is to compare the firm's total revenue at the $58 price with its total variable cost, assuming a production level of 5 units. The total revenue is $290 ($P \times Q$), and the total variable cost is $262.50 ($Q \times$ AVC). Clearly, this revenue is sufficient to cover the firm's total variable cost. Moreover, the amount left over ($27.50) can be used to pay for a part of its fixed cost. Hence, we can also conclude that as long as a firm's total revenue is greater than its total variable cost (or on a per-unit basis, as long as the market price exceeds average variable cost), it is better to operate than to shut down because at least part of its fixed cost will be defrayed. We refer to the amount by which total revenue exceeds total variable cost as the **contribution margin** (see Figure 8.7*a*). You should also recognize that the portion of fixed cost that is *not* covered by the contribution margin is in fact the amount of the firm's loss (i.e., $27.50 − $100 = −$72.50).

It is not always advisable to operate in the short run at a loss. Suppose the market price fell to $50. In this case, even if the firm followed the MR = MC rule, it would still incur a loss greater than it would have to bear by shutting down. This situation is not shown in a separate table but is discussed in relation to the figures in Table 8.4. By literally following the MR = MC rule, the firm would be led to produce 3 units of output. But we can see that at this level, the total revenue of $150 ($50 × 3) would not even be enough to cover the firm's total variable cost of $153.90 ($51.30 × 3), resulting in a negative contribution margin of $3.90. Looking at this situation in terms of the firm's loss versus its fixed cost, we can see that its total loss of $103.90 is clearly greater than the fixed cost of $100 that it would incur if it decided to shut down its operations. (As you can see, the firm's loss is the combination of its fixed cost and negative contribution margin.) Thus, given the market price of $50, the firm would be better off by shutting down its operations. This is illustrated in Figure 8.7*b*.

Also shown in this figure is what economists refer to as the **shutdown point**. At this point, the market price is at a level in which a firm following the MR = MC rule would lose an amount just equal to its fixed cost of production. Expressed in another way, this price would result in a zero contribution margin. At the shutdown point, we assume a firm would be indifferent about operating versus shutting down. However, it would certainly give strong consideration to ceasing to operate in the short run. As you can see, the shutdown point coincides with the point at which the firm's average variable cost is at its minimum.

The Competitive Market in the Long Run

Regardless of whether the market price in the short run results in economic profit, normal profit, or a loss for competing firms, economic theory states that in the **long run**, the market price will settle at the point where these firms earn a normal profit. This is because over a long period of time, prices that enable firms to earn above-normal profit would induce other firms to enter the market, and prices below the normal level would cause firms to leave the market. We just completed a discussion of the rationale for a firm's operating at a loss in the short run. However, in the long run, we assume firms that are losing money would have to seriously consider leaving the market even if they have positive contribution margins. Recall that in the long run, firms have the time to vary their fixed factors of production. This means that they would have sufficient time to liquidate the fixed assets that account for their fixed costs.

We discuss the long-run adjustment process of entering and exiting firms in chapter 3. The entry of firms shifts the supply curve to the right, driving down market price. The exiting of firms shifts the supply curve to the left, placing upward pressure on market price. A firm's motivation to go into or get out of the market can now be examined in greater detail. There is only one price at which firms neither enter nor leave the market. This, of course, is the price that results in normal profits. The long-run process of entering and exiting firms is illustrated in Figure 8.8.

Figure 8.8*a* shows a hypothetical short-run situation in which the price (determined by supply and demand) is high enough to enable a typical firm competing in this market to earn economic profit. (Viewed in another way, given the market price, the firm's cost structure is low enough to enable it to earn economic profit.) Over time, new firms would enter the market, and the original firms would expand their fixed capacity in response to the incentive of economic profit. This would have the effect of increasing the market supply (shifting the supply curve to the right) and reducing the market price. At the point where firms earn only normal profit, this adjustment process would cease. Figure 8.8*b* shows the opposite case, in which a short-run loss incurred by firms in the market causes firms in the long run to leave the market. This causes price to rise toward the level in which the remaining firms would earn a normal profit.

The concept of a long-run "resting point" may seem a bit unrealistic. As much as we try to use real-world examples to support the theory of managerial economics, it is extremely difficult, if not impossible, to find examples of this principle in action. For one thing, in actual market situations, demand does not remain constant while supply adjusts toward the normal price. Tastes and preferences, as well as the number of buyers, incomes, and prices of related goods, are constantly changing. For another, the economic notion of the long run is a theoretical construct, not a period that can be measured in calendar time. If the market price has not reached the normal level, economists can say that the market is still adjusting toward long-run equilibrium. But herein lies the principal relevance of this concept to the real world of business.

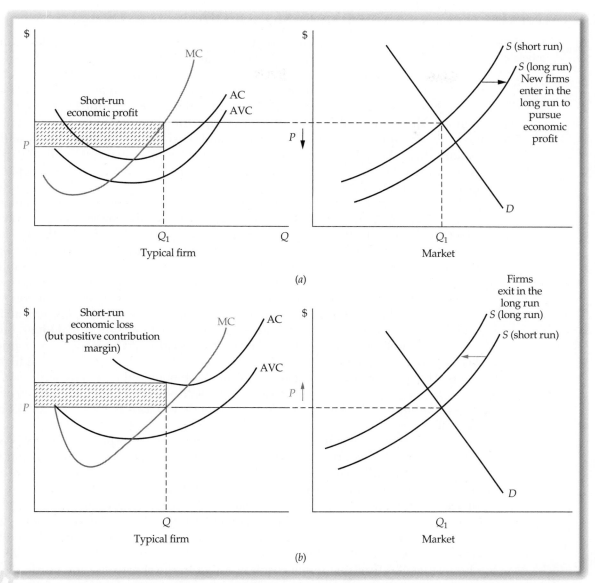

Figure 8.8   Long-Run Effect of Firm's Entering and Exiting the Market

For business decision makers, the process of *adjustment* toward equilibrium is far more important than the equilibrium price itself.

An understanding of the conditions motivating market entry or exit over the long run should lead the firms to consider the following points:

1. The earlier the firm enters a market, the better its chances of earning above-normal profit (assuming a strong demand in this market).

2. As new firms enter the market, firms that want to survive and perhaps thrive must find ways to produce at the lowest possible cost, or at least at cost levels below those of their competitors.

3. Firms that find themselves unable to compete on the basis of cost might want to try competing on the basis of product differentiation instead, although this is extremely difficult in this type of market.

PRICING AND OUTPUT DECISIONS IN MONOPOLY MARKETS

Module 8B
Module 8C

A monopoly market consists of one firm. The firm *is* the market. Examples are gas and electric utilities and firms selling products under protection of U.S. patent laws. Prior to its breakup in 1984, AT&T was considered one of the largest monopolies in the world. The regional companies that were formed after divestiture still represent monopolies in many of the local calling areas within their respective regions. Most monopolies cited previously are closely regulated by government or government-appointed agencies. (A notable exception is companies selling patented products.) Because this regulation severely constrains their ability to choose price and output levels, regulated monopolies are analyzed as a separate group of firms in chapter 14.

In the absence of regulatory constraints, the monopoly stands in counterpoint to the perfectly competitive firm. Firms in perfectly competitive markets have no power to set their prices; the monopoly firm has the power to establish any price that it wants. If you were responsible for setting the price of a product that you alone were selling in the market, how much would you charge? The layperson's answer is usually "as much as I can" or "whatever the market will bear." On the surface, this answer seems reasonable enough. Unfortunately, it is too simplistic to be of much help to the monopolist. In 1948, when Polaroid first offered its camera, it could have charged any price that it wanted. The original price was $85 (which was a considerable sum at that time), but it could just as well have been $850 or $8,500. The market could have borne those prices because some people probably would have been willing to buy the camera at higher levels. The question is *how many* people would have bought the cameras and *when*. As it turned out, Polaroid offered five cameras for sale on the first day and sold them all in several hours. Who knows how long it would have taken them to sell the 5 units at $8,500?

The key point is that a monopoly firm's ability to set its price is limited by the demand curve for its product and, in particular, the price elasticity of demand for its product. (Recall that according to the law of demand, people will buy more as price falls and vice versa.) The price elasticity of demand indicates how much more or less people are willing to buy in relation to price decreases or increases. If we assume the firm's downward-sloping demand curve is linear, we know that as the price of the product falls, the marginal revenue from the sale of additional units falls, reaches zero, and then becomes negative. For purposes of illustration, let us also assume the firm's marginal cost is constant in the short run. The linear, downward-sloping demand curve, the marginal revenue curve, and the constant marginal cost curve for such a firm are shown in Figure 8.9. Notice that if the firm charges too high a price (e.g., P_1), its marginal revenue will exceed its marginal cost; hence, it will be forgoing some amount of marginal profit (shown by the lighter shade). If the firm sets its price at too low a level, its marginal cost will exceed its marginal revenue, and the firm will experience a marginal loss (shown by the darker shade).

The ability of a monopoly to set its price is further limited by the possibility of rising marginal costs of production. If this is the case, then surely at some point the increasing cost of producing additional units of output will exceed the decreasing marginal revenue received from the sale of additional units. This begins at QY shown in Figure 8.10.

In conclusion, the firm that exercises a monopoly power over its price should not set its price at the highest possible level. Instead, it should set it at the *right* level. And what is this "right" level? It is the level that results in MR = MC.

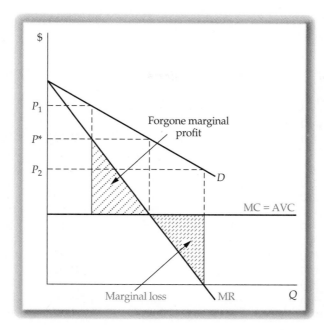

Figure 8.9 Demand, MR, and MC Curves for a Monopoly

To see how the MR = MC rule applies to the monopolist and to the perfect competitor, see Table 8.8. Note that the table presents only the cost data relevant to this example. For purposes of comparison, the same cost figures used in the previous section for the perfectly competitive firm have been selected.[3] But in this case, we assume the firm is the "only game in town." Note that the price is not equal to the marginal revenue because the firm is a price setter and not a price taker. Its demand schedule consists of columns 1 and 2, and the total revenue and marginal revenue schedules are those that normally accompany a downward-sloping demand curve.

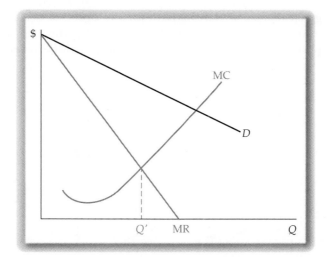

Figure 8.10 Increasing Marginal Costs in Relation to Decreasing Marginal Revenue

---

[3]By maintaining consistency in the cost data, we realize that we are sacrificing some realism because a monopoly would obviously produce more than a perfectly competitive firm. However, this shortcoming can be rectified by simply assuming each unit of output is the equivalent of a larger number of units (e.g., $Q = 1 = 1,000$).

Table 8.8 Using Marginal Revenue and Marginal Cost to Determine Optimal Price and Output: The Case of Monopoly

Quantity (Q)	Price (P)	Total Revenue (TR)	Marginal Revenue (MR)	Average Total Cost (AC)	Total Cost (TC)	Marginal Cost (MC)	Total Profit (π)
0	$180	$ 0			$ 100.00		$-100.00
1	170	170	$170	$155.70	155.70	$ 55.70	14.30
2	160	320	150	102.80	205.60	49.90	114.40
3	150	450	130	84.63	253.90	48.30	196.10
4	140	560	110	76.20	304.80	50.90	255.20
5	130	650	90	72.50	362.50	57.70	287.50
6	120	720	70	71.87	431.20	68.70	288.80
7	110	770	50	73.59	515.10	83.90	254.90
8	100	800	30	77.30	618.40	103.30	181.60
9	90	810	10	82.81	745.30	126.90	64.70
10	80	800	−10	90.00	900.00	154.70	−100.00
11	70	770	−30	98.79	1,086.70	186.70	−316.70
12	60	720	−50	109.13	1,309.60	222.90	−589.60

Starting from the zero output level, let us consider the price, output, marginal revenue, marginal cost, and marginal profit as additional units of output are produced. You can see that as output increases, the marginal revenue associated with each unit exceeds the marginal cost up to 6 units. Beyond this level, the firm actually incurs a marginal loss. As the firm moves beyond this level, total profit is still positive, but it is not at its maximum. In other words, by following the MR = MC rule, a profit-maximizing firm would want to produce 6 units of output per time period. To do so, it would have to set a price of $120.

The way in which the MR = MC rule underlies the monopoly price can perhaps be more clearly seen in a graph. In Figure 8.11, we see that the firm would select P* because, given the particular demand for the product, this is the price that would prompt customers to buy Q*. Q* is the quantity that the firm would want to produce per time period because this is the amount at which the revenue received from the

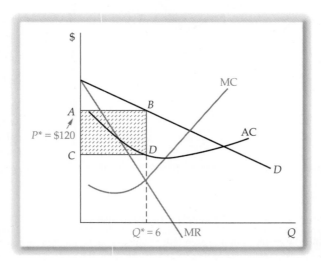

Figure 8.11 Graphical Depiction of MR = MC Rule for a Monopoly

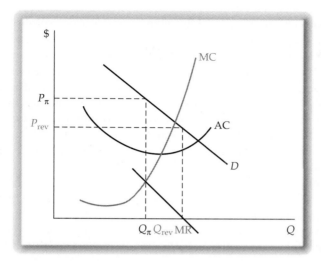

Figure 8.12   Relationship between the Profit-Maximizing and Revenue-Maximizing Price and Quantity

last unit produced is just equal to its cost (i.e., marginal revenue = marginal cost). With the same graphical references to total revenue and total cost as used in the analysis of perfect competition, we arrive at the measure of total profit as the shaded area *ABCD*.

In a perfectly competitive market, the short-run economic profit enjoyed by the monopoly firm in this example would be vulnerable in the long run to the entry of other firms wanting to earn similar amounts of profit. But because we assume it is a monopoly, this firm would not be subject to such threats in the long run. Nonetheless, the preceding illustration is not meant to give the impression that a monopoly automatically earns economic profit in either the short or the long run. Whether or not it does depends on the demand for its product. For example, a company may have a monopoly on a toy for children that is in great demand and consequently enables it to earn the kind of economic profit illustrated in Figure 8.11. But as the market demand is filled or as children begin to tire of the product, the demand could decline (e.g., the demand curve shifts to the left) to the extent that the firm earns only a normal profit or perhaps even incurs a loss.

Suppose a price-setting firm does not want to maximize its short-run profit but instead wants to maximize its revenue. Let us explore this possibility using the data in Table 8.8. The price that maximizes the total revenue can be determined simply by observation. As you can see, by charging $90 for its product, the firm will receive the maximum total revenue of $810. You can also see that this revenue-maximizing price is lower than the one that maximizes the firm's total profit (i.e., $90 < $120). This relationship is illustrated in Figure 8.12. This dichotomy between **pricing for profit** and **pricing for revenue** is discussed in greater detail in chapter 10.

THE IMPLICATIONS OF PERFECT COMPETITION AND MONOPOLY FOR MANAGERIAL DECISION MAKING

After studying this chapter, it might appear to the reader that managers in a perfectly competitive or a monopoly market do not have much of a challenge in deciding on the price and output levels of their firm. In the case of perfect competition, the market price is determined for the managers by the forces of supply and demand. All that they have to do is to decide whether their cost structure will enable their firm to at least earn a normal amount of profit. In the case of monopoly, the fact that the firm has no competition enables its managers simply to follow the MR = MC rule to maximize its profit. We would agree with this view, particularly when the pricing and output challenges of these firms are compared with those in monopolistic competition and oligopoly. This will be evident when reading the next chapter. Nonetheless, as explained earlier, we have presented a detailed analysis of perfect competition and monopoly because those models serve as the basis from which pricing and output decisions in monopolistic competition and oligopoly can be better understood and appreciated. Besides this, we believe that the analysis of firms in perfect competition and monopoly offers lessons to managers that go beyond the routine application of the P = MC or MR = MC rule.

The most important lesson that managers can learn by studying the perfectly competitive market is that it is extremely difficult to make money in a highly competitive market. Indeed, the only way for firms to survive in perfect competition is to be as cost efficient as possible because there is absolutely no way to control the price. Another lesson offered by the perfectly competitive model is that it might pay for a firm to move into a market before others start to enter. This might mean entering a market even before the demand is high enough to support an above-normal price. Spotting these market opportunities and taking the risk of going into these markets are key tasks of a good manager. Of course, the demand may never materialize or the long-run increase in supply might be so great that no one makes any money in this market. But that is all part of the risk that a manager must sometimes take. We see more of the making of pricing and output decisions in highly competitive markets in chapter 9 when we examine the case of monopolistic competition.

In monopoly markets not sanctioned by the government via regulations or patent laws, a monopoly presents a manager with somewhat of a paradox. What happens if the managers of a firm are so successful in beating the competition that the firm in fact becomes a monopoly, or at least one that exercises monopolistic power? An excellent historical example of this was the case of the Department of Justice antitrust suit against IBM in 1969, when IBM dominated the computer hardware business. The suit was dropped in 1982. Some years later, the Department of Justice turned its attention to possible antitrust violations by the software giant Microsoft. Microsoft settled with the Department of Justice in 2001, but the case continued on with separate lawsuits by nine states. In early 2002, AOL Time Warner instigated a new suit against Microsoft on behalf of its subsidiary, Netscape. The suit was settled in May of the following year. As part of the settlement, the two companies agreed to a new royalty-free, seven-year license of Microsoft's browsing technology. In addition, Microsoft agreed to pay $750 million to AOL Time Warner.[4] One of the lawsuits by individual states is finally in the process of being completed as this edition is being prepared. For example, in 2007 Microsoft settled a class action suit with the state of Iowa by agreeing to pay $179,950,000 to parties in that state who purchased certain Microsoft products over a certain period of time.[5]

Microsoft was also a subject of antitrust actions by the European Union. In 2004, European Competition Commissioner Mario Monti ruled that Microsoft had failed to provide to rivals information that they needed to compete fairly in the market for server software, and that the company had been offering Windows on the condition that it come bundled with Windows Media Player, stifling competition. Microsoft was

---

[4]http://www.microsoft.com/presspass/press/2003/may03/05-29msaolsettlementpr.mspx.
[5]http://www.iowamicrosoftcase.com.

fined €497 million. At first, Microsoft appealed the ruling in 2007, but later decided to drop the appeal.[6]

Our personal view on this matter is that a number of past examples indicate that changes in the economics of a business (i.e., customers, technology, and competition), eventually break down a dominating company's monopolistic power, no matter how invincible the company might seem. Shortly after the Justice Department dropped the case against IBM, the company began to lose a considerable amount of business as personal computers, workstations, and client server networks became more important than the mainframe in many aspects of computing. Polaroid, the company that had a virtual monopoly on its instant developing camera, is no longer the company that it once was, thanks to the 1-hour photo developing process, video cameras, and most important, digital cameras. Microsoft has dominated the PC software market since the advent of this industry in the mid-1980s. However, it certainly trails Google in the Internet search engine business.

Perhaps one of the best examples of the vulnerability of a monopoly can be found in the pharmaceutical industry. Until the early 1990s, firms in this industry enjoyed among the highest profit margins and returns on equity of all the companies in the *Fortune* 500. However, a number of recent events have started to erode their profitability. To start with, companies that do not have the patent on a drug that treats a particular illness are coming up with what the industry calls "me-too" products. These are drugs that offer a therapy for the same illness but whose chemical compositions are different enough to come under different patents. Furthermore, patents are beginning to run out on a number of highly profitable drugs and generic drugs are entering the market at far lower prices. Finally, those who make the purchasing decisions are exerting much more market power than ever before. It used to be that the majority of purchasers were fee-based private physicians who wrote prescriptions regardless of price, partly because they knew that their patients would be reimbursed by third-party payers such as insurance companies. Now much more of the purchasing decisions are being made by cost-conscious health maintenance organizations, hospital associations, and networks of retail pharmacies.

The key lesson for managers to learn from the many examples of once-powerful monopolies or near-monopolies that have eventually been affected by changing economics is not to be complacent or arrogant and assume their ability to earn economic profit can never be diminished. This is certainly the case for monopolistic competition and oligopoly, as seen in chapter 9.

GLOBAL APPLICATION: THE BRUTAL ECONOMICS OF THE MARKET FOR BLUEFIN TUNA

A good way to really appreciate what it is like to be a manager in markets subject to the volatility of supply and demand conditions is to look at individual companies in specific markets. The current challenges for owners of sushi restaurants all around the world provide such a case. Sushi restaurants could be considered as operating in monopolistic competition. However, the price of their main input, bluefin tuna, is largely determined by the perfectly competitive forces of supply and demand.

In 2002, one of the authors was invited for a meal in Shanghai by a host who was known for his congeniality and generosity. Understandably, the author expected to be taken to a famous Chinese restaurant. To his surprise, he and his colleagues were

---

[6]For example, see: http://www.news.com/EU-slaps-record-fine-on-Microsoft/2100-1001_3-5178281.html and http://www.msnbc.msn.com/id/20818452.

invited by the host to a popular Japanese restaurant for sushi. Subsequently, the author began to notice a proliferation of sushi restaurants throughout his travels in Europe, particularly in the major cities in France, Germany, and England. In late November of 2006, long lines of customers were observed outside in the cold, waiting to get into a trendy sushi restaurant in Moscow. (A guide told the author that there were hundreds of sushi restaurants in Moscow.) In fact, sushi can also be found in such diverse places as the prepared food section of your local supermarket and the food court of international airports such as the one in Zurich, a busy international airline hub. No doubt readers will be able to corroborate this story with their own experiences, either as consumers of sushi or as simply observers. Japanese sushi has indeed reached the status of a global food.

This global sushi phenomenon has been written about extensively in the popular press. The simple keyword "sushi" on any search engine will produce thousands of such sources of information. One freelance writer of travel magazine articles, Sasha Issenberg, became so interested in the subject that she wrote an entire book on this subject.[7] In her book, Issenberg describes the challenges of maintaining adequate fish stocks because of rising global demand and overfishing by international fleets. Governments of the world have established quotas, but these quotas are difficult to enforce. In an interview with Devin T. Steward, director of the Global Policy Innovations program at the Carnegie Council for Ethics in International Affairs, Issenberg explained that the new members of the Chinese middle class were starting to demand more sushi, in a fashion similar to their economic counterparts in places like Russia and Dubai. Moreover, she pointed out that the reason why China has had such a noticeable impact on the market for seafood served in sushi restaurants is because so many Chinese have experienced rising incomes so quickly.[8]

Suppose you are an owner-manager of a sushi restaurant. Would current market conditions be good or bad for your business? What key managerial decisions would you have to make under these circumstances? Consider the plight of those who started this whole phenomenon: the owners and operators of sushi restaurants in Japan. Outside of Japan, we may consider "sushi" to be an assortment of all types of fanciful dishes such as the "California Roll"[9] (whose name derives from the fact that avocado is part of its mix) and "Rock and Roll" (considered by one of the authors as simply a mix of whatever fish was not sold the day before!). However, in Japan, a restaurant cannot be considered a true sushi restaurant unless bluefin tuna (*maguro* in Japanese, generally called simply "tuna" in the United States) is readily available to customers. One part of the bluefin tuna, the belly (*toro* in Japanese), is considered to be the premium cut, demanded by discriminating Japanese customers and commanding the highest price.[10] So here is the critical challenge for sushi restaurant owners in Japan: The market price for bluefin tuna is skyrocketing for all the reasons cited above. And the problem is that wholesale prices are now so high (prices rose 20 percent in 2007) that Japanese restaurant owners have a difficult time passing on the full cost to their customers. Nonetheless, they continue to offer bluefin tuna on their menus because as

---

[7]See Sasha Issenberg, *The Sushi Economy: Globalization and the Making of a Modern Delicacy*, New York: Gotham, 2007, 323 pp.

[8]From Sasha Issenberg, "How the World Grew a Taste for Sushi," Asia Times Online (http://www.atimes.com/atimes/Japan/IH22Dh01.html), August 22, 2007.

[9]Issenberg's "Chengdu roll" in the above quote was made in satirical reference to our California roll.

[10]In some Japanese sushi restaurants in the United States, we have noticed that there are sometimes two or three grades of *toro*, with the top grade sometimes selling for up to $12 for a sliver about the surface size of a matchbox. This is probably the case in Japan as well.

Izumi Niitsu, manager of the Kihachi restaurant in Tokyo, says: "If you have good tuna, you have a reputation of being a proper restaurant."[11]

In order to offset the low or even negative profit margin of bluefin tuna, sushi restaurant owners in Japan must try to make more profit from other sushi items on the menu. Besides other kinds of raw and prepared seafood, there is now talk among restaurant owners in Japan about offering such foods as raw horse and deer meat. These items were offered in the early 1970s when few people wanted to eat tuna in Japan because of a mercury scare.[12] But some traditional sushi restaurant owners do not place too much hope in such exotic alternatives. Tadashi Yamagata, vice chairman of Japan's national union of sushi chefs, declared, "It's like America running out of steak. Sushi without tuna just would not be sushi."

Yet Mr. Yamagata is also a realist and knows that he cannot just stand by while tuna prices continue to rise and the long-run prospects for survival of this valued fish are uncertain. At his family restaurant, Miyakozushi, which has been in business for four generations, Mr. Yamagata, has been experimenting with more creative tuna alternatives. According to the just cited article in the *New York Times,*

> His [Yamagata's] most successful substitutes were ideas he "reverse imported" from the United States, like smoked duck with mayonnaise and crushed daikon with sea urchin. He said he now made annual visits to sushi restaurants in New York and Washington for inspiration.

As Yamagata said, "We can learn from American sushi chefs. Sushi has to evolve to keep up with the times."[13]

---

[11]Blaine Harden, "Japan's Sacred Bluefin, Loved Too Much," *Washington Post Foreign Service,* November 11, 2007.
[12]Martine Fackler, "Waiter, There's Deer in My Sushi," *New York Times,* June 25, 2007.
[13]Ibid.

The Solution

Armed with all the available figures on the estimated cost and demand for Waterpure, Frank spent the next week trying to come up with an optimal price for the product. The weekly demand for the firm's bottled water product was estimated to be

$$Q_D = 2,000 - 1,000\, P \tag{8.1}$$

where Q_D = Quantity of 12-ounce plastic bottles (in thousands)
P = Price per container

Based on estimates provided by the bottling plant, Frank expressed the cost function as

$$TC = 150 + 0.25Q \tag{8.2}$$

where TC = Total cost per week (in thousands of dollars)
Q = Output of 12-ounce plastic bottles (in thousands)

To find the optimal price on the basis of the MR = MC rule, Frank first found the total revenue and marginal revenue functions based on the data in Equation (8.1). Expressing this equation in terms of price,

$$P = 2 - 0.001Q \tag{8.3}$$

and substituting this into the equation for total revenue (i.e., TR = $P \times Q$), he found total revenue to be

$$TR = 2Q - 0.001Q^2 \tag{8.4}$$

(continued)

(continued)

To find marginal revenue, he took the first derivative of this equation and set it equal to the firm's marginal cost. [Based on Equation (8.2), he knew that the firm incurred a constant marginal cost of $0.25 per unit of the product.] He then solved for the quantity (Q^*) that satisfied the equality. Then he found the optimal price by substituting the value of this optimal quantity into Equation (8.3).

$$MR = \frac{dTR}{dQ} = 2 - 0.002Q$$

$$2 - 0.002Q = 0.25$$

$$Q^* = 875 \ (875{,}000 \text{ units per week}) \qquad \textbf{(8.5)}$$

$$P = 2 - 0.001 \ (875)$$

$$P^* = 1.125$$

$$= \$1.10 \text{ (rounding to the nearest 10 cents)}$$

Figure 8.13 shows Frank's solution on a per-unit basis.

Frank assumed the main distributors of Waterpure would be small retail food establishments, which generally mark up the wholesale price of bottled water by about 100 percent. Therefore, Frank determined the wholesale price that Global Foods could charge the retail stores by simply taking 50 percent of the optimal price of $1.10. For every unit sold, the company would receive $0.55.

Frank then estimated the company's weekly profit from the production and sale of bottled water.

$$TR = \$0.55 \times 875$$
$$= 481.25, \text{ or } \$481{,}250$$

$$TC = 150 + 0.25 \ (875)$$
$$= 368.75, \text{ or } \$368{,}750$$

$$\text{Total profit} = \$481{,}250 - \$368{,}750$$
$$= \$112{,}500$$

Although Frank realized that he had the optimal price for Waterpure, he also knew that there were already companies with established bottled water products in the market that were selling for about $1.25 a bottle. As the new entrant into the market, should Global Foods go along with the price established by the market leaders or should it try to sell it at a lower price? He was going to have to take up this issue with Nicole Goodman.

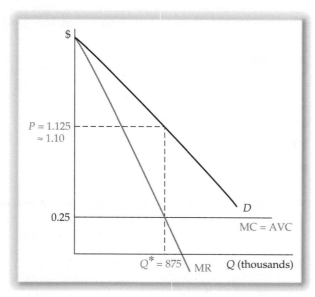

Figure 8.13   Frank's Result for the Optimal Pricing Problem

SUMMARY

This chapter presents a view of the pricing and output decisions facing firms in two extreme situations. In the case of perfect competition, the firm has virtually no power to set the price and is only able to decide to what extent (if at all) it wants to produce in this market, given the going market price. In the case of a monopoly, the firm *is* the entire market supply. This monopoly of supply gives the firm the power to set any price that it desires. In certain cases, this monopoly power is regulated by the government.

We demonstrate that firms wanting to maximize their short-run profit (or minimize their short-run loss) should establish their price and output levels according to the MR = MC rule. For those firms in perfectly competitive markets, MR is in fact equal to the price that has already been established for them by the forces of supply and demand. For these price-taking firms, the only task is to decide what output quantity results in the matching of the market price (i.e., marginal revenue) and the marginal cost of producing the last unit of its output. For the monopoly firm, following the MR = MC rule involves pricing the product at the level whereby the quantity that people purchase is the amount needed to bring MR in line with MC. We now turn to the cases between the two extremes of perfect competition and monopoly. For these "imperfect competitors," the MR = MC rule is an important part of their pricing decision. However, as we show, the actions or reactions of their competitors also play a major role in the pricing of their products.

IMPORTANT CONCEPTS

Contribution margin: The amount of revenue that a firm earns above its total variable cost. According to economic analysis, a firm experiencing a loss may continue operating in the short run if it has a positive contribution margin. A firm experiencing a negative contribution margin must shut down its operations because its revenue cannot even cover its variable costs of operations. (p. 325)

Economic cost: All cost incurred to attract resources into a company's employ. Such cost includes explicit cost usually recognized on accounting records and opportunity cost. (p. 316)

Economic loss: A situation that exists when a firm's revenues cannot cover its accounting cost and its opportunity cost of production. (p. 317)

Economic profit: Total revenue minus total economic cost. An amount of profit earned in a particular endeavor above the amount of profit that the firm could be earning in its next-best alternative activity. Also referred to as *abnormal profit* or *above-normal profit*. (p. 316)

Long run (market analysis):   Firms are expected to enter a market in which sellers are earning economic profit. They are expected to leave a market in which sellers are incurring economic losses. (p. 326)

Market power: The power to establish the market price. (p. 311)

Market structure: The number and relative sizes of the buyers and sellers in a particular market. A "competitive" market structure implies that the number of buyers and sellers in a market is large enough that it is difficult, if not impossible, for any one buyer or seller to determine the market price. (p. 311)

Monopoly: A market in which there is only one seller for a particular good or service. There may be legal barriers to entry into this type of market (e.g., regulated utilities, patent protection). (p. 314)

MR = MC rule: A rule stating that if a firm desires to maximize its economic profit, it must produce an amount of output whereby the marginal revenue received at this particular level is equal to its marginal cost. This implies that those firms with market power must set a price that prompts buyers to purchase this particular level of output. (p. 321)

Normal profit: An amount of profit earned in a particular endeavor that is just equal to the profit that could be earned in a firm's next-best alternative activity. When a firm earns normal profit, its revenue is just enough to cover both its accounting cost and its opportunity cost. It can also be considered as the return to capital and management necessary to keep resources engaged in a particular activity. (p. 316)

P = **MC rule:** A variation of the MR = MC rule for those firms operating in perfectly competitive markets. In such markets, firms are price takers. Thus, the price they must deal with (which has been determined by the forces of supply and demand) is in fact the same as a firm's marginal revenue. Firms using this rule must also be careful that the price is greater than average variable cost as well as equal to marginal cost (i.e., AVC < *P* = MC). If a firm cannot operate at the production level where this condition holds, it should shut down its operations. (p. 321)

Perfect competition: A market with four main characteristics: (1) a large number of relatively small buyers and sellers, (2) a standardized product, (3) easy entry and exit, and (4) complete information by all market participants about the market price. Firms in this type of market have absolutely no control over the price and must compete on the basis of the market price established by the forces of supply and demand. (p. 312)

Price makers: Firms that exercise market power through product differentiation or by being dominant players in their markets. (p. 311)

Price takers: Firms that operate in perfectly competitive markets. (p. 311)

Pricing for profit: The method of pricing that follows the MR = MC rule. (p. 331)

Pricing for revenue: The pricing of a product to maximize a firm's revenue. In this case, the firm would try to price its product to sell an amount of output whereby the revenue earned from the last unit sold would be equal to zero (i.e., MR = 0). Assuming the firm faces a linear demand curve, the price it establishes to maximize revenue would be lower than the price that would maximize its profit. (p. 331)

Shutdown point: The point at which the firm must consider ceasing its production activity because the short-run loss suffered by operating would be equal to the short-run loss suffered by not operating (i.e., the operating loss = total fixed cost). In a perfectly competitive situation, this point is found at the lowest point of a firm's average variable cost curve. If the market price falls to this point, the firm should consider shutting down its operations. Any price lower than this would dictate that the firm should cease its operations. (p. 326)

QUESTIONS

1. What are the main characteristics of a perfectly competitive market that cause buyers and sellers to be price takers? Explain.
2. Explain the importance of free entry and exit in the perfectly competitive market. That is, if free entry and exit did not exist, what impact would this have on the allocation of resources and on the ability of firms to earn above-normal profits over time?
3. "The perfectly competitive model is not very useful for managers because very few markets in the U.S. economy are perfectly competitive." Do you agree with this statement? Explain. Regardless of whether you agree, what lessons can managers learn by studying perfectly competitive markets?
4. Explain why the demand curve facing a perfectly competitive firm is assumed to be perfectly elastic (i.e., horizontal at the going market price).
5. Explain why the demand curve facing a monopolist is less elastic than one facing a firm that operates in a monopolistically competitive market (all other factors held constant).
6. Use the model of perfect competition described in this chapter to explain, illustrate, or elaborate on the following statements.
   a. "Increasing competition from new firms entering the market is good because it means one is in a good business."
   b. "One important difference between an entrepreneur and a manager is that the former gets into a market before demand increases, while the latter gets into the market after the shift."
7. Explain the relationship between *P* > AVC and a firm's contribution margin.
8. Why do economists consider zero economic profit to be "normal"?
9. "Economic profit" is a theoretical concept used to help explain the behavior of firms in competitive markets. Suggest ways in which this concept can actually be measured.

10. Explain why the $P = $ MC rule is the same as the MR $=$ MC rule for perfectly competitive firms.
11. Explain why a price-setting firm will always set its revenue-maximizing price below the price that would maximize its profit.
12. Provide some examples of business cases that a typical firm must consider. If possible, use current examples reported in the business press.
13. How "perfectly" competitive do you think are the following markets: (1) stock market, (2) bond market, (3) foreign exchange market, (4) world sugar market, and (5) world oil market? Explain.
14. Explain how the concept of "economic profit" might help explain the rationale for the government's granting of monopolies to those firms that protect their product with a patent.

PROBLEMS

For certain questions, consult Appendix 8A.

1. Following is the graphical representation of a short-run situation faced by a perfectly competitive firm. Is this a good market for this firm to be in? Explain. What do you expect will happen in the long run? Explain.

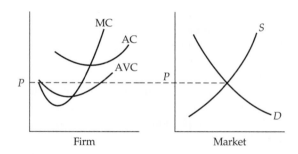

2. Indicate whether each of the following statements is true or false and explain why.
   a. A competitive firm that is incurring a loss should immediately cease operations.
   b. A pure monopoly does not have to worry about suffering losses because it has the power to set its prices at any level it desires.
   c. In the long run, firms operating in perfect competition and monopolistic competition will tend to earn normal profits.
   d. Assuming a linear demand curve, a firm that wants to maximize its revenue will charge a lower price than a firm that wants to maximize its profits.
   e. If $P > $ AVC, a firm's total fixed cost will be greater than its loss.
   f. When a firm is able to set its price, its price will always be less than its MR.
   g. A monopoly will always earn economic profit because it is able to set any price that it wants to.
3. Kelson Electronics, a manufacturer of VCRs, estimates the following relation between its marginal cost of production and monthly output:

$$MC = \$150 + 0.005Q$$

   a. What does this function imply about the effect of the law of diminishing returns on Kelson's short-run cost function?
   b. Calculate the marginal cost of production at 1,500, 2,000, and 3,500 units of output.
   c. Assume Kelson operates as a price taker in a competitive market. What is this firm's profit-maximizing level of output if the market price is $175?
   d. Compute Kelson's short-run supply curve for its product.

4. A manufacturer of electronics products is considering entering the telephone equipment business. It estimates that if it were to begin making wireless telephones, its short-run cost function would be as follows:

Q (Thousands)	AVC	AC	MC
9	$41.10	$52.21	$30.70
10	40.00	50.00	30.10
11	39.10	48.19	30.10
12	38.40	46.73	30.70
13	37.90	45.59	31.90
14	37.60	44.74	33.70
15	37.50	44.17	36.10
16	37.60	43.85	39.10
17	37.90	43.78	42.70
18	38.40	43.96	46.90
19	39.10	44.36	51.70
20	40.00	45.00	57.10

   a. Plot the average cost, average variable cost, marginal cost, and price on a graph.
   b. Suppose the average wholesale price of a wireless phone is currently $50. Do you think this company should enter the market? Explain. Indicate on the graph the amount of profit (or loss) earned by the firm at the optimal level of production.
   c. Suppose the firm does enter the market and that over time increasing competition causes the price of telephones to fall to $35. What impact will this have on the firm's production levels and profit? Explain. What would you advise this firm to do?
5. This same manufacturer of electronics products has just developed a handheld computer. Following is the cost schedule for producing these computers on a monthly basis. Also included is a schedule of prices and quantities that the firm believes it will be able to sell (based on previous market research).

Q (Thousands)	Price	MR	AVC	AC	MC
0	$1,650				
1	1,570	$1,570	$1,281	$2,281	$1,281
2	1,490	1,410	1,134	1,634	987
3	1,410	1,250	1,009	1,342.33	759
4	1,330	1,090	906	1,156	597
5	1,250	930	825	1,025	501
6	1,170	770	766	932.67	471
7	1,090	610	729	871.86	507
8	1,010	450	714	839	609
9	930	290	721	832.11	777
10	850	130	750	850	1,011

   a. What price should the firm charge if it wants to maximize its profits in the short run?
   b. What arguments can be made for charging a price *higher* than this price? If a higher price is indeed established, what amount would you recommend? Explain.
   c. What arguments can be made for charging a *lower* price than the profit-maximizing level? If a lower price is indeed established, what amount would you recommend? Explain.

6. The manufacturer of high-quality flatbed scanners is trying to decide what price to set for its product. The costs of production and the demand for the product are assumed to be as follows:

$$TC = 500{,}000 + 0.85Q + 0.015Q^2$$
$$Q = 14{,}166 - 16.6P$$

a. Determine the short-run profit-maximizing price.
b. Plot this information on a graph showing AC, AVC, MC, P, and MR.

7. The demand and cost function for a company are estimated to be as follows:

$$P = 100 - 8Q$$
$$TC = 50 + 80Q - 10Q^2 + 0.6Q^3$$

a. What price should the company charge if it wants to maximize its profit in the short run?
b. What price should it charge if it wants to maximize its revenue in the short run?
c. Suppose the company lacks confidence in the accuracy of cost estimates expressed in a cubic equation and simply wants to use a linear approximation. Suggest a linear representation of this cubic equation. What difference would it make on the recommended profit-maximizing and revenue-maximizing prices?

8. Overheard at the water cooler: "The demand and cost estimates that were provided at the meeting are very useful [$Q = 90 - 6.5P$ and TC $= 150 + 3.5Q$]. Unfortunately, what we didn't realize at the time was that our fixed costs were underestimated by at least 30 percent. This means that we'll have to adjust our price upward by at least 30 percent to cover the added fixed cost. In any case, there is no way in the world that we can survive by charging less than $9 for our product."

a. Comment on this statement. Do you agree with the speaker? Explain. Illustrate your answer with the use of a graph indicating the firm's short-run cost structure.
b. What price do you think this firm should charge if it wants to maximize its short-run profit?

9. Use the following equation to demonstrate why a firm producing at the output level where MR = MC will also be able to maximize its total profit (i.e., be at the point where marginal profit is equal to zero).

$$P = 170 - 5Q$$
$$TC = 40 + 50Q + 5Q^2$$

10. "In a perfectly competitive market, a firm has to be either *good* or *lucky*." Explain what is meant by this statement. Illustrate your answer with the use of the diagrams shown in Figures 8.5, 8.6, and 8.7.

The Use of Calculus in Pricing and Output Decisions

Thus far, we have discussed the firm's pricing and output decisions with the use of tabular and graphical examples. Using both the "total" approach and the "marginal" approach, we arrived at the MR = MC rule for determining the optimal level of output and price for those firms able to exercise market power. As a supplement, we now explain the MR = MC rule with the use of calculus.

To simplify our illustrations, we assume the firm has a quadratic total cost function, rather than the cubic function used throughout the examples in the previous sections of this chapter.

Perfect Competition

Suppose you are the owner and operator of a perfectly competitive firm with the following total cost function:

$$TC = 2,000 + 10Q + 0.002Q^2 \quad \text{(8A.1)}$$

Further, suppose the current market price is $25. By definition, TR = $P \times Q$, so your total revenue function can be stated as:

$$TR = 25Q \quad \text{(8A.2)}$$

Profit (π) is defined as TR − TC. Therefore, using Equations (8A.1) and (8A.2), your firm's profit function can be expressed as:

$$\pi = 25Q - (2,000 + 10Q + 0.02Q^2) \quad \text{(8A.3)}$$
$$= 25Q - 2,000 - 10Q - 0.02Q^2)$$
$$= -2,000 + 15Q - 0.02Q^2)$$

The optimal output level (Q^*) can be found at the point where your firm's marginal profit is equal to zero. In other words, additional units of output should be produced as long as your firm earns additional profit from their sale. Using calculus, the marginal profit can be expressed as the first derivative of the profit function:

$$\frac{d\pi}{dQ} = 15 - 0.04Q \quad \text{(8A.4)}$$

Setting Equation (8A.4) equal to zero and solving for the optimal level of output (Q^*),

$$15 - 0.04Q = 0 \quad \text{(8A.5)}$$
$$Q^* = 375$$

Returning to the total profit function presented in Equation (8A.3) and substituting Q^* for Q results in the following profit:

$$\pi = -2,000 + 15(375) - 0.02\,(375)^2 \quad \text{(8A.6)}$$
$$= \$812.50$$

We conclude that at the price of $25, the firm will earn maximum economic profit by producing 375 units of output per time period.

An alternative way of finding P^* and Q^* is to set the firm's marginal revenue function equal to its marginal cost function and then solve for Q^*. We already know that MR = P. The marginal cost function is the first derivative of the total cost function:

$$MR = \frac{dTC}{dQ} = 10 + 0.04Q \quad \text{(8A.7)}$$

Setting MR equal to Equation (8A.7) and solving for Q^* gives us

$$25 = 10 + 0.04Q \quad \text{(8A.8)}$$
$$15 = 0.04Q$$
$$Q^* = 375$$

Comparison of Equations (8A.8) and (8A.5) provides a useful and concise explanation of the MR = MC rule. As you can see, using this rule is the mathematical equivalent of finding the level of output that maximizes the total profit function.

Monopoly

As the manager of a product that only your company sells (e.g., a patent-protected product), suppose you are given the following information:

$$TC = 10,000 + 100Q + 0.02Q^2 \quad \text{(8A.9)}$$
$$Q_D = 20,000 - 100P \quad \text{(8A.10)}$$

You can use the same procedure employed in the case of perfect competition to find Q^* and P^*.

First, determine your marginal revenue function. Because you are a price setter and not a price taker, you cannot assume that MR = P. Instead, you must derive the marginal revenue function from your firm's demand function, shown in Equation (8A.10). Because your objective is to find the level of output that will maximize your profit (i.e., Q^*), you must rearrange the terms in the equation so price depends on the level of output:

$$P = 200 - 0.01Q \qquad \text{(8A.11)}$$

By definition, TR = $P \times Q$. So by substitution,

$$TR = (200 - 0.01Q)Q \qquad \text{(8A.12)}$$
$$= 200Q - 0.01Q^2$$

The marginal revenue function is the first derivative of the total revenue function:

$$MR = \frac{d\,TR}{dQ} = 200 - 0.02Q \qquad \text{(8A.13)}$$

From the example of perfect competition, we know that the first derivative of the total cost function is the marginal cost function:

$$MC = \frac{d\,TC}{dQ} = 100 + 0.04Q \qquad \text{(8A.14)}$$

Thus the MR = MC rule is adhered to by setting Equation (8A.13) equal to Equation (8A.14) and solving for Q^*:

$$200 - 0.02Q = 100 + 0.04Q \qquad \text{(8A.15)}$$
$$0.06Q = 100$$
$$Q^* = 1,667 \text{ (rounded to the nearest}$$
$$\text{whole number)}$$

To find P^* we return to Equation (8A.11) and substitute Q^* for Q.

$$P = 200 - 0.01\ (1,667) \qquad \text{(8A.16)}$$
$$P^* = \$183.33, \text{ or } \$183$$

At the rounded price of \$183, your firm can expect to sell 1,667 units of output per time period and earn an economic profit of \$73,333 (rounded to the nearest dollar). From the example on perfect competition, you should be aware of how the profit figure was determined.

***

As you can see from the preceding examples, the use of calculus offers a concise way of explaining the output decision for price-taking firms in perfectly competitive markets and the pricing/output decision for monopoly firms. The same procedures could be applied for those firms in monopolistic competition and even for oligopolistic firms that have clear-cut roles as price leaders in their markets. However, tables and graphs similar to those used in previous sections of this chapter provide the same answers as the calculus method. Our intention is for this appendix to serve as a supplement rather than an advanced treatment of the pricing/output decision.

Break-Even Analysis (Volume-Cost-Profit)

Learning Objectives

Upon completion of the appendix, readers should be able to:

- Understand the concept of break-even analysis.
- Calculate the break-even point and break-even revenue.
- Show how break-even analysis can be combined with demand analysis.

- Explain and apply the concept of degree of operating leverage.
- Describe the benefits and limitations of break-even analysis.

The Situation

October and November of each year are extremely busy months for the department of financial planning at Global Foods, Inc. It is during this period that the financial plan for the next 2 years is prepared. As is customary in business, greater emphasis is always placed on the first of the 2 years. Planning data are collected from all departments—covering projected sales, costs, and expenses. After checking as much as possible to ensure reasonability and accuracy, the department consolidates the numbers to obtain a planned income and expense statement. The plans are prepared along profit center lines, usually by specific flavors of the products.

Suzanne Prescott is the senior analyst responsible for the company's new bottled water product, Waterpure. She and her assistant have worked on this project for 2 weeks and have completed the profit plan, which she will present to the manager of the financial planning department. The first page of the long and detailed presentation shows the summary income statement for the Waterpure profit center for the year 2008 (Table 8B.1).

Suzanne has kept her manager, Dorothy Simon, informed regarding the progress of the plan. As is quite

common during a corporate planning cycle, their final discussion has been delayed several times due to late data, changed numbers, and missed schedules. Thus Suzanne and Dorothy are meeting just 1 day before the results are to be presented to the company's controller. Dorothy agrees with the method with which the plan has been put together and with the results Suzanne has presented. But she expects that the controller will require additional information. She asks Suzanne whether she has performed a sensitivity analysis calculating profit results if sales were to be 10 percent lower or 10 percent higher than planned. She is also interested in the level of sales at which profit would be zero to establish the "worst case." Suzanne admits that this analysis is incomplete due to lack of time. Because the presentation must be ready the next day, there is not enough time to rework the complete plan to obtain the alternative results. Suzanne will therefore have to devise a method by which she can obtain some good estimates for the "what-if" cases, estimates sufficiently reliable to show the controller. She remembers that in graduate school, she learned a method called break-even or volume-cost-profit analysis. Fortunately, she happens to have a few old textbooks in her office.

(continued)

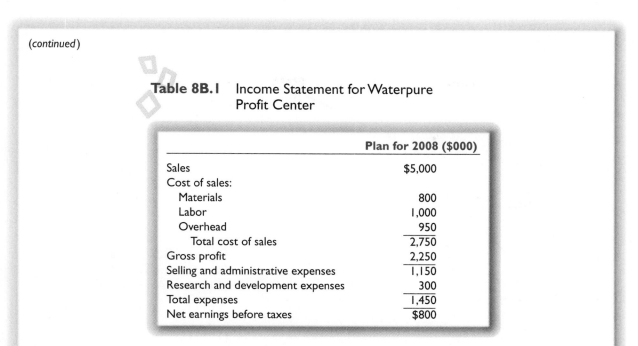

(continued)

Table 8B.1   Income Statement for Waterpure
Profit Center

	Plan for 2008 ($000)
Sales	$5,000
Cost of sales:	
Materials	800
Labor	1,000
Overhead	950
Total cost of sales	2,750
Gross profit	2,250
Selling and administrative expenses	1,150
Research and development expenses	300
Total expenses	1,450
Net earnings before taxes	$800

Introduction

The analysis described in this appendix is derived from price/output decision making in the short run, which is discussed in the body of chapter 8. **Break-even analysis** (or volume-cost-profit analysis), which is used a great deal in actual business situations, is basically a simplification of the usual short-run analysis in economics. The following are the important elements that go into this analysis:

1. It retains the distinction between fixed and variable costs.

2. Typically it uses a straight-line total revenue curve. Thus, it implicitly assumes the existence of perfect competition because the price is considered to be the same regardless of quantity. (This procedure is followed, however, more for convenience than for theoretical reasons and can be changed.)[14]

3. Probably the most important deviation from the analysis in chapter 8 is that break-even analysis employs a straight-line total variable cost curve. This means that marginal cost and average variable cost are both constants and that marginal and average variable costs are equal to one another. Although such an assumption may not seem realistic over large quantity intervals, it may not be unreasonable when a relatively limited range of quantities is considered. The possible existence of constant unit variable costs over a range of quantities has already been mentioned in the discussion of empirical cost estimates.

Figure 8B.1 presents a graph depicting the typical break-even analysis chart.

There are, however, some important differences between customary economic analysis and the break-even method that should not be overlooked:

1. The short-run economic chart shows two points where economic profits are zero, and maximum profit is identified somewhere between these two points. In break-even analysis, there is only one no-profit (break-even) point. As quantities rise beyond this point, profit increases continuously until, presumably, capacity is reached, and no additional quantities of product can be achieved.[15] At this point,

---

[14]It also must be understood that the horizontal (quantity) axis on graphs used in economics tends to measure large quantity intervals. To claim that exact relationships hold over these long intervals is rather unrealistic. It is done for convenience and ease of exposition. But a firm will generally not consider such wide-ranging alternatives. It is much more likely that a company, given a particular level of production, will try to analyze some limited deviations from that level to, say, 5 to 10 percent higher or 5 to 10 percent lower. In such a limited interval, it is quite possible that a significant price change may not be necessary. Thus, even if the particular firm is not in a perfectly competitive market, a straight-line total revenue curve (i.e., no price change) in the relevant range may be close to reality.

[15]Because break-even analysis deals with the short run only, capacity does not change.

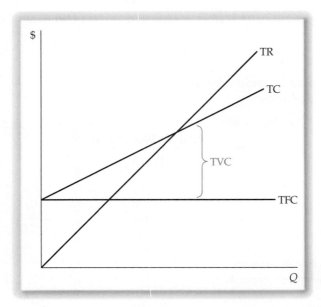

Figure 8B.1 Total Revenue and Cost Curves (Constant Average Variable Cost)

costs become infinitely high, and the total cost line would thus cross the total revenue line.

2. There is also a major difference between the objectives of the two analyses. In chapter 8, interest focused on the question of resource allocation—the effect of a price change or a cost change on the quantity produced. In break-even analysis, the question is what impact does a change in quantity have on variable costs and profit?

3. The third difference lies in the use of the cost concept. Economic costs, as previously discussed, are based on replacement costs and include imputed costs and normal profit. Break-even analysis, as practiced in business, usually relies on accounting costs (often standard costs as used in cost accounting), which include explicit costs only and represent historical data. However, in this case, careful treatment of data could convert accounting data into economic cost data. For instance, as is shown later, a "required" minimum profit, which can represent the normal profit, can be included in the calculation.

Another point to consider is that break-even analysis does not consider the time dimension of business activity. We discussed this dimension in chapter 2 in connection with the maximization of shareholder wealth. In chapter 12 we deal with the question of time and the time value of money as well as risk. We have included a brief discussion in chapter 12 of the calculation of the time value of money and present values in solving for break-evens.

The Break-Even Point

Module 8BA
Module 8BB

The first of the calculations we examine identifies the quantity at which the company will just break even—no profit, no loss. But this is not the point where company executives wish the firm to be. The break-even point merely sets the stage to investigate the relationship between quantity of the product, the cost to produce this quantity, and the profit—hence the name *volume-cost-profit* analysis.

The same abbreviations used in previous chapters are used here:

$P = Price$	$TC = Total\ cost$
$TVC = $ **Total variable cost**	$Q = Quantity\ produced$
$AVC = Average\ variable\ cost$	$TR = Total\ revenue$
$TFC = $ **Total fixed cost**	$\pi = Profit$

The very simple equation for profit is:

$$\pi = TR - TC$$
$$= TR - TVC - TFC$$
$$= (P \times Q) - (AVC \times Q) - TFC$$
$$= Q(P - AVC) - TFC$$

To obtain the **break-even point**, total revenue is set equal to total cost:

$$TR = TVC + TFC$$
$$(P \times Q) = (AVC \times Q) + TFC$$
$$(P \times Q) - (AVC \times Q) = TFC$$
$$Q(P - AVC) = TFC$$

Table 8B.2   Break-Even Analysis

Variables

Price per unit	$5.00
Variable cost per unit	$3.00
Total fixed cost	$20,000

Results

Break-even quantity	10,000
Break-even revenue	$50,000

Units	Fixed Cost	Variable Cost	Total Cost	Revenue	Profit
0	$20,000	$ 0	$20,000	$ 0	$−20,000
5,000	20,000	15,000	35,000	25,000	−10,000
10,000	20,000	30,000	50,000	50,000	0
15,000	20,000	45,000	65,000	75,000	10,000
20,000	20,000	60,000	80,000	100,000	20,000
25,000	20,000	75,000	95,000	125,000	30,000
30,000	20,000	90,000	110,000	150,000	40,000
35,000	20,000	105,000	125,000	175,000	50,000
40,000	20,000	120,000	140,000	200,000	60,000

Thus the break-even quantity is

$$Q = \text{TFC}/(P - \text{AVC})$$

For example, if $P = \$5$, $\text{AVC} = \$3$, and $\text{TFC} = \$20,000$,

$$Q = 20,000/(5 - 3) = 20,000/2 = 10,000$$

This result can be checked as follows:

Total revenue (10,000 × $5)	$50,000
Total variable cost (10,000 × $3)	30,000
Total fixed cost	20,000
Total cost	50,000
Profit	$0

If the quantity produced is larger than 10,000 units, a profit will result. If quantity drops below 10,000, the company will incur a loss. Table 8B.2 illustrates the revenue, costs, and profits resulting from changes in quantity, and Figure 8B.2 graphs the results.[16]

What happens to the break-even point when one or more of the variables change? An increase in the average variable cost will increase the slope of the total cost curve, and increase the break-even

point (a decrease will cause the opposite). A change in the unit price will change the slope of the total revenue curve; a price increase (decrease) will decrease (increase) the break-even point.

An increase (decrease) in fixed costs will cause a parallel shift up (down) in the costs curve and an increase (decrease) in the break-even point.[17]

Break-Even Revenue

Module 8BC

Under certain circumstances, the product price and the unit variable costs may not be available. This will happen—frequently—when more than one product is produced in a plant. Because each of the different products being manufactured side by side has a different price and a different unit variable cost, it is difficult to use the formula of the previous section to establish the break-even point of the plant.

A weighted price and unit cost can be calculated for the products if the various products are produced in constant proportions. If we assume variable costs are a constant percentage of total revenue, then we can calculate **break-even revenue** directly. Again, we are assuming the relationship between

---

[16]The table and graph were generated with a Microsoft Excel program.

[17]The reader should substitute new numbers for those shown in Table 8B.2 and Figure 8B.2, and observe the results. Modules 8BA and 8BB will perform this analysis quickly.

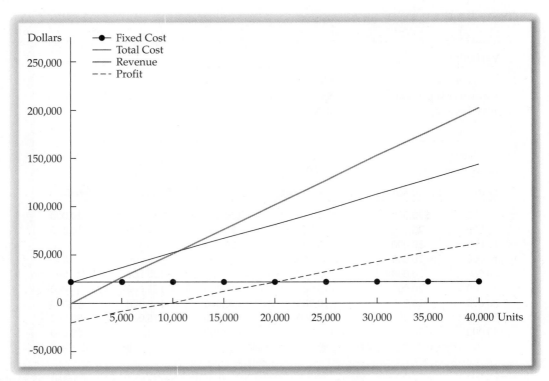

Figure 8B.2   Break-Even Analysis

average variable cost and price for each product remains the same and the quantities of the various products are produced in constant proportions. Such an assumption does not appear to be unrealistic for relatively small changes in total revenue.

Starting with the equation that shows revenue at break-even,

$$TR = TVC + TFC$$

we now convert TVC into a constant fraction of total revenue, $TVC = a \times TR$, where a is a constant less than 1. The break-even total revenue then becomes

$$TR = TFC/(1 - a)$$

For example, if TFC = 20,000 and a = 0.6, then break-even TR equals 50,000, which is the same result as obtained previously, because if P = 5, and AVC = 3, a = 0.6 expresses the same relationship.

Required Profit

If the only objective of this analysis were to find the point at which a plant or a company breaks even, not much would be accomplished. For a company to prosper, it must earn profits, not just break even.

If a firm has a particular dollar profit objective per period, a small adjustment of the break-even equation will provide the appropriate output measure. A specific, fixed dollar amount of **required profit** can be handled as an addition to fixed cost.

Continuing the illustration that has been used throughout this chapter, if the owners of the firm require a $10,000 profit, the equation is altered as follows:

$$\begin{aligned} Q_\pi &= (TFC + \text{Profit requirement})/(P - AVC) \\ &= (20,000 + 10,000)/(5 - 3) \\ &= 30,000/2 = 15,000 \end{aligned}$$

where Q_π stands for break-even with profit requirement.

If a specific profit per unit of product is required, this unit profit must be added to the average variable cost. For instance, suppose the company's objective is 40 cents profit per unit. Then AVC is changed to $3.40, and

$$Q_\pi = 20,000/1.60 = 12,500$$

Earlier in this chapter it was stated that the calculation of cost in volume-cost-profit analysis usually involves the use of accounting data. However, the "required profit" concept can easily be interpreted to represent the implied or opportunity costs that economists find crucial to the analysis of the firm. Thus, the profit measure, whether total or per unit, can be the normal profit, which is the minimum amount necessary to cause the owner to continue operating this business.

Combining Break-Even Analysis with Demand[18]

Until now, we have assumed a specific sales price to obtain our results. Going one step further, we can calculate break-even points at different prices by substituting those prices into our basic formula. We use the same numbers we used before (i.e., TFC = $20,000 and AVC = $3). Table 8B.3 gives us the resulting break-even prices and quantities when we set prices from $3.75 to $8.

The results of Table 8B.3 can now be plotted on a graph (Figure 8B.3). We obtain what we can call a zero profit "iso-profit" curve. Note that the curve approaches the level of average variable cost asymptotically. The curve also approaches the vertical axis at extremely high prices. We have now established the break-even point at a large range of prices.

The next step is to combine the iso-profit curve with the demand curve. The company's economist has estimated the demand curve for this product to be $Q = (8 - P)4,000$. In Table 8B.4, we show quantities and prices. In Figure 8B.4, we combine

the iso-profit curve with the demand curve D. The demand curve intersects the iso-profit curve at two points, at somewhat less than $7 (point A) and at about $4.50 (point B). At these points, there is no profit. At prices between points A and B, there will be a positive profit, whereas above and below the intersections a loss is incurred. The highest profit is obtained where the iso-profit curve is the furthest horizontally to the left of the demand curve.[19]

Degree of Operating Leverage

Module 8BD

Because volume-cost-profit analysis is concerned with the effect of a change in quantity of product on the profits of a firm, we must develop a method to quantify this effect. Such a method, called **degree of operating leverage (DOL)** is, in fact, a type of elasticity formula. The calculation result is a coefficient that measures the effect a percentage change in quantity has on the percentage change in profit.

$$DOL = \frac{\%\Delta\pi}{\%\Delta Q}$$

The percent change in profit can be written as follows:

$$\%\Delta\pi = \frac{\Delta\pi}{\pi} = \frac{\Delta Q(P - AVC)}{Q(P - AVC) - TFC}$$

The percent change in quantity equals $\Delta Q/Q$. Thus, we obtain the result,

$$DOL = \frac{Q(P - AVC)}{Q(P - AVC) - TFC}$$

To better explain the meaning of DOL, let us use the example of the preceding section. At a production of 15,000 units, profit was $10,000. DOL can now be measured at the 15,000 quantity:

$$DOL = \frac{15,000(5 - 3)}{15,000(5 - 3) - 20,000} = \frac{30,000}{10,000} = 3$$

DOL = 3 means that, at $Q = 15,000$, a 1 percent change in quantity will result in a 3 percent change in profit (and a 10 percent change in Q will lead to a

Table 8B.3   Break-Even Prices and Quantities

Price	Quantity
$8	4,000
7	5,000
6	6,667
5	10,000
4.50	13,333
4	20,000
3.75	26,667

[18]This section is based on Jon M. Hawes. Michael F. D'Amico and Thomas L. Baker, "Simultaneous Use of Break-Even and Demand Analysis for Pricing Decisions: A Teaching Method," *Journal of Education for Business*, May/June 1995, pp. 285–89.

[19]We could also plot additional iso-cost curves to the right of the break-even iso-cost curve. Where the demand curve is just tangent to the highest possible iso-cost curve, profit is maximized.

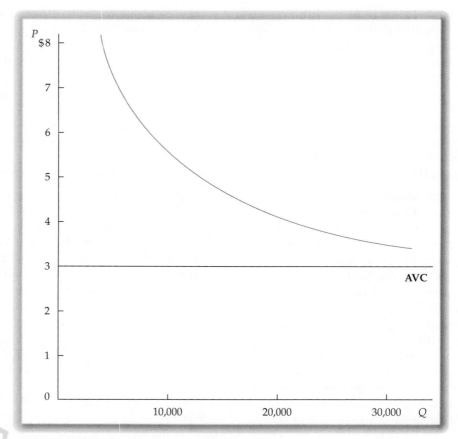

Figure 8B.3   The Zero Profit Iso-Profit Curve

30 percent change in profit). The DOL effect can be seen in terms of an income statement at quantities of 13,500 and 16,500 (a 10 percent decrease and a 10 percent increase):

	$Q = 13,500$	$Q = 15,000$	$Q = 16,500$
Total revenue	$67,500	$75,000	$82,500
Total fixed cost	20,000	20,000	20,000
Total variable cost	40,500	45,000	49,500
Total cost	60,500	65,000	69,500
Profit	$7,000	$10,000	$13,000

At a quantity of 13,500, profit is $7,000, or 30 percent less than at a quantity of 15,000 units. Conversely, at a quantity of 16,500 units, the profit is $13,000, or 30 percent larger.[20]

Table 8B.4   Demand Curve, Prices, and Quantities

Price	Quantity
$8	0
7	4,000
6	8,000
5	12,000
4	16,000
3	20,000
2	24,000
1	28,000
0	32,000

[20]The degree of operating leverage can be calculated at any point in the profit or loss area. However, it cannot be calculated at the break-even quantity because a percentage change in profit from zero does not make sense. (The denominator of the DOL formula is zero at break-even quantity.)

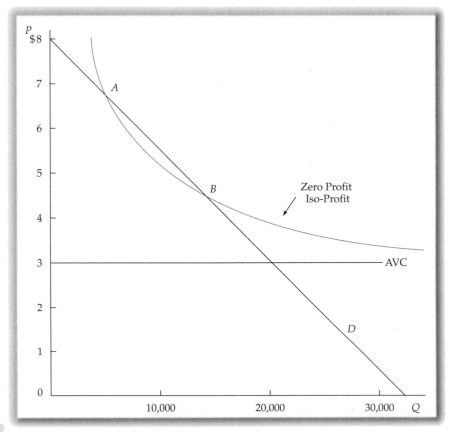

Figure 8B.4   The Iso-Profit and Demand Curves

The importance of the degree of operating leverage is that it reveals to management the effect on profits of a small change in quantity. This construction will hold only, of course, as long as all variables remain the same (i.e., price, average variable cost, and total fixed cost).

The relative sizes of fixed and variable costs influence the level of the DOL coefficient. A plant with high fixed costs and low variable costs will have a higher DOL than a plant with lower fixed costs and higher variable costs. The former plant will also have a higher break-even point. The significance of this relationship is that a firm with high fixed costs—a capital-intensive firm—will usually achieve break-even at a higher quantity, but because it has a higher DOL, its profits will grow at a relatively high rate when production rises above break-even. Its profits will also decline more quickly during downturns in economic activity, and the firm will become unprofitable at a relatively high point of production (since its break-even quantity will be high). In contrast, a

plant with lower fixed costs and higher variable costs—a labor-intensive plant, perhaps somewhat obsolete—will break even at lower quantities, and its profits will tend to rise or fall less quickly when quantity produced moves up or down.

Thus, the break-even quantity and the DOL can have a very significant influence on a firm deciding whether to convert from an old—labor-intensive—manufacturing facility to a more modern, automated (i.e., capital-intensive) plant. For example, using the income statement presented at the beginning of this appendix, let us assume the average variable costs per unit are $2.75 and total fixed costs are $1,450.[21] The break-even point for a $5 price is easily calculated as 644 units (rounded to the nearest integer).

Now suppose additional, more up-to-date machinery were installed in the plant, increasing annual fixed costs to $2,000 and driving average

---

[21]All dollar and unit numbers (except price and variable cost per unit) are in thousands.

Table 8B.5   Break-Even and DOL Data for Old versus Modernized Plants

	Old Plant	New Plant
Price per unit	$5.00	$5.00
Variable cost per unit	$2.75	$2.25
Total fixed cost	$1,450	$2,000
Break-even quantity	644	727
Break-even revenue	$3,222	$3,636
Equal Profit		
Quantity	1,100	1,100
Profit	$1,025	$1,025
Degree of operating leverage at equal-profit quantity	2.41	2.95

variable costs down to $2.25. The break-even point for the modernized plant will have increased to 727 units. Why, then, should the company invest in the new machinery? Because the newly equipped plant enjoys a higher degree of operating leverage, its profits will rise more quickly with increases in production. At some quantity, the modernized plant and the old one will achieve equal profits. In this case, the point of equality is 1,100 units, at which both plants will show a profit of $1,025.[22]

At the production level of 1,100 units, the DOL values for the old and modernized plants are 2.41 and 2.95, respectively. Thus, if more than 1,100 units are to be produced annually in the future, the profit from the modernized plant will be greater. If, however, the quantity is expected to remain at 1,000 units per year as in the company's plan, modernization would not be advisable at this time. The data for the present example are shown in Table 8B.5.

The Uses and Limitations of Volume-Cost-Profit Analysis

Volume-cost-profit analysis is a useful tool under certain circumstances, but its limitations must be understood. When a corporation prepares its financial plan for the next year or even the next 2 years, it usually engages in what is referred to as "bottom-up" planning, a process that is not only time consuming but extremely detailed. Many parts of the corporate organization contribute data on sales forecasts, prices, manufacturing costs, administrative and marketing expenses, and other measures. Data may be generated from every department in the corporation. Consolidating these data and making various changes in them before bringing a final plan up to top management for approval is a mammoth undertaking. A corporation would not use volume-cost-profit analysis for this type of planning.

The main use of this analysis lies in calculating alternative cases in a restricted period of time. It can also be used to make small, relatively quick corrections. In addition, during early stages of the plan, when detailed data are not yet available, estimates using variable and fixed costs can be used to establish some rough benchmarks for the eventual detailed plan.

However, despite its usefulness, break-even analysis has important limitations, some of which have already been mentioned:

1. It assumes the existence of linear relationships, constant prices, and constant average variable costs. However, when the effects of relatively small changes in quantity are measured, linear revenues and variable costs are certainly good approximations of reality.
2. It is assumed costs (and expenses) are either variable or fixed. The existence of fixed costs limits this analysis to the short run. Changes in capacity are ordinarily not considered.

---

[22]This point is calculated as follows:

$$Q(P - AVC_a) - TFC_a = Q(P - AVC_b) - TFC_b$$

where the subscripts a and b denote the old plant and the modernized plant, respectively.

$$Q(2.25) - 1,450 = Q(2.75) - 2,000$$
$$0.5Q = 550$$
$$Q = 1,100$$

The profit for a quantity of 1,100 units is $1,025 for each plant.

3. For break-even analysis to be used, only a single product must be produced in a plant or, if there are several products, their mix must remain constant.

4. The analysis does not result in identification of an optimal point; it focuses on evaluating the effect of changes in quantity on cost and profits.

An Application: The Restaurant Industry

The following is an illustration of the application of break-even analysis to the restaurant industry. Although the numbers that follow are hypothetical, they are based on a survey conducted in conjunction with the National Restaurant Association. The study compared a full-menu restaurant with a fast-food restaurant. Costs and expenses were classified into fixed and variable. It is interesting to note that a large percentage of payroll costs was considered fixed (for skeleton staff necessary to run a restaurant).

	Full-Menu Restaurant	Fast-Food Restaurant
Revenue	$950,500	$622,100
Fixed cost	445,700	260,700
Variable cost	459,500	280,900
Profit	$ 45,300	$ 80,500

From the preceding numbers, several inferences result:

1. The fast-food restaurant has a higher profit margin than the full-menu restaurant, 12.9 percent against 4.8 percent.

2. The break-even points are at revenues of $862,800 and $475,300, respectively.

3. The degree of operating leverage for the full-menu restaurant is 10.8 against the fast-food restaurant's 4.2 at the revenue levels given previously.[23] An increase in the full-menu restaurant's revenue would increase its profits at a much faster rate than a similar revenue increase in the fast-food restaurant's revenue.

Thus, the study concludes that volume-cost-profit analysis "can help you understand your establishment's cost structure, and help improve your decision making by quantifying the effect of specific policy decisions on the bottom line."[24]

---

[23]The formula for the degree of operating leverage is $TR(1 - a)/[TR(1 - a) - TFC]$, where a is the fraction TVC/TR.
[24]Carol Greenberg, "Analyzing Restaurant Performance," *The Cornell H.R.A. Quarterly*, May 1986, pp. 9–11.

The Solution

To calculate results for Waterpure sales of 10 percent more and 10 percent less, Suzanne Prescott needs to make estimates of price per unit, average variable cost, and total fixed cost. She had the production figure and price per case of $5. Breaking up the cost and expense numbers into fixed and variable components was a much more difficult task. Working with her assistant, she arrived at the following estimated breakdown:

Cost of sales ($000)	
Variable materials and labor	$1,800
Variable overhead	500
Fixed overhead	450
Expenses ($000)	
Variable selling and administrative	450
Fixed selling and administrative	700
Fixed research and development	300

Thus, total fixed costs were found to be $1,450, and total variable cost $2,750 or $2.75 per unit.

She calculated the break-even point as follows:

$$\frac{1,450}{5 - 2.75} = 644$$

For the +10 percent and −10 percent, she used the DOL equation:

$$\frac{1,000(5 - 2.75)}{1,000(5 - 2.75) - 1,450} = \frac{2,250}{800}$$
$$= 2.8125$$

For every 1 percent change in quantity, profit will change by 2.8125 percent. Thus, if quantity changes by 100 units (i.e., 10 percent), profit will change by 28.125 percent, from its $800 level down to $575 or up to $1,025.

Suzanne proceeded to prepare the presentation chart showing the planned figures, the two 10 percent variations, and the worst case. Table 8B.6 illustrates the results. She is now ready for the next day's meeting with the controller.

(continued)

(continued)

Table 8B.6   Alternative Plans for Year 2008 ($000)

	Best Estimate	+10%	−10%	Worst Case
Quantity	1,000	1,100	900	644
Sales	$5,000	$5,500	$ 4,500	$ 3,222
Cost of Sales				
Variable mat. & labor	$1,800	$1,980	$ 1,620	$ 1,160
Variable overhead	500	550	450	322
Fixed overhead	450	450	450	450
Total cost of sales	2,750	2,980	2,520	1,932
Gross Profit	$2,250	$2,520	$ 1,980	$ 1,290
Expenses				
Variable selling & admin.	$ 450	$ 495	$ 405	$ 290
Fixed selling & admin.	700	700	700	700
Fixed research & devel.	300	300	300	300
Total expenses	$1,450	$1,495	$ 1,405	$ 1,290
Net earnings before taxes	$ 800	$1,025	$ 575	$ (0)

SUMMARY

Break-even (volume-cost-profit) analysis is a simplification of the economic analysis of the firm. It involves several limiting assumptions, such as constant prices and constant average variable costs. Because fixed costs are an essential component of this technique, it is strictly a short-run tool. Yet, despite these simplifications—and possibly because of them—break-even analysis is a very useful aid to an economic or financial analyst. It is, however, necessary to be aware of the method's limitations.

Several specific tools are discussed. The first is the break-even formula itself stated in terms of quantities of production units. If a single product cannot be identified, then a break-even formula for total revenue can be used.

Because the firm's objective is certainly not to break even but to achieve profitability, an equation was developed to identify the required quantity of production, given a lump-sum profit requirement or a profit-per-unit requirement.

Break-even analysis can also be combined with demand analysis to find the most profitable price and quantity.

To measure the effect of change in quantity on profits, the concept of degree of operating leverage is introduced. This elasticity-like formula measures the relation between a percentage change in quantity sold and a percentage change in profit. This equation is also shown to be useful in comparing two plants employing differing technologies (and therefore having different relationships between fixed and variable costs) or in making decisions on modernizing a plant.

The usefulness of break-even analysis in evaluating alternatives and in making quick corrections is discussed. The limitations in the application of this technique are also pointed out.

IMPORTANT CONCEPTS

Break-even analysis: Also called *volume-cost-profit analysis,* a simplification of the economic analysis of the firm that measures the effect of a change in quantity of a product on the profits of the firm. (p. 345)

Break-even point: The level of output at which the firm realizes no profit and no loss. (p. 346)

Break-even revenue: The amount of revenue at which the firm realizes no profit and no loss. (p. 347)

Degree of operating leverage (DOL):   An elasticity-like formula that measures the percentage change in profit resulting from a percentage change in quantity produced or revenue. (p. 349)

Required profit: Profit that can represent the opportunity cost or the normal profit and that

can be incorporated in the break-even formula. A fixed dollar amount of required profit can be handled as an addition to fixed cost; a specific profit per unit of product can be added to the average variable cost. (p. 348)

Total fixed cost (TFC):   A cost that remains constant as the level of output varies. In a short-run analysis, fixed cost is incurred even if the firm produces no output. Also referred to simply as *fixed cost.* (p. 346)

Total variable cost (TVC):   The total cost associated with the level of output. This can also be considered the total cost to a firm of using its variable inputs. Also referred to simply as *variable cost.* (p. 346)

QUESTIONS

1. Although volume-cost-profit analysis uses graphs similar to those used by economists, the analysis differs in content. Discuss these differences.
2. Does the volume-cost-profit method analyze short-run or long-run situations? Why?
3. What is the difference between fixed costs and constant costs?
4. How realistic is the assumption of constant variable unit costs in volume-cost-profit analysis? Does it detract a great deal from the value of this analysis? Explain briefly.
5. What is the effect on break-even quantity of
   a. A decrease in unit price?
   b. A decrease in average variable cost?
   c. A decrease in fixed cost?
   Assume some numbers and illustrate the effect by drawing graphs showing the break-even point.
6. Business risk is usually defined in terms of variations of return (or profit) to a firm due to changes in activity

resulting from changes in general economic activity. Can the degree of operating leverage therefore be described as a measure of business risk? Why?
7. Would you expect a company whose production is rather stable from period to period and growing slowly from year to year to have relatively high fixed costs?
8. How would you account for required profit in the break-even formula when
   a. Profit is set as a requirement for a time period (e.g., a year)?
   b. Profit is set as a specific monetary amount per unit?
9. Can the degree of operating leverage be measured at the break-even quantity point? Why or why not?
10. Is volume-cost-profit analysis a good planning tool? Discuss briefly.
11. What are some useful applications of volume-cost-profit analysis?

PROBLEMS

1. The Automotive Supply Company has a small plant that produces speedometers exclusively. Its annual fixed costs are $30,000, and its variable costs are $10 per unit. It can sell a speedometer for $25.
   a. How many speedometers must the company sell to break even?
   b. What is the break-even revenue?

   c. The company sold 3,000 units last year. What was its profit?
   d. Next year's fixed costs are expected to rise to $37,500. What will be the break-even quantity?
   e. If the company will sell the number of units obtained in part *d* and wants to maintain the same profit as last year, what will its new price have to be?

2. Writers' Pleasure, Inc., produces gold-plated pen and pencil sets. Its plant has a fixed annual cost of $50,000, and the variable unit cost is $20. It expects to sell 5,000 sets next year.
   a. To just break even, how much will the company have to charge for each set?
   b. Based on its plant investment, the company requires an annual profit of $30,000. How much will it have to charge per set to obtain this profit? (Quantity sold will still be 5,000 sets.)
   c. If the company wants to earn a markup of 50 percent on its variable costs, how many sets will it have to sell at the price obtained in part *b*?

3. Bikes-for-Two, Inc., produces tandem bicycles. Its costs have been analyzed as follows:

Variable Cost	
Materials	$30/unit
Manufacturing labor	3 hours/unit ($8/hour)
Assembly labor	1 hour/unit ($8/hour)
Packing materials	$3/unit
Packing labor	20 minutes/unit ($6/hour)
Shipping cost	$10/unit
Fixed Costs	
Overhead labor	$50,000/year
Utilities	$5,000/year
Plant operation	$65,000/year
Selling price	$100/unit

   a. Calculate the break-even quantity.
   b. Calculate the break-even revenue.
   c. Develop a chart to show profits at quantities of 2,000, 4,000, 6,000, 8,000, and 10,000.

4. Music Makers Company, a wholesale distributor, is considering discontinuance of its line of tapes due to stiff competition from CDs and other new, technologically advanced recordings. The variable cost of its tapes last year was about 40 percent of its tape revenue, and the allocated fixed cost equaled $100,000 per year. Last year's sales were $250,000, but it is expected that in the future, annual revenue will drop by 20 percent and variable costs will rise to 50 percent of revenue (because of price reductions). Will tapes still be profitable for the company?

5. The ABC Company sells widgets at $9 each; variable unit cost is $6, and fixed cost is $60,000 per year.
   a. What is the break-even quantity point?
   b. How many units must the company sell per year to achieve a profit of $15,000?
   c. What will be the degree of operating leverage at the quantity sold in part *a*? In part *b*?
   d. What will be the degree of operating leverage if 30,000 units are sold per year?

6. Two companies, Perfect Lawn Co. and Ideal Grass Co., are competing in the manufacture and sale of lawn mowers. Perfect has a somewhat older plant and requires a variable cost of $150 per lawn mower; its fixed costs are $200,000 per year. Ideal's plant is more automated and thus has lower unit variable costs of $100; its fixed cost is $400,000. Because the two companies are close competitors, they both sell their product at $250 per unit.
   a. What is the break-even quantity for each?
   b. At which quantity would the two companies have equal profits?
   c. At the quantity obtained in part *b*, what is each company's degree of operating leverage?
   d. If sales of each company were to reach 4,500 units per year, which company would be more profitable? Why?

7. Elgar Toaster Co. is contemplating a modernization of its antiquated plant. It now sells its toasters for $20 each; the variable cost per unit is $8, and fixed costs are $840,000 per year.
   a. Calculate the break-even quantity.
   b. If the proposed modernization is carried out, the new plant would have fixed costs of $1,200,000 per year, but its variable costs would decrease to $5 per unit.
      (1) What will be the break-even point now?
      (2) If the company wanted to break even at the same quantity as with the old plant, what price would it have to charge for a toaster?
   c. If the new plant is built, the company would want to decrease its price to $19 to improve its competitive position.
      (1) At which quantity would profits of the old and the new plants be equal (assuming the price of a toaster is $20 for the old plant but $19 for the new)? How much would the profit be at this quantity?
      (2) Calculate the degree of operating leverage for each plant at the quantity obtained in part (1).
      (3) If sales are projected to reach 150,000 units per year in the near future, would you recommend construction of the new plant? Why or why not? (Assume that both plants have the capacity to produce this quantity.)

8. The Saline Company produces and sells rock salt. Its annual fixed cost was $10,000. During the past year, the company sold 8,000 bags of its product. It estimates that at this level of sales its degree of operating leverage is 1.5.
   a. How much was Saline's profit last year?
   b. At which level of production would the company just break even?

9. The Amazing Book Co. sells a selection of paperbacks at an average price of $9. Its fixed costs are $400,000 per year and the unit variable cost of each paperback is $4 on average.
   a. Calculate the company's break-even quantity.
   b. The company's sales target for the year is 100,000 units. What will be its profit?
   c. At the beginning of the year the unit variable cost rises to $5. If the company wants to achieve the same profit as obtained in item *b*, how many books will it have to sell?
   d. At the beginning of the year, the company installs new billing equipment. Its fixed costs rise to $450,000. If the company wants to remain on target to sell 100,000 units and preserve the profit obtained in item *b*, what price will it have to charge per book?
   e. An early review of competitive prices forces the company to drop its average price to $8. If it still targets its sales at 100,000 units and will settle for a profit of $50,000, what is the maximum unit variable cost it can afford? (TFC = $400,000)
   f. If the average price during the year is $8, the unit variable cost remains at $4, how many books must the company sell to achieve the profit obtained in item *b*? (TFC = $400,000)

Pricing and Output Decisions: Monopolistic Competition and Oligopoly

Learning Objectives

Upon completion of this chapter, readers should be able to:

■ Cite the main differences between monopolistic competition and oligopoly.

■ Describe the role that mutual interdependence plays in setting prices in oligopolistic markets.

■ Illustrate price rigidity in oligopoly markets using the "kinked demand curve."

■ Elaborate on how nonprice factors help firms in monopolistic competition and oligopoly to differentiate their products and services.

■ Cite and briefly describe the five forces in Porter's model of competition.

The Situation

In a meeting with Nicole Goodman, Frank Robinson explained the results of his price analysis. "My concern is that we know our optimal price, but do we really know how our competitors are going to react when we launch our product at this price point? Furthermore, I'm not sure the major players really consider us as a threat to their business, at least not yet. Therefore, can we assume they will take us seriously?"

Nicole agreed and suggested conducting further research. "One thing that we need is a complete list of prices of the major brands as well as the smaller brands," she began. "I was at a marketing conference in southern California last week, and I noticed that the hotel that I stayed in had bottled water with the hotel name on the label in its minibar right next to one of the national brands."

"Leave it to California to come out with the trendiest products," Frank retorted.

"Not necessarily," said Nicole. "I heard that private labels are proliferating throughout the country. For example, there is even bottled water with the labels of cities and countries. And you might have heard that even McDonald's has its own bottled water that I understand is selling well in some markets. The other key information that we could use in making our pricing decision is the perception of our product by potential consumers and their view of how much value our product provides them relative to our price. Perhaps it would be worthwhile to hold a few focus groups to find this out."

"Good idea," said Frank. "I'll get on this right away and have a report for you in a couple of weeks."

INTRODUCTION

In this chapter, we examine in detail the pricing and output decisions made by managers in monopolistic competition and oligopoly. Economists also label these markets *imperfect competition*. This is in reference to their relative market power, which you will recall is the economist's main criterion for determining the degree of competition. Perfect competition is, as its name signifies, "perfect" because firms have no market power whatsoever. Monopoly is not competitive because the single firm in the market has absolute market power. Monopolistic competition and oligopoly are considered "imperfect" competition because firms in these markets have the power to set their prices within the limits of certain constraints. This power and these constraints are principal subjects of this chapter.

Table 9.1 provides an overview of the competitive environment by comparing the four market types on the basis of market power, nonprice competition, ease of market entry and exit, and the degree of interaction among competitors when making decisions (referred to as **mutual interdependence**). The key characteristic that separates perfect competition from the other three markets is market power. Firms in perfect competition are price takers, whereas firms in the other three markets are price makers. The key characteristic that separates perfect competition and monopoly from monopolistic competition and oligopoly is nonprice competition. Because product differentiation exists in the latter two markets, firms have reason to compete on the basis of other factors besides the price. Market entry and exit are easiest in perfect competition and relatively easy in monopolistic competition. It is not possible in monopoly and could be difficult in oligopoly, depending on how dominant the leading firms are in that market.

In our view, the most challenging aspect of the competitive environment is the presence of mutual interdependence. It is one thing to know how to use optimization techniques such as the MR = MC rule to set the best price and output levels for the firm. It is entirely another matter when one has to anticipate and judge the possible reaction by competitors to one's decision. The presence of mutual interdependence is the one factor that separates oligopoly from the other markets.

We begin this chapter with monopolistic competition and show how the MR = MC rule that was developed in chapter 8 can be used for firms in this industry. We then proceed to oligopoly. Because of its daunting competitive environment, most of this chapter is devoted to a discussion of the pricing, output, and nonpricing decisions that

Table 9.1   Overview of Competitive Environment, Four Market Types

	Perfect Competition	Monopoly	Monopolistic Competition	Oligopoly
Market power?	No	Yes, subject to government regulation	Yes	Yes
Mutual interdependence among competing firms?	No	No	No	Yes
Nonprice competition?	No	Optional	Yes	Yes
Easy market entry or exit?	Yes	No	Yes, relatively easy	No, relatively difficult

managers in this type of market must make. The topic of game theory constitutes a good part of this discussion. Following the discussion of imperfectly competitive markets, we provide a brief introduction to business strategy. We believe that this is a logical extention of the theoretical analysis of the behavior of firms in imperfectly competitive markets. As you will see, the decisions pertaining to a firm's strategy are particularly important for managers when firms are price makers and are faced with tough price and nonprice competition.

MONOPOLISTIC COMPETITION

Monopolistic competition is a market in which there are many firms and relatively easy entry. These two characteristics are very similar to those of perfect competition. What enables firms to set their prices (i.e., to be monopolistic) is product differentiation. By somehow convincing their customers that what they are selling is not the same as the offerings of other firms in the market, a monopolistic competitor is able to set its price at a level that is higher than the price established by the forces of supply and demand under conditions of perfect competition.

A good example of how product differentiation can turn a product sold in a perfectly competitive market into one in which a seller is able to exercise some degree of market power is the case of the poultry industry. Those readers who live along the East Coast will recognize the Perdue brand of chicken. For a number of years, Frank Perdue, owner of the company that bears his name, appeared on television telling people why his chickens were better. ("It takes a tough man to make a tender chicken," was one of his more memorable slogans.) Of course, Perdue chickens were priced higher than the unbranded poultry products sold in the typical supermarket. But in monopolistically competitive markets, entry by newcomers is fairly easy. Soon after Perdue became a well-known brand, along came Bell and Evans as well as Murray chickens. At first, these newcomers could be found primarily in butcher shops and specialty or gourmet food stores. But soon, many supermarkets began to carry these brands.

Another company that was noted for its ability to differentiate a commodity product such as chicken was Tyson. In the mid-1990s, Tyson was applauded for its ability to differentiate its product and maintain stable premium prices by such actions as pricing by the hen rather than by the pound, and by selling breaded chicken parts.[1] But in recent years, Tyson has been not been profitable, despite its success in differentiating its products. One reason is that it has not been very successful in managing its costs. To be sure, some of these costs, such as high fuel prices and wholesale poultry prices, are not under Tyson's direct control. In response to this, Tyson has been increasing its efforts to reduce costs as well as to continue to innovate with poultry products.[2]

In economic analysis, we assume the monopolistically competitive firm follows the MR = MC rule to maximize its profit (or minimize its loss). Therefore, as a matter of convenience, we employ the same graphical illustration for monopolistic competition that we used for the case of a monopoly market. This is shown in Figure 9.1*a*.

If the firm is in the situation depicted in Figure 9.1*a,* that is, if it is earning above-normal profit, then we can expect newcomers to be attracted to this market.

---

[1]See Gene Walden and Edmund Lawler, *Marketing Masters: Secrets of America's Best Companies,* New York: HarperBusiness, 1993, pp. 12–17.

[2]Tyson CFO: Challenging Times Will Ultimately Benefit Company; Tyson Foods Focused on Creating More Demand Through Innovation, found in: http://www.prnewswire.com/cgi-bin/stories.pl?ACCT=104& STORY=/www/story/09-20-2006/0004437015&EDATE=.

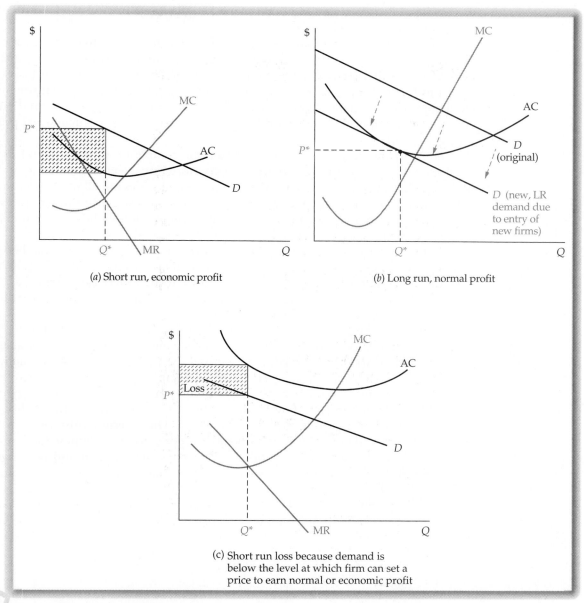

(a) Short run, economic profit

(b) Long run, normal profit

(c) Short run loss because demand is
below the level at which firm can set a
price to earn normal or economic profit

Figure 9.1   Monopolistic Competition

The effect of this added competition on the monopolistic competitor can be seen in
Figure 9.1b. Notice that the entry of new firms causes the original firm's demand
curve to shift downward and to the left. If you are confused by this movement and the
movement of the supply curve in the perfectly competitive market, remember that we
are talking about this change from the point of view of the *individual firm,* not of the
entire market. From an individual firm's perspective, the entry of additional firms in
the market would decrease its market share by reducing the demand for its product.
The leftward shift in the demand curve serves to illustrate this decline in market
share. To be sure, this case assumes the total market demand remains unchanged
while the new firms are entering the market. If the total market demand were

increasing while newcomers entered the market, the direction and extent of the shift in demand would be uncertain.

In the long run, economists hypothesize that the same situation would exist for monopolistic competition as for perfect competition: firms would be earning normal profit. If firms either earned above-normal profit or incurred losses, as shown in Figure 9.1*c*, then the entry or exit of firms, along with the adjustment of fixed capacity by existing firms, would cause each individual firm's demand curve either to increase or decrease until firms in the market earned only normal profit. (See Figure 9.1*b*.)

Some of the best examples of monopolistic competition can be found in the retail trade or in services. Restaurants, grocery stores, dry cleaners, stationery stores, florists, hardware stores, pharmacies, and video rental stores are all markets in which entry is fairly easy and the number of sellers is relatively large. In these businesses, owner-managers may use location, "service with a smile," or a slightly different mix of product offerings to differentiate their business.

In the United States, as well as throughout the world, Japanese sushi has become very popular.[3] In recent years, we have noted a number of Chinese restaurants in New York that have started serving sushi in response to this increasing demand. This increase also points out another important feature of monopolistic competition: relatively easy entry into the market.

In the never-ending effort to keep new and incumbent competitors at bay, a firm in monopolistic competition must constantly strive to maintain product differentiation. An article in the *New York Times* goes well beyond the example of Chinese restaurants selling sushi. In "Borscht, Please, with a Side of Sushi," reporter Sarah Kershaw talks about "Russian sushi, Yemeni fried chicken, Taiwanese fish and chips, Japanese spaghetti and Jamaican jerk chicken with chop suey."[4] In addition, the author has discovered Indian-Chinese restaurants in Queens. These restaurants are owned by Chinese who used to live in India and who are supposed to serve Chinese food exactly as it is prepared in India. Want more? Then try Pakistani-Italian and Norwegian-Cantonese in Brooklyn and Korean soul food in Harlem. There are even restaurants that serve Irish-Dominican, Greek-Irish, and Dominican-Italian food. We could go on and on, but the point of the article from our perspective is what immigrant restaurateurs told Ms. Kershaw: "In the highly competitive world of New York City ethnic food, it pays to branch out, mix, borrow and blend."

OLIGOPOLY

Market Concentration

Oligopoly is a market dominated by a relatively small number of large firms. The products they sell may be either standardized or differentiated. Part of the control that firms in oligopoly markets exercise over price and output stems from their ability to differentiate their products. But market power also comes from their sheer size and market dominance. There are two good sources of information on the degree of concentration that exists in various markets. The Census Bureau's Survey of Manufactures provides a comprehensive account of market share for the major industrial sectors

---

[3]See chapter 8, Global Applications, p. 333.
[4]"Borscht, Please, with a Side of Sushi," *New York Times*, December 21, 2001. One of the authors of this text lives in New York, but the other lives in Phoenix. We do not want to slight the good people of Phoenix so we should say that we know at least one ethnic-fusion restaurant in Phoenix. It is called "Chino-Bandito," and we allow readers to guess what combination of ethnic foods is offered in this establishment.

Table 9.2   Share of Value of Shipments Accounted for by the Four, Eight, and Twenty Largest Companies in the Three-, Four-, Five-, and Six-Digit Levels of Beverage and Tobacco Product Manufacturing and Sugar and Confectionary Product Manufacturing

NAICS Code	Industry Group and Industry	Companies	Value of Shipments ($ millions)	Percent of Value of Shipments			HH Index
				4 Largest	8 Largest	20 Largest	
311	Food manufacturing	21,958	421,737	14.3	22.0	34.8	91.0
3113	Sugar and confectionary product mfg.	1,556	24,114	41.9	56.4	75.0	580.3
31131	Sugar mfg.	49	7,399	64.4	84.0	95.9	1,452.2
311311	Sugarcane mills	34	1,457	56.6	71.4	94.3	1,158.7
311312	Cane sugar refining	12	3,209	98.7	99.9	100.0	D
311313	Beet sugar refining	8	2,732	85.0	100.0	N	1,997.6
312	Beverage and tobacco product mfg.	2,237	96,971	45.1	59.1	72.7	777.2
3121	Beverage mfg.	2,169	60,896	40.9	52.1	66.0	531.5
31211	Soft drink and ice mfg.	1,008	32,587	45.5	53.6	68.8	743.3
312111	Soft drink mfg.	388	31,376	47.2	55.6	70.9	800.4
312112	Bottled water mfg.	109	785	51.7	64.4	80.3	986.6
312113	Ice mfg.	514	424	24.4	31.3	43.1	302.3

N: Does not apply

D: Data omitted because of possible disclosure.

Source: U.S. Census of Manufactures, 1997. (Note: The above data from the 2002 Census are not readily available in the format shown in this table. Thus, we continue to use the 1997 data in this edition for purposes of illustration.)

of the U.S. economy.[5] However, it does not always provide the most current data (the most recent survey was conducted in 2002). For more current data, as well as market share information on specific brands, we recommend the *Market Share Reporter*.[6]

Table 9.2 presents sample information found in the Census Survey. The Census Bureau classifies industries by level of product specificity. The information that we found in the 1997 report begins at the three-digit level (broadest) and goes to the six-digit level (most specific). In 1997, the Census Bureau introduced a new system for classifying companies called the North American Industry Classification System, or NAICS. Previous to that, the Census Bureau had used the Standard Industrial Classification, or SIC. The categories in the two systems are only about 50 percent compatible with each other, so time comparisons on shifting market shares are difficult to make. Notice that as the product classification becomes more specific, the degree of market concentration among sellers tends to increase. This pattern occurs in many other industries but not in any consistent or precise manner.

Besides indicating the degree of market concentration by measuring the market share of the top four, eight, twenty, and fifty largest companies, the Census Survey provides a measure of concentration called the Herfindahl-Hirschman (HH) index. The formula for this index is as follows:

$$HH = \sum_{i=1}^{n} S_i^2$$

---

[5] For a PDF file of the latest survey, go to www.census.gov.

[6] Robert S. Lazich, ed. *Market Share Reporter,* Detroit: The Gale Press, 2007.

where *n* is the number of companies in the industry, and *S* is the *i*th company's market share. The HH index is shown for the fifteen industries in the last column of Table 9.2. The advantages of the HH index relative to concentration ratios are that

1. It uses the market share information about all the firms.
2. The squaring of individual market shares gives more weight to the larger firms.

The maximum HH index is 10,000—when there is just one firm in the industry. Using the prior example, the HH index will differentiate between an industry where four firms equally share the total market (HH = 2,500), and an industry where the top firm has 94 percent and the other three 2 percent each (HH = 8,848). According to U.S. Department of Justice Merger Guidelines of 1982, "unconcentrated" markets are defined as those with an HH of less than 1,000. Table 9.2 shows selected markets relating to the soft drink industry.

The *Market Share Reporter,* the other good provider of data on industry concentration that we recommend, is a compendium of information on market share taken from other sources. For example, this source reported that as of April 15, 2005, the leader in the "Imported Beer" category was Corona Extra with a 29.4 percent share of the market. This brand was followed by Heineken (19.5 percent), Tecate (4.5 percent), and La Batt Blue (4.4 percent). In "Energy Drinks," as of February 2005, Red Bull had a huge lead over its competitors, with a 71 percent share of the market. Monster, Amp, and Sobe Adrenaline Rush followed far behind with 6.3 percent, 4.6 percent, and 3.9 percent shares respectively.

PRICING IN AN OLIGOPOLISTIC MARKET: RIVALRY AND MUTUAL INTERDEPENDENCE

Whether the sellers in an oligopolistic market compete against each other by differentiating their product, dominating market share, or both, the fact that there are relatively few sellers creates a situation where each is carefully watching the other as it sets its price. Economists refer to this pricing behavior as mutual interdependence. This means that each seller is setting its price while explicitly considering the reaction by its competitors to the price that it establishes.

In the 1930s, economist Paul Sweezy provided an early insight into the pricing dynamics of mutual interdependence among oligopoly firms by developing a **kinked demand** curve model.[7] The basic assumption of the Sweezy model is that a competitor (or competitors) will follow a price decrease but will not make a change in reaction to a price increase. Thus the firm contemplating a price change may refrain from doing so for fear that quantities sold will be affected in such a way as to decrease profits.

If a firm lowers its price, this may have an immediate impact on the competition. This firm takes its action to increase sales by drawing customers away from the higher-priced competitors, but when competitors realize what is happening (i.e., their sales are declining), they will quickly follow the price cut to maintain their market share. If this firm undertakes the opposite action—a price increase—incorrectly assuming competitors will follow suit, its sales will drop markedly if competitors fail to do so.

It is easy to demonstrate the "kink" in such a demand curve with the graph in Figure 9.2. Let us assume the original price and quantity are found at point *A*. If the

---

[7]Paul Sweezy, "Demand Under Conditions of Oligopoly," *Journal of Political Economy,* 47 (1939), pp. 568–73.

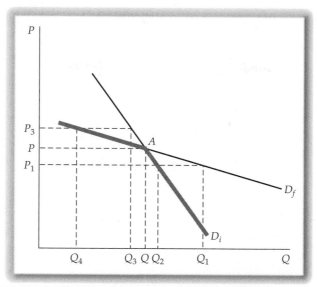

Figure 9.2   Demand Curves for an Oligopoly Considering a Price
Increase/Decrease

firm lowers its price, expecting that quantity demanded will move along the more
elastic demand curve D_f and this result materializes, then it will gain a relatively
large quantity of additional sales for a relatively small decrease in price. If it lowers its
price from P to P_1, it will expect to increase its sales from Q to Q_1. This is the relevant
demand curve for the firm if other companies do not retaliate. Our firm would thus
gain customers at the expense of competition. However, if competitors do react and
match the price cut, our company will increase its sales only to Q_2, along demand
curve D_i; this is the relevant demand curve when all companies in the industry
decrease their price equally. There will be a relatively small increase in sales because
all prices in the industry are lower, but not nearly as much as the company expected
when it reduced its price.

In contrast, suppose our company decides to raise its price, anticipating that
competitors will follow the increase. It thus expects to move along D_i to Q_3 when it
boosts its price to P_3. It would thus sustain some loss in sales while benefiting from a
significantly higher price. However, suppose its competitors refuse to play along and
keep their prices unchanged. The company's situation now becomes more precarious
because its quantity sold drops to Q_4: the demand curve for the firm alone is much
more elastic than if all firms raise their prices in unison.

The prospect of being stung by such action will make the company much
more loath to change its price from P. From that vantage point, it will appear to the
company that the appropriate demand curve is D_i if price is lowered and D_f if
the price is increased. The upper portion of D_f and the lower portion of D_i can be
seen to form a kinked demand curve around point A; thus, the name of Sweezy's
model. These relevant portions of the two demand curves are boldly outlined in
Figure 9.2.

Now that we have developed a demand curve for this oligopolist, we can also
derive a marginal revenue curve. This marginal revenue curve will be discontinu-
ous: there will be a gap at the point where the kink occurs. As we know, a company
will maximize its profits at the point where marginal cost equals marginal revenue.
The two marginal cost curves drawn in Figure 9.3 both imply the same price and

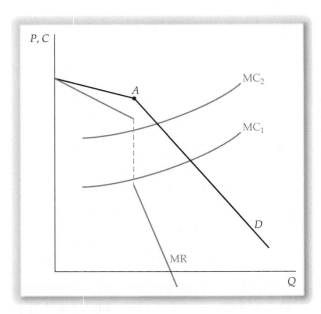

Figure 9.3 The Kinked Demand Curve

quantity at point *A*. Thus a significant change in costs could occur for our firm, but it will not react by changing its price. Actually, the price may remain unchanged even if the demand curve moves to the right or left, as long as the kink remains at the same price level. Hence, it can be concluded that under the circumstances described, a kinked demand curve will result in price rigidities despite changes in demand and cost.

Over the years, the kinked demand curve has been challenged by other economists. In particular, Nobel Prize laureate George Stigler investigated several oligopolistic industries and found little empirical support for Sweezy's model. Stigler found that in these industries, price increases were followed as quickly as were price decreases.[8] Such findings, of course, contradict the existence of the kink. Further, the model does not explain how the price was originally set at the kink. Was it originally set where marginal revenue equaled marginal cost, or was it by some other means, such as tradition?

One commonly held view of how the price at point *A* is determined involves the concept of an industry **price leader**. This is the firm that dares to break out of the pack without fearing the consequences spelled out in the kinked demand model. If this firm decides to raise its price, it assumes all others will follow. If this firm decides to lower its price, it assumes the others may follow but will not go even lower, thereby triggering a price war that would hurt the entire industry.

In oligopoly markets in the United States, the role of the price leader is usually assumed by the company with the largest share of the market. For example, General Motors is often the first to announce price increase for the next year's line of cars and trucks. During its reign as the dominant leader in the mainframe computer market back in the 1960s through the mid-1980s, IBM was always the price leader. The "fringe companies" (as economists sometimes refer to the significantly smaller companies in an oligopoly market) generally set their prices about 10 percent lower than the "umbrella price set by IBM." The undisputed

[8]George J. Stigler, "The Kinky Oligopoly Demand Curve and Rigid Prices," *Journal of Political Economy,* October 1947, pp. 432–39. Similarly, see Julian J. Simon, "A Further Test of the Kinky Oligopoly Demand Curve," *American Economic Review,* December 1969, pp. 971–75.

champion of the general merchandise retail industry is Wal-Mart. At its 2001 annual shareholders' meeting, the executives at the company stressed that they will continue to be the price leader by maintaining a close watch over competitors. Tom Coughlin, president and CEO of the Wal-Mart Stores Division, told meeting attendees that the company conducts price checks in 99.8 percent of Kmart stores and 98.7 percent of Target stores every week.[9]

There also may be nonprice leaders in an oligopoly market. American Airlines was the first to offer frequent flier points to its passengers. All other airlines followed suit. It was also the leader in the co-branding of its name with a credit card issuer. The Citibank-American Airlines credit card is the dominant co-branded card in the industry today. Another interesting form of nonprice competition and leadership is the practice by pharmaceutical companies of "wining and dining" physicians. Drug company sales representatives often invite doctors to lavish weekend retreats and expensive evenings out. But according to an article in the *New York Times*, Merck has instructed its sales representatives that they should "no longer treat doctors to free Broadway plays, weekend trips and other gifts that could be viewed as inappropriate." Other companies may soon be following suit.[10]

COMPETING IN IMPERFECTLY COMPETITIVE MARKETS

Nonprice Competition

The key to the pricing power of firms in monopolistic competition and oligopoly is their ability to differentiate their product so they are not mere price takers who are subject to the tyranny of supply and demand. All efforts to do so are referred to in economics as *nonprice competition*.[11] We have already provided examples of non-price competition in our earlier discussion of monopolistic competition. But we now present this concept in a more formal and systematic manner.

A simple, but useful definition of nonprice competition is "any effort made by firms other than a change in the price of the 'product in question'[12] in order to influence the demand for their product." More specifically, these efforts are intended to influence the nonprice determinants of demand. Here you will see the nonprice determinants of demand (first introduced in chapter 3) and a suggested list of nonprice variables that firms might choose to use to compete in monopolistic competition or oligopoly. *Nonprice determinants of demand* include any factor other than the price of the good in question that causes the demand curve to shift. They are (1) tastes and preferences, (2) income, (3) prices of substitutes and complements, (4) number of buyers, and (5) future expectations of buyers about product price. *Nonprice variables* include any factor that managers can control, influence, or explicitly consider in making decisions affecting the demand for their goods and services. These variables are (1) advertising, (2) promotion, (3) location and distribution

---

[9]Mike Troy, "Wal-Mart Maintains Expansion Strategy," *DSN Retailing Today,* June 18, 2001.

[10]Melody Petersen, "Merck Is Said to Limit Perks in Marketing to Physicians," *New York Times,* January 18, 2002.

[11]This somewhat awkward term is an indication of the heavy emphasis in economic analysis of pricing or market power as the basis for competition. In the ordinary language of business, the term to describe the factors discussed in this section would be considered just a part of "competition." Therefore, outside the confines of economic analysis, a "highly competitive market" is assumed to mean price or nonprice competition or some combination of both.

[12]The use of the term *product in question* is to remind readers about the difference that we made in chapter 4 between *own-price* and *cross-price* elasticity. Companies may use the price of complements or substitutes to try to stimulate the demand for the product in question. But this is considered to be a form of nonprice competition.

channels, (4) market segmentation, (5) loyalty programs, (6) product extensions and new product development, (7) special customer services, (8) product "lock-in" or "tie-in," and (9) preemptive new product announcements.

Readers might recognize the nonprice variables as important tools of marketing. In a typical corporation, the management of these variables (sometimes called the *marketing mix*) is largely the responsibility of the marketing function. A complete discussion of each variable is well beyond the scope of this text and in fact would be found in any marketing text. But we comment briefly on some of these variables in terms of their expected impact on the non-price determinants of demand:

1. ***Tastes and preferences:*** *Advertising and promotion* are intended to influence tastes and preferences.[13] Very often, advertising and promotional campaigns are tied into the building or support of a brand. A common means of enhancing these campaigns is the use of celebrities as a representative of a brand. Brand advertising and promotion are often combined with *market segmentation*. In this case, rather than try to influence tastes and preferences, firms try to target different market segments in which they believe their products will have the greatest appeal. In recent years, efforts to retain customers over the long term have become as important to firms as those designed to win new customers. Thus, *loyalty programs* such as points given for using a credit card, for mileage traveled on an airline, or for staying at a hotel have been an important means of influencing tastes and preferences.

2. ***Income:*** Firms cannot affect income. But *market segmentation* is a way for firms to focus on the income levels that they believe will be most likely to buy their products. If they are selling a "superior" product, then they would try to target higher income groups. The opposite would hold if they believed their products were "inferior." (Refer to chapter 4 for a discussion on the economic meaning of superior and inferior products.) An article in the *Wall Street Journal* pointed out how Volvo (owned by Ford) and Saab (owned by General Motors) have both fallen considerably behind the German and Japanese luxury car brands. In early 2002, they announced that they were going to try to catch up in this market segment by introducing their versions of upscale SUVs.[14] Volvo's SUV has attracted consumer interest and demand. Saab is much less successful today.

3. ***Prices of substitutes and complements:*** Efforts to *lock-in* customers will tend to reduce the effect that changes in the prices of substitutes will have on the products that firms sell. This effort may be fairly aggressive, such as wireless phone companies offering discounts or free mobile phones for long-term contracts but levying a penalty if customers want to get out before the expiration date. In contrast, this effort may be rather subtle. In effect, Microsoft locks in the use of its PC applications such as Word or PowerPoint through the "network effect."

4. ***Number of buyers:*** Firms also can use effective *market segmentation* to increase the number of potential buyers of their product. For example, according to Paul Ballew, a market analyst for General Motors, in 2001, the richest 20 percent of Americans accounted for 46 percent of new car purchases as compared with only 30 percent in 1995. In the words of Paul Ballew, this represents "a phenomenal structural change in [the auto] industry." He goes on to say that "Your primary vehicle buyer is increasingly a dual-income, 40-something-year-old couple where [at least] one member has a college degree."[15] Firms also can increase the number of potential buyers in the market by expanding their operations beyond their borders. For example, both Wal-Mart and Carrefour (a French retail chain similar to Wal-Mart) have made major investments in

---

[13]One must be cautious about the precise nature of advertising's impact on tastes and preferences. As John Wanamaker, founder of the famous Philadelphia department store, once said, "I believe that half of my advertising is effective, the problem is that I don't know which half."

[14]"SUVs Swedish Style," *Wall Street Journal*, January 3, 2002.

[15]Ibid.

China. With the entry of China into the World Trade Organization in 2001, many firms have done the same. It is easy to see why. If we suppose that over the next decade 25 to 30 percent of the Chinese reach a middle-income status similar to the rest of the developed world, then we are talking about a consumer market of about the size of the United States or Western Europe. The population of China is currently about 1.3 billion.

5. *Future expectations:*   Firms may attempt to influence the future expectation of customers about product price and availability through such means as early new product announcements. In the days when IBM dominated the mainframe computer market (late 1960s to mid-1980s), it would sometimes announce its intentions of launching a new product at the same time that its competitors launched their products. This did not change future expectations about prices per se. This preemptive announcement tactic was intended to keep its customers from switching to the competitors' new products. This action may not have had a direct impact on the expectations of the future price of a product, but it did have an effect on the demand for the product. Software companies have also used this tactic, prompting wary analysts who wonder whether there actually will be a new product to use the term "vaporware."

6. *Financing terms and conditions:*   In both consumer and industry markets, sellers can use financing terms and conditions as a way of influencing the demand for their product. This initiative does not quite fit into the set of non-price determinants of demand used in economic theory. But in effect, the use of financing terms and conditions is like changing the price.

Perhaps you have seen advertisements or promotional literature sponsored by electronics stores, furniture stores, or department stores saying "zero interest" or "no monthly payments until next year." This is a way of reducing the price of their products to those who buy on credit without actually lowering the price of the products themselves. Manufacturers of industrial equipment may use the financing arm of the company for this purpose. During the boom years of the telecommunications industry in the 1990s, there were a number of "competitive local exchange carriers" (CLECs) that sprouted up to compete against the incumbent Regional Bell Operating Companies (RBOCs). Much of the equipment sold to them by Lucent was done with the help of Lucent-backed financing. When the technology sector crumbled, a number of these CLECs went bankrupt or failed to meet their obligations to Lucent, thereby causing the company to suffer heavy losses. In 2006, Lucent was bought by Alcatel, the French telecommunications equipment manufacturer.

American auto manufacturers have also used easy credit as a way of promoting sales, and they are now being seriously threatened by this tactic.[16] After September 11, 2001, the financing subsidiaries of the U.S. automakers used interest-free offers to prop up falling demand. However, low-interest rate financing had been a part of the way American auto makers tried to stimulate sales long before September 11. As *New York Times* reporter Daniel Hakim observes:

> Unlike their foreign rivals, which have developed stables of models that buyers actually will pay more for, Ford and GM have relied more on incentives like low-interest loans and cheap leases to attract customers. The automakers have ponied up billions of dollars to their financing units to make up the difference on the below-market financing.[17]

---

[16]Danny Hakim, "All That Easy Credit Haunts Detroit Now," *New York Times,* January 6, 2002. Shortly after this article appeared, the CEO of Ford announced that the company was going to lay off about 30,000 workers and discontinue four product lines, including the Lincoln Continental.
[17]Ibid.

Economic Optimization and Nonprice Competition

We demonstrate how the MR = MC rule helps managers determine the optimal price and output level for their products. As we also explain, the MR = MC rule is actually part of a more general economic concept called "equalizing at the margin," which managers can use to help make an optimal decision. (Recall that we use this concept in the determination of the optimal amount of an input and the optimal combination of inputs in a production function; see chapter 6.) Equalizing at the margin can also be used to decide on the optimal expenditure level of a nonprice factor that influences a firm's demand. For example, let us consider advertising expenditure. Suppose

> MCA = cost of advertising associated with an additional unit of sales
>   of a firm's product
>   = Δ total cost of advertising/delta change in quantity demanded

and,

> MRA = marginal revenue resulting from advertising
>   = Δ total revenue/delta quantity minus delta total cost
>   other than advertising/delta quantity
>   = MR − MC (other than advertising)

We can therefore say that a firm will increase its advertising expenditure up to the point at which MRA = MCA.

Our experience in working with firms on this issue indicates that a number of them use the concepts of discounted cash flow and the time value of money. These concepts are explained in detail in chapter 12. However, we briefly introduce these concepts in the context of this section's subject matter.

Over the past decade, there has been a growing focus among managers, particularly in the market function of a corporation, on the "lifetime" or at least the long-term value of a customer.[18] For example, suppose you are the manager of a wireless telecom company and you and your competition offer free phones to attract customers. These phones may cost up to several hundred dollars. How long does a customer have to use your network for you to break even or make a profit? Suppose you are the manager of a company that issues credit cards. To keep customers from switching to another company, you offer them the chance to get a free airline ticket for a companion if they use your card to buy airline tickets over the next year.

These two examples of promotional efforts involve initial added costs that presumably result in a stream of additional revenue over a long period of time. However, money spent or received over time (e.g., over a 3- to 5-year period) does not have the same value as money spent at the present time because of a concept called "the time value of money." Therefore, marginal revenue and marginal cost has to be adjusted for this time value of money before they can be compared with each other. After adjusting for the time value of money, if marginal revenue exceeds marginal cost, then the promotional effort is justified from an economic standpoint.[19]

---

[18]An undocumented, but well-known story, told to one of the authors about Domino's Pizza serves as a good illustration. Apparently, the employees of the company at one time had banners in their office saying "One customer = $5,000." This was supposedly the average amount that a loyal customer is expected to spend on Domino's Pizza over the course of his or her lifetime.

[19]In our experience, we found that a number of companies use the term *cost–benefit analysis* or *business case* in reference to optimization analysis using the time value of money.

The Reality of Monopolistic Competition and Oligopoly: "Imperfect" Competition

In economic theory, monopolistic competition consists of a large number of relatively small firms that are subject to competitive pressures because of the ease with which newcomers can enter the market and set their own prices. Oligopoly consists of a small number of relatively large firms whose size or power in differentiating their products makes it difficult for newcomers to enter the market. But their size and domination of the market also make it imperative for them to watch each other closely when setting their prices.

However, the distinction between monopolistic competition and oligopoly can sometimes be blurred in actual markets. For example, mutual interdependence can sometimes be found in monopolistic competition, and there is a possibility for new firms to enter oligopoly markets. Consider the following three examples:

1. *The American automobile industry:*   Look at any economics textbook from the 1970s and you will probably find the American automobile market as a prime example of an oligopoly. But today this market has taken on certain key characteristics of monopolistic competition. The increasing dominance of Japanese, German, and, more recently, Korean automakers into the U.S. market make it hard to argue that entry is difficult in this market. In fact, analysts believe that Chinese-made and branded cars will eventually enter the American market. At its peak in the early 1970s, General Motors held more than 50 percent market share. Today it is below 25 percent.

2. *Small retail establishments around the world:*   A frequently used example of monopolistic competition is the retail industry, particularly those dominated by small "mom and pop" establishments. But the competitive landscape of the retail business has changed dramatically in the United States over the past several decades as large "big box" chains, led of course by Wal-Mart, have come to dominate the selling of products and services to consumers. These firms (other examples include Home Depot, Sports Authority, Target, Best Buy) look much more like the giant steel and auto companies originally envisioned by economic theorists as examples of oligopoly.[20] These giant retailers make it increasingly difficult for the traditional mom and pop store to survive. Moreover, the family pharmacist who owns the corner drugstore has also become a relic of the past as chains such as CVS, Rite Aid, and Walgreens increase their presence and domination of this particular retail business.

3. *Global issuers of credit cards: monopolistic competition or oligopoly?*   On the surface, the credit card industry appears to be an oligopoly dominated by Visa, MasterCard, American Express, and Discover. But a look below the surface reveals that Visa and MasterCard are really associations of financial institutions that issue cards and "acquire" merchants who agree to accept the cards as a means of payment. Visa and MasterCard each have thousands of members, most of whom are banks. This would indicate monopolistic competition. But a still closer look indicates that the card-issuing industry has become increasingly more concentrated. On the basis of card holder receivables (i.e., the amount owed by card holders to issuing financial institutions), the top ten account for about 90 percent market share.

As a way of dealing with the possible blurring of these two types of markets, monopolistic competition and oligopoly are sometimes put together into one category called imperfect competition. We introduce this term at the beginning of this chapter. But let us provide a formal definition of this term just to reinforce our points.

---

[20]To give readers a rough idea of exactly how big Wal-Mart is, consider the fact that its annual sales in 2007 of more than $350 billion exceeded the roughly $200 billion in sales of all the world's semiconductor industry. Furthermore, based on revenue, Wal-Mart is the largest seller of apparel and toys in the United States.

Imperfect competition is "a market in which firms are able to exert varying degrees of market power because of their size and/or their ability to differentiate their products from those sold by their competitors."

STRATEGY: THE FUNDAMENTAL CHALLENGE FOR FIRMS IN IMPERFECT COMPETITION

Since the mid-1990s, textbooks in managerial economics have gradually expanded their coverage of strategy. This topic is a principal component of a business curriculum, and entire courses are devoted to its study. There are some important linkages between managerial economics and strategy. Furthermore, within the context of managerial decision making, we believe that no discussion would be complete without some mention of the strategic challenges facing a firm. As the title of this section implies, the decisions pertaining to a firm's strategy are especially critical for managers of firms operating in imperfect competition. Strategic decisions are far less important for perfectly competitive or monopoly firms. The former are price takers, and their strategic decisions are confined primarily to whether they want to remain in a market and how best to survive during the downturns of a market. The latter have no competition, so a strategy is not as critical. Strategy becomes a critical part of the manager's responsibility, primarily when firms are price makers and are faced with tough price and nonprice competition, as well as the threat of new entrants into the market. Such is the case with firms operating in imperfect competition (i.e., monopolistic competition and oligopoly). This is our reason for placing this brief discussion of strategy in this particular chapter of the text.

There are many linkages between managerial economics and strategy because a number of the concepts and tools of analysis used in the making of strategy are rooted in economics.[21] In fact, the two fields of study can be said to be linked almost by definition. In chapter 1, we define managerial economics as "the use of economic analysis to make business decisions involving the best use of an organization's scarce resources."[22] Textbooks abound with a number of definitions of **strategy**.[23] Here is a composite definition of strategy that we can provide using selected sources: "Strategy is the means by which an organization uses its scarce resources to relate to the competitive environment in a manner that is expected to achieve superior business performance over the long run."

The similarities and differences between managerial economics and strategy can perhaps be best seen by comparing the basic questions addressed in the two fields of study. These are the types of questions firms must consider in the study of managerial economics:

1. If we operate in perfect competition, what output level should we set for our product?
2. If we are a monopoly or imperfect competitor, what price (which in turn determines our output level) should we set for our product?
3. If we compete in an oligopoly, what might the reaction of our competitors be to decision 2?
4. Are we prepared to compete as a low-cost producer in the long run as new firms enter the market?

---

[21]Two excellent texts on strategy written by economists and intended for strategy courses with an economics slant are Sharon M. Oster, *Modern Competitive Analysis*, 3rd ed., New York: Oxford University Press, 1999; and David Besank, David Dranova, and Mark Shanley, *The Economics of Strategy*, 3rd ed., New York: John Wiley & Sons, 2003. The latter book has been cited in various other sections of this text and is also used as a reference for this section.
[22]Refer to chapter 1.
[23]See Besank et al., p. 1, for a list of three definitions of strategy provided by leading academics that are very similar to the one we offer. Also, the introductory section of this book "Primer: Economic Concepts for Strategy," pp. 9–40, provides an excellent survey of the economic foundations of strategy.

5. If we are not breaking even, should we shut down our operations?

6. How do we ensure our short-run profit is maximized? If we are losing money, how do we ensure our losses are minimized?

7. If we are operating in monopolistic competition or oligopoly, how can we differentiate our products in such a way that we can command a price that is higher than the rest of the competition?

These are the types of questions that firms must consider in the determination of their strategy:

1. What businesses should we be in? (corporate-level decision)

2. How should we compete in these businesses: product differentiator or cost leader? (group, division, or product-level decision)

3. What are our long-run strategic objectives? How do these relate to our short-run tactics?

4. What geographic segments of the market should we focus on? (local, regional, national, and international)

5. What demographic segments of the market should we focus on?[24]

6. What will be the reaction of our competitors to our decisions? Is there a particular advantage to being a first mover in the market?

7. What are our core competencies and how can we use this to our competitive advantage?

8. In making our strategic decisions, how can we best incorporate the changes that are taking place in the total business environment, which includes suppliers, buyers, potential entrants, substitute products in completely different markets, technology, and macroeconomic factors such as the national business cycle and levels of growth and development around the world?

There are more strategic questions that we could add, but this should be sufficient to show the similarities and differences between the study of managerial economics and the study of strategy.

Our coverage of the linkage between managerial economics and strategy is divided into two sections. The first section deals with industrial organization, a branch of economic study that underlies much of the original work on strategy done by Professor Michael Porter. The second section introduces Porter's basic ideas on strategy.

Industrial Organization

Industrial organization is the branch of economics that studies ways that firms and markets are organized and how this organization affects the economy from the viewpoint of social welfare (i.e., maximizing the well-being of consumers and producers). An important question that affects this discipline directly relates to managerial economics and the study of the behavior of oligopoly firms. *How, if at all, does industry concentration affect the behavior of firms competing in this industry?*[25] Two approaches to the study of industrial organization and to this question in particular have dominated the field. The first, the **structure-conduct-performance (S-C-P) paradigm**, has been predominant since the 1940s until its critics, proponents of the price theory approach, began to challenge it in

---

[24]Demographics refers to such well-known characteristics as age, gender, income or education level, and ethnic background or origin. Marketing strategists also use the term "psychographics," which segments consumers by values and lifestyles.

[25]Industry organization specialists who believe that industry concentration does in fact affect the behavior of firms proceed to explore the social welfare implications of this behavior. This part of their work is not within the scope of this text.

the 1970s. As so often is the case, the two explanations of industrial behavior were advanced by two of the leading schools of economic thought in the United States, Harvard University and the University of Chicago, respectively. A brief coverage of the two analytical methods follows.[26]

The Structure-Conduct-Performance Paradigm

The causality in this theory runs only in one direction. An industry *structure* affects its *conduct*, which in turn affects its *performance*. Hence the label "structure-conduct-performance." We start with structure that is shaped by the demand and supply conditions prevalent in the industry. For instance, if an industry's product demand tends to be inelastic, then market prices would be higher than if demand were more elastic. Growth patterns and substitutability would also affect structure. On the supply side, technology is an important factor. The existence of economies of scale will determine the number of firms that can operate profitably in the industry.

These basic conditions thus determine industry structure: the number of firms in an industry, conditions of entry, and product differentiation. The structure of the industry then directly influences the way the industry operates—its conduct. Conduct entails primarily pricing strategies and other activities such as advertising, product development, legal tactics, and choice of product, as well as the potential for collusion among companies and mergers, which may further endanger the competitive nature of the industry. "The essence of the structuralist approach is a presumption that industries having fewer (and larger) firms will tend to engage in conduct inconsistent with the norms of perfect competition."[27]

The next step in the S-C-P model is to link conduct to performance. As mentioned, the usual normative standard adopted by economists is the maximization of society's welfare. An industry market with great concentration will fall far short of reaching such a goal. Its performance will be marked by both productive and allocative inefficiencies. Prices will be above marginal costs, the choice and quality of products will not be ideal, technological progress may be slowed down, and ultimately profits will be higher than under competitive circumstances. This high level of profitability arises from the industry's pricing policy and not because of any cost advantages.

We have now connected the three parts of the S-C-P model. A necessary corollary of the results of this approach is that high industry concentration becomes a reason for government intervention proceeding against possible mergers and even trying to deconcentrate industries.

The "New" Theory of Industrial Organization

A competing view of industrial organization is offered by a theory stating that there is no necessary connection between industry structure and performance that uniquely leads to maximum social welfare. It argues that the study of industry organization should use and apply microeconomic price theory. Thus, for instance, higher profit levels in more concentrated industries may be caused by economic efficiencies rather than pricing strategies. In other words, a small number of efficient firms can survive better than a larger number of firms that cannot take advantage of economies of scale. In fact, certain industries may not be able to support many firms on an acceptable profit level. Another argument involves the potential for collusion

---

[26]The following discussion is based on two texts on industrial organization: Dennis W. Carlton and Jeffrey M. Perloff, *Modern Industrial Organization*, 2d ed., New York: HarperCollins, 1994; and William E. Shugart II, *The Organization of Industry*, Homewood, IL: Irwin, 1990.

[27]Shugart, *The Organization of Industry*, p. 9.

in concentrated industries. George Stigler concluded that although industry concentration makes collusion more likely, collusive agreements (cartels) are inherently unstable because they are expensive to enforce and because participants have incentives to cheat.[28]

A large number of studies examining the links between industry concentration and profits have been produced. The results, particularly in the earlier studies, appear to point to direct correlation between concentration and profit levels. However, the evidence is at best rather weak. Many later studies cast doubt on the earlier results, showing that what appeared to be a link between concentration and profits was actually due to other industry characteristics and often disappeared over the long run. For instance, one researcher found that cost reductions were significantly greater in increasingly concentrated industries, and even though price reductions to consumers were less than cost savings realized, consumers benefited from considerable price advantages.[29]

Another, more recent, addition to the previous discussion and the notion that industry profits are not necessarily a function of industry structure is Baumol's theory of "contestable markets."[30] The idea is that performance by firms is ultimately influenced not by the presence of competition, but by the threat of potential competition. Contestability comes in several forms. An extreme case is perfect contestability, which implies that entry by new firms is free and exit is costless. In such cases, existing firms will not be able to sell their product at prices exceeding marginal costs. Of course, in industries where entry and exit are difficult and costly, such competitive threat would not be present. Still, if outsiders have access to the industry's technology and if assets are nonspecialized so their costs can be recouped upon exit, such a competitive threat is powerful.

The debate between the advocates of the S-C-P paradigm and the price theory approach has now continued for many years and neither side has gained clear dominance. Market structure is still very important, particularly from a public policy point of view. But other factors must also be considered in deciding what are the important influences affecting social welfare.

Strategy and the Ideas of Michael Porter

In the late 1970s, Michael Porter, an economics professor from the Harvard Business School, began publishing articles on strategy that would have a profound impact on the study of this subject. As with all innovative ideas, his work has been subject to counterarguments and criticism over the years.[31] Nevertheless, many of the terms and concepts that he introduced have become a part of the everyday vocabulary of the business strategist. In our discussion of strategy, we chose to limit coverage to his ideas about strategy because they are most directly related to the study of the economics of the firm and industry economics.

Porter did not dwell on theoretical issues about the links between industry structure, business conduct, and performance and whether a concentrated industry

---

[28]G. J. Stigler, "A Theory of Oligopoly," *Journal of Political Economy,* 72 (February 1964), pp. 44–61. Another argument made by the S-C-P approach is the monopolistic implications caused by tie-in sales. This point is discussed in chapter 10.

[29]S. Peltzman, "The Gains and Losses from Industrial Concentration," *Journal of Law and Economics,* 20 (October 1977), pp. 229–63.

[30]W. J. Baumol, "Contestable Markets: An Uprising in the Theory of Industry Structure," *American Economic Review,* 72 (March 1982), pp. 1–15.

[31]For a good review of Porter's ideas on strategy together with the developments in the entire field of study during the past 30 years, see Henry Mintzberg, Bruce Ahlstrand, and Joseph Lampel, *Strategy Safari: A Guided Tour Through the Wilds of Strategic Management,* New York: The Free Press, 1998.

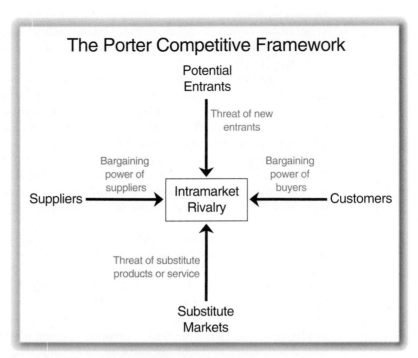

Figure 9.4   The Porter Competitive Framework

structure leads to a misallocation of a country's resources. Instead, he used the concepts of the S-C-P approach to industry economics as the basis for understanding the strategic challenges facing the managers of firms as they seek to maximize their firm's profit. His **Five Forces model**, shown in Figure 9.4, illustrates the various factors that affect the ability of any firm in the industry to earn a profit.

If buyers and suppliers do not exert much market power and there is little threat from either new competitors or the use of substitute products, firms in the industry are likely to earn relatively high returns on their investment. An extreme example of this is the market for operating systems software for personal computers, as long as you think of Microsoft as *the* company in this industry. It is easy to see the influence of the microeconomic theory of the firm on Porter's ideas when you compare the five forces with the characteristics of the different market types shown previously in Figure 8.1. For example, "Entry Barriers" is related to "free entry and exit." If it is easier to enter, firms in the industry are less able to exercise market power, and hence, are less likely to have a relatively high return on investment.

After establishing a model for analyzing the overall profitability of an industry, Porter proceeded to discuss what kind of strategy would enable a specific firm in the industry to earn a return higher than the industry average. This above-average return can be considered akin to "economic" or "above-normal" profit. Porter offers two generic strategies for earning an above-average return on investment. The first is the "differentiation" approach, the second is "cost leadership" approach. There is actually a third approach, in which a firm could exercise either differentiation or cost leadership for a particular market segment rather than for the entire market of potential buyers.

We can also see the influence of the microeconomic theory of the firm in this aspect of Porter's ideas on strategy. The cost leadership approach appears to be based on perfect competition, whereas the differentiation approach can be seen as related to the case of a monopoly or monopolistically competitive market. Recall that in the perfectly competitive market, all firms are price takers. The only way in which a particular firm in this market can earn an economic profit is to keep its cost structure low enough so when $P =$ MC, there is still a positive difference between P and AC. In our view, this is where Porter came up with the idea of the cost leadership approach.

In the case of monopoly or monopolistic competition, product differentiation results in a downward-sloping demand and an MR curve that lies below this demand line. Following the MR $=$ MC rule enables a firm to set a price on the demand line that is higher than its AC, assuming of course the demand curve itself is high enough to allow this to happen. The extreme case of this was shown in the example of pure monopoly. Not only is the product different, but it is also unique. In the case of monopolistic competition, the above-normal profit enjoyed by the differentiating firm may be reduced as the entry of firms in the long run shift a firm's demand curve to the left. But Porter would say that those firms that have a solid differentiation strategy would not be affected by the new entrants as much as those who allow their products to be "commoditized."

Concluding Remarks on the Linkages between Managerial Economics and Strategy

The fundamental link between managerial economics and strategy is the decision regarding the allocation of a company's scarce resources. In this chapter, we also show how the tools of strategic analysis such as Porter's "Five Forces" model and his "differentiation versus cost leadership" approach are linked to the economic study of industrial organization and the economic models of a firm's behavior in different market settings. Interested readers can find a thorough discussion of these and many other examples of the linkages between economics and strategy in the textbooks on the subject previously cited.[32]

GLOBAL APPLICATION: THE WORLD'S MARKET FOR BEER[33]

The market for beer is a good example of how difficult it is to actually label a particular industry using any of the four basic types of economic markets. At the least, we can say that the market for beer is neither pure monopoly nor perfect competition. But to say it is monopolistic competition or oligopoly depends on whether we are looking at the market from the standpoint of a country, a region, a type (e.g., regular vs. light, mass market vs. craft-brewed, domestic vs. imported), or a brand. To complicate the issue further, as you know each beer company can produce or own and distribute many different brands. For example, a visit to the Web site of Anheuser Busch, the leading brewer in the United States, reveals that the company produces or distributes dozens of different brands including its top sellers Budweiser, Bud Light, and Michelob. A leading brewer of craft beer, the Boston Beer Company, produces many other types of beer in addition to its flagship Samuel Adams brand.

In the U.S. market, all of the beer brands and types produced by perennial market leader Anheuser Busch hold about 50 percent market share. The second two

---

[32]See Oster and Besank et al.

[33]This section is based on the following sources: Anne Nugent, "The Global Beer Market: A World of Two Halves," *Euromonitor,* February 25, 2005; Julie Bradford, "Just About Everyone Agrees That the Beer Industry Is Having Problems, But the Troubles Are More Frustrating Than They Are Fatal," *Beverage Dynamics,* September 1, 2005; and "The Global Battle of the Bottled Beer," *Grocer,* July 15, 2006.

companies, SABMiller and Molsen Coors, have a combined market share of around 30 percent. The remaining share comprises second-tier brewers such as Stroh's Brewery, craft brewers such as the Boston Beer Company, and imports such as Corona (which in fact is 50 percent owned by Anheuser Busch). Leading imports include Heineken (based in the Netherlands) and Stella Artois (owned by the global giant InBev). So is the U.S. market an oligopoly? Just looking at the market share held by the top three companies, the answer would seem to be yes.

However, based on pricing power, the answer would seem to be more like monopolistic competition. This is because the U.S. market for beer is very much a mature one. The growth rate in recent years was less than 1 percent and demand for mass market regular beer has been falling about 2 percent per year. Only the increase in consumption of craft and imported beers has kept overall market sales from falling. And as a result of the fall in the demand for mass market brands, even the leading manufacturers such as Anheuser Busch have had to drop their prices. The only way that Anheuser Busch can offset this decline in price is to try to sell more of the higher profit margin imports or craft-brewed beer. Another way that this U.S.-based company can offset the stagnating U.S. beer market is to expand globally. But in this respect, it has been outdone in recent years by two leading global companies based in Europe, Heineken and InBev, and a third global player from South Africa, South African Breweries (SAB), now known as SABMiller.

The Heineken brand is probably well known to American consumers because it is one of the leading imported beers. InBev is the result of the merger of Interbrew, a Belgian company, and AmBev, a Brazilian company. Their popular brands include Stella Artois and Brahma. In 2003, SAB made the headlines by buying Miller Brewing from Philip Morris. At the time, Miller was the third largest beer company in the United States. It still is. The fourth largest, Coors, recently merged with the Canadian company Molsen. The new company is now called Molsen Coors Brewing Company.

All of the leading global giants are trying to expand by acquisition. As they grow, they hope to use the increasing power of economies of scale and scope to reduce their unit cost of production. Also their expansions are typically in areas of the world such as Brazil, China, Russia, and Central Europe, where beer sales are still expanding at rates 3–4 percentage points above the mature markets in the United States and Western Europe. Several recent acquisitions made at the time this text was being prepared illustrate this global trend.

In 2007, SABMiller and Molsen Coors Brewing merged their U.S. units and also bought Royal Grolsch, a Dutch company that is Heineken's closest rival in the Netherlands. In January 2008, Heineken and Carlsberg (a Danish company) announced that they had agreed to buy the largest brewery in the United Kingdom, Scottish & Newcastle, for $15.4 billion. The U.K. brewer is best known for brands such as Foster's and Kronenbourg 1664. Among the key reasons for this acquisition is that Heineken will gain access to Britain's cider market and Carlsberg will gain control of Scottish & Newcastle's holding of the Russian brewer, Baltic Beverages. The cider market in Britain is growing at double-digit rates, and Russia's beer market is expected to grow 5 percent in 2008.[34]

There are still many hundreds of breweries around the world. So it is safe to say that the global market can still be considered monopolistically competitive. However, at the rate that global acquisitions and mergers are being carried out, perhaps even the global market may become more like an oligopoly.

---

[34]Julia Werdigier, "Scottish & Newcastle Agrees to Be Bought and Split," *New York Times,* January 20, 2008.

The Solution

A few weeks later Frank again met with Nicole. He recommended selling Waterpure for $1.00 instead of the $1.10 suggested by the MR = MC analysis. His focus group studies showed that people paid more attention to a 25-cent than a 15-cent difference. The average price of the major national brands was $1.25.

"I believe the 25-cent difference will be really noticeable to the consumer," Frank explained. "After all, we're new entrants into the market and we can use this lower price to attract customers away from the competition. At least they'll be more inclined to give our product a try. But we're not going to sell this product as a private label or discount product. According to your marketing plan, Nicole, we're going to be putting a lot of money into advertising to build brand awareness among consumers."

"That's just it, Frank, we are in fact going to be positioning Waterpure as a premium product, as good as any other national brand, if not better," Nicole responded. "If we're going to position our product in this way, we have got to use our price in support of this. If we set the price at $1.00 and then decide to raise it to $1.25 after it gains customer acceptance, they may not go along with this increase. We have to use promotion and advertising more than price to build our brand in the marketplace. Why don't we just match the competition's $1.25?"

"It makes sense to me," Frank answered. "The one thing we don't want to do is to trigger a price war. If any of our competitors with established brands decides to match or even beat our lower price, then the whole industry might suffer. As it now stands, I guess we're all doing very well if we can get people to pay more than a dollar for a bottle of water."

"Hey, now I've really got you thinking like a marketing person, Frank. Remember, demand is based on the customer's *perception* of value and not the intrinsic value of the product. If we can use advertising to support the price of $1.25, that's going to be the key to our success. Besides, you're right about a price war—I don't even want to think about starting a price war with the likes of Nestlé, Pepsi, and Coke."*

---

*Pepsi's main product is Aquafina, a tap water that is purified with triple filtration and a process known as "reverse osmosis." Nestlé's leading bottled brands are Perrier, Deer Park, Poland Spring, and Calistoga. Coca-Cola's brand is Dasani. It is also a major distributor of branded bottle water.

SUMMARY

This chapter examines the pricing and output decisions faced by firms in monopolistic competition and oligopoly. Oligopoly firms have a more challenging task because of mutual interdependence. However, if oligopoly firms are of sufficient size or are very effective in differentiating their products, they may not have as much competition from new market entrants as those firms operating in monopolistic competition. In both types of markets, non-price decisions are an important part of the competitive environment. A critical part of the success of a firm's operations in imperfectly competitive markets is the development (as well as implementation) of an effective business strategy. Therefore, the final sections of this chapter examined the important elements of business strategy and their linkages to the terms and concepts covered in managerial economics.

IMPORTANT CONCEPTS

Five Forces model: Model developed by Michael Porter that shows the key factors that affect the ability of a firm to earn an economic profit: potential entrants, bargaining power of suppliers, bargaining power of buyers, threat of substitute products or services, and intramarket rivalry. Also referred to as the Porter Competitive Framework. (p. 376)

Kinked demand: A theoretical construction that attempts to explain price rigidities in oligopolistic markets. (p. 364)

Monopolistic competition: A market distinguished from perfect competition in that each seller attempts to differentiate its product from those of its competitors (e.g., in terms of location, efficiency of service, advertising, or promotion).

Good examples of this type of market can be found in small businesses, particularly those in the retail trade. (p. 360)

Mutual interdependence: A situation in which each firm in the market sets a price based on its costs, price elasticity, *and* anticipated reaction of its competitors. This type of pricing situation prevails in oligopolistic markets. (p. 359)

Oligopoly: A market in which there is a small number of relatively large sellers. Pricing in this type of market is characterized by mutual interdependence among the sellers. Products may either be standardized or differentiated. (p. 362)

Price leader: One company in an oligopolistic industry establishes the price, and the other companies follow. Two types of price leadership, barometric and dominant, are discussed in chapter 10. (p. 362)

Strategy: The means by which an organization uses its scarce resources to relate to the competitive environment in a manner that is expected to achieve superior business performance over the long run. (p. 372)

Structure-conduct-performance (S-C-P) paradigm: An approach to studying industrial economics that states that an industry's structure determines an industry's conduct, which in turn affects the industry's performance. The key factors that shape industry structure are the number of firms in the industry, the conditions of entry and exit, and product differentiation. (p. 373)

QUESTIONS

1. Explain the key difference between perfect competition and monopolistic competition.
2. Assume firms in the short run are earning above-normal profits. Explain what will happen to these profits in the long run for the following markets:
   a. Pure monopoly
   b. Oligopoly
   c. Monopolistic competition
   d. Perfect competition
3. In certain industries, firms buy their most important inputs in markets that are close to perfectly competitive and sell their output in imperfectly competitive markets. Cite as many examples as you can of these types of businesses. Explain why the profits of such firms tend to increase when there is an excess supply of the inputs they use in their production process.
4. In the short run, firms that seek to maximize their market share will tend to charge a lower price for their products than firms that seek to maximize their profit. Do you agree with this statement? Explain.
5. Explain why it is sometimes difficult to apply the MR = MC rule in actual business situations.
6. Define *mutual interdependence*.
7. Why do oligopolists often rely on a price leader to raise the market price of a product?
8. How does one determine whether a market is oligopolistic? Is it important for managers to recognize the existence of oligopolistic competitors in the markets in which their companies operate? Explain.
9. In the following list are a number of well-known companies and the products that they sell. Which of the four types of markets (perfect competition, monopoly, monopolistic competition, and oligopoly) best characterizes the markets in which they compete? Explain why.
   a. McDonald's—hamburgers
   b. Exxon Mobil—gasoline
   c. Dell—personal computers
   d. Heinz—ketchup
   e. Procter & Gamble—disposable diapers
   f. Kodak—photographic film
   g. Starbucks—gourmet coffee
   h. Domino's—pizza
   i. Intel—computer chip for the PC

10. Briefly explain the structure-conduct-performance approach to the study of industrial economics.
11. Compare and contrast Porter's Five Forces model with the four basic types of markets first described in chapter 8 in the section "Market Structure."
12. In 2002, Philip Morris sold its Miller Brewing Division to South African Breweries.
    a. What impact do you think this transaction had on the market structure of the beer industry in the United States? In world markets? Explain.
    b. Using the economic concepts presented in chapters 7, 8 and 9, discuss possible reasons why both parties agreed to this transaction.

PROBLEMS

1. A group of five students has decided to form a company to publish a guide to eating establishments located in the vicinity of all major college and university campuses in the state. In planning for an initial publication of 6,000 copies, they estimated the cost of producing this book to be as follows:

Paper	$12,000
Research	2,000
Graphics	5,000
Reproduction services	8,000
Miscellaneous	5,000
Personal computer	2,000
Desktop publishing software	500
Overhead	5,500
Binding	3,000
Shipping	2,000

By engaging in this business, the students realized that they would have to give up their summer jobs. Each student made an average of $4,000 per summer. However, they believed they could keep expenses down by doing much of the research for the book by themselves with no immediate compensation.

They decided to set the retail price of the book at $12.50 per copy. Allowing for the 20 percent discount that retail stores in their state generally required, the students anticipated a per-unit revenue of about $10.00. The director of the campus bookstore advised them that their retail price was far too high, and that a price of about $8.75 would be more reasonable for a publication of this kind.

One of the students, who was a math and statistics major, asked the bookstore manager to provide her with historical data on sales and prices of similar books. From these data, she estimated the demand for books of this kind to be

$$Q = 18,500 - 1,000P$$

where Q = Number of books sold per year
   P = Retail price of the books

a. Construct a numerical table for the retail demand curve, and plot the numbers on a graph. Calculate the elasticity of demand for the interval between $12.50 and $8.00.
b. Do you think the students should follow the store manager's advice and price their book at $8.75? Explain. If you do not agree with this price, what would be the optimal price of the book? Explain.
c. Assuming the students decide to charge the optimal price, do you think they should proceed with this venture? Explain.
d. Assuming the student's demand equation is accurate, offer some possible reasons why the bookstore manager would want to sell the book at the lower price of $8.75.

2. Use the same data presented in problem 1 to answer the following questions:
   a. Explain the impact on the optimal price of designating the "miscellaneous" cost item as fixed versus variable. (Hint: Do the pricing analysis assuming miscellaneous is a fixed cost and compare it with an analysis that assumes it is a variable cost.)
   b. Under what circumstances do you think the average variable cost would *increase* (as is generally expected in the economic analysis of cost)? Do you think the law of diminishing returns would play a role in increasing AVC? Explain.
   c. Under what circumstances do you think the average variable cost would *decrease?* Explain.

3. A firm in an oligopolistic industry has identified two sets of demand curves. If the firm is the only one that changes prices (i.e., other firms do not follow), its demand curve takes the form $Q = 82 - 8P$. If, however, it is expected that competitors will follow the price actions of the firm, then the demand curve is of the form $Q = 44 - 3P$.
   a. Develop demand schedules for each alternative, and draw them on a graph.
   b. Calculate marginal revenue curves for each.
   c. If the present price and quantity position for the firm is located at the intersection of the two demand curves, and competitors follow any price decrease but do not follow a price increase, show the demand curve relevant to the firm.
   d. Draw the appropriate marginal revenue curve.
   e. Show the range over which a marginal cost curve could rise or fall without affecting the price the firm charges.

4. Indicate whether each of the following statements is true or false, and explain why.
   a. A competitive firm that is incurring a loss should immediately cease operations.
   b. A pure monopoly does not have to worry about suffering losses because it has the power to set its prices at any level it desires.
   c. In the long run, firms operating in perfect competition and monopolistic competition will tend to earn normal profits.
   d. Assuming a linear demand curve, a firm that wants to maximize its revenue will charge a lower price than a firm that wants to maximize its profits.
   e. In an oligopoly, the firm that has the largest market share will also be the price leader.
   f. The demand curve facing a firm in a monopolistically competitive market is more elastic than one facing a pure monopoly.

5. A phenomenon in the retail merchandising of food and clothing in the United States and the United Kingdom is the growing popularity of private-label (also called store-brand) products. These products are priced at a lower level than the premium national brands. Use the concepts of price elasticity and relevant cost to explain the profitability of these products from the point of view of
   a. The retail stores that sell these private-label products.
   b. The manufacturers of these private-label products.
   If you were the manager of a national premium brand, what would you do to fight the growing competition of private labels?

6. Suppose three firms face the same total market demand for their product. This demand is

P	Q
$80	20,000
70	25,000
60	30,000
50	35,000

Suppose further that all three firms are selling their product for $60 and each has about one-third of the total market. One of the firms, in an attempt to gain market share at the expense of the others, drops its price to $50. The other two quickly follow suit.
   a. What impact would this move have on the profits of all three firms? Explain your reasoning.

b. Would these firms have been better off in terms of profit if they all had raised the price to $70? Explain.

7. A firm has the following short-run demand and cost schedule for a particular product:

$$Q = 200 - 5P$$
$$TC = 400 + 4Q$$

a. At what price should this firm sell its product?
b. If this is a monopolistically competitive firm, what do you think would start to happen in the long run? Explain.
c. Suppose in the long run, the demand shifted to $Q = 100 - 5P$. What should the firm do? Explain.

8. Suppose there are three firms with the same *individual* demand function. This function is $Q = 1,000 - 40P$. Suppose each firm has a different cost function. These functions are:

Firm 1: $4,000 + 5Q$
Firm 2: $3,000 + 5Q$
Firm 3: $3,000 + 7Q$

a. What price should each firm charge if it wants to maximize its profit (or minimize its loss)?
b. Explain why the answer to the preceding question indicates that two of the firms should charge the same price and the third should charge a higher price.
c. Which firms will be most vulnerable to a price war? Explain.

9. Professor Michael Porter's generic strategy options for competing are the differentiation approach and the cost leadership approach. The first involves competing by having a better product and the second by having a lower cost than one's competitors. Relate this strategy to the monopolistically competitive model presented in this chapter. In particular, use the diagram in Figure 9.1 to explain the rationale for Porter's generic strategies.

Special Pricing Practices

Learning Objectives

Upon completion of this chapter, readers should be able to:

■ Analyze cartel pricing.

■ Illustrate price leadership.

■ Understand price discrimination, and explain how it affects production and prices.

■ Distinguish between marginal pricing and "cost-plus" pricing.

■ Discuss the various types of multiproduct pricing.

■ Explain the meaning of "transfer pricing," and explain how a company should price products that pass from one operating division to another.

The Situation

One of the most difficult challenges in the food and beverage industries is the establishment of effective channels of distribution. Many food-processing and beverage companies rely on food brokers to sell their products to retail outlets such as supermarkets and grocery stores. In the case of bottled water, the product is shipped from the bottling plants to the individual retail establishments. Obviously, there must first be a willingness on the part of these retail businesses to carry a particular product line.

The task of establishing the relationship between Global Foods, Inc., and the retail stores was given to Rebecca James, assistant vice president of marketing of the beverage division. Because the product, Waterpure, was so new, she found considerable resistance among the major supermarket chains to carrying Global's line of bottled water. Thus far, she had been able to sell relatively small volumes to smaller grocery stores, convenience stores, delicatessens, and sandwich shops. Then she learned that a large catering company that provided food service in major airports all across the United States wanted to carry an additional line of bottled water. This firm had put out a request for bids to all the major beverage companies and also to Global Foods. After all, Global had an established reputation in the food business.

Rebecca was eager to land this major account. But she also realized that her bid would have to be considerably lower than that offered to her present customers. However, this lower price would be more than made up by the potential volume of sales, as well as by the creation of a base from which to further penetrate the market for bottled water. But she was not quite sure how to decide on the price she should recommend. She decided to consult with Philip Olds, an executive in the company's foods service division. Philip had considerable experience in preparing bids for large customer contracts.

INTRODUCTION

In chapters 8 and 9, we discuss output and pricing decisions under different market arrangements. We now continue this discussion and apply our knowledge to pricing decisions made in specific situations. We are also confronted by some complications. Whereas we have previously assumed a firm produces only one product, we now have to allow for the pricing of several products simultaneously. The situations we encounter in this chapter usually occur under imperfectly competitive conditions.

CARTEL ARRANGEMENTS

Competition is a very tough taskmaster. To survive in competition in the long run, a company must operate at its most efficient (minimum) cost point, and it will earn no more than a normal return. Thus there is always an incentive for a company to try to become more powerful than its competitors—in the extreme, to become a monopolist. In an oligopolistic type of industry, where there are several powerful firms, it would probably be impossible for one firm to eliminate all the others. So, to reap the benefits of a monopoly (i.e., higher profits, stable market shares and prices, and the general creation of a more certain and less competitive environment), it may be advisable for companies in the industry to act together as if they were a monopoly. In other words, they all agree to cooperate with one another; they form a **cartel**. Cartel arrangements may be tacit, but in most cases some sort of formal agreement is reached. The motives for cartelization have been recognized for many years. Indeed, an early recognition can be found in a passage in Adam Smith's famous book: "People of the same trade seldom meet together, even for merriment and diversion, but the conversation ends in a conspiracy against the public, or in some contrivance to raise prices."[1]

Cartels were made illegal in the United States with the passage of the Sherman Anti-Trust Act of 1890. Thus, most "official" cartels are found in countries other than the United States. Probably the most famous cartel in existence today is the Organization of Petroleum Exporting Countries (OPEC). But there are others, such as the IATA (International Air Transport Association), to which U.S. airlines can belong. Collusive agreements have also existed in the United States. One of the most famous cases of price and market share fixing was in the electrical industry and involved General Electric, Westinghouse, and other large corporations. The case was tried and concluded in 1961 and resulted in prison sentences for several executives and large fines. This case, and other more recent ones are described briefly following a discussion of the characteristics and effects of cartels.

Cartels may not flourish in all oligopolistic markets. Following are some of the conditions that influence the formation of cartels.

1. The existence of a small number of large firms facilitates the policing of a collusive agreement.
2. Geographic proximity of the firms is favorable.
3. Homogeneity of the product makes it impossible for cartel participants to cheat on one another by emphasizing product differences.
4. The role of general business conditions presents somewhat contradictory arguments. Cartels are often established during depressed industry conditions, when companies attempt to forestall what they consider to be ruinous price cutting. However, it also appears that cartels disintegrate as demand for the product falls, and each member

---

[1]Adam Smith, *An Inquiry into the Nature and Causes of the Wealth of Nations,* New York: Modern Library, 1937, p. 128.

thinks it can do better outside the cartel. The cartel may then reestablish itself during the recovery period. Thus cartels can form or fall apart during either phase of the business cycle.[2]

5. Entry into the industry must be difficult. The case of OPEC is a good example. It is impossible for countries that do not possess the basic resource to begin petroleum production and compete for monopoly profits.

6. If cost conditions for the cartel members are similar and profitability thus will not differ greatly among members, cartels will be easier to maintain. Product homogeneity, mentioned earlier, will contribute to cost uniformity.

The ideal cartel will be powerful enough to establish monopoly prices and earn maximum monopoly profits for all the members combined. This situation is illustrated in Figure 10.1. For simplicity, assume there are only two firms in this oligopolistic industry. The total industry demand curve is shown in Figure 10.1c. The marginal revenue curve is constructed for this demand curve in the usual manner. Each of the two competitors (illustrated in Figures 10.1a and b) has its respective average total cost and marginal cost curves, which can differ.

The two individual marginal cost curves are then added horizontally, and the result is plotted on the industry graph (MC_T). Industry output will take place where MC_T equals the industry marginal revenue, and the price charged will be found by drawing a vertical line to the demand curve (point A). This is, of course, the classic monopoly situation, and monopoly profits will be maximized at this point.

The next step is to establish how much each of the two companies will sell at this price. For the entire industry output to be sold, each company will sell that output

Figure 10.1 The Ideal Cartel

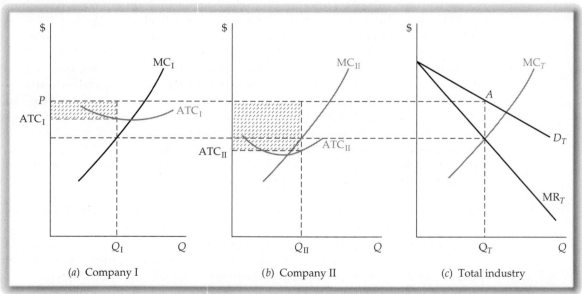

(a) Company I   (b) Company II   (c) Total industry

[2]A very cogent description of this phenomenon can be found in George J. Stigler, *The Theory of Price*, New York: Macmillan, 1949, pp. 274–75. Stigler also puts forward the idea that, regardless of the level of business activity, government action in support of such collusion is an important factor in a cartel's success. An important example is the U.S. National Recovery Act (NRA) of the 1930s, later declared unconstitutional by the Supreme Court.

corresponding to the point at which a horizontal line drawn from the $MC_T = MR_T$ intersection on the industry graph crosses the marginal cost curve of each of the two firms. It can be seen that each firm will produce different quantities and achieve different profits, depending on the level of the average total cost curve at the point of production. Generally, the lower-cost company will be the more profitable one (profits for the two companies are shown by the hatched areas in Figure 10.1). This result, although maximizing combined profits, may also be one of the reasons for the subversion of cartels. A very efficient company with low average costs, and most likely with excess capacity under cartel conditions, may find it profitable to cheat by offering its product at a lower price and capturing a larger share of the total business.

Such a cartel may be unstable. Unless strictly enforced, cartels will have a tendency to break down. Secret price cuts may be extremely profitable because (if the product is undifferentiated) the demand curve for an individual firm in a cartel will be quite elastic. Cartel subversion often occurs during slumps in demand because individual members will be looking to increase their share to avoid significant quantity decreases.

It must also be remembered that collusion is costly. First, there is the cost of forming the cartel. Second, there is a cost of monitoring the actions of the cartel members and of enforcing the rules to minimize cheating. There is also the potential cost of punishment by authorities. Thus, in the end, cartelization may not necessarily be profitable. In short, the additional revenues obtained by cartel members due to collusion must exceed the costs just described. We can, therefore, state that although profit maximization is the incentive that leads to collusion, it may also be the cause of a cartel's breakdown.

Cartels often have agreements specifying the market share of each participant. Such allotments may be based on history, or they can be arranged to give each member a certain geographic area. Collusion can also exist in much more informal ways. Thus, physicians within a geographic area coincidentally charge similar fees for their services. Trade associations are often suspected of collecting and conveying information that will lead to the fixing of prices.

Cases of Price Fixing by Cartels

A classic case of price fixing and market sharing ended in February 1961 in a Philadelphia court, when seven executives of General Electric, Westinghouse, and other companies were sent to prison and fined; twenty-three others were given suspended sentences and fined; and twenty-nine companies were fined a total of approximately $2 million. Starting shortly after World War II, this conspiracy involved a number of heavy electrical equipment products, such as switching gears, circuit breakers, transformers, and turbine engines. The companies involved pleaded guilty and no contest to the federal indictments.

The story of these collusive practices reads like a mystery story.[3] There were meetings in hotel rooms during conventions of the National Electric Manufacturers Association. There were hotel meetings at various locations in which the participants did not register under their company affiliations and recorded trips to other locations in their expense accounts. There were code numbers given to each company. There were telephone calls at the participants' homes and even a conspiratorial round of golf.

---

[3]The description of this case has been obtained from two articles in *Fortune* (April 1961, pp. 132–37 ff, and May 1961, pp. 161–64 ff), and from the *Wall Street Journal*, January 10 and 12, 1962.

A more recent case is that of the Archer Daniels Midland Company (ADM), a large agricultural business with annual revenues of approximately $31 billion in 2003. In October 1996, ADM pled guilty to price fixing of two of its products, lysine, a feed supplement, and citric acid, a food additive. Four Asian firms were implicated in the lysine conspiracy, and four European companies were involved in the citric acid case. The price fixing and division of markets was arranged in a series of secret meetings in many locations, including Mexico City, Paris, Tokyo, and Atlanta. ADM was fined a total of $100 million, and in addition paid approximately $90 million to settle customer and stockholder suits.

Two years later, in September 1998, three ADM executives were convicted of participating in the case. One of them was the former vice chairman, Michael Andreas, son of ADM's chief executive officer and his likely successor. He was sentenced to 2 years in prison and assessed a $350,000 fine.[4]

There is an additional chapter to the saga of Archer Daniels Midland. In 1995, the U.S. Department of Justice began investigating another anticompetitive pricing action involving ADM, Cargill, and two other companies. This investigation concerned the pricing of fructose corn syrup. The plaintiffs comprised some 2,000 companies, including Coca-Cola and PepsiCo. Although the other three companies had settled with the plaintiffs previously (for a total of $31 million), the case was finally closed in June 2004, when ADM agreed to settle by paying $400 million.[5]

In 1997, the U.S. Department of Justice began to investigate possible collusion in setting buying and selling commissions by two leading art auction houses. The two companies, Sotheby's and Christie's, together controlled 90 to 95 percent of the art auction market. Although Sotheby's and Christie's appeared to be active competitors in soliciting business, in 1992 they raised their buyers' commissions to identical rates within 6 weeks of one another. Then in 1995 they took similar action on sellers' commissions, again within 6 weeks of one another. In January 2000, Christie's CEO turned over a large number of documents to the Department of Justice and agreed to cooperate with the department; in return, he and his firm were granted immunity from prosecution. In February 2001, a federal judge accepted Sotheby's guilty plea to conspiracy to fix prices and fined the company $45 million. During the same month, a $512 million class-action suit settlement was reached between the two auction houses and some 130,000 buyers and sellers. In addition, Sotheby's settled with a group of shareholders who claimed that the auction house had misled them about the size of their earnings; the amount was $70 million.

In October 2000, the former chief executive officer of Sotheby's, Diana D. Brooks, pled guilty to conspiracy to violate antitrust laws and agreed to cooperate with federal authorities. In May 2001, a federal grand jury indicted both former chairmen, A. Alfred Taubman of Sotheby's and Sir Anthony J. Tennant of Christie's, for collusion. Mr. Taubman was found guilty by a jury in December 2001. He was sentenced to 1 year and 1 day in prison and fined $7.5 million in April 2002. Mr. Tennant did not stand trial; he did not leave Britain, his home, and the United States cannot extradite him under

[4]N. Millman, "$100 Million Fine in ADM Guilty Plea," *Chicago Tribune*, October 16, 1996; G. Burns, "Three ADM Execs Found Guilty," *Chicago Tribune*, September 17, 1998; S. Kilman, "Jury Convicts Ex-Executives in ADM Case," *Wall Street Journal*, September 18, 1998; S. Kilman, "Ex-Officials of ADM Given 2 Years in Jail," *Wall Street Journal*, July 12, 1999; Julie Forster, "A Different Kind of Andreas at ADM," *BusinessWeek*, July 9, 2001, pp. 62–64.
[5]Kurt Eichenwald, "Archer Daniels Settles Price-Fixing Case," *New York Times*, June 19, 2004.

British law. Ms. Brooks received no prison term, but was sentenced to home detention, probation, community service, and a fine of $350,000.[6]

In 1999, two large drug companies, Roche Holding AG and BASF AG, pled guilty in a case brought by the U.S. Justice Department and were fined $500 million and $225 million, respectively. The fine incurred by Roche was reported to be the largest ever imposed in an antitrust case. The two companies were accused of fixing the prices of a large array of vitamins. In addition, a Roche executive was fined $100,000 and sentenced to 4 months in prison. In succeeding years, the companies also paid another $1 billion in European fines and more than $1 billion to settle civil lawsuits.[7]

A 10-year-old price-fixing case was brought to an end in July 2004, when De Beers SA, the large diamond company, pled guilty and was fined $10 million. This case, which began in 1994, also involved General Electric; however, that company was acquitted some years ago. De Beers admitted conspiring to fix prices in the industrial diamond market in 1991 and 1992. This resolution paved the way for De Beers to reenter the U.S. market directly. It had been barred from doing so and dealt in the United States only through intermediaries. Separately, the company had previously settled a civil case totaling $26 million.[8] Since then, the diamond industry has been transformed. DeBeers has "loosened its grip, and a host of smaller producers are emerging." In the early 1990s, DeBeers produced 45 percent of the world's rough diamonds and sold about 80 percent of the total supply. Today, those numbers are 40 percent and 45 percent, respectively. "The diamond trade is starting to look more like any other ordinary industry."[9]

A DRAM price-fixing conspiracy composed of Korean, Japanese, and German companies was fined more than $730 million in a U.S. court. The companies raised and stabilized prices of DRAM sold to certain OEMs in the United States from 2001 to 2002. The fines were levied from 2004 to 2007. Several executives of Samsung Electronics Co., Ltd. were given prison sentences and fines.[10]

PRICE LEADERSHIP

When collusive arrangements are not easily achieved, another type of pricing practice may occur under oligopolistic market conditions. This is the practice of **price leadership**, in which there is no formal or tacit agreement among the oligopolists to keep prices at the same level or change them by the same amount. However, when a price movement is initiated by one of the firms, others will follow. Examples of such practices abound.

---

[6]Stories about this case appeared frequently in *Wall Street Journal* during the period 2000 to 2001. A few among these were Laurie P. Cohen and Alexandra Peers, "Christie's Davidge Contacted Sotheby's on Pricing," March 20, 2000; Kathy Kranhold, "Judge Backs Guilty Plea from Sotheby's," February 5, 2001; Kathy Kranhold, "Sotheby's $70 Million Settlement of Shareholder Suit Is Approved," February 20, 2001; Kathryn Kranhold, "Sotheby's, Christie's Settlement Is Approved by Judge in New York," February 23, 2001; Kathryn Kranhold, "Ex-Chiefs of Sotheby's, Christie's Indicted," May 3, 2001; Kathryn Kranhold, "Sotheby's Chief Is Convicted of Price-Fixing," December 6, 2001; Jerry Markon, "Sotheby's Taubman is Sentenced to Jail Time, Fined $7.5 Million," April 23, 2002. Also see Devin Leonard, "First: Feud? What Feud?" *Fortune Magazine*, March 20, 2000, p. 36, and Joshua Chaffin, "Ex-Sotheby's Chief Avoids Prison for Price-fixing Role," *Financial Times*, April 30, 2002. A book published in 2004 tells the story of this case: Christopher Mason, *The Art of the Steal: Inside the Sotheby's-Christie's Auction Scandal*, New York, Putnam, 2004.
[7]"Roche and BASF Fined Heavily for Vitamin Price-Fixing in the USA," *Nutraceuticals International*, June 1, 1999; Edward Iwata, "High Court Rebuffs Foreign Price-Fixing Suits," *USA Today*, June 15, 2004; John R. Wilke, "Price-Fixing Investigations Sweep Chemical Industries," *Wall Street Journal*, June 22, 2004.
[8]Mark Williams, "De Beers Pleads Guilty to Price-Fixing Charges," *Deseret Morning News*, July 14, 2004; Margaret Webb Pressler, "De Beers Pleads to Price-Fixing; Firm Pays $10 million, Can Fully Reenter U.S.," *Washington Post*, July 14, 2004; John Reed, "De Beers Poised for U.S. Return," *Financial Times*, August 10, 2004.
[9]"Changing Facets," *The Economist*, February 24, 2007.
[10]Colleen Taylor, "Sixth Samsung Exec Headed for Jail for DRAM Price-Fixing," *Electronic News*, Vol. 53, Issue 18, April 30, 2007, p. 8.

You may have observed that at two or more gasoline stations at the same intersection, prices for each grade of gasoline are either identical or almost the same most of the time. Another example is automobile companies, which in recent years have come up with rebate programs. Surely you have seen advertisements offering "$1,000 cash or 3.9 percent financing." One company is usually the first to announce such a program; the others follow in short order. Another case is IBM. For many years, in the 1950s and 1960s, IBM was considered to be the price leader in the computer industry. In fact, IBM's prices were considered to form an "umbrella" for industry pricing. It was said that IBM would establish a price, and because it was the most powerful and preferred manufacturer and thus could command a higher price (an umbrella over the others), its competitors would tend to set their prices at some slightly lower level for similar equipment.

We just described two major variants of the price leadership phenomenon: barometric and dominant price leadership.

Barometric Price Leadership

There may not be a firm that dominates all the others and sets the price each time. One firm in the industry—and it does not always have to be the same one—will initiate a price change in response to economic conditions, and the other firms may or may not follow the leader. If the **barometric price leadership** model has misjudged the economic forces, the other companies may not change their prices or may effect changes of a different, possibly lesser, magnitude. If the firm has correctly gauged the sentiment of the industry, all the firms will settle in comfortably at the new price level. But if this does not happen, the price leader may have to retract the price change, or a series of iterations may be set in motion until a new price level, agreeable to all, is reached. Such a pattern of price changes has been observed in many industries, including automobiles, steel, and paper.

In more recent years, the airline industry has furnished several examples of price leadership that was not followed. An almost bizarre example occurred in August 1998. First, Delta Air Lines and American Airlines raised leisure fares by 4 percent. When Northwest Airlines refused to match the increase, it was rescinded. A few days later, Northwest raised its fares and was matched by the others. Two days later Northwest rescinded the increase, and within a day other airlines followed. Then Northwest raised some of its fares again, only to pull some of them back, and actually decreased leisure fares in some of its markets. Other airlines then realigned their fares with those of Northwest.[11]

A similar case occurred more recently. Due to the increases in fuel costs in the summer of 2004, American Airlines announced that it was increasing prices on domestic flights by $5 on one-way trips and $10 on roundtrips. Some airlines went along with this increase. However, some low-cost airlines, including Southwest and JetBlue, refused to increase their fares. A day later, American and the other airlines retracted the increases.[12]

Dominant Price Leadership

When an industry contains one company distinguished by its size and economic power relative to other firms, the **dominant price leadership** model emerges. The

---

[11]This sequence of fare changes was reported in several issues of *Wall Street Journal* between August 11, 1998, and the end of August.
[12]"American Air Abandons Proposed Fare Increases," *Wall Street Journal*, August 3, 2004.

dominant company may well be the most efficient (i.e., lowest-cost) firm. It could, under certain circumstances, force its smaller competitors out of business by undercutting their prices, or it could buy them out on favorable terms. But such action could lead to an investigation and eventual suit by the U.S. Department of Justice under the Sherman Anti-Trust Act. To avoid such difficulties, the dominant company may actually act as a monopolist, setting its price at the point where it will maximize its profits, and it will permit the smaller companies to continue to exist and sell as much as they want at the price set by the leader. The theoretical explanation of the dominant price leadership model is quite straightforward and is presented in all microeconomics textbooks. We follow its development in Figure 10.2.

The demand curve for the entire industry is D_T. The marginal cost curve of the dominant firm is MC_D, and the sum of all the marginal cost curves of the follower firms is represented by MC_R. The demand curve for the leader, D_D, is derived by subtracting at each point the marginal cost curve of the followers from the total demand curve, D_T. The reason is that if the small firms supply the product along their combined marginal cost curve, MC_R, then the dominant firm will be left with product demand shown along D_D. When the leader's marginal revenue curve, MR_D, is drawn in the usual manner, the leader can establish its profit-maximizing quantity at point A and its price at point B. This price is then accepted by the smaller firms in the industry, which will supply the rest of the market at this price. The followers are thus actually faced by a horizontal demand curve at price P.

Such an arrangement is satisfactory to the dominant firm. It maximizes profits and at the same time permits the small firms to exist, thus possibly avoiding legal action. In contrast, the followers will be able to assure themselves of a piece of the market without inviting the possibility of a price war, which they would most likely lose.

As in the case of cartels, dominant price leadership arrangements tend to break down. As markets grow, new firms enter the industry and decrease the interdependence among the firms. Technological changes may bring changes in pricing, and in the long run the leadership of the dominant firm is likely to erode.

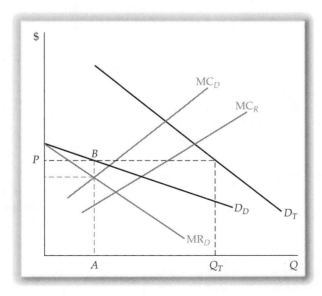

Figure 10.2   Dominant Price Leadership

REVENUE MAXIMIZATION

Module 10A

Another model of oligopolistic behavior was developed some years ago by the American economist William Baumol.[13] Ignoring interdependence, the **Baumol model** suggests that a firm's primary objective, rather than profit maximization, can be the maximization of revenue, subject to satisfying a specific level of profits. He gives several reasons for this objective, among them (1) a firm will be more competitive when it achieves large size (in terms of revenue), and (2) management remuneration may be more closely related to revenue than to profits.

This situation is depicted in Figure 10.3. The figure shows three solid curves. The total revenue curve is the usual one for a firm in imperfect competition, with revenue increasing at a decreasing rate because the firm is faced by a downward-sloping demand curve.[14] The total cost curve is also no surprise; it indicates first decreasing and then, at higher production levels, increasing marginal cost. The third line represents profits. It is simply the vertical difference between the revenue and cost lines.

If the firm were a profit maximizer (the traditional economic objective), production would take place at point Q_P, where the profit line hits its peak. In contrast, should the firm be a pure revenue maximizer, equilibrium would occur at output Q_S, where the total revenue curve reaches its peak. This point, as we learned earlier, occurs where demand elasticity is unity (i.e., marginal revenue equals zero).

However, revenue maximization is subject to the constraint that an acceptable profit level exists. This profit will tend to be at a lower level than the maximum achievable. Assuming this acceptable level is at OP, output will settle at Q_A. This will achieve the highest possible revenue, while satisfying the profit requirement. Thus, total revenue will be higher than would have been attained under conditions of

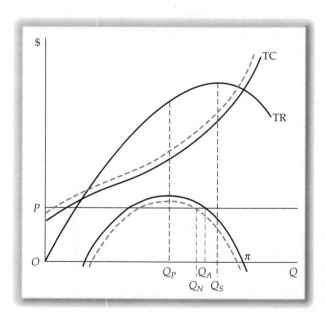

Figure 10.3   Revenue versus Profit Maximization

---

[13]William J. Baumol, *Economic Theory and Operations Analysis*, 3d ed., Englewood Cliffs, NJ: Prentice Hall International Editions, 1972, chapter 13.
[14]Thus each quantity represents a different price.

profit maximization, but lower than if pure revenue maximization (without a minimum profit constraint) had been pursued.

An interesting implication of this model is the effect of a change in fixed costs. Recall that under conditions of profit maximization in the short run, a change in fixed costs will have no effect on price or quantity because neither marginal revenue nor marginal cost is impacted, and thus the maximizing requirement of MR = MC will remain the same. However, in the Baumol model, a rise in fixed costs will raise the cost curve and decrease the profit line. Both new lines will be parallel to the old ones. The two broken lines in Figure 10.3 represent this shift. As can be seen, the existence of the profit constraint will cause output to decrease to Q_N. At this lower output, price will be higher.

Baumol's model is an interesting attempt to present an alternative to the traditional maximization hypothesis. Because his model has not been extensively tested, it is difficult to assess its validity. There have been some empirical studies investigating the relationship between executive pay and revenue (as opposed to profits), but no definitive verdict has been obtained. Some of the studies found a more solid relationship between executive pay and revenue, and others appeared to favor a relationship with profits. Still others arrived at ambiguous answers. One important question remains: Are corporate owners (stockholders) more concerned—and thus determine the market value of a corporation—with revenue or profitability? In the long run, the most likely answer is the latter. Thus it is doubtful that Baumol's model, although possibly applicable to some corporate behavior in the short run, will ever replace the traditional profit-maximizing objective.

PRICE DISCRIMINATION

Up to this point, we assume a firm will sell identical products at the same price in all markets. (When the term *identical* is used in this context, it implies that the costs of producing and delivering the product are the same.) But such is not always the case. When a company sells identical products in two or more markets, it may charge different prices in the markets. Such a practice is usually referred to as **price discrimination**. The word *discrimination* here is not used in a normative sense; there is no judgment being made about whether this practice is good or bad. (The term *differential pricing* could be used instead, but the former term has become part of the everyday language of the economist.)

Price discrimination means one of the following:

1. Products with identical costs are sold in different markets at different prices.
2. The ratio of price to marginal cost differs for similar products.

The practice of price discrimination is not an isolated event. It occurs in many familiar situations. Later in this section, we cite a number of common examples. Here we mention just two to illustrate each general instance just listed. In the first case, price discrimination exists when an adult and a child are charged different prices for tickets (of the same quality and at the same time) at a movie theater. The latter can be illustrated by the selling of cosmetic items, identical except for names on the labels and the quality of packaging, for vastly different prices at department or specialty stores on the one hand and drug and discount stores on the other. The existence of price discrimination is caused by differing demand conditions, not by differences in cost.

Such discriminating price differentials cannot exist under all circumstances. In fact, two conditions are necessary for such a market arrangement:

1. The two or more markets in which the product is sold must be capable of being separated. Specifically, this includes the requirement that there can be no transfer or resale of the product (or service) from one market to the other. That is, there is no leakage

among the markets. Only if the markets are sealed off from one another (by natural or contrived means) will the buyers in the various markets be unable to trade the products among these markets. Only in such a case will the seller be able to charge different prices without the price differential being nullified through competition. If the seller incurs costs in creating separate markets, these costs must be less than the additional revenue obtained from discrimination.

2. The demand curves in the segmented markets must have different elasticities at given prices. Without this condition, price discrimination would be futile.

The reason that companies attempt to engage in price discrimination is that it can enhance profits. From the viewpoint of the consumers of the product, those in the lower-price market may benefit compared with situations where a uniform price is charged. However, consumers in the higher-price market are at a disadvantage.

Economists normally identify three degrees of discrimination. First-degree discrimination is the most profitable for the seller, but it can be enforced only infrequently. Third-degree discrimination, which is not as profitable, is the most commonly observed, and we single it out for brief discussion in the next subsection:

1. First-degree discrimination exists when the seller can identify where each buyer lies on the demand curve and can charge each buyer the price it is willing to pay. Thus, the demand curve actually becomes the marginal revenue curve as faced by the seller. Of course, for the seller—a monopolist[15]—to achieve this advantageous position, it must have considerable information on where each buyer can be found on the demand curve, admittedly a herculean amount of market knowledge rarely attained. It is probably almost impossible to find such a pure case in real life, but let us attempt an example. A consumer purchasing a new automobile will generally bargain with the salesperson until they finally agree on a price. If the automobile dealer were clever enough to figure out the highest price that each individual was willing to pay, she could then conclude a deal with each customer at the maximum price (but only if no other dealer offered a lower price). Thus, each price the dealer obtains is on the buyers' demand curve. In reality, automobile dealers (and we must surely be thankful for this) are usually not endowed with such omniscience. We could stretch this example to apply to certain personal services such as medical or legal, where different customers (i.e., patients and clients) could be charged different fees based, for example, on their incomes.

2. Second-degree discrimination, although encountered somewhat more frequently than first degree, also is not commonplace in real life. It involves differential prices charged by blocks of services. An example is the way some public utilities price. They will charge the highest unit price (e.g., per kilowatt of electricity) for small quantities (at the top of the demand curve) and lower prices as the rate of consumption per period increases.[16] Thus, again, only if the monopolist seller has a great deal of information about the demand curve will it be able to roughly "skim" the curve and exact higher revenues from its customer set. To be able to engage in second-degree discrimination, a firm must be able to meter the services consumed by the buyers.[17]

3. Third-degree discrimination is by far the most frequently encountered. In this case, the monopolist segregates the customers into different markets and charges different prices in each. Such market segmentation can be based on geography, age, gender, product use, or income, for example.

---

[15]The assumption is usually made that a discriminating seller is a monopolist. But price discrimination also commonly exists in markets where competition is not perfect, not just in pure monopoly markets.
[16]The price differential here is not related to pricing at peak versus off-peak periods. Such pricing may be related to the cost of producing the service, and therefore, does not represent discrimination.
[17]Price discrimination can also be achieved by using a "two-part tariff," that is, charging a lump-sum fee and then charging for usage. Thus, buyers with greater demand will pay more. Examples of such charges would be a base fee charged by water and telephone companies.

Third-Degree Discrimination

If the firm can segment markets successfully, it can increase its profits above what they would be if a single price were charged. We show the pricing results with graphs, and subsequently we show a numerical example comparing the profitability of differential pricing versus uniform pricing, as well as a mathematical solution. As shown in Figure 10.4, the company operates in two markets, A and B. In Figure 10.4*a* and *b*, it can be seen that A's demand curve is less elastic than B's. Figure 10.4*c* shows the horizontal summation of both demand and marginal revenue curves to represent the company's total market.

Because we assume the products sold in the two markets are homogeneous, we can draw a marginal cost curve for the firm as a whole, as shown in Figure 10.4*c*. Output will take place at the point where MR = MC. Had a uniform price been charged, it would have been at point C on the aggregate demand curve. However, the firm can increase its profit by differentiating prices between the two markets. By drawing a horizontal line from the MR = MC intersection across the graphs for the two separate markets, we can allocate total production to the two markets. For each market, this will be the point where the horizontal line intersects the marginal revenue curve. Marginal revenue is thus the same for both markets. The price charged in each market can be found by drawing a vertical line at the corresponding quantity to the demand curve. Price will be considerably higher in market A, whose demand elasticity is lower.

A numerical example will illustrate third-degree discrimination.[18] Section A of Table 10.1 presents the demand schedule for two markets, as well as the combined schedule for the entire market. Assume fixed costs are $12,000 per period, and that the average variable cost is constant (and consequently so is marginal cost) at $3 per unit.

Figure 10.4   Third-Degree Price Discrimination

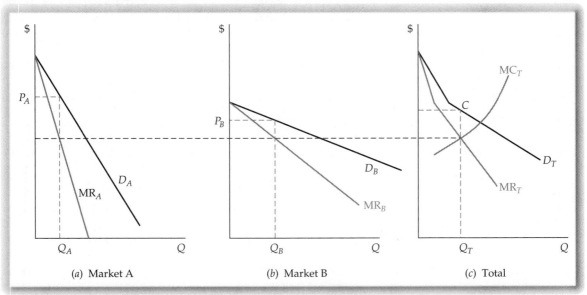

(*a*) Market A   (*b*) Market B   (*c*) Total

---

[18]We have chosen to show a numerical example of price discrimination rather than a mathematical proof. The latter would have been more precise. However, the simpler numerical illustration should be more useful. A brief outline of a mathematical solution is presented in the next subsection.

Table 10.1   Numerical Example of Third-Degree Discrimination

A. Demand Schedules

Price	Market A Quantity	Market B Quantity	Total Quantity
$36	0	0	0
30	475	25	500
24	900	100	1,000
18	1,100	400	1,500
12	1,300	700	2,000
6	1,450	1,050	2,500
0	1,500	1,500	3,000

B. Total Market

Price	Quantity	Total Revenue	Marginal Revenue	Fixed Cost	Aver. Var. and Marginal Costs	Total Cost	Profit
$36	0			$12,000		$12,000	$−12,000
30	500	$15,000	$ 30	12,000	$3	13,500	1,500
24	1,000	24,000	18	12,000	3	15,000	9,000
18	1,500	27,000	6	12,000	3	16,500	10,500
12	2,000	24,000	−6	12,000	3	18,000	6,000
6	2,500	15,000	−18	12,000	3	19,500	−4,500
0	3,000	0	−30	12,000	3	21,000	−21,000

C. Market A

Price	Quantity	Total Revenue	Marginal Revenue	Fixed Cost	Aver. Var. and Marginal Costs	Total Cost	Profit
$36	0			$6,000		$ 6,000	$ −6,000
30	475	$14,250	$ 30	6,000	$3	7,425	6,825
24	900	21,600	17	6,000	3	8,700	12,900
18	1,100	19,800	−9	6,000	3	9,300	10,500
12	1,300	15,600	−21	6,000	3	9,900	5,700
6	1,450	8,700	−46	6,000	3	10,350	−1,650
0	1,500	0	−174	6,000	3	10,500	−10,500

D. Market B

Price	Quantity	Total Revenue	Marginal Revenue	Fixed Cost	Aver. Var. and Marginal Costs	Total Cost	Profit
$36	0			$6,000		$ 6,000	$ −6,000
30	25	$ 750	$ 30	6,000	$3	6,075	−5,325
24	100	2,400	22	6,000	3	6,300	−3,900
18	400	7,200	16	6,000	3	7,200	0
12	700	8,400	4	6,000	3	8,100	300
6	1,050	6,300	−6	6,000	3	9,150	−2,850
0	1,500	0	−14	6,000	3	10,500	−10,500

If the company were to sell at a uniform price in both markets, it would maximize its profits at a price of $18. At that point, its profit would be $10,500. This can be seen in section B of Table 10.1. But if our company can separate the two markets, it can increase its total profit, as shown in sections C and D of the table. If it charges $24 per unit in

Table 10.2   Profits from First-Degree Discrimination

Price	Quantity		Revenue
$30	500		$15,000
24	500		12,000
18	500		9,000
12	500		6,000
6	500		3,000
Total revenue			$45,000
Fixed cost		$12,000	
Variable cost (2,500 × $3)		7,500	
Total cost			19,500
Profit			$25,500

market A and $12 per unit in market B, its profits will be $12,900 and $300, respectively. Thus, it will be able to increase its profit by $2,700.[19]

Had the company been able to carry out first-degree discrimination and sold to all potential customers at the prices they were willing to pay (with the exception of the last 500 units, which would not have been produced), its profits would have risen to $25,500, as shown in Table 10.2.

A Mathematical Solution for Third-Degree Discrimination

We discuss briefly a simple method to solve for prices and quantities in the presence of third-degree discrimination.

1. Assume there are two markets, A and B, and the demand curves are straight lines, that is,

$$Q_A = a_A - b_A P_A \text{ and } Q_B = a_B - b_B P_B$$

2. Reverse these equations so that P is the dependent variable:

$$P_A = \frac{a_A}{b_A} - \frac{Q_A}{b_A} \text{ and } P_B = \frac{a_B}{b_B} - \frac{Q_B}{b_B}$$

3. Now calculate total revenue by multiplying by Q:

$$\text{TR}_A = \frac{a_A Q_A}{b_A} - \frac{Q_A^2}{b_A} \text{ and } \text{TR}_B = \frac{a_B Q_B}{b_B} - \frac{Q_B^2}{b_B}$$

4. Calculate the first derivative of total revenue to obtain marginal revenue:

$$\text{MR}_A = \frac{a_A}{b_A} - \frac{2Q_A}{b_A} \text{ and } \text{MR}_B = \frac{a_B}{b_B} - \frac{2Q_B}{b_B}$$

---

[19]We have arbitrarily divided the fixed costs equally between the two markets. But this has no effect on the total profits of the company or on the levels of sales in the two markets that will lead to profit maximization. Indeed, we could have omitted the fixed costs altogether, and there would have been no impact, except that the profits would have been $12,000 higher in both cases. Also, it should be noted that the quantity sold in this case is somewhat higher than in the one-price case. This is an inaccuracy caused by using discrete numbers in our demand schedule. Had this case been solved mathematically, using calculus, this inaccuracy would not have arisen.

5. Now set the marginal revenue equal to the company's marginal cost, which we assume to be a constant:

$$MR_A = MC \text{ and } MR_B = MC$$

6. Substituting for MR_A and MR_B and solving the two equations gives the quantity sold in each market.

7. From here it is easy to find the contribution profit for the two markets and for the combination of the two. Remember that because MC is a constant, average variable cost is constant also, so total variable cost can be calculated simply by multiplying AVC ($= MC$) by the quantity. Fixed cost, if any, can then be subtracted.

8. If we want to find out what the price would be if a uniform price were charged, we first add the two demand functions found in step 1. We then reverse the resulting equation in terms of price, as in step 2, and obtain marginal revenue. Marginal revenue is then equated to MC, and the price, quantity, and contribution profit are obtained in the same manner as in steps 3 to 7. The quantity sold will be the same as if discrimination existed, but the profit will be lower.

Examples of Price Discrimination

Price discrimination is an extremely common practice encountered in all types of situations. A number of rather common examples follow:

1. In the past, physicians often set their fees in accordance with patient income. In a way, it could be argued that such a fee arrangement was quite equitable: Those who can afford to pay higher prices will do so. However, as stated before, we are not concerned here with the normative aspects of differential pricing. The result of such a practice will still be an increase in the physician's income.

   Presently, medical price discrimination exists in a somewhat different guise. Physicians frequently charge a patient who has health insurance more for the same services than they charge a patient who does not. The difference cannot be explained by the cost incurred by the physician in filing insurance documents. However, the two conditions necessary for differential pricing exist. The elasticities in the two markets (uninsured and insured) are certainly different, and the markets are sealed from each other (either the patient does or does not have insurance).

2. Often, products going into the export market will be priced lower than those sold domestically. A major reason for the differential is that international competition is stronger than that faced by the firm in its (frequently sheltered) domestic markets. Thus demand curves in international markets are more elastic. Japanese electronics and French wines are just two examples of such discrimination.

3. Many pubs and bars have "ladies' hours," and in the past, major league baseball parks had ladies' days on Wednesdays. In both cases, the price for women is lower than that charged their male counterparts.

4. Theaters, cinemas, and sports events often charge lower prices for children occupying equal accommodations as adults. The same arrangement is frequently offered to senior citizens.

5. Public transportation systems commonly offer reduced fares to senior citizens.

6. State universities charge higher tuition fees to out-of-state students, although there is no cost differential to the university between in-state and out-of-state students.

7. Public utilities (electric, gas, telephone) customarily charge higher rates to business customers than to residential customers.

8. University bookstores offer 10 to 15 percent discounts to faculty, while charging full prices to students.

9. Individuals can order publications from publishers at lower prices than those charged to libraries and other institutions. Most professional journals are priced in this way.

10. Advancing technology is creating new avenues for practicing price discrimination, as shown in the following two examples:

   a. Last-minute airline ticket buyers can make special deals through the Web site priceline.com.

   b. New software permits Web-based merchants to identify individual visitors to their Web sites and study their shopping behavior. Price-sensitive customers may be offered lower prices. This new approach is a variation on catalog retailers' policies of sending catalogs with different prices to different zip codes.[20]

We leave it to you to think of additional examples.[21] In all these instances, different prices are charged at the same time. A senior citizen and a person 40 years of age traveling in the subway together will pay different fares. Differential utility charges to business and residential customers are in effect at the same time during the day.

However, there are also price differences that depend on when products or services are consumed:

1. Theaters charge different ticket prices for matinees and evening performances.
2. Theaters charge higher ticket prices on weekends than on weekdays.
3. Daytime telephone rates are higher than nighttime rates.
4. Hotels catering mostly to business travelers charge lower room rates during weekends.

Are these also examples of price discrimination? Many economics texts subscribe to this notion. (Of course, where a firm's costs differ at different times, no price discrimination would be claimed.) However, if these are types of discrimination, they do not really belong with the original examples given. After all, movements, of a demand curve over time will change the prices of many products without the presence of price discrimination. What appears to be the case here is that weekend theater ticket demand, for example, is considerably higher than demand on a Tuesday or a Wednesday, while the supply curve is essentially vertical. Prices change as demand changes. Whether this qualifies as price discrimination is questionable.

Some Recent Examples of Price Discrimination Practices

It was 1995 when California passed a law banning price discrimination based on gender. The legislation was aimed at retail stores, such as dry cleaners and hair salons, which charged higher prices to women than to men for presumably similar services. However, price differentials still appeared to exist. So in 2001, the California legislature passed a law to further discourage price differentials. In addition to increasing monetary penalties, stores are now required to display prices charged for their fifteen most commonly used services. However, differentials due to differences in cost (due to time required or difficulty of service) are still permitted.[22]

---

[20]S. Woolley, "I Got It Cheaper Than You," *Forbes*, November 2, 1998, pp. 82–84.

[21]Fare differentials in the airline industry are often mentioned as a prime example of price discrimination. A ticket bought well in advance, whose price is not refundable and which includes a weekend, is usually considerably cheaper than one that does not possess these characteristics. Vacation (elastic demand) and business (inelastic demand) travel are usually differentiated in this manner, and thus it may not be unusual for two travelers to sit next to one another on a plane and be paying vastly different fares. However, there are also differences in cost and risk to the airline between these two different fares, so the two tickets are really not the same. If the fare differentials occur due to disparities in cost and risk, then this is not an example of price discrimination.

[22]Jim Sanders, "California Lawmakers Pass Bills to Eliminate Retailer Gender Discrimination," *Sacramento Bee*, September 30, 2001.

Several years later, Lavalife, an online dating service, agreed to pay over $700,000 to male customers in California because it charged male customers for their services while it allowed female customers to have free access.[23] And recently, the California Supreme Court permitted four men to bring a suit against a Los Angeles nightclub. The four men claimed that the club charged them a $20 admission charge while women had to pay only $15.[24]

In March 2000, McCormick & Co., the leading marketer of spices in the United States, entered into a consent decree with the Federal Trade Commission for violating the Robinson-Patman Act.[25] It was alleged that McCormick charged higher prices to some retail stores than others in return for obtaining greater shelf space at the expense of smaller stores. McCormick commonly demanded as much as 90 percent of a store's shelf space. This practice is usually referred to as "slotting fees," and is a standard way of doing business in grocery stores and some other industries. Thus, this decision could have much wider implications for the future. The consent order did not impose any monetary penalties but is effective for 20 years.[26]

Gasoline wholesalers in several areas employ a method called "zone pricing." For instance, in the Phoenix, Arizona, metropolitan area there are differentials between, for example, prices in the city of Phoenix and Scottsdale, an affluent suburb. Oil companies do not reveal the details of the zone demarcation. However, it is believed that real estate values (i.e., an indication of income levels) are an important factor. Gas consumption and traffic counts are also potential factors. Another area in which zone pricing has been described is in the Long Island, New York, area. Although it may be a matter of supply and demand, according to Ed Silliere, vice president at Energy Merchant Corporation, "[e]ven the affluence of the community could be a factor, not only because higher real costs mean higher rents and taxes, but because wealthier consumers are deemed less likely to go out of their way to shop for price. . . . You might have a marketplace that can afford to pay more, doesn't mind paying more and is unwilling to drive the distance to get a better price." What he is describing, of course, are differences in demand elasticity.[27]

Toyota Corporation settled several class-action suits alleging price discrimination against Hispanic and African American car buyers. In addition to paying more than $10 million in attorney fees, Toyota also agreed to grant preapproved credit offers to these car buyers, contribute to nonprofit organizations focusing on educating minority consumers, and pay damages to class members.[28] This case illustrates the two necessary conditions for the existence of price discrimination—market segmentation and differences in demand price elasticity.

A study of price discrimination in a Broadway theater showed that the theater's profit was increased by 5 percent compared to uniform pricing. This was largely due to the sale of half-priced tickets at the day-of-performance discount booth.[29]

---

[23]Robert Benzie, "Dating Services Hire Top Lobbyist to Fight Gender Pricing Bill," *Toronto Star*, March 13, 2006.

[24]"Court: Nightclub Can Be Sued for Price Discrimination," *Oakland Tribune*, May 31, 2007.

[25]The Robinson-Patman Act is discussed briefly in chapter 14. This law makes it illegal to charge different prices to different customers, unless justified by cost differentials.

[26]Ira Teinowitz, "FTC, McCormick Reach Accord on Slotting Fees," *Advertising Age*, March 13, 2000, p. 75; Tom Weir, "FTC Raises the Ante with McCormick Order," *Supermarket Business*, April 15, 2000, pp. 45–46.

[27]Max Jarman, "One Key to Gas Price Puzzle," *The Arizona Republic*, June 16, 2004; Tom Incantalupo, "Many Factors Cause Varying Gasoline Prices in Melville, N.Y., Area," *Newsday*, May 20, 2004.

[28]Jared A. Favole, "Toyota Motor Credit Settles Price-Discrimination Lawsuit," *Dow Jones Newswires*, February 6, 2007.

[29]Philip Leslie, "Price Discrimination in Broadway Theatre," *Rand Journal of Economics*, Vol. 35, Issue 3, Autumn 2004, pp. 520–541.

Pricing in the Hotel Industry: Example of Price Discrimination

Differential room rates have existed in the hotel industry for a long time. However, we do not discuss in this section, for instance, the lower weekend rates that are standard at business hotels or the higher rates charged during the busy season by resort hotels. These intertemporal differences appear to be based on different levels of demand. Here we are concerned with different rates charged to different customers at the same time (e.g., same day). In the following discussion, we must remember an important fact attending the operation of a hotel: a large proportion of the cost of running a hotel is fixed. The variable cost of renting an empty room is relatively small. "To paraphrase one general manager, 'If I've got a warm body with money standing in front of me and cold sheets upstairs, I want to make a deal. As long as the customer is willing to pay more than my variable cost to clean that room, I'm going to make money.' "[30] Each additional rented room represents incremental revenue.

This situation leads to different types of price discrimination practices in the hotel industry.

Often a hotel will have several different rates, and the actual rate charged to a particular guest will depend on the bargaining skill of the customer and the knowledge of the innkeeper in estimating the highest price the potential patron is willing to pay. Thus, the revenue of the hotel may be found along the demand curve (if the manager is really proficient at estimating the customer's willingness to pay), and the result may approach first-degree discrimination. Figure 10.5 illustrates this situation with potential scenarios for three different prices.

However, the more typical way of discriminating is to segment the market. The simplest method is to separate leisure travelers from business travelers. The demand of the former is certainly more price elastic because the room price is an important part of the total vacation expense. At the same time, vacation travelers may be willing to make an advance commitment, may stay for a longer time period, and are more flexible in their arrangements. The business travelers' demand is less price elastic; they are much more

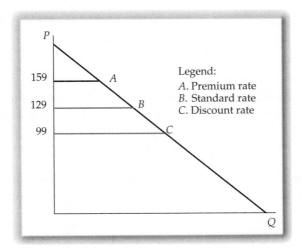

Figure 10.5 First-Degree Discrimination in the Hotel Industry

---

[30]Richard D. Hanks, Robert G. Cross, and R. Paul Noland, "Discounting in the Hotel Industry: A New Approach," *The Cornell H.R.A. Quarterly,* February 1992, pp. 15–23. The discussion in this section is based largely on this article. The quote and all that follow also come from this article.

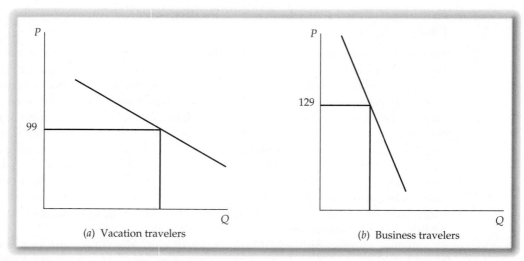

Figure 10.6   Third-Degree Discrimination in the Hotel Industry

inflexible in making their arrangements (they must be in a certain place at a certain time); their commitments often cannot be made far in advance; perhaps most important is that they are in most cases not willing to stay over the weekend, when rates are often lowest. Figure 10.6 shows the two demand curves with possible prices.

"As customers have become more sophisticated in manipulating the current pricing system, hotels will eventually be forced to modify their pricing structure." A new approach being introduced will "fence" customers into different rate categories tailored to specific needs so higher-rate patrons will not be able to "trade down." Among the various methods to segment the customer sets will be the following:

1. Advance reservations and advance purchase
2. Rates differentiated depending on how many days in advance the reservations are made
3. Refundability
4. Flexibility to make changes in arrangements
5. Required time of stay

Hotels will be able to combine and alter these requirements ("fences") depending on the level of demand at any specific time. With these procedures, hotels will be able to penetrate their markets more deeply. However, such a multifaceted program also has its problems. First, to carry out this program effectively, hotels must have sophisticated computer-directed reservation systems and must be able to make rapid adjustments to ensure they do not sell too many rooms at unnecessarily discounted rates. The adminis-tration of such a system may require additional staffing and additional costs, and management must be sure the additional revenue derived from this system more than compensates for this cost.

Tying Arrangements: A Possible Extension of Price Discrimination

A *tying arrangement* (frequently referred to as a *tie-in sale*) exists when a buyer of one product is obligated to also buy a related (usually complementary) product from the same supplier. U.S. antitrust laws take a very dim view of tying arrangements, and a large number of court cases have declared this practice to be illegal. The reasoning behind this is that a firm will use its existing market power in the first (tying) product to suppress previously existing competition in the second (tied) product. The firm will thus extend its monopoly power.

Typically a tying arrangement will involve a major, often durable product and a low-value item that is usually complementary to the former.[31]

The legal argument claiming that tying arrangements cause an extension of monopoly appears flawed. If a company already has market power in the tying product it can maximize its monopoly profit. To tie another product to it may actually dilute its power, in that customers who buy the two complementary products are mainly interested in the total cost of the two products combined. Thus, if a tie-in sale arrangement causes the price of the tied product to increase, it may have to be made up by a decrease in the price of the tying product.

An alternative economic explanation of a tying arrangement is that it is a type of third-degree discrimination. A company may charge identical prices for the tying good. However, purchasers of the tying product may have different levels of demand for its usage. This quantity of demand can be "metered" by the tied product; purchasers who use the product with greater intensity will use a larger quantity of the tied product. Thus, the seller may charge a relatively reasonable price for the major product and collect monopoly profits on the lower-valued complementary product.

One of the more prominent cases in the history of this litigation was the U.S. government suit against IBM.[32] IBM rented its equipment on a monthly basis. All customers paid the same monthly rental whether they used the machine 8 hours a day or 2 hours per week. Those customers who used the equipment with greater intensity had to use a larger number of punch cards. Thus IBM really had a relatively inexpensive way to separate its customers into those who used the rented machines more intensively and those who used them only sporadically. It could practice this discrimination even while charging the same unit price for punch cards to all customers. "It is generally agreed that if the tying and tied goods are complementary in demand, then profit maximization under the price discrimination hypothesis will lead the seller to lower the price of the tying good (below the level that would prevail if the good were sold separately) and sell the tied good at a price above its marginal production cost."[33]

Although price discrimination is a plausible explanation of tying arrangements, other arguments have been advanced:

1. *Quality control.* Firms have argued that tying arrangements are necessary to ensure the integrity of their product so they do not get blamed if an inferior tied good is used.

2. *Efficiencies in distribution.* A total lower cost can be attained if there are savings to the company in delivering both products.

3. *Evasion of price controls.* If there is a ceiling price on one of the two products, then selling the second product at a higher price will circumvent price control.

---

[31]To illustrate, some of the court cases involving tying arrangements have included riveting machines and rivets, computers and punch cards, camera film and film processing, and condominiums and building management services.

[32]*International Business Machines Corporation v. United States,* 298 U.S. 392 (1936).

[33]Meyer L. Burstein, "The Economics of Tie-In Sales," *Review of Economics and Statistics,* 42 (February 1960), p. 69. Much of the preceding discussion is based on William F. Shughart II, *The Organization of Industry,* Homewood, IL: Irwin, 1990, pp. 307–14.

Social Welfare Implications of Price Discrimination

As mentioned previously, U.S. antitrust laws look unfavorably at the practice of price discrimination, which is said to lead to a lessening of competition.

Under monopoly conditions, an industry produces a smaller amount of product at a higher price than under competitive conditions. However, as we have seen, under price discrimination of the first and second degree, a company may produce a larger quantity than a single-price monopoly. Given the conditions of first-degree discrimination, the firm will charge prices along the demand curve all the way to the point where demand equals marginal cost. This, of course, results in a larger quantity than produced by a single-price monopoly. A similar situation would hold for second-degree discrimination. Thus, when price discrimination exists, total production may equal that which would exist under competitive circumstances.

In the case of third-degree discrimination, the situation is more ambiguous. As we have seen, as long as the demand curve for the monopolist is a straight downward-sloping line, the quantity produced will be the same under a single-price and a price-discrimination situation. However, under certain circumstances, production under discriminatory pricing may increase. This situation may occur if the demand curve is not a straight line or if a one-price policy would not be profitable enough for a company to produce the product at all.

In the case of third-degree discrimination, customers in the market with lower price elasticity will pay higher prices, while those in an elastic demand market will pay lower prices than under conditions of a one-price monopoly. The implications here are uncertain because it is very difficult to weigh the benefits bestowed on the latter compared with the costs imposed on the former as to their effect on total economic welfare. However, there is no question that the sellers in the discrimination case will benefit from the higher prices charged at least in a part of the market, thereby increasing their profits.

NONMARGINAL PRICING

Throughout this text, we appear to have assumed all businesspeople calculate demand and cost schedules, obtain marginal revenue and marginal cost curves, equate marginal revenue with marginal cost, and thus determine their profit-maximizing selling price and production quantity. But how many business owners or managers actually know how to make these calculations? Even if they have the knowledge, how many have the time and, even more important, sufficient information to make such calculations?

In fact, it is often claimed (as discussed in chapter 2) that businesses are really not profit maximizers, that they have other objectives. It has been said that management will seek only satisfactory levels of profit for the owners. The term *satisficing* has been used in this context.[34] Other corporate goals may also be important, such as the achievement of a desired market share, a target profit margin (i.e., percent of profits to revenue), or a target rate of return on assets (profit divided by assets) or on equity (profit divided by stockholder equity).

---

[34]See Herbert Simon, "Theories of Decision Making in Economics and Behavioral Science," *American Economic Review,* 49 (June 1959), pp. 253–83. This condition usually prevails in large corporations, where professional managers may not act in conformance with the wishes of stockholders. In the textbooks on corporate finance, considerable attention is accorded this subject, which has been named "agency theory." It is based on a famous article by Michael C. Jensen and William H. Meckling, "Theory of the Firm: Managerial Behavior, Agency Costs, and Ownership Structure," *Journal of Financial Economics,* October 1976, pp. 305–60.

It also appears that one of the most popular pricing methods, believed to be pervasive throughout industry, is the cost-plus or full-cost method, which at first glance seems not to employ the marginal pricing principle. It is this subject that we discuss next.

Cost-Plus Pricing

A researcher questioning a sample of businesspeople on their pricing methods would probably be told by a majority that they simply calculate the variable cost of the product, add to it an allocation for fixed costs, and then add a profit percentage or markup on top of these total costs to arrive at **cost-plus pricing**.[35] Thus, for instance, if the direct (variable) cost of a product is $8, its allocated overhead is $6, and the desired markup is 25 percent, the price of the product will be $17.50 (8 + 6 + 0.25 × 14).[36]

Such a calculation appears to be extremely simple, and the whole method is often described as naive. But this apparent simplicity hides some fairly difficult calculations and assumptions:[37]

1. How are average variable costs calculated?
2. How are fixed costs allocated? Why are fixed costs included in the price calculation? Economic theory tells us that fixed costs do not affect price.[38]
3. How is the size of the markup determined? Usually, it is said that the markup should guarantee the seller a "fair profit," or some target profit margin or target rate of return. If this is the case, are demand conditions taken into consideration?

We discuss these problems, and as we go through this analysis, we may find that cost-plus pricing and marginal pricing have a lot in common.

In cost-plus pricing, costs, both variable and fixed overheads, are usually calculated at some standard or normal quantity, as is done by accountants. These are historical costs and do not appear to include an opportunity cost. But economic theory tells us that unit costs tend to vary with quantity, and the expected quantities may not correspond to those that result.[39] Also, as mentioned, fixed costs should not be used in the determination of prices.

However, if we take these criticisms in turn, the shortcomings of cost-plus pricing may not be as serious as they appear. There is no real reason why accounting costs cannot include some measure of opportunity cost. Even if it is not incorporated, a normal profit (another name for opportunity cost) certainly could easily be included in

---

[35]One of the original studies was R. L. Hall and C. J. Hitch, "Price Theory and Business Behavior," *Oxford Economic Papers,* 2 (May 1939), pp. 12–45.

[36]Markup is ordinarily calculated as a percentage of cost. Profit margin is commonly computed as a percentage of price. Thus, a 25 percentage markup is equivalent to a 20 percent profit margin.

[37]It is said that restaurants usually mark up the food cost four times to arrive at the price of a menu item—a very simple calculation indeed.

[38]Only in the Baumol revenue maximization model does fixed cost enter into price determination.

[39]The accountant's cost for a normal quantity can be shown as one point on the economist's average cost curve:

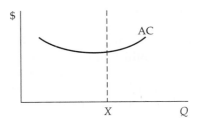

Point X is the "normal" quantity at which costs would be calculated. But other quantities would be produced at different costs.

the markup. Now, it is often said that cost-plus pricing is a long-term concept. If that is the case, then, according to economic theory, all costs are variable; a cost allocation is then an estimate of the additional variable costs in the long run. Further, although economists like to draw nice U-shaped cost curves, it is quite possible that in the longer run the bottom portion of the average cost curve is quite shallow (saucer-shaped) and that over some production range it may appear to be almost horizontal.[40] In that case, as long as a firm is producing in the range at which standard costs are calculated, the problem of costs varying with quantity is obviated. Also, if the curve is relatively horizontal, marginal cost will be identical or almost identical to the average cost in that interval, and pricing on basis of average cost will thus be substantially similar to marginal cost pricing. In addition, economic theory tells us that, under perfect competition, in the long run all but normal profits will disappear. The markup, then, must certainly represent normal profit. It is more likely, however, that competition in the real world is not quite perfect, and the firm will therefore be faced by a downward-sloping demand curve.

This brings us to the question of the demand curve. If a markup is applied to obtain a "fair" profit, the implication is that demand conditions are not taken into consideration. But that would indicate almost complete inflexibility regarding the size of the markup. However, it has been observed in innumerable cases that markup percentages differ among different product lines of the same firm. The fact that a company accepts a lower markup for some products than others indicates that demand conditions and the competitive environment are included in the pricing decision making. As is shown, the markup percentage tends to vary inversely with demand elasticity. This makes obvious sense: when a firm is faced by very strong competition, the demand curve facing it will tend to be nearly or completely horizontal: under those circumstances, the firm will not be able to afford a very large markup.

One other important point must be made. Not only will different markups be applied for different product lines of a given firm, but the markup will probably change on a given product from time to time. Such changes could be caused by changing demand or changing cost conditions. When this occurs, a firm will adjust its markup and thus its price to meet the new circumstances. Its purpose for such action is most probably to increase or protect its profits. As long as a firm changes its prices to "do better" (i.e., increase its profit or minimize its loss), it is acting as if it has knowledge of its demand and cost curves: that is, it is acting consistently with marginal pricing.

It is certainly true that businesspeople do not have sufficient knowledge to estimate marginal revenue and marginal cost curves with any degree of accuracy. Thus, cost-plus pricing can be a substitute for marginal pricing in the absence of sufficient knowledge. But given the proclivity for firms to adjust their markups in response to demand and cost conditions in such a way as to improve profitability, profit maximization and cost-plus pricing can be quite compatible.

Cost-Plus Pricing in Practice

A rather interesting case of cost-plus pricing recently appeared in a *Wall Street Journal* article. It concerns the pricing practices of the Parker Hannifin Corporation, a manufacturer of industrial parts. "For as long as anyone at the 89-year old company could recall Parker used the same simple formula to determine prices of its 800,000 parts." Managers would calculate how much it cost to make and deliver a part, and then add a percentage, much of the time 35 percent.

---

[40]This situation is consistent with constant returns to scale.

In 2001 a new chief executive, Donald Washkewicz, was elected. After reviewing the company's pricing method he decided that prices should not be determined by applying a similar percentage to all products. Rather, prices should be set based on what customers would be willing to pay. (In other words, demand elasticity should be considered.)

With the help of consultants the company classified its products by the amount of competition it faced. It found that a large number of products were priced too low because they were unique or specialized and did not have much competition. The company raised prices on a large number of products an average of 5 percent. There were also some products whose prices were decreased.

Since the introduction of this program, the company has increased its return on invested capital considerably, and the price of its shares has risen faster than the Standard and Poor's 500 index.[41]

An Arithmetic Reconciliation of Cost-Plus and Marginal Pricing

It can be shown mathematically that under certain circumstances, cost-plus pricing can be consistent with profit maximization (i.e., MR = MC).

Most microeconomics textbooks show the mathematical relationship among price, marginal revenue, and demand elasticity as follows.[42]

$$\text{MR} = P\left(1 + \frac{1}{E_P}\right)$$

As profit is maximized when MR = MC, we can rewrite the equation as

$$\text{MC} = P\left(1 + \frac{1}{E_P}\right)$$

Further, under certain conditions, marginal cost will equal average cost. Thus, our equation becomes

$$\text{AC} = P\left(1 + \frac{1}{E_P}\right)$$

and can then be rewritten as

$$\text{AC} = P\left(\frac{E_P + 1}{E_P}\right)$$

To show how price is based on average cost, we can rearrange the equation as

$$P = \text{AC}\left(\frac{E_P}{E_P + 1}\right)$$

---

[41]Timothy Aeppel, "Seeking Perfect Prices, CEO Tears Up the Rules," *The Wall Street Journal*, March 27, 2007.

[42]The equation is derived in the following way: total revenue (TR) equals price times quantity ($P \times Q$). To obtain marginal revenue, total revenue must be differentiated with respect to quantity:

$$\text{MR} = \frac{d\text{TR}}{dQ} = \frac{d(P \times Q)}{dQ} = P \times \frac{dQ}{dQ} + Q \times \frac{dP}{dQ} = P \times 1 + Q \times \frac{dP}{dQ} = P\left(1 + \frac{Q}{P} \times \frac{dP}{dQ}\right)$$

Note that the product inside the parentheses is the reciprocal of elasticity; hence,

$$\text{MR} = P\left(1 + \frac{1}{E_P}\right)$$

Remember that demand elasticity has a negative sign.

Under conditions of cost-plus pricing,

$$P = AC(1 + M)$$

where M stands for the markup percentage. If the two previous equations are comparable, then

$$(1 + M) = \frac{E_P}{E_P + 1}$$

It can be shown that there is an inverse relationship between markup and demand elasticity. For example, if $E_p = -2$, then $(1 + M) = -2/-1 = 2$ and M is therefore 100 percent. If, however, $E_p = -5$, then $(1 + M) = -5/-4 = 1.25$, and markup is only 25 percent. This result is quite reasonable; it indicates that the less elastic the demand curve, the larger will be the markup.

Thus, under the not infrequent conditions where the average cost curve is constant in the relevant range of production, cost-plus pricing may give results identical to those that would be obtained if managers were pursuing profit maximization.

Incremental Pricing and Costing Analysis

We have just discussed the cost-plus method of pricing; it is considered to be a very popular pricing method. We explained that cost-plus pricing and marginal pricing can generally be reconciled. But there are difficulties with implementing marginal pricing in the real world. To do a good job of marginal pricing, a manager would have to have good estimates of the shape of demand and cost curves. Because it may be quite costly and certainly very difficult to estimate marginal quantities, businesses will often use incremental analysis to achieve the objective of profit maximization.

In a way, marginal and incremental analyses are very similar. But although *marginal* implies that we must estimate the revenue and costs created by one additional unit or the additional revenue obtained from one extra dollar of expenses, incremental analysis deals with changes in total revenue and total costs resulting from a particular decision to change prices, introduce a new product, discontinue an existing product, improve a product, or acquire additional machinery or plant. We discuss the question of incremental costs in chapter 7.

The important lesson to learn here is that only those revenues and costs that will change due to the decision should be considered. Thus, it is a mistake to include sunk costs in calculating the outcome. Furthermore, if costs such as fixed overhead are already being incurred and will not change (even though accountants may reallocate these costs), they are irrelevant to the decision. In contrast, if a decision results in a change in revenues or costs of another product (possibly a complementary or substitute good), such an effect must be included in the analysis.

Obviously, this is an important subject to which we are devoting only a small amount of space here. However, incremental analysis is at the heart of the study of long-term investments. This is a subject discussed at greater length in chapter 12.

MULTIPRODUCT PRICING

In economics, much of the analysis makes use of simplifying assumptions. For example, we know that very few products in our economy are produced under conditions of perfect competition. Nevertheless, a large portion of our text—and all other economics texts—is devoted to its discussion. There are good reasons for this practice. First, perfect competition is the simplest of the economic models and is thus a good starting point for the discussion of more complex systems. Second, many markets, although not perfectly competitive (i.e., firms are faced by downward-sloping demand curves), can be analyzed as such because their behavior resembles perfect competition closely enough. Any predictions based on this analysis will be sufficiently accurate to obviate the need for more complex models.[43]

Another simplification frequently made in economic theory is assuming a firm or a plant produces a single product. Up to this point, we have done so in this text. Actually, we first assumed single products were sold in single markets, and later extended our analysis to operations in more than one market (price discrimination). Now we provide a brief treatment of **multiproduct pricing**, cases in which a plant or a firm produces two or more products, which are, of course, the norm rather than the exception.

The various products produced by a firm can be independent of one another. This means that neither the demand for nor the cost of one product is affected by the demand for or cost of another product. In such a case, each product will be produced, as usual, at the level where its marginal revenue equals its marginal cost. The analysis can then proceed as if only one good were produced.

In most cases, however, there is some relationship among products produced by one firm. The relationships can exist either on the demand side or the cost side—or both. We can distinguish (at least) four different interrelationships:

1. Products are complements in terms of demand. One company may produce both personal computers and software, or a fast-food restaurant may sell both hamburgers and soft drinks.

2. Products are substitutes in terms of demand: a company may produce different models of a personal computer, or a soft drink company may bottle both cola and lemon-lime soda.

3. Products are joined in production. The extreme case of joint production occurs when two products are produced in fixed (or almost fixed) proportions, such as cattle production, which involves one skin and one carcass per steer.

4. Products compete for resources. If a company making different products that compete for the available resources produces more of one product, it will have to do so at the expense of producing less of other products. The production of different models of the same computer is an example.

Let us now discuss each case.

Products Complementary in Demand

When two products are complementary, an increase in the quantity sold of one will bring about an increase in the quantity sold of the other. This may be due to an increase in the demand for product A or a price decrease of product A (bringing about an increase in the quantity demanded). Products may be so closely related that they are bought in fixed proportions. An example is kitchen knives, each of which must be made of one wooden handle and one metal blade. Other complementary products are a personal computer and a keyboard, and still another example is an automobile body and a set of four wheels. Somewhat less fixed in proportion but still closely related products are razors and razor blades, tennis rackets and tennis balls,

---

[43]It is the accuracy of the prediction provided by a model that is important to scientists, not the reasonableness or realism of the assumptions. This point has been successfully argued by Milton Friedman in "The Methodology of Positive Economics," contained in his *Essays in Positive Economics,* Chicago: University of Chicago Press, 1953, pp. 3–43.

and computers and software. There are also more remotely related products where the demand for one can easily have a beneficial effect on the demand for the other. For instance, a popular textbook in economics published by a particular company may enhance the sales of a finance textbook by the same publisher.

The important point is that the demand for a product is affected not only by its price, by income, and by tastes, for example, but also very strongly by the prices of related commodities. This subject is discussed in chapter 3, where we define the determinants of the demand curve in general. Here we concentrate on the effects of complementary commodities on the revenues of one firm. Thus, if products A and B are complementary, a change in revenue from A will entail a change in the revenue from B. In both cases, profit maximization will occur at the familiar point where the marginal revenue of each product equals its marginal costs. Because each demand equation will include the prices of both products, the pricing problem will require the solution of simultaneous equations.

If managers had nice, neat demand and cost functions available for each product, they could arrive at the combined profit maximization positions using relatively simple mathematical formulas.[44] However, because in real life the decision maker would most likely not have sufficient data on hand, the maximization process would proceed along a trial-and-error course, where markups (and thus prices) for the products would be adjusted until the optimal combination is reached. Actually, the process would be even more complex in reality because it is not only the complementary relationship between the firm's two products that has an important influence on the firm's revenue (and profit); competitors' products that are substitutes for our firm's products must also be considered in the process of price setting.

There is another instance in which a company must consider these interrelationships. It is not necessary that a firm produce two related products simultaneously. It may just produce one and be in the process of deciding whether to embark on the production of a complementary product. In calculating the profitability of such expansion, the company must include the increase in sales of and profit earned on the earlier product. If it omitted this positive effect, it would be understating the benefits of the new product. It may decide against the product's introduction when in fact the total profits of the company would increase if the new product were brought to market. As an example, suppose a successful producer of television sets is considering whether to introduce a new line of DVD players. In calculating the potential profitability of producing DVD players, the producer must include the possibility of enhanced sales (and profits) from its television line.

Products Substitutable in Demand

A brief treatment of substitutability and pricing will suffice because this case is extremely similar to that of complements. For substitutes, the effect to be considered is the decrease (increase) in revenue and profits of a second product if quantities

[44]For a two-product situation, a manager could calculate the marginal revenue for each interrelated product. Because

$$Q_A = f(P_A, P_B) \text{ and } Q_B = f(P_B, P_A)$$

then

$$\text{MR}_A = \frac{d\text{TR}_A}{dQ_A} + \frac{d\text{TR}_A}{dQ_B} \text{ and MR}_B = \frac{d\text{TR}_B}{dQ_B} + \frac{d\text{TR}_A}{dQ_B}$$

Each marginal revenue would be equated to their respective marginal costs simultaneously:

$$\text{MR}_A = \text{MC}_A \text{ and } \text{MR}_B = \text{MC}_B$$

bought of the first product rise (fall), either because of changes in demand or changes in price. Examples of such cases abound. Two different sizes of personal computers certainly are substitutes for one another. The different automobile models produced by one manufacturer (sedans versus convertibles, Honda Civics versus Accords, Chevrolets versus Pontiacs, etc.) are relatively close substitutes, so it is necessary to price them jointly. Another example is Global Foods' soft drink division, which produces cola-type and non–cola-type sodas simultaneously.

Just as in the case of complementary products, substitution can occur when a new product is introduced. Thus, a computer manufacturer developing a new generation of computers must consider the impact that the introduction will have on similar but less advanced products now being marketed.

The analysis of these cases is basically the same as for complementary commodities. The marginal revenue of one product will be a function of the quantities sold of both commodities, and the prices of the two will be found by solving simultaneous equations. However, in this case, the sales of one product will have a negative impact on the sales of the other.

Joint Products with Fixed Proportions

Certain products will be produced together from one set of inputs. In some instances, the two products will be produced in fixed proportions to one another. Although precisely fixed proportions may not occur often in the real world, relative fixity is commonly encountered, particularly in the short run. The example given earlier involved the products of a beef carcass and a hide (only one of each can be obtained from one steer). Other examples are soybean meal and soybean oil, and coconut milk and coconut meat. In many cases, there is a principal product and one or more by-products.

Assume products A and B are produced jointly in fixed proportions. Only one cost curve can be constructed in this case. However, the demand curves for the two products are independent (e.g., the demand for coconut meat is not related to the demand for its milk). Thus, the two demand curves and their respective marginal revenue curves can be added vertically to obtain a total demand curve and a total marginal revenue curve. Observe, however, that when one of the separate marginal revenue curves goes negative, it becomes irrelevant to the solution of the problem, because no business would produce at a point where marginal revenue is negative. To the right of this point, the total marginal revenue curve will be coincident with the marginal revenue of the product that is still in the positive range. Production will take place (using our usual maximization rule) where total marginal revenue equals marginal cost. The prices of the two separate products can be found at the quantity indicated on their respective demand curves. Figure 10.7 shows the results. D_A, D_B, MR_A, and MR_B are the demand and marginal revenue curves for the two products, and MR_S represents the vertical summation of the two individual marginal revenue curves. (The summed demand curve is actually irrelevant to the solution of the problem and need not be shown.) As can be seen, MR_S becomes identical with MR_B to the right of the point where MR_A becomes negative.

The curve MC represents the marginal cost of the joint product. Production will take place where marginal cost is equal to MR_S, which is at quantity Q on the graph. The prices charged for the two products will be found on their respective demand curves at P_A and P_B. An interesting aspect of this type of construction is that if the optimal production quantity were to the right (i.e., at higher quantities) of the point where one of the marginal revenue curves (in our case, that for product A) becomes negative, it would become profitable for the company to produce this total amount

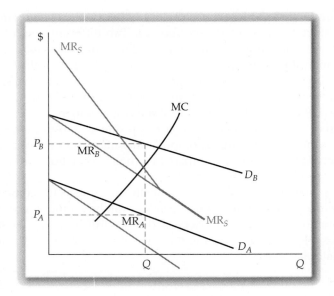

Figure 10.7 Price Determination for Joint Products Made in Fixed Proportions

but not to sell quantities of product A beyond the point where its marginal revenue becomes zero. The company should discard the excess product A.

Another important point is the effect of the change in the demand for one of the two jointly produced products. If the demand for product B rises and the price of B thus increases, there will be a decrease in the price of A (as it will be produced at a lower point on its demand curve).

Joint Products in Variable Proportions

When we relax the limitation of fixed proportions, we have the usual case of joint production. Indeed, when two products are produced from similar resources in variable proportions (i.e., if we produce more of one product we must produce less of the other) the situation is not dissimilar to the general case of production of different products with limited resources. We are essentially describing the "guns or butter" situation. Under short-run conditions, there is a given amount of resources with which the two products can be produced.

Figure 10.8 illustrates this situation. Curve I_1 is an isocost curve; the total cost of production is the same at each point. An essential requisite is that the curve be concave to the origin: as more of one product is produced, progressively larger quantities of the other must be given up. The isocost curve shows the alternative quantities of product A and B that can be produced. If the prices of the two products are constant regardless of quantity (i.e., we are implicitly operating under conditions of perfect competition), then a straight-line isorevenue curve can be drawn. At each point on R_1 in Figure 10.8, identical revenue is obtained. To optimize, the company will produce at the point of tangency between the isorevenue and isocost curves (point M in the figure). This represents the highest revenue that the company can attain for a given total cost. If revenue at this point is greater than cost, economic profit will result.

The company could also move from one isocost curve to another (e.g., from I_1 to I_2 to I_3), and consequently from one isorevenue curve to another, representing the use of additional variable resources. Production would take place at the tangency point that results in the largest difference between total revenue and total

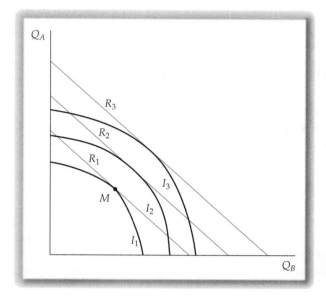

Figure 10.8 Joint Production Using Variable Proportions

cost. This point signifies the maximum economic profit the company can achieve. In the long run, these isocost curves would include changes in all resources, including those (e.g., plant and equipment) that are fixed in the short run. Under conditions of perfect competition, the optimal tangency would occur where total revenue just equals total cost, with no economic profit. At all other points, economic losses would be sustained.

We have limited our discussion to a simple model, using only two products and assuming perfect competition. Much more complex models could be developed, involving more than two products, noncompetitive conditions, and demand interrelationships, for example. The results would be more difficult to obtain, and relatively complicated mathematical models would have to be introduced, but the principles of economic maximization would still apply. Whenever a company takes action in introducing a new product, producing more of one at the expense of another or eliminating a certain commodity from its product line, and when such action is taken to improve its short-run or long-run profitability, the company is guided by the basic principle of equating marginal cost with marginal revenue.

TRANSFER PRICING

In today's complex industrial world, many companies have subdivided their operations into several groups or divisions. As a product moves from its early stages to the point where it is ready to be sold to consumers, it is passed from one operating division of the company to another. In the automobile industry, for example, various auto parts may be produced in different plants and then assembled into the finished product in yet another plant. Computer and peripheral equipment components may be produced in one plant and assembled into different products at other plants. Then, to sell the products, the marketing arm of the company may have to assemble the various individual machines into complete systems.

To continue this analysis, it is necessary to address the notion of *profit center*, a frequently used term that refers to a situation prevalent in large corporations.

The management of each division is charged with a profit objective. Thus, each stage of production must measure its costs and then establish a price at which it will "transfer" its product to the next stage. However, if each intermediate profit center were to set its price to maximize its own profit, the price of the final product may not maximize the profit of the company as a whole, which is the appropriate objective. The price set by the division transferring the intermediate product becomes the cost of the division receiving this product. If that price is set too high, this may start a chain reaction resulting in the final product price being higher than the price which would maximize the company's profit. The **transfer pricing** mechanism must be geared toward maximizing total company profit; therefore, the final pricing policy may be dictated centrally from the top of the corporation.

Such processes can be extremely complicated, particularly if there are more than two steps in the transfer process. Further, the intermediate products may be only for internal usage. In contrast, the producing division may also be selling its product in an external market, and the receiving division may be free to purchase the intermediate product from a competitor, if that would improve the company's profit situation. Let us discuss each case in turn. To simplify matters, we will assume the existence of just two divisions, one that manufactures components (division C), and another that assembles them into the final product and sells it (division A).

No External Markets

If there is no possibility for division A to buy components from a competing firm and no possibility for division C to sell components to other companies, then the two divisions must deal with equal quantities; division C will produce exactly the number of components that will be used by division A for assembly and sales. This situation is illustrated in Figure 10.9. The company will be faced by a demand curve for the final product and two marginal cost curves (D, MC_A, and MC_C). The two marginal cost curves, one for each division, will be summed vertically to obtain total marginal cost (MC), and the company will maximize its total profit by equating the total marginal cost with marginal revenue (MR). Production will take place at that intersection (point B), and the price for the final product will be the corresponding price on the demand curve (point A). The quantity sold is Q_t. The transfer price for the intermediate product is P_C.

Figure 10.9   Transfer Pricing with No Market for Intermediate Product

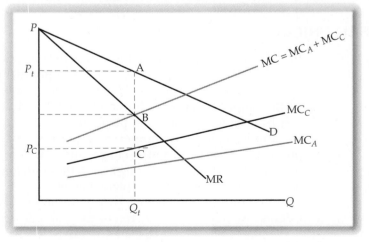

External Markets

It may be possible for division C to sell its (intermediate) product in a competitive market and for division A to purchase division C's product (an identical product) in a competitive market. In that case, the pricing of the product will proceed as follows:

1. Division C will produce at the point where its marginal cost equals the market price. (Because we are assuming the existence of a competitive market, the demand curve is horizontal, resulting in a uniform price regardless of quantity.)

2. The cost of the intermediate product to division A is the market price. This will be added to division A's marginal cost curve to obtain the total marginal cost for the final product.

3. Production will take place at the quantity where the total marginal cost equals the marginal revenue for the final product.

Figure 10.10 shows a case where there is a competitive market for the intermediate product, and division C produces components in excess of those used by division A. Assume the market price for division C's product is P_C. The optimal quantity to be produced by C is Q_C, given its marginal cost MC_C. The marginal cost of division C's product to division A is now P_C and the total marginal cost MC equals MC_A plus P_C. The company will sell its product at optimal price P_t at quantity Q_t. Division C will sell quantity Q_C minus Q_t in the competitive market.

Of course, should division C for some reason attempt to price the intermediate product in excess of the market price, then A would buy all the intermediate product in the external market.

If the optimal output of division C is less than A wants to buy, then A will turn to the external market for the additional units of the intermediate product it needs to maximize company profits. The graph for this situation would be quite similar to Figure 10.10, and we leave it to the reader to illustrate this particular situation.

In this section, we discuss transfer pricing among different divisions of a company when all the divisions are located in the same country. When different parts

Figure 10.10   Transfer Pricing with Competitive Market for Intermediate Product

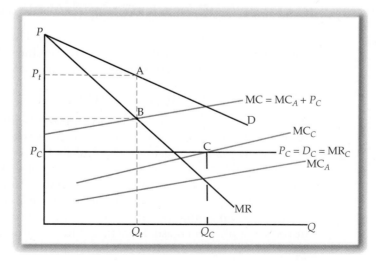

of a corporation are located in different countries and products are shipped across borders, the situation becomes even more complex. We discuss this subject in detail in chapter 13.

OTHER PRICING PRACTICES

Price skimming occurs when a firm is the first to introduce a product. It may have a virtual monopoly, and often will be able to charge high prices and obtain substantial profits before competition enters.

In **penetration pricing** a company sets a relatively low price in order to obtain market share.

Limit pricing exists when a monopolist sets a price below the monopoly price (where MR = MC) to discourage potential competitors from entering the market and competing. At the lower price, the monopolist's profit will be below its maximum. Of course, limit pricing may be based on the monopolist's expectation that its cost will decrease because of the existence of a learning curve, so that ultimately the limit price will become the profit maximizing price.

Another special pricing practice is **predatory pricing**, where a company prices below its marginal cost to cause competitors to exit the market. After the competitors have left the market the company will raise its prices. However, this practice is not seen very often in the United States because it is illegal under the Sherman Antitrust Act. Also, it may create considerable losses to the monopolist and may not be worthwhile in the long run. Further, after the monopolist raises prices a new competitive threat may appear. Thus the company may have to lower prices again and incur new losses.

With **prestige pricing**, demand for a product may be higher at a higher price because of the prestige that ownership bestows on the buyer.

Psychological pricing takes advantage of the fact that the demand for a particular product may be quite inelastic over a certain range but will become rather elastic at one specific higher or lower price. Such a demand curve has the appearance of a step function.

Complete explanations of these pricing practices can be found in many marketing textbooks.

GLOBAL APPLICATION: THE DECLINE OF EUROPEAN CARTELS

European governments have in the past tolerated and supported monopolies, and while pricing cartels have been illegal, they have flourished. But this situation is currently changing. Where monopolies existed, markets are now opening up.

The European Carton-Board Cartel

A case involving nineteen carton-board producers in ten European countries actually resembles the electrical manufacturers' case discussed previously.

In July 1994, the European Commission imposed record fines of $159 million on ninteen producers. The cartel involved a market-sharing agreement and orchestrated 6 to 10 percent price increases each 6 months from 1987 to 1990. Monthly "social" meetings were arranged at luxury hotels (most frequently in Zurich). "The cartel's members then compared the state of their order books to judge when best to introduce a price increase. Sometimes the big producers agreed on temporary plant stoppages to keep production under control."[45] Fake minutes were drawn up to disguise the business that was transacted.

The European Commission acted after complaints by the industry's customers about the continual price increases during a period of sharp economic downturn. In 1991, officials of the commission staged simultaneous raids on the producers and found private notes documenting the dates and amounts of price increases. One of the companies decided to admit to the conspiracy and aided the probe, which resulted in heavy fines.

The European Vitamin Cartel

In November 2001, the European Commission imposed fines totaling more than 850 million euros (approximately $747 million) on thirteen pharmaceutical companies for price fixing of vitamins that had spread over 9 years. Most of the fine was levied on Roche of Switzerland and BASF of Germany. This decision followed 2 years after the United States, who under a similar investigation, had fined the same two companies an amount exceeding $700 million. It was said that the companies had "virtually operated as a single company." The cartels met each month or quarter, exchanged sales and price data, and reviewed quotas allotted to each company. In some cases, "participants even prepared an annual 'budget' to adjust sales according to each company's quota."[46]

The European Copper Pipe Cartel

In September 2004, the European Commission fined eight copper pipe manufacturers 222 million euros for price fixing. The companies fined were located in several European countries, the United Kingdom, Sweden, Finland, Italy, Greece, the Netherlands, and Germany. "The companies operated a classic cartel with code names, meeting in airports and the objective to avoid competition through allocation of production volumes and market shares." According to notes taken from one group "the objective is to keep the prices in the high price level, if possible to increase even more." The case started in 2001 when the commission carried out raids at the firms' headquarters. The commission had received information regarding the cartel from one of the companies involved, Mueller Industries. Mueller was not fined because of its cooperation with the commission.[47]

Other Price-Fixing Cases in Europe

More recently, a large number of price-fixing actions have been pursued in various European countries and in the European Commission. Let us just mention a few decisions. In 2003, the European Commission imposed fines totaling €138 million on several companies involved in fixing the price of sorbates. Also in 2003, the EC fined three companies a total of €79 million for fixing the prices of copper tubing. The three companies, which account for 75 percent to 85 percent of total output, were

---

[45]This discussion and quotation are based on Emma Tucker, "Price-Fixing Cartel Given Record Fine by Brussels," *Financial Times,* July 14, 1994, and Emma Tucker, "Rise and Fall of a House of Cards," *Financial Times,* July 15, 1994.
[46]Francesco Guerrera and Birgit Jennen, "European Groups Face Record Fines for Roles in Price-Fixing," *Financial Times,* November 21, 2001; Francesco Guerrera, "Monti Lashes 'Vitamins AG' Cartel," *Financial Times,* November 22, 2001.
[47]Caroline Merrell, "Price-Fixing Copper Pipe Firms Fined Pounds 159 Million by EU," *Times,* September 4, 2004.

found to have held talks to fix prices and share markets. In 2004, the Dutch anticartel body fined three bicycle producers €30 million for agreeing to raise prices of bicycles between September 2001 and September 2002.[48]

A very recent case of price fixing involved British Airways, which was fined $300 million by the U.S. Department of Justice and $246 million by Great Britain's Office of Fair Trading. British Airways admitted that during the period 2004–2006 it conspired with Virgin Atlantic over surcharges to be added to prices of long-haul flights because of increases in oil prices. Virgin Atlantic was not fined because it reported the action. In a separate case involving price fixing of cargo rates as well as passenger rates, British Airways and Korean Airlines were assessed another $300 million each.[49]

In January 2007, the European Commission fined ten European and Japanese engineering companies a total of €751 million for price fixing of switchgear used to control electricity to homes, offices, and factories. The commission stated that the companies "rigged bids for procurement contracts, fixed prices, allocated projects to each other, shared markets, and exchanged important and confidential information" between 1988 and 2004.[50]

What was called the "largest ever" fine of €992 million ($1.3 billion) in the European Union was levied on five European elevator makers "for operating cartels for the installation and maintenance of lifts and escalators in Germany, Belgium, Luxembourg, and the Netherlands." Of the five companies, the German conglomerate ThyssenKrupp AG received the largest fine, €479 million. The European Commission stated that the cartel rigged bids, fixed prices, and shared markets during the period 1995–2004.[51]

Apparently, price-fixing cartels abound throughout the world. A perusal of the business press will reveal the frequency of cases brought against companies conspiring to fix prices.

Price Discrimination by Airlines

In December 2003, the European Commission asked eighteen European airlines whether they charge different fares on the same flights to residents of different European Union countries. Most of these price differentials occurred in tickets ordered on the Internet and were not connected with different dates of purchase, possibility of changing reservations, or other features that could impact cost. Apparently, this price discrimination existed. After receiving answers from sixteen of the eighteen airlines, the commission ended its action in June 2004 because this pricing practice had been eliminated after the commission's inquiries.[52]

Another case of price discrimination by an airline was reported in 2003. Apparently, foreigners flying domestic routes in Vietnam were charged considerably more (as much as 50 percent) than local fliers. In December 2003, Vietnam's Civil Aviation Administration announced that it would abolish this type of discrimination on January 1, 2004.[53]

---

[48]"EC Imposes Fines Totaling EUR138.4 M on Companies in Sorbates Cartel," *Press Release* (*Chemicals*), December 17, 2003; "Competition: Commission Fines Copper Tubes Cartel," *European Report*, December 20, 2003; "Dutch Regulator Fines Bicycle Producers 30 Min Euro," *Dutch News Digest*, April 22, 2004.
[49]"OFT Fines British Airways GBP121.5M for Price Fixing," *Dow Jones International News*, July 31, 2007; Michael Peele et al., "BA Fined $546m in International Cartel Crackdown," *Financial Times*, August 3, 2007; Corey Boles, "Judge Accepts Korean Airlines Guilty Plea in Price Fixing," *Dow Jones New Service*, August 23, 2007.
[50]Russell Hotten, "Engineering Cartel 'Cheats' Are Given Record Fines," *Daily Telegraph*, January 25, 2007.
[51]"EU Slaps U.S. $1.3 Billion Fine on Four Elevator Makers for Price Fixing," *Canadian Press*, February 21, 2007.
[52]"Air Transport: Suspicion of Price Discrimination Practices," *European Report*, December 24, 2003; "Airlines Put End to Price Discrimination on Basis of National Residence," *Europe Information*, June 9, 2004.
[53]"Vietnam to End Airfare Price Discrimination Jan. 1," *Kyodo News*, December 2, 2003.

The Solution

Rebecca James went to see Philip Olds of the food division to solicit his advice on the bid she intended to make for the bottled water supply contract with the large airport catering company.

"One thing is certain," he said. "You have to bid at a price considerably lower than the price at which you sell to small retail stores. These stores have a leeway in how much they can charge their customers because they are really selling convenience. A small variance in price is not going to change their sales significantly, so they will not stop buying from us as long as our price is not out of line.

"However, your potential new customer intends to give a contract to only one additional supplier, and 10 cents per case will make a large difference when hundreds of thousands of cases are involved. Thus, you will have to shave your markup as much as possible. It may turn out that you will make precious little profit, if any, on this contract."

Philip was telling Rebecca that the demand price elasticity of the large caterer was quite different from that of the small retailers. As a result, Global Foods could sell to these two markets at different prices.

Rebecca is thus confronted with a case of price discrimination. The demand elasticities in the two markets are probably quite different; thus higher prices can be charged in the market displaying lower elasticity. The separation of the two markets (i.e., no cross-selling) represents the second important condition for the existence of price discrimination. Another important consideration for Rebecca is that the price to be charged must enable the company to gain a foothold in this large market (penetration or entry pricing).

Back in her office, Rebecca begins to work on determining the price. She assumes the average cost per case of Waterpure for the two customers is the same. Although this is certainly not quite accurate (the large shipments the company will make to the new customer if the bid is won will probably create some cost savings), the unit cost differences will probably not be significant, so her analysis will lose little if she assumes equality.

She estimates the company's usual markup to be about 50 percent. After some additional consideration, and a review of some data for the industry that she obtained, she feels that a 20 percent markup would put the company in a good competitive position.

Before making this recommendation to her boss, she will consult with the finance and accounting departments to determine what, if any, profit would be realized on this transaction. She will, of course, include this analysis with her recommendation. It is quite possible that at this low price profit will be extremely marginal, and she will then have to argue that obtaining a foothold in this market will have beneficial long-run consequences.

The decision that she has made has some rather important implications for the estimate of demand elasticities for the two classes of customers. The lower the demand elasticity, the higher will be the markup that a company can obtain. Following the equation developed previously,

$$(1 + M) = \frac{E_P}{E_P + 1}$$

(where demand elasticity is a negative number), an elasticity of 3 conforms to a markup of 50 percent, whereas an elasticity of 6 corresponds to a 20 percent markup. Of course, these numbers are approximations, but such an estimate could be of great help to Rebecca in her attempt to set the proper price.

SUMMARY

This chapter is built on the foundation laid in chapters 8 and 9 by applying the principles of pricing and output to specific pricing situations, most under conditions of imperfect competition. Briefly, we learned the following:

1. Cartels are formed to avoid the uncertainties of a possible reaction by one competitor to price and production actions by another. The firms in the industry agree on unified pricing and production actions to maximize profits. However, as history shows, such arrangements are not always stable.

2. Price leadership exists when one company establishes a price and others follow. Two types of price leadership were discussed: barometric and dominant.

3. Baumol's model describes the actions of a company whose objective is to maximize revenue (rather than profits) subject to a minimum profit constraint.

4. Price discrimination (or differential pricing) exists when a product is sold in different markets at different prices. Third-degree price discrimination is the most common. By charging different prices in separate markets that have demand curves with different price elasticities, a firm can increase its profits over what they would be if a uniform price were charged.

5. Cost-plus pricing appears to be a very common method. However, such pricing does not necessarily imply that marginal principles and demand curve effects are not taken into consideration.

6. Multiproduct pricing was examined, because most firms and plants produce more than one product at the same time. Multiple products produced by one firm can be complements or substitutes, both on the demand side and the supply side. Four possible cases were discussed, and it was shown how application of the marginal principle brings about profit maximization.

7. Several other pricing practices were summarized. One was transfer pricing, which is used to determine the price of a product that progresses through several stages of production within a firm.

IMPORTANT CONCEPTS

Barometric price leadership: In an oligopolistic industry, a situation in which one firm, perceiving that demand and supply conditions warrant it, announces a price change, expecting that other firms will follow. (p. 390)

Baumol model: A model hypothesizing that firms seek to maximize their revenue subject to some minimum profit requirement (i.e., the profit constraint). (p. 392)

Cartel: A collusive arrangement in oligopolistic markets. Producers agree on unified pricing and production actions to maximize profits and to eliminate the rigors of competition. (p. 385)

Cost-plus pricing: Also called *full-cost pricing,* a practice in which prices are calculated by adding a markup to total cost. (p. 405)

Dominant price leadership: In an oligopolistic industry, a firm, usually the largest in the industry, sets a price at which it will maximize its profits, allowing other firms to sell as much as they want at that price. (p. 390)

Limit pricing: A monopolist will set price below MR = MC to prevent potential customers from entering the market. (p. 416)

Multiproduct pricing: Pricing that reflects the interrelationship among multiple products of a firm that are substitutes or complements. (p. 409)

Penetration pricing: A company charges a lower price than indicated by economic analysis in order to gain a foothold in the market. (p. 416)

Predatory pricing: A company sets price below its marginal cost to drive competitors out of the market. (p. 416)

Prestige pricing: A perception that charging a higher price will increase quantity sold because of the prestige obtained by the buyer. (p. 416)

Price discrimination: A situation in which an identical product is sold in different markets at different prices. (p. 393)

Price leadership: One company in an oligopolistic industry establishes the price, and the other companies follow. Two types of price leadership are common: barometric and dominant. (p. 389)

Price skimming: The practice of charging a higher price than indicated by economic analysis when a company introduces a new product and competition is weak. (p. 416)

Psychological pricing: The practice of charging, for example, $9.95 rather than $10 for a product, in the belief that such pricing will create the illusion of significantly lower price to the consumer. (p. 416)

Transfer pricing: A method to correctly price a product as it is transferred from one stage of production to the next. (p. 414)

QUESTIONS

1. "If a company sets its prices on the basis of a cost-plus calculation, it cannot possibly suffer a loss on its products." True or false? Comment.

2. Price discrimination is often defended on the basis of equity. What is meant by this statement? Comment on its validity.

3. Which products in each pair would tend to have higher markups in a supermarket?
   a. Cigarettes versus tomatoes
   b. Potatoes versus orange juice

4. Many years ago, a neighborhood lunch counter charged 15 cents for a cup of coffee and 15 cents for a buttered hard roll. One day, a customer ordered the two items and was told that the total price was 35 cents. When the customer asked which of the two items had been raised by 5 cents, the owner's condescending reply was, "Which do you think?" In your opinion, which of the two items was affected and why?

5. Differentiate *barometric* price leadership and *dominant* price leadership.

6. Is there a similarity between cartel pricing and monopoly pricing?

7. What conditions are favorable to the formation and maintenance of a cartel?

8. Can government be a potent force in the establishment and maintenance of monopolistic conditions? Name and describe such occurrences.

9. Describe the properties of the Baumol revenue maximization model. Do you consider this to be a good alternative to the profit maximization model?

10. Telephone companies charge different rates for calls during the day, in the evening, and at night or weekends. Do you consider this to be price discrimination?

11. Is cost-plus pricing necessarily inconsistent with marginal pricing?

12. Airline ticket prices may differ with respect to when the ticket is bought, how long a passenger remains on the trip (e.g., over a weekend) and other variables. Are these differences a case of price discrimination?

13. Does cost-plus pricing necessarily ignore the demand curve?

14. Define and describe (giving examples):
    a. Transfer pricing
    b. Psychological pricing
    c. Price skimming
    d. Penetration pricing

15. Under what circumstances would a discriminating monopolist produce a more socially optimal quantity than a nondiscriminating monopolist? Is there any situation under which a discriminating monopolist could produce the quantity that would be produced under competition?

PROBLEMS

1. There are only two firms in the widget industry. The total demand for widgets is $Q = 30 - 2P$. The two firms have identical cost functions, $TC = 3 + 10Q$. The two firms agree to collude and act as though the industry were a monopoly. At what price and quantity will this cartel maximize its profit?

2. An amusement park, whose customer set is made up of two markets, adults and children, has developed demand schedules as follows:

Price ($)	Quantity Adults	Quantity Children
5	15	20
6	14	18
7	13	16
8	12	14
9	11	12
10	10	10
11	9	8
12	8	6
13	7	4
14	6	2

The marginal operating cost of each unit of quantity is $5. (*Hint:* Because marginal cost is a constant, so is average variable cost. Ignore fixed cost.) The owners of the amusement park want to maximize profits.

a. Calculate the price, quantity, and profit if
    1. The amusement park charges a different price in each market.
    2. The amusement park charges the same price in the two markets combined.
    3. Explain the difference in the profit realized under the two situations.

b. (Mathematical solution) The demand schedules presented in problem 2 can be expressed in equation form as follows (where subscript A refers to the adult market, subscript C to the market for children, and subscript T to the two markets combined):

$$Q_A = 20 - 1P_A$$
$$Q_C = 30 - 2P_C$$
$$Q_T = 50 - 3P_T$$

Solve these equations for the maximum profit that the amusement park will attain when it charges different prices in the two markets and when it charges a single price for the combined market.

3. The Bramwell Corporation has estimated its demand function and total cost function to be as follows:

$$Q = 25 - 0.05P$$
$$TC = 700 + 200Q$$

Answer the following questions either by developing demand and cost schedules (*Hint:* Use quantities from 1 to 14) or by solving the equations.

a. What will be the price and quantity if Bramwell wants to
    1. Maximize profits?
    2. Maximize revenue?
    3. Maximize revenue but require the profit to be a minimum of $300?

b. Now assume the cost function is $TC = 780 + 200Q$, while the demand function remains the same. What will the price and quantity be if Bramwell wants to
    1. Maximize profits?
    2. Maximize revenue?
    3. Maximize revenue but require the profit to be a minimum of $300?

c. Why are the answers the same in $a(1)$ and $b(1)$ but different in $a(3)$ and $b(3)$?

4. The Great Southern Paper Company has the following marginal cost schedule for producing pulp:

Quantity (tons)	Marginal Cost
1	$18
2	20
3	25
4	33
5	43

Pulp can be bought in the open market for $25 per ton. The marginal cost of converting pulp into paper is $MC = 5 + 5Q$, and the demand for paper is $P = 135 - 15Q$. Calculate the marginal cost of paper if the company produces its own pulp. What is the profit-maximizing quantity? Should the company purchase pulp from the outside or produce it in-house?

5. The purchase price of Fancy Shoes, sold by Bradbury Footwear Stores, is $30 per pair. The company's economist has estimated the point price elasticity to be -1.8. What price should the company charge if it wants to maximize its profits?

6. An airplane manufacturer has annual fixed costs of $50 million. Its variable costs are expected to be $2 million per plane. If the manufacturer wants to earn a 10 percent rate of return on its investment of $400 million and expects to produce 100 aircraft this year, what will its markup on total cost have to be? If it expects to produce 150 aircraft, what will its markup have to be?

7. Schultz's Orchard grows only two types of fruit—apples and peaches—and over the years it has been able to chart two production levels and the resulting total cost. The figures are shown in the following table, where quantity produced is given in bushels.

Apples	Peaches	Apples	Peaches
900	0	1,400	0
800	200	1,200	300
600	400	900	600
400	500	700	700
250	550	300	850
0	600	0	900
Total cost: $15,000		Total cost: $25,000	

This year it is expected that the price of apples will be $30 per bushel and that of peaches will be $45 per bushel.

What is the best production level at each cost? How much is the profit at each level?

8. The Prestige Office Equipment Company produces and sells different types of office furniture. One of the important items it sells is a high-quality desk. During the past year, Prestige sold 5,000 of these at a price of $500 each. The contribution profit for this line of furniture last year was $700,000.

A consultant suggests that Prestige decrease the price of each desk by $30. In his opinion, another 500 desks could then be sold, and the total profit would be maintained. A trade publication that employs an economist has estimated price elasticity of office furniture (including desks) to be about -1.8.

Assume the variable unit cost per desk in the coming year will remain the same. Evaluate the consultant's proposal. Be sure to include in your answer the price elasticity assumed by the consultant, as well as the published elasticity estimate.

9. The royalties received by an author for writing a college text are frequently set at a rate of about 15 percent of the publisher's book price. This may create a conflict between the goals of a profit-maximizing publisher and those of a royalty-maximizing author. As a student consumer (assuming you have to pay for your textbooks), whose goal would be more beneficial to you? Why? Demonstrate this situation graphically (assume a downward-sloping demand curve).

10. The Prime Company produces two products, X and Y. They are produced jointly so for each X manufactured a unit of Y is also produced. The joint cost function is

$$TC = 50 + 2Q + .5Q^2$$

Q represents the number of joint units produced. The demand equations for the two products are the following:

$$Q_x = 100 - P_x$$
$$Q_y = 60 - 2P_y$$

a. How many units should the company produce per period?
b. What price should it charge for each of the joint products?
c. What will be the company's profit per period?
Assume the company is a profit maximizer.

11. George's Pants Store sells a particular brand of slacks. It recently decreased the price of a popular brand by 5%. This decrease was followed by a 20% increase in sales. The marginal cost of producing these slacks is $100.
a. What is the point price elasticity of demand for these slacks?
b. What would be the optimal mark-up and price of these items?

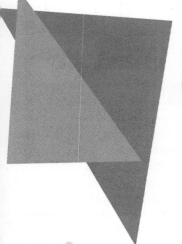

Game Theory and Asymmetric Information

Learning Objectives

Upon completion of this chapter, readers should be able to:

- Define game theory, and explain how it helps better understand mutually interdependent management decisions.

- Explain the essential dilemma faced by participants in the game called Prisoners' Dilemma.

- Explain the concept of a dominant strategy and its role in understanding how auctions can help improve the price for sellers, while still benefiting buyers.

- Explain the key problems that arise in a market where buyers and sellers do not have the same information about a product (i.e., when "asymmetric information" exits between buyers and sellers).

- Briefly explain the concepts of "adverse selection" and "moral hazard" and why they exist in the type of market described in objective 4.

- Explain how "market signaling" can help market participants make better economic decisions when asymmetric information exists between buyers and sellers.

The Situation

Henry Caufield did not want to lower the price of his soft drinks even further because he knew it would start a vicious price war between him and the other two store owners in the vicinity.[1] But he believed that this might be the only way he could restore his share of the market for a product that was an important part of his business's profitability.

To his surprise, his daughter Erica wanted to stay at home and work in the family store over the summer to gain some practical business experience. She had just decided to switch her major from art to economics, so she believed that working in her dad's store would be a useful complement to her studies. But when he confided in her about his dilemma regarding the pricing of his soft drinks, he was a bit puzzled by her reaction. "Dad, what you're faced with is a classic game theory problem," she responded.

"I'm not so sure what you mean, Erica. This is not a game we're talking about. This is the real world of business, and the future of my business could well depend on the outcome of this potential price war over soft drinks. If my competitors get the best of me in the pricing of this product, who knows what they'll do in the pricing of coffee, snacks, and gasoline?"

"Don't worry, Dad, I know this is serious. I know that you probably didn't study this topic when you were in college, but when my professor introduced game theory to us in my managerial economics course, I was fascinated. Moreover, I do believe there are some practical applications of the concepts that may be of help to you in this situation."

"Okay, Erica, what's this game theory stuff all about and how can it help me?"

---

[1]This situation continues from "The Situation" and "The Solution" vignettes presented in chapter 4.

INTRODUCTION[2]

The optimization analysis used throughout this text, such as the use of the MR = MC rule in the setting of price and output, provides the theoretical foundation for managerial decision making. But this type of analysis has two shortcomings when applied to actual business situations. It assumes other factors such as the reaction of competitors or the tastes and preferences of consumers remain constant as the firm sets its optimal price and output according to the MR = MC rule.[3] In reality, managers must often make these decisions in the face of changing competitive reactions and changing consumer tastes and preferences, as Henry Caufield discovered in "The Solution" vignette in chapter 4. Moreover, managers must sometimes make decisions when certain parties have more information about market conditions than others. This chapter presents two theories—game theory and the theory of asymmetric information—that have been incorporated by economists into managerial economics to address the shortcomings of standard optimization analysis. The first part of this chapter talks about **game theory** and shows how this theory can be applied to the setting of prices in oligopolistic markets and can help firms develop their business strategies. The second part presents the basic concepts of the theory of asymmetric information and illustrates when, why, and how managers need to incorporate these particular concepts in the making of their business decisions.

Game Theory

Formally speaking, game theory is concerned with "how individuals make decisions when they are aware that their actions affect each other and when each individual takes this into account."[4] There are numerous ways in which game theory can be applied to economic analysis and decision making. As already stated, game theory can help us better understand the competitive reactions of firms in the pricing of products in the market and gain an insight into the establishment of a firm's long-term strategy. In addition, game theory provides certain insights into the behavior of individuals in such economic situations as the bidding for items in auctions, as well as the negotiations that take place between suppliers and buyers or between union and management.

Figure 11.1 presents a useful taxonomy of the different types of games covered in game theory. As illustrated in Figure 11.1 the various types of games analyzed in game theory can be characterized as zero-sum or non–zero-sum, cooperative or noncooperative, and two-person or *n*-person. In a **zero-sum game**, the gains of one player directly reflect the losses of another player. In a non–zero-sum game, all players may gain or lose, depending on the particular actions that each player takes. Most economic activity can be characterized as a non–zero-sum game. But regardless of which type of game is involved, the essential idea in game theory is to apply the logic of mathematics to arrive at a "solution," or in economic terms, an "equilibrium." Let us look at some examples of specific games that are particularly relevant to economic analysis and decision making.

---

[2]Most of the material in this chapter was originally written by Professor Shannon Mudd. The authors also want to acknowledge the help of Michael Mills in updating the material for this edition.

[3]The kinked demand model presented in chapter 9 tries to explain why prices in oligopoly markets tend to be similar for each competitor, but it does not explain how and why this "administered price" is initially established. Also, in the early 1900s, the French economist Cournot developed a mathematical model to explain how price is determined in a market with only two competitors (i.e., a "duopoly"). However, his model did not take into account possible actions and reactions by the two competitors.

[4]H. Scott Bierman and Luis Fernandez, *Game Theory with Economic Applications*, Reading, MA: Addison-Wesley, 1998, p. 4.

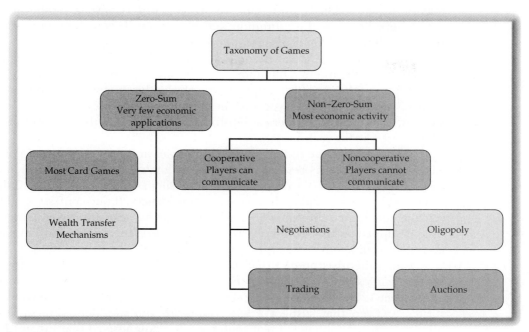

Figure 11.1   Taxonomy of Games

A SELECTED SAMPLE OF GAMES OF PARTICULAR RELEVANCE IN ECONOMICS

Prisoners' Dilemma[5]

Prisoners' Dilemma is one of the most well-known and frequently cited games in economics textbooks. This variation is characterized as a *two-person, non–zero-sum,* **noncooperative game** with a **dominant strategy**. In a *zero-sum game,* one player's gain is the other's loss and vice versa. In a non–zero-sum game, both players may gain or lose, depending on the actions each chooses to take. The noncooperative feature of the game implies that opponents are not allowed to share information with each other. A dominant strategy means that there is one strategy that is best for a person, no matter what the other one does.

The particulars of the prisoners' dilemma are essentially as follows. Two individuals commit a serious crime together and are apprehended by the police. They know that there is insufficient evidence to convict them of the crime. At worst, they risk being charged and convicted of the less serious offense of loitering near the scene of the crime, which involves a lesser prison sentence. The police interrogate them separately. During this procedure, the suspects are not allowed to communicate with each other. If one suspect confesses, then he will get a minimum sentence (that could be suspended) for cooperating with the authorities, while the other will receive the

---

[5]There are numerous versions of the Prisoners' Dilemma story. This one is based on Andrew Schotter, *Microeconomics: A Modern Approach,* Reading, MA: Addison-Wesley, 1997, Ch. 7, and J. R. McGuigan, R. C. Moyer, and F. H. Harris, *Managerial Economics,* 9th ed. Cincinnati, OH: South-Western College Publishing, 2002, pp. 532, 568–69.

maximum sentence. If both talk, then each will receive a moderate sentence somewhere between the minimum and maximum. Given these conditions, what should each suspect do? Game theory provides the answer.

All solutions in game theory involve what economists call an equilibrium condition. In Prisoners' Dilemma, a stable equilibrium is achieved. It is a stable equilibrium in that once the suspects have chosen his/her strategy (in this case, both suspects would choose to confess) neither would want to unilaterally change its strategy.[6] Let us use a numerical illustration to show what the equilibrium situation would look like for each suspect.

Let us assume the options for each prisoner and the consequences of selecting each option can be represented in the payoff matrix seen in Figure 11.2. For each suspect, the options are to confess or remain silent. If they both confess, the matrix indicates that they would each receive 5-year sentences. If one confesses and the other remains silent, then the "stool pigeon"[7] would get a 1-year suspended sentence, while his tight-lipped partner would receive a 14-year prison term. If they both remain silent, then they would both receive an 18-month sentence.

Game theorists predict that ultimately both suspects would decide to confess because confessing is a dominant strategy for both of them. To see this, suppose you are suspect 1. If suspect 2 were to choose to confess, which would be your preferred strategy? Given that suspect 2 has confessed, you would prefer confess (5-year sentence) to not confess (14-year sentence). Suppose instead that suspect 2 were not to confess; you would prefer confess (1-year suspended sentence) to not confess (18-month sentence). In both cases, you prefer to confess. With the payoffs as given in this game, confess is a dominant strategy for you. Because the game is symmetric, confess is also a dominant strategy for suspect 2. When both suspects choose not to confess, it is a stable equilibrium because neither would want to change the strategy after the other has chosen his or her strategy.

Figure 11.2 Prisoners' Dilemma: Payoff Matrix

		SUSPECT I	
		Confess	Not Confess
SUSPECT II	Confess	5 years 5 years	14 years 1 year suspended
	Not Confess	1 year suspended 14 years	18 months 18 months

[6]Economists often refer to this as "Nash equilibrium," after the mathematician John Nash, who first proposed this in 1951 and who received a Nobel Prize in Economics for his work in game theory. John Nash is also the focus of the book by Sylvia Nasar, *A Beautiful Mind,* New York: Simon & Schuster, 1998, recently made into an award-winning movie.

[7]We recognize that there are more current terms for this type of person, but we are hoping that we have some readers who on occasion watch a James Cagney movie on television.

At this point readers might be wondering what the relationship is between alleged criminals and oligopolistic pricing. Instead of alleged criminals, suppose we use two companies competing in a market for a product in which price is a key consideration in the purchasing decisions of consumers. In place of "confess" or "not confess," we can use the options "high price" and "low price." In place of prison sentences, we can use profit.

Figure 11.3 shows two companies, A and B, and the expected revenue that each hopes to gain by charging a high or low price relative to the price charged by the other. It is easy to see that real two-company combinations, such as Coca-Cola and Pepsi-Cola, Dell and Gateway, or Miller and Anheuser Busch, could be used as the A and B companies. As a test of your understanding of the Prisoners' Dilemma, what would be the dominant strategy equilibrium in this version of the game?

If your answer is that both companies would charge the low prices, you would be absolutely right. The low price strategy is a dominant strategy for both firms. However, both firms would prefer to be in the high price/high price situation than in the low price/low price situation. If they both prefer this situation, why was this not the outcome? The problem is that the high price/high price equilibrium is not stable. Once Company B had chosen the high price, Company A would want to change its strategy to the low price. The same holds for Company B; once Company A had chosen the high price, it would want to change its strategy to the low price. Only when both companies have chosen low prices is a stable equilibrium achieved because neither firm would have an incentive to change its strategy on its own. Although the situation in which each company chose high price would be preferred to each choosing the low price, the point of this game is that each would always be thinking of the possibility of the other setting a lower price (i.e., the equivalent of confessing). Therefore, as a sort of "second-best solution," each would choose the more secure situation of the low price, thereby dispensing with the fear of the other gaining an advantage by setting a lower price.

What if we changed the rules to allow them to cooperate? If they could cooperate, they could both choose the high price and both would be better off. This would be *efficient* in that once this equilibrium was achieved there would be no alternative

Figure 11.3   Oligopoly Pricing Using the Prisoners' Dilemma: Payoff Matrix Model

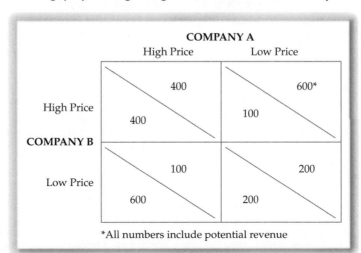

*All numbers include potential revenue

outcome in which at least one player is better off and no player is worse off.[8] But because the rules of the game require noncooperation, the firms end up in an equilibrium that is, from their perspective, suboptimal.

This example shows the value of game theory. By understanding the rules under which players (firms, employers, employees, managers, stock owners, etc.) operate, we can understand why we observe what might be otherwise inexplicable in the marketplace. We may even be able to predict outcomes. In a later section, we look at how managers can use their understanding to strategize, taking advantage of the rules of the game or working around them to achieve better results for their firm or even a more efficient result overall. In the remainder of this section, we examine four additional examples of games and how they can inform us about market interactions. Two of these examples involve pricing, one involves location, and the fourth involves decisions about output.

Beach Kiosk Game

Let us look at other potential equilibriums to better understand stable and unstable equilibriums. The **beach kiosk scenario** is a *two-person, noncooperative, zero-sum game.* There are two potential equilibriums in which the players are equally well off, but only one of them is stable. Suppose two vendors have been granted licenses to provide soft drinks, snacks, and sunscreen to a county beach area that runs north and south for about 200 yards. Every day they roll their kiosks down to the beach and must decide where to set them up. The beachgoers tend to avoid large concentrations and are generally spread out evenly along the beach. They have no preferences for one vendor over the other and will use whichever beach kiosk is nearest. One possibility is for the two vendors to split the market so one locates 50 yards from the north end and the other locates 50 yards from the south end.

The previous situation would not be a stable equilibrium because if the first vendor sets up at 50 yards from the north end, the second vendor can make herself better off by moving closer to the first, perhaps 25 yards farther north (midway between the first vendor and the south end). She can then serve a wider portion of the beach, that is, take away some of the other vendor's customers. Likewise, once the second vendor locates at 75 yards from the south end, the first vendor can make himself better off by moving closer to the first vendor, perhaps 12.5 yards farther south (midway between the north end and the second vendor). Can you see where this is going and define the Nash equilibrium?

The only stable equilibrium is when both vendors locate next to each other at the midpoint, 100 yards from both the South and from the North ends. Only in this situation will neither vendor have an incentive to move given the location of the other vendor. They will split the market just as when they were located 50 yards from the ends. In this case, neither of the two equilibriums is more *efficient* from the vendors' point of view. However, from the beachgoers' point of view, either would be preferable. Have you ever observed this phenomenon? Consider the location of gas stations or the political rhetoric of the two main American parties in a presidential election year. Is there evidence that they tend to position themselves close together? What additional examples can you provide?

---

[8]Note that this definition of efficiency is not consistent with a welfare maximization concept of efficiency. It is efficient only from the point of view of the players. Others not involved in setting the strategy may be made worse off. For example, consumers facing higher prices would be worse off than if no cooperation were possible and both firms chose the lower price. For this discussion, we choose not to consider whether the outcome of a game is economically efficient.

Repeated Games

The beach kiosk example differed from the Prisoners' Dilemma in that decisions were made across time. Let us see what happens when we bring time into our earlier pricing example by changing the rules somewhat. Suppose our two companies described in Figure 11.3 set prices not just once, but every week for an indefinite period; that is, the game is repeated. How will this change the outcome?

Recall that from the players' point of view, the efficient equilibrium is when both charge a high price. But because each has a dominant strategy of choosing a low price, this efficient equilibrium is not achieved. However, when the game is repeated, the threat of retaliation in future periods can offset each firm's incentive to "cheat" by charging a low price while the other firm is charging a high price. In this case, once the high price equilibrium is established, it can potentially be a stable equilibrium.

To see how this works, return to Figure 11.3. Suppose that the high price equilibrium has been established and that each firm receives $400 in revenue in each week. If one firm were to cheat and charge the low price, it would receive $600 in that week, an extra $200. However, the other firm would only be receiving $100 and could retaliate in the next period by also charging the low price. With each firm now charging the low price, for each successive week the firms would earn $200 each. It is apparent that the one-time $200 gain to the first firm would quickly be dissipated by successive weeks in which it earned $200 less than it would have if it had maintained its high price. In repeated games such as this, it is in the interest of each firm to continue with the high price equilibrium and the efficient outcome is achieved.

But there are limits to these rules being able to produce the efficient outcome. What happens if the game is set to end after a certain number of periods? In this case, retaliation for cheating in the last period is not possible, and both players will cheat and charge a low price in the last period. But if both players charge a low price in the last period, retaliation is not possible for cheating in the penultimate period, the next-to-last period. Both will then cheat in the penultimate period. But, if both expect low prices in the penultimate period, then retaliation for cheating is not possible for the period just prior to that. As you can see by such chain logic, once the ability to retaliate in the last period is taken away, the threat of retaliation no longer has any teeth for all previous periods and a self-enforcing mechanism for achieving an efficient outcome is not possible.

When is such implicit cooperation (both charging high prices) most likely to occur? We would expect this to occur more in stable industries. In industries in which cost and/or demand function change often, it is difficult to recognize when a firm cheats because what might be a high price in certain circumstances may be a low price when cost and demand have changed. If one firm charges $30 for its product consistent with its understanding of this being a high price, but a second firm perceives the high price to be $40, the second firm may retaliate against what it perceives to be cheating by the first firm. A price war breaks out, and cooperation ceases because of a difference in perception. In addition, when many firms are in the industry, it may be difficult to detect when a rival firm cheats and begins using a lower price. So, the implicit cooperation of a repeated game is more likely to occur in a stable industry with few firms.

Sequential Games and First Mover Advantage

So far, we have discussed decisions made in games as being made simultaneously by the players (in each round, if repeated). However, we can design games in which decisions are made sequentially. In this situation, strategy may differ. Game theory helps us explain observed practices that can be associated with **first mover advantage**.

Suppose two firms have designed a type of large, specialized printer and are about to go into full-scale production. They must choose and commit to one of two different production processes that vary in their cost schedules and output. One process is more efficient at producing low quantities. The other process is more efficient at producing larger quantities. Suppose that estimated demand and costs are such that the payoff matrix in Figure 11.4 is understood by both companies.

In this example, there is no dominant strategy for either firm. If Company D were to choose a high output, Company C would prefer to choose a low output. However, if Company D were to choose a low output, Company C would prefer to choose a high output. Without further information, it is not possible to predict what would happen in this market. Suppose, however, that one firm, say Company C, could choose first. In that case, it would be to its advantage to choose the high-output production process and a high output. Then, Company B would be better off choosing the low-output production process and earning 75 in profits than choosing a high output and gaining only 50 in profits (unless it considered vengeance—the reduction of the profits of Company C an additional motive). If Company C announces its production plans first, it can gain first mover advantage and increase its profits relative to, and at the expense of, the other firm.

Of course, there also may be gains to moving last. Returning to the beach kiosk example, it is to your advantage to position your kiosk second if once established a kiosk cannot be moved. An article on the two largest producers in the Arizona copper industry demonstrates this further. At the time of the article, world copper prices had fallen precipitously, and the firms were experiencing negative profits from their Arizona mines. Each was trying to decide how much to reduce production. But, as evident in the article, the firms are interdependent and the actions of one firm will have an effect on what the other firm would like to do. In the words of the article:

> Part of the problem . . . is the reluctance of producers such as Asarco and Phelps Dodge to appreciably scale back production. . . . Because it can take months to ramp production back up after a cutback, the two Arizona companies are reluctant to make the first move. A major cutback, such as a mine closing by one of the companies, could leave the other able to take advantage of the resulting higher prices.[9]

These examples of games illustrate how game theory can inform us about observed market pricing, output, or location decision practices in which mutual

Figure 11.4   Hypothetical Payoff Matrix

		Company C	
		High Q	Low Q
Company D	High Q	(D) 50/50 (C)	(D) 200/75 (C)
	Low Q	(D) 75/200 (C)	(D) 100/100 (C)

---

[9]"Meltdown Gets Worse for Copper," *Arizona Republic*, October 21, 2001.

interdependence exists. We return to game theory in the final part of this section in the context of our discussion about the importance and use of strategy in imperfectly competitive markets.

GAME THEORY AND AUCTIONS

An auction is a good way to view the workings of a "noncooperative, non–zero-sum" game. As in any game, the object of each player is to achieve the best possible situation for himself. In this particular type of game, recall that the players cannot communicate or cooperate with each other, but the outcome may very well end up benefiting all parties. Although some parties may benefit relatively more than others, each party believes that under the circumstances the best possible (i.e., optimal) situation has been achieved. Clearly, in an auction, the object of the seller is to sell at the highest possible price and the object of the buyer is to buy at the lowest possible price. The concepts developed in game theory can give us interesting insights into the behavior of the sellers and buyers in an auction as each side strives to achieve optimal outcomes for themselves. In the two examples discussed here, the game theory concept of particular help in understanding the auction process is "dominant strategy." Recall that the dominant strategy is the one that each player in a game deems to be in his best interest, regardless of what his opponent does.

The use of an auction by Google in its 2004 initial public offering (IPO) provides a good example of game theory in action. In this particular case, Google employed what is called a "**Dutch auction**" to maximize the IPO of its shares of stock. Before presenting the particulars of this case, let us review the goals and options of the sellers and buyers. As the company issuing the shares of stock, Google obviously wants to extract the highest possible price. Let us assume for a moment a very simple market where Google is offering a single share to only one of two possible buyers, Buyer A and Buyer B. Assume analysts before the IPO suggest a fair price of $30 for a share of Google's stock. Game theory refers to this price as the "public value" because it is publicly available and independent of the bidders. However, let us assume Buyer A knows he can sell the share to someone else for $40, and Buyer B knows he can sell the share to someone else for $50. These values are known as "private values" because they are not easily inferred and are also dependent on the situation of the individual players. If Google were to sell the share for $30, both buyers would gladly want to purchase it because their private values exceed this amount. We can assume Google would also be satisfied with this price because it at least matches the public value.

However, suppose Google wanted to sell the share for more than the public value and tried to do so by requesting a single written bid from Buyers A and B, with the promise of selling it to the highest bidder. Assuming the private valuations stated previously, what do you think Buyers A and B would do? Without knowing each other's true private value, the two buyers would be faced with a dilemma. For example, if Buyer B bid an amount greater than $40, such as $41, he would win the bid because Buyer A could not be expected to submit a price that is greater than his private value of $40. But because Buyer B does not know this, there would also be the chance that he would bid an amount that is greater than the bare minimum that he needs to win. (Paying more than what one needs to purchase an item of value is sometimes referred to as the "winner's curse.") For example, suppose Buyer B bids $48 thinking that this relatively high price is still below his private value of $50. In so doing, he would be overpaying by $7. One can imagine similar thoughts going through Buyer A's mind. Therefore, in this simple exercise of allowing only one bid price, the *dominant strategy* of both Buyer A and Buyer B would be to avoid the winner's curse by simply submitting a bid of $30, the stated public value. The situation for Google would therefore be no better than the one in which it agreed to pay the public value of $30.

The only way for Google to sell this share above the public value would be by forcing Buyers A and B into paying a price closer to their private valuations. As you will see, this auction process changes the dominant strategy of the two bidders. Let us say that Google's auctioneer interacts with Buyers A and B in a room by opening with a price of $30. Now, instead of just submitting one bid at the public value of $30, both Buyer A and Buyer B are forced to adopt a *new dominant strategy* of bidding incrementally higher until the price reaches their respective private values. Inevitably, Buyer A would drop out of the bidding process once the price hits $40, and Buyer B would take the share with a winning bid of $41. Both Google and Buyer B would be satisfied. Google receives $11 more than the public value, while Buyer B avoids the winner's curse.

The Dutch auction process that Google actually used worked in much the same way that we just described. In a Dutch auction, the seller asks the bidders to state how many shares they want to buy and at what price. Suppose Google wants to sell ten shares to four bidders. Google would then ask the bidders how many shares they would purchase and at what price. Suppose the four bidders respond in the following way to Google's request for information concerning the number of shares and price:

Bidder	Price	Shares
A	$ 5	4
B	6	5
C	8	2
D	10	3

We can see that no single bidder is willing to purchase the entire supply. Furthermore, because each share is identical, Google cannot set a different price for each bidder. In a Dutch auction, Google would find the highest price that can sell all the shares on auction—$6 per share would sell all ten shares. In this particular example, Bidders C and D would be happy with $6 because they would have been willing to pay $8 and $10, respectively. Bidders are heartened when they are told that the seller will be setting the price at the level required to sell all the shares, rather than at the highest level actually bid. This criterion has the effect of encouraging them to bid up the price beyond the public value, while remaining confident that they will not need to go so high as to risk being hit with the winner's curse. As it turned out, the actual auction resulted in a price of $85, far less than Google's originally publicized expectations of between $108 and $135.[10]

Another illustration of how the game theoretic concept of dominant strategy can be used to help understand the economic value of auctions is the case of the Federal Communication Commission's (FCC's) auctioning off of spectrum rights or licenses to operating companies for applications such as wireless telephony. Prior to 1994, the government granted monopoly rights to transmit signals such as radio or television stations through a process of congressional hearings and lotteries. The hearings were intended as a way for the government to determine the "best qualified companies," whereas the lotteries presumably evened the playing field for both small and large competitors for these spectrum rights. In July 1994, the FCC

---

[10]At the time this text is being prepared, it appears that those fortunate enough to purchase shares at the IPO price of $85 are experiencing a sort of "winner's blessing." Google's stock rose to as high as $747.24 per share in early November 2007. As this book goes to print, it is trading in the mid-$500s.

introduced a new method of allocating spectrum rights. It created an auction system by which companies could bid against each other to determine a price for a given portion of the spectrum. Within 2 years, the government had raised more than $20 billion from these auctions.

The FCC spectrum auctions involve multiple rounds of bidding. Rounds last 1 hour each, and each bidder must bid a certain amount of money per round. Several spectrum rights are auctioned concurrently, so bidders must continue to bid on a number of licenses. The auction ends when no bids are received for an entire round because it is assumed the maximum price has been reached.

The spectrum auctions face similar problems of accounting for public and private values discussed in the Google IPO auction. In this case, the future plans of a company factor greatly into their private value of a spectrum right. For example, a cellular phone company seeking to expand into the Midwest would value spectrum rights in Illinois more than would a cellular phone company that operates solely in Maine.

The FCC auction serves as an example of a tight control over the incentive structure for every player. If firms bid on only one item at a time, they could strike bargains with each other. The carrier in Maine could offer not to bid on the spectrum rights in Illinois in return for some equivalent favor further down the road. Within the market itself, they may have no reason to compete and thus can cooperate effectively. Such cooperation could very well price the rights below the public value. By auctioning multiple licenses at once, the FCC has forced the firms into competing against each other. This competition inevitably sparks a bidding war that produces a price much closer to the true private values of the spectrum licenses.

In any auction with a predetermined time limit, every player has a *dominant strategy* to bid as late as possible. If a bidder produces the highest bid at the very last second of an auction, he wins by default, even if other bidders would have been willing to pay more than the final price. (Any reader who uses eBay or similar types of auctions on the Internet would know that the common term for this is "sniping.") Because the FCC auctions have a time limit, it has introduced rules that counteract this incentive. Before entering into any auction, bidders must first place a down payment of a minimum value set by the FCC. In each round, bidders must bid a large percentage of this down payment or they are removed from the auction entirely. They cannot wait until the final rounds of an auction to bid, so the players' dominant strategy becomes one of bidding up prices early on. As in the case of the Google auction, this forces bidders to raise the sale price to a level much closer to their actual private values.[11]

STRATEGY AND GAME THEORY

Earlier in this chapter, we study game theory to see how it can help economists (and policy makers who study industrial organization) better understand the pricing and output decisions of firms competing in oligopoly markets. Game theory can also be applied in a more general way to help managers analyze their firm's position and design better strategies in competing and cooperating with other firms in the marketplace. Recognizing the differences in the various constraints imposed by the "rules of the game" or by the positions of the individual firms can help managers both predict the behavior of other firms and design an appropriate strategy, either

---

[11]Interestingly enough, the resale value of spectrum licenses is rather low, suggesting that the best price for those portions of the spectrum was reached through the auction process. This serves both the FCC and the public. In effect, by using an auction, the FCC has forced bidders into competing against each other with the result that they end up paying as close as possible to their private valuation of the spectrum rights. This produces both an efficient market and a large amount of revenue for the FCC.

in response to their actions or to elicit a preferred response from them. As was evident in the pricing example of Figure 11.3, sometimes the logic of the game may lead players into an inefficient outcome. For managers to achieve a preferred outcome, they must try to overcome the logic of the game by designing strategies to get around the rules or by changing the game. Aspects of game theory can inform managerial decision making in many ways. To give a sample of how it can be helpful, two aspects of strategy, commitment and incentives, are examined in the next two sections.[12] The final section describes an overall framework for using the game theory paradigm in designing strategy.

Commitment

In the noncooperative pricing game of Figure 11.3, the players had dominant strategies that led them to the low price equilibrium. They would have both been better off if both had charged the high price. However, the logic of the game made the low price the dominant strategy for both players. Is it possible to break this logic to achieve the better outcome? We saw before how repeating a game could potentially allow the firms to achieve implicit cooperation (e.g., with both charging the higher price). In this section we explore how commitment, explicit or implicit, can be used by firms to achieve preferred outcomes.

For commitment to be effective as a strategy, it must be credible because the incentive to cheat is apparent. For example, suppose two firms promise each other to charge high prices for their products. The fact remains that one player can cheat and increase its payoff by charging a lower price. With such an incentive to cheat, how can players' promises be credible?

To make a commitment credible, you must make it in your interest to keep to your commitment. Dixit and Nalebuff provide a list of ways in which this can be done. We discuss three of them:[13]

1. Burn bridges behind you.
2. Establish and use a reputation.
3. Write contracts.

"Burning bridges behind you" is a common form of strategy to make one's commitments credible. A hint of how this works can be gleaned by referring back to the sequential game discussed earlier in this chapter. In that game, firms had to choose between two different production processes: one that was more efficient at low quantities and one that was more efficient at high quantities. Given the profit structure of the example, if one firm could choose first, an announcement of its choice of the higher-output production process would leave the second firm with a preferred strategy of producing with the lower-output production process. However, simply announcing its choice may not be sufficient. If the second firm irrevocably commits itself to the high-output production technology, perhaps by licensing the technology or signing a contract with a builder, changing its strategy will clearly be costly. The first firm announced that it is going to employ the high-production technology. However, its commitment is not credible. The second firm knows that there is no cost for it to switch to the low-production technology. If the second firm

---

[12]For a more in-depth discussion of these and other aspects of game theory and strategy, see Avinash Dixit and Barry Nalebuff, *Thinking Strategically: The Competitive Edge in Business, Politics and Everyday Life,* New York: W. W. Norton, 1991.

[13]The other five are (1) cut off communication, (2) leave the outcome to chance, (3) move in small steps, (4) develop credibility through teamwork, and (5) employ mandated negotiating agents.

is committed to producing a high output, this technology and a low output is not its preferred strategy. By committing itself in an irrevocable way, that is, burning its bridges behind it, the second firm can preempt the move of the first and ensure itself a better outcome for itself.

For the second means of changing the rules of the game, "establish and use a reputation," let us look at an example of how a reputation can make a commitment credible between producers and consumers. Branded soft drinks cost more than store or generic brands. Would you ever expect Coca-Cola to degrade its product by using less consistent production processes? Why not? Coca-Cola has an established reputation for producing soft drinks. It has established its reputation partially by its large advertising expenditures. Why does it spend so much money on advertising? Most people in the United States, if not in the whole world, know what Coke is. So advertising is not providing consumers with information. One interpretation of its advertising expenditures is that it is, in effect, posting a bond. The purpose of spending so much money is to convince you that its product will continue to be what you expect it to be. If it were to cheat and reduce its quality consistency, it would forfeit that bond. Its ability to sell product would be diminished, and all that advertising money would be wasted. By continuing to make huge expenditures to maintain its reputation, it is ensuring it is in its interest to produce as expected.

A final example of how to make a commitment credible is to write contracts that are irrevocable and can be enforced, for example, through the courts.[14] When punishments for breach of contract are sufficiently severe, the incentive to cheat is dampened. As pointed out by John McMillan, recognition of the importance of enforceable contracts is apparent in the wording of legislation passed by the British Parliament in 1834 when it conferred on companies the "privilege" of suing and being sued.[15]

Although often useful, contracts are not always appropriate. One issue is that in a world in which outcomes are uncertain, it may be difficult to include in the contract clauses to deal with all possible outcomes, that is, contingencies. Returning to the pricing example of Figure 11.3, suppose the two firms could write a contract specifying that each charge a high price and providing penalties to any party that cheats and charges a low price. Consider an extreme case. In the event of a war, prices may rise with a general inflation. A contract between two parties that obligates them to charge what is a high price in normal times may turn out to be a low price in such an inflationary environment. It may be possible to write such a contingency into the contract. But, it is impossible to write into the contract responses to all possible contingencies. The costs of designing such a contract would be enormous, and it is still unlikely that all contingencies could be imagined. So, contracts are necessarily incomplete. In addition, there are often legal restrictions on the types of agreements that can be made. In particular, it is illegal in the United States for competitors to discuss pricing.

Commitment is a useful concept in a wide range of business activities. Negotiation is often viewed in a game-theoretic way. Making a "take it or leave" offer in a negotiation can be quite advantageous to you. However, it will only work as a bargaining tool if you are committed to walk away if the offer is not accepted. Of course, most important for its success is that the other party believes your commitment is credible. Reputation, burning bridges behind you, and other means, as in the previous examples, can help make such commitments credible.

---

[14]One possible explanation for the rise of organized crime in Russia was its ability to enforce contracts when the court system was powerless to do so.

[15]John McMillan, *Games, Strategies and Managers: How Managers Use Game Theory to Make Better Business Decisions,* New York: Oxford University Press, 1992, p. 27.

Incentives

In the pricing example of Figure 11.3, each firm has a dominant strategy that leads to an outcome (low price/low price) that is different from the preferred outcome (high price/high price). The U.S. auto and airline industries have faced a similar situation in recent history as they engaged in price wars that were hurting profitability. The problem they faced was how to break the logic of the dominant strategies that each faced.

In both cases, the dominant strategy arose because large numbers of customers were willing to switch from one provider to another when prices were lowered. If it were possible to develop incentives for customers to remain loyal to a single provider, the returns to one firm for lowering its price while others remained at the high price would be diminished, that is, it would change the payoff structure. How did the airlines accomplish this? They instituted frequent flyer programs that encouraged customers to stick to a single airline for their business. This decreased the payoff to other firms of lowering prices because the responsiveness to prices by customers was diminished.

How did the auto industry respond in a similar situation in the early 1990s?[16] At that time, end-of-year rebates and dealer discounts had become entrenched. Competing car manufacturers were stuck with imitating these programs or losing customers to other manufacturers. As customers grew to expect these programs, they tended to delay purchases until the end of the year when they were offered. The auto industry was stuck in a low price equilibrium.

GM came up with a strategy to change the payoffs by offering a credit card that allowed customers who charged purchases to use 5% of their charges, up to $500, to apply toward the lease or purchase of a GM vehicle. The program was incredibly successful for GM. In 2 months, it had opened 1.2 million accounts. In 2 years, it had opened 8.7 million accounts. The GM card program replaced other incentive programs. Because of the nature of the new incentives, GM could decrease its end-of-year rebates and still keep its card holders as customers because other cars were effectively more expensive to them. Because GM decreased its rebate program, other manufacturers could reduce theirs also without worrying about losing as much customer base.

Note that other manufacturers followed GM's lead. When games are thought of as zero sum, such imitation is expected to diminish the success of the strategy. However, in this case, it was not a zero-sum game. All firms gained because it changed the dynamic of the game and allowed the manufacturers to move to a better outcome, that is, a high price/high price outcome.

Let us look at another example of how the use of incentives can change a game. In general, when one player has more information than another, it can use that information to its advantage. Are there ways for the other players to diminish this advantage? One possibility is to change the rules in a way that provides incentives for players to reveal their information.

A standard example comes from the health insurance industry. Insurance companies make money by pooling risk and charging individuals the expected payout on their insurance claims. However, if they could discern high-risk from low-risk individuals, they would like to extract higher premiums from the high-risk individuals. Individuals necessarily know more about their own health than insurance companies. Is there a way for insurance companies to get individuals to reveal which group they

---

[16]This example is drawn from Avinash Dixit and Barry Nalebuff, "The Right Game: Use Game Theory to Shape Strategy," *Harvard Business Review,* July/August 1995, pp. 58–59.

are in? Insurance companies often provide a menu of options to individuals as they choose their health care. A primary feature of these options is a choice of the level of the deductible. High-risk individuals expect to have to pay the full deductible. Low-risk individuals expect to be healthy and do not expect to pay the full deductible on average. Insurance companies can design the pairs of premiums and deductibles offered in such a way that the expected cost of a high-deductible/low-premium plan is lower for low-risk individuals and the expected cost of a low-deductible/high-premium plan is lower for the high-risk individuals. Insurance companies elicit the information on the individual's riskiness by allowing them to self-select into the two different plans. This allows them to charge a higher premium to the high-risk individuals and a lower premium to the low-risk individuals.

A General Framework

The many examples provided so far illustrate two fundamental aspects of game theory: interdependence and uncertainty. First, players are interdependent. There are interactions between your decisions as a manager and the decisions of other people. Decisions that you make as a manager affect other players; decisions that other players make affect you. The second fundamental aspect of the game arises from uncertainty. Actions by other players affect you, but you are not certain what their actions will be, and they may not be certain what your actions will be. This uncertainty arises because other players' actions are not entirely predictable; because information is dispersed, you may not have all the information about the other player's context to help you predict their decision; or the other players may be making decisions without full information. Because of this interdependence and uncertainty, managers must act strategically, that is, make decisions based on what they predict other players are going to do and how those other players are going to react to his or her decision.

Studying game theory equips managers with a paradigm for studying a situation, for predicting players' actions, and for making strategic decisions. The PARTS framework developed by Brandenburger and Nalebuff is one such paradigm.[17] PARTS is an acronym for **P**layers, **A**dded Value, **R**ules, **T**actics, and **S**cope. By examining the game through this paradigm, the authors believe a manager can design a better strategy for his or her personal success and for the success of the firm. The basic elements of the paradigm are as follows:

Players: *Who are the players and what are their goals?* For a particular firm, it would be customers, suppliers, and those that produce complementary or substitute products. It could also be people who work for the company. *What are the players' goals?* For example, an individual may not have profit as the primary motive. *What alternative opportunities do they have? How important is it to them to move quickly? Can they make irrevocable commitments?*

Added Value: *What do the different players contribute to the pie?* For success in the business world, the primary question is often not how to take a greater slice of the pie, at the expense of your competitors, but how to take a bigger slice of a bigger pie. Understanding what each player contributes is key. Ideally, a strategy will work to raise your value added or lower the value added of the other players.

Rules: *What is the form of competition?* It could be price, output, cost, quality, R&D, marketing, or some combination of these. *What is the time structure of the game?* For example, it could be repeated or sequential. *Does one player face higher costs for a lengthy negotiation than another? What is the information structure of the game? How much do the players know about one another's positions?*

---

[17]McMillan, p. 180.

> *Tactics:*   *What options are open to the players? Are there possibilities for credible commitments (i.e., those that remove uncertainty)? Can incentives be offered to change the dynamics of the game?*
>
> *Scope:*   *What are the boundaries of the game?* For example, it could be the products, the players, or the region or country. *Is it possible these boundaries can be expanded or shrunk?*

The discussion in this section provides an introduction into how game theory can help managers design successful strategies. We encourage you to explore this further in your own reading or in coursework devoted to a more complete discussion of its many aspects. For useful examples of strategic challenges and decisions of firms in the highly competitive and rapidly changing semiconductor industry, see chapter 15.

Asymmetric Information

The four types of markets in which firms compete are distinguishable from each other based on size and number of firms, market entry and exit, degree of product differentiation, and existence of mutual interdependence among competitors. But regardless of the market type, economists assume buyers and sellers have perfect information about market products and prices. The condition of perfect (or at least near-perfect) market information does not always exist. When this occurs, it poses the problem of what economists call **asymmetric information**. This is a market situation in which one party in a transaction has more information than the other party. For a manager, it is important to understand the potential problems of asymmetric information both because it can directly affect a firm's strategy and because such market failures are often used by governments to regulate industries.

Asymmetric information can lead to poorly functioning markets: too much or too little of a good may be produced. Contracting can be difficult. Fraud is possible. Consumers may fear purchasing goods when they know that the seller knows more about the quality or attributes of a good than they do. In the worst-case scenario, a market may cease to exist or a contractual agreement may never be fulfilled. Many institutions and practices have arisen to mitigate the problems of asymmetric information. Still, for any transaction, when one party has more information than another, the party with more information can use that to its advantage in negotiations. To develop an appropriate strategy for problems of asymmetric information, firms must be aware of any information advantages or disadvantages and what options are available to help it in their position.

The next section describes the two problems that arise with asymmetric information. It is followed by a discussion of various responses that have been devised to address these problems.

MARKETS WITH ASYMMETRIC INFORMATION

Asymmetric information can cause two problems for markets and for those engaging in transactions in a market. The first problem of asymmetric information is called **adverse selection,** and it occurs before a transaction takes place. Prior to a transaction's occurrence, one party may know more about the value of a good being offered than the other. This can complicate the transaction if it is impossible for the information to be credibly conveyed to the other party or if there is a risk of cheating. The negotiated price will be affected, or the transaction may not even take place.

The second type of asymmetric information problem arises after a transaction has occurred. This problem occurs because it is difficult for one party to a transaction to monitor the second party. If the transaction itself changes the incentives of the second party, the problem of **moral hazard** may arise.

For example, suppose "LoudNoises Stereo Systems" enters into a contract to purchase speaker components from "BigBang Audio." BigBang Audio may determine that it is in its interest to reduce the quality of its speaker components to increase its profits. If LoudNoises Stereo Systems recognizes that it cannot adequately monitor or enforce a quality level after the contract is signed, it may choose not to undertake the transaction to avoid the risk of BigBang's cheating.[18]

Example: Adverse Selection—The Market for Lemons

The market for lemons, that is, bad used cars, is a famous example of adverse selection. George Akerlof, who developed this example, was awarded the Nobel Prize in Economics in 2001 for his work in the problem of asymmetric information.[19]

Consider the market for used cars. If I am selling a used car, my experience with it gives me a lot of information about its value, for example, whether it is dependable, whether the air conditioning can handle very hot temperatures on long drives, whether the windshield leaks, whether the battery works consistently, and whether regular maintenance has been performed and recommended repairs made. The buyer does not have this information and is uncertain how to value this car. How much should the buyer pay?

Assume a world in which there are two kinds of used cars: high quality and low quality ("lemons"). If there is perfect information (i.e., both the buyer and the seller could identify whether a used car was a good used car or a lemon), we would simply have two separate markets. There would be a demand for good cars and a supply of good cars. Demand and supply would interact to produce an equilibrium price. The same would work for lemons; supply and demand would interact to produce an equilibrium price and quantity for these cars. We would expect the price for good used cars to be higher than the price for lemons.

Suppose instead the owner of the car knows the quality, but the buyer does not, and the owner cannot credibly convey that information. Suppose also the number of cars that are of high quality (which are worth $4,000 each) and the number that are of low quality (worth $1,000 each) is the same. How much should the buyer pay? The buyer has a 50 percent chance of a purchased car being high quality and 50 percent chance of the purchased car being of low quality. Suppose the buyer is risk neutral and simply offers the expected value of $2,500 (EV = 50% × $4,000 + 50% × $1,000 = $2,500).[20] But if the seller of a high-quality car can only get $2,500, she may choose not to sell the car. What happens? Because some sellers of high-quality cars choose not to sell them for $2,500, there will be fewer high-quality cars offered. The probability of purchasing a high-quality car will decrease and the price will drop. In the worst case, no high-quality cars will be offered and the price drops to $1,000. This is inefficient because no buyer is able to buy a high-quality car and no owner of a high-quality car is able to obtain its true value. The market falls apart because the information cannot be conveyed.

As you may know from personal experience, a market for used cars does exist—and they are not all lemons. What practices have arisen to help this market avoid failure? We discuss this in the next section. But first, let us look at an example of moral hazard.

---

[18]For more discussions of issues of supply chain management, see chapter 7.

[19]George A. Akerlof, "The Market for 'Lemons': Quality Uncertainty and the Market Mechanism," *Quarterly Journal of Economics*, August 1970, pp. 488–500.

[20]*Expected value* is the weighted average of the value of all possible outcomes with the weights equal to the probabilities of those outcomes. For an additional discussion of risk and uncertainty, see chapter 12.

Example: Moral Hazard—Insurance

The second problem that arises because of information asymmetries is moral hazard; this is a problem of asymmetric information that arises *after* a transaction takes place. It is particularly common in insurance because the firm cannot completely monitor the activities or condition of the insured and the behavior of the insured may affect the probability of a payout.

For instance, consider the decisions faced by an insurance company and an owner of a warehouse that is worth $100,000. The premium charged by the insurance company is based on the expected loss from a fire: the probability of loss times the dollar amount of the loss. However, the probability of a fire can be affected by the institution of a fire prevention program. Suppose if the fire prevention program were fully implemented it would reduce the probability of fire from 1 percent (.01) to 0.5 percent (.005) but would cost the firm $50. Furthermore, suppose if a fire did occur, the warehouse would suffer a complete loss of its value.

Value of warehouse: $100,000
Probability of fire   *Premium = Expected loss*
   1% with no fire prevention program   *$1,000*
   0.5% with $50 fire prevention program   *$500*

If the fire prevention program were fully implemented, the insurance company would sell the insurance at a premium of $500 (the expected loss of $0.005 \times \$100,000$). However, once the policy is purchased, the insured firm has no incentive to institute the program. It will be fully covered for a loss due to fire whether or not it institutes the program. Because the program is costly ($50), there is no gain to the firm in implementing it. If the insurance company cannot observe implementation, it cannot make a clause in its contract that it will only pay if the fire prevention program is implemented. It then faces a dilemma of what premium to charge.

How have insurance companies tried to mitigate this problem? One practice is to require co-payments or deductibles in the event of a loss. If the firm must pay out some of its own money in the event of a fire, it may consider the cost of the fire prevention program acceptable. Note that because a loss also becomes costly to the insured, it reduces the problem of moral hazard.

MARKET RESPONSES TO ASYMMETRIC INFORMATION

Let us return to the problem of asymmetric information: how can a buyer learn whether the quality of a product is good? One way is to try to obtain information from other sources. For example, *Consumer Reports* provides information on the average reliability of various models and years of used cars. This can help the buyer determine the probability that a given car is a good-quality car.

In some markets, it is possible to buy information. For example, bond-rating agencies can provide information on a particular bond about the likelihood that the company will be able to meet its contractual obligations. A limited amount of this information is freely available, but more detailed information is provided at a cost. However, the amount of information is, in general, not as extensive as it could be. This is because information is costly to provide and information suffers from the "free rider" problem. Investors may be able to obtain information without paying for it. Because information providers do not receive compensation from these free riders, the amount of information they produce is less than if all users paid for the information.

REPUTATION

Another way in which a buyer can make educated guesses about the reliability of a good is by relying on the reputation of the seller. Suppose a seller makes a high-quality product. It is able to charge a higher price to reflect its higher costs only if the buyer expects a higher level of quality from the seller. Over time, or with specific advertising, a seller may be able to develop a reputation for producing high-quality goods. However, if it cheats and starts to sell low-quality goods at high-quality prices, the seller will lose its reputation and buyers will no longer be willing to pay for the higher level of quality. It is in the interest of the seller to maintain that reputation and not sell low-quality goods at high-quality prices if it wants to stay in the high-quality market.

Example: Reputation in eBay Auctions

Online auctions suffer from information asymmetries. The buyer cannot directly observe the product and must rely on the seller's description to determine its value. The quality of the information that the seller provides is not directly verifiable. As the auction provider does not usually offer any guarantee, the buyer has difficulty determining the value of the good and the probability that the seller will actually deliver. However, online auctions such as eBay have developed a practice to mitigate this problem of asymmetric information. Sellers may develop reputations in online auctions through feedback from previous buyers. In fact, online auctions report reputational indicators of the seller on the screen for each auction item.

What is the value of a reputation? Melnik and Alm studied this question using eBay auction data on recently issued gold coins.[21] They chose to examine a single homogeneous coin, the 1999 $5 U.S. gold coin. Their results confirm that reputation has a small, but consistent, statistically significant effect on the price received for the good. During the period examined, the coins sold for $32.73 on average. Reputation indicators, constructed by simply subtracting the number of negative feedback comments from the sum of positive feedback comments, ranged from 3 to 3,583, with a mean value of 452. Their results indicate that a doubling of the indicator from 452 to 904 would increase the price received by a seller by $0.18.

STANDARDIZATION

Another institution that has arisen to mitigate adverse selection problems is standardization of products.[22] The success of McDonald's restaurants is a good example of the use of standardization. In your neighborhood, you have a good idea about the quality of eating establishments around you, either from your own experience or word of mouth. However, when you travel, you do not know as much. When you see a McDonald's sign, you know exactly what you will get. All McDonald's restaurants are supplied with the same food inputs, and they maintain a level of training for the staff that ensures consistency. There may be a terrific little cafe around the corner whose food you would have found to be better. But you did not know what to expect and chose what you knew. With McDonald's, because of the company's strict policy of standardization, you know exactly what to expect.

---

[21]Mikhail Melnik and James Alm, "Does a Seller's eCommerce Reputation Matter? Evidence from eBay Auctions," *Journal of Industrial Economics,* 50, Issue 3, 2002, pp. 337–339.
[22]This example is based on Robert S. Pindyck and Daniel L. Rubinfeld, *Microeconomics,* 5th ed., Upper Saddle River, NJ: Prentice Hall, 2001, pp. 599–600.

MARKET SIGNALING

Another important mechanism for combating asymmetries of information is signaling. **Market signaling** can occur if it is less costly for high-quality agents to invest in the signal than low-quality agents. Michael Spence, who shared the 2001 Nobel Prize in Economics with George Akerlof and Joseph Stiglitz, was cited for his interesting work on signaling.[23] The primary example comes from the labor markets.

Example: Education as a Signal in Labor Markets

Envision a simplified world in which there are two kinds of workers: high productivity and low productivity. The characteristics that contribute to these designations are how hard the person works, his or her portfolio of skills, level of responsibility, leadership capabilities, and so forth. At the time of hiring, a firm may not know which type of worker a person is. If the type of worker was immediately identifiable after a person was hired, the firm could immediately discharge low-quality workers. However, many jobs require a large amount of initial training, and it may not be apparent which type a person is for some time. This can be quite costly if the firm is paying wages, payroll taxes, training costs, and other employee benefits. In addition, there are often obstacles that restrict the ability of a firm to fire an employee once that employee has been hired. A firm may have to justify its action and/or pay severance to the fired employee. Can potential employees convey information about themselves, that is, signal to potential employers whether they are high- or low-productivity workers? Donning a suit instead of ragged jeans and a T-shirt is one potential signal. But a low-quality worker can do this as easily as a high-quality worker. To be strong, a signal must be relatively more costly for the low-productivity worker.

Education is considered a strong signal by many employers. To attend school successfully requires a certain amount of perseverance, a level of general skill or intelligence, and so forth, qualities that mark a high-productivity worker and a successful student. A firm may be able to judge some of a person's work capabilities by looking at the person's grade point average, the reputation of the school attended, degrees obtained, and length of time in school.

It may be that the school actually contributed to the worker's productivity and provided a signal. As a student, you would certainly like to think this. Although investing in education as a signal is certainly valuable, it may not serve as a sufficient motivator to continue to work hard in school, especially if you plan to work for yourself or for a family member.

However, there is scant evidence that education is anything more than a signal. Performing statistical tests to separately identify the value of an education in improving productivity from its value as a signal is tricky. A classic study by Finis Welch examined the performance of family farms to demonstrate the productivity of schooling.[24] If a young person leaves the farm for college and then returns having earned a degree, the value of the college education as a signal is zero, or at least very small, because the person is already known to the family. Are college-educated farmers more productive? According to the study, those with more education do tend to be more successful. They were able to adapt and respond more quickly, especially in an environment of changing technology.

Even if education is not productive, it can serve as a strong signal if it is more costly for low-quality workers to do well than for high-quality workers. A good signal is one in which success at one activity is closely correlated with success at another activity.

---

[23]Michael Spence, *Market Signaling*, Cambridge, MA: Harvard University Press, 1974.
[24]Finis Welch, "Education in Production," *Journal of Political Economy*, January–February, 1970, pp. 35–59.

Example: Guarantees and Warranties

Guarantees and warranties can serve as a signal because it is more costly to maintain them on low-quality goods than on high-quality goods. A product with a longer warranty is a signal that it is probably of higher quality. Of course, you also may need to have information on the reputation of the seller. The warranty is not worth much if it takes 2 years for something to get fixed or it does not get fixed. An interesting example of how a firm can use warranties as a strategy is found in the book *The Reckoning* by David Halberstam.[25] In this history of the motor industry, Halberstam discusses how a warranty was used to change a firm's internal operations. As he tells it, when Lee Iacocca arrived at Chrysler as chief executive officer, the firm had an awful reputation for quality, and for good reason. Iacocca decided to reinstitute the 5-year/50,000-mile warranty that had been used several years before. The other Chrysler managers believed that the policy would be ruinous. They knew the cars were badly constructed and that the program would be very expensive. Iacocca understood that under the current firm systems, the incentives to produce quality cars simply were not there. The indicators by which divisional performance was judged were designed by finance people who had little knowledge of cars. The statistics that they examined had to do with speed of the line, quantity of cars, volume of steel used, and so forth. By instituting the warranty, Iacocca forced the company to pay attention to quality to survive. For 2 years, there was no change in the number of claims and problems reported by dealers. However, in the third year claims began to come down. The quality of cars had begun to improve.

A FINAL EXAMPLE: TWO BANKING SYSTEMS AS RESPONSES TO INFORMATION ASYMMETRIES

Banking systems are classic examples of the problem of asymmetric information. Banks and other lending institutions know less about a borrower's ability and willingness to pay than the borrower. This leads to both problems of asymmetric information: adverse selection and moral hazard. Adverse selection arises because financial institutions charge interest rates that are partially based on their assessment of the ability and willingness of the borrower to pay. Because the assessment is based on an expected number of defaults from low-quality borrowers, the rates may be considered high by high-quality borrowers who may choose to self-finance and not borrow. This produces a tendency for only low-quality borrowers to seek loans, that is, adverse selection.

Moral hazard arises because once a loan is made the borrower may choose to change behavior. For example, a plumber may intend to borrow money to buy a machine to help unclog drains. But once he or she receives the loan, it may seem easier to take the money and bet on a horse based on a "good" tip. If the bank had known that this is what the money was going to be used for, it probably would not have made the loan. Moral hazard arises after the loan is made because a borrower may choose not to pay or to engage in activities that the lender would not have agreed to.

There are many ways that banks and other financial institutions, as well as potential borrowers, can try to mitigate these problems. Rajan and Zingales describe two different banking systems that can be seen as alternative responses to the problems of asymmetric information: *arm's length banking,* as is typically practiced in the United States, and *relationship banking,* as is typically practiced in Japan and Korea.[26] This

---

[25]David Halberstam, *The Reckoning,* New York: Morrow, 1986.
[26]Raghuram G. Rajan and Luigi Zingales, "Which Capitalism? Lessons from the East Asian Crisis," *Journal of Applied Corporate Finance,* Fall 1998, pp. 40–48.

description will try to differentiate the two systems, although elements of both systems can be observed in all countries.

Relationship banking systems are characterized by the financier having some control over the borrower. This is typical of the Japanese Keiretsu and Korean Chaebol systems. In these systems, a banking institution is related to a group of other firms through mutual ownership and cross-holding of shares. When the bank lends to one of the members of its Keiretsu or Chaebol, it has inside information about the firm's ability and willingness to pay. This mitigates the problem of adverse selection. In addition, its ownership relationship allows the bank to monitor and exercise some control over its borrower's behavior, avoiding the problem of moral hazard.

In arm's length systems, the banking institution and the borrower may not have had any prior knowledge of each other. When the bank considers whether to extend a loan, it asks for information from the borrower about his business history and runs a credit check. In addition, it may require collateral. Practices such as these help to mitigate the problem of adverse selection by making it easier to distinguish high from low-quality borrowers.

In addition, in arm's length systems, the lender and borrower sign a contract. The contract often includes restrictive covenants, clauses that limit the behavior of the borrower. For example, a borrower may be required to provide periodic financial statements. Or it may be required to maintain its deposits at the bank. The bank can then monitor the firm's activities and performance by examining the reports and the levels of its deposits to determine whether the business is performing as expected. In addition, the firm may be required to put up collateral, for example, purchase a certificate of deposit (CD) which the bank holds until the loan is paid off. The loss of the CD provides the firm with an incentive to make its payments.

The essential characteristics of the two systems are summarized in the following table.

RELATIONSHIP VERSUS ARM'S LENGTH BANKING

Relationship Banking	Arm's Length Banking
Defining Characteristics	
Financier has power over borrower	Market for funds is competitive
Low transparency in business environment, information not freely available	Well-developed disclosure rules
Methods for Lessening Problems of Adverse Selection	
Financier has inside knowledge about borrower	Collateral requirements, borrower must have some capital
	Historical data on firm performance to predict ability to pay
	Credit reports to assess willingness to pay
Methods for Lessening Problems of Moral Hazard	
Financier has some control of borrower	Enforceable loan contract has covenants that restrict use of funds by borrower
Financier and borrower are linked in the long term; difficult for borrower to cheat and disappear	Loans have reporting requirements to assist financier in monitoring
Financier control allows direct monitoring of borrower activity	Collateral requirements backed up by rule of law impose cost on borrower from cheating

Is either system superior? Perhaps it is better to say that the business environment of a country may be more conducive to one or another. In countries in which contract enforcement and information disclosure laws are not well developed, the relationship banking system may be more appropriate. However, even in the United States, relationship banking is important. Firms may prefer to stay with one bank over time because they can develop a reputation as a good borrower. Plus, it is costly to provide information and to convince a lender that a business project will offer the expected return. By building trust and understanding in the relationship, customers are often offered lower interest rates than they would receive if they went to a new bank unfamiliar with its business and its business practices.

There are advantages and drawbacks to both systems. Relationship banking allows lenders and borrowers to take a longer-term view of the relationship. Financial institutions in a relationship banking system may be more willing to compromise in the short term to maintain the relationship and future venues in the long term. However, as relationships and agreements become more complicated and inward looking, interest rates become less and less based on credit risk and other typical market factors. This severely hampers the bank's risk management and can impact its profitability and the prudent construction of its loan portfolio.

Rajan and Zingales point to this as one of the causes of the financial distress currently being experienced in Japan and Korea. They also point to the interaction of the two systems, Western arm's length banking systems lending to Southeast Asian relationship banking systems, as being one contributor to the East Asian financial crisis of the late 1990s. Western arm's length lenders recognized that information disclosure and contract enforcement laws were not as developed as their own systems. To reduce the risk in lending to Southeast Asian firms, the Western banks tended to make short-term loans. The fact that short-term lending can quickly be withdrawn made these countries vulnerable to large outflows of capital when the perceived risk associated with such lending increased.

The Solution

"Let me understand you on this, Erica. You're telling me that I should construct some sort of payoff matrix to determine the possible consequences to me and my competitors of future price wars?"

"That's it, Dad. As I was explaining to you with the Prisoners' Dilemma example, if we can come up with what it might be worth to keep the prices constant versus lowering these prices, perhaps we can come up with a solution that will be helpful to you and your competitors."

"I get it. That's what we noneconomists sometimes call a 'win–win' situation. But I don't think that it is realistic to create a payoff matrix, as you call it. Whatever I put down, it'll just be simply made up. Please don't think I'm criticizing this theory. Just like you, I find this fascinating. In fact, some of the concepts that I learned when you talked about game theory and auctions actually have given me an idea. I've been thinking for some time now that I want to sell this business and retire. Maybe I should consider auctioning off my business to my two closest competitors. They of all people would know that I'm situated in a great location, which is worth as much as my store itself, maybe more. I could get an assessment of my property and building, and use that as . . . what term did you use . . . was it 'public value'? Yes, and that could be the starting point for the auction. I think the dominant strategy of both my competitors would be to bid up the price closer to their private value, which I know would be much higher than any appraised value that I could get."

"How do you know this, Dad? You sound pretty sure of yourself," Erica remarked.

"Well, I have some friends in the Rotary Club, and they're telling me that they heard from very reliable sources that Wal-Mart wants to open a superstore in this area and that my property and the land right next to mine offer a potential location for them. If these friends have heard this rumor, maybe my competitors have, too. So they'll be thinking that they could resell my land to Wal-Mart for a good price when the time comes."

(continued)

(continued)

"That's a great idea, Dad, and by the way, that's a good use of the game theory concept of dominant strategy. But why don't you simply wait and sell your land directly to Wal-Mart when the time comes?"

"Well, perhaps you learned in your economics class other concepts besides those used in game theory, such as good old-fashioned *risk*. What if our town, like a few others, decides to try to block Wal-Mart from opening a new superstore and is in fact successful? What if Wal-Mart decides to open up in another location and still worse, another location *close* to ours . . . you get the picture?"

"Hey, Dad, I'm pretty impressed with your foresight. But what will you do when you retire?" Erica asked.

"Well, I've always wanted to be a teacher. I'm thinking of going back to the university to get an MBA as a sort of credential. Then, I'm sure there are colleges around here that believe their students would benefit from my 35 years of business experience."

SUMMARY

This chapter is an important complement to all of the topics on managerial decision making discussed in the first 10 chapters of this book. Game theory sheds light on various situations in which managers must deal with possible reactions by competitors to the decisions that they make. The theory of asymmetric information provides insights into how participants in a market adjust for situations in which complete market information is not available. Game theory is particularly applicable to discussions of strategy and pricing in oligopolistic markets. The theory of asymmetric information reminds us that the market cannot always be relied upon as the best mechanism for establishing a product's price or for determining the optimal allocation of scarce resources among competing uses.

IMPORTANT CONCEPTS

Adverse selection: A situation resulting from asymmetric information in which parties may not come to an agreement on a transaction because of distrust on the part of the party with incomplete market information about such factors as the quality or reliability of a product that is being offered in the market. (p. 440)

Asymmetric information: A market situation in which one party in a transaction has more information than the other party. (p. 440)

Beach kiosk scenario: An example of a two-person, noncooperative, zero-sum game. Typically, the solution or "equilibrium" point in this situation ends up not being the optimal condition for both parties. (p. 430)

Dominant strategy: A strategy that is considered to be the best for a player in a game no matter what the other players do. (p. 427)

Dutch auction: An auction in which the auctioneer starts at the highest asking price and the bidders contiuously lower prices. The auction ends when the seller accepts a particular bid or a predetermined minimum price is reached. (p. 433)

First mover advantage: This is the advantage of a player who makes the first move in a game in which the decisions are made sequentially rather than simultaneously. (p. 431)

Game theory: A formal mathematical approach to the study of how individuals make decisions when they are aware that their actions affect each other and when each individual takes this into account. (p. 426)

Market signaling: A way of conveying information to other parties in situations where asymmetric information exists. For example, level of education completed can be considered a way of signaling to employers about the potential productivity of a job applicant. (p. 444)

Moral hazard: This is the risk that the behavior of one party may change to the detriment of another after a contract has been agreed upon. It can happen because of asymmetric information between the two parties in the contract. (p. 440)

Noncooperative game: A situation in a game in which the opponents are not allowed to share information with each other. (p. 427)

Prisoner's Dilemma: The classic example of a two-person, non–zero-sum, noncooperative game with a dominant strategy. This game typically ends with a stable equilibrium or solution. (p. 427)

Zero-sum game: A game in which the gains of one player directly reflect the losses of the others, as opposed to a non–zero-sum game in which all players may gain or lose, depending on the particular actions that each player takes. (p. 426)

QUESTIONS

1. It is difficult for older people to buy private medical insurance at almost any price. Although it is true that older people have a much higher probability of illness and therefore file more claims against insurance, why do insurance companies not offer policies to older individuals at a higher price to reflect this?

2. Because credit card companies and banks must charge the same interest rate on credit cards to all borrowers, there is an adverse selection problem with credit cards. How does a credit card company or firm know whether a person will be a high-quality borrower (i.e., one who pays the debts) or a low-quality borrower (i.e., one who does not pay debts)? Describe
    a. how the restriction of a single rate leads to an adverse selection problem, and
    b. at least two potential means that credit card companies can use to try to lessen this problem.

3. Suppose the Sri Lankan government awarded contracts to private companies to rebuild the country's infrastructure damaged by the tsunami and based its contracts on a percentage of the cost of the reconstruction. Would this constitute a moral hazard? If so, what would the government need to do to prevent such a problem?

4. This chapter discussed how a game called Prisoners' Dilemma could be used to show how two competing firms might establish their prices. What other variables besides price might be considered in this particular type of analysis? What are some limitations to using this analysis in actual business situations?

PROBLEM

1. a. You and a competing firm are the only sellers of a new product. You are engaged in an intense battle for initial market share. You both realize that the one who captures most of the market share will be the one who spends the most on advertising and promotion. You are the marketing manager and you have up to $1 million for advertising and promotion for all your products. You have to decide how much of your budget you should allocate to the marketing of the new product. Construct a payoff matrix similar to the one shown in Figure 11.3. Notice in Figure 11.3 that price is the variable designated as being "high" or "low." What variable would you use in this example? The numbers in Figure 11.3 represent potential revenue. What might they represent in this example?
   b. What challenges do you think there are in using this type of analysis in an actual business situation?

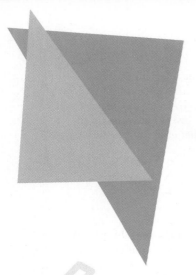

Capital Budgeting and Risk

Learning Objectives

Upon completion of this chapter, readers should be able to:

- Identify the types of capital budgeting decisions.
- Show how to calculate the net present value and the internal rate of return, and understand the difference between the two.
- Identify different types of cash flows, and explain how they fit into the capital budgeting calculation.
- Define the cost of capital, and demonstrate how it is calculated.
- Explain the meaning of the capital budgeting model.
- Define capital rationing.
- Define risk and uncertainty.
- Describe and calculate various measures of risk, such as the expected value, standard deviation, and coefficient of variation.
- Explain the meaning of the risk-adjusted discount rate and certainty equivalents.
- Distinguish between sensitivity analysis and scenario analysis.
- Describe how to calculate simulations and decision trees.
- Explain how real options can improve capital budgeting calculations.

The Situation

George Kline, the manager of Global Foods' capital planning department, is responsible for analyzing capital budgeting projects. When the analysis is completed, George and his staff of five make presentations up the company hierarchy—to the treasurer (George's boss) and the vice president of finance. If the proposal is large enough, it may finally have to be approved by the Corporate Management Committee (a group composed of top executives).

George has in front of him a new project proposal that requires extensive analysis by his staff. It is the proposed expansion of company activities into a new geographic region. Global is investigating the possibility of entering a new region where its soft drink and bottled water products have not been marketed previously. Potential annual sales for this area have been estimated at 100,000,000 cases. A 4 percent annual increase in total consumption is forecast. The market research people have estimated that, given an extensive advertising campaign, the first year's market share could reach 1 percent, and it might grow to some 5 percent 4 years later.

(continued)

(continued)

For the company to compete in this new area, it must establish a plant. An unused, somewhat obsolete bottling plant is available in the area for $5 million. The total costs of rebuilding and renovating the plant, and purchasing and installing the new equipment, are expected to amount to $2 million. During the first year, the company will incur expenses of recruiting a new workforce and an extensive advertising and promotion campaign. These expenses are estimated at $750,000.

If Global Foods actually achieves a 1 percent share of the market, it will sell 1 million cases. Each case sells for $5. Production costs will be $2.50 per case. General and administrative expenses will be $650,000 during the first year. Of this amount, $500,000 is fixed; the remainder is a function of sales revenue. Distribution and selling expenses will be 60 cents per case. Advertising expenses will be 5 percent of sales.

The total cost of the plant, renovation, and new equipment and their depreciation schedule is as follows:

- Land—$500,000, not depreciable
- Plant—$3,500,000, depreciated straight-line over 31 1/2 years
- Machinery—$3,000,000, depreciated by the Modified Accelerated Cost Recovery System (MACRS) over 7 years

Global also expects that it will have to increase the size of its working capital by $750,000 to cover the additional inventory, accounts receivable, and cash for transactions.

The analysis will span 7 years, including the first year of expenditures and 6 years of operations. This is a relatively conservative assumption—if the company cannot make a viable business of this plant over a 7-year time period, it would consider the operation too risky to undertake. Two other important pieces of information needed to complete the analysis are the following:

The company's marginal income tax rate (federal, state, and local) is 40 percent.
The cost of capital for this project will be 15 percent.

After George completes the evaluation, he will perform a risk analysis to consider potential upside and downside risk. George knows that there are various ways to account for risk. He decides that, although he will make an extensive assessment, he will keep it relatively simple so management will be comfortable in making the final decision.

INTRODUCTION

When we discussed the long-run cost curve, we accepted that each point on the horizontal axis represented a different plant size. We did not ask how the company got from one point to the other. The subject of capital budgeting addresses the question of how a company decides to make investments in additional capacity or in new products, and to replace worn-out fixed assets. We now analyze how a company makes decisions to commit funds for future periods, leading to the maximization of shareholders' wealth.[1]

Although capital budgeting is a subject taught at great length in corporate finance courses, we provide a brief treatment in this text. We see that capital budgeting applies the tools of incremental and marginal analysis that we encountered in previous chapters. Capital budgeting is microeconomic analysis extended to multiperiod problems.

In the latter part of this chapter, we turn to a discussion of risk. Throughout this text, we implicitly treated all quantities as if they were certain. However, risk is always present in any decisions managers make because future events are not known with any degree of certainty. We explore the various methods of incorporating risk into economic analysis.

---

[1]See the discussion on the maximization of shareholder wealth in chapter 2.

THE CAPITAL BUDGETING DECISION

Capital budgeting describes decisions where expenditures and receipts for a particular undertaking will continue over a period of time. These decisions usually involve outflows of funds (expenditures) in the early periods, and the inflows (revenues) start somewhat later and continue for a significant number of periods.[2]

The following figure is a simple illustration of the components to be considered in making capital budgeting decisions. The figure shows one outflow at the beginning of the project and five inflows in subsequent periods. This model could represent the purchase of a new machine that will last 5 years and provide new revenues (or savings, if it decreases the cost of production) during that time. We could have shown an example with outflows occurring during, say, the first 3 years. Such flows could represent a company's decision to build a new plant and equip it with new machines, with inflows beginning in year 4.

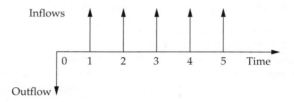

Types of Capital Budgeting Decisions

Now that we have described the general characteristics of a capital budgeting decision, we can list types of projects that fit this category:

Expansion of facilities.   Growing demand for a company's products leads to consideration of a new or additional plant, sales offices, or warehouses.

New or improved products.   Additional investment may be necessary to bring a new or changed product to the market.

Replacement.   Replacement decisions can be of at least two types: (1) replacement of worn-out plant and equipment or (2) replacement with more efficient machines of equipment that is still operating but is obsolete.

Lease or buy.   A company may need to decide whether to make a sizable investment in buying a piece of equipment or to pay rental for a considerable time period.

Make or buy.   A company may be faced with deciding whether to make a significant investment to produce components or to forgo such investment and contract for the components with a vendor. Outsourcing, which has become extremely important during the past decade or so, is discussed in chapter 2 and elsewhere.

Other.   A capital budgeting problem exists whenever initial cash outflows and subsequent cash inflows are involved. For instance, an advertising campaign or an employee training program would lend itself to the same method of analysis.

Safety or environmental protection equipment.   Such investments may be mandated by law and therefore are not necessarily governed by economic decision making. However, if there are alternate solutions, capital budgeting analysis may be helpful in identifying the most cost-efficient alternative.

---

[2]Note that the term *flows,* meaning inflows or outflows, is used in this chapter. In capital budgeting decisions, the quantities considered are the actual expenditures and receipts of cash, not quantities adjusted by accounting conventions, such as accruals. Cash flows are quite objective—either cash goes out or it comes in—and there are no allowances made for when revenues and expenses are recognized in the company's books of account.

TIME VALUE OF MONEY

Because capital budgeting involves cash flows occurring at various times in the future, we must make them equivalent at a particular point in time. This involves the use of the **time value of money**. All this term really means is that a dollar today is worth more than a dollar tomorrow. As long as there is an opportunity to earn a positive return on funds, a dollar today and a dollar a year from now are not equivalent.

Thus to put cash flows originating at different times on an equal basis, we must apply an interest rate to each flow so they are expressed in terms of the same point in time. In capital budgeting calculations, cash flows are usually brought back from various points in the future to the beginning of the project—time zero. It is then said that all cash flows are discounted to the present to obtain a present value. This is a useful convention, although we could discount or compound the flows to any date.

Those of you who are unfamiliar with time value of money calculations or whose memory on this subject is rather hazy will benefit from reading the time value of money material on the Companion Website.

METHODS OF CAPITAL PROJECT EVALUATION

Various methods are used to make capital budgeting decisions, that is, to evaluate the worth of investment projects. Two methods that have been used for many years are mentioned only briefly. They are the payback method and the accounting rate of return method. Although they are still often used in the business world, they have generally been judged to be inadequate.

The **payback** method calculates the time period (years) necessary to recover the original investment. The **accounting rate of return** is the percentage resulting from dividing average annual profits by average investment.[3] Among the many drawbacks of these methods is the fact that neither applies the criterion of the time value of money in its computations.[4] Readers who are not familiar with these two measures and are interested in learning about them will find more lengthy descriptions in any basic corporate finance textbook.

The two major methods that do discount cash flows to a present value are **net present value (NPV)** and **internal rate of return (IRR)**.[5] Both techniques satisfy the two major criteria required for the correct evaluation of capital projects: use of cash flows and use of the time value of money.

Net Present Value

The net present value of a project is calculated by discounting all flows to the present and subtracting the present value of all outflows from the present value of all inflows. In simple mathematical terms,

$$\text{NPV} = \sum_{t=1}^{n} \frac{R_t}{(1 + k)^t} - \sum_{t=0}^{n} \frac{O_t}{(1 + k)^t}$$

[3]Note that the accounting rate of return uses profits, rather than cash flows, in its calculation.
[4]Another version of payback, the discounted payback method, uses time value of money calculations. But it does not consider cash flows received after the payback period has been reached.
[5]A third calculation method using discounted cash flows is called the *profitability index* or *index of present value*. This is a derivative of the other two methods and is discussed briefly in this text. You should refer to any of the leading textbooks in managerial finance.

where t = Time period (e.g., year)
n = Last period of project
R_t = Cash inflow in period t
O_t = Cash outflow in period t
k = Discount rate (cost of capital)

Some of these terms must be explained further. Inflows are shown from period 1 to period n; however, inflows may not occur in all periods. If the project under consideration is the construction of a plant, the time elapsed before the first shipment of product, and thus the first inflow, may not occur until a later period. Remember that in George Kline's expansion project, inflows will not begin until the second period.

Outflows are shown starting in period 0 (i.e., at the very beginning of the project). Indeed, the only outflow may occur in period 0 if the proposal being evaluated is the purchase of a machine that will begin to produce cash inflows upon installation.

The **discount rate**, k, is the interest rate used to evaluate the project. This rate represents the cost of the funds employed (the opportunity cost of capital) and is often called the **cost of capital**. It can also be referred to as the *hurdle rate,* the *cut-off rate,* or the *minimum required rate of return.*[6]

To illustrate the NPV method, we use a simple example. A proposed project requires one initial investment of $100. The project will last 3 years, and the cash inflows will be $40, $60, and $30 in years 1 to 3, respectively. The cost of capital is 12 percent.

Inflow, year 1	40 × 0.8929	$ 35.72
Inflow, year 2	60 × 0.7972	47.83
Inflow, year 3	30 × 0.7118	21.35
		$104.90
Outflow, year 0		100.00
Net present value		$ 4.90

All the estimated cash inflows have been brought back (discounted) to the present at the 12 percent cost of capital and then added. (The factors by which each of the cash flows is multiplied have been obtained from Table A.1c in Appendix A at the end of this text.) The total present value of cash outflows is deducted. In this case, there is only one outflow occurring at period 0 (now); thus no discounting is necessary. The net present value equals $4.90. Should this proposal be accepted?

The answer is yes. The net present value for this program is positive. Stated somewhat differently, if we add all the cash inflows discounted at the cost of capital and deduct the cash outflow, we still have something left over. We expect to earn more than the cost of capital (i.e., the cost of financing this project). The proposal earns what the suppliers of capital require plus an additional amount.

---

[6]The term *cost of capital* often applies to the overall average cost of funds for a corporation. This cost may differ from the rate used for a specific division of the company or for a particular capital budgeting proposal. One of the major reasons for the difference is risk (both business and financial risk). The corporation's cost of capital represents an average for the whole entity, but specific areas of the business may be more or less risky than the average and thus require higher or lower discount rates. Thus, the discount rate may differ from area to area or project to project within the same company.

If the NPV is positive, the project is financially acceptable. If NPV is negative, rejection is indicated. If NPV is exactly zero, this proposal is just earning the cost of capital; we are on the borderline. However, because the return just equals the required rate of return, the project appears to be acceptable.[7]

Internal Rate of Return

Rather than looking for an absolute amount of present-value dollars, as in the NPV analysis, we solve for the interest rate that equates the present value of inflows and outflows:

$$\sum_{t=1}^{n}\frac{R_t}{(1+r)^t} = \sum_{t=0}^{n}\frac{O_t}{(1+r)^t}$$

or

$$\sum_{t=1}^{n}\frac{R_t}{(1+r)^t} - \sum_{t=0}^{n}\frac{O_t}{(1+r)^t} = 0$$

The r term in the equations is the internal rate of return—the unknown variable for which we solve. Actually, the IRR solution is only a special case of the NPV technique; the internal rate of return of a project is the discount rate that causes NPV to equal zero (which occurs when the project is just earning its cost of capital).

The calculation of the IRR can be easily accomplished with a handheld business calculator or a computer (using, for instance, an Excel function), and this is what most people do. However, for our purposes, we use the tables in Appendix A at the back of the text. In this case, the calculation may become rather cumbersome. Unless all cash inflows are uniform and there is only one outflow (in which case we can simply employ the annuity formula), it is necessary to find the answer by trial and error. One must first choose an applicable interest rate—and this may be no more than an educated guess—and then iterate until the correct answer is obtained.

Turn to the example used previously. We found in the NPV analysis that, with a 12 percent cost of capital, net present value is positive ($4.90), so the internal rate of return must be greater than 12 percent. We first try 14 percent.

The result is still positive, so we try the same calculation with a 15 percent interest rate.

	At 14 percent		At 15 percent	
Inflow, year 1	40 × 0.8772	$ 35.09	40 × 0.8696	$ 34.78
Inflow, year 2	60 × 0.7695	46.17	60 × 0.7561	45.37
Inflow, year 3	30 × 0.6750	20.25	30 × 0.6575	19.73
		$101.51		$ 99.88
Outflow, year 0		100.00		100.00
Net present value		$ 1.51		−$.12

NPV is now negative; 15 percent is too high. Thus the result lies somewhere between 14 percent and 15 percent. It is readily seen that the IRR is much closer to 15 percent than to 14 percent. A more precise answer can be obtained using linear interpolation; this would result in an internal rate of return of about 14.9 percent.

---

[7]This case is similar to one encountered in chapter 8. Production takes place at the point where marginal cost equals marginal revenue. If discrete quantities are involved, the cost of the "last" unit produced is the same as the revenue received from it; it earns no economic profit, but only normal profit. In capital budgeting, the situation is really the same: the "last" proposal that would be accepted is the one that just earns the rate required by the suppliers of capital.

The accept/reject criterion for the internal rate of return is based on a comparison of the IRR with the cost of capital of the project. If the internal rate of return is larger than the cost of capital—the required rate of return—of the proposal, it signals acceptance. If IRR < k, the proposed project should be rejected. If IRR = k, although it could be said that decision makers would be indifferent on whether to undertake the project, an argument can be made that the project is earning its cost of capital and therefore should be accepted at the margin.

The Profitability Index

There is a third method for evaluating projects, which supplements the previous two methods. It is called the **profitability index (PI)**. Its formula is

$$PI = \text{Present value of cash inflows/Initial investment}$$

The project will be financially acceptable if PI is greater than 1 and not acceptable if PI is less than 1.

 Module 12A

NPV versus IRR

Should one of the preceding methods be preferred to the other? In a large majority of cases, both NPV and IRR will indicate the correct accept/reject decision because when

$$NPV > 0, IRR > k, PI > 1$$
$$NPV = 0, IRR = k, PI = 1$$
$$NPV < 0, IRR < k, PI < 1$$

Thus, either of the three measures gives the correct answer. In some cases, however, problems may arise.

When **independent projects** are being analyzed, both IRR and NPV criteria give consistent results. "Independent" implies that if a company is considering several projects at the same time, they can all be implemented simultaneously as long as they pass the NPV or IRR tests and as long as funds are not limited. The adoption of one independent project will have no effect on the cash flows of another.

However, proposals may be **mutually exclusive projects**. This occurs when two solutions for a particular proposal are offered, only one of which can be accepted. Suppose Global decides to acquire a new depalletizer. At this point, sales representatives from two manufacturers of these machines descend on the company, and each offers a new version. But the company needs only one depalletizer. NPV analysis may suggest purchase of machine A, but IRR indicates machine B. Such disparate signals can occur if one or both of the following conditions are present:

1. The initial costs of the two proposals differ.
2. The shapes of the subsequent cash inflow streams differ; for instance, one alternative may have large early inflows with the other exhibiting increasing inflows over time.

The reason for the differences between IRR and NPV results is the implicit reinvestment assumption. In the NPV calculation, as inflows occur, they are automatically assumed to be reinvested at the cost of capital (the project's k). The IRR solution assumes reinvestment at the internal rate of return (the project's r).

Conflicting accept/reject signals may not occur frequently in capital project analysis, but they do occur, and they may cause the analyst some anxious moments.

An Example

As mentioned previously, conflicting results can be caused by a difference in project size. Table 12.1 shows such a case. Project A involves an original outlay of $1,500; its

Table 12.1   Two Mutually Exclusive Projects That Differ in Size

Project	t = 0	t = 1	t = 2	t = 3	t = 4	t = 5
A	$(1,500)	$580	$580	$580	$580	$0
B	$(1,000)	$400	$400	$400	$400	$0
Cost of capital			15.0 %			

	<Internal Rate of Return>				<Net Present Value>	
Project A		20.1 %			$156	
Project B		21.9 %			$142	
Delta Project						
(A − B)	(500)	180	180	180	180	0
Internal rate or return	16.4 %		Net Present Value			14

Project Evaluation as Several Discount Rates

	0.00 %	5.00 %	10.00 %	15.00 %	20.00 %	25.00 %
Project A	$820	$557	$339	$156	$ 1	$(130)
Project B	600	418	268	142	35	(55)

cash inflows are $580 per year for 4 years. Project B (which is a substitute for A) is somewhat less expensive—only $1,000—but the four cash inflows are also smaller, at $400 each. Each project has a 4-year life and no salvage value. The cost of capital is 15 percent. The IRR of project B exceeds the IRR of project A. However, the NPV of project A is greater than that of project B.

To resolve this dilemma, we calculate the NPV and IRR for an "incremental" (or *delta*) project. That is, we take the differences between the two project cash flows and create a delta project. If we undertake A rather than B, we must incur an additional original cash outflow (at $t = 0$) of $500 and receive in turn additional cash inflows of $180 for each of the next 4 years. Such a project, evaluated separately, would have an NPV of $14 and an IRR of 16.4 percent. This means that the additional outlay of $500 provides an incremental positive NPV ($14) and an internal rate of return that exceeds the 15 percent cost of capital. Thus both criteria indicate that the additional investment of $500 is worthwhile. It follows that the NPV rule, which suggested project A, was the correct indicator, and that project A should be chosen over project B.

Figure 12.1 illustrates the relationship between the two projects. At the bottom of Table 12.1, the two projects have been evaluated at six different discount rates, and their respective NPVs have been plotted on the graph. When the discount rate is 0, the NPV is merely the sum of all the cash flows. This is shown on the vertical axis. On the horizontal axis, the projects' NPVs become 0 at their respective IRRs. The two projects' NPVs cross at $111, at a discount rate of 16.4 percent, which is the IRR of the incremental project. To the left of this intersection, project A's NPV exceeds that of project B's, which creates a conflict because project B's IRR (21.9 percent) is always higher than project A's (20.1 percent). Had the cost of capital been higher than 16.4 percent, project B would have been preferred under both methods because it also would now have the higher NPV.

The second instance when the two measures may give conflicting rankings occurs when the shapes of the cash inflow streams differ significantly. Although the initial outlays for both mutually exclusive projects may be the same, one of the projects has a cash flow pattern that starts slowly and builds up, whereas the other has cash inflows that are initially large but decline over time. Readers can verify that this is so by entering data into Module 12A and calculating results.

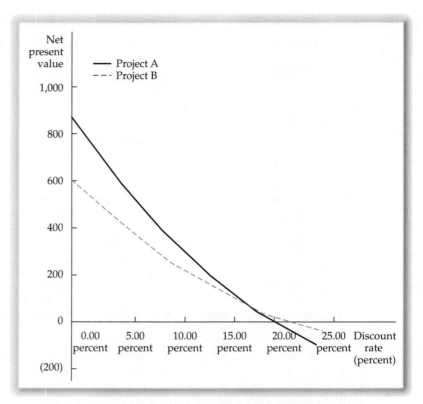

Figure 12.1   Net Present Value Profiles for Projects of Different Size

Another problem that may occur concerns the case of nonconventional cash flows. Conventional cash flows occur when cash outflows are followed by a series of cash inflows for the remainder of the project's life. In other words, over time, there is only one change from negative flows (outflows) to positive (inflows). But suppose there are two or more changes. If a project starts with a cash outflow followed by a series of cash inflows and then ends up with a cash outflow (i.e., two changes in sign), two different rates of return will result. Such an answer is obviously not satisfactory. If NPV analysis is used, a single answer will be obtained.

Writers of financial and economic literature almost unanimously recommend NPV as the theoretically more correct measure. Arguments to support this choice are

1. The financial objective of the firm is the maximization of stockholder wealth. Projects with the largest NPVs will add up to the highest present value for the business.
2. The NPV reinvestment assumption, at k, appears to be more realistic in most cases than reinvestment at r of a particular project.[8]

---

[8]There is a method that has gained favor and that corrects some of the problems encountered with the internal rate of return. It is called the *modified internal rate of return* (MIRR) and is calculated by discounting, at the cost of capital, all cash outflows to year zero and compounding all inflows to the end of the project. The discount rate that equates the sum of the ending values to the sum of the beginning values is the MIRR. Using this method reinvests the cash flows at the cost of capital. Also, the possibility of obtaining more than one solution (nonconventional cash flows) is eliminated. However, accept/reject signal conflicts with NPV can still occur. For a longer explanation, see Eugene F. Brigham, Louis C. Gapenski, and Michael C. Ehrhardt, *Financial Management: Theory and Practice,* 9th ed., Fort Worth, TX: Dryden, 1999, pp. 440–41.

Capital Budgeting in Practice

According to numerous surveys, payback and accounting rate of return have been the popular methods in the past. Over the past 40 years numerous surveys of capital budgeting practices have been conducted. During this period there has been a significant increase in use of the more sophisticated methods—NPV and IRR. This is particularly true among large companies. IRR has been the favored method, despite what financial experts have recommended. Why? Businesspeople are probably more comfortable with a percentage figure rather than a dollar figure that is not immediately recognizable.

A 2001 study of 392 companies found that about 75 percent used the IRR and NPV methods "always or almost always." Large firms (with sales of more than $1 billion) emphasized discounted cash flow analysis even more. Payback was more prominent among small firms.[9]

Another study covered 232 small manufacturing companies (defined as those with sales of less than $5 million per year and with fewer than 1,000 employees). Here the payback and accounting rate of return methods were most frequently used, while IRR and NPV lagged far behind.[10]

A more recent study investigated capital budgeting practices of very small firms, those with 249 employees or fewer. There were 792 companies in the sample. Here, as should be expected, the use of the older methods was predominant. Actually, the most frequent answer—of 26 percent of the firms in the sample—was "gut feel." This was followed by the payback period with 19 percent and the accounting rate of return with 14 percent. Discounted cash flow analysis was used by only 12 percent of the companies surveyed.[11]

In summary, as one looks at the numerous surveys that have been conducted over the last 30 or so years, there is an unmistakable significant upward trend in the use of the more sophisticated capital budgeting analysis methods.

CASH FLOWS

Module 12B
Module 12C

Up to this point, the discussion has concentrated on the methods and mechanics of the capital budgeting process. Cash flows were assumed and put into the appropriate formulas for processing. The term *cash flow* has been used in abundance but has not been explained thoroughly.

When confronted with a capital budgeting proposal, the analyst's most difficult task is to enter the best estimates of cash flows into the analysis. Because all the inflows and outflows are in the future, their amounts and timing are uncertain. Some of them can be assessed with relative certainty such as the cost of the new machine. But as the analyst tries to assess future annual benefits and costs, the amount of uncertainty increases.

In most cases, capital budgeting analysts do not generate the inputs for the model. They obtain the estimates from other parts of the organization, such as market research, marketing, manufacturing, engineering, or service. These data have to be examined for potential bias. Market forecasts may be too high because the people who prepare them

[9]John R. Graham and Campbell R. Harvey, "The Theory and Practice of Corporate Finance: Evidence from the Field," *Journal of Financial Economics*, 61 (2001), pp. 1–53.

[10]Stanley Block, "Capital Budgeting Techniques Used by Small Business Firms in the 1990s," *The Engineering Economist*, Summer 1997, pp. 289–302.

[11]Morris G. Danielson and Jonathan A. Scott, "The Capital Budgeting Decision of Small Businesses," *Journal of Applied Finance*, Fall/Winter 2006, Vol. 16, Issue 2, pp. 45–56.

are interested parties. Costs often are underestimated. In general, estimated cash flows tend to be optimistic and must be adjusted to make them more realistic.[12]

The person organizing the data must understand the following points:

1. All revenues and costs must be stated in terms of cash flows.

2. All cash flows should be incremental. Only those flows that will change if the proposal is accepted should be recorded.

3. Sunk costs do not count. Costs incurred prior to the time the project is being evaluated and that cannot be recouped should be omitted from consideration.

4. Any effect on other parts of the operation must be taken into account. If the introduction of a new diet soda will have an adverse impact on sales of current soft drinks, this amount must be subtracted from the cash flows planned for the new product. In contrast, impact may be positive. For example, if the company also sells alcoholic beverages, the introduction of a "light" tonic could enhance sales of the company's gin. These are, of course, examples of the familiar cases of substitutes and complements.

5. Generally, in capital budgeting analysis, interest paid on debt is not considered. Because interest is included in the discount rate, showing it as a cash outflow would amount to double counting.

Types of Cash Flows

Cash flows come in many varieties. Some of the most common and important types are discussed next.

Initial Cash Outflows

Cash flows occur at the inception of the project. If a new machine is installed, this represents a one-time outflow. But initial outflows can also be spread over a period of time, as mentioned previously.

Operating Cash Flows

When a new project goes online, it begins to generate cash inflows (revenues). Of course, it also generates cash outflows (costs and expenses), which must be subtracted from the inflows. In the early years of operations, outflows can exceed inflows; thus the annual net outflow can continue even after the initial investment stage.

One expense that is recorded by accountants on income statements is depreciation. However, depreciation does not represent a cash flow. The cash flow occurred when the fixed asset was acquired, and depreciation is an accounting entry that shows the decrease in its value. But although no cash flow occurs when depreciation is recorded, it decreases the profits reported to tax authorities and thus qualifies for a tax deduction. Therefore, in capital budgeting analysis we must add depreciation back to the aftertax profit to arrive at cash flow. Here is a simple example:

Sales	$100
Costs and expenses	50
Depreciation	20
Total costs and expenses	$ 70
Net profit before tax	30
Income tax	12
Net profit after tax	$ 18
Depreciation	20
Net cash flow	$ 38

---

[12]Stephen W. Pruitt and Lawrence J. Gitman, "Capital Budgeting Forecast Biases: Evidence from the *Fortune* 500," *Financial Management*, Spring 1987, pp. 46–51.

For each period (years), operating cash flows have to be calculated and the results discounted to the present.

Additional Working Capital

In the case of an expansion proposal, in addition to new plant and equipment, increased working capital may be required. Inventories may be larger, accounts receivable may grow, and more cash may be needed to finance transactions. Investing in working capital is a cash outflow that is similar in nature to an investment in brick and iron. We must account for it. When the proposed project comes to the end of its life, inventories will be used up, accounts receivable will be collected, and the additional cash will no longer be needed. So the same amount that was expended at the beginning of the program may be returned at the end—with one big difference: The cash outflow occurs at or near the beginning of the operations, whereas the inflow of the same amount occurs at the end and must be discounted to the present.

Salvage or Resale Values

At the end of the project's life, a machine that has been completely depreciated (i.e., has an accounting book value of zero) may turn out to have a residual resale value or some scrap value. If cash can be obtained for it, a cash inflow will result.

But care must be exercised in including this cash flow. If the market value is greater than the book value, a profit will result, with inevitable tax consequences. The formula for computing the cash flow in such a case is

$$\text{Cash flow} = SV - (SV - BV)\ T$$

where SV = Salvage or resale value
BV = Book value
T = Tax rate

Noncash Investment

Sometimes a new project involves an investment that does not require a cash flow. For instance, suppose an old, fully depreciated machine is standing on the factory floor. This machine is not needed for present production requirements. But then a new expansion proposal is accepted, allowing this old machine to be used. Does it represent a cash outflow? Yes, if the machine has a salvage value; no, if it has no market value. Thus, as in all cases of capital budgeting decisions, the alternatives have to be considered.

COST OF CAPITAL

In each capital budgeting decision described, a certain cost of capital was assumed. Its derivation has not been explained. Much space is usually devoted to this subject in finance textbooks—an entire chapter or more. Such an exposition is beyond the scope of this text. However, a brief explanation of this important concept is essential.

To invest in capital projects, a company must obtain financing. Financing, of course, comes from different sources. There is debt, either short term or long term. Then there is equity. A company may retain earnings, which then become part of its equity, or it can issue new shares. Each type of financing must be paid for; each has its cost. It is these costs that establish a company's cost of capital. When all the costs have been identified, they are combined to arrive at an average cost of capital for a given debt/equity mix.[13]

---

[13]Admittedly, there are other financial instruments with which a company obtains funds, such as preferred stocks or convertible bonds. However, this short description limits itself to debt and common equity.

Debt

The cost of debt is easier to explain. It is simply the interest rate that must be paid on the debt. But because interest expense is tax deductible, the actual cost of the debt to the company is the aftertax cost. The expression for the cost of debt is

$$\text{Interest rate} \times (1 - \text{Tax rate})$$

Which interest rate should be used? If a company already has debt outstanding, it pays a certain rate. But the rate being paid on past debt is not relevant. What is important to the company in measuring its cost of capital is the interest it would have to pay if it were to borrow today. Thus, the present rate being charged in the market for the kind of debt the company would issue (e.g., life to maturity, risk category) determines the company's cost of debt.

Equity

 Module 12D

The cost of equity is more difficult to obtain. A large body of literature exists on this subject, and there are different methods to arrive at this cost. Two of these are described here.

The Dividend Growth Model

Because we discussed the derivation of the **dividend growth model** in chapter 2, we will just repeat the formulas here. If the annual dividend remains the same each year, then the formula for the price of a share is

$$P = D/k_e$$

where P = Present price of stock
  D = Annual dividend
  k_e = Discount rate (the cost of capital)

If, however, we expect the dividend to grow at a constant rate each year, the equation becomes

$$P = D_1/(k_e - g)$$

where D_1 = Dividend to be paid in the coming year
  g = Dividend's annual growth rate

Because it is the cost of capital that we seek, the equation can be written in terms of k_e as

$$k_e = \frac{D_1}{P} + g$$

Thus, this construction states that the cost of equity capital (k_e) equals the dividend in year one divided by today's stock price—the dividend yield—plus the expected growth rate in the dividend. This formula is often referred to as the Gordon model, so named for Myron J. Gordon, an economist who has done a great amount of work in this area and who is credited with a major role in developing this model.[14]

---

[14]See, for instance, Myron J. Gordon, *The Investment, Financing, and Valuation of the Corporation*, Homewood, IL: Irwin, 1962.

The dividend growth model just presented is generally applicable when a company reinvests the earnings that have not been paid out as dividends. If a company issues new stock in the financial markets, it incurs an additional cost. The proceeds from the sale of the stock will be less than the current market price, P, due to the cost of underwriting the issue. If these costs, often referred to as *flotation costs, f*, are expressed as a percentage of P, the Gordon model converts to

$$k_0 = \frac{D_1}{P(1 - f)} + g$$

Obviously, the cost of external equity capital will be higher for newly issued stock than for retained earnings.[15]

Although the Gordon model formula appears rather simple, it requires a forecast of growth. Forecasts, as we have found out, are always tenuous. Thus, the calculation of the cost of capital can be only as good as the estimates entered into it.

The Capital Asset Pricing Model

The **capital asset pricing model (CAPM)** had its birth in the 1960s.[16] It is based on the principle that there is a relationship between risk and return. The more risky the investment, the higher will be the required return. Only a brief description of this model is given here.

An important conclusion of this model is that the required rate of return[17] on a stock is a function of the volatility (market risk) of its returns relative to the return on a total stock market portfolio. This volatility is referred to as *beta* (β) and is calculated by regression analysis. The variability of the individual stock's return is the dependent variable, and the variability of the market return is the independent variable. The higher the volatility of the individual stock's return compared with the market return, the higher the beta. A beta of 1.0 signifies that the stock's return is as volatile as the market's. If the beta is greater than 1.0, the stock's return is more variable and, therefore, the stock is more risky; the reverse situation holds when beta is less than 1.0.

One other item is included in this model, the riskless interest rate, usually represented by interest paid on U.S. Treasury securities. The beta coefficient is used to

---

[15]The assumption of constant growth may not always be realistic. For a variable growth rate, the growth rate must be estimated for each period and the entire equation solved for k_e. For example, in the case of a company that expects rapid growth at first, then a slowdown, and finally some "normal" constant growth, the equation becomes somewhat complicated:

$$P_0 = \sum_{t=1}^{n} \frac{D_t}{(1 + k_e)^t} + \frac{D_{n+1}}{k_e - g}\left[\frac{1}{1 + k_e}\right]^n$$

where n = Number of years of nonconstant growth
  g = Expected annual growth rate during the constant growth period
  D_t = Dividend expected in each year t of the nonconstant growth period
 D_{n+1} = Dividend in first period of constant growth

For additional information on this construction, see any finance textbook; for instance, Brigham, Gapenski, and Ehrhardt, *Financial Management,* pp. 339–42. This method of calculation is employed later in this chapter in "The Value of a Corporation" section (Appendix 12A).

[16]See, for instance, William F. Sharpe, "Capital Asset Prices: A Theory of Market Equilibrium under Conditions of Risk," *Journal of Finance,* 19 (September 1964), pp. 425–42.

[17]The rate of return for a period is defined as

$$\frac{\text{Dividend} \pm \text{change in stock price}}{\text{Stock price at the beginning of the period}}$$

arrive at the risk premium of the individual stock relative to the difference between the average return for the market portfolio and the riskless rate.

The required rate of return on an individual stock is calculated as follows:

$$k_j = R_f + \beta (k_m - R_f)$$

where k_j = Required rate of return on stock j
R_f = Risk-free rate
k_m = Rate of return on the market portfolio

This model has experienced immense popularity—and also criticism. Probably one of the most serious objections is that the model tries to predict the present and future costs of equity capital with past data. It assumes, therefore, the past relationship between stock return and market return will continue into the future.

Another criticism of CAPM lies in the fact that betas are not always stable. They vary, depending on the time period used in making the analysis, and they are affected by the specific statistical method used. Thus, again, the cost-of-capital estimate is only as good as the data used in the computation and the method used. It is obvious that there is much work yet to be done to improve the estimates of the equity cost of capital.

The Weighted Cost of Capital

 Module 12E

Despite the fact that the measurements of the components of capital costs are not entirely satisfactory, they are the best available at the present, and they are used in obtaining an overall cost of capital of the firm. This is achieved by weighting the various costs by the relative proportion of each component's value in the total capital structure.

When the **weighted average cost of capital (WACC)** is calculated, the weights should reflect the actual market value of the components rather than book values as shown on the balance sheet.

If debt makes up 20 percent and equity 80 percent of a company's financial structure, and their respective costs are 6 percent and 14 percent, the weighted cost of capital is

$$0.2\ (0.06) + 0.8\ (0.14) = 0.012 + 0.112 = 0.124 = 12.4 \text{ percent}$$

Because the cost of debt capital is usually lower than that of equity, this formula would indicate that a company can decrease its cost of capital (and thus increase the value of the firm) by increasing the ratio of debt to equity. This is misleading, however. As the proportion of debt increases (i.e., as leverage rises), the financial community will view the company as more risky. Consequently, the cost of both components, debt as well as equity, will rise, causing the weighted average to rise also. There is probably some point where the combination of components is optimal and the weighted cost of capital of a particular firm is at a minimum.

THE CAPITAL BUDGETING MODEL

In the arena of corporate decision making, capital budgeting is an application of the marginal revenue-marginal cost principle. Figure 12.2 illustrates this principle.

Assume a company is faced with a menu of seven independent capital budgeting proposals. The capital planning department has analyzed each of them and has calculated the internal rate of return, which is the evaluation technique the

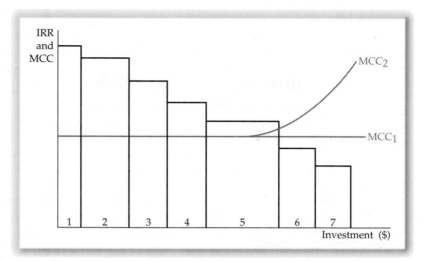

Figure 12.2   The Capital Budgeting Decision

company uses. In Figure 12.2, the projects have been ranked by IRR from highest to lowest. Each proposal is represented by a bar; its height represents the IRR, and the width indicates the size of the investment. If a line were drawn connecting the tops of the bars and then smoothed, it would be a curve representing the internal rate of return on successive doses of investment—a marginal investment opportunity curve.

If the company can obtain new funds at a constant cost of capital, then the horizontal marginal cost of capital (MCC_1) curve would be valid. However, it is more likely that as the company needs additional funds to finance its projects, it may incur higher capital costs. Thus, MCC_2 is probably the more realistic situation.

Thus, as the costs of both debt and equity rise, the marginal weighted cost of capital will show an increase as the corporation increases its demand for capital funds. Hence, it is considerably more realistic to draw the weighted marginal cost of capital as a rising curve (MCC_2), particularly after the capital budget of a certain size is reached.

The company will reach the optimal investment budget at the point where the marginal investment opportunity curve and marginal cost of capital curve intersect. This is, of course, the principle that was applied in the one-period case. In our example, the conclusion is that projects 1 through 5 should be accepted, and those with lower IRRs (projects 6 and 7) should be rejected.

There is one other important point that must be made. We have just concluded that to arrive at an optimal capital budget, a company will accept all projects with positive NPVs (an exception, capital rationing, is discussed in the next section). However, if a firm operates in a competitive market, then in the long run, all NPVs will be reduced to zero. This is consistent with our discussion of competition in chapter 8, where we conclude that in a long-run equilibrium firms will earn only their normal profit. Of course, in reality, continuous changes in demand and supply conditions may prevent a static long-run equilibrium from ever being reached. Nevertheless, competitive forces will require companies to continue to innovate to maintain their market advantage or to attempt to create noncompetitive (monopolistic) conditions to produce economic profits—and positive NPVs—in the long run.

CAPITAL RATIONING

The marginal rule indicates that the company should invest in every project whose IRR exceeds the marginal cost of capital or whose net present value is positive. However, some corporations impose an absolute limit on capital spending during a particular interval, and not all projects that pass the IRR or NPV test will be accepted. This situation, referred to as **capital rationing**, occurs when management may not be willing to obtain external financing. There are various reasons for such a practice. For instance, there may be a reluctance to incur increasing levels of debt. Alternatively, management may not want to add to equity in fear of diluting control. Thus, under capital rationing conditions, a company may have to reject otherwise acceptable projects to remain within its expenditure limit.

Assume a corporation has evaluated five independent capital projects, with the results shown in Table 12.2. Each project has a positive net present value and therefore should be undertaken under the usual rule. To embark on these five projects, the company would have to incur cash outflows of $250 and would obtain a net present value of $120.

However, the management of this firm has decreed that only $100 will be spent on capital projects at this time. Which projects should it select? To create the most value it can under the circumstances, it will choose the combination of projects that will give the highest net present value within the spending constraint. This leads to the selection of projects A, C, and D. These three projects together will require an outlay of just $100 and will have a combined net present value of $60. No other combination of projects within the $100 spending constraint will achieve a net present value as high as $60.

Although the imposition of capital rationing does not appear to be rational maximizing behavior, it nevertheless occurs quite frequently. The final judgment on capital rationing is that it does not permit a company to achieve its maximum value.

RISK VERSUS UNCERTAINTY

In economic or financial theory, the two terms **risk** and **uncertainty** have somewhat different meanings, even though they are often used interchangeably. Although no future events are known with certainty, some events can be assigned probabilities, and others cannot. Where future events can be defined and probabilities assigned, we have a case of risk. Thus, for instance, a company's sales manager estimates that next year's sales of diet cola have a 25 percent probability to be 5 million cases, a 50 percent probability to be 6 million, and a 25 percent probability to be 7 million. If there is no way to assign any probabilities to future random events, we are addressing pure uncertainty. Even though this distinction is theoretically important, many writers omit it as a matter of convenience. We follow this practice.

Table 12.2 Investment Choices under Capital Rationing

Project	Original Investment	Net Present Value
A	$50	$25
B	70	30
C	20	25
D	30	10
E	80	30

Probabilities can be classified as *a priori* or *statistical*. The former can be obtained by repetition. Thus, if a true two-sided coin is flipped an infinite number of times, tails will come up on half the tosses and heads on the other half. Instead of throwing the coin an infinite number of times, we can specify the frequency based on general mathematical principles.

In everyday business, a priori probabilities cannot be specified. To assign probabilities to various outcomes, businesspeople must rely on statistical probabilities. These may be obtained empirically, based on past events. For instance, if a particular event has occurred once every ten times in the past, a 10 percent probability would be assigned to it. Alternatively, probabilities obtained from past events can be adjusted to reflect changed expectations for the future.

SOURCES OF BUSINESS RISK

What are the sources of risk faced by a businessperson?

➤ *Economic conditions:* Firms face rising and falling phases of the business cycle. Although forecasting can help prepare a business for changes, it cannot completely predict timing and volatility of economic activity.

➤ *Fluctuations in specific industries:* Such fluctuations may not always coincide with the overall economy.

➤ *Competition and technological change:* When competitors improve a product or new technologies are introduced, sales of particular companies or industries are impacted.

➤ *Changes in consumer preferences:* Successful products for one year may become the discarded, unwanted items of the next. The fashion industry is a good example of changing styles.

➤ *Costs and expenses:* Labor and material costs are subject to change, sometimes unexpectedly. Oil prices are an excellent example of such an uncertainty.

THE MEASURES OF RISK

When outcomes are uncertain, two measures that take risk into consideration are used.

First, not just one outcome but a number of outcomes is possible. Each potential result will have a **probability** attached to it. In making estimates of a future cash inflow, for example, the analyst must decide on the probability of each possible result and construct a probability distribution.

A **probability distribution** describes, in percentage terms, the chances of all possible occurrences. When all the probabilities of the possible events are added up, they must total 1 because all possibilities together must equal certainty. Thus, we may assign probabilities to various possible cash flows as shown in Table 12.3. We estimate

Table 12.3   Probability Distribution for Cash Inflows

Cash Inflow	Probability
$3,000	0.1
4,000	0.2
5,000	0.4
6,000	0.2
7,000	0.1

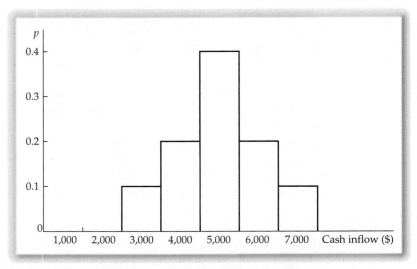

Figure 12.3   Bar Graph of Data from Table 12.3

that possible cash flows from a project during the coming year will be $3,000, $4,000, $5,000, $6,000, or $7,000. If all conditions are favorable, the cash flow will be $7,000; if unfavorable conditions prevail, the cash flow will be only $3,000. Table 12.3 can also be translated into a bar chart, shown in Figure 12.3.

The assigned probabilities indicate that there is only a 10 percent chance that all the unfavorable predictions will materialize. Similarly, there is only one chance in ten (i.e., 10 percent) that all the favorable conditions will prevail. It is much more likely that some favorable and some unfavorable influences will ensue. Therefore, the probabilities for the intermediate cash flows are the highest.

Once we have established a probability distribution, we are ready to calculate the two measures used in decision making under conditions of risk.

Expected Value

Module 12F

From the numbers given in Table 12.3, we calculate the **expected value** of possible outcomes. The expected value is simply the average of all possible outcomes weighted by their respective probabilities.

$$\overline{R} = (3,000 \times 0.1) + (4,000 \times 0.2) + (5,000 \times 0.4) + (6,000 \times 0.2) + (7,000 \times 0.1)$$
$$= 300 + 800 + 2,000 + 1,200 + 700$$
$$= 5,000$$

where $\overline{R}$ represents the expected value. The generalized expression for expected value is as follows:

$$\overline{R} = \sum_{i=1}^{n} R_i P_i$$

where $\overline{R}$ = Expected value
R_i = Value in case i
p_i = Probability in case i
n = Number of possible outcomes

Now that the weighted average—the expected value—has been obtained, we can determine the second measure, the one that specifies the extent of the risk.

The Standard Deviation

In economics and finance, risk is considered to be the dispersion of possible outcomes around the expected value. The greater the potential differences from the average, the greater the risk. Thus, to measure risk, we must find some yardstick that reflects the variation of possible outcomes from this average. A concept prominent in elementary statistics is used for this purpose—the standard deviation.[18]

The **standard deviation** is the square root of the weighted average of the squared deviations of all possible outcomes from the expected value:

$$\sigma = \sqrt{\sum_{i=1}^{n} (R_i - \overline{R})^2 p_i}$$

where σ is the standard deviation. For the example in Table 12.3, the standard deviation is calculated in Table 12.4.

What is the meaning of a standard deviation of 1,095? First, because our probability distribution is symmetric, there is a 50 percent chance that the outcome will be larger than the expected value and a 50 percent chance that it will be less. Based on statistical theory describing the normal curve (which is discussed more fully later), about 34 percent of all possible occurrences will be within one standard deviation of the mean, on each side of the mean, 47.7 percent within two standard deviations, and 49.9 percent within three standard deviations. Thus, given the expected value of 5,000 and standard deviation of 1,095, we conclude the following: there is 34 percent probability that the cash flow will be 3,905. In other words, there is a 16 percent probability that our cash flow will be 3,905 or lower. Further, because two standard deviations are equal to 2,190, there is a 2.3 percent probability that the cash flow will be 2,810 or lower. It is almost certain that the cash flow will not fall below 1,715. The same reasoning leads us to conclude that chances are almost nil that the cash flow will exceed 8,285. There is a 16 percent probability that it will exceed 6,095, and so on.

Table 12.4   Calculation of Standard Deviation for Table 12.3

R_i	p_i	$(R_i - \overline{R})$	$(R_i - \overline{R})^2$	$(R_i - \overline{R})^2 p_i$
$3,000	0.1	−2,000	4,000,000	400,000
4,000	0.2	−1,000	1,000,000	200,000
5,000	0.4	0	0	0
6,000	0.2	1,000	1,000,000	200,000
7,000	0.1	2,000	4,000,000	400,000
				1,200,000

$$\sigma = \sqrt{1,200,000} = 1,095$$

[18]If you want to review the concept of standard deviation more thoroughly, consult any college statistics textbook.

The combination of the expected value and the standard deviation aids in making a decision between two projects. Suppose we have to choose between project 1 (shown in Tables 12.3 and 12.4) and another, called project 2. Data for project 2 are the following:

Cash inflow	Probability
$2,000	0.10
3,500	0.25
5,000	0.30
6,500	0.25
8,000	0.10

When the expected value and standard deviation are calculated, the results will be 5,000 and 1,710, respectively.

Because the expected values of the two proposals are identical, the decision will be made on the basis of the standard deviation. Project 2, with the greater standard deviation (1,710), is the riskier of the two. Generally, businesspeople are averse to risk; therefore, project 1, which has the lower risk, would usually be accepted.

Discrete versus Continuous Distributions and the Normal Curve

The frequency distributions discussed so far are known as discrete.[19] The potential outcomes have been limited to just five numbers for each of the two projects. However, it is quite likely that other outcomes could occur—for instance, 4,679 or 6,227. If all possible outcomes are considered, we have a continuous distribution. The possible outcomes on a continuous distribution are often described by a bell-shaped curve, referred to as a *normal curve*. It is only on this type of curve that the properties of the standard deviation previously explained apply strictly. The two normal curves, shown in Figure 12.4, peak at the center, at the expected value, and are symmetrical on either side. Actually, the curves approach but do not reach zero at either end of the *X*-axis. Curves of this kind are called *asymptotic*.

With projects 1 and 2 drawn as continuous standard normal probability functions, project 1 exhibits a tighter curve, whereas project 2's curve is spread out over a much larger horizontal distance.

The probabilities for any other range of numbers can be easily obtained from a table of values of the areas under the standard normal distribution function (see Table A.2 in Appendix A at the end of this text). If, in assessing project 1, we want to find the probability that the cash flow will be between, for example, 3,200 and 5,000, we can apply the following formula:

$$Z = \frac{X - \overline{R}}{\sigma}$$

where Z = Number of standard deviations from the mean
X = Variable in which we are interested

---

[19]They are also symmetrical, which means that the observations to the left and to the right of the mean have the same probabilities and the same deviations from the mean.

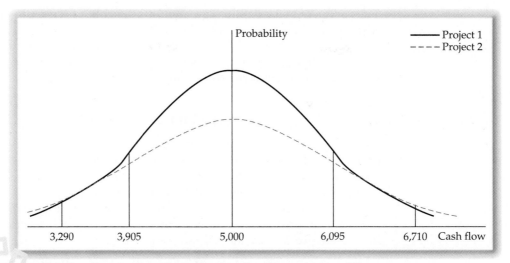

Figure 12.4   Continuous Distributions for Projects 1 and 2

Thus,

$$Z = \frac{3,200 - 5,000}{1,095} = \frac{-1,800}{1,095} = -1.64$$

The quantity 3,200 is 1.64 standard deviations below the mean. Looking up 1.64 in Table A.2, we find the value to be 0.4495. Thus the probability that the cash flow will be between 3,200 and 5,000 is 45 percent. Because the left half of the normal curve represents 50 percent of all probabilities, we can also state that the chance of the cash flow being below 3,200 is 5.0 percent.

The Coefficient of Variation

When the expected values of two projects are equal, or at least close to one another, the standard deviation is a proper measure of risk. But because the standard deviation is an absolute measure, it may not serve our purposes if the two projects being compared have divergent expected values. For example, compare the two following hypothetical projects:

	Expected Value	Standard Deviation
Project A	$100	30
Project B	50	20

Project A has both the larger expected value and the larger standard deviation.

Thus an absolute measure of risk may not give an adequate answer. In such cases, another concept is introduced, the **coefficient of variation**, which measures risk relative to expected value. The simple formula for the coefficient of variation is

$$CV = \sigma/\overline{R}$$

For the two projects,

$$CV_A = 30/100 = 0.30$$
$$CV_B = 20/50 = 0.40$$

The coefficient of variation is greater for project B. Because project A's expected value is greater and relative risk is smaller, project A is preferable.

The coefficient of variation will provide a satisfactory solution in most cases. However, when it does not, the businessperson will have to make a choice based on the perception of whether the risk is worth the potential return.[20]

CAPITAL BUDGETING UNDER CONDITIONS OF RISK

So far the discussion of expected value and risk has been limited to the results of one period only. However, the assessment of risk is even more important when plans span a term of several years. So we now turn to the question of how to deal with a capital investment proposal when we include risk in the calculation.

The first task is to calculate the net present value of the expected values obtained in each year, or the expected net present value. For a 3-year project with one initial investment, we can use the following equation:

$$\overline{NPV} = \frac{\overline{R}_1}{1 + r_f} + \frac{\overline{R}_2}{(1 + r_f)^2} + \frac{\overline{R}_3}{(1 + r_f)^3} - O_0$$

where $\overline{NPV}$ = Expected net present value

$\overline{R}_i$ = Expected values of the annual cash inflows

O_0 = Initial investment

r_f = Risk-free interest rate

It should be noted that the expected cash flows are discounted at the riskless interest rate. Because risk is considered separately (in calculating the standard deviation), discounting at a rate that includes a risk premium could result in double counting risk.[21]

The standard deviation of the present value is

$$\sigma = \sqrt{\sum_{t=1}^{n} \frac{\sigma_t^2}{(1 + r_f)^{2t}}}$$

where σ = Standard deviation of NPV

σ_t = Standard deviation of each year's cash flow

Note that the exponent in the denominator of the expression is $2t$. Thus, the first year's σ will be discounted at $(1 + r_f)^2$, the second at $(1 + r_f)^4$, and so on.

A simple numerical example concludes this section. Table 12.5 shows that for a 2-year project with a cash flow distribution and probabilities as specified, and with an

---

[20]The economic theory of the marginal utility of money can also provide a way to incorporate risk in decision making. Although such an approach is quite elegant, it is somewhat doubtful that it can be used in most practical situations. To apply this approach, one would have to know the utility function of the decision maker, or of the stockholders the decision maker represents. This appears to be a rather monumental task. However, in the final analysis, it is the decision maker's perception of risk that determines the shape of the utility function. Thus, the decision is subjective. For a more detailed explanation of utility, see, for example, Haim Levy and Marshall Sarnat, *Capital Investment and Financial Decisions*, 5th ed., Hertfordshire, England: Prentice Hall International, 1994, p. 221 ff. This exposition is based on the famous work of John Von Neumann and Oskar Morgenstern, *Theory of Games and Economic Behavior*, 2d ed., Princeton, NJ: Princeton University Press, 1953.

[21]Actually, the use of the proper discount rate is subject to some controversy. In discounting at the risk-free rate, we have followed the method recommended in several finance books. However, other books suggest that the company's (or the specific unit's or project's) risk-adjusted discount rate is more appropriate.

Table 12.5   Capital Budgeting under Risk

	Expected Value				
	Year 0	Year 1		Year 2	
		p	R	p	R
	-500	0.2	$300	0.25	$400
		0.6	500	0.50	500
		0.2	700	0.25	600
$\overline{R}$			500		500

$$r_f = 0.05$$
$$\overline{NPV} = 500/1.05 + 500/1.05^2 - 500$$
$$= 476 + 454 - 500 = 430$$

Standard Deviation

	Year 1				Year 2		
p	$(R - \overline{R})$	$(R - \overline{R})^2$	$(R - \overline{R})^2 p$	p	$(R - \overline{R})$	$(R - \overline{R})^2$	$(R - \overline{R})^2 p$
0.2	-200	40,000	8,000	0.25	-100	10,000	2,500
0.6	0	0	0	0.50	0	0	0
0.2	$+200$	40,000	8,000	0.25	$+100$	10,000	2,500
			$16,000				$5,000

$$\sigma = \sqrt{16,000/1.05^2 + 5,000/1.05^4}$$
$$= \sqrt{14,512 + 4,114} = \sqrt{18,626} = 136$$

initial investment of $500, the expected net present value is $430, and the standard deviation is 136.

The preceding calculations are generally valid when the cash flows over the years are independent, that is, if in the case depicted in Table 12.5, the results in year 2 are not influenced by those of year 1.

TWO OTHER METHODS FOR INCORPORATING RISK

Two other techniques of accounting for risk are commonly used. Both make the risk adjustment within the present-value calculation (without the use of the standard deviation) so the final result is just one number: the net present value adjusted for risk. The two methods are

1. The **risk-adjusted discount rate (RADR)**, in which the risk adjustment is made in the denominator of the present-value calculation
2. The **certainty equivalent**, in which the numerator of the present-value calculation is adjusted for risk

The Risk-Adjusted Discount Rate

When we discussed the cost of capital (k) earlier in this chapter, we actually included a risk factor in our calculation. The cost of capital is composed of two components, the risk-free rate (r_f) and the risk premium (RP):

$$k = r_f + RP$$

The risk-free rate ideally represents the pure time value of money. It is usually represented by the yield on a short-term U.S. Treasury bill. The risk premium is a judgment as to the additional return needed to compensate for risk.

A company's cost of capital is the average required rate of return for all its parts combined. However, a company is composed of divisions (or even projects within a division) with different levels of risk. For example, a company with an average cost of capital of 10 percent may be composed of two same-size divisions (A and B) whose required rates of return are 8 percent (less risky division) and 12 percent (riskier division), respectively. It would be a mistake for the company to apply the 10 percent rate to all projects being considered in the two divisions. Thus a project with an IRR of 9 percent would be acceptable in division A, whereas a project with an IRR of 11 percent should be rejected in division B.

Of course, it must be recognized that developing RADRs involves a large amount of judgment. But even if such adjustments are necessarily judgmental, they are very important. Companies with staffs capable of such refinements have developed some methods for differentiating discount rates.[22]

Certainty Equivalents

In calculating the RADR, the inclusion of risk in the calculation of present value is accomplished by altering the discount rate or the cost of capital, that is, the denominator of the discounting equation. Another technique for including risk in the calculation of present values is to work through the numerator of the cash flow fraction; that is, the cash flow itself is adjusted to account for risk. Basically, this is accomplished by applying a factor to the cash flow to convert a risky flow into a riskless one. To accomplish this, the risky cash flow must be reduced by some amount, or multiplied by a number smaller than 1. We refer to this adjustor as the *certainty equivalent factor.*

Just as in the case of the RADR, certainty equivalents require a significant amount of judgment. The size of the certainty equivalent factor depends on the decision maker's attitude toward risk. Thus, if he decides that an expected risky cash flow of $100 is equivalent to a risk-free cash flow of $95, the certainty equivalent factor equals 0.95.

So, for each risky cash flow, R_t, a certainty equivalent factor a_t is assigned. If risk increases as a function of time, the certainty equivalent factors will decrease as we move into the future. For instance, a project could have the following cash flows and certainty equivalent factors:

Period	R_t	a_t	$a_t R_t$
1	$100	0.95	$ 95
2	200	0.90	180
3	200	0.85	170
4	100	0.80	80

The risk-free cash flows, $a_t R_t$, are obviously smaller than the risky flows, R_t, as would be expected for a risk-averse investor. These risk-free cash flows are then discounted at the risk-free interest rate to obtain the present value of the cash flows.

---

[22]See Grenville S. Andrews and Colin Firer, "Why Different Divisions Require Different Hurdle Rates," *Long Range Planning*, 20, 5, 1987, pp. 62–68.

Present Value Break-Even Analysis

In Appendix 8B we introduced break-even analysis. However, in that case we used accounting data and arrived at an accounting profit. Now that we have learned about the calculation of present values, we can show a break-even analysis using this method. Present value break-even analysis can be used as an adjunct to sensitivity analysis. It tells us in terms of cash flows how much production we need to break even.

We now include the investment in equipment and depreciation in our calculations. We also have to consider taxes. Assume the following data:

Investment	$10,000
Annual fixed costs (TFC)	3,000
Sales price per unit (P)	10
Variable cost per unit (AVC)	3
Discount rate (cost of capital)	10%
Tax rate (t)	35%
Straight line depreciation over 5 years	

In order to put our investment on an annual basis we have to use a tool called *annual equivalent cost (AEC)*. We do that by converting the original investment into an annuity. We divide the investment by the present value factor of an annuity at 10 percent for 5 years, or 10000/3.7908 = 2638.

The formula for the present value break-even is as follows:

$$BE = \frac{AEC + TFC(1 - t) - \text{Depreciation} \times t}{(P - AVC)(1 - t)} = \frac{2638 + 3000(0.65) - 2000(0.35)}{(10 - 3)(0.65)}$$

$$= (2638 + 1950 - 700)/4.55 = 3888/4.55 = 855$$

The quantity of 855 will create a break-even situation. Had we used the accounting method the break-even point would be lower.[23]

SENSITIVITY AND SCENARIO ANALYSIS

Sensitivity analysis and scenario analysis are both pragmatic ways to estimate project risk.

Sensitivity analysis involves the changing of a key variable to evaluate the impact that the change will have on the results of the capital budgeting analysis.

A simple example illustrates this procedure. Assume we are analyzing a 10-year capital investment project that will require an investment of $50,000. Our best estimate of net cash inflows per year is $10,000, and our cost of capital is 10 percent.

Our best (base) estimate may, however, be incorrect. The cash flows from the project may be higher or lower, depending on such factors as the economy, inflation, and competition. So we make two more forecasts, a pessimistic one and an optimistic one. We estimate that under the worst circumstances our annual net cash inflows will be $8,000, and if all circumstances are favorable, they will be $12,000.

---

[23]Using the accounting method, we would add depreciation to the fixed cost. After all, depreciation is a fixed cost. The result would have been: (3000+2000)/(10−3) = 5000/7 = 714.

Table 12.6   Sensitivity Analysis

Estimates	Pessimistic	Base	Optimistic
Initial investment	$50,000	$50,000	$50,000
Net cash flows	8,000	10,000	12,000
Present value	$ −843	$11,446	$23,735

Table 12.6 shows the results of our calculation. If the pessimistic conditions prevail, then the project will not be acceptable. At this point, it will be necessary for management to decide what is the probability of the worst case. If it is relatively small, then the project would probably be implemented. A shortcoming of sensitivity analysis is that it considers only the change in one variable.

Scenario analysis is similar to sensitivity analysis but corrects the latter's shortcoming. It takes into consideration the changes in several important variables simultaneously. Thus, in the case of "The Situation" vignette at the beginning of the chapter, we could consider possible changes in the sales quantity, sales price, production costs, and the cost of capital, to name just a few. George Kline will consider these potential variations, and we discuss their impact on the capital project in "The Solution" vignette later in this chapter.

Sensitivity analysis and scenario analysis are commonly used in business. Their outcomes can be displayed in a simple, straightforward manner. These analyses permit analysts (and their managers) to evaluate each important variable and examine the trade-offs among them. They can easily use a spreadsheet program to generate alternative results quickly.

SIMULATION

Although the sensitivity and scenario analysis techniques are popular with business, they do not make use of probability distributions. There is one method that does: simulation. In **simulation analysis**, each key variable is assigned a probability distribution. Let us say that we have estimated the sales revenue for a particular project. We can then assign it a probability distribution that will show the probabilities of the estimated value and deviations from it:

Deviation from Estimate Value (%)	Probability	Cumulative Probability
−30	0.1	0.1
−15	0.2	0.3
0	0.4	0.7
+15	0.2	0.9
+30	0.1	1.0

The column of cumulative probabilities indicates that there is a 10 percent chance that sales will be 30 percent lower than the base case. Furthermore, the probability is 30 percent that sales will be at least 15 percent below the base case, 70 percent that sales will not exceed the base estimate, and so on. Similar distributions would be estimated for the other important variables.

The device of random number is used to "simulate" a possible outcome. Suppose a random number generator with numbers from 1 to 100 is used. For this case, we can assign numbers from 1 to 10 to represent the −30 percent case. Any number between 11 and 30 (which has a 20 percent chance of being drawn) would stand for a −15 percent sales situation. All numbers between 31 and 70 would represent 0 percent deviation (the base case estimate) and so on.

We also assign probability distributions to other key variables, such as production costs, expenses, and capital investment. The next step is to generate a random number for each key variable, obtain the appropriate values, and calculate an NPV figure. This process will then be repeated a large number of times, each time generating another NPV figure. The NPVs thus generated will form a probability distribution and also enable the analyst to calculate a standard deviation as well as a z-statistic.[24] A large number of iterations can be obtained quickly and effortlessly by using a computer.

Simulation can be a good tool for decision making. However, the illustration used here is severely simplified and may not be sufficient for the solution of complex business problems. In obtaining the preceding solution, we made at least two assumptions that may have omitted some important relationships among the variables. First, we assumed the deviations obtained with the use of random numbers remain the same in each year for which estimated cash flows were calculated. This need not be the case. A set of different random number calculations for each year may have been more appropriate. With the use of a computer, such calculations could have been taken care of quite efficiently.

Even more important, it has been assumed here that the variables are statistically independent. It is much more likely that the various factors are interrelated. For example, a shortfall in market demand may have a negative effect on the price. An unexpected increase in sales may have an effect on costs: in the short run, cost per unit may rise as plant employees work overtime at increased wages. If such interdependencies actually exist, they must be included in the simulation model. Such a model would, of course, be considerably more complex. That is the reason why, in the past, simulation analysis was not generally used by business. However, more recently, a number of software packages have been introduced that significantly facilitate such an analysis. Two of the more popular programs are @Risk and Crystal Ball. Both of these can be added to Excel programs.

Even though such models present the manager with a significant amount of useful information, the final decision, as in all cases, would still have to be based on the decision maker's judgment. In other words, no amount of data and information will substitute for mature business thinking.

DECISION TREES

One other method for making decisions under conditions of risk is the **decision tree**. This technique is especially suitable when decisions have to be made sequentially, for instance, if a decision 2 years hence depends on the outcome of an action undertaken today. The use of a tree diagram facilitates the process because it illustrates the sequence in which decisions must be made. It also compares the values (e.g., NPVs) of the various actions that can be undertaken.

The best way to explain the technique is to use a relatively uncomplicated example. A company has an opportunity to purchase a patent for the manufacture of a new product for $200,000. It has three possible choices:

➤ It does not purchase the patent.
➤ It purchases the patent at the above price.
➤ It spends an additional $50,000 on a feasibility study before purchasing the patent.

---

[24]The simulation procedure discussed here is based on a technique introduced by David B. Hertz in "Risk Analysis in Capital Investment," *Harvard Business Review*, January–February 1964, pp. 95–106, and "Investment Policies That Pay Off," *Harvard Business Review*, January–February 1968, pp. 96–108.

The company analysts have developed the following estimates:

➤ Probability that additional research will find the product to have good potential is 60 percent. If the research results are favorable, there is an 80 percent probability that the product will net the company $1 million; a 20 percent probability that income will be only $150,000. If the research results are unfavorable, there is a 90 percent probability that income will be $100,000 and a 10 percent probability that it will be $800,000.

➤ If the company purchases the patent without further research, the income estimates are as follows: 30 percent probability—$1 million, 40 percent probability—$500,000, and 30 percent probability—$150,000.

Figure 12.5 illustrates the decision tree with the resulting calculations. The first step in the analysis is to set up all the "branches" of the decision tree. As we move from left to right on the diagram, we are faced with decision points and with chance events. On the diagram, decision points are designated with squares and chance events with circles. When the entire tree is completed, the procedure is to move back from right to left, calculate the value of each branch, and where appropriate combine or eliminate branches.

Starting with the highest branch, which represents the situation in which research is conducted before purchasing the patent and the research results are favorable, the expected income is $830,000 (0.8 × $1,000,000, plus 0.2 × $150,000). We then subtract the cost of the patent and research, $250,000, and arrive at a final figure, $580,000. Because not buying the patent if the market research is favorable would result in a net loss of $50,000 (the cost of research), we eliminate that particular decision. Now, if the result of the research is unfavorable, the company would not proceed with the purchase of the patent because the loss is only $50,000 compared with a loss of $80,000 if the company does purchase it.

Figure 12.5   Decision Tree

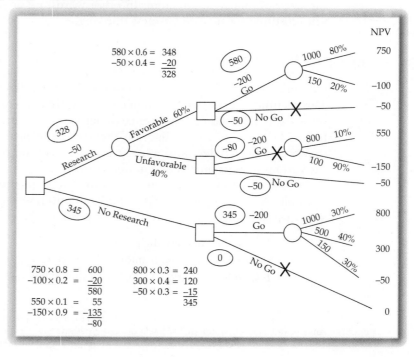

Thus, if the company does the research, the resulting NPV is $328,000 because there is a 60 percent probability of favorable results and 40 percent unfavorable $(0.6 \times 580{,}000 + 0.4 \times -50{,}000 = \$328{,}000)$.

Next we look at the results of not doing research. Proceeding the same way as we did previously, if the company buys the patent the expected NPV will be $345,000, whereas if it does not go ahead, the result is, of course, an NPV of $0.

Thus, purchasing the patent without additional research appears to be the better alternative.

The preceding solution is not quite complete because the decision is being made on the basis of expected NPV alone. There has been no calculation of standard deviations, so we have, in effect, ignored the differences in risk between purchasing the patent with or without additional research. As mentioned in note 19 of this chapter, risk can also be measured by the use of utility analysis. Each outcome could have been assigned an expected utility, and instead of maximizing NPV, as we did in this example, the objective would have been to maximize utility.

REAL OPTIONS IN CAPITAL BUDGETING

The subject of decision trees, just discussed, points to a possible event we have not addressed previously: a capital budgeting decision does not have to be set in concrete at the beginning of the project.

Up to now, in analyzing capital budgeting decisions, we made estimates of costs, cash flows, life of the project, and probabilities of outcomes, and then proceeded to calculate the NPV or the IRR. But we did not consider that there might be an opportunity for making changes in some aspects of the project while it is in progress or to make adjustments even before the project is started. The ability to make changes is commonly referred to as **real options** that are embedded in the capital project.[25]

These real options may increase the value of a project above that resulting from a straightforward discounted cash flow calculation. The value of the option is the difference between the project's value with and without the option. We can represent this result with the following simple equation:

$$\text{Value of the project} = \text{NPV} + \text{option value}$$

Indeed, if such an option is taken into consideration, it may result in the acceptance of a project that was considered unacceptable without the option. (In other words, it can convert a project with a negative NPV to one with a positive NPV.)[26]

There are various forms of real options:

1. *Option to vary output.*   Some projects can be structured to permit operations to expand if demand rises above expectations (this is usually called a *growth option*), or to contract operations if demand falters. It may even allow for a temporary shutdown of production.

2. *Option to vary inputs—flexibility.*   A plant may include the possibility of operating with different types of fuel. Although the original cost of the plant may be higher, switching

---

[25]Real options have a similarity to financial options, which are an important subject in managerial finance. An option gives the holder the right, but not the obligation, to take an action in the future.

[26]For a more detailed introduction to real options, consult the following articles: A. K. Dixit and R. S. Pindyck, "The Options Approach to Capital Investment," *Harvard Business Review,* May–June 1995, pp. 105–15; and N. Kulatilaka and A. J. Marcus, "Project Valuation Under Uncertainty; When Does DCF Fail?" *Journal of Applied Corporate Finance,* 5, 3 (fall 1992), pp. 92–100. A leading book in this field is Lenos Trigeorgis, *Real Options,* Cambridge, MA: MIT Press, 1997. For an article on this subject, see P. Coy, "Exploiting Uncertainty," *BusinessWeek,* June 7, 1999, pp. 118–24.

from a more expensive fuel to a less expensive one may make the project more favorable. Another potential flexibility is that of taking advantage of different technologies, depending on input costs.

3. *Option to abandon.*   If, after the project has been started, results turn sour, it is possible that abandoning the project will improve its payoff. If the project can be sold for a price higher than the present value of its expected cash flows, or if its facilities can be used more favorably in another part of the company, then abandoning the project will enhance its value.

4. *Option to postpone.*   An oil company may profit by postponing the extraction of oil from its field if current prices are low but are expected to rise in the future. A company may postpone the introduction of a new product pending completion of market research to better evaluate the product's potential.

   In both of these cases there is, of course, a cost involved in the postponement, whether it is the cost of delaying cash inflows or of incurring the expense of market research. However, the benefits of the postponement may exceed these costs, and thus create a positive value for the postponement option.

   Another reason for postponement may be the expectation of decreases in interest rates. Lower interest rates would decrease the project's required rate of return and thus increase its present value. It must be remembered, however, that by postponing action, the company may lose the "first-mover" advantage.

5. *Option to introduce future products.*   A company may be willing to launch a product with a negative NPV if doing so gives it an option to gain an advantage when later versions of the product are introduced.

Real Options in Practice

It is generally recognized that real option analysis enhances the making of investment decisions over the usual capital budgeting calculations because it allows for the flexibility of changing decisions during the project's life. Classic net present value analysis may result in an understatement of a project's value. Thus, it is rather surprising that real options have not become more popular with large corporations. A recent study of 279 corporations (taken from the 1,000 largest *Fortune* companies) showed that only 40—or 14.3 percent—employed real option analysis. Technology and energy firms were the most frequent users of real options. The companies that did not use real options gave various reasons for their nonuse. The most frequent ones were lack of top management support; discounted cash flow being a proven method; and real option analysis being too sophisticated. However, a large number of nonusers expected to begin using real options in the future.[27]

An Abandonment Option

We conclude this brief introduction to real options with a simple example. By including the option to abandon the project, we can convert a project with a negative NPV to a positive one.

The data for this project are as follows (all dollar amounts are in thousands):

1. The life of the project is 2 years.
2. The original cash outflow is $8,000.
3. The potential cash inflows in year 1 are $3,000 or $6,000, each with a probability of 50 percent.

---

[27]Stanley Block, "Are 'Real Options' Actually Used in the Real World?" *The Engineering Economist,* Vol. 53, Issue 3, 2007.

4. If the first year's cash inflow is $3,000, the second year's cash inflows will be either $2,000 or $4,000, each with a probability of 50 percent.

5. If the first year's cash inflow is $6,000, the second year's cash inflows will be $5,000 or $7,000, each with a probability of 50 percent.

6. The project can be abandoned at the end of year 1. The expected abandonment value is $3,500.

7. The project's discount rate is 10 percent.

The calculations are shown in Table 12.7. The upper third of the table shows the NPV calculation if abandonment is not included. The cash flows and their present value at period 0 are shown. Then the probabilities are calculated. Each

Table 12.7   An Abandonment Option

Expected Net Present Value Calculation									
Period 1		**Period 2**		**Total**					**Expected**
CF	**PV$_0$**	**CF**	**PV$_0$**	**PV$_0$**	**P$_1$**	**P$_2$**	**P$_1$ × P$_2$**		**PV$_0$**
		$2,000	$1,653	$4,380		0.5	0.25		$1,095
$3,000	$2,727				0.5				
		4,000	3,306	6,033		0.5	0.25		1,508
		5,000	4,132	9,587		0.5	0.25		2,397
6,000	5,455				0.5				
		7,000	5,785	11,240		0.5	0.25		2,810
				Total expected present value					$7,810
				Initial investment					−8,000
				Expected net present value					$−190

Present Value of Period 2 Cash Flows at End of Period 1			
Period 2 **CF**	**PV$_1$**	**P$_2$**	**Expected** **PV$_1$**
$2,000	$1,818	0.5	$ 909
4,000	3,636	0.5	1,818
			$2,727
5,000	4,545	0.5	2,273
7,000	6,364	0.5	3,182
			$5,455

Net Present Value with Abandonment			
Period 1 **CF**	**PV$_0$**	**P$_1$ × P$_2$**	**Expected** **PV$_0$**
$3,000	$5,909*	0.5	$ 2,955
	9,587	0.25	2,397
6,000			
	11,240	0.25	2,810
Total expected present value			$ 8,161
Initial investment			−8,000
Expected net present value			$ 161

*(3,000 + 3,500)/1.1 = 5,909

potential outcome has a probability of 25 percent. The present value of the cash flows is $7,810, and the expected NPV is a negative $190. Thus, the project would be rejected.

In the second third of the table, we show the present value at the end of period 1 of the year 2 cash inflows. We can see that if the first year's cash inflow was $3,000, and the second year's were either $2,000 or $4,000, the PV of these two cash flows at the end of year 1 is $2,727, less than the abandonment value. The expected PV_1 of the two higher cash flows is $5,455, well above the abandonment value.

In the last section of Table 12.7, we substitute the abandonment value of $3,500 into the calculation, and compute the expected PV_0. The expected PV_0 is now $8,161, which gives us a positive NPV of $161. With the abandonment option included, this has now become an acceptable project. The value of the option to abandon is $351.

We did not calculate the standard deviation for this problem. However, had we done so, it would have been lower when the option was considered than when we calculated a straight NPV without the option. Thus, inclusion of the option did not only increase the NPV of the project, but it also decreased its riskiness.

GLOBAL APPLICATION:

Political Risk

Political risk can be defined as an action by a foreign government that is detrimental to the firm. Four types of such action can be enumerated:

1. *Regulation:*   Such actions can include changes in taxes, labor law rules, minimum wages, and price controls. It should be noted that such regulation can also affect local companies in the foreign country.
2. *Discrimination:*   Potential actions include restrictions on the repatriation of dividends, special labor conditions, tariff and nontariff barriers, and also imposition of administrative rules (red tape) that will make operations prohibitively expensive. Such actions are probably the most frequent.
3. *Expropriation:*   A government takes over foreign property, usually with the intention of operating the business itself. Expropriation can be done with fair compensation and with inadequate or no compensation.
4. *Wars and disorders:*   These can lead to destruction of a firm's property.

It is important for a company to attempt to forecast political risk using the best information and advice that it can obtain. There is also the potential of insuring through the U.S. government–owned Overseas Private Investment Corporation. This insurance can be obtained in dealing with developing countries and covers inconvertibility, expropriation, war, and political violence. Furthermore, a company can also reduce political risk by negotiating agreements with the government of the foreign country. There are also operating and financial strategies a company can adopt to decrease political risk. This brief discussion of financial risk cannot go into the details of such strategies; thorough descriptions can be obtained from books dealing with multinational corporate finance.[28]

We discuss political and economic risk further in chapter 13.

---

[28]Two of the books on this subject, which have been mentioned previously, are David K. Eiteman, Arthur L. Stonehill, and Michael H. Moffett, *Multinational Business Finance,* 11th ed., Boston, MA: Addison-Wesley, 2007, chapter 17, and Dennis J. O'Connor and Alberto T. Bueso, *International Dimensions of Financial Management,* New York: Macmillan, 1990, chapters 6 and 11. Materials in these two texts have been used in this narrative.

A Political Risk Index

Alliant Emerging Markets publishes a political risk index of 190 countries. In early 2007, this survey showed that political risk had risen by nearly 5 percent from 2006. One of the major reasons for this increase was the possibility of the expropriation of U.S. assets, especially those in the energy sector, in South America. The top political risks were the following:

➤ Expropriation and government breach of contract in Ecuador, Bolivia, Argentina, and Venezuela targeting foreign companies

➤ Expropriation and government breach of contract in Central Asia, targeting foreign investors in energy and mining sectors

➤ Civil war and terrorism in Georgia

The review listed the "top ten hot spots" for political and economic risk: Ecuador, Bolivia, Argentina, Turkmenistan, Georgia, Thailand, Turkey, Venezuela, Hungary, and Ukraine.[29]

Containing International Risk

Operating internationally entails some additional risk, but a company can manage these exposures (and possibly benefit) by diversifying its operations and finances.

Suppose that due to a temporary disequilibrium, costs of production among different countries diverge. The company may be able to shift its production and sources of materials and components from one country to another. Or, if product prices and profitability shift among countries, so can a company's marketing efforts. If temporary deviations occur in interest or exchange rates, a company may find it possible to decrease its cost of capital by moving its financing sources. Finally, a diversification strategy may avoid some of the dangers of political risk.[30]

Capital Budgeting in Practice

Finally we include here two examples of capital budgeting practices in countries other than the United States.

Capital Budgeting in Croatia[31]

The authors surveyed 59 companies in both nonfinancial and financial sectors to find the most commonly used capital budgeting methods. The responses were grouped into four categories: always, often, sometimes, never. Here are the results in percentage terms:

	Always	Often or Sometimes	Never
Internal rate of return	59%	22%	19%
Payback period	56	27	17
Net present value	42	34	24
Discounted payback	27	38	36
Profitability index	22	32	46

---

[29]"Alliant Index Shows Political Risk up 5% in 2006," *Alliant Emerging Markets,* March 13, 2007.
[30]A more complete discussion of this subject can be found in Eiteman, Stonehill, and Moffett, op cit, pp. 310–312, 436.
[31]Lidija Dedi and Silvije Orsag, "Capital Budgeting Practices: A Survey of Croatian Firms," *South East Europen Journal of Economics and Business,* Vol. 2, Issue 1, April 2007, pp. 59–67.

Again, as we mentioned previously, the IRR method is preferred to NPV, contrary to the viewpoint of financial experts. Also, the payback period is still very much in use.

Forecasting Errors in Capital Budgeting in Portugal[32]

Capital budgeting analysis is always an estimate of the future. So it is quite interesting to investigate whether the actual results correspond to the estimates. The authors had access to companies' applications for investment subsidies that were presented with the data they needed to do this study. The study examined a sample of 264 companies of different sizes and different industries. The results showed that on average, forecasted sales exceeded the actual by about 9 percent. The forecasts of costs appeared to be quite accurate, with the exception of personnel costs, which were understated by about 3 percent. Thus, profits were severely affected, showing that earnings before interest and taxes (EBIT) decreased by some 42 percent.

The authors state that there is a potential bias in the results. There is the possibility that in applying for subsidies the companies may have overstated profitability in order to improve the probability of approval.

 Module 12G

The Solution

George Kline is now ready to put some numbers together. He assumes the market forecast of 100 million cases pertains to Global's first year of production. Because the market research people expect, rather optimistically, that market share will grow to 5 percent after 4 years, George sets market share at 2, 3, and 4 percent for the interim years. He calculates the Modified Asset Cost Recovery System (MACRS) depreciation for the equipment according to the 1986 tax law. The depreciation percentages using this method will be 14, 25, 17, 13, 10, 9, 9, and 3 percent for years 1 to 8, respectively. Depreciation will start in year 2; thus the equipment will not be fully depreciated after 6 years. George assumes the remaining book values will be the market value at the end of year 7. He also decides that of the original $750,000 investment in working capital, 80 percent will be recovered as cash at the end of year (there will be some uncollectible accounts receivable and obsolete inventory). The 20 percent loss is tax deductible. To simplify the worksheet, George combines product and distribution costs into one line; he also combines variable General and Administrative expenses and advertising expenses.

George now prepares his worksheet (Table 12.8). The column labeled "Constant" contains the parameters established originally. They can be changed. Most numbers in this table are self-explanatory. The start-up expenses are tax deductible; thus the cash outflow is $450.

When the cash flows are obtained and discounted at the 15 percent required rate of return, the resulting NPV is a positive $3,552,000. The IRR is 24.2 percent—considerably above the required rate.

George could therefore recommend the acceptance of this expansion project. However, because all the cash flows are future estimates, there is probably considerable uncertainty about their accuracy. He decides to perform a risk analysis. He settles on using scenario analysis for his presentation to management. The chart he presents to management (Table 12.9) will show three summary estimates—worst case, base case, and best case. The worst case will show all important variables on the unfavorable side and the best case on the opposite. Because of the newness of the expansion and severe competition, probably the riskiest of the forecasts are sales volume and sales price, particularly on the downside. So, he decreases the base estimates by 20 percent for the worst case and increases them by only 5 percent for the best case. He further estimates that production and distribution costs and variable expenses should deviate from the base case by 10 percent.

Table 12.8 includes two columns that will help him make his calculations quickly. He enters the deviations from the bases case in the "Sensitivity Factor" column (e.g., 0.8 would indicate a 20 percent decrease from the base case) to produce the "New Constant."

(continued)

---

[32]Joao Oliveria Ssoares, Maria Cristina Coutinho and Carlos V. Martins, "Forecasting Errors in Capital Budgeting: a Multi-Firm Post-Audit study," *Engineering Economist*, Vol. 52, Issue 1, 2007, pp. 21–39.

Table 12.8   Expansion Project

	Constant	Sensitivity Factor	New Constant	Year 0	Year 1	Year 2	Year 3	Year 4	Year 5	Year 6	Year 7
Total market	4.0 %	1.00	4.0 %			$100,000	$104,000	$108,160	$112,486	$116,986	$121,665
Market share						1.0 %	2.0 %	3.0 %	4.0 %	5.0 %	5.0 %
Company sales	1.00	1.00	1.00			1,000	2,080	3,245	4,499	5,849	6,083
Expenditures				$-5,000	$-2,000						
Working capital					-750						
Start-up expense	750	1.00	750		-450						
Sales	5.00	1.00	5.00			$5,000	$10,400	$16,224	$22,497	$29,246	$30,416
Prod. & dist.cost	3.10	1.00	3.10			3,100	6,448	10,059	13,948	18,133	18,858
Variable expenses	8.0 %	1.00	8.0 %			400	832	1,298	1,800	2,340	2,433
Fixed costs	500	1.00	500			500	500	500	500	500	500
Depreciation (plant)	3,500	1.00	3,500			111	111	111	111	111	111
Depreciation (equipment)	3,000	1.00	3,000			420	750	510	390	300	270
Total Cost & Expense						4,531	8,641	12,478	16,749	21,384	22,173
NEBT						469	1,759	3,746	5,748	7,863	8,244
Income tax	40.0 %	1.00	40.0 %			188	704	1,498	2,299	3,145	3,298
NEAT						281	1,055	2,248	3,449	4,718	4,946
Add Depreciation						531	861	621	501	411	381
Operating cash flow						812	1,916	2,869	3,950	5,129	5,327
Remaining values											
Land	$500	1.00	$500								500
Plant	2,833	1.00	2,833								2,833
Equipment	360	1.00	360								360
Working capital	1.00	0.80	0.80								660
Total cash flow				$-5,000	$-3,200	$812	$1,916	$2,869	$3,950	$5,129	$9,680
NPV	15.0 %										3,552
IRR											24.2 %

The worst case turns out to have a very negative NPV and an IRR close to zero. (See Table 12.9.) To further prepare his presentation, George calculates several cases for which NPV is near zero. He is thus able to show the magnitude of errors that would cause the company to be indifferent to this proposal. These are shown in Table 12.10. Many other calculations could have been made, but at this point George believes that he has a good handle on his presentation.

Table 12.9   Three Possible Scenarios

	Worst Case	Base Case	Best Case
Percentage differences			
Sales	-20	0	+5
Sales price	-15	0	+5
Prod. & distr. costs	+10	0	-10
Variable expenses	+10	0	-10
Net present value ($000)	-3,909	3,552	8,093
Internal rate of return	1.6 %	24.2 %	33.9 %

(continued)

(continued)

Table 12.10   Additional Scenarios

	Case 1	Case 2	Case 3
Percentage differences			
Sales	−10	−5	−7
Sales price	−6	−7	−5
Prod. & distr. costs	+5	+7	+7
Variable expenses	0	+5	+4.5
Net present value ($000)	−8	−2	0
Internal rate of return	15.0 %	15.0 %	15.0 %

When the time for the presentation to top management arrived, George, accompanied by the treasurer, brought all his charts to the conference room. George proceeded with his discussion, summarizing the forecasts and estimates and arriving at the recommended solution. He reviewed with management his sensitivity analysis, and the treasurer completed the presentation by recommending that the company go ahead and begin production in the new region.

George believed that his presentation went well, and the treasurer commended him for a good job. But a few days later, the treasurer called George into his office and told him that management had, at least for the time being, decided not to go ahead with expansion. He explained that management believed that this was not the right time to expand, given the economy's somewhat cloudy future. Also, they considered the strength of their competition and decided that this was not the time to make the investment. Sensing George's disappointment, the treasurer assured him that he had done an excellent job with the data he had. Actually, the treasurer said, the vice president of finance had told him to commend George for his substantial effort. "But that's the way things go in a large corporation," he continued. "You see, decisions are not always made on the basis of figures, however thoroughly they were developed. You must remember that in business, once the data have been put together, there is still the judgment factor that must be applied by management. After all, that's what top management gets paid for. I am sure that in the future, this or a similar project will be considered again."

SUMMARY

In this chapter, we expand the economic concept of profit maximization to multiperiod projects.

Capital budgeting involves the evaluation of projects in which initial expenditures provide streams of cash inflows over a significant period of time. The process of evaluating capital proposals includes the following:

1. Estimating all incremental cash flows resulting from the project
2. Discounting all flows to the present
3. Determining whether a proposal should be accepted

Two methods are recommended for evaluating capital budgeting proposals—NPV and IRR. These two criteria are compared as to their validity. It was found that, from a theoretical viewpoint, NPV is the more valid. However, there is much to recommend the use of IRR, and business, in fact, favors this technique. In most cases, both methods lead to the same answer.

The concept of the cost of capital was then developed, and methods of arriving at a weighted cost of capital are discussed. Capital rationing was also discussed.

We then turn to the second subject of this chapter, risk analysis as applied to capital budgeting. The most common measures of risk are discussed: standard deviation, coefficient of variation, and the z-statistic. We use the concepts of expected value and standard deviation to obtain the expected NPV for a multiperiod project.

Two additional calculations incorporating risk in capital budgeting are presented: risk adjusted discount rate and certainty equivalents. Although both methods can be employed, the former is simpler to use and is much more popular in business.

Additional techniques are discussed. Two similar methods are sensitivity analysis and scenario analysis. The latter is used in "The Situation" and "The Solution" vignettes. We further present a brief discussion of simulation analysis and decision trees. Simulation analysis is capable of obtaining expected value and standard deviation, whereas decision trees lend themselves to sequential decision making.

Although many techniques of accounting for risk were discussed in this chapter, it is obvious that none of these methods is completely satisfactory. However, the important lesson of this chapter is that risk is everpresent in business, and anyone engaging in business planning must be aware of the dangers of risky outcomes and be able to cope with the uncertainty of future events. Thus, the awareness of a risky situation may be more important than familiarity with any of the specific methods illustrated in this chapter.

IMPORTANT CONCEPTS

Accounting rate of return: **Also known as the** *return on investment* (ROI) or *return on assets* (ROA), a method for evaluating capital projects. It is obtained by dividing the average annual profit by the average investment. (p. 453)

Capital asset pricing model (CAPM):   A financial model specifying relationships between risk and return. An important part of the CAPM is the development of beta, which measures the market risk of a security and is a necessary ingredient in determining a stock's required rate of return. (p. 463)

Capital budgeting: An area of business decision making that concerns undertakings whose receipts and expenses continue over a significant period of time. (p. 452)

Capital rationing: The practice of restricting capital expenditure to a certain amount, possibly resulting in the rejection of projects that have a positive net present value and should be accepted to maximize the company's value. (p. 466)

Certainty equivalent: A certain (risk-free) cash flow that would be acceptable as opposed to the expected value of a risky cash flow. (p. 473)

Coefficient of variation: A measure of risk relative to expected value that is used to compare standard deviations of projects with unequal expected values. (p. 471)

Cost of capital: Also often referred to as the required rate of return, the hurdle rate, or the cutoff rate, the rate of return a company must earn on its assets to justify the using and acquiring of funds. (p. 454)

Decision tree: A method used with sequential decision making in which a diagram graphically points out the order in which decisions must be made and compares the value of the various actions that can be undertaken. (p. 477)

Discount rate: The rate at which cash flows are discounted. It is the required rate of return or cost of capital. (p. 454)

Dividend growth model: A method to arrive at the value of a security. Given the price of the security, it calculates the company's cost of equity as the dividend divided by the current stock price plus the growth rate in dividends (assumed to be constant). It is an alternative method to CAPM in calculating the equity cost of capital. (p. 462)

Expected value: An average of all possible outcomes weighted by their respective probabilities. (p. 468)

Free cash flow: Funds that are available for distribution to investors. It includes operating cash flow after taxes minus (plus) increases (decreases) in operating working capital and fixed assets investment. (See Appendix 12A.) (p. 495)

Independent projects: A situation in which the acceptance of one capital project does not preclude the acceptance of another project. (See *mutually exclusive projects*.) (p. 456)

Internal rate of return (IRR): One method of evaluating capital projects by discounting cash flows. The IRR is the interest rate that equates the present value of inflows with the present value of outflows, or, in other words, causes the net present value of the project to equal zero. (p. 453)

Mutually exclusive projects: A situation in which the acceptance of one project precludes the acceptance of another. (p. 456)

Net present value (NPV): A method of evaluating capital projects in which all cash flows are discounted at the cost of capital to the present and the present value of all outflows is subtracted from the present value of all inflows. (p. 453)

Payback: A method of evaluating capital projects in which the original investment is divided by the annual cash flow. It tells management how many years it will take for a project's cash inflows to repay the original investment. (p. 453)

Probability: An expression of the chance that a particular event will occur. (p. 467)

Probability distribution: A distribution indicating the chances of all possible occurrences. (p. 467)

Profitability index: A method of evaluating capital budgeting projects by dividing the present value of cash inflows by the original investment. (p. 456)

Real option: An opportunity to make adjustments in a capital budgeting project in response to changing circumstances potentially resulting in improved results. (p. 479)

Risk: Refers to a situation in which possible future events can be defined and probabilities assigned. (p. 466)

Risk-adjusted discount rate (RADR): A value equal to the riskless (risk-free) interest rate plus a risk premium. The risk-free rate ideally is the pure time value of money, and the risk premium represents a judgment as to the additional return necessary to compensate for additional risk. (p. 473)

Scenario analysis: A method for estimating project risk. Key important variables are identified and changed simultaneously to measure the impact of their changes on results of a capital budgeting proposal. (p. 476)

Sensitivity analysis: A method for estimating project risk that involves identifying a key variable that affects results and then changing it to measure the impact. (p. 475)

Simulation analysis: A method that assigns a probability distribution to each key variable and uses random numbers to simulate a set of possible outcomes to arrive at an expected value and dispersion. (p. 476)

Standard deviation: The degree of dispersion of possible outcomes around the mean outcome or expected value. It is the square root of the weighted average of the squared deviations of all possible outcomes from the expected value. (p. 469)

Time value of money: Very basically, this means that a dollar today is worth more than a dollar tomorrow because today's dollar will earn interest and increase in value. (p. 453)

Uncertainty: Refers to situations in which there is no viable method of assigning probabilities to future random events. (p. 466)

Weighted average cost of capital (WACC): The expected average cost of funds. It is found by weighting the cost of each capital component by its proportion to the total capital structure. (p. 464)

QUESTIONS

1. What is the objective of capital budgeting?
2. Define the *time value of money*.
3. How is NPV calculated? What is the decision rule for NPV? How is the internal rate of return calculated? What is the decision rule for IRR?
4. Under which circumstances can the NPV and IRR calculations lead to conflicting results? What is the major reason for the difference? Which of the two methods is preferable? Why?
5. What are the major types of cash flows to be included in a capital budgeting analysis? Describe each.
6. Why is depreciation important in the analysis of a capital budgeting proposal?
7. You are analyzing a potential capital investment project involving a new product. As you are compiling the relevant data for your analysis, you are informed of an expenditure that occurred during the prior year. The marketing research department of your company conducted an assessment of the demand for this new product. The cost of this research was

$100,000 and was part of the company's expenses during the previous year. Is this relevant to your present analysis? Why or why not?

8. How is the company's optimal capital budget determined? Does the decision-making process in this case resemble the procedure used in determining the price and quantity of output? How?

9. How is the weighted average cost of capital determined?

10. Define *beta*. How is it used to compute the required rate of return on a company's stock (the equity cost of capital)?

11. Why is capital rationing not considered to be rational maximizing behavior?

12. Enumerate causes of business risk.

13. You are comparing two potential mutually exclusive investment projects. You have calculated the expected NPV of project A to be $3,758 and that of project B to be $3,114. Can you be certain that you should recommend to your management to implement project A?

14. Would a risk-averse person prefer a project whose distribution of potential outcomes can be drawn as a continuous normal curve with a very high peak and a steep decline around the peak?

15. Define *coefficient of variation*.

16. "All our projects are discounted at the same interest rate," says the treasurer of a large company. Would you dispute the advisability of such a procedure?

17. Why do companies use the RADR method much more frequently than the certainty equivalent method?

18. Describe and give examples of
    a. Sensitivity analysis
    b. Simulation analysis

19. Why does the use of "real options" improve capital investment analysis? Under which circumstances would you recommend using real options?

PROBLEMS

1. Jay Wechsler agrees to purchase a car from a local dealer, the Con Car Co. The purchase price is $15,000. Jay has the cash to pay the entire amount and wants to do so. Con's sales manager uses the following argument to convince him to finance the car: "All we require is a down payment of $3,000. Then you can borrow the $12,000 from our finance company at 12 percent. You will make monthly payments of $266.93 for 5 years (60 months), a total of $16,015.80. If you do that, you get to keep your $12,000. Now suppose you keep this money in a money market account that pays you 8 percent compounded quarterly. In 5 years, the $12,000 will grow to $17,831.40. That means that you will be better off by $1,815.60 than if you pay the $12,000 in cash."

   Assume all the numbers are correct. Does the offer sound too good to be true? Why? (This is an argument often used by automobile dealers. One of the authors encountered it not too long ago.)

2. Your firm has an opportunity to make an investment of $50,000. Its cost of capital is 12 percent. It expects aftertax cash flows (including the tax shield from depreciation) for the next 5 years to be as follows:

Year 1	$10,000
Year 2	20,000
Year 3	30,000
Year 4	20,000
Year 5	5,000

   a. Calculate the NPV.
   b. Calculate the IRR (to the nearest percent).
   c. Would you accept this project?

3. You own a large collection of fine wines. You now decide that the time has come to consider liquidating this valuable asset. However, you predict that the value of your collection will rise in the next few years. The following are your estimates:

Year	Estimated value
Today	$70,000
1	88,000
2	104,000
3	119,000
4	132,000
5	142,000
6	150,000

If you assume your cost of capital to be 10%, when should you sell your collection to maximize your NPV?

4. The Glendale construction company is considering the purchase of a new crane. Its cost would be $500,000. If it were to make the purchase, the company would sell an old crane, which still has a book value of $100,000 and which it could probably sell in the second-hand market for $70,000. If the tax rate is 40 percent, what would be the actual cash investment in the new crane?

5. As capital investment analyst for the Parkhurst Printing Corporation, you have been asked to evaluate the advisability of purchasing a new printing press to accommodate projected increases in demand. This new machine is expected to last 5 years, and you will be calculating the cash flows of the project for that period.

   The purchase price of the press is expected to be $140,000; in addition, it will cost $10,000 to install it. The press will be depreciated on a straight-line basis over 5 years to a zero salvage value. However, it is expected to have a market value of $10,000 at the end of 5 years.

   The press is expected to generate the following cash revenues and cash costs and expenses:

	Year 1	Year 2	Year 3	Year 4	Year 5
Cash revenue	$50,000	$80,000	$80,000	$80,000	$40,000
Cash cost and expense	25,000	40,000	40,000	40,000	20,000

Because of increased production, additional working capital of $15,000 will be needed at $t = 0$ (today) and will be returned at the end of the project (5 years from now). The income tax rate is 40 percent, and the company's cost of capital is 12 percent. Calculate the net present value. Should the press be purchased?

6. The Thunderbird Quick Delivery Company needs a truck and is evaluating two alternatives for meeting its needs for the next 10 years.

   Choice A: Buy a used Ford truck for $6,000. It will be depreciated straight-line over a 5-year life to a salvage value of zero. However, it is expected that the truck will be sold after 4 years for $800. At this point, another used Ford truck will be bought for $12,000. It will last 6 years and will have no market value at the end of this period. This truck will also be depreciated over 5 years on a straight-line basis.

   Choice B: Buy a new Chevrolet truck for $16,000. The truck will last the entire 10 years and will have a market value of $1,000 at the end. Again, 5-year straight-line depreciation will be used.

   Other information: Income tax rate 34%

   Cost of capital 12%

Which of the two choices is preferable?

7. The Colgate Distributing Company has the choice of furnishing its sales representatives with a car or paying a mileage allowance for the use of the representatives' own cars. If the company furnishes the car, it will pay all expenses connected with it, including gasoline for business mileage. The estimates are as follows:

> *Cost of car: $15,000*
> *Estimated life: 4 years*
> *Depreciation method: Straight-line over 4 years (assuming no salvage value)*
> *Expected sales value of car at end of 4 years: $2,500*
> *Estimated annual operating costs:*

Gasoline	$900
License and insurance	600
Garaging	300
Maintenance	
Year 1	250
Year 2	350
Year 3	450
Year 4	600

If the sales representatives use their own cars, the company will reimburse them at 35 cents per mile; the company estimates that each representative will drive 18,000 miles per year for business purposes. The company's cost of capital is 10 percent, and its income tax rate is 40 percent.

Should the company buy cars for its sales representatives or pay them a mileage allowance? Use the NPV method in your calculation.

8. A company's common stock is currently selling at $40 per share. Its most recent dividend was $1.60, and the financial community expects that its dividend will grow at 10 percent per year in the foreseeable future. What is the company's equity cost of retained earnings? If the company sells new common stock to finance new projects and must pay $2 per share in flotation costs, what is the cost of equity?

9. A company has 1,000,000 shares of common stock outstanding, and the current market price is $50 per share. The company has also issued 20,000 bonds ($1,000 maturity value each), which are presently selling in the market at $980 each. The bonds are selling at a yield of 11 percent; the company expects to pay a dividend of $3 per share in the coming year, and the dividend is expected to grow at 8 percent per year. The company is in the 40 percent tax bracket. What is the weighted average cost of capital?

10. A company has a beta of 1.3. The risk-free interest rate today is 8 percent, and the return on a market portfolio of stocks is 14 percent. (Therefore, the market risk premium is 6 percent, the difference between the market return and the risk-free return.)
    a. What is the required return (equity cost) on the company's stock?
    b. If the risk-free rate rises to 9 percent, what will be the required rate of return on the company's stock?
    c. If the beta of this company were 0.8, what would be its required rate of return?

11. Two mutually exclusive alternatives, projects C and D, have the following investments and cash flows:

	Project C	Project D
Investment at period $t = 0$	$40,000	$40,000
Cash inflow at $t = 1$	10,000	20,500
Cash inflow at $t = 2$	10,000	20,500
Cash inflow at $t = 3$	47,000	20,500

a. Calculate the NPV and IRR of each project. The company's cost of capital is 12 percent.

b. Which of the two projects would you accept? Explain.

c. Sketch the two projects' NPV profiles.

12. The Berkshire Resort Hotel has planned several improvement projects. However, it has decided to restrict its capital expenditures to $340,000 during the next year. The following are the projects it has on its drawing board:

	Original Investment	Net Present Value
Additional tennis court	$ 20,000	$ 5,500
Kitchen renovation	50,000	14,000
New children's playground	60,000	12,500
New bungalows	100,000	22,500
New golf clubhouse	120,000	32,500
Olympic-size swimming pool	140,000	45,000
New theater arena	150,000	40,000

Which projects should it undertake?

13. The Quality Office Furniture Company has compiled the year's revenue expectations and their probabilities:

Sales ($000)	Probabilities
240	0.05
280	0.10
320	0.70
360	0.10
400	0.05

Calculate

a. The expected revenue

b. The standard deviation

c. The coefficient of variation

14. The Learned Book Company has a choice of publishing one of two books on the subject of Greek mythology. It expects the sales period for each to be extremely short, and it estimates profit probabilities as follows:

Book A		Book B	
Probability	Profit	Probability	Profit
0.2	$2,000	0.1	$1,500
0.3	2,300	0.4	1,700
0.3	2,600	0.4	1,900
0.2	2,900	0.1	2,100

Calculate the expected profit, standard deviation, and coefficient of variation for each book. If you were asked which of the two to publish, what would be your advice?

15. The Cactus Corporation is considering a 2-year project, project A, involving an initial investment of $600 and the following cash inflows and probabilities:

Year 1		Year 2	
Probability	Cash Flow	Probability	Cash Flow
0.1	$700	0.2	$600
0.4	600	0.3	500
0.4	500	0.3	400
0.1	400	0.2	300

a. Calculate the project's expected NPV and standard deviation, assuming the discount rate to be 8 percent.

b. The company is also considering another 2-year project, project B, which has an expected NPV of $320 and a standard deviation of $125. Projects A and B are mutually exclusive. Which of the two projects would you prefer? Explain.

16. The Grand Design Corporation uses the certainty equivalent approach in making capital budgeting decisions. You are given the following data for a particular project:

Year	Cash Flow	Certainty Equivalent Factor
0	$-20,000	1.00
1	5,000	0.90
2	5,000	0.90
3	5,000	0.90
4	15,000	0.70

The risk-free discount rate is 4 percent, and the RADR is 12 percent. Calculate the NPV. Would you accept this project?

17. Project A has an expected NPV of $500 and a standard deviation of $125. Project B has a standard deviation of $100 and an expected NPV of $300. Which of the two projects would you select? Explain why.

18. Global Industries has calculated the return on assets (ROA) for one of its projects using the simulation method. By simulating the operations 1,000 times, they obtained an ROA of 16.7 percent and a standard deviation of 6.2. The results of the simulation conform quite closely to a normal curve.

a. Draw a probability distribution using the given data.

b. The company's objective is to achieve an ROA of 12 percent. What is the probability that the project will achieve at least that level?

c. What is the probability of ROA being nonnegative?

19. The Great Pine Forest Corporation is analyzing an expansion project with the following information:

Initial investment:	*$120,000*
Depreciation life:	*5 years—straight-line*
Project life:	*5 years*
Additional working capital at t = 0	*$20,000*
Working capital returned at t = 5	*$20,000*
Expected salvage value at t = 5	*$15,000*
Tax rate:	*34 percent*
Cost of capital:	*12 percent*

	Year 1	Year 2	Year 3	Year 4	Year 5
Revenue	$50,000	$80,000	$80,000	$80,000	$40,000
Cash costs	30,000	30,000	25,000	25,000	25,000

a. Calculate the NPV of this project.

b. Now conduct a scenario analysis as follows:

1. Assume the best case to have revenue 10 percent higher than just stated, costs 5 percent lower than given, and salvage value twice the amount given.

2. Assume the worst case to have revenue 10 percent lower than given, costs 5 percent higher than given, and salvage value to be 0.

Show the results for the best case, the most likely case, and the worst case.

20. Sam Parkington has a nontransferable option to mine for gold on a certain piece of land. He has three choices of action:
    a. He can start mining immediately.
    b. He can conduct further tests to see whether there is a good promise of finding gold.
    c. He can drop the option.

    The cost of the test would be $45,000, and the cost of mining would be $150,000. If he finds gold, he expects to net $600,000.

    He estimates the following probabilities. If he starts mining without further tests, he estimates that the probability of finding gold is 55 percent. He expects that the probability of the test being successful is 60 percent. If the test is favorable, the probability is 85 percent that there is gold in the ground, but if the test is not favorable it is only 10 percent. Using a decision tree, make a recommendation.

21. It has been your secret wish to own and operate an amusement park when you can afford to make the investment. That time has now arrived. There is a large empty lot at the outskirts of Phoenix, Arizona, owned by the city. The city is willing to lease one-half of this lot for 5 years with an option to lease both it and the other half for the next 5 years. In return for charging you a reasonable rent, the city will take ownership of your equipment at the end of the 5 or 10 years.

    You have estimated your original investment to be $250,000. You expect your net cash flows (after lease payments, all other expenses, and taxes) to be $55,000 for each of the first 5 years. If you exercise your option to continue with both parts of the property at the end of year 5, you will need to invest another $150,000 (for additional equipment and a miniature golf course). Because your cash flow estimates are now far into the future, you estimate a 50 percent probability that your annual cash flows will remain the same ($55,000) and a 50 percent probability that they will rise to $100,000 per year for the second 5 years. Your cost of capital is 12 percent.
    a. Is the first 5-year project acceptable?
    b. What is the value of the total project if you exercise your option? What is the value of your option?

22. You have been offered an investment, which, according to your calculations, has the following possible rates of return:

Probability	Rate of return
0.2	−5%
0.6	+10%
0.2	+25%

You can also use your funds to buy a U.S. Treasury note, which will earn a certain 3.5%. In which of these two alternatives will you invest your money?

The Value of a Corporation

We have just learned how to calculate the present value of a project given cash inflows and outflows over a period of time, and discounting these to the present using a discount rate, the cost of capital.

A similar method of computation can be employed to value a corporation as a whole. Of course, if the corporation's stock trades on a stock exchange and its debt is composed of publicly owned bonds, its market value can easily be established from published data. However, assume you are one of the founders of a relatively small private corporation. You and the other owners are now planning to carry out an "initial public offering" (usually referred to as an IPO). How would you go about estimating what your company is worth?[33] To determine some kind of a reasonable value figure, you will have to estimate your cash inflows and outflows several years into the future. To do a complete valuation job, it would be necessary to project your income statements and balance sheets. We try to condense our procedure here by selecting the essential data we need to make our computation without constructing complete financial statements.

To accomplish our objective we must start with the concept of **free cash flow**.[34] Free cash flow consists of funds that would be available to investors from operating cash flows after we subtract investments in working capital and fixed assets needed to operate and grow the company. These terms are defined as follows:

1. Operating cash flow = EBIT × (1 − T) + Depreciation

   where EBIT = Earnings before interest and tax (also frequently called operating profit)

   T = Tax rate

2. New investment in operating working capital represents the annual increases in certain parts of current assets less increases in accounts payable.

3. Increases in fixed assets are increases in land, property, and equipment before subtracting depreciation (i.e., the gross increases in fixed assets).

Let us construct a simple example to illustrate the valuation method. Assume in 2004, the following were the relevant numbers (in $000):

EBIT	$ 60
Depreciation	20
Operating working capital	80
Gross fixed assets	120

Your company expects to have rather rapid growth during the next 3 years because of a new product you are bringing to the market. You expect, however, that after 3 years your competition will have caught up with you. Because you are not certain what new products you will introduce then, you make the conservative judgment that your company's free cash flow will increase at 6 percent per year for the foreseeable future. To calculate the free cash flow for the years 2005, 2006, and 2007, you have estimated the following:

	2005	2006	2007
EBIT	$ 90	$110	$125
Depreciation	30	35	40
Operating working capital	110	135	155
Gross fixed assets	160	190	220

EBIT and depreciation give us the two components of free cash flow. To calculate the other two, we must compute the year-to-year changes to obtain the cash outflow arising from an increase in those investments. Thus,

	2005	2006	2007
Operating working capital	$30	$25	$20
Gross fixed assets	40	30	30

We expect the income tax rate to be 40 percent in each of the years. Now we are ready to calculate the free cash flows for the 3 years:[35]

	2005	2006	2007
EBIT $\times (1 - T)$	$54	$66	$75
+ Depreciation	30	35	40
− Increase in operating working capital	30	25	20
− Increase in gross fixed assets	40	30	30
Free cash flow	$14	$46	$65

The next step is to calculate the present value of the free cash flows. At this point we must establish the discount rate—the cost of capital. We estimate it to be 12 percent. Therefore, the present value of the above three cash flows at the end of 2004 will be the following (again using data from Appendix Table A.1c):

Year 2005	14 $\times$ 0.8929	$12.5
2006	46 $\times$ 0.7972	36.7
2007	65 $\times$ 0.7118	46.3
Total		$95.5

Now we must account for the cash flows after the first 3 high-growth years. We had previously assumed we would expect the normal long-term growth rate in free cash flow to be 6 percent. We can use the constant growth formula (Gordon model) to give us the answer. If free cash flow grows by 6 percent in 2008, then it will amount to 65 $\times$ 1.06 = $68.9. Because the cost of capital is 12 percent and the growth rate is 6 percent, our calculation will proceed as follows:

$$68.9/(0.12 - 0.06) = 68.9/(0.06) = 1,148.3$$

---

[35]It is quite common for a new, small, and growing company to have negative free cash flows in its early years. Even though its EBIT is positive, it will have substantial cash outflows as it builds up its working capital and fixed asset base. To simplify matters, we have assumed positive free cash flows in each year.

The answer is the present value of all future cash flows at the beginning of year 2008 (or the end of 2007). To bring this amount back to the end of 2004, we must discount the amount for 3 years, or 1148.3 $\times$ 0.7118 = 817.4. The last step is to add the present value of the first 3 years to the present value of the growing perpetuity: 95.5 + 817.4 = 912.9.

We have thus estimated the total value of your business to be $912,900. But as one of the owners of the business, you are interested in how much you could receive for your stock. We must now deduct any bank debt and long-term debt that you have on your balance sheet. Suppose you had borrowed $300,000. Then the estimate of your stock value is $612,900. Let us assume you and the other present owners want to retain 20 percent of the stock ownership of the firm. This means you could expect to obtain $490,320 from your IPO.

Some cautions are in order. The result that we calculated is extremely sensitive to all the estimates we had made for cash flows, tax rates, and discount rates. The final results could differ substantially from our calculations. It would most likely be useful to do one or more additional calculations, using more optimistic and pessimistic assumptions, to help establish a range of potential outcomes.

You would perform a similar calculation, if instead of an IPO you were to consider a buyout offer by a large established firm in your industry. You would then be interested in determining the price at which you would be willing to sell your company. Again it would be useful to make several calculations to arrive at a desirable selling price. Further, if the acquiring firm should be able to achieve some synergies from taking over your firm, then the value of your company could be higher. That firm certainly made calculations similar to yours, and because of the synergies, they may have arrived at a higher figure. Thus, after you have bargained with the large firm, you may end up with a larger amount. If you were lucky enough to have two large firms competing to acquire you, you may indeed strike a good bargain.

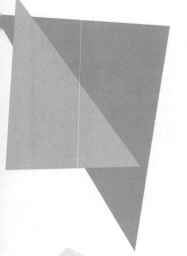

The Multinational Corporation and Globalization

Learning Objectives

Upon completion of this chapter, readers should be able to:

- Describe the meaning of the term *globalization* and discuss the arguments for and against it.
- Define the exchange rate and identify several methods of hedging.
- Understand multinational capital budgeting and explain how it differs from capital budgeting of a domestic corporation.
- Show how changing transfer prices can benefit a corporation.

The Situation

Global Foods has ceased to be a strictly domestic corporation. It has opened production facilities that produce both its soft drinks and its bottled water in several countries in Western Europe and the Pacific Rim. It is now ready to make an investment in one of the countries that was formerly part of the Soviet sphere. Management has been investigating in which of the countries to locate. It turned out that it favored the Czech Republic. This country is centrally located, has a skilled labor force, has been very active in privatizing industry, and has a fairly stable government. Its labor costs are relatively low.

After an investigation of various locations within the Czech Republic, the company found a plant not presently in use but rather well maintained just outside the town of Pelhřimov, in southeastern Bohemia, not too far from the border of Moravia. It is about 115 kilometers from Prague, the capital city. The town itself has about 17,000 inhabitants. Pelhřimov has some light industry including wood processing, food, textile, and clothing.

George Kline, manager of Global Foods' capital planning (we met George earlier), has been given the task of preparing a capital budgeting evaluation. He consults with the marketing and manufacturing departments. He discusses the Czech economic situation with the company's economist. He obtains estimates of Czech and U.S. inflation rates, and the exchange rate of the Koruna (KCZ) against the U.S. dollar. He further acquaints himself with the corporate tax rate in the Czech Republic. Armed with this information, he begins to put down the assumptions with which he will work.

He expects that the fixed investment by Global Foods, U.S.A., will be $4 million, and that another $400,000 will be invested in working capital. The fixed investment will be depreciated straight-line over 8 years. Because the plant is in very good condition, only the installation of machinery will be needed for the plant to begin operating rather quickly.

To be very conservative, cash flows for only 4 years will be estimated, with a terminal value estimated at the end of the 4 years. His marketing people think that first year's sales will be 400 million KCZ and that the volume will increase by 6 percent each year. Production costs in the first year will be 190 million KCZ. The parent company will

(continued)

(continued)

be providing various supplies and services to the subsidiary starting at 110 million KCZ and will grow at the same rate as volume. A license fee of 3 percent of sales will be paid by the Czech subsidiary to the parent corporation. General and administrative expenses will be 12 percent of sales revenue. The following are estimates of annual price level changes in the United States and the Czech Republic:

General price level in the United States	2.0%[1]
General price level in the Czech Republic	3.5%
Sales price in Czech Republic	4.0%
Cost of production in Czech Republic	4.0%

Today's exchange rate is 27 KCZ/$1. The exchange rate is expected to change in relation to the inflation rates in the two countries.[2] The income tax rate in the Czech Republic is 31 percent, whereas it is 35 percent in the United States. After the initial infusion of working capital into the project, the subsidiary will require that working capital be 10 percent of sales. Fifty percent of this additional requirement will be financed internally (profits and increase in current liabilities), and the other 50 percent will be financed externally by the subsidiary.

Global Foods' cost of capital for projects of average risk is 15 percent. However, to account for the additional risk faced by operating in a foreign country that just recently embraced free trade (although still regulated), a 4 percent risk margin will be added so the discount rate for the parent company will be 19 percent. The cost of capital for similar enterprises in the Czech Republic is 22 percent.

The profit calculated on the parent's shipments of supplies to its subsidiary will be computed at 5 percent. This appears reasonable and should not be questioned by U.S. or Czech tax authorities.

The subsidiary will remit 50 percent of its aftertax profits to the parent.

With all this information, George will now input the data into an Excel spreadsheet that he specifically prepared for this project. He will have to organize his work into five separate exhibits. First, he will calculate the profit of the subsidiary. Second, he must compute the additional working capital investment made by the subsidiary. The third exhibit will be a cash flow statement for the subsidiary with a calculation of the NPV and IRR. The fourth exhibit may appear somewhat complicated. It translates the dividend by the subsidiary to the parent from KCZ into U.S. dollars; this involves a process called "grossing up" to ascertain the tax for which the parent may be liable because the Czech tax rate is lower than that in the United States.[3] Last, the parent company must compute the NPV and IRR of all cash flows received from the subsidiary.

INTRODUCTION

Most of our discussion in this book does not differentiate between domestic and international businesses. We touch briefly on aspects of international business in the "Global Application" sections that are found at the end of most chapters. However, the opportunities and problems faced by American corporations in foreign countries occupy many recent headlines and articles in the business media. Therefore, we devote a chapter to this increasingly important topic—the multinational corporation.[4]

A multinational corporation (usually abbreviated as MNC or MNE for multinational enterprise) is faced with the same opportunities and problems as the domestic corporation. It must concern itself with the forces of supply and demand. It must consider demand elasticity for its products and seek to achieve profit optimization by

---

[1] The price of supplies and services from the United States will also increase at 2 percent.
[2] Because inflation in the United States is 2 percent and in the Czech Republic 3.5 percent, the KCZ will depreciate each year by 1.5 percent.
[3] The process of grossing up is explained later in this chapter.
[4] Some of the topics discussed in this chapter may have been mentioned in some of the previous chapters. However, this chapter tries to tie the various strings together into a unified whole. This chapter benefited a great deal from Michael H. Moffett, Arthur I. Stonehill, and David K. Eiteman, *Fundamentals of Multinational Finance,* 2nd ed. Boston: Pearson Addison Wesley, 2006.

applying the marginal principle, given business and financial risks. All these concerns are discussed thoroughly in this text. But a company operating globally faces additional challenges. It must take into account different currencies, rules and regulations of different countries, different tax systems, tariffs and other restrictions, different costs of production, and different cultures. Each challenge presents new risks (and opportunities) with which an MNC must cope.

GLOBALIZATION

Before specifically describing the activities of an MNC, we discuss the term **globalization**, which has become a very popular word. It is praised by some and condemned by others. Globalization can be defined in various ways.

One author depicts globalization as a transition process. At the beginning, a corporation limits its transactions strictly to its home country, both in its sales and its purchases.[5] But to compete and grow, the company will begin to import products it needs to manufacture and export its final products to foreign countries. This may be called the "international trade" phase. Dealing internationally introduces the corporation to new considerations. It must now concern itself with foreign exchange and exchange rates, and with credit evaluation of potential customers in countries with varying business practices and legal systems, different languages, and cultures.

The next step occurs when the company establishes a presence in a foreign country. It may start by opening a sales and/or service office abroad. It may enter into licensing agreements. Finally, it will establish operations there. This could be the result of a joint venture, acquisition of a foreign company, or the erection of a manufacturing facility (the latter is usually called a "greenfield investment"). This is the third phase in the transition process—the "multinational phase." Here a company encounters new opportunities—the ability to serve a world market—and new problems. It must now consider differing traditions and cultures, as well as local laws and tax systems.[6]

Another definition deals with the final result of companies' expansion into the world market. It also considers the financial aspects of globalization: "closer integration of the countries of the world—especially the increased level of trade and movements of capital—brought on by lower costs of transportation and communication."[7] Recently we have seen what may be another step in the progression of globalization, from the multinational corporation to what has been referred to as a *globally integrated enterprise*. "This is an enterprise that shapes its strategy, management and operations in a truly global way. It locates operations and functions anywhere in the world based on the right cost, the right skills and the right business environment. And it integrates those operations horizontally and globally."[8] This statement comes from a speech by Samuel J. Palmisano, the chief executive officer of IBM Corporation. Thus, for instance, IBM now has 74,000 employees in India, about 19 percent of its labor force. Further, the company recently moved its chief procurement officer, John Patterson, to Shenzen, China. He is the first head of a company-wide function to be based outside the United States. Other top executives may follow.[9]

---

[5]Even a strictly domestic company is affected by international trade. It may be exposed to competition from foreign companies exporting to the company's home country or from other companies in its industry that engage in international trade.

[6]Michael H. Moffett et al., op. cit., pp. 5–8.

[7]http://www.wwnorton.com/stiglitzwalsh/economics/glossary.htm.

[8]Samuel J. Palmisano, "Leadership, Trust and the Globally Integrated Enterprise," *INSEAD Global Leader Series*, INSEAD Business School, Fontainbleau, France, October 3, 2006.

[9]"Hungry Tiger, Dancing Elephant," *The Economist*, April 7, 2007, pp. 67–69.

Another example of this new level of globalization—albeit on a smaller scale—can again be found at IBM. A team of 50 programmers around the world is charged with making IBM's WebSphere software work with code written in other programming languages. The team is made up of 20 programmers in Hursley, England, 20 in Bangalore, India, and 10 in Ottawa, Canada. The project is divided into small pieces, which requires constant communication among the team members. The manager of this team estimates that it can decrease the time required to revise such a product to 4 months from 18 to 24 months a few years ago.[10]

IS GLOBALIZATION GOOD OR BAD?

Globalization has become a controversial topic, with strong arguments made by both sides. Many of these arguments are emotional rather than based in fact. We remember presidential candidate Ross Perot's warnings in 1992 about the "great sucking sound" that would materialize if the North American Free Trade Agreement were to be enacted. By that he meant that a large number of manufacturing jobs would be exported to Mexico. Today, we hear strong arguments about the **outsourcing (offshoring)** of white-collar jobs, such as programmers, to India and China. How valid are these?

Before we discuss the contemporary arguments about the benefits and drawbacks of globalization, we should look at similar episodes of the past not necessarily created by international trade. In the mid-twentieth century, textile plants moved from New England to the south of the United States to take advantage of lower wages, leaving behind a significant number of unemployed workers in the Northeast. As economies progressed and innovations spurred improvements in technology, certain occupations and industries disappeared to be replaced by new ones. An example that goes back a century is the horse and buggy industry that was supplanted by the automobile industry. A more recent example is the decline of the typewriter industry with the advent of computers. Another example, a very current one, is that, in 2003, digital cameras outsold film cameras in the United States. Thus film may become a thing of the past, a victim of the new technology. We are sure you can think of many more examples. The point is that improvements in technology, creating new industries and devastating old, have been with us for centuries. This process has been named "creative destruction" by Josef Schumpeter, a famous economist.

In the long run, innovations have undoubtedly raised living standards and increased employment. However, it must be recognized that in the short run, these changes have injured large numbers of individuals whose jobs just simply disappeared. The resistance to the results of technological change has historically been quite strong, resulting in government regulation and union rules. Violent and destructive outbreaks have also been common.

PROGLOBALIZATION ARGUMENTS

Among the arguments favoring globalization are the following:

➤ Consumers benefit when globalization opens new markets and thus offers consumers a greater choice.

➤ Consumers benefit when competition due to the expansion of markets tends to lower prices. Products and services are produced in lower-cost locations.

---

[10]Phred Dvorak, "How Teams Can Work Well Together from Far Apart," *Wall Street Journal*, September 17, 2007.

➤ Advances in communication allow goods, services, and capital to flow more freely, and thus contribute to growth and greater productivity.

➤ The quality of products and services is enhanced due to increased worldwide competition.

➤ The globalization of financial markets leads to a more efficient allocation of resources worldwide. Because of the mobility of capital, production can be more easily moved to geographic locations where it is most efficient (where the location has a comparative advantage).

➤ Globalization can improve the living conditions in poorer developing nations when production is moved from highly developed countries. When demand increases for labor in poorer countries, wage levels will rise as new employment opportunities arise.

➤ With the improvement in wages in poorer countries, new demand for goods is generated and may create export opportunities for other, more developed, countries.

➤ When MNCs invest abroad, they tend to pay higher wages than are paid locally and maintain better working conditions. They also create new employment opportunities.

➤ By creating higher living standards globalization may increase the society's willingness to devote resources to the environment and other social goals.[11]

ANTIGLOBALIZATION ARGUMENTS

The following are some of the arguments against globalization:

➤ By operating in foreign countries, MNCs in developed countries create competition for their home country workforces. This leads to the lowering of wages (and thus standard of living) in home countries.

➤ "Large corporations with international undertakings stand accused of social injustice, unfair labour practices—including slave labour wages, living and working conditions—as well as a lack of concern for the environment, mismanagement of natural resources and ecological damage."[12]

➤ Technological advances in industrial countries decrease demand for workers, thus causing insecurity in the workforce. This is particularly the case in manufacturing industries, resulting in a shift to service industries where wages are on average lower. But more recently, there has been a tendency to transfer service jobs to lower-wage countries, causing a loss of jobs in the service industry.

➤ Capitalism ignores social welfare of individuals and destroys cultures.

➤ Companies shift operations to countries where they can produce at lowest costs, thus achieving high profits.

➤ Companies will shift their operations to countries where taxes are low, thus eroding the tax base worldwide.

➤ Globalization tends to weaken national sovereignty and national identity.[13]

It is most likely the pro- and antiglobalization lists are incomplete. However, they should impart a flavor of the various arguments.

---

[11]These arguments can be found in various sources. See, for instance, International Chamber of Commerce, *ICC Brief on Globalization,* 22 November 2000; Thomas Grennes, "Creative Destruction and Globalization," *Cato Journal,* 2003, 22, 3, pp. 543ff; International Monetary Fund, *Globalization: Threat or Opportunity?* April 12, 2000 (corrected January 2002); Bradford J. DeLong, *"Globalization" and "Neoliberalism,"* 1999, http://econ161.berkeley.edu/EconArticles/Reviews/alexkafka.html; Murray Weidenbaum, "Weighing the Pros and Cons of Globalization," Woodrow Wilson International Center for Scholars, March 5, 2003.
[12]Canadian Security Intelligence Service, *Anti-Globalization—A Spreading Phenomenon,* Report #2000/08, August 22, 2000.
[13]These arguments can found in Ibid; Kevin Danaher, *Economics 101, Globalization and the Downsizing of the American Dream,* Global Exchange (updated September 15, 2003), http://www.globalexchange.org/campaigns/econ101/americanDream.html; International Labour Organization, *World Commission Says Globalization Can and Must Change, Calls for Urgent Rethink of Global Governance,* February 24, 2004, http://www.ilo.org/public/english/bureau/inf/pr/2004/7.htm.

GLOBALIZATION AND THE FUTURE

There are strong and valid arguments on both sides of this question. So, where do we go from here?

Despite a great deal of opposition, including protests and some violence, the globalization process will continue. Even though it has brought about some great advantages for many countries and people, it must be recognized that the progress has not been even and that although there are great benefits to globalization, there are also drawbacks. It is certainly true that globalization has engendered the possibility of easing the transfer of technology and its increase. But as mentioned previously, the process of technological advance has been with us for centuries. There is no question that it has caused upheavals and hardships for parts of the population. However, in the long run it has led to economic progress and improved standards of living. Although there was always fear of declining employment due to technological advances, the world has seen increases in the labor force and in employment. And so it is with globalization. Some segments witness great improvements, whereas others may be left behind, at least in the short run.

Let us first look at the impact of globalization on different parts of the world. A large number of developing countries have done very well and have moved toward the levels found in developed countries. This is especially true of countries in East Asia. These countries have opened themselves to globalization and have benefited from it. In contrast, many African countries have lagged behind, and the differences in per capita income between them and developed countries have widened.

For these lagging developing countries to be included in the advances that globalization can provide, certain conditions have to be present:

➤ An effective government that will encourage governance and economic stability through responsible fiscal policies
➤ Policies to encourage foreign investment
➤ Progress toward domestic competition
➤ Improvements in health, education, and training

But the poorer developing countries cannot accomplish these advances by themselves. Developed countries must take various actions to make this possible rather than impeding developing countries' progress. They must encourage free trade, not hide behind tariff and nontariff barriers and export subsidies. Further, they must encourage flow of private capital to developing countries. Another important matter is for corporations in developed countries to promote good governance practices in their own organizations. This is crucial because recent problems arising from various ethical shortcomings and loose accounting practices on the part of large corporations have created distrust of large business in general, and consequently, of globalization. Large corporations must exhibit concern over environmental and social problems, and must act upon them.

With this said, we turn to consider whether globalization hurts labor forces in developed countries. The more recent phenomenon of the transfer of white-collar jobs—particularly in software development—has stirred a great deal of controversy and concern. Both U.S. political parties have decried offshoring of these jobs, and the issue became a hot potato in the 2004 presidential election campaign. Indeed there has been talk of "Benedict Arnold CEOs" who ship jobs to India (and also to China) at the expense of American workers.

Although there appears to be a great fear that offshoring is a danger to workers, particularly in the information technology industry, a recent study[14] has shown that only a small portion of layoffs is due to work moving across a country's border. The figure for the United States was 4 percent of total layoffs, and this number includes both manufacturing and service jobs. During the period of this study, 2004–2005, the United States was experiencing robust growth in employment while the percentage of unemployed workers was decreasing. For the EU-15 (the fifteen countries of the European Union prior to its recent expansion) the same study found that offshoring was about 5 percent of total layoffs. A recent study by the Work Foundation showed that only 5.5 percent of all jobs lost in Europe were due to offshoring in the first quarter of 2007.[15] Of course, offshoring will continue in the future. Proponents of offshoring cite its various benefits: decrease in costs leading to greater competitiveness on the part of U.S. (and other developed countries) industries and to lower prices benefiting consumers, and thus possibly, increasing their wealth. But according to proponents, benefits of offshoring go beyond cost savings. "Outsourcing certain functions . . . can free up company resources to pursue core activities," and in some cases result in increased productivity.[16] They point out that the jobs being lost tend to be of a more routine nature, while there is a high demand for (and shortage of supply of) more specialized and technically advanced jobs. In addition to lower costs, other advantages offer great flexibility, 24/7 schedules, and access to more expertise.

Although globalization may have depressed wages in Western industrialized countries, particularly wages of low-skilled workers, wages in some developing countries have been rising at a rapid rate, thus neutralizing one of the major reasons for offshoring. "'Reverse offshoring' remains unusual, [but] it points to a broader belief in the U.S. technology industry that the savings that drove software engineering jobs to India's technology capital [Bangalore] are quickly eroding."[17] Actually, in a few cases Indian companies have been recruiting American workers to work in the United States. In a very recent action, Tata Consultancy Services, an Indian company, has announced plans to open two computer service centers in Cincinnati, Ohio. The company's chief executive stated that the centers "would help the company to attract highly educated talent from U.S. universities and to qualify for IT outsourcing work that can only be done onshore, such as government contracts."[18]

However, even those who see benefits in offshoring recognize that businesses face some additional challenges when they send work to foreign countries. There are additional costs to managing distant facilities that may include the need for additional supervision and more detailed instructions, particularly when offshore projects are of an advanced technical nature. In some cases, productivity may be lower. Communication with distant locations is more difficult, and cultural differences may create problems. Further, even though workers in India are highly educated and speak English well, communication with Americans is not always easy. This may be particularly true in the case of call centers where a misunderstanding

[14]Jacob Funk Kirkegaard, "Offshoring, Outsource and Production Relocation—Labor Market Effects in the OECD Countries and Developing Asia," *Working Papers Series, WP 07-2*, Peter G. Peterson Institute for International Economics, April 2007.

[15]"Offshoring Threat to Jobs 'Exaggerated,'" *Reuters News*, July 8, 2007.

[16]Rodd Zolkos, "Cost Savings Only the Beginning of Offshoring Advantages," *Business Insurance*, June 18, 2007, Vol. 41, Issue 25, pp. A16–17.

[17]Richard Waters, "Bangalore Wages Spur 'Reverse Offshoring,'" *Financial Times*, July 2, 2007.

[18]Steve Hamm, "Guess who's Hiring in America," *BusinessWeek*, June 25, 2007, p. 47; Joe Leahy, "TCS Plans Outsourcing Centre in Ohio," *Financial Times*, October 17, 2007.

in the transmission of information may occur. Another drawback is the risk of security breaches and the appropriation of trade secrets.[19]

As discussed previously, the outsourcing (offshoring) of jobs from developed countries is, of course, one of the greatest concerns of those who do not view globalization as beneficial. Opponents have called for restrictions on free trade to protect the industries that have been affected. However, although such actions may help certain classes of workers in the short run, they impose costs on the economy as a whole. The imposition of steel tariffs in the United States in 2001 improved labor's conditions in the steel industry, but resulted in increasing prices in steel-using industries and thus has decreased demand for workers in these industries.[20] To promote the benefits of globalization, developed countries must develop policies to mitigate their problems. These may involve government action in areas of education and training to create opportunities for workers who have been displaced and to enable new workers in the labor force to find employment in new endeavors created by globalization.

In addition, these policies should include a safety net to help those whose jobs have emigrated and need assistance during the transition to new employment.[21] Undoubtedly, the public debate about the merits of globalization will continue. Meanwhile, the reality is that MNCs find themselves having to cope with the risks brought on by an increasingly globalized world. Let us now review some of these risks.

RISKS FACED BY A MULTINATIONAL CORPORATION

All companies, whether domestic or international, face risk. As discussed previously, risk can be defined as the chance that business results will be different from those that are expected. Because most businesspeople are risk averse, they are mostly concerned with downside risk. An MNC must deal with risks faced by domestic industries; however, it is faced with risks that are present only because it transacts business across national borders, that is, **multinational corporation risk**.

One of the important concerns for a corporation is **exchange rate risk** resulting from changes in exchange rates. We discuss these concerns later in this chapter. Here we touch on various other risks faced by the MNC:

Blockage of funds and capital controls: A country may prohibit the repatriation of funds. Such action can lead to a corporation investing its funds less than optimally.

Differences in cultural and religious philosophies: These may create potentially hostile attitudes toward foreign corporations.

Ownership restrictions: Complete ownership of subsidiaries may not be permitted. Thus, the MNC may be restricted to minority participation.

Human resource restrictions: Rules and regulations regarding employment practices may differ from those in the home country. Companies may be required to hire only local workers. In some countries, labor laws and union contracts make hiring and firing more rigid. In some countries, there may be restrictions regarding the hiring and promotion of female employees.

Intellectual property: In some countries, it may be difficult to enforce protection of intellectual property, such as software, textbooks, and films.

---

[19]Ann Bednarz, "The Downside of Offshoring," *Network World,* July 5, 2004, pp. 33–35; Jennifer Mears, "The Promise of Offshoring," *Network World,* July 5, 2004, pp. 28–29, 40.

[20]Remember our discussion of derived demand in chapter 4.

[21]Much of this section has been taken from International Monetary Fund Staff, *Globalization: Threat or Opportunity?* April 12, 2000 (corrected January 2002). http://www.imf.org/external/np/exr/ib/2000/041200.htm.

Discrimination: Governments may impose special regulations and taxes on foreign corporations, while subsidizing domestic business.

Red tape and corruption: Such problems exist in most countries, in some to a greater extent than in others. As an example, Transparency International publishes a "Corruption Perceptions Index" ranking 163 countries. This index is based on the perception of the degree of corruption as seen by businesspeople, academics, and risk analysts. The scores can range from 0 (most corrupt) to 10 (least corrupt). In the 2006 index Finland, Iceland, and New Zealand ranked the highest (each with a score of 9.6), followed by Denmark (9.5) and Singapore (9.4). Haiti came in last (1.8), preceded by Guinea, Iraq, and Myanmar (each scoring 1.9). The United States ranked twentieth (7.3).[22]

Internal and external wars: These can occur at any time.

Changes in government: A friendly government may be replaced by a hostile one. At the extreme, the new government may expropriate foreign property.

These are just some of the risks that an MNC must take into consideration. No listing can be entirely complete.

The PRS Group, Inc., publishes the "International Country Risk Guide." Its composite index combines three measures of risk: political, economic, and financial. Each component rates countries on a large number of risk categories. The publication has ranked 140 countries for many years. The highest achievable rating (i.e., the lowest risk) is 100, the lowest is 0. In a recent issue, Norway (91.5), Switzerland (90.5), and Luxembourg (90.0) topped the list, whereas Zimbabwe (45.0) and Somalia (16.8) were last.[23]

EXCHANGE RATES

One important risk that an MNC faces has to do with exchange rates. Companies that sell in or buy from foreign countries and receive or make payments later in foreign currencies must always consider the possibility that exchange rates may turn unfavorable during the period between the setting of the price and the time when payment is made.

An **exchange rate** is the price of one country's currency in terms of another country's. An exchange rate may be quoted in terms of the domestic or foreign currency. If we want to measure the euro in terms of the U.S. dollar, and at a given time the euro is worth $1.40, then we write the exchange rate as €1/$1.40. If we want to express the exchange rate in terms of the euro, then we write it as $1/€0.714.

Assume a U.S. exporter sells goods worth €100,000 to an importer in Germany when the exchange rate is €1/$1.40. At today's exchange rate, the shipment would be worth $140,000. When the payment becomes due in 60 days, the exchange rate is quoted at €1/$1.35. The euro has weakened during this interval. The U.S. exporter will receive only $135,000.

Now let us look at the exchange rate risk faced by an importer. The U.S. company purchases goods from a German exporter in the amount of €100,000, at a time when the exchange rate is €1/$1.40. The shipment is worth $140,000. Sixty days later, when the payment becomes due, the exchange rate is quoted at €1/$1.45; the dollar has weakened, and now the U.S. importer will have to pay $145,000. Of course, if the exchange rate movement had been opposite, the U.S. company would have gained.

---

[22]Transparency International, *Corruption Perception Index 2006,* http://www.transparency.org.
[23]The PRS Group, Inc., *International Country Risk Guide,* January 2007.

EXCHANGE RATE HEDGING

Exchange rate hedging refers to various ways that companies can protect themselves from such a potential loss. Of course, a U.S. company could attempt to have all transactions denominated in U.S. dollars. This, however, is not always possible.

Offsetting Transactions

A U.S. company could export goods of the same amount to the same country from which it had imported goods spanning the same period of time. Thus a change in the exchange rate would be offset. Although such transactions may be the easiest way to hedge against possible exchange rate losses, this is not always possible or practical.

The Forward Market

A company wanting to protect itself against adverse exchange rate fluctuations can enter the forward market. Although the spot exchange rate is the price of currency today for immediate delivery, a forward contract permits a company to buy or sell currency at a specific rate at a specific time.

Assume a U.S. importer owes €1 million to a French exporter 60 days from now. If the importer does not want to be affected by a sudden strengthening of the euro, it may execute a contract to buy €1 million 60 days forward. Thus it assures itself of a specific price that it will have to pay in 60 days.[24] In contrast, a U.S. exporter who expects to receive a payment of €1 million 60 days from now may contract to sell the euros 60 days from now, thus protecting itself against an unexpected weakening of the euro.

Both London and New York have extensive forward markets. Forward transactions are usually executed by commercial banks, and sometimes by currency brokers. Contracts are usually available for amounts of $1 million or greater and can be made for 30 to 360 days, and sometimes longer.

The Futures Market

Futures contracts are similar to forwards. However, there are several differences.

Futures contracts are made for standard amounts, and they mature on certain days (on Wednesdays of specific months). When a future is purchased, a certain amount—called the margin—must be deposited. The contracts are marked to market each day and transaction fees are negotiated. The largest futures market in the United States is the International Monetary Market of the Chicago Mercantile Exchange. Again, as in the case with forwards, if a person or a company expects the foreign currency to rise, the futures will be purchased. If a weakening of the foreign currency is expected, the futures will be sold.

Currency Options

A currency option is a contract that gives the buyer the right to buy or sell a certain amount of currency at a specified price during a certain period of time. A call option gives the purchaser the right to buy the foreign currency, whereas a put option represents the right to sell. The price of the option for each unit of currency is called the premium, and the exercise (or strike) price is the price that must be paid when the

---

[24]Of course, if the euro were to weaken during the next 60 days, the importer could have made a gain. But again, we must remember that most people are risk averse, and thus prefer to assure themselves that they will not incur a loss.

option is exercised. Each contract specifies the expiration date of the option—the last day on which the option can be exercised.[25]

A company will purchase a call option if it has an obligation to pay in a foreign currency in the future. If during the period before expiration the price of the foreign currency rises above the strike price, the company will exercise the option. If, however, the foreign currency remains below the strike price, the company will let the option expire. As mentioned previously, the purchase of an option gives the buyer the right to exercise the option; however, it has no obligation to do so.

Here is a brief example of a U.S. company that will have to pay a French supplier in 90 days. The present exchange rate is $1.40 for €1. Because the company wants to obtain euros to pay the French company, it buys a 90-day call option with a strike price of $1.42/€ at a premium of $0.015 (1.5 cents) per option. If at the expiration date the exchange rate is $1.44/€, the company will exercise the option. It will gain 2 cents per option, and after deducting the cost of the premium it will have a net gain of $0.005 per option. If a €1 million option had been purchased, the net gain would have been $5,000. Even if the exchange rate 3 months hence is only $1.43/€, the company would still exercise the option. It will only lose $0.005 per option because it would recover a part of the premium. If the exchange rate is less than $1.42/€ the company would let the option lapse. In this case it will lose only what it originally paid for the option.

Similarly, when a company expects to receive funds in the future, it can protect itself against a decline in the value of a foreign currency by purchasing a put. Options are traded on various exchanges, for instance, the Chicago Mercantile Exchange.

Currency Swaps

A currency swap can occur when two companies in two different countries expect a cash flow from other companies in their respective countries. Assume U.S. company A sells its products to customers in the United Kingdom and will receive payment in pounds sterling (£), whereas company B, located in the United Kingdom sells its product to companies in the United States and expects payment in U.S. dollars. However, each company wants to receive its own currency. In that case, the two companies can arrange a currency swap to receive payment in their own currencies. Such transactions can be negotiated directly or through a bank. Thus, both companies can be sure to receive payments denominated in their own currencies and avoid a possible exchange rate loss.

FOREIGN DIRECT INVESTMENT

As corporations move into their multinational phase, they expand their operations into foreign countries. These operations may involve the licensing of foreign companies or joint ventures. But in creating a permanent presence abroad, they will begin to invest in real assets. They may do this by acquiring fixed assets, buying out existing firms, or establishing foreign subsidiaries with their own infrastructure. This is called **foreign direct investment (FDI)**.

The main reason for a company's foreign investment is of course to increase its earnings and increase the value of the company. Companies that experience heavy competition in their domestic market may seek a competitive advantage in foreign markets. Their domestic market may have become saturated and their growth potential can only be realized by entering new previously unexplored markets. In contrast, a

---

[25]An American option can be exercised at any time prior to the expiration date, whereas a European option can be exercised only on the expiration date.

corporation may have a competitive advantage in its home country and by moving abroad will be able to exploit this advantage worldwide. Another reason for FDI may be that a foreign country imposes restrictions on imports; by establishing itself in that country, the company will avoid these restrictions and may even be welcomed there if it contributes to the country's balance of payments by exporting its products to another country. The company may also be able to take advantage of economies of scale, as well as lower production and transportation costs.

Before making a foreign investment, whether it is to purchase a company, establish a subsidiary, or undertake a large project, the company will have to conduct a capital budgeting analysis to ascertain whether the project will be profitable (i.e., whether it will have a positive NPV or whether its return on the investment will exceed the cost of capital). We turn to this subject next.

MULTINATIONAL CAPITAL BUDGETING

The method of capital budgeting for an MNC proceeds along the same lines as for a domestic corporation. We must identify the investment made in a project, estimate the cash flows, establish a discount rate, and then solve for NPV and/or IRR. However, in addition to the complications encountered in doing a capital budgeting analysis for a domestic corporation, there are several other variables that must be taken into consideration when we deal with **multinational capital budgeting**.

Intercompany Fund Flows

There will be cash flows going from the parent to the subsidiary and vice versa. The parent will tend to finance, at least partially, large projects in a subsidiary. It may provide equity investment or loans. As the project gets under way, the subsidiary will most likely begin to remit cash payments—dividends—to the parent. Further, the subsidiary may also pay license fees or royalties (e.g., for the use of the parent's patents used in the products made by the subsidiary). The parent may also ship certain products, such as components, to be assembled and marketed by the subsidiary for which the subsidiary must pay the parent.[26]

Inflation Rates

The rates of inflation in the country of the parent corporation and of the subsidiary may differ. The sales price and the cost of production in the subsidiary country may change at a different rate from those of the home country. Therefore, expected inflation must be included in the calculation.

Exchange Rates

The exchange rate between the parent and subsidiary country will change during the project period. This change may be based on the differential inflation between the two countries. Because the subsidiary may remit its profits, or part of the profits, and other payments to the parent, it is extremely important that expected changes in exchange rates be considered in the analysis. Of course, unexpected changes cannot be predicted. The company may engage in hedging to avoid losses from unexpected changes in the exchange rate. However, because a capital project will span over many years, long-term hedges are needed. They are available for certain leading currencies (euro, yen, etc.); however, many of the world's currencies cannot be hedged for longer periods of time.

---

[26]This brings up the question of the price the parent should charge the subsidiary. Transfer pricing is an important aspect of the parent–subsidiary relationship and is discussed later in this chapter.

Tax Differences

Tax rates differ between the two locations and this has to be taken into account when a capital project is under consideration. But differences in income tax rates are not the only problems that may be encountered. A country may not only have a tax on profits made locally, but may also charge an additional tax on remittances to the parent's country. This withholding tax can be levied on remitted profits (dividends), as well as license fees, royalties, or interest payments made by the subsidiary to the parent; the tax rates can differ among the various payments.

Another complication arises. When the parent receives payments from the subsidiary that are taxable to it, it could be open to double taxation because taxes have already been paid in the subsidiary's country. To avoid double taxation, most countries permit the parent to credit tax payments in the subsidiary's home country. How the tax credits are treated may differ among countries. Generally, if the tax in the parent country turns out to be higher than in the subsidiary country, the parent will have to pay the difference. As a rule, the tax credit is limited to the amount of taxes that would have been paid in the parent's country.[27]

To calculate the foreign tax credit, a calculation called "gross up" must be performed. The dividend by the subsidiary must be "grossed up" to a before-tax amount. This is done by dividing the dividend received by $1 - t$ (1 minus the tax rate in the subsidiary's country). Then the tax to be paid by the parent using the parent's tax rate must be calculated. The calculation is illustrated in "The Solution" vignette of this chapter, using the example posed in "The Situation" vignette.

Differences in Cash Flows

Because of the various differences mentioned previously, the cash flows received and recorded by the parent may differ substantially from those in the subsidiary's country. Thus, capital budgeting calculations must be made at both locations to determine whether the project meets the company's criteria.

Cost of Capital

When projects are evaluated both from the parent's and the subsidiary's viewpoint, they must be discounted at the cost of capital. But here again, there could be a difference between the two. Because the project may be financed partially in the subsidiary's country and because of different tax rates, as well as the possibility of obtaining subsidized loans locally, the subsidiary's cost of capital may differ substantially from that applied by the parent to the cash flows from the subsidiary. The parent company presumably uses a specific cost of capital for its investments and adjusts this rate up or down to take account of project risks. Thus, because of certain uncertainties that exist in making a cross-border investment, the company may adjust the capital cost of such a project higher than the company's weighted average cost of capital. Political risk is certainly one of those that must be considered in setting that rate.

The Final Project Valuation

As mentioned previously, the cash flows and discount rates used may differ substantially between those of the parent and those of the subsidiary. It can easily happen that the differences are so significant that the project may be deemed acceptable (i.e., positive

---

[27]In the United States, an excess foreign tax credit can be offset against tax liabilities owed by the parent on income from other subsidiaries, as long as the income is of a similar nature.

NPV, or IRR exceeding the cost of capital) in one calculation and not acceptable in the other. Which of the two measures should prevail, the parent's or the subsidiary's?

Most financial practitioners would agree that the results from the parent's point of view should dominate. The cash flows from the subsidiary are those that add to or detract from the value of the company and the company's goal of maximizing shareholder value. Although the results from the parent's viewpoint appear to be theoretically more correct, this may not be the case in practice. Many companies appear to prefer to determine acceptability of a project based on the results in the subsidiary.

THE REPOSITIONING OF FUNDS

For an MNC, the movement of funds among countries may contribute to greater profitability and an enhancement of the company's value. The positioning of funds may affect a company's tax liabilities, earnings on excess funds, and its cost of capital. Several methods of achieving this are outlined briefly. One of the methods, transfer pricing, is discussed at greater length.

Royalties and license fees can be used to channel funds to those areas of the company where they may be used most profitably.

Dividend payments to the parent are another method of controlling the positioning of funds. Because the parent company pays dividends to stockholders, dividends paid by subsidiaries to the parent are influenced by the size of the parent's dividend payout. However, other considerations enter. First, there are tax implications. Some countries apply different tax rates to distributed and undistributed earnings. Second, some countries levy a tax on dividends that are transmitted to the parent.

However, if a particular subsidiary has the opportunity to reinvest its earnings profitably (i.e., more profitably than other parts of the company), it may be asked to remit a smaller portion of its earnings, whereas subsidiaries with less favorable investment opportunities may be required to remit larger percentages of their earnings. In addition, a corporation must consider political risk and potential changes in exchange rates in shaping its dividend remittance policies. If a subsidiary must make payments to its parent or other subsidiaries (e.g., for goods purchased from the parent or another subsidiary), they can be postponed if the subsidiary that is to pay can earn higher yields than the parent or subsidiary that is supposed to receive the payment. Borrowing (interest) rates may also determine when the payment will be made.

Reinvoicing centers can be established by the company to manage the cash flows among the parent and its subsidiaries. They can direct funds to where they would earn the most.[28]

MULTINATIONAL TRANSFER PRICING

 Module 13A

The theory of transfer pricing is discussed in chapter 10. Ensuring a company sets prices that will optimize profits when products are transferred from one division to another within the same company and within the same country is difficult enough. When products are transferred across borders, additional complications arise. **Multinational transfer pricing** involves products or services that are transferred from the parent company to the subsidiary or among subsidiaries.

---

[28]However, caution must be exercised lest the company could be accused by a government of profit shifting.

An MNC can affect a transfer of funds from one unit to another by charging high or low prices. If a transfer is made at low prices, this will basically shift funds to the country receiving the product. This may be profitable for a company if investment opportunities are higher in the receiving country than they are in the shipping country.

However, charging specifically high or low transfer prices may have an effect on a corporation's tax liability. The reason for this is that different countries, as we already mentioned, have different tax systems and different tax rates. Thus a company can try to take advantage of these differentials by setting its transfer price at a level to minimize its taxes.

Let us use a simple example to show how this can happen.

Multinational Transfer Pricing Example

An MNC has a components plant in its parent country, P. It ships these components to its subsidiary in country S, where other components are produced and then assembled into a final piece of electronic equipment that will then be sold in S.[29] Assume that during one year P ships 100,000 units with a production cost of 2 per unit to S. Operating expenses in P are 35,000 per year while in S they are 25,000. Additional costs to complete the product and bring it to market in S are 1 per unit. P sets a transfer price of 3.20 per unit and S will sell the final product at 5.00 per unit. The income tax rate in P is 25 percent and in S 35 percent. In Table 13.1 we calculate the profit in each country, the combined profit and the combined income tax.

Table 13.1   The Effect of Taxes on Profit in Transfer Pricing

	Parent		Subsidiary
Income tax rate	25.0 %		35.0 %
Revenue	320,000		500,000
Cost of production	200,000		420,000
Gross profit	120,000		80,000
Operating expenses	35,000		25,000
Profit before taxes	85,000		55,000
Income taxes	21,250		19,250
Profit after taxes	63,750		35,750
Combined result:	Taxes	40,500	
	Profit	99,500	
Revenue	360,000		500,000
Cost of production	200,000		460,000
Gross profit	160,000		40,000
Operating expenses	35,000		25,000
Profit before taxes	125,000		15,000
Income taxes	31,250		5,250
Profit after taxes	93,750		9,750
Combined result:	Taxes	36,500	
	Profit	103,500	

---

[29]To make this example simple, let us assume that the exchange rate between the currencies of the two countries is 1P = 1S. This will permit us to explain the example without the complication of translating the values of the currencies.

As shown in the first half of Table 13.1, the cost to the subsidiary is the revenue received by the parent (320,000) plus 100,000 of its own production cost. The combined profit for the two entities is 99,500, and their combined tax liability is 40,500. However, because the tax rate in S is higher than in P, the company would gain if the parent retained a higher portion of the profit at the expense of the subsidiary. In the second half of Table 13.1, the transfer price per unit has been increased to 3.60. The parent's profit now rises to 93,750 while the subsidiary's profit declines to 9,750. Because of the lower tax rate in S, the combined profit has risen by 4,000 to 103,500, and the tax liability has decreased by the same amount to 36,500.

If the income tax rate had been higher in the parent country than in the subsidiary, the corporation could have increased its profits (and cut its tax liability) by lowering the transfer price.[30] If a tariff is imposed by the importing country, this will offset, at least to some extent, the advantage of a high transfer price.

A simple equation can be used to ascertain the effect on the tax liability due to a change in the transfer price:

$$\Delta T = (Q \times \Delta P \times t_e) - (Q \times \Delta P \times t_m)$$

where ΔT = Change in the total tax bill

Q = Quantity of products shipped by E (exporter) to M (importer)

ΔP = Change in the price of the product

t_e and t_m = Tax rate in the exporting and importing counties, respectively

If $t_e > t_m$, combined income would increase if transfer prices are lowered, and if $t_e < t_m$, combined incomes would rise if transfer prices are increased.

Transfer Pricing in Practice

The potential for decreasing the tax liability is a subject that is attracting a great deal of attention by tax authorities in many countries.

In the United States, Section 482 of the U.S. Internal Revenue Code gives the Internal Revenue Service (IRS) the authority to "shift around income and expense figures to arrive at what the government considers a more equitable result."[31] In such cases, the burden of proof is on the taxpayer to prove that the IRS has been incorrect in reallocating income.

The IRS requires that transfer pricing be done on an "arm's length" relationship. There are several methods of calculating such a relationship; however, the best evidence is that prices resemble those that would be established between two independent companies.

Despite the fact that transfer price proceedings have been a prominent activity of the IRS, a recent study estimated that the cost in tax revenue to the U.S. government due to transfer pricing, both from importing and exporting, was $53.1 billion in the year 2001. The largest losses were incurred in our trade with Japan and Canada.[32]

Although regulations regarding transfer pricing have been present in industrialized countries for many years, as globalization becomes even more prominent, developing countries are now becoming active in this area. For instance, the

---

[30]Readers can calculate similar results by turning to Module 13A.
[31]C. Carroll, "IRS Target Local Company in 'Transfer Pricing' Case," *Houston Business Journal*, February 3, 1997.
[32]Simon J. Pak and John S. Zdanowicz, *U.S. Trade with the World*, October 31, 2002.

government of Vietnam amended its tax laws on January 1, 2004, to include specific rules regarding transfer pricing. The Income Tax Department of India issued its first transfer pricing orders in 2004, asking some MNCs in India to pay additional taxes.[33]

Here are just a few examples of transfer pricing actions taken by governments. In January 2004, the IRS notified GlaxoSmithKline (GSK), the prominent pharmaceutical company, that it owes the government $5.2 billion ($2.7 billion in back taxes and $2.5 billion in interest charges). The IRS claims that GSK has "used development and production of drugs outside the U.S. to improperly avoid taxes due" since 1989. In 2006 GSK agreed to pay the Internal Revenue Service $3.4 billion to settle the case.[34] This settlement was the largest in the IRS's history.

In Canada, in three separate tax disputes, the government alleged that Canadian subsidiaries of European drug companies deducted improperly about $160 million in costs through transfer pricing practices. The chemicals were produced in "relatively tax-friendly countries, such as the Bahamas and Ireland." In one of the cases, the government contended that the drug company had paid up to $1,650 per kilogram for ranitidine HCL (an ingredient in an ulcer medicine) made in Switzerland, when the price should have been closer to $250.[35] Pharmaceutical companies appear to be a frequent target of tax authorities. In October 2006, the Canada Revenue Agency issued a notice of assessment to Merck Frost Canada (the Canadian subsidiary of Merck & Co.) for US$1.7 billion relating to pricing practices connected with Merck's asthma drug Singular. By July 2007 the dispute had not yet been resolved.[36] In 2006, Symantec Corporation, a large antivirus software producer, agreed to settle one dispute with the Internal Revenue Service for $36 million. In another claim the IRS has charged Symantec about $1 billion. This amount relates to transactions by Veritas Software Corporation (which Symantec acquired in 2005) with its subsidiary in Ireland.[37]

A 2003 survey by Ernst & Young reported that 59 percent of all MNCs with revenues of US$5 billion or more and 71 percent of all U.S.-based MNCs were subject to audit since 1999. The survey also reported that 40 percent of the transfer pricing adjustments resulted in double taxation. Transfer pricing audits are predominantly brought about in cases of tangible goods transactions; however, the percentage of audits relating to service and intangible property transactions has been on the rise. In a more recent report Ernst & Young, in a poll of 476 companies in 22 countries, found that nearly two-thirds have been challenged over the tax treatment of internal transactions over the last three years. "More than 40 percent of these audits resulted in adjustments by the tax authorities."[38]

---

[33]"Finance—Vietnam Tightens Management on Multinationals' Transfer Pricing," *Vietnam News Brief Service,* January 16, 2004; "I-T's First Transfer Pricing Order to Demand More Tax from MNCs," *Economic Times,* February 18, 2004, p. 5.

[34]David Firn, "GSK Faces $5.2 Claim for Tax and Interest," *Financial Times,* January 7, 2004; David S. Hilzenrath, "Glaxo to Pay IRS $3.4 Billion; Tax Settlement Is Biggest in Agency's History," *Washington Post,* September 12, 2006.

[35]Colin Freeze, "Taxman Targets Drug Firms Government Alleges Offshore Purchases Were Inflated to Dodge Canadian Taxes," *The Globe and Mail,* July 7, 2001.

[36]Dale Hill, "Transfer Pricing and the Pharmaceutical Industry: The Lessons from 2007," *Mondaq Business Briefing,* July 19, 2007.

[37]"Symantec Faces $1B Tax Demand," *Reuters Technology News,* June 30, 2006; "IRS Hits Symantec with $1 bn Tax Bill for Irish Arm," *Irish Independent,* April 19, 2006.

[38]"Transfer Pricing Is the Most Important International Tax Issue According to New Ernst & Young Survey," *Business Wire,* November 5, 2003; Vanessa Houlder, "Tax Authorities Step Up Pressure on Multinationals," *Financial Times,* November 16, 2005.

GLOBAL APPLICATION: "FROM HERE TO THE MOON IN SIX MONTHS"

This entire chapter is devoted to international business, so we decided to present an example that is a bit different from those in previous chapters. Part of the move from the expansion of firms from "international" to "multinational" is the greater demand on staff to operate on a global basis. Today it is common for a manager to have "virtual teams" of people who live in all parts of the world. While meeting face to face perhaps only several times per year, these teams of people carry out their work via e-mail or conference calls at all hours of the day or night. Furthermore, the relocation of employees for international assignments of 3 to 4 years has become less common. It is very expensive for a company to send an employee and his or her family on such an assignment. For example, it could cost a company about $1 million per year to support a typical American family in Tokyo. For this reason, as well as shifting human resource policies, companies are trying much harder to develop and promote local staff to positions that in the past would have been filled by employees from countries in which the corporate headquarters resides. Instead, people with global responsibilities fly back and forth from their home base to international locations, or at the most work at these locations on projects lasting shorter periods of a few weeks or a few months.

An example of this trend is the story of an executive of a software company. In 1997, he logged about 240,000 miles—the distance between earth and the moon—in 6 months between his home in Seattle and London. In addition, he also did a lot of traveling within Europe. He learned how to cope with this situation, and he has advice for international travelers—sleep and drinking water are the best ways to get through these long flights, and stay away from coffee and alcohol.[39]

The Solution

With all the data at hand, George Kline begins to input the information into the Excel spreadsheet he had prepared (Table 13.2).

At the top of the sheet, he enters the percent volume change and the price level changes. He could have entered different numbers for each year, but he chose not to.

He then enters today's exchange rate in year 0. The new exchange rates are calculated automatically based on the relationship between U.S. and Czech inflation.

He enters the fixed asset investment and the working capital in the year 0 column. Next he enters the various factors in the "Constant" column. In the "depreciation" line he obtains the annual depreciation by dividing 1 by the depreciation life of the property. He sets the terminal value at 100 million KCZ. Any of these inputs can be easily changed if his assumptions change and new iterations of the solution are desired.

He also enters the sales revenue, production cost and imports in year 1. George now goes over the results of his calculations. The NPV for the subsidiary is positive and the IRR exceeds the cost of capital. Thus it would appear that the project is acceptable from the subsidiary's viewpoint. George notes, however, that the IRR is just barely above the cost of capital and NPV is relatively small. Any small adverse change in his assumptions would probably cause the NPV to turn negative.

He next looks at the results from the parent company's viewpoint. Here the NPV is negative (and the IRR substantially below the cost of capital). George is very familiar with the opinion of most of the experts in the financial area—that the parent's results are the ones that should be considered primarily.

George arranges for a meeting with the company's executives, including the vice presidents (VPs) of finance, marketing, and manufacturing, to present his results. He recommends that the project should be shelved at this time. However, he points out that the various assumptions he made may be subject to change, and proposes to consult the various departments in 3 months and repeat the analysis. The VP of manufacturing suggests that better results could possibly be obtained if the company were to build a new more efficient plant (i.e., to make a greenfield investment) and

(continued)

---

[39]Joe Sharkey, "Coping with the Rigors of Global Flights," *New York Times*, March 30, 2004.

(*continued*)

thus improve the profitability of the project. He asks George to make another calculation with new assumptions. However, the VPs of marketing and finance argue that this would probably only make the results worse. They have several reasons for this. From the marketing viewpoint, the VP points out that this is not a new product in Europe and that the company would face stiff competition. Because the demand for the product is probably quite price elastic, the company would have to be very careful in its pricing. The VP of finance adds that even though a brand new plant may be more efficient, the advantage of purchasing the existing plant is the relatively low price, resulting in lower depreciation charges.

The final decision is to hold off on this project. However, George is asked to review his numbers with the various staffs and report back to the executives in about 2 months.

Table 13.2   Capital Project Evaluation

	Constant	Year 0	Year 1	Year 2	Year 3	Year 4
		Assumptions				
Volume change			6.0%	6.0%	6.0%	6.0%
Price level %Δ in						
United States			2.0%	2.0%	2.0%	2.0%
Price level %Δ in						
Czech Republic			3.5%	3.5%	3.5%	3.5%
Sales price %Δ in						
Czech Republic			4.0%	4.0%	4.0%	4.0%
Cost %Δ in						
Czech Republic			4.0%	4.0%	4.0%	4.0%
Exchange rate—KCZ/$		27.00	27.41	27.82	28.23	28.66
Fixed-asset investment						
($000)		4,000				
Working capital ($000)		400				
Cost of capital						
United States	19.0%					
Cost of capital						
Czech Republic	22.0%					

Income Statement for Czech Subsidiary
(Thousands of KCZ)

		Year 1	Year 2	Year 3	Year 4
1. Sales revenue		400,000	440,960	486,114	535,892
2. Production costs—					
Czech Republic		190,000	209,456	230,904	254,549
3. Imports from					
United States		110,000	120,716	132,476	145,381
4. License fees	3.0%	12,000	13,229	14,583	16,077
5. G&A expense	12.0%	48,000	52,915	58,334	64,307
6. Depreciation	12.5%	13,500	13,500	13,500	13,500
7. EBIT		26,500	31,144	36,317	42,078
8. Income taxes	31.0%	8,215	9,655	11,258	13,044
9. NEAT		18,285	21,489	25,059	29,034
10. Cash dividend	50.0%	9,143	10,745	12,529	14,517

(*continued*)

(continued)

(continued)

Working Capital Requirements
(Thousands of KCZ)

	Constant	Year 0	Year 1	Year 2	Year 3	Year 4
1. Required at $t = 0$		10,800				
2. Year-end requirement (as percent of sales)	10.0%		40,000	44,096	48,611	53,589
3. Required additions			29,200	4,096	4,515	4,978
4. Financed internally in Czech Republic	50.0%		14,600	2,048	2,258	2,489
5. New WC required			14,600	2,048	2,258	2,489

Cash Flows for Czech Subsidiary
(Thousands of KCZ)

	Constant	Year 0	Year 1	Year 2	Year 3	Year 4
1. NEAT			18,285	21,489	25,059	29,034
2. Depreciation			13,500	13,500	13,500	13,500
3. Terminal value	100,000					100,000
4. WC additions			−14,600	−2,048	−2,258	−2,489
5. Original investment by U.S. parent		−118,800				
6. Net cash flow		−118,800	17,185	32,941	36,301	140,045
7. NPV		626				
8. IRR		22.2%				

Calculation of Dividends Received
by Parent from Subsidiary

(KCZ in 000)			Year 1	Year 2	Year 3	Year 4
1. Cash dividend paid			9,143	10,745	12,529	14,517
2. Dividend percent of tax paid			4,108	4,827	5,629	6,522
3. Grossed-up dividend			13,250	15,572	18,158	21,039
($ in 000)						
4. Grossed up dividend			483	560	643	734
5. Income tax in United States	35.0%		169	196	225	257
6. Credit for sub's taxes			150	174	199	228
7. Additional tax due in United States			19	22	26	29
8. Cash dividend paid to parent			334	386	444	507
9. Aftertax div. rec. by parent			314	364	418	477

(continued)

(continued)

(continued)

(continued)

Cash Flows Received by U.S. Parent						
	Constant	Year 0	Year 1	Year 2	Year 3	Year 4
(KCZ in 000)						
1. License fees from Czech subsidiary			12,000	13,229	14,583	16,077
2. Profit on exports to Czech subsidiary	5.0%		5,500	6,036	6,624	7,269
3. Total receipts from Czech subsidiary			17,500	19,265	21,207	23,346
($ in 000)						
4. Total receipts from Czech subsidiary			639	693	751	815
5. Income tax in United States			223	242	263	285
6. Aftertax receipts			415	450	488	530
7. Aftertax dividend			314	364	418	477
8. Project cost		−4,400				
9. Terminal value						3,490
10. Net cash flows		−4,400	729	814	906	4,496
11. NPV		−432				
12. IRR		15.1%				

SUMMARY

A multinational corporation must compete not just domestically but worldwide. As we discuss in previous chapters, managers must always be concerned with the economic environment facing them. They must inform themselves about the demand for their products, the cost of supplies and components, the productivity of their machinery and labor force, and changes in technology. They must digest this information to try to maximize the corporation's profitability (in a broader definition, the corporation's market value). We have learned that to achieve best results, corporate managers must be aware that any increase in revenue must be greater than costs when the corporation grows; in other words, they must apply the concepts of marginal revenue and marginal cost.

An MNC must consider these factors and many others:

➤ *Economic factors:* Exchange rates and exchange rate changes; differences in cost of capital; economic stability of the foreign country, production costs in foreign country influencing the choice of sourcing locations

➤ *Political factors:* Stability of government institutions, different tax systems, restrictions on foreign ownership, blockage of fund transfers, laws regarding employment and wages, bureaucracy and corruption, attitude of government toward multinational corporations, expropriation, war, terrorism

➤ *Social and cultural factors:* Religious differences, differences in the hiring of and promotion of female employees, different attitudes toward profit maximization.

We describe in detail the differences in capital budgeting between a domestic and a multinational corporation. We specifically direct our attention at differences in taxation, consideration of differential rates of inflation and their influence on the exchange rate, and differences in the cost of capital. We also discuss the question of whether the decision to make an investment should be based on the results in the subsidiary or the parent.

Finally, we addressed the extremely important topic of transfer pricing. A corporation can achieve higher profits (and lower taxes) by manipulating the prices charged for products or services flowing from the parent to a subsidiary or among subsidiaries. Governments are becoming very wary of these practices and, in many cases, corporations have been required to pay additional taxes.

IMPORTANT CONCEPTS

Exchange rate: The price of one country's currency in terms of another. (p. 505)

Exchange rate hedging: Actions that a company can employ to protect itself from exchange rate fluctuations. Among these are forward contracts, futures, currency options, and currency swaps. (p. 506)

Exchange rate risk: The possibility that exchange rates will change to the detriment of an MNC. (p. 504)

Foreign direct investment (FDI):   Investment in real assets by an MNC, including the acquisition of fixed assets, purchase of a foreign plant, or establishment of a subsidiary. (p. 507)

Globalization: The changes in the activities of a corporation as it moves from solely domestic to worldwide operations. (p. 499)

Multinational capital budgeting: Decision making by an MNC when it seeks to undertake a long-term project in a foreign country. (p. 508)

Multinational corporation risk: Risks that are faced by a multinational corporation not directly faced by a domestic corporation. These include economic, political, and social and cultural risks. (p. 504)

Multinational transfer pricing: The pricing of goods and services when these are transferred across borders. These decisions are affected by different tax rates between countries and import tariffs. (p. 510)

Outsourcing (offshoring):   The transfer of production of goods and services by one company to another (independent) company when potential cost savings are possible. Offshoring occurs when outsourcing is conducted across national borders. (p. 500)

QUESTIONS

1. Opponents of globalization argue that offshoring leads to a loss of jobs in the country that transfers jobs to lower-wage countries. Evaluate all aspects of this argument.
2. Supporters of globalization argue that offshoring benefits a country's economy. Evaluate.
3. What is the difference between a futures contract and a forward contract?
4. A U.S. importer who owes a Belgian company €500,000 payable 30 days from today expects that the US$ will weaken during this period. What would you advise the importer to do? What would happen if the US$ were to strengthen during this period?
5. A U.S. importer purchases a currency option. If the foreign currency does not rise to the strike price, what should the importer do?
6. Describe the additional complications facing an MNC compared with a domestic corporation when it is evaluating a capital budgeting project.
7. Why should an MNC's capital budgeting decision be based on the parent's results rather than those of the subsidiary?
8. Is an MNC generally faced with incurring double taxation on its profits in the subsidiaries country? Why or why not?
9. Why should a government be concerned with the pricing of products that a company transfers to an affiliate in another country?

PROBLEMS

1. The Great Computer Company, a U.S. corporation, has a subsidiary in the Netherlands. It is deciding whether to invest $2 million of its (the parent's) funds in a 3-year project in the Netherlands.

   The aftertax cash flows to the subsidiary are estimated to be as follows (in euros):

Year 1	€500,000
2	800,000
3	900,000

   The entire cash flows of the subsidiary are remitted to the parent annually. There is no additional tax (nor credit) in the parent country.

   The exchange rate today is €1/$1.20. The exchange rate forecast for the next 3 years is the following:

Year 1	€1/$1.15
2	€1/$1.10
3	€1/$1.05

   The cost of capital for both the parent and the subsidiary is 13 percent.
   a. What is the NPV of this project to the Netherlands' subsidiary?
   b. What is the NPV of this project to the U.S. parent?
   c. Should the project be accepted?

2. The XYZ Multinational Corporation has manufacturing facilities in country A and an assembly plant in country B. The company ships manufactured units from its plant in A to its assembly plant in B.
   a. In April 2008, the company will ship 1,000 units with a production cost of 650 per unit to its plant in country B. Its operating expenses in A are 15,000 for the month. The income tax rate in A is 20 percent and in B 40 percent. The company plans to have a transfer price of 100 per unit. The final product can be sold in B for 1,400. B's operating expenses are 10,000 during the month. How much will the combined profits be of the two operations in April 2008?
   b. Could the company benefit by changing the transfer price to 120?
   c. Now, suppose the income tax rate in A is 40 percent, while in B it is 20 percent. What will the combined profit be if all other numbers are the same as in **a**?
   d. What would be the result in **c** if the company decreased its transfer price to 900?

3. Today the XYZ Corporation shipped goods valued at €1 million to a customer in Belgium. Payment is due in 90 days, and the Belgian firm will make the payment in euros. Today's spot rate is €1/$1.40. The 90-day forward rate is €1/$1.38.
   a. How many dollars would XYZ receive if payment were made today?
   b. If XYZ sells €1 million forward for 90 days, how much is it assured to receive 90 days from now?
   c. If XYZ had not hedged in the forward market and the spot rate 90 days from now is €1/$1.39, how much would XYZ receive (in U.S. dollars)?
   d. If the U.S. dollar were to weaken in the 90 days and XYZ did not hedge, would it benefit or lose?

4. The ABC Company expects to receive payment in euros from a German company in 60 days. To protect itself from a decline in the value of the euro, it purchases a put option with a strike price of $1.42/€ at a premium of $0.015 (1.5 cents) per option.
   a. If the exchange rate 60 days from now is $1.40/€, should ABC exercise the option? How much will it gain or lose on the transaction?
   b. If the exchange rate is $1.41/€, what should the company do and why?
   c. At what exchange rate will the company break even?

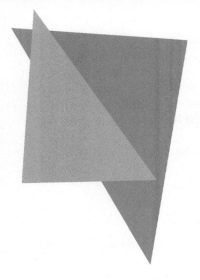

Government and Industry: Challenges and Opportunities for Today's Manager

Learning Objectives

Upon completion of this chapter, readers should be able to:

■ Cite the five major functions of government in a market economy.

■ Explain the reasoning of the Coase theorem in its contention that government involvement may not be necessary to deal with market externalities.

■ Explain why firms merge and why, in particular, firms have chosen to merge in markets that have experienced government deregulation.

■ Briefly explain the process that a private firm must follow in securing a government contract.

The Situation

Bill Adams, the CIO of Global Foods, was faced with a serious problem. Four years ago, his company had decided to outsource its entire voice and data communications operations to AT&T. A 10-year contract had been negotiated, but the terms and conditions of the contract were subject to a review after 5 years, and Global Foods had the option to discontinue services if it was not satisfied with AT&T's work.

It had been an interesting 4 years. When he first put out the RFP (request for proposal), he was surprised at the number and diversity of responses. He thought that there would just be the usual cast of characters such as AT&T, Verizon, and Sprint. But in addition, his local telecommunications company, along with a consortium of big consulting companies such as EDS and IBM Global Services, also put in bids. It was then that Bill realized that the deregulation of the telecommunications industry had provided customers with many more options to choose from. In the end, Global Foods went with AT&T because it had recently bought IBM's data network and because it was the most experienced company in the telecommunications outsourcing business. After 4 years of experience, he was not so sure he had made the right choice. He asked his staff to prepare a complete assessment of the situation and to recommend whether the company should continue using AT&T's services for the balance of the 10-year contract.

INTRODUCTION

The primary objective of this chapter is to discuss the impact of government policies on managerial decision making. When the government is involved in the market economy, it generally controls the behavior of buyers and sellers through a process of "indirect command." That is, rather than ordering buyers and sellers to allocate resources in a particular way, the government uses market incentives or disincentives. This "visible hand" of the government can take such forms as price controls, rules and regulations, taxes, and subsidies. In using the incentive of profit or the disincentive of loss, the government does not change the basic system of rewards and punishments used in the market. Instead, it simply alters the reward structure of a laissez-faire market so resources are allocated more in accordance with government policy than with the actions of individual buyers and sellers.

In the following section, we elaborate on the different roles that government plays in the market economy and the justification for such roles. We then describe what it is like to do business with the U.S. government, which after all is one of the largest buyers of goods and services in the world. That section is written by Sylvia Von Bostel, a member of the staff of Booz-Allen & Hamilton, one of the world's top consulting companies. Its client list includes a number of agencies and departments of the federal government.

THE RATIONALE FOR GOVERNMENT INVOLVEMENT IN A MARKET ECONOMY

There are five major functions the government can perform in a market economy such as that of the United States. First, it provides a legal and social framework within which market participants buy and sell the goods and services produced by the economy's scarce resources. For example, the Food and Drug Administration (FDA) seeks to ensure food and pharmaceutical companies sell products that meet certain standards of safety and quality.

Second, the government strives to maintain competition in markets for goods and services by trying to ensure no one seller dominates the market in an unfair manner. Third, the government may decide to play a role in the redistribution of income and wealth. It can do so through the tax system (particularly through income taxes), and also through various types of government subsidies and grants for special-interest groups. For example, one of the major subsidies for middle and upper income in the United States is the ability to deduct interest payments on residential mortgages.

The fourth market-related function of government is the reallocation of resources. According to economic theory, a misallocation of resources results whenever a market has certain externalities or spillovers. That is, some of the benefits or costs associated with the production or consumption of a particular product accrue to parties other than the buyers or sellers of a product.

The fifth major function of government in a market economy is the stabilization of the aggregate economy. The market economy is prone to periodic upswings and downswings in economic activity. As you have probably already studied in a course in macroeconomics, governments can employ monetary and fiscal policy to deal with the problems of unemployment and inflation, which usually occur at different stages of the cycle.

One government function that does not quite fit into any of the five main categories is the regulation of natural monopolies. The economic definition of a **natural monopoly** is an industry in which a single firm can serve customers more efficiently than many smaller competing firms because of the predominance of economies of scale. Examples of natural monopolies are electricity and gas utilities and telephone services. However, over the past decade or so, there has been a movement by governments throughout the world to reduce the government ownership or regulation of these natural monopolies. Let us elaborate a bit further on three of the five main functions of government: providing a competitive framework for market participants, the reallocation of resources in the presence of market externalities, and the stabilization of the aggregate economy.

Providing a Legal Framework for Competition: The Antitrust Laws

A thorough interpretation of antitrust laws would carry us beyond the scope of this book.[1] Thus, we provide a brief review of the subject. The beginning of antitrust legislation in the United States dates back to the late nineteenth century in response to the formation of large corporations and the so-called "merger-to-monopoly" wave. While under common law various anticompetitive actions (e.g., price fixing) were not enforceable; therefore, stronger positive legal action appeared necessary. The first law to be passed was the Sherman Anti-Trust Act, followed by several others.

The Sherman Anti-Trust Act (1890)

The two important sections of this law were the following:

> Section 1: . . . every contract, combination in the form of trust or otherwise, or conspiracy, in restraint of trade or commerce among the several states, or with foreign nations, is declared to be illegal . . .
>
> Section 2: . . . every person who shall monopolize or attempt to monopolize any part of the trade or commerce among the several states, or with foreign nations, shall be deemed guilty of a felony . . .

Section 1 outlawed explicit cartels. Section 2, which appeared to outlaw monopoly, was interpreted by the courts as a prohibition of "bad acts" and not monopoly per se.

The Clayton Act (1914)

The Clayton Act was intended to strengthen and widen the application of antitrust enforcement, and specifically enumerated four forbidden practices:

> Section 2: prohibits price discrimination that would "substantially lessen competition . . ." It exempted price differentiation due to differences in quality, quantity, and costs of selling and transportation.
>
> Section 3: Prohibits the use of tying or exclusive contracts that would lessen competition.
>
> Section 7: Prohibits the acquisition of other companies through purchase of stock if this lessens competition.
>
> Section 8: Restricts interlocking directorates.

The Clayton Act also provided for the recovery of treble damages by the injured party.

---

[1]A large number of texts on industrial organization treat this topic thoroughly. An example is Dennis W. Carlton and Jeffrey M. Perloff, *Modern Industrial Organization*, 2d ed., New York: HarperCollins, 1994, chapter 20.

The Federal Trade Commission Act (1914)

This law set up a new agency, the Federal Trade Commission (FTC), to investigate violations, enforce antitrust laws, and determine what actions constitute "unfair method of competition," which the law declared unlawful. The Wheeler-Lea Act (1938) extended the FTC's authority to the protection of consumers.

Subsequent Acts

The Robinson-Patman Act (1936) strengthened the price discrimination provisions of the Clayton Act to include not only the lessening of competition, but also injury to or prevention of competition "with any person who either grants or knowingly receives the benefits of such discrimination, or with customers of either of them." This act was the result of political pressure by small independent grocery stores to make it difficult for large grocery chains to buy and sell at lower prices.

The Celler-Kefauver Act (1950) corrected some omissions of the Clayton Act. Specifically, it applied the law to mergers accomplished through asset acquisition (the Clayton Act applied only to acquisition of stock).

The Hart-Scott-Rodino Act (1976) imposed a premerger notification requirement on large firms (where the acquiring firm has at least $100 million in assets and $10 million in annual sales).

Government Antitrust Policy in Action: The Case of Microsoft

Over time, the interpretation and enforcement of antitrust laws has varied a great deal. Before leaving this subject, we briefly discuss the two main schools of thought regarding the purpose of antitrust laws and comment on perhaps one of the most publicized antitrust cases in recent years: the U.S. government versus Microsoft Corporation.

One school of thought suggests that the main purpose of antitrust laws is economic efficiency. The laws act against practices that restrict output and raise prices. But not all mergers and agreements will create economic inefficiencies; instead, they may lead to greater efficiency and lowering of costs. Thus courts should interpret such actions case by case. The final goal of policy should be to enhance consumer welfare.

The opposing school of thought argues that the purpose of antitrust laws is actually to limit the power of large firms and protect smaller independent firms, regardless of the effects on efficiency. This seemed to be particularly evident in the case of the Robinson-Patman Act, which was explicitly aimed at the protection of small grocery businesses. Obviously, this is an extremely complex issue that has not yet been solved, and probably will not be for many years to come. An excellent contrast between these two schools of thought is illustrated in the case of the failed attempt by GE to take over Honeywell in 2001. This move was approved by American regulators but rejected by their European counterparts. (See the "Global Application" section at the end of this chapter for details.)

One of the highest-profile antitrust cases in recent years is the U.S. government's case against Microsoft Corporation. In a nutshell, the U.S. government has charged that Microsoft has used its monopolistic powers to compete unfairly against the Netscape Communications Corporation in the Web browser market. (Microsoft was also accused of unfair practices against other companies; however, we confine ourselves here to the government's case regarding Netscape.) After Microsoft bundled its own product, Internet Explorer, with its Windows operating system, the government charged that the company gained an illegal competitive advantage against Netscape's Navigator. The thrust of the government's arguments rested on two points: (1) Microsoft indeed has monopolistic powers that violate current antitrust laws, and (2) Microsoft used these powers to unfairly restrict Netscape's ability to compete.

Readers can well expect that top economists were among the cast of expert witnesses called in to testify on behalf of either side. In a dramatic display of "you've got your expert and I've got mine," the government called in prominent economist Franklin M. Fisher of the Massachusetts Institute of Technology (MIT), and Microsoft countered with Richard L. Schmalensee, also of MIT. By coincidence (or perhaps not), Professor Fisher was Professor Schmalensee's Ph.D. thesis advisor.

Professor Fisher challenged the fairness of Microsoft's decision to imbed its browser into its Windows operating system, which has more than a 90 percent share of the market. Professor Schmalensee countered by saying that this is like saying that "consumers will be made better off if they are deprived, by court order, of Web-browsing functionality that Microsoft wishes to provide at zero marginal cost and that consumers are free to ignore or replace."[2] Professor Fisher argued, saying that the threat is not merely that Microsoft will wrest the browser market away from the current leader, Netscape, but worse, that Microsoft might well use browser domination to eliminate competition in operating systems. He further charged that Microsoft's decision to give away its browser constituted an extreme form of "predatory pricing," designed to drive a competitor out of business.[3]

In late 2001, Microsoft settled with the Justice Department. This settlement is very controversial. Antitrust enforcers from nine states are not satisfied and have decided to pursue the case on their own. U.S. District Judge Coleen Kollar-Kotelly suggested in late 2001 that the case could proceed on parallel tracks. Under the requirements of the Tunney Act, the Justice settlement is subject to additional review. Meanwhile, the states could continue preparing for a final round in court.[4] The concerns raised by the state antitrust enforcers and many other critics are quite involved. Essentially, these critics believe that the settlement will not prevent Microsoft from continuing to use the same type of monopolistic tactics that brought the suit on it in the first place.[5]

There is also an international aspect to government antitrust action against Microsoft. In 1999, following a complaint by Sun Microsystems, the European Commission began an investigation of Microsoft's business practices. The investigation revealed two questionable practices:

➤ Nondisclosure of interface documentation precluding rivals from making their software work well with Microsoft Windows

➤ The bundling of Microsoft's Windows Media Player with the Windows 2000 operating system

After five years, in March 2004, the Commission concluded that Microsoft broke the European Union competition law and fined the company €497 million, at that time the Commission's largest penalty. It gave Microsoft 90 days to offer Windows without the Media Player and 120 days to release "complete and accurate" information to rivals in the server market. The U.S. Department of Justice's antitrust department reacted very negatively, stating that "sound antitrust policy must avoid chilling innovation and competition by 'dominant' companies. A contrary approach risks protecting competitors, not competition, in ways that may ultimately harm innovation and consumers

[2]"Trial's War of Economists Pits Student Against Teacher," *New York Times*, January 25, 1999.
[3]Readers should have no trouble finding material in the popular press about this case. However, two good sources are "As Microsoft Struggles with Antitrust Case, Tactical Errors Emerge," *Wall Street Journal*, February 18, 1999, and "For Microsoft, Humbled May Not Mean Defeated," *New York Times*, February 28, 1999.
[4]"States Find Flaws in Deal with Microsoft," *Wall Street Journal*, November 5, 2001.
[5]There are numerous articles about the controversial settlement besides the one cited previously. For example, see "Commentary: Settlement or Sellout?" *BusinessWeek*, November 19, 2001.

that benefit from it." In 2005 the Commission threatened additional fines because Microsoft had missed its deadlines and in the summer of 2006 it levied an additional fine of €280 million. Microsoft paid the fine but appealed both fines. The decision was then left to the European Union Court of First Instance.

In 2007 the Commission stated that Microsoft had continued to obtain a larger proportion of the server market, increasing from 35–40 percent in 1999 to 75–80 percent. Also, it said that Microsoft was charging royalties that were too high for the information it revealed to its competitors. The Commission wanted the information released at little or no cost.

On September 17, 2007, the Court upheld the Commission's decision on both parts of the case, saying that Microsoft unfairly withheld code from competitors at a reasonable price. Microsoft considered appealing to the European Union's highest court, the European Court of Justice. However, on October 22, Microsoft decided not to appeal, agreed to obey key parts of the 2004 antitrust ruling, and agreed to slash the charges for revealing the interface information.[6] The results of this case seem to confirm the different interpretation of antitrust laws between the European Union and the United States. The decision here again appeared to favor the protection of competitors.

Dealing with Market Externalities: Another Key Function of Government in the Market Economy

In the microeconomic theory of the firm, on which much of managerial economics is based, it can be shown that under conditions of perfect competition, an economy's scarce resources will be most efficiently allocated and social welfare will be maximized. This situation prevails when all costs are fully accounted for in the price of the product. However, there are frequent cases when not all costs are included in the price or when not all costs are compensated. Such situations give rise to externalities and result in market failure.

A **benefit externality** is one where not all costs are compensated. In other words, certain benefits accrue to third parties. For instance, a beautiful private garden will benefit people who walk by, but this will not compensate the owner. Benefit externalities (sometimes called positive externalities) also arise in the case of information (several people can read the same newspaper) or from innovations that benefit many people. Because producers of these products cannot appropriate all the revenue, too little may be produced.

But **cost externalities** are the ones with which economists are mostly concerned. These are the cases where a producer does not pay all the costs generated by the product. The most popular example of cost externalities (also called negative externalities) in economic literature is pollution. A factory will produce both the product and pollution. But if it does not have to pay for the cost of the pollution it has created, the product will be priced based only on the "private" production costs. Thus, the product's price will be lower than if it had been fully costed, and too much of the product will be produced. This can be shown on a simple graph for a competitive industry, shown in Figure 14.1.

The marginal cost curve of the product is shown as MC_p. The price of the product will be P_1 and the quantity produced will be Q_1. The cost of pollution is not considered in this result. The marginal cost of pollution is shown as MC_{pol}.

---

[6]The above information was obtained from a large number of newspaper articles, items from the Associated Press, AFX International Focus, and several other sources.

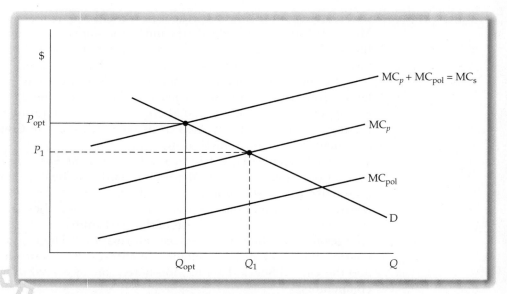

Figure 14.1 Impact of the Marginal Cost of Pollution on Price

The total cost of the product to the economy, the "social cost," is the vertical summation of MC_p and MC_{pol}, or MC_s. If this cost had been included in the pricing of the product, then equilibrium would have been at P_{opt} and Q_{opt}. Obviously, there will always be some pollution. If pollution were to be completely eliminated, then this industry would have to shut down and produce nothing. But this would not be an ideal situation because there is demand for the product. The **socially optimal price** will occur at P_{opt}, where the price of the product is equal to marginal social cost. Note that at this point less pollution will be produced (and less of the product also) than under strictly competitive conditions where only MC_p was priced into the product.

How can the optimal equilibrium be attained? The usual prescription is for government to act in one of two ways.[7] The first would be to restrict production to Q_{opt}. The other method is taxation. Ideally, this tax would be equal to the MC_{pol} curve. If such a tax were levied, then "externalities would be internalized." A third, rather new way, under the 1990 Clean Air Act, is for the government to set maximum pollution levels, and then sell licenses to companies to give them the right to pollute.

The Coase Theorem: An Alternative Treatment of Externalities

In 1960, Ronald Coase advanced the idea that government intervention to eliminate the effect of externalities is not necessary if property rights are correctly and clearly defined.[8] This is often referred to as the **Coase theorem**. Who has the right to pollute, and who has the right to keep pollution low? If it were originally decided who owns the property in question, then bargaining between the two parties would result in an optimal solution, without government intervention, at the level that would have been brought about with a correct taxation policy.

---

[7]The entire subject of externalities and government intervention was first treated fully by a famous English economist, A. C. Pigou. See *The Economics of Welfare,* 4th ed., London: Macmillan, 1932.
[8]Ronald Coase, "The Problem of Social Cost," *Journal of Law and Economics,* 3 (October 1960), pp. 1–44. This is a long and complex article. For an excellent brief summary, see George J. Stigler, *The Theory of Price,* 4th ed., New York: Macmillan, 1987.

Various examples of such a situation can be given. Let us assume a stream on which we find a chemical plant and a fishing establishment. If the property rights to this stream go to the chemical plant, the fishing company will have to pay the plant to reduce the dumping of its waste into the stream. It will pay just up to the point where the marginal benefit to the fishermen (from harvesting more and healthier fish) will be equal to the cost incurred by the chemical plant (in dumping its waste at a less convenient and more expensive location, or actually decreasing its production). In contrast, if the fishing company has the property rights, the plant will have to pay the fishermen to permit the plant to dump waste. In both cases, the final result will be the same and will take place at the optimal point that would have been achieved if a correct tax policy (i.e., taxes equal to the marginal cost of polluting) had been imposed.

Other examples of this kind abound. Coase, in his famous article, described the case of farmers growing grain in unfenced fields until a cattle rancher, whose cattle tend to damage the farmers' crops, arrives in the area. In addition, in his article, Coase cited a number of legal cases spanning back to the nineteenth century where the assignment of property rights was crucial in the decision.

The Coase theorem poses interesting questions regarding the need for government interference, but it is important to look at its limitations. For instance, although optimal production levels are reached regardless of which party is assigned property rights, income distribution will be affected. In our example, if the chemical plant was awarded property rights, it will gain at the expense of the fishing industry. Thus, normative issues are not addressed by Coase.

But there are additional limitations. First, if transaction costs—i.e., the cost of obtaining an agreement between the two parties—are high, then bargaining may not be an ideal solution. Second, if one company engages in unfair bargaining, no reasonable agreement may be reached. Third, neither side may have complete information regarding the costs and benefits of arriving at the optimal solution.[9]

STABILIZATION OF THE AGGREGATE ECONOMY: MONETARY AND FISCAL POLICY

Monetary and fiscal policy are mentioned previously as government activities designed to stabilize the economy. In light of the 2001 recession in the United States, this function has become a much more important part of the role of government in the market economy. We discuss each of these briefly.

Monetary Policy

Monetary policy is carried out by the Federal Reserve System (the Fed) through its control of the quantity of money in the economic system and/or interest rates. It is directed at attaining certain goals such as economic growth or price stability. Over the years, the specific methods used by the Fed have differed. At one time, its primary concern was the quantity of money. More recently, monetary policy has concentrated on influencing interest rates, specifically the Federal Funds rate.

Banks are required to keep certain cash reserves with the Fed. On any given day, some banks' reserves may exceed requirements. Federal Funds is the name given to these excess reserves, which can be borrowed by banks whose reserve balances are deficient. Most of these loans are extremely short term, mostly overnight. It is the rate on these loans that the Federal Reserve targets. Depending on the condition of the

---

[9]A. M. Polinsky, "Controlling Externalities and Protecting Entitlements: Property Right, Liability Rule, and Tax-Subsidy Approaches," *Journal of Legal Studies*, 8, 1979, pp. 1–48.

economy, the Federal Funds rate target can be lowered, raised, or left alone. This determination is made by the Fed's Open Market Committee, which meets eight times each year.

During the downturn of the U.S. economy in 2001, the Federal Funds rate target was lowered eleven times, by either a quarter or a half of a percentage point each time. This was done to apply the brakes to the economic skid. From a level of 6.5 percent at the end of 2000, the rate declined to 1 percent in January 2003. The 1 percent rate remained in effect until June 2003. At this point the economy had been growing rather quickly and to prevent it from overheating and causing an inflationary trend, the Federal Reserve began to raise the federal funds rate. It raised the rate by 0.25 percent in each of the next 17 meetings of the Open Market Committee, until the rate reached 5.25 percent in June 2006. As we are writing this edition, a recession seems to be possible. The economy has been slowing down, the value of the dollar has been falling, and the decline in housing prices, accompanied by the problems in the subprime mortgage market leading to a record number of foreclosures, all appear to be signaling a potential downturn in the economy. In order to ease this situation the Federal Reserve has reversed its policy and has begun to decrease the rate. Starting with a half-percent drop in September 2007, it lowered the rate two more times by the end of 2007, bringing it to 4.25 percent. In early 2008, the Fed cut the rate to 2 percent. As this edition is being prepared, there do not seem to be any moves by the Fed to lower the rate further.

Of course, the announcement of a lower target rate may not always be sustained automatically. To bring the rate to its desired level, the Fed may have to engage in open market operations to raise or lower the quantity of money in the economy. Open market operations involve the purchase of government securities in the market to increase the money supply. At other times, when the economy threatens to overheat, resulting in inflation, the Fed may sell securities in the market to decrease the money supply and push interest rates up.

Fiscal Policy

The U.S. government collects taxes to finance expenditures for goods and services, as well as transfer payments that have been legislated by the U.S. Congress. Such expenditures are generally based on long-term goals. However, fiscal policy—the changes in the level of taxation and spending—is designed to achieve macroeconomic goals relating to output (gross domestic product) and employment.

By manipulating receipts or expenditures, a surplus or deficit is created. To stimulate the economy, the government—through Congress—will either decrease taxes or increase expenditures (or both) and create a deficit in the federal budget. Although both actions may stimulate an economy that has descended into a recession, the result of an increase in spending is to enlarge the role of the U.S. government in the economy, which may be considered unfavorable by the part of the population that believes in limited government. However, another part of the population looks at such actions favorably, believing that increased government actions may be beneficial. Again, the actions in the year 2001 present us with good examples of changes in fiscal policy.

One of the new administration's primary goals was to lower the level of taxes in the long run, thus decreasing the government's role in our lives. During 2001, Congress passed a law that decreased income taxes gradually over the next 10 years (other provisions were also included, such as the phasing out of the estate tax). However, because the economy appeared to be turning downward, the Congress included a provision that gave immediate refunds of up to $600 to most taxpayers. This was, of course, intended to give the economy a quick shot in the arm. As the economy appeared to continue its decline toward the end of the year, the administration and Congress embarked on trying to pass an "economic stimulus" package composed of certain tax cut and spending increases. It was passed by Congress and signed by the president in March 2002. Congress enacted further tax cuts in the Jobs and Growth Tax Relief Reconciliation Act of 2003.

As this edition is being prepared, it appears that the economy is either heading into or already in a recession. The cut in the Fed Funds rate mentioned in the previous section is part of the government's attempt to deal with this problem. In terms of fiscal policy, President Bush proposed and Congress approved of a tax rebate stimulus package in early 2008.

Lags

Although both policies can affect the movement of the economy, it must be recognized that in both cases the effect is not immediate. In fact, there are significant lags in the consequences of both monetary and fiscal actions. First, there is usually a delay in recognizing that a problem exists. Although both the Fed and the U.S. government have a large amount of economic data available, they may not be timely, or different data may give conflicting signals. (As already mentioned in chapter 5, the onset of the most recent recession was dated March 2001, but this was not announced until December 2001.) Second, after the problem is recognized, there is a delay in implementation. This interval is particularly present in fiscal policy where the action must go through a political process that may be excruciatingly slow. The action can be realized more quickly in the case of monetary policy. Third, even when action is taken, there is a substantial lag for it to work itself into the economy and become effective.

Various economists have tried to estimate these lags. Although there is no agreement on the precise size of the lag, we know that it can last more than 6 months and may at times be as long as 1 year or more. Thus, it is quite possible that either monetary or fiscal action will actually turn out to be counterproductive. It may become effective when the economy has actually righted itself on its own, and the policy action may either add fuel to an already growing economy or aggravate a decline. The stimulus package passed in 2002 may be just such a case. Even without it, the economy appeared to have bottomed out in early 2002, and any stimulus that it may provide could be too late and could become effective at a time when the economy no longer needs it.

DOING BUSINESS WITH THE U.S. GOVERNMENT

Nowhere else do government policies and procedures have greater impact than on market segments where the government *is* the buyer.[10] Such a market is sometimes described as a **monopsony**, or a market in which the product or service of a number of sellers is sought by only one buyer. In this section, we focus on the U.S. government because of its size, reach, and impact on the U.S. economy. Conversely, we also illustrate that a market economy can have a great impact on how the U.S. government acts as a buyer. The challenges of doing business with local and state governments are similar, although there may be specific differences in policies and procedures from those followed by the federal government.

The U.S. government is arguably the single biggest client in the world. In fiscal year 2004, federal receipts totaled $1.9 trillion. Total outlays were $2.2 trillion.[11] Each

---

[10]This section is written by Sylvia Von Bostel, on the staff of Booz-Allen & Hamilton.
[11]"The Budget System and Concepts," *Budget of the United States Government, Fiscal Year 2004,* Washington, DC: U.S. Government Printing Office, 2004.

year, the federal executive branch purchases more than *$200 billion* in goods and services.[12] According to the Federal Procurement Data Center, part of the U.S. General Services Administration, every 20 seconds of each working day the U.S. government awards a contract with an average value of $465,000.[13] In such a market, government policies fundamentally shape the ways in which businesses behave.

The Government Market

Doing business with the federal government is highly complicated. Entire industries have emerged to explain how to be successful in this marketplace. Some companies choose not to do business with the government due to special accounting and reporting requirements, potential liabilities, profit limitations, and other statutory and regulatory controls. In contrast, many companies have learned how to operate and prosper in this environment.

For the purposes of this discussion, we approach this subject with three basic questions of *what? when?* and *how?* First, businesses look at *what* they believe the government will buy. This determines the way in which businesses define their product or service offerings. Related to this question is that of *when* the government plans to buy. This is a critically important factor and has an impact on whether short- or long-term investments are required. Third, businesses carefully monitor changes in federal acquisition policies that govern *how* the government will buy. This affects the way in which they develop their bidding strategies. Let us take a closer look.

What the Government Buys

What the U.S. government buys is influenced by government strategic plans, budget and program input from federal departments and agencies, priorities set by the president, the availability of appropriated funds, congressionally mandated requirements, whether the federal budget is in surplus or deficit, and lots of politics. Businesses monitor this ever-changing environment, their government clients, and the entire federal budget process carefully. Although perhaps 80 to 90 percent of the president's budget request is usually enacted, individual programs or projects can be eliminated, cut back, restricted, or limited in other ways. Sometimes Congress adds funding that was not requested. Any of these actions can have a significant impact on a business that has or is seeking a contract with the government.

The federal government's fiscal year begins on October 1, ends on September 30, and is named by the year in which it ended. Fiscal year 2005, for example, began on October 1, 2004, and ended on September 30, 2005. Each January, the president announces priority initiatives and proposed funding in the president's State of the Union address. The formal budget process begins with release of the *Budget of the United States Government* to Congress, which the president is required to submit to Congress by the first Monday in February.[14]

In reality, federal departments and agencies begin building their budgets 2 years in advance and, in addition to the fiscal year in question, look at "out years," or 5 to 6 years into the future. The White House, bipartisan commissions, independent panels, interagency councils, inspectors general, the General Accounting Office (the investigative arm of Congress), congressional committees, and federal departments and agencies themselves conduct many reviews that influence budget requests. The Office of Management and Budget (OMB) provides detailed instructions to federal

---

[12]Retrieved February 3, 1999, from Federal Procurement Data System, General Services Administration Web site: https://fpds.gsa.gov.
[13]"FPDS . . . the Competitor's Edge," retrieved February 3, 1999 from https://fpds.gsa.gov/fpds/compete.
[14]"Citizen's Guide to the Federal Budget," *Budget of the United States Government, Fiscal Year 2000.*

departments and agencies about how to put their budgets together in *OMB Circular A-11,* "Preparation and Submission of Budget Estimates," a document that is updated annually to reflect changes in law. OMB collects the budget requests, "scrubs" the numbers, and puts together the president's budget.

Ultimately, it is the U.S. Congress that authorizes and appropriates the funds that can be obligated and expended for the purchase of goods and services. Once the president's budget is submitted to Congress, the annual appropriations process begins in earnest. There are thirteen appropriations bills. Some years they are enacted separately. In others, due to lack of time or breakdowns in negotiations between the White House and Congress on major programs or policy issues, some or all appropriation bills are bundled in a large catchall piece of legislation. Appropriation bills or some stopgap legislation, referred to as "continuing resolutions," must be enacted by October 1 or parts or all the federal government may be forced to "shut down."

When the Government Buys

When the government plans to purchase goods or services is a critical factor in many ways. Learning about a major procurement when the government publishes an RFP usually means it is too late to be a player. Competitors who have been tracking the procurement, devising a strategy, and negotiating with teaming partners will have an advantage. For companies that develop and build prototypes and manufacture high-cost items requiring substantial long-term investment, serious delays can threaten their very survival and even lead to merger or acquisition. Unanticipated cancellations due to budget cutbacks or major government shutdowns can result in layoffs, plant closings, and cash flow problems. One need only look at the consolidations that have been occurring in the defense and aerospace industries since the end of the Cold War to see the impact of changes of federal government budgets on private industry.

How the Government Buys

How the government purchases goods and services has a major impact on bidding strategies. Government acquisition is controlled by two basic laws, the Armed Services Procurement Act, applicable to the Army, Navy, Air Force, Coast Guard, and NASA, and the Federal Property and Administrative Services Act, applicable to the General Services Administration and all other agencies. The Federal Acquisition Regulation System codifies and publishes uniform policies and procedures for acquisition by all federal agencies. It consists of the Federal Acquisition Regulation (FAR), which is the primary governmentwide document, and agency acquisition regulations that supplement the FAR. The Office of Federal Procurement Policy, part of the OMB, provides overall direction.[15]

Companies doing business with the government must comply with requirements and controls that do not exist in commercial transactions. These include competition requirements, profit restrictions, audits, bid protest rules, accounting system requirements, prohibitions against gratuities and certain hiring practices, and socioeconomic programs. The FAR is divided into fifty-three parts. Part 15 deals exclusively with negotiated contracts. Parts 19 to 26 of the FAR are dedicated to socioeconomic programs, for example, small business programs, the application of labor laws to government acquisitions, environment, conservation, occupational safety, and drug-free workplace, protection of privacy and freedom of information, foreign acquisition, the Native American incentive program, and historically black colleges and universities and minority institutions. Part 30 sets forth cost accounting standards and part 31 deals with

---

[15]"Authority·Policy·Laws·Regulations·Selling to the Federal Government," *Government Contracts Reporter,* Commerce Clearing House, June 14, 1989.

contract cost principles and procedures. Part 52 is a long list of solicitation provisions and contract clauses, and includes a matrix listing of FAR provisions and clauses applicable to each principal contract type, for example, fixed-price supply or cost reimbursement research and development. Part 53 provides examples of standard forms, optional forms, and agency-specific forms.[16]

The Government and the Market Economy

As stated, the market economy has a great impact on how the U.S. government acts as a buyer as well. During the 1980s, it became apparent that the annual federal deficit and total national debt were reaching unacceptable levels, the Cold War was ending, and the nation was entering a new Information Age. Laws were enacted to enforce budget discipline, and the federal government sought ways in which to become more efficient and cost effective. It did this by adapting for its use successful business practices in the private sector, such as total quality management, business process reengineering, downsizing, rightsizing, mergers, streamlining acquisitions, and shedding excess infrastructure. From the height of the defense buildup in the mid-1980s until around 1998, the Department of Defense reduced force structure by 35 to 40 percent.[17] Four Base Realignment and Closure (BRAC) Commissions between 1988 and 1995 proposed the closure or realignment of 152 major installations and 235 smaller installations.[18] Although not all actions have occurred, approximately $14 billion to $15 billion in savings were achieved by 1998.[19]

In the 1990s, the federal government accelerated steps to further streamline its acquisition processes, adopt commercial practices, get away from detailed government specifications, buy commercial off-the-shelf items whenever possible, and emphasize performance- or results-based management. Table 14.1 highlights some of the laws enacted during the 1990s.

One of the major impacts of these acquisition reforms of the 1990s was the increased use of the Federal Supply Schedules as a preferred way of doing business. Under the Federal Supply Schedules administered by the General Services Administration (GSA), companies apply to provide certain types of commercial items and services and are placed on a list of approved vendors, together with their price lists, which are posted on the GSA's Web site. Qualified vendors are able to market their products and capabilities to federal agencies. Federal agencies are able to find vendors on the list and use streamlined acquisition procedures to meet their requirements. Commercial items and services and off-the-shelf commercial items are also exempt from significant statutory and regulatory requirements, both at the contract and subcontract levels.

Around 1995, under the auspices of the National Performance Review, another phenomenon, sometimes referred to as *entrepreneurial government,* emerged. This brought the adaptation of commercial practices to a new level by actively sanctioning government "franchising," employee stock ownership programs (ESOPs) composed of former government employees, public–public competition, and public–private competition. The Government Management Reform Act/Federal Financial Management Act of 1994, cited in Table 14.1, established a franchise fund pilot program in six executive agencies. The fund is used to provide common administrative support services to the designated

---

[16]*Federal Acquisition Regulation* as of January 1, 1998, Commerce Clearing House, 1998.
[17]William S. Cohen, Secretary of Defense, "The Secretary's Message," *Report of the Quadrennial Defense Review,* May 1997.
[18]William S. Cohen, Secretary of Defense, *Annual Report to the President and Congress,* 1998, p. 176.
[19]William S. Cohen, Secretary of Defense, Testimony before the House Armed Services Committee, "Hearing on the President's Fiscal Year 2000 Budget," February 2, 1999.

Table 14.1   Selected Laws Adopting Commercial Practices

Year	Public Law	Key Provisions
1990	Chief Financial Officers Act	• Required the establishment of agency CFOs and designated a governmentwide CFO
1993	Government Performance and Results Act	• Established strategic planning and performance measurement requirements for federal agencies
1994	Government Management Reform Act, which contained the Federal Financial Management Act	• Required agencies and the government as a whole to produce annual audited financial statements • Mandated direct deposit electronic funds transfers for all federal wage, salary, and retirement payments
1994	Federal Acquisition Streamlining Act	• Expanded the types of commercial items and services that the government could purchase using streamlined procedures • Simplified payments for small purchases by increasing the use of governmentwide credit cards
1996	Federal Acquisitions Reform Act	• Expanded the definition of commercial items and services, and exempted them from the requirement for certified cost or pricing data and the federal government's cost accounting standards
1996	Information Technology Management Reform Act	• Required capital planning and investment control or information technology • Called for the designation of a chief information officer at each executive agency

Sources: *Chief Financial Officers Act of 1990*, Public Law 101–576, November 15, 1990; *Government Performance and Reform Act of 1993 (GPRA)*, PL 103–62, August 3, 1993; *Government Management Reform Act of 1994 (GMRA)*, PL 103–356, October 13, 1994; *Federal Acquisition Streamlining Act of 1994 (FASA)*, PL 103–355, October 13, 1994; *Federal Acquisition Reform Act of 1996 (FARA)*, PL 104–106, February 10, 1996; *Information Technology Management Reform Act of 1996 (ITMRA)*, PL 104–106, February 10, 1996.

agency, but can also be used to provide services to other agencies on a competitive basis. As of July 1997, the Environmental Protection Agency, the departments of Commerce, Health and Human Services, Interior, Treasury, and Veterans Affairs were participating in the franchise fund program. Data centers at these six agencies gave up their operating budgets but recovered their expenses by charging their own agencies and other government entities for the work they do.[20] US Investigations Services, Inc. (USIS) is an ESOP formed in July 1996 by former federal civil servants in the Office of Federal Investigations, part of the Office of Personnel Management. USIS is the first employee-owned enterprise that involved a former federal agency, and has become the largest private investigations company in North America.[21]

In May 1997, the Federal Aviation Administration (FAA) awarded its Integrated Computing Environment-Mainframe and Networking (ICE-MAN) contract, worth up to $250 million over 8 years, to the U.S. Department of Agriculture (USDA) computer

[20]"Battle Lines Drawn on FAA Contract," *Washington Technology*, July 10, 1997, p. 1.
[21]"Live Long and Prosper," edited with permission from an article appearing in *Government Executive*, Web site of Foundation for Enterprise Development, http://www.fed.org/leadingcompanies/nov97/harper.html.

center in Kansas City, Missouri. Under that contract, the USDA operates the FAA's computer systems for payroll, personnel, and flight safety. Competitors included major corporations such as IBM, Unisys, Computer Sciences, and Lockheed Martin and at least one other government agency, the Defense Information Systems Agency.[22]

Federal policy regarding the performance of commercial activities is set forth in *OMB Circular A-76,* first promulgated by the Bureau of the Budget in 1955 and reissued and revised many times since then, most recently in 2003. Circular A-76 states that in the process of governing, the government should not compete with its citizens and shall rely on commercially available sources to provide commercial products and services. When commercial performance of a government commercial activity is appropriate, A-76 requires that the cost of private sector versus government performance be compared to determine who will do the work. It also states that certain functions are so intimately related to the public interest as to mandate performance only by federal employees.[23]

In 1998, the Federal Activities Inventory Reform Act (FAIR) required federal agencies to review, inventory, and publicly list those functions that are not inherently governmental and that could therefore be performed by commercial entities. At the same time, FAIR statutorily sanctioned competition between federal agencies and the private sector. To address long-standing concerns in the private sector that government bids in public–private competitions do not fully reflect all costs, FAIR also required the OMB to issue guidance on conducting such competitions. To ensure realistic and fair cost comparisons, FAIR further directed federal agencies to ensure all costs, including the costs of quality assurance, technical monitoring of the performance of a function, liability insurance, employee retirement and disability benefits, and all other overhead costs, be considered.[24]

These changes over the past 20 years are altering client relationships and redefining what it means to do business with the federal government. Much more business is being conducted using the Federal Supply Schedules. More A-76 competitions are being held to determine whether commercial activities should be performed by the government or by commercial entities. There have been major reforms to reduce bid protests and long procurement cycles. The potential value of large federal information technology contracts more frequently reaches or exceeds $100 million. The federal government has created "franchises" and ESOPs. Government agencies are competing against each other to perform administrative services, and companies find themselves bidding against their government clients to provide computer services. In the words of Aldous Huxley, this government market is a "brave new world," one that will certainly bring fascinating challenges in the years to come.

GOVERNMENT DEREGULATION, MERGERS, AND ACQUISITIONS

For various historic, political, and economic reasons, certain major industries in the United States were subject to considerable government regulation. Telecommunications, electric and gas utilities, airlines, and commercial banks are perhaps the best examples. Beginning in the late 1970s and continuing on through the 1990s, the U.S. government in effect eliminated most if not all regulatory control that it had exercised over firms in

---

[22]"FAA, $150M Iceman Cometh to USDA," *Federal Computer Week,* May 12, 1997, p. 1; "When the Government Hires the Government, FAA Awards Big Systems Contract to USDA, but to Private Contractors, It Doesn't Compute," *Washington Post,* May 22, 1997; "Battle Lines Drawn on FAA Contract," *Washington Technology,* July 10, 1997, p. 1
[23]*QMB Circular A-76,* March 1996.
[24]*Federal Activities Inventory Reform Act (FAIR),* Public Law 105–270, October 19, 1998.

these industries. Regardless of the original reasons for their regulation, the government has assumed that by deregulating these industries, consumers will be better served by lower prices, better service, or more rapid introduction of technology that would ostensibly stem from a more competitive environment.

However, in recent years, the deregulation has apparently resulted in such a fiercely competitive environment that a number of companies in these industries have sought to merge or acquire other companies in order to survive and grow. This is somewhat ironic because one of the great concerns of antitrust policy in the United States has been the level of merger activity. As companies merge, is there a danger that their greater size makes them monopolistic and a threat to free competition? If so, then the very actions of the government to make certain industries more competitive may require it to assert its role as the arbiter of what constitutes "competition."

In commercial banking, the mergers (the combination of two firms or the acquisition of one firm by another) that have grabbed most of the headlines have been among the leading financial institutions. Citicorp merged with Traveler's Insurance to form Citigroup. Chemical Bank and Chase Manhattan merged to become the Chase Bank, which then merged with JP Morgan to become JP Morgan Chase. Bank of America merged with Nations Bank, and then later acquired Fleet Bank. In 2004, Bank One (which had earlier merged with First Chicago) merged with JP Morgan Chase.

In the market for local telecommunications service, the seven Regional Bell Operating Companies that were formed by the breakup of AT&T have been reduced to three: at&t, Verizon, and Qwest. The "new AT&T" (which now uses the lowercase "at&t" on its logo) consists of SBC, Pacific Telesis, Ameritech, and, most recently, Bell South. In each merger, SBC was the dominant company. The "old AT&T" was also bought by SBC. SBC renamed itself at&t shortly before acquiring Bell South. Verizon is the result of a merger with two original Baby Bells, Nynex and Bell Atlantic, plus GTE, a long distance and local company that had remained independent of the original Bell System of AT&T. U.S. West is now called Qwest, since the latter bought out the former.

From a historical perspective, it is interesting to see what has happened to the original dominant long-distance companies over the past decade. MCI WorldCom broke into two separate entities, MCI (essentially the voice communications business) and WorldCom (essentially the data communications business). But after the financial scandals surrounding the company, the company filed for bankruptcy. It recently remerged as MCI. In 2002, AT&T sold its cable TV business to Comcast, and in 2004 it sold its wireless voice business to Cingular. Also in 2004, AT&T decided to retreat from the consumer voice business and concentrate only on providing communications services to large customers (e.g., multinational corporations). Finally in early 2005, SBC announced that it was seeking to buy AT&T for $16 million. Shortly after that, Verizon announced its intention to buy MCI. Both purchases were completed in 2006.

The airline industry in the United States also has experienced some merger and acquisition activity, although not quite as much as in the financial and telecommunications industries. In 2000, United Airlines tried to buy U.S. Airways but was prevented from doing so by the government. However, in 2001, the government allowed American Airlines to acquire TWA. After the approval of this acquisition, two additional mergers occurred. In 2006, U.S. Airways merged with America West. In 2008, Delta joined forces with Northwest.

Why Firms Merge

The recent increase in mergers in the deregulated industries is nothing new. The U.S. economy has passed through a number of merger waves since the end of the nineteenth century. During the 1980s and early 1990s, many mergers were motivated by low valuations of the target firms, which had been underperforming. In addition to mergers, this period also saw a large number of leveraged buyouts (LBOs), where public companies were taken private by groups of investors, using large amounts of debt to finance the transaction.[25] In the mid- and late 1990s, mergers have been motivated primarily by the necessity to obtain greater efficiencies—economies of scale or scope—to be able to compete in a global economy. This impetus for merging with or acquiring companies is relevant for any industry where the intensity of competition has increased.

As we have just pointed out, deregulated industries are perhaps the most dramatic example of situations where there is a sharp increase in competition, but certain other industries that have never been regulated have also undergone significant upheaval. In the automobile industry, mergers and acquisitions that made the news include the merger of Daimler-Benz with Chrysler, the Ford Motor Company's purchase of Jaguar and of Volvo's motor vehicle divisions, and BMW's purchase of Rover. In 2000, after several years of owning Rover, BMW lost so much money that it decided to sell it off to a group of private investors. In 2007, Daimler Benz followed in BMW's footsteps by selling Chrysler to another private equity group.

Another well-known example of a merger in an industry not subject to deregulation is the case of Hewlett-Packard and Compaq. The major reasons for this merger were the economies of scale by combining the two companies' PC business and, most important, the critical size that Carly Fiorina, the CEO of HP, believed was needed to compete against the likes of IBM and EDS in the information technology services business. After three years of operating as one company, the new HP was able to cut its costs by about $1 billion. (The anticipated cost savings at the time of the merger was about $500 million.) Thus the value of the merger due to economies of scale was quite evident. However, the new HP was still unable to generate more revenue than HP and Compaq were each able to generate on its own prior to the merger. Largely because of this factor, Ms. Fiorina was forced by HP's Board of Directors to step down as head of the company in February 2005.[26]

There are many reasons behind merger activity. The basic motivation for mergers is to increase the value of the combined firms compared with their separate valuations. This simple idea is usually expressed with the following equation:

$$V_{A+B} > (V_A + V_B)$$

where V stands for total market value, and A and B are the two companies involved in the merger.

Among the incentives to merge, some result in increased economic efficiency, but others do not. A partial list of incentives follows:

1. *Synergies in production.* If synergies exist, then the value of the combined companies should exceed the value of the two separately. Among the synergistic results, we would find the following:

   a. *Revenue enhancements.* For example, a better distribution system for products when two companies combine may increase sales.

   b. *Operating economies.* These results would include economies of scale and/or scope. Economies could also be achieved through improved research and development (because of complementarities in technical skills resident in the two companies) or

---

[25]The ultimate goal was, of course, to streamline these companies, make them more efficient (possibly by disposing of some parts of the company), and eventually bring them back as publicly owned companies.
[26]For example, see December 13, 2004, Ben Elgin, "HP: Corroding Carly's Clout," *BusinessWeek*, January 24, 2005, and Cliff Edwards, "Where Fiorina Went Wrong," *BusinessWeek*, February 9, 2005.

"management meshing," where the skills of the management of the companies complement each other. For instance, one company has strong marketing management while the other's managers have technical superiority.

   c. *Financial economies.* The combined company may be able to lower its cost of capital.

2. *Improved management.* In some cases, the acquired firm may lack good management skills, while the acquiring firm has a relative abundance of skilled managers. The merger will create an opportunity for improving the overall management level of the new company by eliminating poor managers.

3. *Tax consequences.* Although a merger may not result in increased economic efficiency, it may reduce the tax bill of the two combined companies. If a company has been incurring losses, it will not be paying taxes. It will carry tax losses forward and may reduce its tax liabilities in the future when it becomes profitable. By merging with a profitable company, it will be able to save taxes immediately and increase the combined companies' cash flow, even in the absence of any synergies.

    Taxes will also be decreased for a company with much cash and no great investment opportunities. If this company were to pay a large dividend, then its stockholders would pay taxes immediately; or if the company were to buy back its stock, stockholders could be liable for capital gains taxes. By using its cash to acquire another company, it will avoid creating tax liabilities.

4. *Managerial power.* Mergers may occur when the acquiring company's managers are seeking to increase their span of authority. Although the acquisition of another company may expand the power of managers, it will, in many cases, not result in enhanced efficiency.

5. *Diversification.* During the 1960s, diversification was the ostensible motivation for a large number of mergers. Mergers among companies in unrelated fields of activity predominated. It was said that diversification could decrease the variability of sales and earnings, and thus be of benefit to stockholders, even if no synergistic effects were present. This is a flawed argument. There is no reason why stockholders cannot achieve their own diversification by investing in both companies. This would be accomplished much more cheaply because it would avoid the significant costs that would be incurred in completing the merger.

6. *Market power.* The combination of two or more powerful firms could lead to a decrease of competition in the industry. The result could be lower production, higher prices, and a negative effect on the efficient functioning of the economy. It is with these potential effects that U.S. antitrust laws are concerned.

A large number of studies have investigated the effects of mergers on stockholders and the economy. We summarize their results as follows:

1. There is general agreement that stockholders of the target companies are the big winners, gaining between 20 and 30 percent when their company is acquired. In contrast, the stockholders of the acquiring firms gain very little because their stock prices, on average, remain constant. Overall, there appears to be an increase in the value of the combined companies.

2. The evidence regarding increased profitability of merged firms is rather mixed.

3. Merger activity does not appear to have increased the level of industry concentration.

4. There appears to be no decrease in research and development activity of merged firms, contrary to the opinion of some commentators.[27]

Two recent studies have generally reinforced the summary of findings above. One, by Robert F. Bruner, surveyed over 120 studies that have been conducted over

[27]For an excellent review of recent mergers and acquisitions, including those in industries that we discuss in this chapter, see "Oligopolies Are on the Rise as the Urge to Merge Grows," *Wall Street Journal,* February 25, 2002.

the last three decades.[28] Essentially, Bruner examined the following outcomes: value conserved, value created and value destroyed, using three forms of measurement:

➤ **Weak form:** Did share prices rise?

➤ **Semi-strong:** Did the firm's returns exceed a benchmark (such as S&P 500 Index)?

➤ **Strong:** Are shareholders better off after the deal than they would have been if the deal had not occurred?

While the strong form would have been the most valid measurement, such results are not observable. Thus, the semi-strong form is used in summarizing results. The result of a large number of market-based return studies confirmed that the returns to stockholders of target firms are significantly positive. However, when the results for the acquirer are investigated, the results are not clear. Bruner summarized at least fifty studies and concluded that "abnormal returns to buyer shareholders from M&A activity are essentially zero," and that buyers "essentially break even." When the returns to the buyer and target firms are combined, most of the studies report positive returns.

However, Bruner points out that, from an economist's viewpoint, breaking even does not represent failure. Even though no new value is created, such mergers have a present value of zero, which means that stockholders are earning at least their opportunity cost of capital. An economist would consider failure only if value is destroyed.

Several studies investigated longer term effects. A majority of these studies reported negative returns. However, in these cases there is a possibility that the outcomes are not caused by the transaction itself but that there are other reasons for these results. Bruner mentions two possible plausible explanations:

➤ The buyer's shares were overvalued at the time of the merger.

➤ Industry conditions after the merger have influenced results.

The studies that investigated the results of mergers have identified a number of factors that are influential in determining the success (or lack of success) of mergers and acquisitions. Among those that are instrumental in enhancing value are:

➤ Expected synergies

➤ Mergers that look for value

➤ Restructuring that includes divestitures of underperforming businesses

➤ Tender offers (as compared to friendly mergers)

Those that do not create value include:

➤ Glamour acquisitions (based on book-to-market ratios)

➤ Mergers to build market power

➤ Mergers to use excess cash

The other study examined the performance of over 12 thousand publicly listed U.S. acquiring firms during the 1990s.[29] These acquiring firms appear to have outperformed the market by 50 percent. While most prior studies have analyzed the performance of companies after acquisition, this paper appears to find that

---

[28]Robert F. Bruner, *Applied Mergers and Acquisitions*, John Wiley, 2004, Chapter 3.
[29]Michael Bradley and Anant Sundaram, "Do Acquisitions Drive Performance or Does Performance Drive Acquisitions?" Paper presented at a seminar at Thunderbird, the Garvin School of International Management in October 2004. An earlier version was presented at the 2004 European Finance Association meeting in Maastricht Netherlands.

companies that undertake acquisitions show a significant stock price increase in the year before the acquisitions. These increases are greater when the acquisition target is a non-public rather than a public company. Also, the pre-announcement run-up is greater when stock rather than cash is used to complete the acquisition. After the acquisition is completed, stock prices tend to decline; however, this decrease does not erase the pre-announcement increases. The authors find that the findings of previous studies that "targets gain and acquirers break even" are too simplistic. Most acquisitions appear to bring about positive gains. The only category that confirms the previous findings is the acquisition with stock of large, public target companies.

GLOBAL APPLICATION: THE FAILED ATTEMPT TO MERGE BY GENERAL ELECTRIC AND HONEYWELL

The failed attempt by General Electric to merge with Honeywell in the first half of 2001 provides an excellent example of the international dimension of the role of government in a market economy. What it really illustrates is two opposite philosophies of antitrust held by American and European regulators and government officials. In October 2000, the General Electric Company proposed to merge with Honeywell International, Inc. Prior to this move, Honeywell was in the process of merging with the United Technologies Corporation. After GE topped United's bid, Honeywell and GE prepared for their merger.

The U.S. Department of Justice approved the merger in May 2001. During the past 20 years, the American interpretation of the antitrust laws has been moving in the direction of making decisions on the basis of a merger's effect on consumer welfare. The GE–Honeywell merger appeared to promise production and distribution efficiencies. However, because the merger would affect business in Europe, it had to be approved by the European Commission. After investigation and conferences during the first half of 2001, the European Commission ruled against the merger, despite various concessions made by GE. The basis for the rejection was the merger's potential threat to competitors.

Two major issues appeared to influence the commission's decision:

1. GE and Honeywell, if combined, could "bundle" their products. GE is a major producer of aircraft engines, whereas Honeywell produces avionics and aerospace products. The merged company would now be able to offer discounts to "customers who bought a package of components and services from GE–Honeywell."[30] Thus, the merged company's competitors would be injured. Several competing companies actively opposed the merger; among them were United Technologies, Rolls-Royce, and Rockwell.

2. GE Capital Aviation Services (GECAS) is one of the world's largest buyers of commercial aircraft, which it sells or leases to airlines. The commission feared that GECAS could require aircraft manufacturers to install GE–Honeywell products on the aircraft ordered by it.[31]

Based on this case, we can say that U.S. government officials appear to favor the demand side of the market (i.e., the buyers of aerospace and related products), whereas their

---

[30]Andrew Hill and Deborah Hargreaves, "How Monti Turned GE-Honeywell into a Flight of Fancy," *Financial Times*, July 6, 2001.
[31]In addition to the article quoted in footnote 30, several other articles appeared in the press on this subject. Among these were Mike France, "Europe: a Different Take on Antitrust," *BusinessWeek*, June 25, 2001, p. 40; Gary Becker, "What U.S. Courts Could Teach Europe's Trustbuster," *BusinessWeek*, August 6, 2001, p. 20; Bryan M. Carney, "Blame the EU's Antitrust Rules—Not Monti," *Wall Street Journal*, July 7, 2001; Philip Shishkin, "Barred Merger Signals U.S.-EU Divergence," *Wall Street Journal*, July 5, 2001.

European counterparts tend to favor the supply side (i.e., the firms that produce these products). We think that the concern about the loss in jobs that inevitably follows such mergers is probably what tilts the Europeans toward the supply side.

The Solution

___

The staff report that Bill was reviewing was very revealing. Outsourcing is not necessarily the panacea for cost control that everyone seems to imagine. It is true that the vendor's total charge for services is less than the cost that the company believes it would incur by staying "in-house." However, the company has to have a staff to monitor and work with the vendor to ensure the various services are carried out according to the service level agreement, or SLA. A large and complex contract such as the one that Global Foods signed with AT&T has multiple SLAs.

After giving the matter considerable thought in consultation with his staff, Bill decided to continue the relationship with AT&T. His reasons were as follows:

1. Both Global Foods and AT&T were relatively new at the outsourcing game and were only just beginning to accumulate the experience and skills to make the relationship pay off.
2. In certain instances where AT&T was not providing satisfactory service, it was because Global Foods was itself not very clear about its requirements. Rather than throwing out the proverbial "baby with the bathwater," Bill felt that a reevaluation and possible revision of certain SLAs would be more effective than changing vendors.
3. The competitive environment in the telecommunications industry had been changing over the past few years. Right after the 1996 Telecommunications Act was passed, there were a slew of new telecom companies eager to gain entry into the market who were bidding for contracts at very low prices. This had put downward pressures on pricing in the entire industry and had made outsourcing a lot more attractive strictly from a standpoint of cost (versus the quality of service). There had ben a drastic shakeout in the market since that time, and many of the smaller competitive local exchange carriers (CLECs) had gone out of business. This gave the remaining telecom companies, including the incumbent giants such as AT&T, MCI, Verizon, and SBC, slightly more breathing room as far as pricing was concerned. In fact, Bill had read in a recent *Wall Street Journal* article that the telecommunications industry, as well as a number of other industries, had become more oligopolistic as smaller companies dropped out or companies of all sizes had begun to merge. One statistic cited in the article was that at the end of 2000, there were 330 CLECs challenging the incumbent companies such as Verizon and SBC. A year later, only 150 of them were left.[32] Therefore, the number of alternative vendors and their cost differential were a lot smaller today than they were a few years ago.

Shortly after Bill's staff announced to AT&T that the contract would be continued, he got a call from AT&T's senior account relationship manager for the Global Foods account.

"Hey, Bill, there's a fabulous new Asian-French restaurant that has just opened up downtown. The chef is actually featured on the Food Channel. I'd love to take you and your entire staff there to try out the food, which I understand is fabulous."

"That's really nice of you," Bill responded. "But to be honest, I'm on a diet. Maybe some other time."

SUMMARY

We illustrate specifically how various business decisions can be influenced by government involvement in the market economy. As we discuss in chapter 1, the primary advantage of the market process over the command and traditional processes is the efficient manner in which market participants allocate a country's scarce resources. Throughout this text, we try to show how managers, equipped with an understanding of the major factors of the market process (supply, demand, production, cost, and competition) and various quantitative tools of analysis are able to make optimal decisions to help their firms maximize economic profit.

___

[32]"Oligopolies Are on the Rise . . . " The situation and solution are completely fictitious, but interestingly enough, in early 2005 SBC announced its intention to buy AT&T. Shortly afterward, Verizon bid for MCI.

However, managers must often take government involvement into account in the making of an optimal decision. This is particularly true when managers operate on a global basis and must deal with the laws and regulations of different governments. A case in point is the failed attempt by GE to merge with Honeywell discussed in this chapter's "Global Application." Government laws and regulations can reduce a firm's profits. But at the same time, as we show, the government itself is a major customer and so businesses can profit by being suppliers to the government's demand for various goods and services. Today's manager must be equally versed in matters of government and private industry.

IMPORTANT CONCEPTS

Benefit externalities: Benefits that accrue to individuals other than those who have paid for a particular good or service, also referred to as *positive benefits, spillover benefits, third-party benefits,* and *social benefits.* The demand for products with external benefits tends to be understated in the market. (p. 525)

Coase theorem: The idea, developed by Ronald Coase, that government intervention to eliminate the effect of externalities is not necessary if property rights are correctly and clearly defined. (p. 526)

Cost externalities: Costs incurred by individuals other than those who produce a particular good or service, also referred to as *negative costs, spillover*

costs, and *social costs.* The supply of goods whose production involves cost externalities tends to be overstated in the market. A good example of cost externalities is environmental pollution. (p. 525)

Monopsony: A market in which there is only one buyer. The government procurement office is often cited as a good example of a monopsony. (p. 529)

Natural monopoly: An industry in which a single large firm can serve customers more efficiently than many smaller ones because of economies of scale. (p. 521)

Socially optimal price: The price of a good or service that is equal to its marginal cost of production. (p. 526)

QUESTIONS

1. What is the rationale for government involvement in the market economy? (Cite the five points presented at the outset of this chapter.)
2. Define *benefit* and *cost externalities.* Explain why situations involving benefit externalities tend to result in an underallocation of society's scarce resources, and why situations involving cost externalities tend to result in an overallocation of society's scarce resources.
3. What is the role of government in dealing with benefit externalities? With cost externalities?
4. Suppose a chemical company was fined for violating certain antipollution laws. As the spokesperson for the Environmental Protection Agency, how would you explain the economic reasons for these actions to angry customers of this company who were forced to pay more for the chemicals as a result of this government action?
5. "The reason the government has to step in and 'internalize' benefit and cost externalities is because people are basically selfish." Do you agree with this statement? Explain.
6. Briefly discuss the Coase theorem. What does this theory imply about the role of government in dealing with market externalities?
7. Based on the competitive challenges that Microsoft faces from Google, do you think it still has "monopoly powers"? Explain.
8. Discuss the economic justification for a merger. In particular, how might these reasons apply to companies now merging in the following industries: oil, automobiles, telecommunications, electric power, and commercial banks?

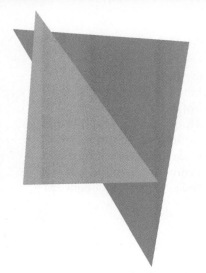

Chapter 15

Managerial Economics in Action[1]

The Case of the Refreshment Beverage Industry[2]

Learning Objectives

Upon completion of this chapter, readers should be able to:

- Describe the market structure of the beverage industry and cite the main factors that affect the degree of competitiveness in this industry.

- Cite specific ways that the activities in the beverage industry illustrate the major economic concepts presented in this text (e.g., supply and demand, cost function, production function, forecasting).

- Cite ways that the activities involved in creating an annual plan in the beverage industry illustrate the major economic concepts presented in this text.

- Describe the "changing economics" of the soft drink industry and explain how Coca-Cola, Inc. and PepsiCo, Inc. have adjusted their strategy in the beverage market accordingly.

The Situation

Amy Roberts, newly appointed brand manager of Spritz soda, one of Global Foods' most recent acquisitions, was wrapping up her status meeting with her boss, Fred Duchesne. The last item on her update list was the most important—it was time to begin Spritz's annual business plan for the upcoming fiscal year.

"As you know, Amy, Spritz has been in the market for over a decade, well before Global Foods bought us out. We have been a steady cash cow until recently. It's a solid brand but over the past 2 years we have seen a gradual decline of both sales and market share," Fred explained. "That's why we have hired you. Even though you're new to this industry, you have a proven record of using your marketing skills to turn things around at your former company. We figured that

(continued)

---

[1]The authors are very grateful to Amy Roman, who co-authored this chapter. She also conducted the interviews with beverage industry executives (see Appendix 15A) and did most of the background research for this chapter. Moreover, the details about the planning process are based on her considerable experience as a senior product manager for several global businesses in the consumer goods and health care industries.
[2]The term *refreshment beverage* is commonly used in the industry to describe nonalcoholic drinks.

(continued)

if you could increase sales in soap, you could do it in soft drinks (chuckle). But seriously, we have to find a way to reignite top-line growth while maintaining the brand's profit margin. In other words, I want Spritz to demonstrate *profitable growth.*[3] I'm getting a lot of pressure from Bob Burns [recall CEO Bob Burns from chapter 1's Situation] himself to turn this brand around. There are rumblings at the board level that maybe Spritz is another Quaker Oats–Snapple story.[4] We certainly don't want the stock analysts thinking this."

Amy was certainly motivated by the task her new boss had given her, although she realized it wouldn't be easy. To begin with, she had a lot of catching up to do on understanding the soft drink business. To be sure, soap and beverages are in the general category of personal consumables.[5] But every product has its own unique characteristics. She would first do an industry review, including an analysis of trends and the competitive landscape, and then she'd work out her business plan. This meant more than just a few sleepless nights. But she looked forward to the challenge.

INTRODUCTION

As we state in chapter 1 of this text, microeconomics is about the study of how scarce resources are allocated among competing uses. Managerial economics is essentially the study of how managers go about making choices regarding the allocation of scarce resources in the best interest of their firm. In making these choices, managers must decide on the answers to the questions listed as follows in abridged form:

1. What are the economic conditions in a particular market in which we are or could be competing? In particular,
   a. Market structure
   b. Supply and demand condition
   c. Technology
   d. Government regulations
   e. International dimensions
   f. Future conditions
   g. Macroeconomic factors
2. Should we be in this business?
3. If so, what price and output levels should we set in order to maximize our economic profit or minimize our losses in the short run?
4. How can we organize and invest in our resources (land, labor, capital, managerial skills) in such a way that we maintain a competitive advantage over other firms in this market?
   a. Cost leader?
   b. Product differentiation?
   c. Focus on market niche?
   d. Outsourcing, alliances, mergers, acquisitions?
   e. International dimension—regional or country focus or expansion?
5. What are the risks involved?

---

[3]The term *profitable growth* is a commonly used expression in business. Conduct a Google search and you will find numerous books and articles using this term. There is even a consulting company named Profitable Growth Partners.
[4]Refers to the famous case in which Quaker Oats bought Snapple in 1994 for $1.7 billion. When combined with its Gatorade sports drink, this acquisition catapulted Quaker Oats to the third largest producer of noncarbonated refreshment beverages, behind PepsiCo and Coca-Cola, Inc. Unfortunately, Quaker did not manage its star acquisition very well and ended up selling it to Triac Companies, Inc. for $300 million only 3 years later.
[5]In Europe, particularly in the United Kingdom, marketing managers like to use the acronym "FMCG" ("fast moving consumer goods") for this type of market.

The basic premise of this text is that economic concepts and tools of analysis help managers to find answers to these questions that are in the best interest of their firms.

Standard & Poor's produces a series of *Industry Surveys* that we consider one of the best sources of independent and objective information about the major industry groups evaluated by stock analysts. The S&P's industry category that most closely relates to our Global Foods is "Food and Non-Alcoholic Beverages." This is using actual industry information to help summarize what we have been trying to show throughout this text with our hypothetical "Situations" and "Solutions": Economic tools and concepts can indeed help managers in the real world to analyze business problems and make sound business decisions. The comments and remarks that we have inserted in the following excerpt from the S&P survey of the food and nonalcoholic beverage industry will help you recall some of the key concepts that we have discussed throughout the text.

ECONOMIC OVERVIEW OF THE INDUSTRY[6]

Industry Trends

Food, Beverage Companies Go Healthy

With rising commodity prices and a shift in consumer preferences, U.S. food and beverage companies face a challenging environment. In response, we see businesses continuing to focus on cost reductions and the introduction of healthier offerings. At the same time, companies are supporting their brands with increased marketing expenditures and are pursuing growth opportunities in developing overseas markets, such as Russia, China, and India.

> *Comment:* How do these two factors, rising commodity prices and a shift in consumer preferences, affect the supply and demand for food and beverages? It is interesting to note the responses that firms must take in response to these shifts. An important part of this response is the continuing expansion into global markets.
>
> *Reference:* Review chapter 3, "Supply and Demand," chapter 7, "The Theory and Estimation of Cost," and chapter 13, "The Multinational Corporation and Globalization."

Prices Are Rising

The U.S. Department of Agriculture reported that in October 2007, its index for crop prices was up 31 percent from the year-ago level, including sharp increases for food grains (62 percent), oil-bearing crops (55 percent), and commercial vegetables (56 percent). Food grains obviously have a bearing on various baked goods, while oil crops, such as soybeans, are used in a variety of applications. Corn prices soared during 2006 and early 2007, reaching more than $4 a bushel in some markets, compared to a typical price of less than $3 between 1999 and 2005. In part, we believe this was due to growing demand for corn in the production of ethanol, which is an alternative fuel. However, in 2007, as U.S. farmers saw recent market prices at high levels, they sharply increased the amount of acreage targeted for corn production. We believe this has contributed to a recent decline in corn prices. In early November 2007, the cash

---

[6]Information from *Industry Surveys: Standard & Poor's,* December 4, 2007, pp. 1–7.

price had dropped back to about $3.60 per bushel, which was still about 9 percent above where it was one year earlier. Corn prices have an impact on various parts of the production chain for both foods and beverages, as corn is utilized in such areas as feed for meat-producing farm animals and in high fructose corn syrup for soft drinks.

> *Comment:* This is a good example of a "long run" or "guiding function" of price. Over time, producers respond to higher prices by shifting their resources into the market with relative higher prices. Also notice the repercussion that higher corn prices have on the cost of food and beverages.
>
> *Reference:* Chapter 3, "Supply and Demand," and chapter 7, "The Theory and Estimation of Cost."

Meanwhile, the October 2007 meat price index was flat compared to a year ago, and chicken (broiler) prices were up only about 8 percent. However, the price of dairy products had surged, with its index up 56 percent from the year-ago level. We have seen dairy prices putting pressure on production costs for items such as cheese and chocolate. While commodity costs tend to be a relatively small part of the overall price paid by consumers for food, increases of a high magnitude can still be significant for food manufacturers. Although they can lock in some future costs through advance purchases, we believe that it has become increasingly important for manufacturers to reduce other costs or to raise prices to customers in order to offset commodity cost pressure and be able to maintain profit margins.

In the second half of 2007, we believe that input cost pressure (largely commodities) on various food manufacturers has accelerated. In some cases, the manufacturers have not fully offset the input cost pressure by raising prices or reducing other expenses. Overall, we believe that increases in farm prices have been running ahead of the prices charged by manufacturers, which, in turn, have increased more than food prices at the retail level. In the first half of 2008, we expect to see a catch-up effect in some categories, with more of the commodity cost increases showing up in the price tags that consumers see in the store.

> *Comment:* Regardless of the type of market, firms must try to reduce costs when demand and prices for their product fall. However, their ability to pass on higher costs by increasing their output prices depends on the type of market they are competing in. The greater the competition, the more difficult is to raise prices. What does this tell you about the nature of competition in the food and beverage market?
>
> *Reference:* Chapter 3, "Supply and Demand," chapter 8, "Pricing and Output Decisions: Perfect Competition and Monopoly," and chapter 9, "Pricing and Output Decisions: Monopolistic Competition and Oligopoly."

In November 2007, the USDA was forecasting that overall consumer food prices would rise 3.0 percent to 4.0 percent in 2008, down modestly from the 3.5 percent to 4.5 percent increase forecast for 2007. More specifically, upward pricing pressure on meats, poultry, fish and seafood, and dairy products was expected to ease in 2008, and the price of eggs was forecast to decline modestly after a sharp expected rise in 2007. However, the USDA forecasts that price increases for fresh vegetables, fats and oils, and cereals and bakery products will accelerate in 2008.

In 2007, we expect that a shift of farmers toward planting more corn acreage has reduced the amount of land allotted to other crops such as soybeans and wheat. We believe that this contributed to sharply higher farm prices for wheat and soybeans in the latter part of 2007. With some commodities, we expect higher prices are also due partly to increased demand from foreign markets.

> *Comment:* This is a good example of how analysts utilize the determinants of supply and demand to forecast market prices.
>
> *Reference:* Chapter 3, "Supply and Demand," and chapter 5, "Demand Estimation and Forecasting."

Restructuring Programs Implemented

During the past decade, in an effort to bolster profits, we have seen various companies implement restructuring programs, which included such initiatives as plant closings (consolidations) and workforce reductions. In our view, publicly owned companies face particular pressure to grow their profits as a way to potentially boost their stock price and please shareholders. At H.J. Heinz Co., for example, we believe that criticism from a shareholder group contributed to the initiation and/or magnitude of a major growth and cost reduction plan that Heinz announced in June 2006.

Corporate cost reduction programs are focusing on a variety of areas. We have seen a particular emphasis on what are called supply chain improvements—more efficient or less costly ways of getting products to customers. This can range from centralized, more economical purchasing of commodities to better utilization of manufacturing plants.

> *Comment:* This is a good example of how and why companies use improvements in supply chain management to reduce their costs.
>
> *Reference:* Chapter 6, "The Theory and Estimation of Production."

Aiming at Healthier Consumption

Food and beverage companies are adjusting to changing consumer preferences, many of which relate to a desire for healthier consumption. With an aging population in the United States, we anticipate that wellness and nutritional concerns will be taking on an increasingly prominent role in decisions related to product formulations and introductions. We see a growing overlap between the food and health care industries, as consumers and companies are increasingly looking at the impact that food and beverages can have on health. This includes efforts to make traditional products healthier through reformulations, as well as the introduction of new products that may offer such features as vitamin fortification or antioxidant ingredients to potentially combat disease or aging.

Reformulations may include reductions in the fat, sodium, or sugar content of a product, with obesity, high blood pressure, and diabetes being among the health-related concerns of consumers. To justify the investment in reformulations and new products, companies may need to inform or educate consumers about the prospective benefits. We see marketing and clear labeling of products as being increasingly important for such communication.

Also, we see food companies' interest in nutrition being reflected in industry acquisition activity, especially by a pair of large European businesses—Switzerland-based Nestlé S.A., which is the world's biggest food and beverage company, and

France's Groupe Danone SA, one of the world's largest dairy food producers. In July 2007, Nestlé bolstered its already sizable presence in the health care or wellness categories with a $2.5 billion purchase of Novartis Corp.'s medical nutrition business, which provides various tube and oral nutrition products and devices that are used in such settings as hospitals and nursing homes, and also independently by consumers at home. Meanwhile, Groupe Danone is seeking to acquire Dutch company Royal Numico NV for about $17.8 billion. Numico's products include infant milk formula and nutritional products or services for people with specific needs, such as conditions related to diseases or disorders.

We expect that food and beverage companies will be looking for new ways to meet consumers' health consciousness. In October 2007, the Coca-Cola Co. announced the opening of a research center at the China Academy of Chinese Medical Sciences, in Beijing, China. The research center is expected to focus on beverages using Chinese herbal ingredients and formulas.

Focus on Functional Foods

We see food and beverage companies increasingly focusing on what are sometimes called functional foods—nutraceuticals. These are products that are intended to provide added health benefits, such as lowering cholesterol, replacing vitamin deficiencies, or combating disease. We expect that a growing overlap between the food and beverage industry, the health care industry, and the cosmetics industry will continue, as scientists and product development teams discover new applications for various ingredients. However, as this occurs, we project that product labeling will become an increasingly important issue, and that new regulatory authority and standards may be needed to monitor, test, or approve new products.

Healthier Products in the Spotlight

We have seen various efforts to improve the healthiness of existing products. For example, in an effort to maintain taste while still cutting sodium, Campbell Soup Co. incorporated sea salt, which is naturally lower in sodium than table salt, into a number of products in August 2006. PepsiCo's Frito-Lay snack food unit eliminated trans fats from its snacks in 2002 and 2003 and began using sunflower oil in the production of all its potato chips, including Lay's and Ruffles, in May 2006. (Sunflower oil contains no trans fats and has 50 percent less saturated fat than other oils, according to the company.) Relatively new Frito-Lay products include Flat Earth fruit and vegetable crisps, which contain the equivalent of a half serving of fruit or vegetables in each ounce.

Ketchup-maker H.J. Heinz Co. has introduced additional versions of its flagship condiment, including organic and lower-sugar varieties. Kraft Foods, best known for its processed cheeses like Velveeta, has introduced meals and snacks based on the popular South Beach diet.

Companies are also trying to make it easier for consumers to identify healthful fare. Products such as Quaker Oats oatmeal and Baked Doritos chips carry PepsiCo's Smart Spot logo. Kraft's Sensible Solution logo is on foods such as Kraft light mayonnaise and 100-calorie packs of Lorna Doone cookies. To qualify for Kraft's Sensible Solution and PepsiCo's Smart Spot logo, products must contain a beneficial nutrient (e.g., fiber, protein, or calcium) or have low or reduced quantities of sugar, sodium, or fat. Manufacturers have found success with 100-calorie portions of snacks, which have proven popular with consumers looking to enjoy a treat without consuming too many calories. Kraft and PepsiCo have rolled out numerous versions, including 100-calorie bags of Chips Ahoy! cookies and Doritos chips.

To mitigate criticism leveled against food makers for the rising obesity rates in the United States, companies have raised the profile of their healthier products through advertising and new packaging. Companies have also supported restricting children's access to junk food in schools. In May 2006, the largest soft drink companies, including Coca-Cola Co., agreed to sell only water, juice, tea, and low-calorie drinks in elementary and middle schools in the United States starting in the 2008–09 school year. In October 2006, five major snack makers, including PepsiCo Inc., signed a pledge to provide schools with snacks that are more healthful. However, some critics want even stricter limitations on junk food. In April 2007, the Institute of Medicine of the National Academies, a nonprofit research organization, called for a ban on most junk foods in schools, including the sale of candy for fundraisers.

Organic Food Sales Jump

Consumers are also concerned about how their food is produced or grown. Organic foods, which are more likely to be produced by farmers who emphasize the use of renewable resources and soil and water conservation, are growing in popularity. To be considered organic, meat, poultry, and eggs must come from animals that are given no antibiotics or growth hormones. Organic produce is grown without conventional pesticides, bioengineering, or ionizing radiation, and without the use of fertilizers that contain synthetic ingredients or sewage sludge.

In 2002, the US Department of Agriculture (USDA) allowed food makers to label goods as "USDA-Organic" if they contain 95 percent to 100 percent organic ingredients. Foods that contain at least 70 percent organic ingredients can indicate that they contain organic ingredients. Use of the USDA-Organic seal on products is voluntary. Based on retail estimates from the Organic Trade Association (OTA), we expect that organic food sales in the United States are growing about 20 percent annually and account for perhaps 3 percent of all food and beverage sales.

In response to consumer demand, we believe that supermarkets are bolstering their lineups of organic foods. Wal-Mart Stores Inc., the world's largest retailer and one of the largest supermarket operators in the United States, began selling organic produce in its stores in 2006. Many of the large food companies offer organic foods under smaller brands. General Mills, Inc. owns the Cascadian Farm and Muir Glen labels; Kellogg Co. has the Kashi brand; and Kraft Foods owns the Boca and Back to Nature brands. Large food makers also have rolled out organic versions of some of their best-known products. For example, Campbell offers organic V8 juice, while Kraft sells organic macaroni and cheese.

Some companies have built themselves with a major emphasis on organic or "natural foods." (Keep in mind that "natural" lacks the USDA definition and certification of "organic.") For example, The Hain Celestial Group Inc., which has grown partly through acquisitions, had sales of $900 million in the fiscal year ended June 2007. Hain Celestial is represented in various natural or organic food or beverage categories with brands that include Celestial Seasonings, Terra Chips, Garden of Eatin', and Earth's Best. Hain Celestial has increasingly moved into the personal care area, where its brands include Jason, Avalon Organic Botanicals, and Alba Botanica. Organic or alternative products have been a growth driver for Dean Foods, the largest U.S. processor and distributor of milk and other dairy products. Dean's product line includes Horizon Organic dairy products, as well as the Silk Soymilk business. With regard to organic milk, after an earlier period of industry shortage, many dairy farms recently rushed to convert to organic operation before the imposition of new, more stringent U.S. government regulations in June 2007. This has led to a sharp increase in organic milk supply, which, we believe, has led to heightened competition among suppliers. In October 2007, Dean Foods said that it expected organic milk oversupply to continue to hurt results for the balance of 2007 and into at least the first half of 2008.

Meet the "Localvores"

In addition to an increasing interest in organic or natural foods, we have seen a growing emphasis among both retailers and consumers in locally produced products, which offer such potential advantages as freshness; lower transportation costs and related fuel usage; and support for the local economy. People buying food from close to home may be known as "localvores." We see the appeal of locally grown food reflected in a group of people that has focused on only buying or gathering food from within 100 miles of where they live.

According to the Web site 100milediet.org, Canadians James MacKinnon and Alisa Smith started an experiment in 2005, aiming to spend one year basing their food and beverage choices on this geographic restriction. Subsequently, the Web site says, dozens of other groups or individuals have embarked on similar programs aimed at locally available food. The two founders indicate on the Web site that they have largely stayed with locally produced food. However, they acknowledge that some "long-distance favorites" have returned to their cupboard, such as chocolate and beer. For most consumers, the food supply chain includes substantial amounts of transportation. For North American consumers, according to 100milediet.org, food ingredients typically travel 1,500 miles en route to the dinner table.

We see the interest in local foods as partly resulting from increased concerns about preserving the environment. This includes encouraging the protection of renewable resources and the reduction of carbon-based fuels usage. In our view, both individuals and businesses are participating in a "going green" movement, which is part of being a good global citizen.

Changing Population Mix

We also see food tastes being influenced by changing U.S. demographics. We believe that the growing variety of foods and flavors found in grocery stores and restaurants is partly due to increases in the portion of the population that has Hispanic or Asian roots. In areas with a significant or growing Muslim population, food companies may increasingly seek to provide products deemed halal (Islamically permissible). Looking ahead, we expect that an aging U.S. population, with its growing concern about health, is likely to shift its food intake toward fruits, vegetables, and fish, and away from some fried foods, dairy products, and items that contain large amounts of sugar.

Growing Concern about Food Safety and the Environment

Due to various factors, we see increasing concern about the safety of the U.S. food supply. A number of foods have been affected by product recalls, related to such health concerns as *E. coli* bacteria (beef) and salmonella. In addition, we expect increased wariness about the quality of foods coming from overseas, especially following problems with imported pet food in 2007.

In November 2007, according to the *Wall Street Journal*, the Bush administration was seeking new regulatory measures to ensure the safety of imports. If a plan were implemented, it would potentially create a stronger emphasis on the prevention of food safety problems related to imported goods. This could include requirements that producers and importers comply with federal standards. However, the adoption of new federal authority over imported products may require congressional approval.

Companies Look Overseas for Growth

With considerable competition in the relatively mature U.S. food market and limited population growth expected, major food manufacturers are turning to the emerging markets of Eastern Europe and Asia. The economies of both regions are growing quickly as consumer incomes rise and countries in these regions increasingly participate in world trade. In addition, the pervasiveness of electronic media, especially Western media, is making overseas consumers more aware of Western tastes and products.

Economic gains should be particularly dramatic in Asia. By 2030, more than 600 million people in East Asia will earn enough to be considered middle class, up from just over 100 million in 2000, according to a World Bank estimate. In addition, with the U.S. dollar weak against worldwide currencies, including the euro, overseas sales translate into bigger revenues for U.S. companies when they are converted into U.S. dollars. More supermarkets and hypermarkets are opening in Asia, increasing the likelihood that consumers will buy packaged foods and beverages. Over time, we expect that larger format chain stores will increasingly take market share away from smaller, "traditional" shops, similar to trends in the United States.

We expect that demand for packaged goods in emerging markets will be influenced by an increasing availability of refrigeration and other types of storage space in homes. However, for consumers lacking the ability to preserve and keep larger quantities, U.S. companies can look to sell smaller packages, whose portions can be consumed more quickly.

Large U.S. packaged foods companies continue to look overseas for growth. For example, in July 2007, Campbell presented an entry strategy and product plans for Russia and China, which it said are the world's two largest soup consumption markets. According to the company, soup consumption in Russia and China far exceeds that in the United States on an overall and a per capita basis. However, Campbell says that in both Russia and China, nearly all of the soup consumed is homemade. To deal with this and to change consumer behavior, the company said that that it would introduce both products that can be used as the foundation for local recipes. In both markets, Campbell was expected to have a distribution partner that already has a considerable presence there.

In some food categories, the magnitude of China's food consumption is huge. In September 2005, the USDA said that China, with a population of 1.3 billion, consumes 51 percent of the world's pork production, 33 percent of its rice, and 19 percent of both ice cream and poultry production. The USDA said that only 30 percent of food consumption in China was processed products (versus 80 percent in Western countries). However, the market for processed foods was growing, especially in urban areas, where busy consumers were seeking some of the same features (e.g., convenience, healthier choices, variety, and quality) that are valued in the United States.

Overseas markets are still areas of growth for the big beverage companies. In 2007's third quarter, PepsiCo's overall international revenue (excluding Canada) was up 22 percent, year to year, and profits increased 19 percent, helped by strong snacks and beverage growth. Roughly 13 percentage points of the revenue growth came from either currency fluctuations or the net impact of acquisitions and divestitures. PepsiCo said that its international beverage volume was up 8 percent, led by double-digit growth in Pakistan, China, the Middle East, and Russia. Carbonated soft drink volume grew at a high single-digit rate, compared to a 3 percent decline in North America.

U.S. Agricultural Trade on the Rise

The dollar value of U.S. agricultural trade has risen sharply in recent years, which we believe is partly due to rapid growth in some overseas economies and consumers' interest in expanding the variety of their diets. According to the USDA, in the 11 months ended August 2007, the value of U.S. agricultural exports totaled $74.3 billion, up 19 percent from the year-ago level. Meanwhile, the value of such imports was up 9.5 percent, to $64.6 billion. On a calendar-year basis, U.S. agricultural exports totaled $70.9 billion in 2006, up 19 percent from three years earlier, while imports amounted to $65.3 billion, up 38 percent from what they were in 2003. The significance of Asia in world trade is indicated by agricultural imports for China, which totaled an estimated $30.6 billion in 2006, while agricultural exports totaled $20.9 billion, according to the USDA. From the United States, agricultural exports to China totaled $6.7 billion in 2006, compared to $2.3 billion of imports from China to the United States.

Changing Consumer Preferences

For the last several years, carbonated soft drinks (CSDs) have been losing market share to bottled water and other beverages such as sports drinks. In our view, consumers are turning away from traditional sodas because of health concerns as well as an interest in some added features that other drinks provide such as the addition of vitamins and new flavors. Even diet soda, which was previously more of a growth category, saw relatively flat sales. Smaller beverage companies have found success with products that are either unique or have caught consumers' fancy. For example, privately owned Energy Brands Inc. (also known as Glacéau) introduced its vitaminwater brand of "enhanced" water in 1996. The colorful beverages come in clear plastic containers and blend water with vitamins and minerals in varieties including "endurance," which includes vitamin E, and "revive," which has potassium and B vitamins. Glacéau's success with this and other products did not go unnoticed by its larger rivals. In June 2007, Coca-Cola acquired the company for about $4.1 billion.

Meanwhile, Hansen Natural Corp., which makes fruit-flavored sodas, ready-to drink teas, and energy drinks such as Monster Energy, had a year-to-year revenue increase of 74 percent in 2006, to $606 million. In 2007's first nine months, the company's revenue was up 43 percent from the year-ago level.

Coca-Cola and PepsiCo have already acquired a string of smaller beverage firms. In September 2006, PepsiCo purchased IZZE Beverage Co., a maker of sparkling fruit juices. Drinking eight ounces of Izze provides one serving of fruit, according to Pepsi. The company bought Naked Juice, a maker of juices and fruit smoothies that contain no added sugar or preservatives, in January 2006. Coca-Cola bought Fuze, which produces juices and teas infused with vitamins, in March 2006. Terms of the deals were not disclosed.

The largest beverage companies are also trying to get a piece of the alternative beverage action with their own products. In March 2006, PepsiCo's SoBe unit unveiled SoBe Life Water, which offers vitamins C and E, as well as B complex vitamins. In January 2007, Coca-Cola and partner Nestlé SA introduced Enviga, a green-tea drink containing caffeine that Coca-Cola claimed would burn calories.

Still, the beverage makers have not completely given up on carbonated beverages. Coca-Cola has scored a success with its Coke Zero, a diet soda formulated to taste similar to regular Coke. Introduced in late 2005, the soda is the "most successful launch in 20 years," said Coca-Cola CEO Neville Isdell in April 2007. In 2006, Coke Zero had a 0.5 percent market share, according to Beverage Digest's Fact Book 2007. Also, in April 2007, sales began of Diet Coke Plus, a diet soda with added vitamins and minerals. Meanwhile, Pepsi is offering Diet Pepsi Max, with more caffeine than regular Diet Pepsi. Pepsi Max is targeted at soda drinkers aged 25 to 34 who are looking for extra energy to get through busy days.

Comment: This section provides good examples of how actual companies respond to changing market conditions. We provide similar examples, both real and hypothetical, in the "Situation" and "Solution."

Reference: Chapter 9, "Pricing and Output Decisions: Monopolistic Competition and Oligopoly," and chapter 15, "Managerial Economics: The Case of the Food and Nonalcoholic Beverage Industry."

ANALYSIS OF THE REFRESHMENT BEVERAGE INDUSTRY

Americans spend around $100 billion on refreshment beverages every year.[7] Table 15.1 shows the breakdown of the industry by major product category. As you can see, there are a variety of nonalcoholic beverages, including carbonated soft drinks, bottled water, fruit beverages, sports drinks, energy drinks and ready-to-drink (RTD) coffee and tea.[8]

The refreshment beverage industry in the United States is relatively mature and is growing at about a rate that is roughly half the rate of growth of nominal GDP. In such mature markets, companies have to grow either by introducing new products or by acquisition. Both activities have been important to this industry.[9] But without acquisitions, each company's organic growth[10] in a mature market must essentially be done at the expense of its competitors. And if this market is very large, then even small shifts in market share can result in considerable gains or losses. In the case of the $100 billion U.S. refreshment beverage industry, half "a point" market share (1/2 of 1 percent) equals about $500 million in sales. Interestingly enough, those in the beverage industry assume that each person can only consume a certain amount of liquid per day regardless of the type (water, milk, beer, coffee, etc.). So sometimes you will hear industry people refer to market share as "share of stomach." In any case, let us elaborate briefly on the top beverages: carbonated soft drinks (CSDs) and bottled water.

Carbonated Soft Drinks (CSDs)

Until the beginning of this decade, CSDs were the unchallenged leader of the industry. However, their dominance has been offset by the emergence of bottled water. Over the past decade, per capita consumption of CSDs in the United States has been falling, because consumers have been switching to bottled water as well as to the other non-CSDs

Table 15.1   U.S. Liquid Refreshment Beverage Market Volume by Segment 2005–6

| | MMs of Gallons | | % Chg | Share of Volume | |
Segment	2005	2006	05/06	2005	2006
CSDs	15,271.6	15,103.6	−1.1%	52.9%	50.9%
Bottled water	7537.1	8253.1	9.5%	26.1%	27.8%
Fruit beverages	4119.0	4020.1	−2.4%	14.3%	13.5%
Sports drinks	1207.5	1348.8	11.7%	4.2%	4.5%
RTD tea	555.9	701.5	26.2%	1.9%	2.4%
Energy drinks	152.5	227.4	49.1%	0.5%	0.8%
RTD coffee	38.9	43.0	10.4%	0.1%	0.1%
TOTAL	28,882.5	29,697.6	2.8%	100%	100%

Source: *Beverage Marketing Corporation Reports*, March 8, 2007. Reprinted with permission from Beverage Marketing Corporation, 850 Third Avenue, 18th Floor, New York, NY 10022. www.beveragemarketing.com

---

[7]The American Beverage Association reported $92.9 billion of spending in 2004 for this product sector. See Beverage Industry Basics (http://www.ameribev.org).

[8]RTD coffee and tea are very popular in Asia and have started to gain market share in the United States. Vending machines in Asia, particularly in Japan, have a tremendous variety of coffees and teas in cans available for purchase.

[9]It was this rapid growth that helped to give the authors the idea of Global Foods and its move to enter the carbonated soft drink market. This "Situation," spelled out in chapter 1, is the same situation that we presented in the very first edition of this text. (See Paul Keat and Philip Young, *Managerial Economics: Economic Decisions for Today's Decision Makers*, Prentice-Hall, 1992, 1st ed., chapter 1.)

[10]*Organic growth* is a commonly used term to describe a company's growth in revenue, not including any revenue growth from acquired companies.

Table 15.2   CSDs Volume, Growth, and Per Capita Consumption, 1999–2005

Year	MMs of Cases*	% Chg	Gal per capita
1998	N/A		54.9
1999	9,953.3	–	54.8
2000	10,003.3	0.5	54.5
2001	10,053.3	0.5	54.3
2002	10,134.7	0.8	54.2
2003	10,172.3	0.4	53.8
2004	10,244.8	0.7	53.7
2005	10,183.3	−0.6	52.9

I case is equal to 192 fluid oz. of product.

Source: *Beverage Marketing Corporation Reports,* March 8, 2007. Reprinted with permission from Beverage Marketing Corporation, 850 Third Avenue, 18th Floor, New York, NY 10022. www.beveragemarketing.com

shown in Table 15.1. Table 15.2 shows per capita consumption steadily declined from 54.9 gallons in 1998 to 52.9 gallons in 2005. Total consumption, measured in millions of cases, rose throughout this period because of the increase in the population of consumers. But by 2005, even this figure fell. Incidentally, just to give an idea of the magnitude of these figures, regardless of their direction of change, consider this: Based on the conversion ratio of 128 fluid oz. to 1 gallon, we figure that the per capita consumption of carbonated soft drinks in the United States is easily over 560 12-oz can equivalents per year.[11]

Within the CSD category, diet soft drinks are the most important segment. This subcategory comprises almost 30 percent of total CSD volume. In recent years, diet CSD has been a bright spot in the general product category. However, in 2005, even the sales of the leading diet colas suffered. During that year, Diet Coke's sales were flat and Diet Pepsi fell by 1.9 percent. As a result, total sales in the entire category fell by six-tenths of a percent (see Table 15.2).

The leading CSD brands and their corporate owners are shown in Table 15.3. Although the general market is made up of approximately 3,000 companies, there has been strong consolidations, mainly through the acquisition of noncola brands and smaller-niche companies by the two dominant companies: Coca-Cola and PepsiCo.[12] When added to their already dominant sizes, particularly in CSDs, these acquisitions have helped both companies to continue to hold more than 50 percent of the total market share of refreshment beverages and to maintain their brands within the top 10 in the industry. Cadbury Schweppes, the number 3 player, is the only other company to have a brand in the top 10. Only a few other companies have annual revenues in excess of $500 million and the rest are local or regional players with annual revenues less than $100 million (www.marketresearch.com).

Bottled Water

This category became the second largest segment in 2003 and has exhibited strong growth since then.[13] In the glowing words of this product's trade journal, *Bottled Water*

---

[11]Of course, per capita includes every man, woman, and child. Some people do not consume or consume very few carbonated soft drinks. Therefore, this implies a larger amount of soft drinks consumed per day among the regular users of this product.

[12]Acquisitions have been going on for some time. Coca-Cola bought the Minute Maid Company way back in 1960. Pepsi-Cola bought Tropicana from Seagram's in 1998. More recent examples of acquisitions are cited by Coke and Pepsi executives in their interviews presented in this chapter's appendix.

[13]Global Foods entered the bottled water market in the previous edition of this text.

Table 15.3   Leading Liquid Refreshment Beverage Trademarks in the United States[*] 2005–6

		MMs of Gal		% Chg	Share of Volume	
Brand	Company	2005	2006	05/06	2005	2006
Coca-Cola	Coca-Cola	4848.2	4727.0	−2.5%	16.8%	15.9%
Pepsi	PepsiCo	3125.0	3028.0	−3.1%	10.8%	10.2%
Mountain Dew	PepsiCo	1309.1	1324.8	1.2%	4.5%	4.5%
Dr Pepper	Cadbury Schweppes	1168.2	1193.6	2.2%	4.0%	4.0%
Gatorade	PepsiCo	958.0	1072.9	12.0%	3.3%	3.6%
Sprite	Coca-Cola	993.7	958.6	−3.5%	3.4%	3.2%
Tropicana[**]	PepsiCo	706.1	778.8	10.3%	2.4%	2.6%
Minute Maid[**]	Coca-Cola	672.0	614.9	−8.5%	2.3%	2.1%
Aquafina	PepsiCo	504.4	614.7	21.9%	1.7%	2.1%
Dasani	Coca-Cola	448.0	538.0	20.1%	1.6%	1.8%
All Others	–	14149.9	14846.2	4.9%	49.0%	50.0%
TOTAL		28882.5	29697.6	2.8%	100.0%	100.0%

[*]*Includes all trademark volume (e.g., all types of Coca-Cola, including Diet Coke, Caffeine-Free Coca-Cola, etc.)*
[**]*Includes both fruit beverages and carbonated soft drink volume*

Source: *Beverage Marketing Corporation Reports,* March 8, 2007. Reprinted with permission from Beverage Marketing Corporation, 850 Third Avenue, 18th Floor, New York, NY 10022. www.beveragemarketing.com

Reporter (April 2006), "US residents now drink more bottled water annually than any beverage other than CSDs. The gap between the two top categories is narrowing as bottled water ceaselessly advances and CSDs either barely grow or decline." Table 15.4 shows this trend.

Not surprisingly, it was the global food companies, Nestlé and Danone, that first helped to build the bottled water market in the United States when they launched their premium brands, Poland Spring and Evian, respectively. We say "not surprisingly," because all too often companies that dominate a market with highly successful products, as Coca-Cola and PepsiCo have with CSD, and orange juice are slow to recognize potential new consumer demand in other niches of the market. And so after

Table 15.4   U.S. Bottled Water Market Volume, Producer Revenues, and Per Capita Consumption Revenues, 2001–2005

	Volume		Revenues		Per Capita Consumption	
	MMS of Gallons	% chg	MMs of $	% chg	Gallons per Capita	% chg
2001	5185.3	–	6880.6	–	18.7	–
2002	5795.7	11.8	7901.4	14.8	20.7	10.8
2003	6269.8	8.2	8526.4	7.9	22.1	7.0
2004	6806.7	8.6	9169.5	7.5	23.8	7.6
2005	7357.1	10.7	10,012.5	9.2	26.1	9.6

Source: Beverage Marketing Corporation, information reprinted in *Bottled Water Reporter* (April 2006). Reprinted with permission from Beverage Marketing Corporation, 850 Third Avenue, 18th Floor, New York, NY 10022. www.beveragemarketing.com

Nestlé and Danone proved that there was indeed a good business to be had in bottled "spring water," Pepsi came up with the idea of a bottled water that was not spring water, but a highly filtered water that offered consumers the similar value of purity as well as convenience. Following PepsiCo's launch of Aquafina, Coca-Cola introduced its own competing filtered bottled water, Dasani.

Currently in the bottled water market, volume continues to grow but revenue growth is slowing due to the more widespread and increased frequency of price promotions. These price promotions were once confined to the West Coast, but have now spread throughout the rest of the country.[14] Fortunately for the industry, a segment of the market referred to as "enhanced water" has become an important part of this product category. Sales of this type of product have grown from virtually nothing in 1998 to over $300 million in 2003.[15] The leading brand in this segment is Pepsi's Propel, which is part of its Gatorade operation. Pepsi also has Aquafina Flavor Splash, Aquafina Alive, and SoBe Life Water. This last product is "vitamin-enhanced" water and was one of PepsiCo's recent acquisitions. Coca-Cola counters with its Dasani Flavored and Glacéau (one of its recently acquired brands).[16] Even the food companies have their versions. Kraft has Fruit$_2$O and Nestlé has Pure Life Flavored.

Manufacturing and Distribution

There are three basic forms of output in the beverage industry.

1. Concentrates: flavoring ingredients and possible sweeteners used to prepare finished syrups or beverages.
2. Syrups: the beverage ingredients produced by combing concentrates with sweeteners and water. Among this group, fountain syrups are sold to fountain retailers, such as restaurants, which use dispensing equipment to mix the syrups with sparkling or still water at the time of purchase for immediate consumption in cups or glasses.
3. Finished products: packaged products that are ready for immediate consumption.

The production of CSDs typically involves a two-tier process. In the first tier, a CSD manufacturer produces and sells concentrates and syrups to bottling companies. In the second step, these bottlers take the concentrate, add carbonation, package them in cans or plastic bottles and then distribute them to retail stores. A similar two-step process can be seen when the manufacturers produce syrups and then sell them to fountain wholesalers and fountain retailers.[17] Typically, only one step is required in the production of non-CSD beverages. In this case, the same company manufacturers and distributes the liquid refreshment.

Understanding the reasons behind the different tiers provides a fascinating insight into the industry's manufacturing process. For companies with huge production volume such as PepsiCo, Coca-Cola, and Cadbury Schweppes, the two-tiered structure is very cost-efficient. This is because the main ingredient, water, is expensive to ship and is readily available at local sources. Therefore, instead of shipping the finished product to locations all over the country (as well as all over the world), these large companies need only ship the concentrate. In turn, the local

---

[14]*Bottled Water Reporter,* April/May 2005.
[15]*Soft Drink International,* April 2005.
[16]One cannot help but notice the penchant in the industry for using Italian- and French-sounding names for bottled water.
[17]This activity is discussed in greater detail in our interviews with the executives from Coca-Cola and Pepsi-Cola presented in this chapter's appendix.

bottlers simply add the carbonated water, package the liquid, and then distribute the final product to local wholesale and retail stores. But there is a bit more to this than weight and cost. The bottling of CSDs is a fairly simple process and the global manufacturers feel confident that local bottlers can maintain the quality and continuity of supply of the final product (with the global companies' oversight, of course). In contrast, the making of CSD concentrate is usually more complicated and is therefore made by the global manufacturers themselves. The same can be said about non-CSD beverages. Therefore, both CSD concentrate and non-CSD beverages are typically bottled and distributed by the manufacturer rather than local bottlers.[18]

The relationship between manufacturers of CSD concentrate and the bottlers is solidified under a bottler agreement. This is a contract that designates the territory within which the bottler has the exclusive right to make, sell, and distribute the manufacturer's product. It is very important for manufacturers to maintain a good relationship with their bottlers. Manufacturers do not have direct control over the price that bottlers charge their customers. Moreover, a bottler may package and distribute products from competing brands. Therefore, although not required by contract, manufacturers of the concentrate often invest in the infrastructure and marketing of their bottlers in order to help increase their likelihood of success. Bottling is such an important part of the production process that some manufacturers may decide to have full or part ownership in a certain number of bottling facilities.

Competition

The type of competition that exists in the refreshment beverage industry depends on the level or focus of analysis. In the United States, if we start at the national level for all types of liquid refreshment beverages, then the market is clearly dominated by a handful of giant global beverage or food companies. (See Table 15.5.) We also showed in Table 15.3 that Coca-Cola and PepsiCo own 9 out of the top 10 brands of refreshment beverages. But keep in mind that the combined revenue of the top 5 companies in 2006 of about $28 billion is still only a little more than one-fourth of the total U.S. beverage market of about $100 billion. This implies that there are still independent bottlers and makers of niche beverage products in the marketplace.

Table 15.5   Top 5 U.S. Refreshment Beverage Companies, Estimated 2006 Revenues

	Estimated Revenues ($MM)
Pepsi-Cola NA	9565
Coca-Cola NA	7015
Cadbury Beverages NA	4525
Nestlé Waters Beverages	4180
Kraft Foods	3200
NA = North America	

Source: *Beverage Marketing Corporation Reports,* March 8, 2007. Reprinted with permission from Beverage Marketing Corporation, 850 Third Avenue, 18th Floor, New York, NY 10022. www.beveragemarketing.com

---

[18]The two-tier production process is explained in greater detail in Hoovers.com's description of the beverage industry.

Moreover, entry for additional newcomers is relatively easy. A good example of ease of entry by newcomers is the case of Nantucket Nectar, started back in 1985 by two graduates from Brown University. They became very successful and were eventually bought out by Cadbury Schweppes.[19] Therefore, we believe that the economic term that best describes this entire U.S. refreshment beverage market is *monopolistic competition.*

However, if we focus only on the firms that produce and sell carbonated soft drinks, then the market starts to look more like an oligopoly. If we further focused only on cola CSDs, the predominance of Coca-Cola and PepsiCo definitely makes this market an oligopoly and it could actually be considered, for all intents and purposes, a duopoly.[20] The competitive landscape differs somewhat outside the United States, but in general there are various types of competition just as there are in the United States, depending on the country, region, or market area.

Consumer Demand

In economic theory, consumers demand and so producers supply. In marketing, this is also the case, except that skilled marketers should also be able to figure out what consumers need or want, even if consumers themselves may not really know. Because of increasing health consciousness among American consumers, it is understandable why the demand for sweetened carbonated as well as noncarbonated beverages has been negatively affected and why Americans have steadily increased their demand for bottled water. However, do we really need so many different brands and types? A casual look at what is available in today's market shows spring water, triple filtered water, reverse osmosis water, vitamin enhanced water, diet colas with caffeine and ginseng, diet colas without caffeine, colas with fruit juice added, fruit juice with carbonation, fruit juice with herbal enhancements, and nutrient-enhanced sports drinks.

It is not our place to answer the question of whether consumers demand such an array of beverages first or whether the producers supply these products and then convince consumers to buy them. This is an ongoing debate. We simply point out that demand in the refreshment beverage market has been changing due to the "changing tastes and preferences" of consumers, and that producers have apparently responded by increasing the number and variety of different beverage products in order to satisfy these consumers. Firms that want to survive and grow in this highly competitive, mature market must be prepared to act accordingly.

Besides health concerns, another reason for changing consumer tastes and preferences in the U.S. refreshment beverage market is the changing lifestyles and patterns of work. According to industry analysts, this may have something to do with the current popularity of energy drinks. This segment is a booming, multi-billion-dollar market with a growth rate that outperformed all other categories in 2006, although they still make up only about 3 percent of the total retail volume of CSDs.[21] Most energy drinks have about the same amount of caffeine as coffee, so many people are now turning to these to start their day. And according to *Soft Drinks International,*

---

[19]According to Wikipedia, the two college friends, Tom First and Tom Scott, known as "Tom and Tom" or the "Juice Guys," are no longer involved in the day-to-day operations of the business.

[20]To review monopolistic competition and oligopoly, go back to the material covered in chapter 9. The term *duopoly* is used by economists to describe a market in which only two firms compete. Although there are Canadian-owned Cott Beverages, makers of RC Cola, and various private label colas (mostly bottled and distributed by Cott), Coke and Pepsi clearly dominate the CSD cola market in the United States as well as in the rest of the world. Pure duopolies can best be found in niche markets. For example, in the airline industry certain point-to-point routes have only two carriers.

[21]Find source from citation in original draft

"Although hip youths are the most visible targets of energy drink marketers, the beverages also appeal to overworked executives and truck drivers, among others."[22]

For beverage companies, energy drinks are not only an important source of incremental revenue, they are highly profitable as well. In 2007, the price of a 4-pack was selling for as much as $9.99. The category leader is Red Bull, established back in 1997. Examples of new entrants include SmartPower and Bombilla & Gourd's line of matés.[23]

The Solution: Spritz Soda's Annual Business Plan[24]

Introductory Note

The annual business plan is an important document that guides all brand-related activities over the next year including revenue and profit objectives, advertising and promotion programs, allocated R&D resources, and manufacturing schedules. Although the format may vary from company to company, it generally addresses these key issues:

1. Historical results and key lessons learned
   a. What is the brand's current business situation?
   b. What are the key factors that affect its rate of growth?
2. Goals and objectives
   a. Financial (e.g., increase revenue by 5 percent)
   b. Nonfinancial (e.g., develop closer ties with distributors)
3. Strategies and tactics to achieve objectives
4. Selection of key measures to monitor progress and assess performance
5. Risks
6. Opportunities not addressed by the plan

The product manager is responsible for developing the plan. This is often done by involving people from other functional areas of the business as well as the manager's own team. Following is a summary of Amy's business plan for Spritz Soda. As is the case in all previous chapters, the "Situation" and "Solution" are fictional but based on actual business examples and cases. Spritz Soda is not a real product, but the background information and the considerations and thoughts of Amy Roberts are based on actual business experience. Following is an abridged hypothetical version of a typical business plan, including parts of a five-year plan. An actual plan would have more detailed data.

Spritz Soda's Annual Business Plan (Assumed to Be Part of a 5-Year Plan)

1. Historical Results and Key Lessons Learned

a. The Brand's Current Situation
In order to plan for the brand's future, Amy knew she needed a solid understanding of its current situation and how it got there. Her first task was to assess key performance measures over the last five years. She would start with the big picture, the overall beverage category, and work her way down into key brand performance drivers. Based on the

(continued)

---

[22]*Soft Drinks International,* April 2005.
[23]*Beverage Digest,* April 17, 2007. Maté is a type of tea drink originating in Argentina. It was and continues to be a favorite drink among the Argentine cowboys in the Pampas.
[24]This "Solution" is considerably longer than those in the rest of the text because it incorporates concepts and terms that are related to managerial economics but are more commonly presented (in considerable detail) in marketing and strategy courses. Also, typically, product managers are responsible for a one-year plan. And very often, companies treat the one-year product plan as part of an overall long-term plan (usually five years) of the general product category. In this "Solution," we we assume that Amy has to do a one-year and a five-year plan for Spritz.

(continued)

information from the industry survey, Amy knew that overall consumer demand for beverages was relatively flat. But this was due mainly to CSDs' slight decline. Other categories such as enhanced bottled water have been experiencing rapid growth. She hypothesized that Spritz, as a traditional CSD product, was losing its "share of stomach" not to rival CSD brands but to bottled water and other new segments such as sports and energy drinks.

A closer look at the market indicated that growth of the bottled water segment was led by newcomer Drench[25]—a midpriced brand that did a significant amount of business in flavored waters. In the sports drink segment, Quench, a new brand that stressed that it contained energy-boosting ingredients such as ginseng and caffeine, was making some inroads against existing brands. Finally, in the energy drinks, YouthCola Boost, a product line extension of YouthCola and EnerMax, a new energy brand that boasted "twice the caffeine of other leading energy brands," showed significant increases. She noted that EnerMax was owned by one of Global Foods' main rivals in the beverage business.

b. Key Factors Affecting Spritz's Growth

Given the industry's current situation, Amy now needed to hone in on the key factors influencing these changes in consumer demand; that is, the nonprice determinants of demand. Fortunately, she was able to use a major study recently completed by a major consulting firm that her boss, Fred, had hired to provide more detailed information about Spritz's past performance. The report showed that overall brand awareness (how many consumers are aware of the brand) remained relatively strong for Spritz, but that there was slight decline among younger consumers (ages 18–29). The study also showed a decline in a marketing indicator referred to as BUMO or "Brand Used Most Often," particularly among those 18–29 years of age.[26] It was apparent that Spritz Soda's consumers were bringing new drinks into their core beverage repertoire.[27] Finally, trial figures (number of consumers trying your product for the first time) showed significant declines, particularly among this same category of younger consumers. Given this information, Spritz's lackluster performance was not hard for Amy to figure out. Simply put, the brand was falling out of favor among younger consumers. In addition to the demographic factor, Amy wanted to know the extent to which Spritz, like all other CSDs, was being hurt by the health and fitness trend. Unfortunately, there was nothing in the consultant's report that was able to tie this directly into declining sales of Spritz. However, she had no reason to believe that Spritz was any different from the other competing CSDs in this respect.

To gain further insight into the determinants of the demand for Spritz, Amy decided to investigate data on the various channels of distribution. What she found was a slight decline in the channel called "Food and Mass Merchandiser Stores" (FMMS) and an even more significant decline in the "Convenience" channel. She first looked at sales and pricing data in the FMMS and noticed that Spritz Soda's promotional dollar sales rose as prices were discounted but only up to the point of a 15 percent reduction. At discounts greater than 15 percent, the response by consumers in buying more units of product was apparently not enough to offset these price cuts. Hence, dollar sales actually fell when discounts of greater than 15 percent were offered. She recalled her managerial economics class and the professor's discussion about elasticity coefficients dropping below unity as price declined to a certain point and wondered if this had anything to do with it.[28] To learn more about why the drop in dollars sales was so dramatic in the convenience channel, Amy called the salesperson in charge of the convenience channel, Joe Simpson. In his conversation with Amy, Joe explained that Spritz was seen as a solid brand but one that was oriented toward the late 20s/early 30s age group. He further explained that the majority of the convenience channel beverage sales were driven by the younger age segment. He said his team was doing their best to promote Spritz sales but the convenience store buyers just didn't have the patience to wait for these promotions to increase the quantity demanded. Convenience stores have relatively limited floor and refrigeration space and they have to generate a very high turnover to cover the high rent that must obviously be paid for convenient locations. So they would much rather stock their shelves and refrigerators with the types of beverages that their main customers, young consumers, want the most.

(continued)

---

[25]In keeping with the spirit of our "Situations" and "Solutions," this brand and others cited in this section are fictional.

[26]This is a common measure (and acronym) of brand loyalty that is used by marketing professionals.

[27]See the interview with Coca-Cola executive Chris Lowe in the appendix. This is considered a vital indicator of consumer behavior in the refreshment beverage industry. What three or four beverages do *you* drink on a regular basis?

[28]Readers should review chapter 4 for a discussion of this topic.

(continued)

Finally, Amy looked at Spritz's financials over the past two years and was surprised by the decrease in gross profit margin. She decided to talk to Robert Rodriguez, the plant manager, to find out more about the situation. Robert explained that, due to the unit sales decline, Spritz lines were operating well below capacity. The plant's production process was as efficient as any plant of its type in the industry. He indicated that the average variable cost was in fact lower than the industry average. But the problem was that the decline in volume meant that the plant's fixed cost was being spread over a smaller number of units and this in effect increased the average total cost of production. Hence the rising cost of goods sold. This issue was exacerbated by the fact that declining volumes meant they qualified for fewer volume discounts from their suppliers and so material costs were also going up.[29]

After reading the consultant's report and talking to key people in the company, Amy was a bit discouraged. But she came across one section in the consultant's report that made her day. It was about a survey that the consultant had conducted on what the consumer marketing professionals call a "taste profile." When asked what they considered when shopping for a beverage, the consultant's survey revealed that most consumers listed *brand first,* followed by flavor/ingredients and finally type of drink (e.g., CSD vs. water vs. energy drink). In surveys conducted five years ago, the report noted that consumers said they shopped first for the type of drink, followed by brand, and then by flavor/ingredients. "Okay," she thought to herself, "I think I can still play the 'brand' card."

But before pursuing the implications of that survey, she decided to conduct a SWOT analysis of her brand's current situation. She and her team spent a full day doing so at an off-site location (she gave explicit orders to her team to put away their BlackBerries), and they came up with the following.[30]

SWOT Analysis of Spritz Soda

Strengths:

➤ Strong share position and among the top three "white soda" (the industry jargon for noncola) brands
➤ Strong brand awareness and loyalty among older consumers
➤ Potentially high operating profit margin

Weaknesses:

➤ Slow but steady decline of brand attractiveness among younger consumers
➤ Loss of distribution in some convenience chains due to poor fit of brand image
➤ Declining gross profit margin due to growing manufacturing inefficiencies

Opportunities:

➤ Room for new entrants in the growing water, sports, and energy drink segments
➤ Take advantage of growing consumer interest in health and wellness
➤ Solidify and regain distribution in the convenience channel

Threats:

➤ New product introductions in the water, sports, and energy drinks segments are sourcing volume from Spritz Soda and the CSD segment

2. Goals and Objectives

There was really no need for Amy to dwell on her goals and objectives. Her boss, Fred, had pretty much told her the objective. In his words, he wanted Spritz to show "profitable growth." But then Amy began to mull over some key thoughts on this objective. The problem is that there is no generally accepted measure of this profitable growth. How much growth? How much profit? Furthermore, when did he expect Spritz to achieve this? Given Spritz's financial situation, the

(continued)

---

[29]For useful background references to these points, see Appendix 8B on break-even analysis and chapter 7 on economies of scale.
[30]SWOT stands for "Strengths, Weaknesses, Opportunities, and Threats." This topic is usually not covered in managerial economics courses but readers should be familiar with this analytical technique from their marketing and strategy courses. A SWOT analysis helps managers to develop a strategy that takes into account both the current competitive environment and the relative competencies of the firm itself.

(*continued*)

achievement of profitable growth, however it is measured, would be virtually impossible by the end of next year. In any case, she decided to go ahead and offer specific financial goals and objectives. These are presented in part 4 below.

3. Strategies, Tactics, and Measures

The big question, of course, was how was she planning to achieve these ambitious financial targets, which represent profitable growth? Drawing on all her research from sources such as interviews, off-site brainstorming sessions, consultants' studies, and her own experience, Amy decided that the profitable growth strategy for Spritz must entail the development of a brand extension into a growth segment of the market. She decided that Global Foods needed to invest in the development and launching of a premium "white soda" high-energy drink. This new product would combine the strength of the Spritz brand and the booming demand for energy drinks, particularly among younger consumers. She was not quite sure what this new product would be called. Names such as Spritz-Heavy (an obvious play on words to the various "lite" nonalcoholic as well as alcoholic beverages) or PowerSpritz came to mind. But she would seek the help of her company's advertising agency for this task.

But in any case, she proceeded to outline the specific tactics and courses of action that she would take to launch, sustain, and grow this product extension of Spritz. Most of these tactics involved working with the ad agency to develop a youth-oriented campaign in both traditional print and television as well as on the development of impressions of various sorts strategically placed on various Web sites and Web pages. Also included was her plan to spend money to upgrade the packaging design and quality in order to properly project a premium image of this product worthy of a higher price point.[31]

4. Selection of Key Measures to Monitor Performance

As the key measure of performance, she decided to focus on profitable growth.[32] Her strategy called for Spritz to attain this goal in the third year of her plan. At first revenue would start to grow by a few percentage points and gradually build up to an annual growth rate of 4 to 5 percent (about 1 to 2 percentage points greater than the current growth rate of the entire beverage industry). In the first few years, the gross profit margin was expected to stabilize and the operating profit margin was going to decline slightly. But then, from the third year on, operating profit would be growing at a rate higher than the revenue growth rate (about 6 to 7 percent). Furthermore, by year 3 of her plan, gross profit margin as well as operating profit margin would start to improve. She knew that if she could achieve this, her boss as well as the CEO would be very happy.

5/6. Risks and Opportunities Not Addressed by the Plan

To summarize this section of her plan, Amy wrote about the possibility that consumers would not be convinced that a noncola or "white soda" could really be a high energy drink because of the strong mental association of colas or "brown soda" with caffeine. As far as opportunities that were not addressed by the plan, her only thought was that perhaps Global Foods should divest itself of Spritz before the brand lost any further value. She thought that perhaps a company that focused entirely on beverages would be able to do a better job of managing this brand than a company like Global Foods, which produced both food and beverages. However, she decided that if this idea was going to gain any traction in the company, it should be initiated by someone else. Besides, she certainly did not want to be the one to recommend the divestiture of her own product![33]

Preparing for the Big Presentation

Before Amy presented her plan to the senior management team, she ran through it with her boss, Fred. She knew that it was rather aggressive but she felt strongly that the activities she planned were necessary to stop the decline of

(*continued*)

---

[31]Although this story about Spritz is entirely fictional, it does contain some elements of actual business challenges in the beverage industry. In the 1990s, Cadbury Schweppes' major CSD was ginger ale. It had two brands: Schweppes and Canada Dry. The company recognized that ginger ale was considered by many young people to be something their parents or grandparents drank (perhaps as a mixer with whiskey). To dispel this notion, the company introduced ginger ale mixed with fruit flavors such as raspberry and lemon. The idea was to suggest to young consumers that ginger ale was a "fun drink."

[32]For a useful introduction to this term, see Ram Charan, *Profitable Growth Is Everyone's Business: 10 Tools You Can Use on Monday Morning,* New York: Crown Business, 2006.

[33]In case any "value-based" readers are wondering, our fictional Amy's thought on this matter is entirely fictional! In the real world, no one really thinks this way.

(continued)

the Spritz Soda business. At the end of her presentation, Fred gave her useful feedback. "I have to admit that I am surprised by your plan. Spritz Soda has been a longstanding cash cow of ours, so I expected you to come up with a plan to stabilize top-line sales while effectively driving down costs. Instead, you've presented some truly innovative ideas that could potentially put the brand back into a growth phase. Your plan involves some risk, but I like where you're headed. One concern that I do have is the decline in gross margin despite the introduction of a premium-priced line extension. And because of the heavy upfront marketing costs the operating margin will fall still further. What are your thoughts on that?"

Amy nodded in agreement. "My plan does anticipate a slight decline in gross margin and a small decline in operating margin as well, but these indicators should start to increase in the third year of the plan. However, our manufacturing folks tell us that once we develop some experience in using the new packaging, our variable unit production costs (AVC) will go down. Furthermore, if this new product takes off as we expect, then higher production levels should enable us to keep our total unit production costs down, because our fixed cost will be spread over more units of production. Also our hope is that we won't have to put as much into marketing, once this product captures a critical market share."

"Overall I think we should move forward with what you've laid out here," Fred continued. "However, given the increased risk, we'll need to have several checkpoints to ensure we stay on track. Also, I think the numbers you gave me were good enough to give me the big picture. But when we go to the management committee, there will be some pretty tough people there, particularly our division's finance person. He is a newly minted MBA, and he's always asking for hard data. I don't just want a pro-forma P&L. I'd like you to do a quant-based business case. Give me some ROI numbers. Also, if possible, perhaps you could back up your ideas about the key drivers of demand for your new product with some statistical analysis. For example, doing a regression analysis of consumer demand would certainly be impressive. Once you get these accomplished, I think we'll really be ready for the management committee pitch. Good job so far and keep up the good work!"[34]

SUMMARY

In this capstone chapter, we provided you with background information and the business challenges of actual companies in the food and beverage industry. As you can see, many of the economic concepts that we have discussed throughout this entire text play an important part in understanding the daily challenges of companies in this industry. For example, as you read through this chapter you will have clearly noted such terms as *supply, demand, cost management, supply chain management, changing consumer tastes and preferences, price competition, rising costs of inputs, strategic focus on different market segments.* As a fitting close to this chapter as well as to this text, we provide in the following appendix interviews with business executives of the two leading global refreshment beverage companies: Coca-Cola and PepsiCo. Economic concepts are an integral part of their responses to our questions. We have annotated their interviews with occasional remarks in order to reinforce key teaching points that we have tried to make throughout this text.

QUESTIONS FOR FURTHER STUDY

The refreshment beverage industry is closely watched by the business press and financial analysts. The two leading global companies, Coca-Cola and PepsiCo, are frequently in the news. We hope that this chapter has motivated you to follow this fast-moving industry. Moreover, we are sure that this industry and its products are well covered in your marketing classes. As a way

---

[34]Readers who want to get an idea of the type of statistical analysis that Amy might use to understand and forecast the demand for "Spritz Soda" should review Chapter 5 and, in particular, the appendix to this chapter.

of reinforcing your understanding of the economic concepts discussed in this chapter, as well as throughout the book, consider the following:

1. What impact does the price of oil and gasoline substitutes made from corn have on the cost of producing soft drinks?
2. What impact will the "green" movement have on this industry? (For example, consider the concerns about both the production and disposal of aluminum and plastic used in packaging.)
3. How will the industry respond to continuing changes in consumer tastes and preferences? (For example, Coca-Cola and PepsiCo have both vowed to stop advertising to children under the age of 12 all over the world by the end of 2008.)

Interview with Key Beverage Industry Executives[35]

(Margin notes are the authors' comments showing linkages to key concepts presented in various chapters of this textbook.).

Interview with Chris Lowe, President, Foodservice, Coca-Cola

AUTHORS: Tell us a little about your role at Coca-Cola.

CHRIS: I lead Coca-Cola's Foodservice division, which handles the production, sale, and distribution of Coca-Cola products to both our domestic and international foodservice customers.

AUTHORS: What are the main factors influencing consumer demand for beverages?

This is a good assessment of the nature of consumer "tastes and preferences." (See chapter 3.)

CHRIS: We have found that most people have a tight repertoire of approximately 3–4 beverages that accounts for 75 percent of their beverage consumption. They are usually willing to try new and different beverages for the other 25 percent of their purchases. The key for manufacturers is to try to move their product from their variety-seeking segment into their basic core of regularly consumed beverages.

AUTHORS: How has this demand changed in the last few years?

CHRIS: There are many more dimensions to the consumer demand equation than ever before. Recent changes have mainly been fueled by consumers' curiosity in, as well as the media's focus on, health and wellness issues. Currently, two hot topics are the safety of aspartame [authors' note: This is a common artificial sweetener] and the cause of, and cure for, obesity. Another factor is consumers' increasing desire for variety in flavors and packaging.

AUTHORS: How are these consumer trends affecting the beverage industry?

This is a good example of monopolistic competition, whereby new firms with differentiated products enter the market over the long run. See chapter 9.

CHRIS: We are seeing a proliferation of new beverage products as well as smaller beverage houses, such as Glaceau, which we recently acquired. These new entrants into the market build new brands to scale and then often get bought out by larger manufacturers. In addition, the traditional beverage manufacturers such as Coca-Cola are more focused on innovation. Consequently, we have probably seen more new product innovation in the last 24 months than perhaps the previous 20 years. The question is whether these new categories of beverages can scale into levels of sustainability. A 2 to 2.5 percent volume share is a significant sustainable business. However, many new brands never reach this critical threshold. After entry into the market, they only manage to attain 1 to 1.5 percentage volume share; then they fall back.

---

[35]The authors are very grateful to Messrs. Lowe and Rodrigo for agreeing to be interviewed for this edition of our text. We recognize the fierce competition between the two companies whom they represent so the order of presentation of their interviews was determined by the flip of a coin.

AUTHORS: How is Coca-Cola responding to the health and wellness trend?

CHRIS: We continue to expand our product portfolio through both acquisition and internal new product innovation. Our fast-paced innovation cycle requires us to continually bring in new marketing professionals and researchers to address these issues and generate new ideas. Our juice business is one of the best places for us to introduce added nutrients. Because it is a denser product with a strong flavor profile, it is easier to mask the taste of the additives than with sparkling beverages. To address the issue of elevated cholesterol among our consumers, a few years ago we introduced orange juice with phytosterols with the launch of Minute Maid Heartwise.[36] We have also looked at calcium fortification to support bone health. We introduced Enviga, which invigorates your metabolism to gently increase calorie burning. Overall, we continue to experiment with the beverage functionality that consumers say they want—less calories, fat, sodium, etc. We have also made several significant advances in sweeteners, because although consumers want benefits in their beverages, they also want them to taste just as good as the original version.

AUTHORS: Does the government have an impact on the beverage industry?

A good example of the impact of government regulation on business costs. (See chapter 14.)

CHRIS: Government regulations are shaping both delivery (packaging) and form (ingredients used in the beverage itself). Most of the current discourse is around the environmental impact of water and polyethylene. [Authors' note: Polyethylene is the main material in plastic bottles.]

AUTHORS: What role does foodservice play in Coca-Cola's overall beverage strategy?

CHRIS: Foodservice is a unique business within the beverage industry. People generally consume beverages with food. In fact, in our business we consider the number one "beverage occasion" to be when people are having a meal, either at home or away from home in places such as restaurants. As I mentioned earlier, people are creatures of habit and 75 percent of their consumption is limited to a small selection of products. This repertoire is even more limited with regards to what consumers are willing to pair with their food. Being a regular part of a person's meal is extremely important to building a brand. Three out of four restaurants in the U.S. feature Coca-Cola products.

AUTHORS: To what do you attribute Coca-Cola's strength in foodservice?

Note how global differences in the cost of inputs (i.e., water) affect production activity. (See chapter 7.)

CHRIS: In the U.S., the eating and drinking business grew up around the dispensed (fountain) form of the product versus the packaged (bottle/can) form. This has not been the case in some international markets where water quality may not be as good, so fountain beverages (also called "post-mixed beverages") are not as popular. We have a high share in the U.S. foodservice business because we have traditionally invested a lot to support this segment of the marketplace.

AUTHORS Can you give us a few examples of the types of investment that you've made?

CHRIS Sure. We've funded various market research projects to try to understand more about consumer behavior in various eating and drinking situations.

---

[36]Authors' note: Sterol is a naturally occurring component of certain fruits, vegetables, nuts, seeds, cereals, legumes, vegetable oils, and other plant sources. Research indicates that a certain amount in one's daily diet can lead to lower levels of cholesterol. For further information see http://www.ific.org/publications/factsheets/sterolfs.cfm.

We have a program with the Culinary Institute of America to develop beverages that complement certain meal items. We have also developed technology which offers our customers space, efficiency, and economy when using our equipment and our whole system of providing post-mixed product. Our equipment is often the most reliable equipment in our customers' restaurant; but in addition, we have made sure that our customers are supported by a nationwide service network. Finally, we have a strategy to partner with our customers to maximize their revenue-producing capabilities from soft drinks. We have marketers that work directly with our customers to drive their soft drinks sales.

AUTHORS   Revenue is good, but how about profit?

CHRIS   Our customers' gross profit margin on post-mixed beverage sales is 85–90 percent. This means that they buy a gallon of syrup for five to six dollars and then sell it for about $60. On average, a post-mixed beverage will make up 20 to 25 percent of the bottom line sales of a quick service restaurant. May I add that Coca-Cola is the #1 preferred beverage with food, followed by Diet Coke. This means that our customers can sell more drinks with Coca-Cola because there is more built-in demand for our brand.

AUTHORS: How has the decline of carbonated soft drinks or CSDs and growth of non-carbonated drinks or NCBs affected Coca-Cola's foodservice business?

CHRIS: Although still beverages are growing, sparkling beverages continue to account for about 80 percent of the foodservice business. Of the remaining 20 percent, half of that is juice products, which are sold at breakfast. Certain food items such as burgers, hot dogs, or pizza just lend themselves to a sparkling beverage, and consumers don't want to sacrifice taste when they're paying a premium for the meal occasion.

AUTHORS: You're right. We can't imagine drinking orange juice with pizza! We've observed various upward pressures in the price of your inputs. How is this affecting your business?

CHRIS: High fructose corn syrup or HFCS is a major sweetener and its cost is rising dramatically. The wet milling operation that makes HFCS also produces ethanol. In both situations, corn goes in the front door and, depending on market conditions, HFCS or ethanol is produced. Therefore, we expect continued volatility with our #1 sweetener. On the juice side, Hurricane Katrina and other weather conditions have caused rising fruit costs. In addition, apples are usually the #1 juice ingredient in juice-flavored products and are mainly sourced from China. Given that China is expected to consume a lot more apples internally, we expect rising fruit costs to continue. We also expect transportation costs to rise in parallel with increasing oil prices. We have factored all of these cost issues into our future growth and earnings expectations.

AUTHORS: Can you comment on Coca-Cola's international business?

CHRIS: A large portion of our business comes from outside the United States and, therefore, we have benefited from the falling value of the dollar. Our global presence gives us a strong vantage point from which to track changing consumer trends and tastes as they move across the globe. We have the ability to see and react to trends as they are occurring and be on the edge of where the consumer is going. For example, obesity is not just a key U.S. issue but also an important global issue; and we expect caloric consumption to continue to be an important part of the global social discourse.

AUTHORS: How do you respond to these different and changing international market conditions?

CHRIS: We have the ability to move resources to those world markets which offer the greatest opportunity at a given point in time. From a product perspective, we have made significant efforts to balance our international beverage portfolio to best meet the needs of our consumers. Certain brands, such as Coca-Cola, have a core strength in the international aspect of the brand and the consistency of its identity. It is often the same product in the United States as in China and Africa with the only difference being the use of a different sweetener based on governmental requirements. On the other hand, brands such as Fanta are modified to be more suited to local tastes and to make the product more competitive with a local product that has a preestablished and stronger position than we do. In some markets, Fanta Orange contains real juice and in others, we modify the color to be lighter or darker or the flavor to be stronger or milder to meet local tastes.

Good example of how consumer tastes and preferences can vary in different countries or regions of the world. (See chapter 3.)

Interview with Claudio Rodrigo, Vice President, Foodservice Operations, US PepsiCo

AUTHORS: Tell us a little about your role at PepsiCo.

CLAUDIO: I lead the operations function for PepsiCo's U.S. Foodservice division, which handles the distribution of PepsiCo products sold to any foodservice arena, such as Subway, Dunkin' Donuts, and 7–Eleven. Our division generates $3.7 billion of revenue, approximately 10 percent of total PepsiCo revenues. We handle both food and beverage brands including Frito-Lay, Quaker Foods, Pepsi-Cola, Gatorade, and Tropicana. Our beverage business is divided into two key areas: (1) bottles-to-go— ready-to-drink products that are sold to the consumer from a refrigerated case, and (2) fountain beverages—syrup concentrates that are mixed with carbonated water at our foodservice customer and sold in a cup. The latter of these two involves managing the purchase, installation, and service of beverage equipment as well as the operations of our Dallas call center, which receives orders and schedules product deliveries.

When asked a general question about their business, most executives begin with total revenue and the breakdown of revenue by product or line of business. (See chapter 10 on Baumol's revenue maximization model.)

AUTHORS: How has consumer demand for beverages changed recently?

CLAUDIO: The proliferation of choice for consumers continues to drive the beverage business. Consumers are increasingly specific about what they want to drink and are willing to pay more for a product that satisfies their tastes, comes in a convenient package, and is readily available. Noncarbonated products are growing much faster than traditional carbonated soft drinks. Teas, juice drinks, isotonics, New Age beverages such as SoBe, and bottled water are driving growth in the industry. Consumers are also on the go more. As a result, we are seeing growth in the drive-through venue as well as more portable packaging such as the distribution of bottles-to-go in quick-serve restaurants, establishments where only fountain beverages were available not too long ago.

Changes in tastes and preferences play an important part in understanding the demand for soft drinks. In turn, these changes in preferences can be influenced by such things as changes in lifestyles. (See chapter 3.)

The carbonated soft drink market is clearly an oligopoly. As explained in chapter 9, within this type of market "highly competitive" refers to the intensity of the rivalry among a relatively small number of large companies. However, as Claudio points out, the entrance of relatively small, but entrepreneurial companies that focus on specialty products has increased the degree of competition more in line with economic theory. In fact, if these smaller firms are added, the soft drink market becomes more like monopolistic competition.

Recall that technology becomes a factor in the economic theory of the firm primarily by reducing the unit cost of production. (See chapters 6 and 7.) In this case, technology is cited as a factor in improving the quality of the product.

AUTHORS: What is the beverage industry's competitive situation?

CLAUDIO: We operate in a highly competitive environment. Outside of our traditional key competitor, Coca-Cola, we are also seeing many new products from entrepreneurial companies that started as grass-roots ideas. PepsiCo has an entrepreneurial culture, which encourages risk-taking and allows us to see the tremendous potential of smaller players such as SoBe and IZZE. This strategy has enabled us to successfully develop a strong NCB (noncarbonated beverage) portfolio.[37]

AUTHORS: What role does technology play in this industry?

CLAUDIO: Technology is a key driver of this industry, especially within the foodservice division. Bottled and canned beverages are manufactured at high speeds in huge plants that have strong product quality controls. In contrast, fountain beverages are prepared at the foodservice customer with all the same complexity on a very small scale. We have less control over variables such as water filtration (to eliminate chlorine) and product temperatures (the colder the product, the more carbon dioxide you can get into it). As a result, fountain beverages were flatter or less fizzy than that of their bottled and canned counterparts. We continually strove to improve the quality of our fountain beverages so that it would match bottle/can quality standards and, in 2002, we developed and patented our IntelliCarb technology. Through improved temperature control, it allows us to have greater control over the carbonation level of our products with the ability to match bottle and can levels. In addition we have developed an auto ratio valve with the ability to control and monitor the ratio of syrup to carbonated water and thereby deliver the correct sweetness and flavor profile that better emulates our bottle and can products. The story behind this new technology is so strong that is has allowed us to win new customers. Note that when foodservice customers enter into a supply relationship with a beverage manufacturer, they usually sign exclusive contracts, which last a minimum of several years, so each customer we win is a significant accomplishment.

AUTHORS: What is the role, if any, of government regulation on the refreshment beverage industry? The government does not enforce sustainability; this was done out of corporate responsibility. The government regulates through the local board of health and the FDA (Food and Drug Administration) on some products such as teas, dairy, juices, and other low-acid products.

CLAUDIO: One of PepsiCo's top three priorities is the environment. Our president, Indra Nooyi, is from India, a country where water conservation is of utmost importance. Years ago, the industry may have taken the presence of water for granted but we certainly do not do so today. Our goal is to get to a 1:1 ratio where we use 1 gallon of water to make 1 gallon of finished product. Because we are so proactive in this respect, we tend to stay ahead of the requirements that a governmental agency such as the EPA (Environmental Protection Agency) may issue. A greater challenge is the development of new ingredients that are monitored by the FDA. We are constantly developing new artificial and preferably natural sweeteners and flavor ingredients. This is confidential and likely

---

[37]PepsiCo acquired SoBe (which stands for South Beach Beverage Company) in 2000 and Izze in 2006. Both brands are good examples of the trend in noncarbonated "alternative drinks."

See chapter 14 for a review of government regulations' impact on business activities. In what way does the government affect Pepsi's production function and consumer demand?

sensitive. Our goal is not only to meet FDA standards but also to embrace consumers' move to healthier lifestyles. For example, many consumer groups are concerned about obesity and the quality of foods offered to kids in schools. We recognize our responsibility in achieving this and have partnered with the Clinton Foundation to address school nutrition, seek guidance from Dr. Hornish and the Cooper Clinic in modifying our product portfolio, and invest in programs that help educate people about health and encourage them to be more active.

AUTHORS: What role does foodservice play in PepsiCo's overall beverage strategy?

CLAUDIO: Foodservice is a unique environment that we see as an opportunity to build brands, especially at major restaurant operations, which offer breadth and scale of impressions. PepsiCo's foodservice business has been accretive to our overall beverage business. To a lesser degree, foodservice is a sampling venue in that we have the opportunity to capture consumers who might not normally gravitate to our product. For the restaurateur, our fountain products are a very cost-effective means to provide beverages to consumers. They usually make significantly higher margins on the beverage versus food items they sell. Fountain drinks are often the most lucrative item our foodservice customer sells.

AUTHORS: How has the decline of carbonated soft drinks (CSDs) and the growth of noncarbonated drinks (NCBs) affected PepsiCo's foodservice business?

CLAUDIO: We have embraced the shift to more NCBs. In fact we have used innovative technologies to expand our NCB sales in restaurants. For example, we developed the "variety valve," which is a proportioning valve that fits a typical fountain unit but allows the server to pour three NCB flavors in the space of one valve. With this technology, typical 8-valve dispensing machines can now dispense 10 flavors, including three NCB flavors. We are utilizing this technology not only to gain new customers but also to increase the satisfaction levels of our existing customers. For example, we retrofitted all Taco Bell stores to include the variety valve.

AUTHORS: Because CSDs have such high profit margins, has your move to NCBs affected your overall profitability?

CLAUDIO: Fountain NCBs are typically Tropicana lemonade and fruit punch. These are still profitable "bag in box" products that have relatively low juice content. Cost of goods on these items may be marginally but not significantly higher than that of CSDs. Plus, our strategy of portfolio diversification has helped keep our margins strong. For example, we offer premium products that tend to have more profit margin built into them from the beginning. Two examples are our FCBs (frozen carbonated beverages), which are in stores such as 7-Eleven, as well as our premium NCBs, such as our SoBe line.

Even though Pepsi and Coke may be "price makers" in their oligopoly market, they can be "price takers" in the markets in which they have to buy their inputs. What factors have caused the increase in high fructose corn syrup? (See chapter 3.)

AUTHORS: You also have to deal with rising input costs, don't you?

CLAUDIO: Yes, we have seen some modest increases to foodservice equipment costs but the biggest impact has been made by rising high fructose corn syrup costs. This has and is expected to continue to exert pressure on our pricing structures. In the past year, we issued a price increase to our PepsiCo national account customers and many of our local bottlers have done the same. My division is limited by the fact that some of our customer contracts have price protection built into them.

AUTHORS: Can you comment on PepsiCo's international business?

CLAUDIO: In the mid-1990s, international was a very small piece of the PepsiCo business. Since then we have significantly ramped up our international efforts via acquisitions as well as activities that drive organic growth. Overall, our competitor, Coca-Cola, has a much higher share internationally. However, there are certain regions or countries where we are stronger, such as the Middle East. There we have a high share and are seeing strong year over year growth.[38]

AUTHORS: What is your strategy to build your international business?

CLAUDIO   We are selective about which markets we enter rather than trying to compete and win in every market. We identify markets where we have a reason to succeed and then invest practically and sufficiently. We also look for markets where there is consumer spending capability that is adequate and growing. China and India are considered to be two of PepsiCo's major growth markets. When competing in an international market, our approach is to leverage global brands, resources, and capabilities, but then modify to accommodate local tastes. For example, we provide our consumers in Southeast Asia with seaweed-flavored potato chips.

This is a good example of a global company catering to the specific types of tastes and preferences in local markets. (See chapter 3.)

---

[38]One of the author's recent travel experiences seemed to support this. On a trip to Dubai in November 2007, he went to two different restaurants that served only Pepsi. In the corporate cafeteria that he visited, Pepsi was served exclusively.

Statistical and Financial Tables

Table A.1*a*   Future Value of $1 at the End of *n* Periods

Period	1%	2%	3%	4%	5%	6%	7%	8%	9%	10%
1	1.0100	1.0200	1.0300	1.0400	1.0500	1.0600	1.0700	1.0800	1.0900	1.1000
2	1.0201	1.0404	1.0609	1.0816	1.1025	1.1236	1.1449	1.1664	1.1881	1.2100
3	1.0303	1.0612	1.0927	1.1249	1.1576	1.1910	1.2250	1.2597	1.2950	1.3310
4	1.0406	1.0824	1.1255	1.1699	1.2155	1.2625	1.3108	1.3605	1.4116	1.4641
5	1.0510	1.1041	1.1593	1.2167	1.2763	1.3382	1.4026	1.4693	1.5386	1.6105
6	1.0615	1.1262	1.1941	1.2653	1.3401	1.4185	1.5007	1.5869	1.6771	1.7716
7	1.0721	1.1487	1.2299	1.3159	1.4071	1.5036	1.6058	1.7138	1.8280	1.9487
8	1.0829	1.1717	1.2668	1.3686	1.4775	1.5938	1.7182	1.8509	1.9926	2.1436
9	1.0937	1.1951	1.3048	1.4233	1.5513	1.6895	1.8385	1.9990	2.1719	2.3579
10	1.1046	1.2190	1.3439	1.4802	1.6289	1.7908	1.9672	2.1589	2.3674	2.5937
11	1.1157	1.2434	1.3842	1.5395	1.7103	1.8983	2.1049	2.3316	2.5804	2.8531
12	1.1268	1.2682	1.4258	1.6010	1.7959	2.0122	2.2522	2.5182	2.8127	3.1384
13	1.1381	1.2936	1.4685	1.6651	1.8856	2.1329	2.4098	2.7196	3.0658	3.4523
14	1.1495	1.3195	1.5126	1.7317	1.9799	2.2609	2.5785	2.9372	3.3417	3.7975
15	1.1610	1.3459	1.5580	1.8009	2.0789	2.3966	2.7590	3.1722	3.6425	4.1772
16	1.1726	1.3728	1.6047	1.8730	2.1829	2.5404	2.9522	3.4259	3.9703	4.5950
17	1.1843	1.4002	1.6528	1.9479	2.2920	2.6928	3.1588	3.7000	4.3276	5.0545
18	1.1961	1.4282	1.7024	2.0258	2.4066	2.8543	3.3799	3.9960	4.7171	5.5599
19	1.2081	1.4568	1.7535	2.1068	2.5270	3.0256	3.6165	4.3157	5.1417	6.1159
20	1.2202	1.4859	1.8061	2.1911	2.6533	3.2071	3.8697	4.6610	5.6044	6.7275
21	1.2324	1.5157	1.8603	2.2788	2.7860	3.3996	4.1406	5.0338	6.1088	7.4002
22	1.2477	1.5460	1.9161	2.3699	2.9253	3.6035	4.4304	5.4365	6.6586	8.1403
23	1.2572	1.5769	1.9736	2.4647	3.0715	3.8197	4.7405	5.8715	7.2579	8.9543
24	1.2697	1.6084	2.0328	2.5633	3.2251	4.0489	5.0724	6.3412	7.9111	9.8497
25	1.2824	1.6406	2.0938	2.6658	3.3864	4.2919	5.4274	6.8485	8.6231	10.835
26	1.2953	1.6734	2.1566	2.7725	3.5557	4.5494	5.8074	7.3964	9.3992	11.918
27	1.3082	1.7069	2.2213	2.8834	3.7335	4.8223	6.2139	7.9881	10.245	13.110
28	1.3213	1.7410	2.2879	2.9987	3.9201	5.1117	6.6488	8.6271	11.167	14.421
29	1.3345	1.7758	2.3566	3.1187	4.1161	5.4184	7.1143	9.3173	12.172	15.863
30	1.3478	1.8114	2.4273	3.2434	4.3219	5.7435	7.6123	10.063	13.268	17.449
40	1.4889	2.2080	3.2620	4.8010	7.0400	10.286	14.974	21.725	31.409	45.259
50	1.6446	2.6916	4.3839	7.1067	11.467	18.420	29.457	46.902	74.358	117.39
60	1.8167	3.2810	5.8916	10.520	18.679	32.988	57.946	101.26	176.03	304.48

Table A.1a   (continued)

Period	12%	14%	15%	16%	18%	20%	24%	28%	32%	36%
1	1.1200	1.1400	1.1500	1.1600	1.1800	1.2000	1.2400	1.2800	1.3200	1.3600
2	1.2544	1.2996	1.3225	1.3456	1.3924	1.4400	1.5376	1.6384	1.7424	1.8496
3	1.4049	1.4815	1.5209	1.5609	1.6430	1.7280	1.9066	2.0972	2.3000	2.5155
4	1.5735	1.6890	1.7490	1.8106	1.9388	2.0736	2.3642	2.6844	3.0360	3.4210
5	1.7623	1.9254	2.0114	2.1003	2.2878	2.4883	2.9316	3.4360	4.0075	4.6526
6	1.9738	2.1950	2.3131	2.4364	2.6996	2.9860	3.6352	4.3980	5.2899	6.3275
7	2.2107	2.5023	2.6600	2.8262	3.1855	3.5832	4.5077	5.6295	6.9826	8.6054
8	2.4760	2.8526	3.0590	3.2784	3.7589	4.2998	5.5895	7.2058	9.2170	11.703
9	2.7731	3.2519	3.5179	3.8030	4.4355	5.1598	6.9310	9.2234	12.166	15.917
10	3.1058	3.7072	4.0456	4.4114	5.2338	6.1917	8.5944	11.806	16.060	21.647
11	3.4785	4.2262	4.6524	5.1173	6.1759	7.4301	10.657	15.112	21.199	29.439
12	3.8960	4.8179	5.3502	5.9360	7.2876	8.9161	13.215	19.343	27.982	40.037
13	4.3635	5.4924	6.1528	6.8858	8.5994	10.699	16.386	24.759	36.937	54.451
14	4.8871	6.2613	7.0757	7.9875	10.147	12.839	20.319	31.691	48.756	74.053
15	5.4736	7.1379	8.1371	9.2655	11.974	15.407	25.196	40.565	64.359	100.71
16	6.1304	8.1372	9.3576	10.748	14.129	18.488	31.243	51.923	84.954	136.97
17	6.8660	9.2765	10.761	12.468	16.672	22.186	38.741	66.461	112.14	186.28
18	7.6900	10.575	12.375	14.463	19.673	26.623	48.039	85.071	148.02	253.34
19	8.6128	12.056	14.232	16.777	23.214	31.948	59.568	108.89	195.39	344.54
20	9.6463	13.743	16.367	19.461	27.393	38.338	73.864	139.38	257.92	468.58
21	10.804	15.668	18.822	22.574	32.324	46.005	91.592	178.41	340.45	637.26
22	12.100	17.861	21.645	26.186	38.142	55.206	113.57	228.36	449.39	866.67
23	13.552	20.362	24.891	30.376	45.008	66.247	140.83	292.30	593.20	1178.7
24	15.179	23.212	28.625	35.236	53.109	79.497	174.63	374.14	783.02	1603.0
25	17.000	26.462	32.919	40.874	62.669	95.396	216.54	478.90	1033.6	2180.1
26	19.040	30.167	37.857	47.414	73.949	114.48	268.51	613.00	1364.3	2964.9
27	21.325	34.390	43.535	55.000	87.260	137.37	332.95	784.64	1800.9	4032.3
28	23.884	39.204	50.066	63.800	102.97	164.84	412.86	1004.3	2377.2	5483.9
29	16.750	44.693	57.575	74.009	121.50	197.81	511.95	1285.6	3137.9	7458.1
30	29.960	50.950	66.212	85.850	143.37	237.38	634.82	1645.5	4142.1	10143
40	93.051	188.88	267.86	378.72	750.38	1469.8	5455.9	19427	66521	*
50	289.00	700.23	1083.7	1670.7	3927.4	9100.4	46890	*	*	*
60	897.60	2595.9	4384.0	7370.2	20555	56348	*	*	*	*

* > 99,999

Table A.1b   Sum of an Annuity of $1 per Period for *n* Periods

Number of Periods	1%	2%	3%	4%	5%	6%	7%	8%	9%	10%
1	1.0000	1.0000	1.0000	1.0000	1.0000	1.0000	1.0000	1.0000	1.0000	1.0000
2	2.0100	2.0200	2.0300	2.0400	2.0500	2.0600	2.0700	2.0800	2.0900	2.1000
3	3.0301	3.0604	3.0909	3.1216	3.1525	3.1836	3.2149	3.2464	3.2781	3.3100
4	4.0604	4.1216	4.1836	4.2465	4.3101	4.3746	4.4399	4.5061	4.5731	4.6410
5	5.1010	5.2040	5.3091	5.4163	5.5256	5.6371	5.7507	5.8666	5.9847	6.1051
6	6.1520	6.3081	6.4684	6.6330	6.8019	6.9753	7.1533	7.3359	7.5233	7.7156
7	7.2135	7.4343	7.6625	7.8983	8.1420	8.3938	8.6540	8.9228	9.2004	9.4872
8	8.2857	8.5830	8.8923	9.2142	9.5491	9.8975	10.260	10.637	11.028	11.436
9	9.3685	9.7546	10.159	10.583	11.027	11.491	11.978	12.488	13.021	13.579
10	10.462	10.950	11.464	12.006	12.578	13.181	13.816	14.487	15.193	15.937
11	11.567	12.169	12.808	13.486	14.207	14.972	15.784	16.645	17.560	18.531
12	12.683	13.412	14.192	15.026	15.917	16.870	17.888	18.977	20.141	21.384
13	13.809	14.680	15.618	16.627	17.713	18.882	20.141	21.495	22.953	24.523
14	14.947	15.974	17.086	18.292	19.599	21.015	22.550	24.215	26.019	27.975
15	16.097	17.293	18.599	20.024	21.579	23.276	25.129	27.152	29.361	31.772
16	17.258	18.639	20.157	21.825	23.657	25.673	27.888	30.324	33.003	35.950
17	18.430	20.012	21.762	23.698	25.840	28.213	30.840	33.750	36.974	40.545
18	19.615	21.412	23.414	25.645	28.132	30.906	33.999	37.450	41.301	45.599
19	20.811	22.841	25.117	27.671	30.539	33.760	37.379	41.446	46.018	51.159
20	22.019	24.297	26.870	29.778	33.066	36.786	40.995	45.762	51.160	57.275
21	23.239	25.783	28.676	31.969	35.719	39.993	44.865	50.423	56.765	64.002
22	24.472	27.299	30.537	34.248	38.505	43.392	49.006	55.457	62.873	71.403
23	25.716	28.845	32.453	36.618	41.430	46.996	53.436	60.893	69.532	79.543
24	26.973	30.422	34.426	39.083	44.502	50.816	58.177	66.765	76.790	88.497
25	28.243	32.030	36.459	41.646	47.727	54.865	63.249	73.106	84.701	98.347
26	29.526	33.671	38.553	44.312	51.113	59.156	68.676	79.954	93.324	109.18
27	30.821	35.344	40.710	47.084	54.669	63.706	74.484	87.351	102.72	121.10
28	32.129	37.051	42.931	49.968	58.403	68.528	80.698	95.339	112.97	134.21
29	33.450	38.792	45.219	52.966	62.323	73.640	87.347	103.97	124.14	148.63
30	34.785	40.568	47.575	56.085	66.439	79.058	94.461	113.28	136.31	164.49
40	48.886	60.402	75.401	95.026	120.80	154.76	199.64	259.06	337.88	442.59
50	64.463	84.579	112.80	152.67	209.35	290.34	406.53	573.77	815.08	1163.9
60	81.670	114.05	163.05	237.99	353.58	533.13	813.52	1253.2	1944.8	3034.8

Table A.1b   (continued)

Number of Periods	12%	14%	15%	16%	18%	20%	24%	28%	32%	36%
1	1.0000	1.0000	1.0000	1.0000	1.0000	1.0000	1.0000	1.0000	1.0000	1.0000
2	2.1200	2.1400	2.1500	2.1600	2.1800	2.2000	2.2400	2.2800	2.3200	2.3600
3	3.3744	3.4396	3.4725	3.5056	3.5724	3.6400	3.7776	3.9184	4.0624	4.2096
4	4.7793	4.9211	4.9934	5.0665	5.2154	5.3680	5.6842	6.0156	6.3624	6.7251
5	6.3528	6.6101	6.7424	6.8771	7.1542	7.4416	8.0484	8.6999	9.3983	10.146
6	8.1152	8.5355	8.7537	8.9775	9.4420	9.9299	10.980	12.136	13.406	14.799
7	10.089	10.730	11.067	11.414	12.142	12.916	14.615	16.534	18.696	21.126
8	12.300	13.233	13.727	14.240	15.327	16.499	19.123	22.163	25.678	29.732
9	14.776	16.085	16.786	17.519	19.086	20.799	24.712	29.369	34.895	41.435
10	17.549	19.337	20.304	21.321	23.521	25.959	31.643	38.593	47.062	57.352
11	20.655	23.045	24.349	25.733	28.755	32.150	40.238	50.398	63.122	78.998
12	24.133	27.271	29.002	30.850	34.931	39.581	50.895	65.510	84.320	108.44
13	28.029	32.089	34.352	36.786	42.429	48.497	64.110	84.853	112.30	148.47
14	32.393	37.581	40.505	43.672	50.818	59.196	80.496	109.61	149.24	202.93
15	37.280	43.842	47.580	51.660	60.965	72.035	100.82	141.30	198.00	276.98
16	42.753	50.980	55.717	60.925	72.939	87.442	126.01	181.87	262.36	377.69
17	48.884	59.118	65.075	71.673	87.068	105.93	157.25	233.79	347.31	514.66
18	55.750	68.394	75.836	84.141	103.74	128.11	195.99	300.25	459.45	700.94
19	63.440	78.969	88.212	98.603	123.41	154.74	244.03	385.32	607.47	954.28
20	72.052	91.025	102.44	115.38	146.63	186.69	303.60	494.21	802.86	1298.8
21	81.699	104.77	118.81	134.84	174.02	225.03	377.46	633.59	1060.8	1767.4
22	92.503	120.44	137.63	157.41	206.34	271.03	469.06	812.00	1401.2	2404.7
23	104.60	138.30	159.28	183.60	244.49	326.24	582.63	1040.4	1850.6	3271.3
24	118.16	158.66	184.17	213.98	289.49	392.48	723.46	1332.7	2443.8	4450.0
25	133.33	181.87	212.79	249.21	342.60	471.98	898.09	1706.8	3226.8	6053.0
26	150.33	208.33	245.71	290.09	405.27	567.38	1114.6	2185.7	4260.4	8233.1
27	169.37	238.50	283.57	337.50	479.22	681.85	1383.1	2798.7	5624.8	11198.0
28	190.70	272.89	327.10	392.50	566.48	819.22	1716.1	3583.3	7425.7	15230.3
29	214.58	312.09	377.17	456.30	669.45	984.07	2129.0	4587.7	9802.9	20714.2
30	241.33	356.79	434.75	530.31	790.95	1181.9	2640.9	5873.2	12941	28172.3
40	767.09	1342.0	1779.1	2360.8	4163.2	7343.9	22729	69377	*	*
50	2400.0	4994.5	7217.7	10436	21813	45497	*	*	*	*
60	7471.6	18535	29220	46058	*	*	*	*	*	*

*> 99,999

Table A.1c   Present Value of $1 Received at the End of *n* Periods

Period	1%	2%	3%	4%	5%	6%	7%	8%	9%	10%
1	0.9901	0.9804	0.9709	0.9615	0.9524	0.9434	0.9346	0.9259	0.9174	0.9091
2	0.9803	0.9612	0.9426	0.9246	0.9070	0.8900	0.8734	0.8573	0.8417	0.8264
3	0.9706	0.9423	0.9151	0.8890	0.8638	0.8396	0.8163	0.7938	0.7722	0.7513
4	0.9610	0.9238	0.8885	0.8548	0.8227	0.7921	0.7629	0.7350	0.7084	0.6830
5	0.9515	0.9057	0.8626	0.8219	0.7835	0.7473	0.7130	0.6806	0.6499	0.6209
6	0.9420	0.8880	0.8375	0.7903	0.7462	0.7050	0.6663	0.6302	0.5963	0.5645
7	0.9327	0.8706	0.8131	0.7599	0.7107	0.6651	0.6227	0.5835	0.5470	0.5132
8	0.9235	0.8535	0.7894	0.7307	0.6768	0.6274	0.5820	0.5403	0.5019	0.4665
9	0.9143	0.8368	0.7664	0.7026	0.6446	0.5919	0.5439	0.5002	0.4604	0.4241
10	0.9053	0.8203	0.7441	0.6756	0.6139	0.5584	0.5083	0.4632	0.4224	0.3855
11	0.8963	0.8043	0.7224	0.6496	0.5847	0.5268	0.4751	0.4289	0.3875	0.3505
12	0.8874	0.7885	0.7014	0.6246	0.5568	0.4970	0.4440	0.3971	0.3555	0.3186
13	0.8787	0.7730	0.6810	0.6006	0.5303	0.4688	0.4150	0.3677	0.3262	0.2897
14	0.8700	0.7579	0.6611	0.5775	0.5051	0.4423	0.3878	0.3405	0.2992	0.2633
15	0.8613	0.7430	0.6419	0.5553	0.4810	0.4173	0.3624	0.3152	0.2745	0.2394
16	0.8528	0.7284	0.6232	0.5339	0.4581	0.3936	0.3387	0.2919	0.2519	0.2176
17	0.8444	0.7142	0.6050	0.5134	0.4363	0.3714	0.3166	0.2703	0.2311	0.1978
18	0.8360	0.7002	0.5874	0.4936	0.4155	0.3503	0.2959	0.2502	0.2120	0.1799
19	0.8277	0.6864	0.5703	0.4746	0.3957	0.3305	0.2765	0.2317	0.1945	0.1635
20	0.8195	0.6730	0.5537	0.4564	0.3769	0.3118	0.2584	0.2145	0.1784	0.1486
25	0.7798	0.6095	0.4776	0.3751	0.2953	0.2330	0.1842	0.1460	0.1160	0.0923
30	0.7419	0.5521	0.4120	0.3083	0.2314	0.1741	0.1314	0.0994	0.0754	0.0573
40	0.6717	0.4529	0.3066	0.2083	0.1420	0.0972	0.0668	0.0460	0.0318	0.0221
50	0.6080	0.3715	0.2281	0.1407	0.0872	0.0543	0.0339	0.0213	0.0134	0.0085
60	0.5504	0.3048	0.1697	0.0951	0.0535	0.0303	0.0173	0.0099	0.0057	0.0033

Table A.1c   (continued)

Period	12%	14%	15%	16%	18%	20%	24%	28%	32%	36%
1	0.8929	0.8772	0.8696	0.8621	0.8475	0.8333	0.8065	0.7813	0.7576	0.7353
2	0.7972	0.7695	0.7561	0.7432	0.7182	0.6944	0.6504	0.6104	0.5739	0.5407
3	0.7118	0.6750	0.6575	0.6407	0.6086	0.5787	0.5245	0.4768	0.4348	0.3975
4	0.6355	0.5921	0.5718	0.5523	0.5158	0.4823	0.4230	0.3725	0.3294	0.2923
5	0.5674	0.5194	0.4972	0.4761	0.4371	0.4019	0.3411	0.2910	0.2495	0.2149
6	0.5066	0.4556	0.4323	0.4104	0.3704	0.3349	0.2751	0.2274	0.1890	0.1580
7	0.4523	0.3996	0.3759	0.3538	0.3139	0.2791	0.2218	0.1776	0.1432	0.1162
8	0.4039	0.3506	0.3269	0.3050	0.2660	0.2326	0.1789	0.1388	0.1085	0.0854
9	0.3606	0.3075	0.2843	0.2630	0.2255	0.1938	0.1443	0.1084	0.0822	0.0628
10	0.3220	0.2697	0.2472	0.2267	0.1911	0.1615	0.1164	0.0847	0.0623	0.0462
11	0.2875	0.2366	0.2149	0.1954	0.1619	0.1346	0.0938	0.0662	0.0472	0.0340
12	0.2567	0.2076	0.1869	0.1685	0.1372	0.1122	0.0757	0.0517	0.0357	0.0250
13	0.2292	0.1821	0.1625	0.1452	0.1163	0.0935	0.0610	0.0404	0.0271	0.0184
14	0.2046	0.1597	0.1413	0.1252	0.0985	0.0779	0.0492	0.0316	0.0205	0.0135
15	0.1827	0.1401	0.1229	0.1079	0.0835	0.0649	0.0397	0.0247	0.0155	0.0099
16	0.1631	0.1229	0.1069	0.0930	0.0708	0.0541	0.0320	0.0193	0.0118	0.0073
17	0.1456	0.1078	0.0929	0.0802	0.0600	0.0451	0.0258	0.0150	0.0089	0.0054
18	0.1300	0.0946	0.0808	0.0691	0.0508	0.0376	0.0208	0.0118	0.0068	0.0039
19	0.1161	0.0829	0.0703	0.0596	0.0431	0.0313	0.0168	0.0092	0.0051	0.0029
20	0.1037	0.0728	0.0611	0.0514	0.0365	0.0261	0.0135	0.0072	0.0039	0.0021
25	0.0588	0.0378	0.0304	0.0245	0.0160	0.0105	0.0046	0.0021	0.0010	0.0005
30	0.0334	0.0196	0.0151	0.0116	0.0070	0.0042	0.0016	0.0006	0.0002	0.0001
40	0.0107	0.0053	0.0037	0.0026	0.0013	0.0007	0.0002	0.0001	*	*
50	0.0035	0.0014	0.0009	0.0006	0.0003	0.0001	*	*	*	*
60	0.0011	0.0004	0.0002	0.0001	*	*	*	*	*	*

*The factor is zero to four decimal places.

Table A.1d   Present Value of an Annuity of $1 per Period for *n* Periods

Number of Payments	1%	2%	3%	4%	5%	6%	7%	8%	9%
1	0.9901	0.9804	0.9709	0.9615	0.9524	0.9434	0.9346	0.9259	0.9174
2	1.9704	1.9416	1.9135	1.8861	1.8594	1.8334	1.8080	1.7833	1.7591
3	2.9410	2.8839	2.8286	2.7751	2.7232	2.6730	2.6243	2.5771	2.5313
4	3.9020	3.8077	3.7171	3.6299	3.5460	3.4651	3.3872	3.3121	3.2397
5	4.8534	4.7135	4.5797	4.4518	4.3295	4.2124	4.1002	3.9927	3.8897
6	5.7955	5.6014	5.4172	5.2421	5.0757	4.9173	4.7665	4.6229	4.4859
7	6.7282	6.4720	6.2303	6.0021	5.7864	5.5824	5.3893	5.2064	5.0330
8	7.6517	7.3255	7.0197	6.7327	6.4632	6.2098	5.9713	5.7466	5.5348
9	8.5660	8.1622	7.7861	7.4353	7.1078	6.8017	6.5152	6.2469	5.9952
10	9.4713	8.9826	8.5302	8.1109	7.7217	7.3601	7.0236	6.7101	6.4177
11	10.3676	9.7868	9.2526	8.7605	8.3064	7.8869	7.4987	7.1390	6.8052
12	11.2551	10.5753	9.9540	9.3851	8.8633	8.3838	7.9427	7.5361	7.1607
13	12.1337	11.3484	10.6350	9.9856	9.3936	8.8527	8.3577	7.9038	7.4869
14	13.0037	12.1062	11.2961	10.5631	9.8986	9.2950	8.7455	8.2442	7.7862
15	13.8651	12.8493	11.9379	11.1184	10.3797	9.7122	9.1079	8.5595	8.0607
16	14.7179	13.5777	12.5611	11.6523	10.8378	10.1059	9.4466	8.8514	8.3126
17	15.5623	14.2919	13.1661	12.1657	11.2741	10.4773	9.7632	9.1216	8.5436
18	16.3983	14.9920	13.7535	12.6593	11.6896	10.8276	10.0591	9.3719	8.7556
19	17.2260	15.6785	14.3238	13.1339	12.0853	11.1581	10.3356	9.6036	8.9501
20	18.0456	16.3514	14.8775	13.5903	12.4622	11.4699	10.5940	9.8181	9.1285
25	22.0232	19.5235	17.4131	15.6221	14.0939	12.7834	11.6536	10.6748	9.8226
30	25.8077	22.3965	19.6004	17.2920	15.3725	13.7648	12.4090	11.2578	10.2737
40	32.8347	27.3555	23.1148	19.7928	17.1591	15.0463	13.3317	11.9246	10.7574
50	39.1961	31.4236	25.7298	21.4822	18.2559	15.7619	13.8007	12.2335	10.9617
60	44.9550	34.7609	27.6756	22.6235	18.9293	16.1614	14.0392	12.3766	11.0480

Table A.1d   (continued)

Number of Payments	10%	12%	14%	15%	16%	18%	20%	24%	28%	32%	36%
1	0.9091	0.8929	0.8772	0.8696	0.8621	0.8475	0.8333	0.8065	0.7813	0.7576	0.7353
2	1.7355	1.6901	1.6467	1.6257	1.6052	1.5656	1.5278	1.4568	1.3916	1.3315	1.2760
3	2.4869	2.4018	2.3216	2.2832	2.2459	2.1743	2.1065	1.9813	1.8684	1.7663	1.6735
4	3.1699	3.0373	2.9137	2.8550	2.7982	2.6901	2.5887	2.4043	2.2410	2.0957	1.9658
5	3.7908	3.6048	3.4331	3.3522	3.2743	3.1272	2.9906	2.7454	2.5320	2.3452	2.1807
6	4.3553	4.1114	3.8887	3.7845	3.6847	3.4976	3.3255	3.0205	2.7594	2.5342	2.3388
7	4.8684	4.5638	4.2883	4.1604	4.0386	3.8115	3.6046	3.2423	2.9370	2.6775	2.4550
8	5.3349	4.9676	4.6389	4.4873	4.3436	4.0776	3.8372	3.4212	3.0758	2.7860	2.5404
9	5.7590	5.3282	4.9464	4.7716	4.6065	4.3030	4.0310	3.5655	3.1842	2.8681	2.6033
10	6.1446	5.6502	5.2161	5.0188	4.8332	4.4941	4.1925	3.6819	3.2689	2.9304	2.6495
11	6.4951	5.9377	5.4527	5.2337	5.0286	4.6560	4.3271	3.7757	3.3351	2.9776	2.6834
12	6.8137	6.1944	5.6603	5.4206	5.1971	4.7932	4.4392	3.8514	3.3868	3.0133	2.7084
13	7.1034	6.4235	5.8424	5.5831	5.3423	4.9095	4.5327	3.9124	3.4272	3.0404	2.7268
14	7.3667	6.6282	6.0021	5.7245	5.4675	5.0081	4.6106	3.9616	3.4587	3.0609	2.7403
15	7.6061	6.8109	6.1422	5.8474	5.5755	5.0916	4.6755	4.0013	3.4834	3.0764	2.7502
16	7.8237	6.9740	6.2651	5.9542	5.6685	5.1624	4.7296	4.0333	3.5026	3.0882	2.7575
17	8.0216	7.1196	6.3729	6.0472	5.7487	5.2223	4.7746	4.0591	3.5177	3.0971	2.7629
18	8.2014	7.2497	6.4674	6.1280	5.8178	5.2732	4.8122	4.0799	3.5294	3.1039	2.7668
19	8.3649	7.3658	6.5504	6.1982	5.8775	5.3162	4.8435	4.0967	3.5386	3.1090	2.7697
20	8.5136	7.4694	6.6231	6.2593	5.9288	5.3527	4.8696	4.1103	3.5458	3.1129	2.7718
25	9.0770	7.8431	6.8729	6.4641	6.0971	5.4669	4.9476	4.1474	3.5640	3.1220	2.7765
30	9.4269	8.0552	7.0027	6.5660	6.1772	5.5168	4.9789	4.1601	3.5693	3.1242	2.7775
40	9.7791	8.2438	7.1050	6.6418	6.2335	5.5482	4.9966	4.1659	3.5712	3.1250	2.7778
50	9.9148	8.3045	7.1327	6.6605	6.2463	5.5541	4.9995	4.1666	3.5714	3.1250	2.7778
60	9.9672	8.3240	7.1401	6.6651	6.2492	5.5553	4.9999	4.1667	3.5714	3.1250	2.7778

Table A.2   Areas Under the Normal Curve

Z	.00	.01	.02	.03	.04	.05	.06	.07	.08	.09
0.0	0.0000	0.0040	0.0080	0.0120	0.0160	0.0199	0.0239	0.0279	0.0319	0.0359
0.1	0.0398	0.0438	0.0478	0.0517	0.0557	0.0596	0.0636	0.0675	0.0714	0.0753
0.2	0.0793	0.0832	0.0871	0.0910	0.0948	0.0987	0.1026	0.1064	0.1103	0.1141
0.3	0.1179	0.1217	0.1255	0.1293	0.1331	0.1368	0.1406	0.1443	0.1480	0.1517
0.4	0.1554	0.1591	0.1628	0.1664	0.1700	0.1736	0.1772	0.1808	0.1844	0.1879
0.5	0.1915	0.1950	0.1985	0.2019	0.2054	0.2088	0.2123	0.2157	0.2190	0.2224
0.6	0.2257	0.2291	0.2324	0.2357	0.2389	0.2422	0.2454	0.2486	0.2517	0.2549
0.7	0.2580	0.2611	0.2642	0.2673	0.2704	0.2734	0.2764	0.2794	0.2823	0.2852
0.8	0.2881	0.2910	0.2939	0.2967	0.2995	0.3023	0.3051	0.3078	0.3106	0.3133
0.9	0.3159	0.3186	0.3212	0.3238	0.3264	0.3289	0.3315	0.3340	0.3365	0.3389
1.0	0.3413	0.3438	0.3461	0.3485	0.3508	0.3531	0.3554	0.3577	0.3599	0.3621
1.1	0.3643	0.3665	0.3686	0.3708	0.3729	0.3749	0.3770	0.3790	0.3810	0.3830
1.2	0.3849	0.3869	0.3888	0.3907	0.3925	0.3944	0.3962	0.3980	0.3997	0.4015
1.3	0.4032	0.4049	0.4066	0.4082	0.4099	0.4115	0.4131	0.4147	0.4162	0.4177
1.4	0.4192	0.4207	0.4222	0.4236	0.4251	0.4265	0.4279	0.4292	0.4306	0.4319
1.5	0.4332	0.4345	0.4357	0.4370	0.4382	0.4394	0.4406	0.4418	0.4429	0.4441
1.6	0.4452	0.4463	0.4474	0.4484	0.4495	0.4505	0.4515	0.4525	0.4535	0.4545
1.7	0.4554	0.4564	0.4573	0.4582	0.4591	0.4599	0.4608	0.4616	0.4625	0.4633
1.8	0.4641	0.4649	0.4656	0.4664	0.4671	0.4678	0.4686	0.4693	0.4699	0.4706
1.9	0.4713	0.4719	0.4726	0.4732	0.4738	0.4744	0.4750	0.4756	0.4761	0.4767
2.0	0.4772	0.4778	0.4783	0.4788	0.4793	0.4798	0.4803	0.4808	0.4812	0.4817
2.1	0.4821	0.4826	0.4830	0.4834	0.4838	0.4842	0.4846	0.4850	0.4854	0.4857
2.2	0.4861	0.4864	0.4868	0.4871	0.4875	0.4878	0.4881	0.4884	0.4887	0.4890
2.3	0.4893	0.4896	0.4898	0.4901	0.4904	0.4906	0.4909	0.4911	0.4913	0.4916
2.4	0.4918	0.4920	0.4922	0.4925	0.4927	0.4929	0.4931	0.4932	0.4934	0.4936
2.5	0.4938	0.4940	0.4941	0.4943	0.4945	0.4946	0.4948	0.4949	0.4951	0.4952
2.6	0.4953	0.4955	0.4956	0.4957	0.4959	0.4960	0.4961	0.4962	0.4963	0.4964
2.7	0.4965	0.4966	0.4967	0.4968	0.4969	0.4970	0.4971	0.4972	0.4973	0.4974
2.8	0.4974	0.4975	0.4976	0.4977	0.4977	0.4978	0.4979	0.4979	0.4980	0.4981
2.9	0.4981	0.4982	0.4982	0.4983	0.4984	0.4984	0.4985	0.4985	0.4986	0.4986
3.0	0.4987	0.4987	0.4987	0.4988	0.4988	0.4989	0.4989	0.4989	0.4990	0.4990

Table A.3a   Critical Values for the *F*-Distribution ($\alpha = .05$)

Degrees of Freedom for Denominator	Degrees of Freedom for Numerator								
	1	2	3	4	5	6	8	10	15
1	161.4	199.5	215.7	224.6	230.2	234.0	238.9	241.9	245.9
2	18.51	19.00	19.16	19.25	19.30	19.33	19.37	19.40	19.43
3	10.13	9.55	9.28	9.12	9.01	8.94	8.85	8.79	8.70
4	7.71	6.94	6.59	6.39	6.26	6.16	6.04	5.96	5.86
5	6.61	5.79	5.41	5.19	5.05	4.95	4.82	4.74	4.62
6	5.99	5.14	4.76	4.53	4.39	4.28	4.15	4.06	3.94
7	5.59	4.74	4.35	4.12	3.97	3.87	3.73	3.64	3.51
8	5.32	4.46	4.07	3.84	3.69	3.58	3.44	3.35	3.22
9	5.12	4.26	3.86	3.63	3.48	3.37	3.23	3.14	3.01
10	4.96	4.10	3.71	3.48	3.33	3.22	3.07	2.98	2.85
11	4.84	3.98	3.59	3.36	3.20	3.09	2.95	2.85	2.72
12	4.75	3.89	3.49	3.26	3.11	3.00	2.85	2.75	2.62
13	4.67	3.81	3.41	3.18	3.03	2.92	2.77	2.67	2.53
14	4.60	3.74	3.34	3.11	2.96	2.85	2.70	2.60	2.46
15	4.54	3.68	3.29	3.06	2.90	2.79	2.64	2.54	2.40
16	4.49	3.63	3.24	3.01	2.85	2.74	2.59	2.49	2.35
17	4.45	3.59	3.20	2.96	2.81	2.70	2.55	2.45	2.31
18	4.41	3.55	3.16	2.93	2.77	2.66	2.51	2.41	2.27
19	4.38	3.52	3.13	2.90	2.74	2.63	2.48	2.38	2.23
20	4.35	3.49	3.10	2.87	2.71	2.60	2.45	2.35	2.20
21	4.32	3.47	3.07	2.84	2.68	2.57	2.42	2.32	2.18
22	4.30	3.44	3.05	2.82	2.66	2.55	2.40	2.30	2.15
23	4.28	3.42	3.03	2.80	2.64	2.53	2.37	2.27	2.13
24	4.26	3.40	3.01	2.78	2.62	2.51	2.36	2.25	2.11
25	4.24	3.39	2.99	2.76	2.60	2.49	2.34	2.24	2.09
26	4.23	3.37	2.98	2.74	2.59	2.47	2.32	2.22	2.07
27	4.21	3.35	2.96	2.73	2.57	2.46	2.31	2.20	2.06
28	4.20	3.34	2.95	2.71	2.56	2.45	2.29	2.19	2.04
29	4.18	3.33	2.93	2.70	2.55	2.43	2.28	2.18	2.03
30	4.17	3.32	2.92	2.69	2.53	2.42	2.27	2.16	2.01
40	4.08	3.23	2.84	2.61	2.45	2.34	2.18	2.08	1.92
50	4.03	3.18	2.79	2.56	2.40	2.29	2.13	2.03	1.87
60	4.00	3.15	2.76	2.53	2.37	2.25	2.10	1.99	1.84
70	3.98	3.13	2.74	2.50	2.35	2.23	2.07	1.97	1.81
80	3.96	3.11	2.72	2.49	2.33	2.21	2.06	1.95	1.79
90	3.95	3.10	2.71	2.47	2.32	2.20	2.04	1.94	1.78
100	3.94	3.09	2.70	2.46	2.31	2.19	2.03	1.93	1.77
125	2.93	3.07	2.68	2.44	2.29	2.17	2.01	1.91	1.75
150	3.90	3.06	2.66	2.43	2.27	2.16	2.00	1.89	1.73
200	3.89	3.04	2.65	2.42	2.26	2.14	1.98	1.88	1.72
∞	3.84	3.00	2.60	2.37	2.21	2.10	1.94	1.83	1.67

Table A.3b Critical Values for the F-Distribution ($\alpha = .01$)

Degrees of Freedom for Denominator	Degrees of Freedom for Numerator								
	1	2	3	4	5	6	8	10	15
1	4052	4999	5403	5625	5764	5859	5981	6056	6157
2	98.50	99.00	99.17	99.25	99.30	99.33	99.37	99.40	99.43
3	34.12	30.82	29.46	28.71	28.24	27.91	27.49	27.23	26.87
4	21.20	18.00	16.69	15.98	15.52	15.21	14.80	14.55	14.20
5	16.26	13.27	12.06	11.39	10.97	10.67	10.29	10.05	9.72
6	13.75	10.92	9.78	9.15	8.75	8.47	8.10	7.87	7.56
7	12.25	9.55	8.45	7.85	7.46	7.19	6.84	6.62	6.31
8	11.26	8.65	7.59	7.01	6.63	6.37	6.03	5.81	5.52
9	10.56	8.02	6.99	6.42	6.06	5.80	5.47	5.26	4.96
10	10.04	7.56	6.55	5.99	5.64	5.39	5.06	4.85	4.56
11	9.65	7.21	6.22	5.67	5.32	5.07	4.74	4.54	4.25
12	9.33	6.93	5.95	5.41	5.06	4.82	4.50	4.30	4.01
13	9.07	6.70	5.74	5.21	4.86	4.62	4.30	4.10	3.82
14	8.86	6.51	5.56	5.04	4.69	4.46	4.14	3.94	3.66
15	8.68	6.36	5.42	4.89	4.56	4.32	4.00	3.80	3.52
16	8.53	6.23	5.29	4.77	4.44	4.20	3.89	3.69	3.41
17	8.40	6.11	5.19	4.67	4.34	4.10	3.79	3.59	3.31
18	8.29	6.01	5.09	4.58	4.25	4.01	3.71	3.51	3.23
19	8.18	5.93	5.01	4.50	4.17	3.94	3.63	3.43	3.15
20	8.10	5.85	4.94	4.43	4.10	3.87	3.56	3.37	3.09
21	8.02	5.78	4.87	4.37	4.04	3.81	3.51	3.31	3.03
22	7.95	5.72	4.82	4.31	3.99	3.76	3.45	3.26	2.98
23	7.88	5.66	4.76	4.26	3.94	3.71	3.41	3.21	2.93
24	7.82	5.61	4.72	4.22	3.90	3.67	3.36	3.17	2.89
25	7.77	5.57	4.68	4.18	3.85	3.63	3.32	3.13	2.85
26	7.72	5.53	4.64	4.14	3.82	3.59	3.29	3.09	2.81
27	7.68	5.49	4.60	4.11	3.78	3.56	3.26	3.06	2.78
28	7.64	5.45	4.57	4.07	3.75	3.53	3.23	3.03	2.75
29	7.60	5.42	4.54	4.04	3.73	3.50	3.20	3.00	2.73
30	7.56	5.39	4.51	4.02	3.70	3.47	3.17	2.98	2.70
40	7.31	5.18	4.31	3.83	3.51	3.29	2.99	2.80	2.52
50	7.17	5.06	4.20	3.72	3.41	3.19	2.89	2.70	2.42
60	7.08	4.98	4.13	3.65	3.34	3.12	2.82	2.63	2.35
70	7.01	4.92	4.07	3.60	3.29	3.07	2.78	2.59	2.31
80	6.96	4.88	4.04	3.56	3.26	3.04	2.74	2.55	2.27
90	6.93	4.85	4.01	3.53	3.23	3.01	2.72	2.52	2.24
100	6.90	4.82	3.98	3.51	3.21	2.99	2.69	2.50	2.22
125	6.84	4.78	3.94	3.47	3.17	2.95	2.66	2.47	2.19
150	6.81	4.75	3.91	3.45	3.14	2.92	2.63	2.44	2.16
200	6.76	4.71	3.88	3.41	3.11	2.89	2.60	2.41	2.13
∞	6.63	4.61	3.78	3.32	3.02	2.80	2.51	2.32	2.04

Table A.4   Critical Values for the *t*-Distribution

One-Tail α =	0.10	0.05	0.025	0.01	0.005
Two-Tail α =	0.20	0.10	0.05	0.02	0.01
df = 1	3.078	6.314	12.706	31.821	63.657
2	1.886	2.920	4.303	6.965	9.925
3	1.638	2.353	3.182	4.541	5.841
4	1.533	2.132	2.776	3.747	4.604
5	1.476	2.015	2.571	3.365	4.032
6	1.440	1.943	2.447	3.143	3.707
7	1.415	1.895	2.365	2.998	3.499
8	1.397	1.860	2.306	2.896	3.355
9	1.383	1.833	2.262	2.821	3.250
10	1.372	1.812	2.228	2.764	3.169
11	1.363	1.796	2.201	2.718	3.106
12	1.356	1.782	2.179	2.681	3.055
13	1.350	1.771	2.160	2.650	3.012
14	1.345	1.761	2.145	2.624	2.977
15	1.341	1.753	2.131	2.602	2.947
16	1.337	1.746	2.120	2.583	2.921
17	1.333	1.740	2.110	2.567	2.898
18	1.330	1.734	2.101	2.552	2.878
19	1.328	1.729	2.093	2.539	2.861
20	1.325	1.725	2.086	2.528	2.845
21	1.323	1.721	2.080	2.518	2.831
22	1.321	1.717	2.074	2.508	2.819
23	1.319	1.714	2.069	2.500	2.807
24	1.318	1.711	2.064	2.492	2.797
25	1.316	1.708	2.060	2.485	2.787
26	1.315	1.706	2.056	2.479	2.779
27	1.314	1.703	2.052	2.473	2.771
28	1.313	1.701	2.048	2.467	2.763
29	1.311	1.699	2.045	2.462	2.756
30	1.310	1.697	2.042	2.457	2.750
40	1.303	1.684	2.021	2.423	2.704
50	1.299	1.676	2.009	2.402	2.678
60	1.296	1.672	2.000	2.390	2.660
70	1.294	1.667	1.994	2.381	2.648
80	1.292	1.664	1.990	2.374	2.639
90	1.291	1.662	1.987	2.368	2.632
100	1.290	1.660	1.984	2.364	2.626
125	1.288	1.657	1.979	2.357	2.616
150	1.287	1.655	1.976	2.351	2.609
200	1.286	1.653	1.972	2.345	2.601
∞	1.282	1.645	1.960	2.326	2.576

Table A.5a   Durbin-Watson Statistic: Significance Points for d_l and d_u (One-Tail Test, $\alpha = .05$)

	k = 1		k = 2		k = 3		k = 4		k = 5	
n	d_l	d_u	d_l	d_u	d_l	d_u	d_l	d_u	d_l	d_u
15	1.08	1.36	0.95	1.54	0.82	1.75	0.69	1.97	0.56	2.21
16	1.10	1.37	0.98	1.54	0.86	1.73	0.74	1.93	0.62	2.15
17	1.13	1.38	1.02	1.54	0.90	1.71	0.78	1.90	0.67	2.10
18	1.16	1.39	1.05	1.53	0.93	1.69	0.82	1.87	0.71	2.06
19	1.18	1.40	1.08	1.53	0.97	1.68	0.86	1.85	0.75	2.02
20	1.20	1.41	1.10	1.54	1.00	1.68	0.90	1.83	0.79	1.99
21	1.22	1.42	1.13	1.54	1.03	1.67	0.93	1.81	0.83	1.96
22	1.24	1.43	1.15	1.54	1.05	1.66	0.96	1.80	0.86	1.94
23	1.26	1.44	1.17	1.54	1.08	1.66	0.99	1.79	0.90	1.92
24	1.27	1.45	1.19	1.55	1.10	1.66	1.01	1.78	0.93	1.90
25	1.29	1.45	1.21	1.55	1.12	1.66	1.04	1.77	0.95	1.89
26	1.30	1.46	1.22	1.55	1.14	1.65	1.06	1.76	0.98	1.88
27	1.32	1.47	1.24	1.56	1.16	1.65	1.08	1.76	1.01	1.86
28	1.33	1.48	1.26	1.56	1.18	1.65	1.10	1.75	1.03	1.85
29	1.34	1.48	1.27	1.56	1.20	1.65	1.12	1.74	1.05	1.84
30	1.35	1.49	1.28	1.57	1.21	1.65	1.14	1.74	1.07	1.83
31	1.36	1.50	1.30	1.57	1.23	1.65	1.16	1.74	1.09	1.83
32	1.37	1.50	1.31	1.57	1.24	1.65	1.18	1.73	1.11	1.82
33	1.38	1.51	1.32	1.58	1.26	1.65	1.19	1.73	1.13	1.81
34	1.39	1.51	1.33	1.58	1.27	1.65	1.21	1.73	1.15	1.81
35	1.40	1.52	1.34	1.58	1.28	1.65	1.22	1.73	1.16	1.80
36	1.41	1.52	1.35	1.59	1.29	1.65	1.24	1.73	1.18	1.80
37	1.42	1.53	1.36	1.59	1.31	1.66	1.25	1.72	1.19	1.80
38	1.43	1.54	1.37	1.59	1.32	1.66	1.26	1.72	1.21	1.79
39	1.43	1.54	1.38	1.60	1.33	1.66	1.27	1.72	1.22	1.79
40	1.44	1.54	1.39	1.60	1.34	1.66	1.29	1.72	1.23	1.79
45	1.48	1.57	1.43	1.62	1.38	1.67	1.34	1.72	1.29	1.78
50	1.50	1.59	1.46	1.63	1.42	1.67	1.38	1.72	1.34	1.77
55	1.53	1.60	1.49	1.64	1.45	1.68	1.41	1.72	1.38	1.77
60	1.55	1.62	1.51	1.65	1.48	1.69	1.44	1.73	1.41	1.77
65	1.57	1.63	1.54	1.66	1.50	1.70	1.47	1.73	1.44	1.77
70	1.58	1.64	1.55	1.67	1.52	1.70	1.49	1.74	1.46	1.77
75	1.60	1.65	1.57	1.68	1.54	1.71	1.51	1.74	1.49	1.77
80	1.61	1.66	1.59	1.69	1.56	1.72	1.53	1.74	1.51	1.77
85	1.62	1.67	1.60	1.70	1.57	1.72	1.55	1.75	1.52	1.77
90	1.63	1.68	1.61	1.70	1.59	1.73	1.57	1.75	1.54	1.78
95	1.64	1.69	1.62	1.71	1.60	1.73	1.58	1.75	1.56	1.78
100	1.65	1.69	1.63	1.72	1.61	1.74	1.59	1.76	1.57	1.78

Note: n = number of observations, k = number of regressors

Table A.5b   Durbin-Watson Statistic: Significance Points for d_l and d_u (Two-Tail Test, $\alpha = .05$)

	k = 1		k = 2		k = 3		k = 4		k = 5	
n	d_l	d_u	d_l	d_u	d_l	d_u	d_l	d_u	d_l	d_u
15	0.95	1.23	0.83	1.40	0.71	1.61	0.59	1.84	0.48	2.09
16	0.98	1.24	0.86	1.40	0.75	1.59	0.64	1.80	0.53	2.03
17	1.01	1.25	0.90	1.40	0.79	1.58	0.68	1.77	0.57	1.98
18	1.03	1.26	0.93	1.40	0.82	1.56	0.72	1.74	0.62	1.93
19	1.06	1.28	0.96	1.41	0.86	1.55	0.76	1.72	0.66	1.90
20	1.08	1.28	0.99	1.41	0.89	1.55	0.79	1.70	0.70	1.87
21	1.10	1.30	1.01	1.41	0.92	1.54	0.83	1.69	0.73	1.84
22	1.12	1.31	1.04	1.42	0.95	1.54	0.86	1.68	0.77	1.82
23	1.14	1.32	1.06	1.42	0.97	1.54	0.89	1.67	0.80	1.80
24	1.16	1.33	1.08	1.43	1.00	1.54	0.91	1.66	0.83	1.79
25	1.18	1.34	1.10	1.43	1.02	1.54	0.94	1.65	0.86	1.77
26	1.19	1.35	1.12	1.44	1.04	1.54	0.96	1.65	0.88	1.76
27	1.21	1.36	1.13	1.44	1.06	1.54	0.99	1.64	0.91	1.75
28	1.22	1.37	1.15	1.45	1.08	1.54	1.01	1.64	0.93	1.74
29	1.24	1.38	1.17	1.45	1.10	1.54	1.03	1.63	0.96	1.73
30	1.25	1.38	1.18	1.46	1.12	1.54	1.05	1.63	0.98	1.73
31	1.26	1.39	1.20	1.47	1.13	1.55	1.07	1.63	1.00	1.72
32	1.27	1.40	1.21	1.47	1.15	1.55	1.08	1.63	1.02	1.71
33	1.28	1.41	1.22	1.48	1.16	1.55	1.10	1.63	1.04	1.71
34	1.29	1.41	1.24	1.48	1.17	1.55	1.12	1.63	1.06	1.70
35	1.30	1.42	1.25	1.48	1.19	1.55	1.13	1.63	1.07	1.70
36	1.31	1.43	1.26	1.49	1.20	1.56	1.15	1.63	1.09	1.70
37	1.32	1.43	1.27	1.49	1.21	1.56	1.16	1.62	1.10	1.70
38	1.33	1.44	1.28	1.50	1.23	1.56	1.17	1.62	1.12	1.70
39	1.34	1.44	1.29	1.50	1.24	1.56	1.19	1.63	1.13	1.69
40	1.35	1.45	1.30	1.51	1.25	1.57	1.20	1.63	1.15	1.69
45	1.39	1.48	1.34	1.53	1.30	1.58	1.25	1.63	1.21	1.69
50	1.42	1.50	1.38	1.54	1.34	1.59	1.30	1.64	1.26	1.69
55	1.45	1.52	1.41	1.56	1.37	1.60	1.33	1.64	1.30	1.69
60	1.47	1.54	1.44	1.57	1.40	1.61	1.37	1.65	1.33	1.69
65	.149	1.55	1.46	1.59	1.43	1.62	1.40	1.66	1.36	1.69
70	1.51	1.57	1.48	1.60	1.45	1.63	1.42	1.66	1.39	1.70
75	1.53	1.58	1.50	1.61	1.47	1.64	1.45	1.67	1.42	1.70
80	1.54	1.59	1.52	1.62	1.49	1.65	1.47	1.67	1.44	1.70
85	1.56	1.60	1.53	1.63	1.51	1.65	1.49	1.68	1.46	1.71
90	1.57	1.61	1.55	1.64	1.53	1.66	1.50	1.69	1.48	1.71
95	1.58	1.62	1.56	1.65	1.54	1.67	1.52	1.69	1.50	1.71
100	1.59	1.63	1.57	1.65	1.55	1.67	1.53	1.70	1.51	1.72

Note: n = number of observations, k = number of regressors

Index

Note: Page numbers followed by f indicate figures; numbers followed by t indicate tables; numbers followed by b indicate boxes; numbers followed by n indicate footnotes.